MW01244983

# *Art's* Ultimate SPOT *Cleaning*

## Your Care Guide for
## Synthetic/Blended Carpets and Rugs

## By Arthur D. Colo'n

Produced for Arthur D. Colo'n by Barbara Earl and Associates and Wilson/Wilson Designs

## *Dedication*

I want to dedicate this guide to the most important people in my life.

First, to the Lord, my God, who gave me the patience, tenacity and wisdom to acquire the knowledge, along with the desire, to create something that I truly believe will help my fellow man and fellow woman, if but in a small way.

Secondly, to my spectacular wife, whose delicate hands did most of this guide's word processing prior to its editing. Her hard work and devotion allowed me to concentrate on the exhaustive research and development necessary to make it the most comprehensive book on carpet spot treatment.

To my children, whose precious little souls inspired and motivated me to complete this task so that I might spend the time with them they so very much need and deserve.

To my Mom and Dad, who taught me that with a lot of ambition and hard work, I could accomplish anything I put my mind and heart into. I thank them also for the many other important lessons they taught me that have allowed me to continually grow into the man I've always wanted to be.

To my Grandmother and Grandfather, with whom I spent many summers as a boy. From them is where I learned most of my work ethic and entrepreneurial skills as I memorized the things they did to keep their business growing and prosperous.

And lastly, to my editor, Barbara Earl, and my creative director Linda Wilson. Their experience, creativity and desire for excellence transformed my words and vision into a more comprehensive and valuable carpet care guide for you.

I am eternally grateful to all of you.

## Author's Disclaimer

**PLEASE NOTE:** The information and instructions in this guide are the result of years of experience and study. They were carefully written so your spot treatment efforts can be as safe, effective and easy as possible, but I cannot guarantee how successful they will always be. There are too many conditions that can or do affect the outcome of the spot removal process.

These can include, but are not limited to, the type of fibers in your carpet, the design and quality of the carpet, whether or not the carpet was treated with carpet protectors and the type and quality of protector, if treated what is the protector's current condition, the age of the carpet, the carpet's condition as far as wear and cleanliness, the type, size and age of the spot, whether someone has already tried to treat the spot using other methods, the temperature and amount of humidity and sunlight present, the type of spot treatment equipment you have available and how carefully and correctly you follow the treatment steps, etc.

I've done my best to guide you in the right direction regarding effective spot treatments and carpet care, but there are so many variables and unknowns over which I have no control that I cannot be held responsible for any damages that may result from any particular application of a procedure outlined in these pages.

# SECTION I

## Chapter I. Identifying Your Carpet Fiber

Section I Contents

## *Chapter 2. Your Spotting Kit*

## *Chapter 3. Spot Treatment Techniques*

## *Chapter 4. Identifying Your Spot, Stain Or Discoloration*

## *SECTION II*

## *Chapter 5. Spot Treatment Instructions*

## SECTION III - Tips From The Tradesman

## *Chapter 6. How Does One Carpet Fiber Compare To Another?*

## *Chapter 7. How Often Should My Carpet Be Cleaned?*

Section III Contents

## *Chapter 8. What Is The Best Way To Clean My Carpet?*

## Chapter 9. Does My Carpet Need A Carpet Protector After Cleaning?

## *Chapter 10. How Do I Find A Quality Carpet Cleaning Professional?*

## *Need Additional Books*

Section III Contents

# Introduction And Preview

## *Hello.*

### My name is Arthur D. Colo'n and I am a "Certified Carpet Cleaning Specialist".

Basically, that means I've learned how to remove all kinds of carpet spills, spots, stains and discolorations. I did this by taking many classes, doing extensive self study and gaining lots of experience over the years cleaning many types of floor coverings, including restoring what seemed to be hopelessly dirty carpets and rugs.

In 1987 I began a fascinating study of the chemistry of carpet cleaning and the specialized removal of common, and not so common, household spills and disasters. I used that information to start my own company in Texas where we specialized in cleaning and restoration work on carpets, all types of rugs including oriental, and upholstery. Our work is done in homes, businesses, airplanes, boats, cars, recreational vehicles and wherever there is carpet to be found.

**I discovered early in my career that many of my customers were buying spot cleaning products from a variety of sources.**

These included their local grocery store or discount warehouse, by mail, from door-to-door salespeople and in some cases from professional carpet cleaning firms.

They bought these spot cleaners because they wanted to be able to handle the little carpet messes caused by family, friends, pets and others rather than live with the spotted carpet or spend the money that a professional would charge to remove the problem. (When I say "problem" here, I'm referring to the spot itself - not Rover or the kids or whomever made the spot in the first place.)

— 2 —

**Unfortunately, many of these off-the-shelf spot cleaners and "professional" spotting kits caused more problems than they solved.**

These problems were caused by cleaners and kits that:

• Did not remove the spot.

• May have removed the spot, but in some cases created additional problems like residue buildup and continuous re-soiling of the spill area.

(If you've used the wrong spot remover, the job is not necessarily finished when the spot itself is gone. These spot removers leave residues that can become so sticky they attract soil to the spot area, making it look worse than the spot itself did. Plus, the residues of the high pH chemical soaps in some cleaners can damage the carpet fibers and discolor the dye over time. **Hint:** See "Hydrogen Peroxide" in "Chapter 2. Your Spotting Kit" for the recommended treatment if you have already used one of these problematic cleaners.)

• Caused the spot to "set" so even a professional had great difficulty removing - or in some cases could not remove - what might otherwise have been a relatively easy spot for the pro's heavy duty equipment and special cleaners. (The worst I saw was when the cleaner not only set the spot so it couldn't be removed, but also caused new discolorations in the carpet.)

• Did not include any instructions or did not give specific, detailed instructions for their correct use.

• Contained strong chemicals that in my opinion should not have been used by anyone other than a trained professional because of their possible safety hazards and potential to damage the carpet, if used wrongly.

**Caution:** Synthetic carpet fibers (nylon, olefin, polyester, acrylic) and 100% natural carpet fibers (wool, cotton) do **not** respond exactly the same way to spots, spotting chemicals or spotting techniques. What works well to remove a spot on a synthetic carpet or a synthetic/natural fiber blend may not work on the same type of spot on a 100% wool or cotton carpet or may even damage the natural carpet. If you have a problem with an all natural fiber carpet, call a professional as soon as possible and make sure that he or she has a lot of successful experience with natural fibers!

3

**There are many books of helpful cleaning tips on the market, but they offer limited amounts of information on spot cleaning carpets.**

Instead, these everything-you-ever-wanted-to-know-about-cleaning-everything books want to be your one-stop resource for every type of cleaning problem. Their main shortcomings are that they:

- Give information about removing only a small number of the 100's of different types of spills you may encounter.

- Advise the use of as many as a dozen or more cleaning products to be used on both hard and soft surfaces - not just what is needed for carpets.

- Do not give you all the necessary practical instructions. They don't tell you the exact amounts of cleaning chemicals to use, the correct use of tools, the proper application and spot penetration techniques, etc., etc.

- Over simplify carpet spot removal by giving a one-size-fits-all removal recipe for a variety of different types of spots.

- Leave out information about what are realistically your limitations for successful home spot removal and when you are better off calling a pro. (These limitations include the type of carpet you have and the type and/ or size of spill.)

**Most people don't realize that successful carpet spot treatment isn't the result of just dumping any old cleaner on the carpet.**

It's more complex than that because when removing a spot, you must:

- Minimize the amount of spot material to be removed, if possible, before you apply cleaning chemicals (spotting agents).

- Break up the spot matter so the cleaning chemicals can penetrate it and begin to break it down.

- Use the right type and amount of cleaning chemicals on the spot.

- Keep the cleaners and the spot matter at the top of the carpet fibers throughout the removal process.

- Remove the spot debris, if any. The wrong chemicals or too much of a chemical or pushing the spot matter and the chemicals down into the carpet fibers and/or carpet backing can make removing the spot difficult to impossible, even for the professional.

And, if you really want the best spot treatment results, the method you use for removing a specific spot depends not only on the type of spot, but also on whether the spot is old/dried or fresh/wet and the type of tools you have available.

— 4 —

**I wrote this guide because I wanted my customers and others to be able to properly and safely care for their carpets.**

By sharing my knowledge, I hope to help you make the best decisions for you and your carpets whether you are treating a spot, making the major investment of buying new carpet, deciding the most effective method for cleaning your carpet, finding an experienced carpet cleaning professional (or determining if the one you are talking to really knows his stuff or is telling you the facts) or trying to decide if you really need that carpet protector the carpet cleaner is recommending.

## Preview of the Guide

**Note:** Over 85% of today's carpets are made of synthetic fibers which are much easier to treat for spots than natural fiber carpets. So, to keep things simple, this guide is written for treating spots on synthetic fiber carpets.

**The first two sections of the guide tell you everything you need to know to make your spot treatments as easy and effective as possible.**

### Section I - Chapters 1 - 4

This Section is the only part of the guide that I strongly advise you to read completely. It will give you all the basic knowledge you need to do successful spot treatments yourself. The information in these Chapters includes:

• How to identify the type of fibers your carpet is made of if you don't already know. (As long as you have a synthetic or synthetic/natural fiber blend, the method of treating the spot is the same no matter what type carpet fiber you have. The type of fiber can affect your results, however.)

• How to put together your own spot cleaning kit made up of:

  - Several common household items;

  - Three effective, safe, non-problematic cleaning chemicals (also referred to as "spotting agents") that you probably already use at home for other purposes;

  - A spot cleaning machine, if you want to be really effective.

• Proper application techniques that ensure the spotting chemicals penetrate the surface of the spot so they can be most effective, but do not soak the carpet or push the spot material deeper into the carpet fibers.

• Steps for identifying a spot that suddenly appears so you can properly treat the problem when no one will confess or tell you exactly what they spilled.

## Section II - Chapter 5

It is not necessary to read any of this Section except for the Introduction and other white pages at the beginning of the chapter, plus the instructions for specific spots you wish to treat. Read those pages carefully before you begin any spot removal to ensure you have all the information needed.

You will find that the directions are specific, easy to understand, easy to do instructions for removing over 800 different spots, stains and discolorations, including:

- The conditions such as type, size or age of spot, etc., that will facilitate your successful treatment of the spot or require your calling a professional instead.

- Any special comments or cautions regarding treatment of this kind of spot.

- The correct method of treating the spot based on whether the spot is old/dried or fresh/wet and whether or not you have a spot machine.

- The proper sequence for applying the spotting agents and the exact amounts to apply so the spotting agents break down the spot without soaking the carpet.

- The right ways to ensure that the spotting agents penetrate the surface of the spot, so they can be most effective without pushing the spot material deeper into the carpet fibers.

- Any necessary follow-up steps.

**In Section III "Tips From The Tradesman" (Chapters 6 - 10), I share information that is often only available to the cleaning professional.**

This Section, like Section II, is read on an "as needed" basis, unless you are curious about the topics covered here. These include:

- A comparison of the different types of synthetic and natural carpet fibers to help you decide which best fits your needs next time you are buying carpet.

- How often your carpets should be cleaned based on the type and amount of traffic your carpet receives and your environment.

- A comparison that tells the pros and cons of each of the different types of carpet cleaning methods, including do-it-yourself cleaning. I also describe the routine maintenance that will prolong the life and the good appearance of your carpet.

- The truth about whether or not you really need that carpet protector the carpet cleaner is recommending.

- How to find a real carpet cleaning professional - not just someone in the business.

# Chapter 1
# Identifying Your Carpet Fiber

## Introduction

In this Chapter, we will look at the different carpet fibers and how to identify the type (or types) in your carpet. The last part of the Chapter describes how the various synthetic carpet fibers are affected by different types of spots. This information will tell you the kinds of spills that could be especially problematic for your carpet.

**QUESTION:**

**The only thing you need to know before going any further with your spot removal efforts is, "Can you use my safe, easy techniques to do successful spot removal at home?"**

**ANSWER:**

The answer to this is based entirely on the type of fiber or fibers the face yarns (pile) of your carpet are made of:

- **YES: A synthetic fiber (nylon, olefin, polyester, acrylic), a blend of synthetic fibers, or a blend of a synthetic and a natural fiber.**

- **NO:** A 100% natural fiber - wool
  (Cotton is a natural fiber but it is used mainly for rugs and is rarely used in carpets.)

---

My methods are easy, safe,
and effective on all 100% synthetic and
on a blend of synthetic and natural fiber carpets.

---

**Caution:** If you have a 100% natural fiber carpet (or rug), home spot removal is a risky business. I don't recommend that you even try it.

Art's Ultimate Spot Cleaning • **Chapter 1 - Page 1**

As I said in the "Introduction And Preview", synthetic fibers and natural fibers do not respond exactly the same way to spots, spotting solutions or spotting techniques. The process that successfully removes a spot on a synthetic carpet or a synthetic/natural fiber blend carpet:

1. May not work on the same type of spot on a 100% wool carpet; and

2. Could even damage the natural fiber carpet. (Some of the chemicals that are perfectly harmless when used on synthetics can damage wool.)

**Note:** My spot treatment methods can be safely used on synthetic/natural fiber blend carpets. This is because the percentage of natural fiber in each blended yarn is low compared to the amount of synthetic fiber, and my treatments use relatively gentle chemicals and application methods. (Let me repeat, however, "Please do not try them on 100% wool carpets.")

**Best Practice:** Knowing the type(s) of fibers your carpet is made of is important even if you want to call a professional carpet cleaner. Not all "professionals" have the in-depth knowledge necessary to successfully remove spots from natural fibers and/or remove the more difficult types of spots from different synthetic fibers. If you can tell the pro what type of carpet you have when you call and know a few of the right questions to ask, you may save yourself time, trouble and heartache by avoiding people who aren't qualified to help solve your spot problem. (See "Chapter 10. How Do I Find A Quality Carpet Cleaning Professional?" for more information on how to find an ethical, well-trained professional carpet care technician.)

## Carpet Fiber Types

The yarns (called the "face yarns") that make up the surface or pile of your carpet may be made of a single synthetic material, a blend or combination of different types of synthetics, a single natural fiber or a blend of natural and synthetic fibers.

The following describes the different types of materials used for carpet fibers and gives some important facts about each.

### Synthetic Fibers

More than 85% of today's carpets are made entirely of synthetic materials. Synthetic carpet fibers are manmade materials that are created in large vats, then extruded in thin filaments or threads. The filaments are twisted into fibers or yarns that are cut into short lengths. In tufted carpets these "face" yarns (your carpet pile) are then inserted into a primary carpet backing that these days is another synthetic material, polypropylene (olefin). Latex is used to "glue" the yarns to the primary backing. Latex also binds the primary backing to a secondary backing (also polypropylene) that makes the carpet stronger and more durable.

Until the early 80's, carpet backing was normally made of a natural fiber, jute, for all carpet types. Jute could be subject to mildew problems when the carpets were cleaned using the old steam cleaning, especially when done by a poorly trained technician. The polypropylene used today on all carpets but 100% wool ones (they still have jute backings) does not mildew, so the more effective cleaning methods using water and chemicals do not affect the carpet backing when properly applied.

**There are four main types of synthetic carpet fibers** used in home, office, automobile and other carpets:

- **Nylon** - This is by far the most common carpet fiber. Nylon carpets, which are available in a variety of carpet styles or weaves, make up more than 65% of the carpets on the market. There are two types of nylon - type 6 or "regular" which is the original nylon and a newer, better version called type 6,6 or "solution dyed". Nylon, especially the type 6, 6 which better resists sun fading, is also being used more and more for auto carpets.

- **Olefin (or Polypropylene)** - Olefin or Polypropylene is more commonly known by its trade names Herculon® and Astroturf®. It is normally used in looped home carpets such as berbers and in commercial carpets.

- **Polyester** - Polyester is often blended with nylon when used in carpet fibers. It is also used in auto carpets because of its resistant to sun and fading.

- **Acrylic** - Acrylic was originally designed to be the synthetic substitute for wool and to eliminate all of wool's negative characteristics. It is the least used of the synthetic carpet fibers and is usually found in berber (looped) styles and blended with nylon.

## *Natural Fibers*

Natural fibers are those found in nature. Less than 5% of the total carpet sales in the U.S. are natural fibers, so you are more likely to have natural fiber rugs rather than carpets. There are two main types encountered by most consumers:

- **Wool** - Wool is the most expensive and luxurious of the carpet fibers.

- **Cotton** - Cotton is rarely used for face yarns in carpeting and is more commonly found in rugs.

**Note:** Though I strongly recommend you have a professional do spot treatments on natural fiber carpets and this book is about treating synthetics, you need to know a little about natural fibers so you will be an educated carpet cleaning and spotting consumer. (See "Chapter 6. How Does One Carpet Fiber Compare To Another?" in Section III for more information on the characteristics of the natural fibers.)

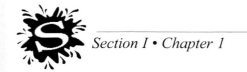

### *Blends or Combinations*

"Blends" are carpets made of two or more different types of fibers. For example: Nylon/Polyester (most often seen in saxony weaves), Nylon/Acrylic (most often seen in berber carpet), Acrylic/Wool, etc.

## How to Identify Your Carpet Fiber(s)

There are several ways to learn exactly what type of fibers were used in your carpet:

- Contact the store that sold you the carpet. This works best if you bought the carpet. (If you inherited it when you bought or rented your home or business, you may not know when/where it was purchased.)

- Look at the sales receipt for the carpet. (It may or may not have all the details.)

- Check the label on the back of the carpet sample the store gave you. (You may or may not have samples for each type and color of carpet in your home or office.)

- Ask your carpet cleaning company. If you have a regular, well-trained carpet cleaner, they keep this kind of record, and they have correctly identified all the types of carpet in your home or office.

- Do your own "fiber test". This is the quickest and most accurate way to identify your carpet fibers if you don't have accurate information from another source.

**Note:** Regarding the two different types of nylon - A fiber test will only identify if your carpet fiber is nylon or some other fiber. It won't tell you if it's the "regular" nylon (type 6) or the "solution dyed" (type 6,6). (You must get that information from the carpet salesperson. Not even your trusted carpet cleaner can identify one from the other.)

**But, all you really need to know is, "Is it a synthetic fiber?".** The steps for treating a spot are the same - no matter what type of synthetic, or type of nylon. The main benefit to knowing which type of nylon you have is that you can normally predict that the results of your spot treatments will probably be better if you have the "solution dyed" fibers.

# How to Do Your Own Fiber Test

Different types of fibers react differently when they are exposed to a flame. By analyzing the results carefully, you can usually identify your carpet fibers.

**Note:** Blends can cause conflicting test results when you do fiber testing. If you get what looks like a combination of results, look closely at the Fiber Identification Chart on page 7 and try to decide what fibers you could be testing. It may require burning a few more fibers than if your carpet is made of only one material.

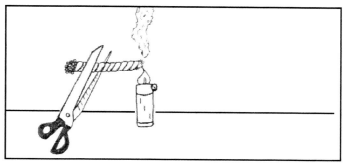

Illustration by Arthur D. Colo'n

## *Materials Needed*

• Pair of scissors - not your best ones

• 2 - 3 yarns cut from each carpet that is a different color, texture or style. Cut these yarns from the edge of the carpet along a wall or at the back of a closet. Cut them off at the base where they go into the primary carpet backing so you have full length yarns.

• Butane lighter - Do not use matches; the sulfur odor will taint the test results.

• "Fiber Identification Chart - Burn Test Characteristics", page 7.

## *Location*

• Kitchen or bathroom sink. This is the safest place to do the test.

## *Fiber Test Steps*

**Caution:** Make sure there are NO children or teenagers present. I'm sure you've heard the saying, "Monkey see; monkey do".

1. Assemble your materials at the kitchen or bathroom sink.

2. Review the "Fiber Identification Chart - Burn Test Characteristics" so you will be familiar with the different things you will be observing and how different fiber types burn. (The Chart is laid out in the order that you will observe the burn characteristics.) Keep the Chart nearby so you can refer to it as needed.

3. Put the first set yarn between the tips of the scissors and hold it over the sink.

4. Light the butane lighter on low flame and slowly begin to burn the tips of the yarn until they hold a flame. Be sure to burn only the carpet yarn and not any latex nodules that are sometimes present at the yarn's base.

5. After the fibers have ignited, carefully watch the color of the flame and how it burns for about 2 - 4 seconds. Notice whether the fibers continue to burn or self extinguish. DO NOT TOUCH the burning fibers.

6. Gently blow out the flame.

7. Observe the smoke, if any.

8. Wait about 2 - 3 seconds.

9. Carefully smell the odor of the smoke. **Do Not Directly Inhale the Smoke.** It could irritate your nose!!!

10. Wait 15 seconds for the ends of the burned fibers to cool.

11. Look at the ash luster, shape and color. Then feel for hardness or brittleness.

12. Match your results to the "Fiber Identification Chart - Burn Test Characteristics".
    **Note:** Remember, blended yarns may create conflicting results. These could be a flame color that does not correspond to the flame action or the appearance of smoke or lack of it. If or when you encounter such strange results, be aware that you are probably dealing with a blend and may not be able to determine exactly what type of fibers your carpet is made from. (Again, as long as the fibers are synthetics or a synthetic/natural blend, it will not make a difference in how you treat a spot.)

13. Write down the carpet location and yarn content(s) for future reference. (See the **Hint** below.)

14. Repeat the test for each carpet yarn sample you have collected.

**Hint:** There is a form called the "New Carpet Purchase / Installation Form" in Section III at the end of "Chapter 6. How Does One Carpet Fiber Compare To Another?". Make enough copies so there is one for each type of carpet you have. Fill out as much information as you can. Put the forms where you can easily find them, the information will be readily available when you need it.

# Fiber Identification Chart

| Burn Test Characteristics | | | | | | |
|---|---|---|---|---|---|---|
| **Fiber** | Nylon | Olefin | Polyester | Acrylic | Wool | Cotton |
| **Flame Characteristics** | | | | | | |
| **Color** | Blue base, Orange tip | Blue base, Orange tip | Orange | Orange | Orange | Orange |
| **Action** | Even | Rapid, Even | Sputters | Sputters | Sputters Out | Even |
| **Smoke** | None | None | Dense Black | Black | None | None (Ember only) |
| **Odor Characteristics** | | | | | | |
| **Smell** | Celery | Asphalt | Sweet, Fruity | Burned Meat | Burned Hair | Burned Paper |
| **Ash Characteristics** | | | | | | |
| **Luster** | Shiny | Shiny | Shiny | Dull | Dull | Dull |
| **Shape** | Round | Round to Oval | Round | Irregular, Crusty | Irregular | Slender |
| **Color** | Tan to Black | Tan to Brown | Jet Black | Dull Black | Gray-Black | Light to Dark Gray |
| **Hardness** | Hard | Hard | Hard | Crumbles, Hard Nub | Crumbles to a Coarse Powder | Crumbles to a Soft, Very Fine Powder |

Section I

# Synthetic Fiber Spotting / Staining Characteristics

No matter what type of synthetic fiber or synthetic/natural fiber blend in your carpet, the spot treatment steps will be the same; but, each type of synthetic fiber has its own characteristics that determine how it reacts to spot causing substances (and how it responds to the cleaning agents as well).

The type of fiber helps determine how effectively the treatment will remove the spot, and influences the probability of recurring spot problems.

## *Nylon Spotting / Staining Characteristics*

As mentioned earlier, there are two types of nylon fibers:

- **Type 6** (which we will refer to as **"regular" nylon**) - This is the original nylon, developed in 1938. "Regular" nylon is easily dyed when the color is applied to the fibers after they have been made. This is because the fibers have "dye sites", which are positively charged surface areas. Negatively charged dyes adhere to the sites when the two come in contact. Unfortunately, these dye sites also make "regular" nylon easier to stain, bleach, wear and fade than the other type of nylon - type 6,6.

- **Type 6,6** (which is also referred to as **"solution dyed"**) - This type of nylon was developed later and has some important differences from the original. The main one is that it is always solution dyed. The dye pigment is mixed with the hot liquid polymer and is literally put inside the fiber - just like olefin, polyester and acrylic. This makes it more difficult to stain, bleach, wear or fade than "regular" nylon. **Note:** If you have "solution dyed" nylon carpet in one room of your home or business, you may find that certain spills are easily removed, while in another room with "regular" nylon carpet, the same type of spill is difficult to impossible to treat successfully.

How nylon carpet reacts to different spots may or may not be affected by whether it is type 6, "regular" nylon or type 6,6 "solution dyed":

- Most major manufacturers use various soil/stain-resist or repellent protective coatings on both types of nylon fibers. These coatings, which are used on their higher quality carpets, are bonded to the nylon fibers or applied during the carpet manufacturing process. The coatings slow down the absorption of spills by the nylon fibers, but they do not prevent it. (Even though "solution dyed" nylon is already resistant to many types of stains and the coating further enhances its stain resistance and durability, it too can be stained by some spills if they are left on the carpet long enough.)

**Note:** These stain-resist or repellent coatings are not permanent and will wear off over time. The freshly cleaned carpet will usually need to be treated with protector by its 3rd year of use if you want to keep the stain resistant quality.) (See "Chapter 9. Does My Carpet Need A Carpet Protector After Cleaning?" in Section III for more information on carpet protectors.

- Varies in its resistance to acid dyes:

  - "Regular" (type 6 nylon) is easily stained by spills that contain acid dyes such as the kind in fruit juices, wine, Kool-Aid®, etc., especially if your carpet does not have carpet protector applied.

  - "Solution dyed" (type 6,6) resists stains by spills containing the acid dyes listed above, even when the carpet protector begins to wear off.

- Is mildly "oleophilic" or oil loving, especially with petroleum-based products such as engine lubricants, tar, asphalt, etc. These types of spots may become permanent and cause the fibers to yellow if the petroleum-based spot is left on the carpet for prolonged periods of many months. (Problem areas may include traffic areas coming from a home garage, auto repair shop bays or a parking lot.)

- Generally resists most other spot contaminants such as cooking oils, greases, tea, coffee or cola. ("Solution dyed" nylon has an even greater resistance than "regular" nylon.) These spots are removed with little effort when treated within a reasonable amount of time using the proper technique and type / quantity of chemical spotting agents.

- Will yellow with prolonged exposure to chlorine bleach. But, "solution dyed" nylon will not lose its color easily when exposed to chlorine bleach, because the color is inside the fiber. Unfortunately, the carpet color in "regular" nylon is usually removed instantly.

- Resists strong solvents such as acetone and paint thinner, acids found in white vinegar, alkalines in liquid soaps and a variety of cleaning chemicals. (Unfortunately, the dye on the type 6, "regular" nylon fibers may not be so resistant.)

- Dissolves in the presence of formic acid, but unless you have a chemistry lab or a colony of ants (whose bite produces formic acid) in the house, this is an unlikely problem.

## Olefin Spotting / Staining Characteristics

Olefin is always solution-dyed. The dye pigment is mixed with the hot liquid polymer and is literally put inside the carpet fiber where it cannot be contacted by bleaches. This makes it extremely colorfast.

**Olefin:**

- Does not have "dye sites" like "regular" nylon. This makes it almost impossible to stain or discolor.

- In rare instances, coloring from very hot or boiling liquids like coffee can permeate olefin fibers. This creates a difficult to remove problem.

- In rare instances, products with strong concentrations of Benzoil Peroxide like acne medicines can penetrate olefin and discolor the dye pigment within the fibers, if not discovered quickly and removed. This is an irreversible problem.

- Is very "oleophilic" or oil loving, especially with petroleum-based products such as engine lubricants, tar, asphalt, etc. These types of spots may become permanent and cause the fibers to yellow if the petroleum-based spot is left on the carpet for prolonged periods of many months. (Problem areas may include traffic areas coming from a home garage, auto repair shop bays or a parking lot.)

- Is resistant to strong alkalines or bleaches or any other types of household cleaners you are likely to use near the carpet.

- Is the most heat sensitive of the synthetics. (If you have olefin carpet with candle or other wax spots, you will appreciate how my suggested removal method eliminates the potential carpet fiber melting that sometimes occurs when you try to heat the wax with a hot iron.)

## *Polyester Spotting / Staining Characteristics*

Polyester is normally dyed with "disperse" dyes. A disperse dye is one that distributes evenly within the carpet filament itself rather than being on the outside. This makes polyester fibers very colorfast.

**Polyester:**

• Is excellent in terms of spot and stain removal.

• May be stained by organic dyes such as coffee, cola drinks, beer and the yellow dye (turmeric) in mustard, herbal tea, soup mixes, etc.

• In rare instances, products with strong concentrations of Benzoil Peroxide like acne medicines can penetrate polyester and discolor the dye pigment within the fibers if not discovered and removed quickly. This is an irreversible problem.

• Is moderately "oleophilic" or oil loving like olefin, especially with petroleum-based products such as engine lubricants, tar, asphalt, etc. These types of spots may become permanent and cause the fibers to yellow if the petroleum-based product is left on the carpet for prolonged periods of many months. (Problem areas may include traffic areas coming from a home garage, auto repair shop or a parking lot.)

• Is difficult to stain with spills containing acid dyes. (Most foods and beverages contain acid dyes).

• Resists most household cleaners you are likely to use, including strong alkalines such as floor stripper or oven cleaner, and most chlorine and hydrogen peroxide bleaches.

- 11 -

*Art's Ultimate Spot Cleaning • **Chapter 1 - Page 11***

## *Acrylic Spotting / Staining Characteristics*

Acrylic is always solution-dyed. The dye pigment is mixed with the hot liquid polymer and is literally put inside the carpet fiber where it cannot be contacted by bleaches. This makes it extremely colorfast.

**Acrylic:**

• Does not have "dye sites" like "regular" nylon so it is almost impossible to stain or discolor.

• Is very resistant to staining.

• In rare instances, products with strong concentrations of Benzoil Peroxide like acne medicines can penetrate acrylic and discolor the dye pigment within the fibers, if not discovered and removed quickly. This is an irreversible problem.

• Very resistant to most household cleaners you are likely to use, including strong alkalines such as floor stripper or oven cleaner, and most chlorine and hydrogen peroxide bleaches.

## *Blends Spotting / Staining Characteristics*

Depending on the combination of fibers and the type of spill, blends may or may not play a role in your successful spot removal efforts. They are worth mentioning, though, because blends can produce some curious spot removal results. Example: If you have a "regular" type 6 nylon/acrylic blend carpet, you may notice that after working on a stain such as fruit juice containing acid dye, a portion of the yarn cleaned up just fine, while the other portion is still stained.

**Hint:** If staining persists on a portion of the blended fibers after home treatment has been exhausted, calling a pro may be your only viable option.

**Caution: Do not attempt to treat the spot using stronger or different products from those listed in this guide.** Other treatments, including several popular off-the-shelf spotters, could damage or discolor one or both of the blended fibers, especially if one is a natural fiber.

## *Natural Fiber Spotting / Staining Characteristics*

(See "Chapter 6. How Does One Carpet Fiber Compare To Another?" in Section III for information on how 100% wool and cotton yarns are affected by various type of spills.)

# *Chapter 2* **Your Spotting Kit**

## *Introduction*

In this Chapter I will show you the tools, equipment and chemicals (also called "spotting agents" or "spotters") needed for doing effective spot removal at home. This includes the most valuable spot removal tool you can have - a spot machine.

We will briefly look at how to use these tools and spotters to do your spot treatments in the easiest, safest and most efficient manner. (Specific instructions about which tool and/or spotter to use, and when and how to use them, are in the treatment instructions for each type of spot in Chapter 5 in Section II.)

Fortunately for your wallet, you already have many of these tools and spotting agents lying around. Before you buy new ones, first look around the house and garage.

**Caution:** There are many "professional" spotting kits available from commercial sources. While they may look impressive, they are not usually a good investment for the lay person. *"Why?"* you ask, since they have such fine advertising or strong "professional" recommendations. There are several reasons, but the main ones in my experience are:

• Most kits are incomplete and do not contain any tools or information about what equipment is needed to do safe and effective spot and stain removal.

   Since the type of tools and the way they are used in the spotting process has as much to do with the effectiveness of the treatment as the chemicals themselves, this omission may doom you to failure from the start.

• They can contain chemicals that require extensive instruction on 1) the safe, proper way to use them, 2) when not to use them, or 3) how much of them to use if you are to avoid problems. You may also need to practice specific safety precautions when using them, but unfortunately, this information is not always included with the kit.

(As I will say several times throughout this guide, safety is a main consideration in my work. If critical information on the proper way to use their chemicals is missing or incomplete, then I don't think the producers of these kits have done their best to protect you, the user, or given you the information you need to do the most effective spot treatment.)

Section I

— 2 —

# *Putting Together Your Spotting Kit*

Your spot treatment will be easier if you have a spotting kit that contains all the tools, equipment and spotting agents in one place, ready to use at a moment's notice. **An effective spotting kit contains the following:**

## *Tools / Equipment*

- **1 Ruler** - 6 or 12 inch plastic ruler.

- **2 Plastic mop buckets** - 1 - 2 gallon size with handles.

- **4 Trigger spray bottles** - Plastic, 8 - 12 ounce size; must be high quality; have an adjustable spray tip that will spray both a mist and a stream and can be twisted completely closed.

- **1 Metal spoon** - Needs a sturdy handle; can be a table or serving spoon - no smaller or larger.

- **1 Hard cushion hair brush** - Bristles are stiff and tips are usually coated with plastic nodules; bristles are spaced apart with large gaps between them.

- **1 Soft cushion hair brush** - Bristles are soft, numerous and do not have nodules on the bristle tips.

- **1 Metal dinner knife** - Should be the type of knife used for buttering bread or cutting softer foods - not a steak knife, no little teeth on the cutting edge.

- **1 Pair scissors**

  - Option 1: Professional duck-bill shears (carpet spotting scissors) - Recommended if you can get them; usually available at a commercial carpet supply store.

  - Option 2: Regular type scissors - Small pair no longer than 5 to 6 inches in overall length; are all metal, extra heavy duty; have short stubby blades that are clean, sharp; absolutely no play between the blades when they are closed.

- **1 Pair of rubber gloves** - Heavy duty dishwashing type.

- **Viscose rayon chamois** - A synthetic chamois like the ones used for car care or household cleaning.

- **Cotton towels** - An assortment of washcloths and hand-sized cotton towels (a small bath towel or two can be useful for very large spills); thick, white color preferred; can be used towels in good condition.

- **Vacuum cleaner** - A regular upright vacuum cleaner with a flexible extension hose (or cleaning wand) to vacuum spot debris.

**Optional, but strongly recommended as the tool that will do more than any other to make your spot removal efficient and effective:**

- **Spot machine (power spotter or deep cleaner)** - Needs these features: small, hand-held size; a clean water tank and a dirty water recovery tank; a flexible vacuum and solution hose; a carpet/upholstery cleaning/rinsing attachment **Note:** For reasons described in detail on page 11 under "Spot Machine", this is the most valuable item in your spotting kit.

## *Miscellaneous Items*

The following household items are only used for treating specific spots, so they are not part of your regular spotting kit. (The Materials Needed information in the spot treatment instructions in Chapter 5 in Section II will tell you when you need these special items.)

These miscellaneous items include:

- **Disposable towels or tissues** - Paper towels for spots such as candle wax or varnish. Facial, toilet or other flushable tissue for removing nasty spots such as feces.

- **Shop Vacuum** - Borrow it from the garage as needed.

- **Broom and Dust Pan** - Borrow them from the broom closet.

- **Protective Mask and Eye Wear** - Optional, extra protection along with your gloves, when you are treating spots like blood or feces.

- **Pair of Pliers** - Regular tool kit pliers.

- **Hair Dryer** - Needs a HIGH heat and HIGH fan setting.

## *Spotting Agents*

- **Isopropyl Alcohol - 70% (rubbing alcohol)** - The type you buy at the pharmacy or grocery store, used full strength.

- **Ammonia** - Plain, unscented, uncolored, type; if available, diluted 1 part ammonia to 3 parts water.

- **Hydrogen Peroxide 3% $H_2O_2$ U.S.P.** - The type you buy at the pharmacy or grocery store used full strength.
  **Caution:** The 6% kind from the beauty supply store is too strong.

### *Miscellaneous Spotting Agents*

The following household products are used in the treatment of specific spots so they are not part of your regular spotting kit. (The Materials Needed information in the spot treatment instructions in Chapter 5 Section II will tell you when you need these special items.)

These miscellaneous spotting agents include:

• **WD-40 with red spray tube** - used for removing chewing gum.

• **Undiluted lemon juice from concentrate (not fresh)** - used for treating rust spots.

More information on the tools, equipment and spotting agents and a brief description of how they are used follows.

## *Tools and Equipment - Detailed Descriptions*

**Caution:** After using your tools to remove a spot, it is important to clean, rinse and dry them before putting them away. Old spot matter can be hard to remove from the tools later. Plus, you don't want to attack a spot, only to find your tools are dirty and could make the problem worse by adding a new contaminant to the carpet.

**Hint:** After spotting is complete, always take your dirty tools to the sink and clean them with the same spotting agents used to treat the spots on the carpet.

**As I promised earlier in this Chapter, the following are more detailed descriptions of the spotting tools and equipment:**

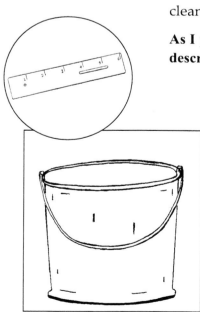

### Ruler

A 6 or 12 inch plastic ruler for measuring the diameter of the spot (or spots) to determine if you can successfully treat it is the first tool needed for most spot treatments. The ruler's size is not as important as the fact that it is made of plastic and can be thoroughly cleaned if it comes in contact with the spot while you are measuring.

### Plastic Mop Buckets With Handles

2 plastic mop buckets (1 - 2 gallon size) of the same size and shape with handles help you stay organized and keep dirty towels or debris from re-contaminating the carpet. These buckets can be bought at a local discount store for about $1.99 to $2.99 each.

- The first bucket (the "Tools" bucket) is used to hold all the spotting tools and spotting agents in your kit. This easy-to-grab unit can be easily stored away from children and pets. Put this bucket into the second one so they are together when you need your spotting kit.

- The second bucket (the "Contaminates" bucket) is used to hold dirty or wet towels or spot debris you remove from the carpet during the spotting process. Remember to clean and dry the contaminated bucket after each use.

**Trigger Spray Bottles**

Four (4) high quality, plastic trigger spray bottles (8 - 12 ounce size) with adjustable tips that can be twisted to produce a mist or a stream or to close completely are your next tools. The spray bottles, filled with your spotters, will enable you to efficiently treat spots where precision application of spotting agents is required.

- Three of the bottles are used to hold spotting agents. **Hint:** Label each spray bottle with its spotting agent (alcohol, ammonia, peroxide) and always refill with the same solution. If in doubt, thoroughly rinse the bottle and trigger sprayer with water; then refill with the correct solution.

- The fourth bottle is used as a spare. **Hint:** As soon as you need the spare bottle, buy a new spare. The sprayer usually wears out first, and it seems once the sprayer on one bottle stops working, the others will soon stop also.

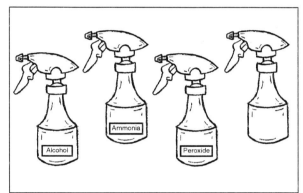

- The bottles need an adjustable tip that can be twisted to the OFF position or twisted so it will spray a mist (not just a stream) of spotting agent.

  - When you are not using the spotting agent, being able to close the tip will slow down the evaporation and loss of effectiveness of your spotting agents.

  - When you are applying a spotting agent, you will adjust the spray to the mist setting. This allows you to apply the spotting agent uniformly and in lesser amounts to minimize the risk of over-wetting or forcing the spot material further into the carpet.

Good spray bottles can be bought in a discount store in the cleaning or lawn and garden sections for between $1.00 and $1.50 each.

**Cautions:**
- Never leave filled spray bottles unattended where small children or pets can get to them. Twist the tips to the OFF position and put the spray bottles back in the bottom of the plastic bucket after spotting is completed.

- Occasionally check to make sure the sprayers are screwed tightly to the bottles.

Section I

## Metal Spoon

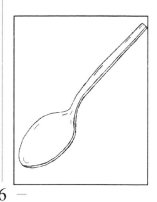

A metal serving or tablespoon with a sturdy handle that does not bend easily is a multipurpose tool. (A smaller or larger sized spoon is not as useful or easy to use.) The spoon can shovel or scoop up spills such as pancake batter, pieces of wet food or other chunks of wet or dry spot matter. It can also scrape out candle wax or be used as a hammering tool for breaking up hardened mud, candy or even hardened concrete. The spoon handle may be used to agitate spotting agents into tiny spots too small for other tools to work properly.

Generally, the cost is little or nothing if you have an extra spoon or can buy one at a thrift shop or garage sale.

— 6 —

## Hair Brush - Hard Cushion

The first type of hair brush in your kit is called a "hard cushion" brush. It has stiff bristles that are spaced far apart. The tips of the bristles are usually coated with plastic nodules. (If these nodules are missing from an old or new brush, do not worry. It is the stiffness of the bristles that is important.)

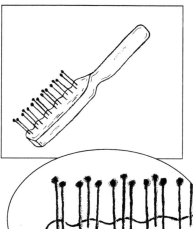

This brush is used to break up spots like dry mud, vomit or any other dried or crusty spot matter prior to applying a spotting agent. It is also used to agitate (a brushing action) a spot after a spotting agent has been applied. The agitation helps physically break up tough spots so the spotting agent (alcohol, ammonia or hydrogen peroxide) can better penetrate the spot material. It also speeds up the chemical reaction that further breaks down the spot.

A new hard cushion hair brush costs about $2.00 at the discount store if you don't already have an old brush at home.

## Hair Brush - Soft Cushion

The second type of hair brush is called a "soft cushion" brush. It has many soft bristles, spaced close together. This type of brush does not have plastic nodules on the bristle tips.

The soft brush is mostly used for tamping (a hammering action) the spot area after the spotting agents have been applied to help them better penetrate and to speed up the chemical process.

A new soft cushion hair brush also costs about $2.00 at the discount store if you have to buy one.

## Metal Dinner Knife

The type of knife in your spotting kit is the kind used for buttering bread or Sunday morning muffins or for cutting softer foods. It is not a steak knife and it is better if it does not have the little teeth on the cutting edge. (You have to be very careful when using a knife with the little teeth because they can fray the carpet fibers.)

Your dinner knife can be used to gently scrape spots like crayon or dried, raw egg off the carpet surface so you don't have to use as much spotting agent or time for treatment. It can also be used to cut and section spots like candle wax. This makes removing the rest of the spot with another tool easier. The knife is also used to break up spots like dried, crusty detergent spills so you can vacuum up much of the spot matter.

If you don't have an old dinner knife lying around, a new one can be bought for about a dollar or less.

Section I

### Scissors

Scissors are used to snip off tiny dried nail polish drips or ink spots off the ends of the carpet fibers. They are also used to poke holes in dried bubble gum to allow the spotting agent to get underneath the gum to make it easier to remove. There are two types of scissors that will work:

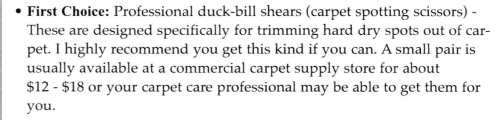

- **First Choice:** Professional duck-bill shears (carpet spotting scissors) - These are designed specifically for trimming hard dry spots out of carpet. I highly recommend you get this kind if you can. A small pair is usually available at a commercial carpet supply store for about $12 - $18 or your carpet care professional may be able to get them for you.

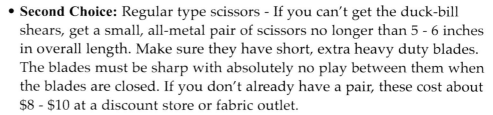

- **Second Choice:** Regular type scissors - If you can't get the duck-bill shears, get a small, all-metal pair of scissors no longer than 5 - 6 inches in overall length. Make sure they have short, extra heavy duty blades. The blades must be sharp with absolutely no play between them when the blades are closed. If you don't already have a pair, these cost about $8 - $10 at a discount store or fabric outlet.

**Hint:** Your scissor blades must be absolutely clean. Otherwise, the carpet yarns will stick to the scissors and you won't get a clean cut or spot matter may transfer from the blades to the carpet. Keep your scissors dry and rust-free by placing them in a dry towel at the top of your spotting kit bucket after each use. Lubricate them with WD-40 from time to time and wipe off any excess. Also have them professionally sharpened when they become dull.

### Rubber Gloves

In my carpet cleaning business, several things have always been important to me - satisfied customers and the safety and health of my customers, my employees and myself. A good pair of heavy duty, dish washing type rubber gloves keeps your hands from making contact with the carpet contaminants you are trying to remove. This is especially important when you are removing feces or blood or other bodily fluids that can be full of bacteria and other pathogens.

Rubber gloves cost about $2.97 - $3.97 at any discount or grocery store. Before you buy, ask a store person if you can try them on so you can be sure to get a snug, correctly fitting pair.

**Hint:** If you are in the middle of a spot treatment (especially a nasty one) and the phone rings or the kids start calling you from another part of the house, pull the top of each glove down over the hand and fingers so the gloves are nearly turned inside out and the fingers are completely covered by the top three-fourths of the glove. Carefully pinch and gently pull the end of each finger slightly to loosen the glove. Then grasp the end of the fingers through the glove and finish pulling it off.

Put the gloves in the extra bucket and go handle the emergency or the phone. Your hands will be clean and you will not cross contaminate other people or items in the house or office by touching them with dirty hands. When you are ready to resume spotting, carefully put the gloves back on, pull the tops of the gloves back up your arms and continue the treatment.

**Hint:** When you are finished using them, wash and thoroughly dry your gloves while they are still on your hands. Turn them inside out to ensure they dry on the inside as well.

### Viscose Rayon Chamois

The new-high tech synthetic viscose rayon chamois is an extremely useful tool, especially when you're treating large liquid spills. A chamois can absorb up to 20 times its weight or more in liquid, which makes it far more absorbent than several cotton towels. It can draw out liquid spots and stains that have penetrated into the carpet pile, almost as if the spots or stains had been vacuumed out.

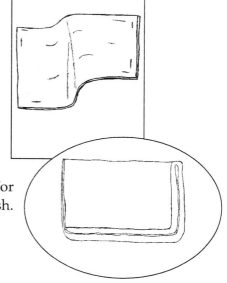

In addition, this durable, washable tool only costs about $7.00 for a good sized sheet that can be cut into smaller pieces if you wish.

(For more information on how to purchase this very useful product, visit our Web site at: www.artsspotcleaning.com)

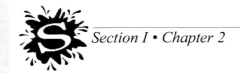
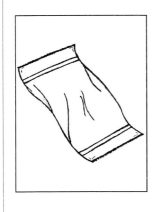

**Cotton Towels**

Cotton towels are one of the most versatile tools in your spotting kit. You need a variety of sizes including several wash cloths and hand towels and possibly a small bath towel or two. A wash cloth can be placed over the palm of your hand to collect spot debris as you scrape them from the carpet. It can also be used to treat a minor spot. A hand towel can be folded several times and then pressed over a spot to absorb liquid spills. A large bath towel is handy when you have a very large spill. The towels are also used to cover and protect a spot or keep it in check until a professional arrives.

The spotting towels should be white or at least faded enough so that coloring from the spot can easily be distinguished from the towel's color when you are blotting a spot. If the towels are used ones, they should be thick, sturdy and not falling apart. If the towels are new, they should be washed and dried at least once to eliminate the lint that may transfer to the carpet.

**Vacuum Cleaner**

An ordinary upright vacuum cleaner is also part of your spotting kit whether you have a spot machine or not.
The vacuum must have a:

- Flexible extension hose or cleaning wand, and

- Rotating brush (also called a "beater bar" brush) in the opening underneath the vacuum.

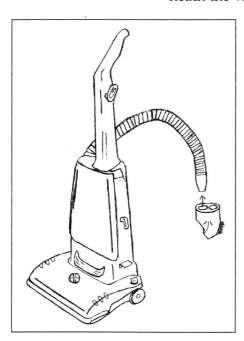

If you don't have a spot machine, the hose or cleaning wand is used to suck up dry spot debris as you loosen the spot from the carpet fibers. After the initial vacuuming with the hose or wand, the rotating brush may be used to vibrate additional debris loose from the carpet face fibers. **Caution:** The rotating brush should **not** be used unless you are specifically told to do so in the spot treatment instructions. The brush can smear wet or semi-wet spots and cause dry, fine particle spots to sift deeper into the carpet.

If you have a spot machine, the vacuum cleaner is used for initial removal of large, dry, powdery spills (like detergent, salt or baby powder) or small spills of soot or ashes.

**Caution:** This type of vacuum cleaner (called a "dry system") should **never** be used to vacuum wet or greasy spots or spotting agents from the carpet. Unless the spot matter is completely dry and not sticky, the debris could clog the vacuum hose.

**Best Practice:** Read the instructions for each spot carefully before starting your spotting. They will tell you exactly when and how to use your vacuum cleaner during spot treatment. Normally, you will use just the end of the vacuum cleaner hose with the attachment removed.

**Caution:** Some fine powder spills such as copier toner can be forced further into the carpet fibers if you start your vacuuming with the rotating beater bar brush. (Check your vacuum cleaner's instructions to see if you can temporarily disable the beater bar when treating these fine powder types of spots.)

You can buy a good vacuum cleaner with everything needed for spot treatments and routine carpet maintenance for $150.00 to $300.00. This vacuum will work as well or better than some costing five to seven times that much. The important things to look for are:

- 12 amp motor

- HEPA filter or some sort of microfiltration bag or both

- Flexible extension hose that is long enough that the vacuum won't topple over on you when you are using it on a spot

- Electrical cord that is at least 25 feet long so you don't have to keep moving the vacuum cleaner plug to a new electrical outlet when doing regular vacuuming

**Spot Machine - the # 1 most valuable tool in your spotting kit**

A spot machine, or "spotting" machine, "power spotter" or "deep cleaner" as it is sometimes called, is the single most valuable tool in your kit. A spot machine is the most effective and efficient way to remove spots and stains. You will be able to clean up a broader range of spots and stains, and it will make it possible for you to remove larger spots as well. (Plus, your higher success rate at spot removal with the spot machine will mean that you don't have to call a professional as often.)

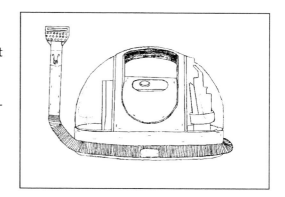

**A spot machine increases your effectiveness because:**

• You can vacuum up larger fresh liquid spills, thus possibly avoiding penetration into the carpet backing or pad;

• Fresh spots like beer, coffee and soft drinks can often be flushed and extracted using water only or with minimal spotting agents;

• Dried spots can be pre-softened and spotting agent cleaning action can be accelerated by the rinse water temperature;

• Even after the spot material has been blotted, scraped, vacuumed, treated and agitated, the job isn't done until anything that remains of the spot has been rinsed and the spot residue extracted. A spot machine can do this easily and effectively.

**Not having a spot machine limits the size and type of spots you can successfully treat at home.** This is because spot removal without the machine is not as effective. A chamois or towel cannot flush out and extract spot materials. Even the viscose rayon chamois, which can absorb many times what a towel can, is not able to remove as much liquid as the spot machine. The chamois or towel is also not able to remove more solid spot matter as effectively as the spot machine.

Your spot machine should be simple, yet versatile enough to do the job it was designed for - rinsing and extracting. It needs to have these features: A small, hand-held size makes it easier to transport to the spot area; a clean water tank where you put only fresh, clean water and nothing else (unless told to do so in the spot removal instructions in Chapter 5 in Section II of this guide); a dirty water recovery tank where the extracted contaminants are stored until dumped; a flexible vacuum and solution hose; and a carpet/upholstery cleaning/rinsing attachment.

**Caution:** If you need to buy a spot machine, make sure that it has the features listed above. There are some machines that look like glorified dust busters that do not have a hose or the vacuum or rinse power adequate to spot clean carpet.

A quality spot machine can be purchased at a local discount store for about $70.00 to $120.00 depending on how many added bells and whistles you want. My best advice, however, is to keep it simple, and therefore as inexpensive as possible. (As I mentioned earlier in this guide, having a professional come to your home or office to remove a single spot is $50.00 to $70.00 and up, depending on the difficulty of removal. Being able to avoid a couple of calls to the professional by using this machine and the instructions in this guide should come very close to paying for it and a small spotting machine.)

## *Miscellaneous Items*

In addition to the essential tools and equipment mentioned earlier, treating specific spots may require one or more of the following household items:

- **Disposable Towels or Tissues**

  **Paper towels:** These are better for removing nasty spots where you want to throw away the towel rather than wash it. Disposable towels are better than cloth ones for spots such as varnish or candle wax. Varnish will ruin the towel, and wax on a cloth towel could contaminate other articles in your washer or dryer when you clean it.

  **Facial or toilet tissue:** Facial or toilet tissue may be your first choice for the initial removal of those really nasty spots such as feces where you want to flush the evidence rather than throw it in the trash can. Make sure you have lots of tissues available to contain the spot matter as you remove it.

- **Shop Vacuum (or Wet-Dry Shop Vac)** - If you don't have a spot machine or an upright vacuum cleaner, a wet-dry shop vac can be used instead for vacuuming any size of dry spot debris and for dry vacuuming up large liquid spills. A shop vac, if you have one, is also a safer choice when treating spots such as fresh cottage cheese or raw or soft-cooked eggs that could clog the hose of a regular vacuum cleaner.

- **Broom and Dust Pan** - Very large spills of dry powders such as detergents or flour, are easier to remove if you first get up as much as possible with a broom and dust pan.

- **Protective Mask and Eye Wear** - Because spots like feces contain large quantities of bacteria and other pathogens, you may choose to wear your gloves and other protective gear when removing these contaminants.

- **Pair of Pliers** - A regular pair of pliers works well when you have spots such as dry blobs of concrete that may be too hard to break up using only your knife or spoon.

- **Hair Dryer** - Spots like wax must be melted in order to be removed. A hair dryer with a HIGH HEAT / HIGH SPEED setting is a much safer way to soften the wax than using an iron and a piece of paper as is so often suggested.

Using the hair dryer lets you melt the wax gradually and you can both see and blot the wax as it melts. The slower melting makes it less likely that the oil and dye in the wax will separate and penetrate the carpet fibers, making an even bigger mess. The hair dryer method also avoids the danger of burns to the person treating the spot, curious children or pets. And, it prevents the melted carpet that happens when you get the iron too hot or too close. (Even if you are one of the few people who has used the iron/paper method successfully, I urge you to try the hair dryer method instead.)

Section I

## Spotting Agents - Detailed Descriptions

The new generation of spotting techniques described in this guide are used in conjunction with three very basic chemicals or spotting agents. These recommended spotting agents are inexpensive products you probably already have in your medicine cabinet or under the kitchen sink, but they are a very important part of efficient and successful spot treatment. (Spotting agents are also called "spot cleaning agents", "spot cleaning solutions", "spot cleaners" or "spotters".)

**The primary spotting agents you will be using on synthetic or synthetic/natural blend carpet fibers are:**

— 14 —

- **Isopropyl Alcohol - 70% (also known as rubbing alcohol) - full strength**

- **Ammonia (clear, unscented, if available) - diluted**

- **Hydrogen Peroxide 3% - full strength**

Isopropyl alcohol, ammonia and hydrogen peroxide have many positive attributes and no negative ones when diluted, if needed, and applied as recommended. These include:

- They are available in all grocery and large discount stores.

- They are cheaper to buy and they work as well or better than 99% of all popular brand-name spot cleaners on the market.

- They require little or no mixing and are easy to use.

- They are self-neutralizing and do not leave strong pH levels behind that can damage carpet fiber or the carpet dye (like many off-the-shelf spotters).

- They completely evaporate and leave no residue that can cause re-soiling of the carpet (like many off-the-shelf spotters).

- They do not need to be rinsed out of the carpet. (When the spot treatment instructions tell you to rinse the spot with your spot machine, it is because there is spot matter that needs to be removed from the carpet, not because the spotting agents need to be rinsed away.)

- They readily destroy odor-causing bacteria.

- They combine safely and synergistically with each other to produce accelerated and enhanced results.

- **Unlike many of the brand name spot removers, they:**

  - **Will not set a spot (no matter what kind it is) when used as instructed;**

  - **Will not remove, discolor or move the carpet dye;**

  - **Will not make it more difficult for a pro to treat a spot if you are unable to completely remove it yourself.**

**Is it safe for the carpet and for the person doing the cleaning to use these chemicals together?** It is safe to use isopropyl alcohol, ammonia and hydrogen peroxide together on a spot.

- **Always follow the instructions exactly when treating a spot.** Use the spotters in the amounts and in the sequence described in the spot treatment pages in Chapter 5.

- Keep the spotters in **separate** spray bottles. Do **not** mix your spotting agents in the same bottle. It is safe, but it lessens their effectiveness at breaking down the spot if you do that.

- **Always read the labels. Use them as directed and do not mix them with other chemicals.**

  *"Why?"* you ask. Several years ago I was cleaning the carpets for a new customer who had just bought her first home. Because she wanted everything perfectly clean and disinfected, she decided to clean the very dirty vinyl floor in the laundry room with ammonia and chlorine bleach. (The labels on both products tell you **never** to do this because the gasses created when you mix these two are very dangerous.)

  She instantly began choking and gasping for breath. I realized what was happening and quickly carried her outdoors to fresh air and safety. The gas caused by the combination of the two chemicals can damage the lungs and possibly kill you. Fortunately, I was there and got her out right away so she was okay after a few minutes of fresh air. It may have been the first time a certified carpet cleaning specialist has literally saved someone's life. The lesson is: Remember to use chemicals together **only** as directed.

**How are these spotters used?**

These spotters are used in a variety of ways during your spot treatments. (When and how much of the spotting agents to use is described in detail in the instructions under the spot treatment steps in Chapter 5 in Section II.)

- A spotter may be used by itself for specific spots that require a specific type of cleaning action.

- Two spotters may be applied one right after the other so they combine on the spot to achieve a synergistic result.

- All three spotters may be applied in a specific sequence in order to break down the separate components of a particular drink or food or other type of "recipe" of ingredients.

**Caution:** Do **not** mix the spotting agents in one bottle in an attempt to simplify the treatment process. Each spotter works best on specific aspects of different types of spots and the order in which they are applied has a lot to do with how effectively they break down a spot.

### How do these spotting agents work?

For the chemists in the group, the three spotting agents work by providing one or more of these four categories of chemical action: Solvent - Alcohol, Self-neutralizing alkaline - Ammonia, Self-neutralizing acid and Oxygen action - Hydrogen Peroxide.

For the rest of us, just know that:

• They work very well both independently and in combination to chemically break down your spots.

• There is no danger in using these three chemicals together, as there are in mixing other household or professional chemicals.

• They do not have to be rinsed out of the carpet. (All rinsing done with the spot machine is to remove spot debris, including coloring - not to rinse out your spotting agents.)

• If you are unable to completely remove a spot, these chemicals will not "set" the spot as many of the off-the-shelf spot treatments can do if used on the wrong type of spot or used incorrectly. If you have to call a professional for help after using your alcohol, ammonia and/or peroxide, you will not have made the professional's job more difficult or even impossible because you used these three spotting agents. (Many off-the-shelf cleaners, including spot treatments and especially all-purpose cleaners and cleaners formulated to remove pet accidents, have a very high pH or alkaline level. This high alkaline level means that these products can weaken or fade carpet dyes or cause chemical reactions that may cause some spots to set.)

**In case you are curious:**

**What causes the off-the-shelf spotting agents that supposedly work on every kind of spot to be so prone to set spots rather than remove them?**

All of the following have the potential to cause the spot to set:

- The lack of instructions on the bottle telling you exactly how much to use on each spot means that you may be using much more chemical than is needed.

- You may be applying an alkaline when the spot you are treating really should be misted with an acid.

- The off-the-shelf spotter does not break certain spot materials down completely. It just thins the spot matter so it soaks further down into the carpet fibers rather than removing it.

## *Isopropyl Alcohol (Rubbing Alcohol) - 70% Solution*

Isopropyl Alcohol, also known as rubbing alcohol, is a "solvent" which means it begins the breakdown of spots that contain oil or grease.

### *Benefits / Attributes*

Isopropyl Alcohol is an excellent spotter, because it:

- Will totally evaporate after use.

- Does not have to be rinsed from the carpet fibers.

- Does not leave a residue behind to collect soil later.

- Is a solvent - neither alkaline nor acid - so it can be used with little concern for fiber shrinkage, dye bleeding, cellulosic browning, alkaline browning or carpet fiber damage. (See "Chapter 4. Identifying Your Spot, Stain Or Discoloration" for more information about cellulosic and alkaline browning.)

## Isopropyl Alcohol - cont.

### Uses

• Works very well at dissolving oil-based spots such as motor oil, some make-ups and fats.

• Lubricates and suspends certain types of particulate matter, such as carbon or pigment.

• Is an excellent disinfectant because it kills a wide variety of bacteria.

• Helps defoam residues left by soaps and detergents or the wrong types of spotting agents (including the ones that claim to "resolve" your spots and stains). This breakdown of the foam in the soapy residue is necessary so it can be removed from the carpet.

• When used with ammonia, it produces a highly synergistic cleaning action.

### Cautions

• Read the directions on the original container about safe and proper handling.

• Be careful when working with Isopropyl Alcohol on large spots near an open flame source like a gas oven, hot water heater or fireplace where a fire is burning. (Isopropyl Alcohol has a very low flash point or Vapor Ignition Point and will not catch fire easily, but it is better to avoid even the possibility.). It may be best to call a professional to remove spots that need Isopropyl Alcohol near these areas.

• Be careful about spotting in small or enclosed areas where there is poor ventilation that might cause breathing problems. Call a professional to remove spots that need Isopropyl Alcohol in these enclosed areas.

• Always fill your spotter spray bottles over the sink and be sure that all spotter bottle tops are properly tightened before use. Isopropyl Alcohol (like any other solvent) can weaken the latex in the carpet backing (or your synthetic throw rugs) if a large quantity of alcohol is spilled and allowed to soak into and remain in the carpet or rug.

**Hint:** If a spill does occur, place one of your cotton towels over the spill area and step on the towel with your full weight. Repeat 15 - 30 times using a clean part of the towel each time until no more absorbs. Or, dry vacuum the spill using your spot machine or shop vac. Then place a fan about 4 feet from the spill area and run it on the highest setting until the spot is dry.

## *Source*

Isopropyl Alcohol can be bought already premixed in solutions of 50%, 70% and/or 91% at any grocery store or pharmacy. I suggest that you use the 70% solution, but the others will also work well.

## *Mixing / Refilling*

- Do not dilute the Alcohol. Use it straight.

- Pour the alcohol into its own spray bottle (be sure to do this over the sink). Close the nozzle to avoid evaporation or spillage. Label the spray bottle.

- Always refill the Alcohol spotting bottle over the sink. Twist the nozzle completely closed.

## *Storage*

Put the alcohol spray bottle in the bottom of your spotting kit. Store it in an indoor environment out of the reach of children, pets and flames.

## *Before Using*

- Check the top to make sure it is properly tightened before each use to avoid spillage or evaporation.

- Always be sure the nozzle is properly adjusted to the mist setting by spraying a small amount into your sink, a towel or the extra bucket before you begin treating a spot.

## *Ammonia - Household*

Use the clear (whitish colored), unscented, ammonia made for household cleaning chores, if available. The yellow coloring in the lemon-scented may stain your carpet.

### *Benefits / Attributes*

Ammonia is an excellent spotter, because it:

- Is an alkaline that has the advantage of being "self-neutralizing". Self-neutralizing means that this spotting agent starts out as an alkaline, but as it dries, its pH returns to a neutral state, so it is neither alkaline nor acid.

- Will evaporate completely, when mixed as recommended, so it does not have to be rinsed from the carpet.

- Leaves no residue to degrade dyes or fibers like many off-the-shelf spotters.

- Leaves no residue to cause re-soiling of the treatment area.

- When diluted as I instruct you to do, it does not leave a smell in the carpet when it dries.

### *Uses*

- Neutralizes vinegar and stomach acids found in vomit due to its alkalinity.

- Removes urine stains if caught early. Unfortunately it does nothing about the carpet discoloration or loss of color often associated with old urine stains.

- Removes food spots, many proteins, ground-in soil, some dyes, some water soluble inks, magic marker and some cosmetics.

- Is an excellent disinfectant.

- Creates a synergistic cleaning action when combined with isopropyl alcohol or hydrogen peroxide.

## Cautions

- Read the directions on the original container about safe and proper handling. (Ammonia, used as I tell you to do it, is safe when handled properly. It can be very dangerous, however, if mixed with some other household chemicals.)

- Be careful about spotting in small or enclosed areas where there is poor ventilation that could cause breathing problems. Call a professional to remove spots that need ammonia in these areas.

## Source

Ammonia is readily available at the local grocery store.

## Mixing / Refilling

- Ammonia should be mixed in a ratio of 1 part ammonia to 3 parts tap water and no stronger. Examples:

  A. If your spray bottle is an 8 ounce size, you would mix 2 ounces of ammonia with 6 ounces of tap water. (Or, if you prefer, mix 1/4 cup of ammonia with 3/4 cup of tap water.)

  B. If the spray bottle is a 12 ounce size, you would mix 3 ounces of ammonia with 9 ounces of tap water. (Or, if you prefer, mix 3/8 cup of ammonia with 1-1/8 cups of tap water.)

- Mix the ammonia and water in its spray bottle in the sink. Close the nozzle to avoid spillage or evaporation. Label the spray bottle.

- Always refill the ammonia spotting bottle over the sink. Close the nozzle.

## Storage

Put the ammonia spray bottle in the bottom of your spotting kit. Store it in an indoor environment out of the reach of children and pets.

## Before Using

- Check the top to make sure it is properly tightened before each use to avoid spillage or evaporation.

- Always be sure the nozzle is properly adjusted to the mist setting by spraying a small amount into your sink, a towel or the extra bucket before you begin treating a spot.

Section I

— 22 —

## Hydrogen Peroxide (Labeled "Hydrogen Peroxide Solution - 3% H₂O₂ U.S.P.")

Hydrogen Peroxide is a clear, colorless, virtually odorless liquid. Peroxide really begins working as it begins evaporating. A spot treated with it is neutralized and often just "disappears".

### Benefits / Attributes

Peroxide is an excellent spotter because it:

- Is self-neutralizing. This spotting agent starts out slightly acidic; but as it dries, its pH returns to a neutral state, meaning it is neither acid nor alkaline.

- Will evaporate completely so it does not have to be rinsed from the carpet.

- Leaves no residue to cause re-soiling of the treatment area.

- Creates an accelerated release of oxygenating effect when used in combination with ammonia. This accelerated release makes your spot treatment faster, easier and more effective, because it requires less agitation and rinsing and removes more spot color.
  **Note:** Only use these two together when you are instructed to do so.

- Its spotting action is accelerated by heat. Putting hot or warm water in your spot machine as you are told to do for specific spots provides the heat that will increase peroxide's spotting action.

### Uses

By itself, peroxide:

- Works great on acid dyes found in jelly, grape juice, red wine, and organic dyes such as tannin found in coffee, tea and cola.

- Can also reduce the appearance of old, oxidized stains.

- May help neutralize the high alkalinity in some soaps because of its slight acidity. This neutralization will help decrease the potential of discoloration to your carpet dye.

- It works as well as any other oxygen product and it is much less expensive. (It also does not set the spot or affect the carpet dye.)

- Can help you determine if a recurring spot is caused by soil-collecting soap residue from the off-the-shelf spot treatment you may have used before you read this guide.

**Hint:** Spray some hydrogen peroxide on a recurring spot problem. Agitate it and then scoop up some of the residue with a spoon and watch to see if it foams. Peroxide's high oxygen content causes the soapy residue in poorly formulated spotting agents and other cleaners to foam up profusely. (If you do find that soapy residue is your problem, see the spot treatments "Detergents, Soaps and Cleaners - Liquid or Gel" and "Detergents, Soaps and Cleaners - Powder" in Chapter 5 for information on how remove the residue.)

Sugar in the makeup of a spot can also cause recurring spot problems. If spraying the hydrogen peroxide on the spot and agitating does not cause foaming, sugar may be the culprit. In that case, see the instructions for the types of spills containing sugar that most likely caused your spot.

- Does not work well on inorganic dyes found in Kool-Aid®, punch drinks or medicines. It will **not**, however, create any problems with these types of stains if mistakenly used on them and may help lessen the stain's appearance.

## Cautions

- Read the directions on the original container about safe and proper handling.

- Hydrogen Peroxide is also available from barber and beauty supply distributors in a 6% concentration. Do **not** use this stronger concentration for carpet spotting because it can weaken or break down carpet dyes.

## Source

Hydrogen Peroxide (labeled Hydrogen Peroxide Solution 3% $H_2O_2$ U.S.P.) is sold as an antiseptic in the first aid area of the health and beauty care section of any grocery store or pharmacy. It comes in a brown, non-transparent plastic bottle in a concentration of 3%.

## Mixing / Refilling

- No dilution with water is needed. Hydrogen Peroxide comes ready to use right off the shelf.

- When it is time to treat a spot, pour the peroxide into its own labeled spray bottle (be sure to do this over the sink). See "Storage" below for more information on handling hydrogen peroxide.

— 23 —

## Storage

- Put the peroxide spray bottle in your spotting kit. Store it in an indoor environment out of the reach of children and pets.

- The hydrogen peroxide bottle itself should be kept tightly closed and stored in a controlled room temperature of about 59° - 86°F / 15° - 30°C. Otherwise shelf life is reduced by exposure to sunlight and elevated temperature.

Hydrogen peroxide is loaded with oxygen and may lose that oxygen in a short time (2 - 3 months) if stored in a spray bottle at room temperature, even with the nozzle closed. To keep the oxygen from escaping, (thus extending the product life up to a year if you don't use it all before then), you can do one of the following:

- Fill your spray bottle with just enough peroxide to use for one spot treatment. If there is any peroxide left in the spray bottle after spotting, pour it back into the brown bottle and tighten the cap. Refill the spray bottle when needed for a spot treatment.

- Pour the entire contents of the peroxide bottle into the spray bottle and put the cap from the brown peroxide bottle onto the spray bottle. The cap should fit. Tighten the cap as tight as possible. (If you use this method, keep the peroxide from as much exposure to light as possible.) When you need to use the peroxide for spotting, replace the cap with the sprayer.

## Before Using

- Check the top to make sure it is properly tightened before each use to avoid spillage or evaporation.

- Always be sure the nozzle is properly adjusted to the mist setting by spraying a small amount into your sink, a towel or the extra bucket before you begin treating a spot.

## Miscellaneous Spotters

The following household items are used to help remove specific spots:

- **WD-40 with red spray tube** - Use WD-40 to help remove chewing gum. The treatment instructions for gum tell exactly how much to use and when and how to use it.

  **Note:** When using the WD-40, for each 1 inch diameter of spot, press the spray button 2 times for 1/2 second each time.

- **Bottled, undiluted lemon juice from concentrate** - Use the juice (without pulp) from a bottle, not the freshly squeezed juice, for treating rust spots. The treatment instructions for rust tell exactly how much to use and when and how to use it.

# *Please Be Safe!*

In closing out this chapter, I want to reemphasize that it is very important to never leave your spotting kit tools, equipment or spotting agents unattended at any time when small children or pets are present. If you have to leave your spotting mid-removal, move your spotting kit someplace out of reach until you return. After spotting is completed and the tools and equipment have been cleaned, store the kit in a designated area inside the home or business out of the reach of children or pets and away from open flames to ensure safety.

Illustration in Chapter 2 were created by Arthur D. Colo'n

# Chapter 3
# Spot Treatment Techniques

## Introduction

Successful carpet spot treatment requires the 5 "Rights":

1. Right tools

2. Right chemicals (spotting agents)

3. Right amounts

4. Right sequence

5. Right treatment techniques

In "Chapter 2. Your Spotting Kit", you learned about the tools and chemicals you'll use when treating a spot using my easy, effective methods. In "Chapter 5. Spot Treatment Instructions", detailed steps tell you exactly how and when each of the tools, chemicals and treatment techniques are needed for your particular spot.

In this Chapter, I'll describe my spot treatment techniques – the most effective ways to blot, rinse, scoop, scrape, vacuum, etc., using the different tools in your spotting kit. Both photographs and detailed instructions show you exactly how to do each treatment technique. (All of these techniques are very, very easy to do, but since I can't be with each of you to demonstrate, I want to be sure you have all the information you need.)

**Caution:** The off-the-shelf, one-size-fits-all spotters would have you believe that the chemical you use is the only thing that's important in a spot treatment. True, the spotting agent(s) you apply is/are important in treating a spill. But, the treatment techniques you use 1) before applying spotting agents and 2) throughout the rest of the process until the spill's been satisfactorily removed, are equally critical to your success.

### Keeping It Simple

I know, it may seem simpler to treat every kind of spot by just dumping that off-the-shelf chemical on the carpet and stirring it up a bit – instead of using specific application techniques tailored to the particular type of spot you're treating with your alcohol, ammonia and/or hydrogen peroxide spotters. However, what may seem simpler is not always the most effective way to treat a spot and the one-way-treats-all-spills may result in a permanent spot – not a removed one.

Section I

— 2 —

**The general rule is to keep spot removal simple by keeping the problem at the surface of the carpet yarns and not letting it penetrate further into the carpet.**

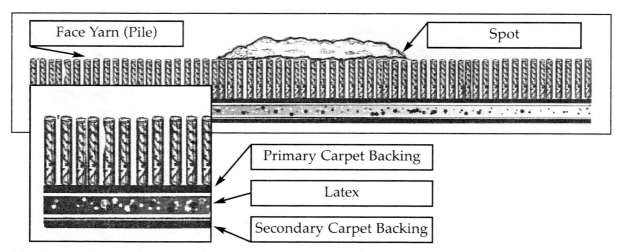

Face Yarn (Pile)

Spot

Primary Carpet Backing

Latex

Secondary Carpet Backing

You have a better chance of doing this by removing the spot gradually. This includes doing the least invasive procedures first before applying spotting agents. Scooping up, scraping out, vacuuming or blotting excess spot matter can lessen the possibility of its spreading or becoming absorbed into the carpet.

Examples: The step-by-step treatment instructions in this guide tell you to:

• Scrape or brush loose or dry debris; then dry vacuum.

• Scoop up pastry or soft debris; then blot with a dry cloth or wet vacuum with a spot machine.

• Blot liquid spills with an absorbent chamois or towel or dry vacuum with a spot machine.

• Trim out small spots of gummy or hard substances with scissors; then dry vacuum.

**Note:** Another benefit of doing these things before applying the spot removal agents is that it may not be necessary to use chemicals at all.

Example: Dry, Powdered Kool-Aid® – This will normally come right out when dry vacuumed first. If the spot is treated with a wet solution before vacuuming, the spot will spread and permanent staining could take place. What was a relatively easy-to-remove spot is transformed into a tough-to-remove stain simply by adding a little moisture.

The treatment techniques also allow you to use as little spotting agent as possible. Spotters must be applied in the recommended amounts and kept at the surface of the carpet. Rinsing, extracting and/or blotting between spotter applications gradually remove the spot and help avoid over-treatment.

**Caution:** Not doing the initial treatment techniques or continuing to apply more spotting agent than needed to speed things up will only cause further dispersion of the spot material over a larger area, deeper penetration of the spot into the carpet fibers, and/or saturation of the carpet backing – problems that are far worse than the one you started with. (The deeper the spot goes into the carpet, the more likely that it won't all be removed during treatment. The remaining spot material wicks up the carpet fibers and continues to reappear as a recurring spot.)

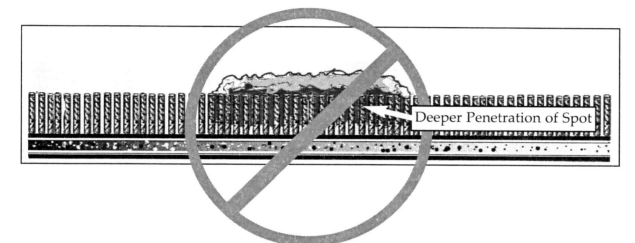

Deeper Penetration of Spot

Section I

## *List of Spot Treatment Techniques*

The following is a list of all the treatment techniques and the page numbers where you'll find them in this Chapter.

- The techniques are grouped under the name of the tool(s) they require.
  *Example:*

### <u>Spoon</u>

- If a technique uses more than one tool, it's listed under both tool names.

- The names of the techniques are based on what the treatment steps tell you to do.

  Example: The first treatment step for removing a butter or margarine spot says, "Using your spoon, scoop as much of the spot as possible onto the towel."

  The technique name is "Scoop Spot onto Towel Using Spoon"

**Don't Panic!**

Even though the list of techniques looks like a long one, **You Don't Have to Read or Use Most of Them!** This list has ALL the techniques you would use if you had to treat EVERY type of spot named in Chapter 5. Though it looks like a lot of information:

- Most homes and businesses tend to have a very small number of different types of spots. Most of their spot treatments are repeats of this small number of different spots. Example: You have a puppy so most of your spot treatments are for pet accidents – urine, feces or vomit.

- Most spot treatments only use 3 – 5 different techniques.

- You only need to look at any techniques you've not used before if you're treating a new type of spot.

- The techniques are so easy to do that when you've done one once, you probably won't need to read it again, unless you just want a little refresher. (You'll see just how easy when you look at the photos and read the descriptions.)

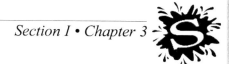

# List of Spot Treatment Techniques

5

## Scissors

## Spoon

## Spot Machine

## Spray Bottles - Spotting Agents

## Towel, Washcloth, Chamois

## Vacuum Cleaner / Wet/Dry Shop Vac

Section I

# Descriptions of Spotting Techniques

The following text and photos describe each of the spotting techniques specified in the spot treatment pages.

## Brush – Hard

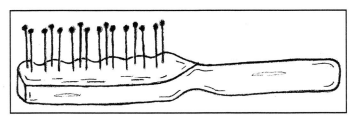

### Agitate Spot with Hard Brush

**Purpose:** To help spotting agents penetrate a dried or sticky spot, such as alcoholic beverages, by stirring the spot with the bristles of the hard brush after the agents have been applied.

**Step 1**                                         **Step 2**

**To do:**

1. Hold the hard brush by the handle with the bristles pointed down.

2. Slightly penetrate the spot with the bristles at the end of the brush. (If the spot is pencil eraser size or smaller, use only one or two groups of bristles at the end of the brush.)

3. Move the bristles from side-to-side and forward-and-back on the surface of the spot. (You can also use a circular motion, if desired.) The bristles should barely penetrate the tips of the carpet yarns and should always stay within the spot area to avoid contaminating clean areas of the carpet.

4. Continue until the entire surface of the spot has been well agitated. (A spot has been well agitated when the spotting agents have penetrated the spot and are not beading or puddling up on the surface of it or the carpet.)

5. Carefully put the dirty brush into your Contaminants bucket.

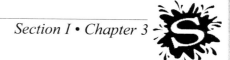

## *Rake Spot onto Towel with Hard Brush*

**Purpose:** To start the removal of stringy, moist spot matter, such as cooked pasta like spaghetti or noodles, by raking it up off the carpet with the hard brush and putting it in a towel.

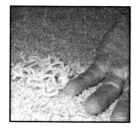

**Step 1**     **Step 2**     **Step 4**     **Step 5**

9

**To do:**

1. Lay one hand, palm up, on the carpet at the edge of the spot.

2. Cover your palm with a small towel.

3. In the other hand, hold the hard brush by the handle with the bristles pointed down.

4. Place the brush so the bristles are resting on the carpet at the edge of the spot furthest from your towel-covered hand.

5. Using only enough downward pressure to graze the brush bristles over the surface of the carpet, carefully rake the pasta up and into the towel with the brush. (Keep the pasta and dirty parts of the towel away from the carpet and change towels as needed to prevent contaminating clean areas of the carpet.)

6. Remove from the brush any large pieces of pasta, meat, vegetables or stringy sub-stances that could fall onto the carpet. (Any sauce, butter, etc., doesn't need to be removed until you clean the brush just before putting it away.)

7. Starting at a slightly different place on the spot's edge, rake the bristles across the spot to the towel.

8. Repeat raking up and dumping into the towel until no more pasta will remove.

9. If needed, use your spoon to scoop any remaining bits of pasta into the towel.

10. Carefully put the dirty towel and pasta into your Contaminants bucket.

Section I

# Brush - Soft

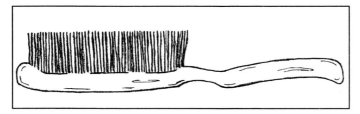

## *Agitate Spot with Soft Brush*

— 10 —

**Purpose:** To help spotting agents penetrate a fresh/wet spot, such as bodily fluids, by stirring the spot with the bristles of the soft brush after the agents have been applied.

**Step 1**

**Step 2**

**Step 3**

**To do:**

1. Hold the soft brush by the handle with the bristles pointed down.

2. Slightly penetrate the spot with the bristles at the end of the brush. (If the spot is pencil eraser size or smaller, use only one or two groups of bristles at the end of the brush.)

3. Move the bristles from side-to-side and forward-and-back on the surface of the spot. (You can also use a circular motion, if desired.) The bristles should barely penetrate the tips of the carpet yarns and should always stay within the spot area to avoid contaminating clean areas of the carpet.

4. Continue until the entire surface of the spot has been well agitated. (A spot has been well agitated when the spotting agents have penetrated the spot and are not beading up or puddling up on the surface of it or the carpet.)

## Brush Spot in a Circular Motion with Soft Brush

**Purpose:** To further rough up the surface of dry, brittle or crusty spots, such as lignin browning. Brushing through the spot in a circular pattern dislodges more spot matter from all sides of the carpet yarns. This technique has a slightly different effect on the spot than the side-to-side brushing motion.

**Step 1**

**Step 2**

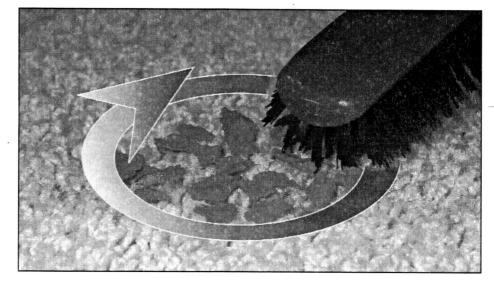

**Step 3**

**To do:**

1. Hold the soft brush by the handle with the bristles pointed down.

2. Barely penetrate the spot with the bristles at the end of the brush. (If the spot is pencil eraser size or smaller, use only one or two groups of bristles at the end of the brush.)

3. Move the bristles in a circular motion clockwise and then counterclockwise on the surface of the spot until the entire spot area has been brushed the specified number of times. The bristles should barely penetrate the tips of the carpet yarns. Always stay within the spot area and be careful to not fray the carpet yarns.

## Brush Spot Side-To-Side with Soft Brush

- Or -

## Brush Spot Side-to-Side with Soft Brush - Gently

**Purpose: Brush** - To rough up the surface of dry, brittle or crusty spots, such as lignin browning.

**Gently Brush** - To lightly rough up the surface of dry, soft spots, such as mouthwash or coffee or tea with/without milk.

This roughing up is done by moving the bristles of your soft brush back and forth through the spot. This dislodges spot matter from the carpet yarns and enhances initial removal. It also allows the spotting agents to more easily and fully penetrate the spot when they're applied.

**Step 1**

**Step 2**          **Step 3**

**To do:**

1. Hold the soft brush by the handle with the bristles pointed down.

2. Barely penetrate the spot with the bristles at the end of the brush. (If the spot is pencil eraser size or smaller, use only one or two groups of bristles at the end of the brush.)

3. Move the bristles from side-to-side on the surface of the spot until the entire spot area has been brushed the specified number of times. (You can also use a forward-and-back or a circular motion, if desired.) Always stay within the spot area and be careful to not fray the carpet yarns.

   • **Brush:** The bristles should barely penetrate the tips of the carpet yarns.

   • **Gently Brush:** The bristles should barely graze the tips of the carpet yarns and the brush should be gently moved through the carpet.

---

## *Tamp Spot with Soft Brush - Tamp*

- Or -

## *Tamp Spot with Soft Brush - Gently Tamp*

- Or -

## *Tamp Spot with Soft Brush - Firmly Tamp*

**Purpose:** To help spotting agents penetrate all types of spots and the carpet yarns as much as possible. This is done by using the bristles at the end of the soft brush as if they were the head of a hammer to tamp or press the agents into the spot matter.

**Step 1**          **Step 2**          **Step 3**

**To do:**

1. Hold the handle of the brush loosely so it floats between your thumb and middle finger with the bristles pointed down.

2. Barely penetrate the spot with the bristles at the end of the brush. (If the spot is pencil eraser size or smaller, use only one or two groups of bristles at the end of the brush.)

3. Move the brush up and down with almost a flicking motion, as if you were using the bristles to gently tap or hammer a nail into the spot. Use only enough force so that the bristles penetrate the carpet surface no more than:

   • **Gently Tamp:** About 1/16th of an inch deep in the spot area.

   • **Tamp:** About 1/8th of an inch deep in the spot area.

   • **Firmly Tamp:** About 1/4th of an inch deep in the spot area.

4. If needed, move the brush to another area of the spot and tamp.

5. Continue until the entire spot area has been tamped at least 3 - 4 times. (Or until the spotting agent has penetrated the spot and the spot appears to be breaking up.)

Section I

## Knife -Dinner

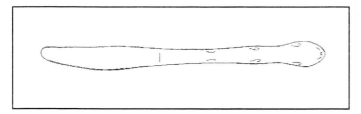

### Break Up Spot with Dinner Knife using Chopping Action

— 14 —

**Purpose:** To break up dried, brittle or crusty spots, such as dried flour or other dry goods or dried feces, that were semi-liquid when wet. This is done by chopping the surface of the spot with your knife as if you were chopping vegetables.

**Step 1**          **Step 2**

**To do:**

1. Hold the dinner knife by the handle as if you're going to use it to cut food.

2. Chop down on the spot with the knife blade using enough pressure to break the spot up into smaller portions and/or separate it from the carpet fibers. **Caution:** Do not chop so hard that you drive the spot matter further into the carpet.

3. Repeat until the entire surface of the spot has been broken up.

4. Carefully put the dirty knife into your Contaminants bucket

### Scrape Out Spot using Dinner Knife or Tip of Dinner Knife

**Purpose:** To start or continue the removal of thick, moist or gooey spots, such as fresh paste shoe polish, waxy cosmetics or putty, by scraping the spot matter off the carpet yarns with your knife tip, one small portion at a time. This technique works especially well on berber type carpets. **Note:** You have more control and are less likely to accidentally smear or drop spot matter on the clean carpet if you use only the tip of the knife for scraping - even if the treatment steps do not specify it.

*Section I*

## Scrape Out Spot using Dinner Knife or Tip of Dinner Knife, continued

**Step 1**   **Step 2**   **Step 3**   **Step 4**   **Step 5**

— 15 —

**To do:**

1 . Lay a small towel next to the spot. (It will be used to wipe the dirty knife blade after each scrape.)

2 . Turn the knife so the cutting edge of the blade is facing up. About halfway down the blade, grasp the knife between your thumb and index finger as if it were a pencil you were going to write with.

3 . Place the tip of the knife so it is resting on the surface of the carpet just outside the edge of the spot furthest from you.

4. Pull the knife tip towards you, applying enough downward pressure so the tip is just underneath the spot matter. Move the tip just far enough to scrape up a portion of the spot matter about the size of the tip of the knife. (The carpet yarns should lie down slightly as you drag the knife across them.)

5. Wipe the dirty knife blade on a clean part of the towel. (Keep the dirty parts of the towel away from the carpet and change towels as needed to prevent contaminating clean areas of the carpet).

6. Starting at a slightly different place on the spot, scrape the knife tip across a small part of the spot. Wipe the knife tip on the towel.

7. Repeat scraping from different directions and wiping until no more spot matter removes.

8. Carefully put the dirty towel and knife into your Contaminants bucket.

## Scrape Spot into Disposable Towel with Dinner Knife

**Purpose:** To start the removal of most types of fresh/wet glue by using your knife blade to scrape the glue off the carpet yarns and onto a towel.

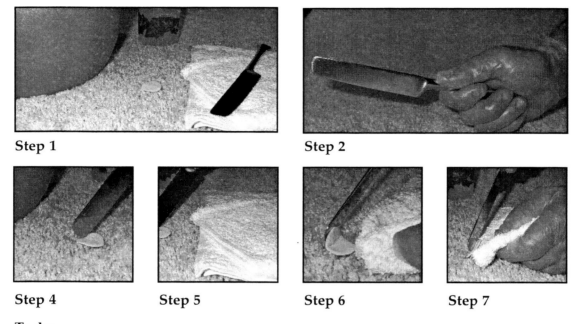

**Step 1**        **Step 2**

**Step 4**    **Step 5**    **Step 6**    **Step 7**

**To do:**

1. Put the dinner knife, alcohol spray bottle, the Contaminants bucket and several disposable towels next to the spot.

2. Hold the dinner knife by the handle as if you were going to use it to cut food.

3. Place the knife inside the bucket and mist both sides of the blade with alcohol.

4. Place the knife so the edge of the blade is resting on the carpet at the edge of the spot furthest from you. The knife blade should be tilted back at a 45° angle or less to the carpet. **Caution:** If you hold the blade perpendicular to the carpet's surface, the scraping action could spread the spot unless you're very careful.

5. With the other hand, hold a disposable towel at the edge of the spot furthest from the knife.

6. Pull the tilted blade across the spot towards the towel. Apply only enough downward pressure to keep the edge of the blade just underneath the spot matter so it is scraped off the carpet and moves up onto the knife blade. (The carpet yarns should lie down slightly as you drag the knife across them.)

7. At the edge of the spot, scrape the spot matter onto the towel.

    

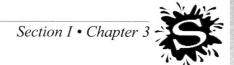

**Scrape Spot into Disposable Towel with Dinner Knife, *continued***

8. Wipe the dirty knife blade on a clean part of the towel. (Keep the dirty parts of the towel away from the carpet. Change towels as needed to prevent contaminating clean areas of the carpet and carefully put the dirty towel into the Contaminants bucket.)

9. Re-mist the knife blade with alcohol. Starting at a slightly different place on the spot's edge, scrape the knife blade across the spot to the towel. Wipe the blade on the towel.

10. Repeat misting, scraping and wiping until no more spot matter removes. Carefully put the dirty towel and knife into your Contaminants bucket.

## Scrape Surface of Spot using Dinner Knife

– 17 –

**Purpose:** To break up and dislodge the spot matter, such as dried blood or other bodily fluids, by scraping it from side-to-side with your knife blade.

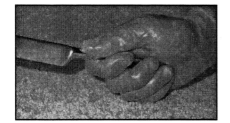

**Step 1**          **Step 2**          **Step 3**

**To do:**

1. Hold the dinner knife by the handle as if you were going to use it to cut food.

2. Place the knife so the blade is resting in the middle of the spot.

3. Holding the blade at a 90° angle to the carpet, scrape the edge of the blade across the spot in a side-to-side motion. Apply enough downward pressure to penetrate the surface of the spot. (The carpet yarns should lay down slightly as you scrape the spot. Be careful to not fray the carpet yarns.)

4. Repeat scraping action in a forward and back pattern and/or scraping in one direction.

5. Repeat scraping until all sides of the carpet yarns have been scraped and no more spot matter is dislodged.

6. Carefully put the dirty knife into your Contaminants bucket.

*Section I*

## Scrape Up Spot using Dinner Knife

**Purpose:** To start the removal of crayons or pastels by using your knife blade to scrape the spot matter off the carpet yarns.

**Step 1**

**Step 2**

— 18 —

**Step 3**

**Step 4**

**Step 5**

**Step 6**

**To do:**

1. Lay a small towel next to the spot. (It will be used to wipe the dirty knife blade after each scrape.)

2. Hold the dinner knife by the handle as if you were going to use it to cut food.

3. Place the knife so the edge of the blade is resting on the carpet at the edge of the spot furthest from you. The knife blade should be tilted back at a 45° angle or less to the surface of the carpet. **Caution:** If you hold the blade perpendicular to the carpet's surface, the scraping action could spread the spot unless you're very careful.

4. Pull the tilted blade across the spot. Apply only enough downward pressure to keep the edge of the blade just underneath the spot matter so it is scraped off the carpet and moves up onto the knife blade. (The carpet yarns should lie down slightly as you drag the knife across them.)

5. Stop scraping at the edge of the spot.

6. Wipe the dirty knife blade on a clean part of the towel. (Keep the dirty parts of the towel away from the carpet and change towels as needed to prevent contaminating clean areas of the carpet.)

7. Starting at a slightly different place on the spot's edge, scrape the knife blade across the spot. Wipe the blade on the towel.

8. Repeat scraping from different places on the spot's edge and wiping the knife until no more spot matter removes.

9. Carefully put the dirty towel and knife into your Contaminants bucket.

## *Separate Yarns using Dinner Knife and Scissors*

**Purpose:** To break up a dried, crusty spot, such as dried blood, into small pieces of spot matter at the end of each carpet yarn. This helps spotting agents penetrate the spot better than if it is a solid mass. The tip of your knife blade is used to hold some of the yarns in the spot area in place while you use the point of one of the scissors' blades to move other nearby yarns away from the knife tip.

**Step 1**   **Step 2**   **Step 3**   **Step 4**   **Step 5**

— 19 —

**To do:**

1. Open the scissors and lay them on your hand so the place where the blades meet is lying on the skin between your thumb and pointer finger. (The narrower blade of the scissors should be resting on your extended pointer finger, and your thumb should be lying on top of the blade.)

2. In the other hand, hold the knife as if it's a pencil and you're going to write on the carpet with the tip of the blade. (The blade should be turned so the cutting edge is up.)

3. Put the tip of the knife blade at the edge of the spot to hold the yarns in place.

4. With the point of the scissors' blade, puncture the spot near the knife.

5. Gently move the point of the scissors' blade away from the knife tip just enough so the carpet yarns are separated and the spot is broken apart.

6. Continue puncturing the spot and moving the dirty yarns with the scissors' blade until all dirty yarns near the knife tip have been separated from each other.

7. Move the tip of the knife to a new place in the spot area and repeat puncturing and separating with the scissors' blade.

8. Repeat moving the knife and puncturing/separating yarns with the scissors' blade until all yarns in the spot area have been separated from each other and the spot is broken into tiny pieces.

9. Carefully put the dirty knife and scissors into your Contaminants bucket.

*Section I*

## Separate Yarns using Dinner Knife (or Tip of Dinner Knife) and Finger

**Purpose:** To break up a dried spot, such as glue stick, into small pieces of spot matter at the end of each carpet yarn. This helps spotting agents penetrate the spot better than if it is a solid mass. The tip of your finger is used to hold some of the yarns in the spot area in place while you use the tip of the knife blade to move other nearby yarns away from the finger. **Note:** You have more control if you use the tip of the knife for separating - even if the treatment steps do not specify it.

 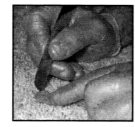  

**Step 1**          **Step 2**          **Step 3**

**To do:**

1. Hold the knife as if it's a pencil and you're going to write on the carpet with the tip of the blade. (The blade should be turned so the cutting edge is up.)

2. Put the tip of your other hand's pointer finger at the edge of the spot to hold the yarns in place.

3. With the tip of the knife blade, puncture the spot near your finger tip. Gently move the tip of the knife blade away from the finger tip just enough so the carpet yarns are separated and the spot is broken apart.

4. Continue puncturing the spot and moving the dirty yarns with the knife tip until all dirty yarns near the finger tip have been separated from each other.

5. Move your finger to a new place in the spot area and repeat puncturing and separating with the knife tip.

6. Repeat moving your finger and puncturing/separating yarns with the knife tip until all yarns in the spot area have been separated from each other and the spot is broken into tiny pieces.

7. Carefully put the dirty knife into your Contaminants bucket.

*— 20 —*

## *Separate Yarns using Tip of Dinner Knife and End of Spoon Handle*

**Purpose:** To break up a dried spot, such as dried pancake syrup, cough syrup or floor wax, into small pieces of spot matter at the end of each carpet yarn. This helps spotting agents or rinse water from a spot machine penetrate the spot better than if it is a solid mass. The end of a spoon handle is used to hold some of the yarns in the spot area in place while you use the tip of your knife blade to move other nearby yarns away from the spoon.

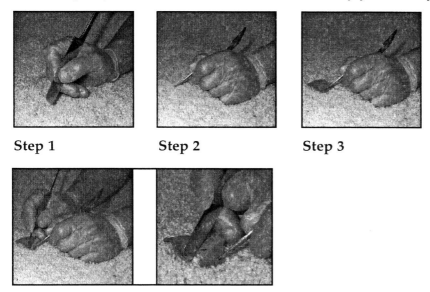

**Step 1**          **Step 2**          **Step 3**

**Step 4**

**To do:**

1. Hold the knife as if it's a pencil and you're going to write on the carpet with the tip of the blade. (The blade should be turned so the cutting edge is up.)

2. In the other hand, hold the spoon as if it's also a pencil and you're going to write on the carpet with the end of the handle.

3. Put the end of the spoon handle at the edge of the spot to hold the yarns in place.

4. With the tip of the knife blade, puncture the spot near the spoon handle. Gently move the knife blade away from the spoon handle just enough so the carpet yarns are separated and the spot is broken apart.

5. Continue puncturing the spot and moving the dirty yarns with the knife until all dirty yarns near the spoon handle have been separated from each other.

6. Move the end of the spoon handle to a new place in the spot area and repeat puncturing and separating with the knife.

7. Repeat moving the spoon and puncturing/separating yarns with the tip of the knife until all yarns in the spot area have been separated from each other and the spot is broken into tiny pieces.

8. Carefully put the dirty knife and spoon into your Contaminants bucket.

Section I

## *Pliers*

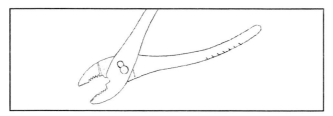

### Crush Spot with Pliers

**Purpose:** To crush small, very hard pieces of spot matter, such as dried cement or putty, into smaller pieces (or preferably into powder) with a pair of pliers, so the debris can be vacuumed up during initial spot removal.

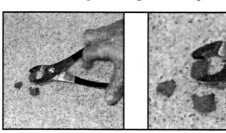  

**Step 1**                          **Step 2**

**To do:**

1. Put the jaws of a pair of regular pliers (not channel lock ones) around one of the small pieces of spot matter.

2. Slowly squeeze the pliers, applying enough pressure to crush the spot into smaller pieces.

3. Repeat until all the spot matter has been crushed into powder - or at least into very small pieces.

4. Carefully put the dirty pliers into your Contaminants bucket.

22

# Scissors

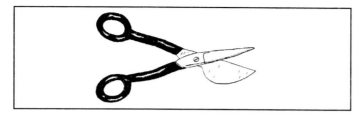 

## Scissors Techniques - General Facts about Snipping Spots from Carpet Fibers

Some spots, such as dried glue or nail polish, wet or dry hard candy, mascara, etc., don't respond so well to scraping, rinsing or other techniques. The initial treatment step for these says to snip the spot matter from the tips of the carpet yarns. Any remaining spot matter is then much easier to treat. **Caution:** To use this technique successfully, the spot must be on the surface of the carpet pile -- not absorbed into it. Your goal is to remove the spot matter and as little of the carpet fiber as possible.

Trimming only the very tips of the fibers minimizes the indention caused by removing the spot. **Note:** Though regular scissors can be successfully used for this technique, the professional duck-bill shears (carpet spotting scissors) are easier to use and more effective. Whichever type of scissors you use, they must have sharp, clean blades to get the best results.

**Best Practice:** Remove as little carpet fiber as possible when you cut off the spot matter. (If you cut too deep, it's very hard to disguise the hole.) To have the most control over the amount of carpet fiber removed, do this technique slowly and cut very small sections (less than half of the spot) at a time. The smaller the amount of the spot removed each time, the more control you have.

**Caution - Looped Carpet:** Avoid trimming spots from any looped carpet, including berber, commercial grade level loop, glue down, etc. If done wrong, a cut loop may completely unravel and look frayed.

If your spot is on a looped carpet, my first recommendations would be:

1. Skip the treatment step that tells you to "trim the spot from the tips of the fibers, then rough up and trim the fibers around the spot area". Instead, go to the next step, if any, and continue the treatment as written. Always try to remove the spot with your spotting agents first before trimming on a looped carpet.

- OR -

2. Wait until your next carpet cleaning and have a professional trim the spot, if he/she can't remove it.

### *Scissors Techniques - General Facts about Snipping Spots from Carpet Fibers, continued*

**Possible Exceptions:** Two situations where you **might** decide to trim a spot on a looped carpet are:

• You're very experienced at successfully trimming out spots,

-Or-

• It's very obvious the spot is only on the outside fibers at the top of the loop(s). If spot matter is only on the outer edge at the top of the loop, then trimming small bits from it shouldn't show. **Caution:** If you try to trim a spot inside the loop, it's very easy to cut through the entire loop. Then the loop unravels and can be seen. (If this happens, you can trim the excess yarn length so it's the same as the rest of the carpet pile. It's harder -- but not impossible -- to see the loop has been cut. I really want to discourage your trimming looped carpet when you shouldn't and then having to use this type of repair.)

**Best Practice:** If you have any doubt about your ability to successfully trim the spot out without damaging the looped carpet, call a professional for options instead

## *Snip Hardened Parts of Spots from Tips of Carpet Fibers with Scissors*

**Purpose - Cutting:** To remove spots, such as dried glue or nail polish, wet or dry hard candy, mascara, etc., from the surface of the carpet pile. This is done by using your scissors to trim the spot matter from the very tips of the carpet fibers. **Caution:** Do **not** try scissors removal of spots from any type of looped carpet (berber, commercial glue down, etc.), unless the spot is only on the outside fibers of the loop(s). If in doubt, call a pro for options as soon as possible.

### *Snip Hardened Parts of Spots from Tips of Carpet Fibers with Scissors, continued*

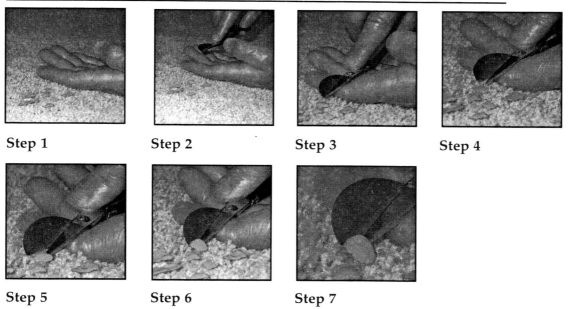

Step 1        Step 2        Step 3        Step 4

Step 5        Step 6        Step 7

- 25 -

**To do:**

1. Put your non-cutting hand on the carpet next to the spot, with your palm facing up.

2. Pick up the scissors with your other hand.

3. Rest the lower blade of the unopened scissors on the index finger of the hand laying on the carpet.

4. Open the blades to no more than half the size of the spot or less. (The smaller the amount cut at one time, the better.)

5. Slide the more slender, pointed blade of the scissors directly down the center of the spot, right under the spot matter.

6. Squeeze the handles and clamp the blades around a small portion of the spot. Do **not** begin cutting yet.

7. Push the blades up with your index finger until they're just beneath the spot matter.

8. Close the blades and cut the spot matter off from the very tip of the carpet fibers.

9. Keep cutting small parts of the spot until it has been completely removed.

10. If you don't need to do Pile Height Blending around the spot area, carefully put the dirty scissors into your Contaminants bucket. If you do need to blend the surrounding carpet yarns, put the scissors in the bucket when you finish.

*Section I*

*— 26 —*

**Snip Hardened Parts of Spots from Tips of Carpet Fibers with Scissors, continued**

**Purpose - Pile Height Blending, also known as Trim, Rough Up, Level:** To make the slight indention where the spot matter was trimmed out less obvious. This is done by trimming very small amounts from the tips of the carpet yarns surrounding the spot area. The spot and surrounding area are gently "roughed up" by rubbing the tips of the closed scissors blades back and forth across the fibers. Any taller fibers are then trimmed so the carpet looks more level. **Note:** Smaller spots rarely go below the surface of the carpet, so pile height blending rarely needs to be done for them. **Caution: Never** do pile height blending on looped carpets. It doesn't work.

**Step 1**            **Step 2**            **Step 4**

**To do:**

1. Trim a few of the yarns around the edge of the removed spot. **Caution:** Gradually remove a little at a time off the top of the fibers so they blend well with the rest of the carpet surface.

2. Slightly rough up the trimmed carpet fibers by rubbing the tips of your closed scissors back and forth across the surface of the fibers.

3. Stop rubbing every few seconds to check that only fiber blending is occurring - not fraying.

4. Trim any taller, roughed up fibers so they are equal in height (level) with the rest of the carpet. (Over time normal wear and tear should take care of the rest of the carpet surface.)

## *Separate Yarns - Using Dinner Knife and Scissors*

A description of this technique is under the above title on page 19 in the "Knife - Dinner" section of this Chapter.

# *Spoon*

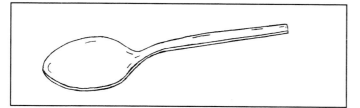

## *Agitate Spot with End of Spoon Handle*

- Or -

## *Agitate Spot with End of Spoon Handle - Gently*

**Purpose: Agitate** - To help spotting agents penetrate a sticky spot, such as asphalt, by stirring the spot with the end of a spoon handle. Because of the denser nature of this type of spot, the stirring must be done with a bit more force than for lacquer or similar spots. **Gently Agitate** - To carefully help spotting agents penetrate a spot, such as lacquer, that may spread easily when fresh/wet by gently stirring the yarns within the spot area with the end of a spoon handle. **Note:** The end of the spoon handle may catch on the loops in berber and other looped carpets. Gently pull it out of the loop and keep stirring.

**Step 1**          **Step 2**

**To do:**

1. Hold the spoon handle as if it's a pencil and you're going to write on the carpet with the end of the handle.

2. Barely penetrate the middle of the spot with the end of the handle.

3. Move the end of the handle from side-to-side and forward-and-back on the surface of the spot. (You can also use a circular motion, if desired.) Always stay within the spot area to avoid contaminating clean areas of the carpet.

   • **Agitate:** The end of the handle should **only penetrate to the depth of the spot - no deeper**.

   • **Gently Agitate:** The end of the handle should **barely graze the tips of the carpet yarns** as it is moved **gently** through the spot.

4. Continue until the entire surface of the spot has been well agitated. (Or gently, but well agitated for spots such as lacquer.) (A spot has been well agitated when the spotting agents have penetrated the spot and are not beading up or puddling up on the surface of it or the carpet.)

5. Carefully put the dirty spoon into your Contaminants bucket.

**Section I**

## Scoop Spot onto Towel using Spoon

- Or -

## Scrape Spot onto Towel using Spoon

**Purpose:** To start the removal of moist, semi-solid to solid spots, such as fresh guacamole, cake icing or paste food coloring, by scraping it towards you with your spoon. Then, scooping it up and dumping it in a towel. (The treatment steps say to use disposable tissues when the spot is a particularly nasty one like wet feces or one that could ruin your towel, like wet paint or fresh grease. **Caution:** Use enough tissues at one time so the spot matter does not soak through the tissue and drip on the carpet.)

– 28 –

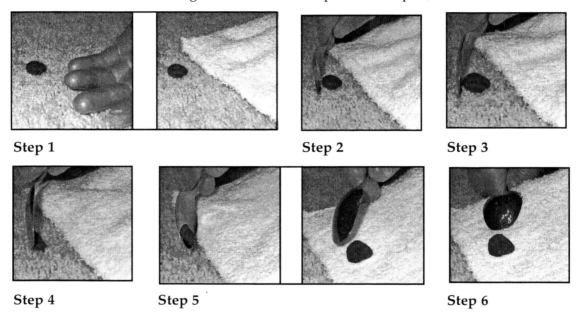

**Step 1**          **Step 2**          **Step 3**

**Step 4**     **Step 5**          **Step 6**

**To do:**

1. Lay one hand palm up on the carpet at the edge of the spot. Cover your hand with a small towel.

2. In the other hand, hold the spoon handle so the bowl (the scooping part) of the spoon is at a 90° angle to the carpet.

3. Place the spoon so the edge of the bowl is resting on the carpet at the edge of the spot furthest from your towel-covered hand.

4. Pull the edge of the spoon across the spot toward the towel, applying only enough downward pressure to get the edge of the spoon just under the spot matter. (The carpet fibers should lie down slightly as you drag the spoon across them.)

5. When the spoon reaches the opposite edge of the spot, carefully scoop the spot matter up with the spoon and dump it into the towel.

6. Wipe the dirty spoon on a clean part of the towel. (Keep the dirty parts of the towel away from the carpet. Change towels as needed to prevent contaminating clean areas of the carpet.)

Section I

### *Scoop Spot onto Towel using Spoon, continued*

7. Starting at a slightly different place on the spot's edge, scrape the spoon across the spot and scoop the spot matter into the towel. Wipe the spoon on the towel.

8. Repeat scraping, scooping and wiping until no more spot matter removes.

9. Carefully put the dirty towel and spoon into your Contaminants bucket.

## *Scrape Edges of Spot towards Center using Spoon*

**Purpose:** To remove chewing gum without spreading it to clean areas of the carpet after you have applied WD-40 to the spot as directed. Instead of using your spoon to scrape the spot matter towards the outside of the spot, you scrape it towards the middle until it has peeled off the carpet and can be scooped up with the spoon.

 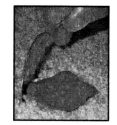  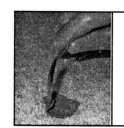 

**Step 1**        **Step 2**        **Step 3**        **Step 4**

**To do:**

1. Hold the spoon handle so the bowl (the scooping part) of the spoon is at a 90° angle to the carpet.

2. Place the spoon so the edge of the bowl is resting on the carpet at the edge of the spot.

3. Pull the edge of the spoon across the spot toward the center of the spot, applying only enough downward pressure to get the edge of the spoon just under the spot matter. (The carpet fibers should lie down slightly as you drag the spoon across them and the spot matter should begin to peel up from the carpet.)

4. Stop at the middle of the spot and lift the spoon off the carpet.

5. Starting at a slightly different place on the spot's edge, scrape the spoon under the gum and across to the middle of the spot.

6. Repeat scraping until the gum has been peeled off the carpet pile.

7. Carefully scoop the gum up with your spoon and put it and the dirty spoon into your Contaminants bucket.

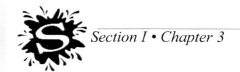 

Section I

## Scrape Out Spot using Spoon

**Purpose:** To start the removal of a semi-dry to dry / semi-solid to solid spot, such as avocado, cooked fruits/vegetables, soft cheese or liquid or gel soaps, by scraping your spoon across the surface of the spot to break it up.

**Step 1**　　　　**Step 2**　　　　**Step 3**　　　　**Step 4**

— 30 —

**To do:**

1. Hold the spoon handle so the bowl (the scooping part) of the spoon is at a 90° angle to the carpet.

2. Place the spoon so the edge of the bowl is resting on the carpet at the opposite edge of the spot from your body.

3. Pull the edge of the spoon across the spot toward you, applying only enough downward pressure to get the edge of the spoon just under the spot matter. (The carpet fibers should lie down slightly as you drag the spoon across them.)

4. When the spoon reaches the edge of the spot, stop and lift the spoon off the carpet.

5. Starting at a slightly different place on the spot's edge, scrape the spoon across the spot.

6. Repeat scraping until no more spot matter removes.

7. Carefully put the dirty spoon into your Contaminants bucket. (**Note:** If you are treating a Class III avocado, fruit or vegetable spill, clean the spoon just before using it to scoop up spot matter after spotting agents have been applied.)

## *Scrape Up Spot using Spoon*

**Purpose:** To start the removal of thick, gooey matter such as old bacon grease, shortening or other types of greases, by using your spoon to scrape the spot matter off the carpet yarns and wipe it onto a towel.

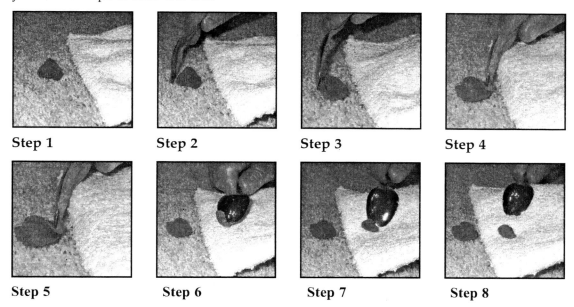

**Step 1**   **Step 2**   **Step 3**   **Step 4**

**Step 5**   **Step 6**   **Step 7**   **Step 8**

**To do:**

1. Hold a small folded towel next to the edge of the spot. (The towel will prevent the grease from falling onto clean areas of the carpet and will be used to wipe the spoon.)

2. In the other hand, hold the spoon handle so the bowl (the scooping part) of the spoon is at a 90° angle to the carpet.

3. Place the spoon so the edge of the bowl is resting on the carpet at the edge of the spot furthest from the towel.

4. Pull the edge of the spoon across the spot toward the towel, applying only enough downward pressure to get the edge of the spoon just under the spot matter. (The carpet fibers should lie down slightly as you drag the spoon across them.)

5. Stop scraping when the spoon reaches the opposite edge of the spot.

6. With a careful scooping / flipping motion, bring the spoon of spot matter up off the carpet and turn it over into the towel.

7. Wipe the spot matter onto the towel.

8. Wipe the dirty spoon on a clean part of the towel. (Keep dirty parts of the towel off the carpet. Change towels often to prevent contaminating the clean carpet.)

9. Starting at a slightly different place on the spot's edge, scrape the spoon across the spot and scoop / flip the spot matter onto the towel. Wipe the spoon on the towel.

10. Repeat scraping, scooping / flipping and wiping until no more spot matter removes.

11. Carefully put the dirty towel and spoon into your Contaminants bucket.

### *Separate Yarns - Using Tip of Dinner Knife and End of Spoon Handle*

A description of this technique is under the above title on page 21 in the "Knife - Dinner" section of this Chapter.

### *Slam or Tamp Edge of Scoop Part of Spoon Down onto Spot*

**Purpose:** To break up hard pieces of spot matter, such as dried cement or mud, into smaller pieces by hitting them with the edge of the scoop part (bowl) of a spoon, so the debris can be vacuumed up during initial spot removal.

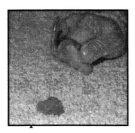 

**To do:**

1. Hold the spoon by the handle with the bowl (the scooping part) at a 90° angle to the carpet.

2. Hit the spot with the edge of the bowl of the spoon, using enough downward pressure to break it up into smaller portions and/or separate it from the carpet fibers.

   • **Slamming Firmly:** Hit the dried cement as hard as needed to break it up.

   • **Tamping:** Hit the dried mud with only enough force to break it up, but not drive it into the carpet.

3. Repeat for the specified number of times or until the entire surface of the spot has been broken up into pieces as small as possible. (Very hard spots like cement may also require crushing the pieces with a pair of pliers.)

4. Carefully put the dirty spoon into your Contaminants bucket.

# *Spot Machine*

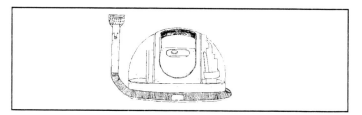

## *Spot Machine Techniques - General Facts*

Carefully read and follow your spot machine's instructions for how to operate your specific machine. Before your first spot treatment, learn how to:

- Vacuum up spot debris or excess rinse water using the "dry" stroke.

- Release a spray of clean water into the spot area when you are using one of the rinse strokes - the "single" stroke or "chop" stroke.

**Before each spot treatment:**

- Fill the clean water tank with water at the temperature listed in the "Materials Needed" section of the spot treatment page for your spot in Chapter 5. **Caution:** Ignore the following instructions in your spot machine owner's manual/user's guide -

  1) Do **not** fill the clean water tank with HOT water (unless that's the water temperature listed on the treatment page), and

  2) Do **not** add the cleaning solutions that came with your machine, or were purchased later, to the clean water tank. They can interfere with the action of your spotting agents and could cause the spot to be set permanently.

- Test the unit by spraying some water in the sink or a bucket.

- Take the spot machine (if it's working properly) and your spotting kit to the spot area to begin treatment.

**After each spot treatment:**

- Clean and store your spot machine and its attachments following the instructions for your particular machine.

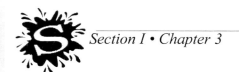

Section I

## Dry Vacuum Stroke

**Purpose:** To begin the initial removal of fresh, wet spots such as beer, fruit juice or liquid dye, or to remove as much moisture as possible from the carpet after the single stroke or chop stroke technique has been used to rinse spot matter out of the carpet yarns. This is done by pulling the spot machine brush tool across the spot in a series of parallel, over-lapping dry vacuum passes.

 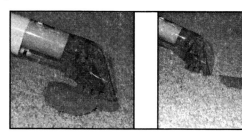 

**Step 2**          **Step 3**                                        **Step 4**

**To do:**

1. Attach the brush tool to the spot machine hose.

2. Firmly press the tool into the carpet pile just above the upper left edge of the spot. Do **not** press the spray trigger or spray water over the spot.

3. Slowly pull the tool toward you, dragging the bristles across the carpet, at about 1 inch per second. Continue until you've pulled the tool just past the lower edge of the spot.

4. Lift the tool off the carpet.

5. If the spot is wider than the width of the tool, again place the tool just beyond the upper edge of the spot. This time, move the tool to the right of the original area vacuumed. (You want your next dry vacuum stroke to overlap the area previously covered by 1 inch.)

6. Repeat firmly pressing and slowly pulling the tool towards you in overlapping passes until the entire spot area has been vacuumed the number of times specified in the treatment instructions. **Hint:** If the recommended number of dry strokes does not remove all the moisture in a larger spot, dry stroke the spot area several more times from a different angle using a backward and forward motion. Continue to dry vacuum the spot area until no more moisture removes.

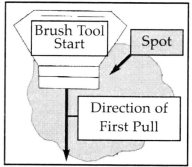 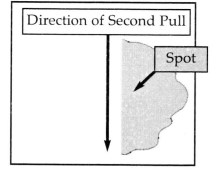 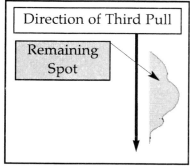

— 34 —

## *Rinse Spot using Single Stroke*

**Purpose:** To continue the removal of wet spots, such as bodily fluids or liquid or gel soaps after any solids have been scooped off the carpet, and/or the removal of other types of spots that don't need the additional scrubbing action of the chop stroke after spotting agents have been applied. This rinsing out of spot matter is done by pulling the spot machine brush tool across the spot in a series of slow, parallel, overlapping passes with the spray trigger depressed.

**Step 2**          **Step 3**          **Step 4**          **Step 5**

**To do:**

1. Attach the brush tool to the spot machine hose.

2. Firmly press the tool into the carpet pile just above the upper left edge of the spot.

3. Press and hold the spray trigger as you slowly pull the tool toward you, dragging the bristles across the carpet, at about 1 inch per second. Continue until you've pulled the tool just past the lower edge of the spot.

4. Just past the lower edge of the spot, release the spray trigger and continue to pull the tool toward you another 1 inch, using the dry vacuum stroke.

5. Lift the tool off the carpet.

6. If the spot is wider than the width of the tool, again place the tool just beyond the upper edge of the spot. This time, move the tool to the right of the original area rinsed. (You want your next rinse stroke to overlap the area previously covered by 1 inch.)

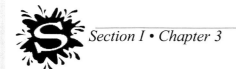

### *Rinse Spot using Single Stroke, continued*

7. Again, firmly press and slowly pull the tool towards you as you press and hold the spray trigger just past the edge of the spot. Then release the trigger and finish with the dry vacuum stroke for 1 inch.

8. Repeat all steps in overlapping passes until the entire spot area has been rinsed at least the number of times specified in the treatment instructions. (If needed, additional passes will not hurt the carpet, as long as you remove the added moisture with the dry stoke after each pass.)

— 36 —

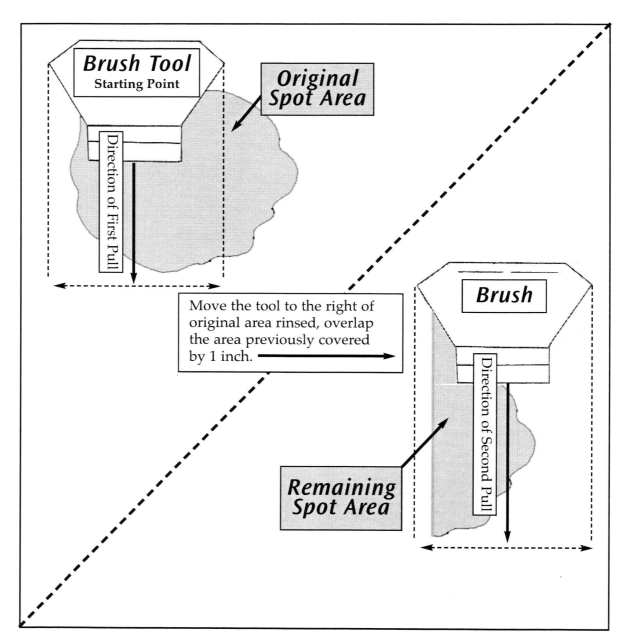

## *Rinse Spot using Chop Stroke*

**Purpose:** To start the removal of fresh, wet spots, such as cough medicine and dried spots like alcoholic beverages. It is also used in most of the treatments to rinse the spot matter out of the carpet after spotting agents have been applied. This rinsing is done by pulling/pushing the spot machine brush tool across the spot in a series of slow, parallel, overlapping passes with the spray trigger depressed. The additional scrubbing action of the chop stroke removes more difficult spot matter from the yarns, and is better able to reach spot matter that is below the surface of the carpet pile.

**Step 2**    **Step 3**    **Step 4**    **Step 5**

- 37 -

**To do:**

1. Attach the brush tool to the spot machine hose.

2. Firmly press the tool into the carpet pile just above the upper left edge of the spot.

3. Press and hold the spray trigger as you slowly pull / push the tool across the spot area towards you using the Pull / Push Pattern described on the next page. Move the tool at about 1 inch per second, dragging the bristles across the carpet.

   **Pull / Push Pattern:** (See drawing on next page)

   From just above the upper edge of the spot, pull the tool toward you 1 inch.

   Push it back to just above the upper left edge of the spot.

   Pull it toward you 2 inches.

   Push it back 1 inch.

   Pull it toward you 2 inches.

   Continue the push-tool-back-1-inch / pull-it-toward-you-2-inches until you have reached the lower edge of the spot.

   At that point push the tool back 1 inch and pull it toward you 1 inch.

   **Note:** If the spot is 2 inches or less, pull / push the tool across the whole spot, rather than using the 1 inch / 2 inch pattern.

4. Just past the lower edge of the spot, release the spray trigger and continue to pull the tool toward you another 1 inch, using the dry vacuum stroke.

5. Lift the tool off the carpet.

Section I

– 38 –

## Chop Stroke Pattern

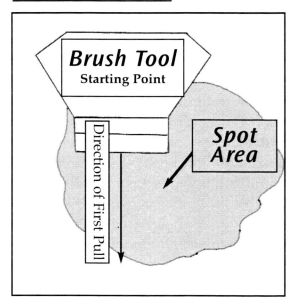

Starting Point

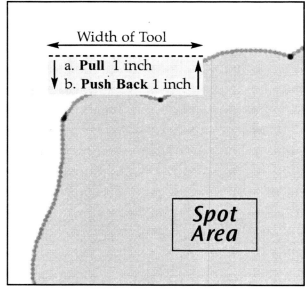

First Pull - **Pull** 1 inch - **Push** 1 inch

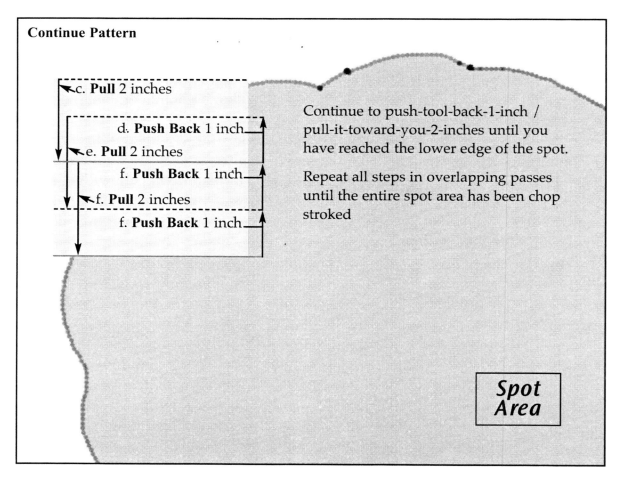

**Continue Pattern**

c. **Pull** 2 inches

d. **Push Back** 1 inch

e. **Pull** 2 inches

f. **Push Back** 1 inch

f. **Pull** 2 inches

f. **Push Back** 1 inch

Continue to push-tool-back-1-inch / pull-it-toward-you-2-inches until you have reached the lower edge of the spot.

Repeat all steps in overlapping passes until the entire spot area has been chop stroked

### *Rinse Spot using Chop Stroke, continued*

6. If the spot is wider than the width of the tool, again place the tool just beyond the upper edge of the spot. This time, move the tool to the right of the original area rinsed. (You want your next rinse stroke to overlap the area previously covered by 1 inch.)

7. Slowly repeat the pulling / pushing pattern with the tool as you press and hold the spray trigger until just past the edge of the spot. Then release the trigger and finish with the dry vacuum stroke for 1 inch. (After you've rinsed the entire spot one time, you may want change direction. Start the pull / push pattern from the side of the spot and chop stroke it at a 90° angle from the original passes. Depending on the type of spot and your pile design, chop stroking from different directions can expose more sides of the yarns to the rinsing/scrubbing action.)

8. Repeat all steps in overlapping passes until the entire spot area has been chop stroked at least the number of times specified in the treatment instructions. (If needed, additional passes will not hurt the carpet, as long as you remove the added moisture with the dry stoke after each pass.)

---

**Pull / Push Pattern (Shown on page 38):**

  a. From just above the upper edge of the spot, pull the tool toward you 1 inch.

  b. Push it back to just above the upper left edge of the spot.

  c. Pull it toward you 2 inches.

  d. Push it back 1 inch.

  e. Pull it toward you 2 inches.

  f. Continue the push-tool-back-1-inch / pull-it-toward-you-2-inches until you have reached the lower edge of the spot.

At that point push the tool back 1 inch and pull it toward you 1 inch.

**Note:** If the spot is 2 inches or less, pull / push the tool across the whole spot, rather than using the 1 inch / 2 inch pattern.

---

Section I

## *Vacuum Debris with Spot Machine*

**Purpose:** To remove the debris left after scraping dry spots, such as dried banana, asphalt or soft cheese, by dry vacuuming them out of the carpet yarns with the spot machine before you apply spotting agents. **Note:** You may be able to see the spot better and have more control over the area being vacuumed if you remove any attachments from the hose. But, you can use the crevice tool attached to the hose, if you wish, as long as the sizes of the spot particles are all small enough to fit through the opening of the tool. Clean the hose or tool thoroughly after removing the debris.

— 40 —

  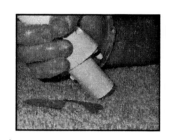

**Step 1**  **Step 2**  **Step 3**

**To do:**

1. Lay the hose on the carpet with the opening near the outside edge of the spot furthest from you. (If you are using a crevice tool, the opening would be just outside the edge of the spot.)

2. Holding the hose at a 45° angle to the surface of the carpet, slowly pull the hose toward you till it reaches the opposite side of the spot. (The bottom edge of the hose opening or crevice tool should scrape across the surface of the carpet as you pull. This scraping action will loosen more spot matter.)

3. Lift the hose opening off the carpet.

4. Move the hose opening to a slightly different place on the outside edge of the spot and slowly pull the hose towards you.

5. Repeat placing the hose opening at a slightly different place on the outside edge of the spot and pulling it towards you until the entire spot area has been vacuumed and no more spot matter removes.

# Spray Bottles - Spotting Agents

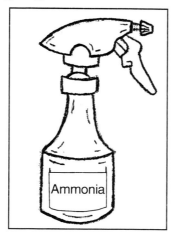

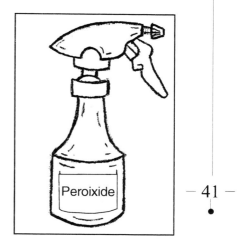

## *Spotting Agent Techniques - General Facts*

Spray bottles have two settings -- a stream setting and a mist setting. **Caution:** Always use the mist setting. You can apply spotting agents more uniformly and in lesser amounts. It also reduces the chances of over-wetting the spot and spreading it or washing spot matter further down into the carpet.

For more information on spotting agents, see "Spotting Agents - Detailed Descriptions", beginning on page 14 of "Chapter 2. Your Spotting Kit".

**Before each spot treatment:**

• Do the following for each spray bottle of spotting agent:

1. Refill with the proper chemical, if needed - Alcohol, Ammonia (diluted 1 part ammonia to 3 parts water) or Hydrogen Peroxide.

2. Check the spray unit to make sure it's properly tightened on the bottle to avoid spills or evaporation.

3. Adjust the spray setting. Turn the spray tip on the nozzle from OFF to the MIST setting.

4. Spray a small amount of spotter into your sink, towel or the extra bucket to be sure the nozzle is properly adjusted and primed.

### *Spotting Agent Techniques - General Facts, continued*

- Measure the spot's diameter with your ruler. This diameter number helps determine how many times you spray the spot with the spotting agent. The amount of spotting agent required for different sized spots of the same type of spill varies because:

  - **Smaller spots** - Their overall volume is less. They cover a smaller surface area of the carpet. Plus, they normally stay close to the top of the carpet pile. Smaller spots need less spotting agent to penetrate and break down the spot matter.

  - **Larger spots** - Their overall volume is greater. Not only do they cover a bigger area on the carpet surface, but they often go deeper into the pile. More spotting agent is needed to penetrate their bigger volume and to get deeper into the carpet.

### During each spot treatment:

**Caution:** Always use only the amount - "small" or "generous" - specified in the treatment step. (The amount of spotting agent needed to successfully treat different types of spots is based on many spot attributes - not just spot size. These include: How fresh or how old is it? Is it liquid, gel or powder? How thin or how thick? What is the makeup of the spot - dense oils, coarse proteins, etc.? How sensitive is it to this specific spotting agent?)

**Best Practice:** Always apply the minimum amount of spotting agent necessary. It's much easier to rework a spot that's been under-treated than to try to fix one that's been over-wetted.

### After each spot treatment:

1. Pour the hydrogen peroxide back into its brown bottle to prolong its effective shelf life.

2. Turn the spray tip of each bottle to the OFF position.

3. Check the spray units to make sure they're properly tightened on the bottles.

4. Put the spray bottles in the bottom of your spotting kit bucket.

## *Mist on a Generous Amount*

**Purpose:** To apply the appropriate amount of spotting agent by spraying it on a spot. This is usually followed by tamping or agitation to enhance the spotter's contact with the spot matter. The spotting agent is then allowed to work undisturbed for a specified length of time. During this soaking or "dwell" time, the agent penetrates the spot, breaks it down and softens its structure. **Caution:** Use only the amount specified in the treatment step.

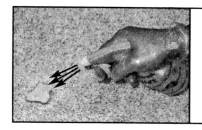

**Step 1**                              **Step 2**

**To do:**

1. Hold the spray tip of the properly adjusted and primed spray bottle about 3 - 4 inches above the spot.

2. Firmly squeeze the spray trigger till it stops. Spray the spot the required number of times, based on its diameter. A "generous amount" = 2 sprays for each 1 inch of the spot's diameter. (See the Generous Amount Examples below.) If more than one spray is required, mist a different area of the spot each time until the proper amount has been disbursed

---

**Generous Amount Examples:**

- **1/2 inch spot diameter: 1 spray**
  (1/2 inch x 2 sprays per inch = 1 spray)

- **1 inch spot diameter: 2 sprays**
  (1 inch x 2 sprays per inch = 2 sprays)

- **1-1/2 inch spot diameter: 3 sprays**
  (1-1/2 inches x 2 sprays per inch = 3 sprays)

- **2 inch spot diameter: 4 sprays**
  (2 inches x 2 sprays per inch = 4 sprays)

- **3 inch spot diameter: 6 sprays**
  (3 inches x 2 sprays per inch = 6 sprays)

---

Section I

## *Mist on a Small Amount*

**Purpose:** To apply the appropriate amount of spotting agent by spraying it on a spot. This is usually followed by tamping or agitation to enhance the spotter's contact with the spot matter. The spotting agent is then allowed to work undisturbed for a specified length of time. During this soaking or "dwell" time, the agent penetrates the spot, breaks it down and softens its structure. **Caution:** Use only the amount specified in the treatment step.

**Step 1**

**Step 2**

**To do:**

1. Hold the spray tip of the properly adjusted and primed spray bottle about 3 - 4 inches above the spot.

2. Firmly squeeze the spray trigger till it stops. Spray the spot the required number of times, based on its diameter. A "small amount" = 1 spray for each 1 inch of the spot's diameter. (See the Small Amount Examples below.) If more than one spray is required, mist a different area of the spot each time until the proper amount has been disbursed.

---

**Small Amount Examples:**

- **1/2 inch spot diameter: 1/2 spray**
  (1/2 inch x 1 spray per inch = 1/2 spray)

- **1 inch spot diameter: 1 spray**
  (1 inch x 1 spray per inch = 1 spray)

- **1-1/2 inch spot diameter: 1-1/2 sprays**
  (1-1/2 inches x 1 spray per inch = 1-1/2 sprays)

- **2 inch spot diameter: 2 sprays**
  (2 inches x 1 spray per inch = 2 sprays)

- **3 inch spot diameter: 3 sprays**
  (3 inches x 1 spray per inch = 3 sprays)

---

# Towel, Washcloth, Chamois

## *Towel, Washcloth, Chamois - General Facts*

The pressure used for blotting a spot is determined by the size and type of spot you're treating. Generally, the larger the spot -- especially more liquid ones which penetrate further into the carpet, the more pressure is used to remove it. Very thick liquids containing heavy dye or globular spots such as wet blood require that you barely touch them with the towel. This prevents your spreading the spot or forcing it deeper into the carpet pile. Other dye spots like those made by carbon paper require a gentle blot for the same reason. The treatment instructions tell you how much pressure to use when blotting the spot. If no specific amount of pressure is listed, you can blot at a pressure you can comfortably apply.

A washcloth or smaller piece of chamois is usually easier to control when barely touching or gently blotting a spot. A hand towel (or washcloth, depending on the size of the spot) or similar size chamois works best for blotting or firmly blotting. A bath towel or larger piece of chamois is usually best when blotting by stepping on the towel.

**Caution:** Always use a different clean, dry part of the towel each time you blot the spot. Change towels as often as needed. Your spot will be absorbed faster and better, plus it helps avoid spreading the spot to clean areas of the carpet or re-contaminating the area you've already blotted.

Section I

## Blot Spot by Barely Touching It with Edge of Towel

**Purpose:** To start the removal of small, thick, wet/fresh spots, such as blood, by barely touching the spot with the edge of a small towel so the spot will wick up into the towel.

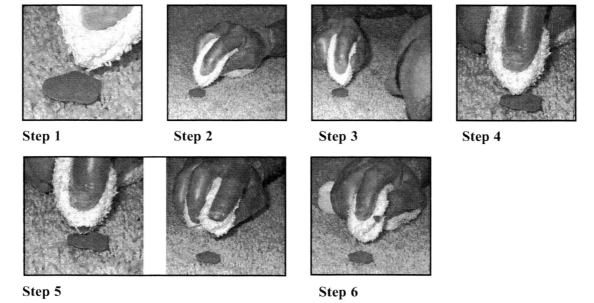

**Step 1**         **Step 2**         **Step 3**         **Step 4**

**Step 5**                    **Step 6**

**To do:**

1. Hold a folded washcloth in your hand with a single edge or corner hanging down slightly.

2. Place the wrist of the hand holding the cloth on the carpet next to the spot.

3. Bend over so your head is almost down on the carpet and you are looking at the spot and cloth from the side.

4. Very slowly move the cloth down until the edge or corner is just barely touching the top of the spot. **Caution:** Do **not** press the washcloth down on the carpet surface.

5. Wait a few seconds until absorption appears to stop and then lift the cloth off the spot.

6. Refold the cloth so you have a clean, dry edge or corner to blot with and then barely touch the spot.

7. Repeat refolding the washcloth and barely touching the spot in different areas until no more is absorbed. (Replace the cloth as needed to aid blotting and avoid spreading the spot or re-contaminating the spot area.)

8. Carefully put the dirty cloth into your Contaminants bucket.

## *Blot Spot with Towel*

- Or -

## *Gently Blot Spot with Towel*

- Or -

## *Firmly Blot Spot with Towel*

**Purpose: Blot** - To help remove most types of liquid, semi-liquid or oily spots at the start of treatment, or during treatment after more solid matter has been removed and/or after spotting agents have been applied.

**Gently Blot** - To start the removal of small, sensitive spots, such as carbon paper using a very gentle touch.

**Firmly Blot** - To help remove sticky spots such as tree sap or asphalt or messy spots like berries at the start of treatment or to remove spot matter after you have applied and agitated spotting agents into the spot.

This removal is done by placing your towel-covered finger or fingers on the spot, letting the spot begin to transfer to the towel and then finishing with a twisting rub on the spot as you remove the towel. The pressure placed on the towel and during the twisting rub depends on the type of spot being treated.

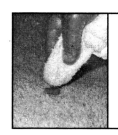

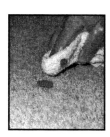

**Step 1**      **Step 2**      **Step 3**      **Step 4**

**To do:**

1. Put a small towel or washcloth over your extended pointer finger and grasp the rest of the towel or washcloth into your palm with the other fingers. (If the spot is a larger one, use two extended fingers.)

2. Put the towel-covered finger(s) on the spot and keep it/them there at the appropriate pressure for about 2 seconds.

   • **Blot:** Press the towel into the spot so it penetrates into the upper portion of the carpet pile, but do not put the full force of your weight on your fingers. Be careful to not press the spot matter further into the carpet pile.

   • **Gently Blot:** Place your towel-covered finger so the cloth is gently touching the tops of the carpet yarns in the spot area.

   • **Firmly Blot:** Leaning forward so your full weight is on your fingers, press the washcloth or towel into the spot so it penetrates into the upper portion of the carpet pile. If you are unable to put much pressure on your fingers, lay the towel on the spot and use your fist to press it into the spot.

### *Blot Spot with Towel* - Or - *Gently Blot Spot with Towel* - Or - *Firmly Blot Spot with Towel,*

#### *continued*

3. At the end of the 2 seconds, quickly turn your hand and finger(s) about 45° to produce a slight twisting rub on the yarns in the spot area and immediately lift your towel-covered fingers from the carpet surface.

   - **Blot or Firmly Blot:** Rub the carpet yarns.

   - **Gently Blot:** Gently rub across the tips of the carpet yarns

4. Reposition the towel on your finger(s) so you have a clean, dry area to blot with. (If you are laying the towel on the spot and using your fist to firmly blot, refold the towel so there's a clean, dry area over the spot.)

5. Blot the spot again using the appropriate amount of pressure for the type of spot you are treating.

6. Repeat repositioning the towel and using the appropriate pressure to blot the spot in different areas until no more absorbs. (Replace the towel as needed to aid blotting and avoid spreading the spot or re-contaminating the spot area.)

7. Carefully put the dirty towel into your Contaminants bucket.

## *Blot Spot by Stepping On Towel*

**Purpose:** To start the removal of larger liquid spots like alcoholic beverages, by stepping on the chamois or towel-covered spot. **Caution:** Wear plastic or rubber soled shoes when doing this type of blotting. Do not go barefoot and do **not** wear leather-soled shoes because the liquid from the spot can cause the dye in the leather to run and cause a bigger problem than your original one.

  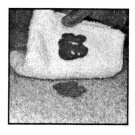 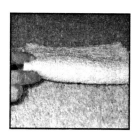

**Step 1**　　　　　**Step 2**　　　　　**Step 3**　　　　　**Step 4**

**To do:**

1. Place a folded chamois, bath towel or several hand towels over the spot.

2. Step on the chamois or towel-covered spot with your full body weight for about 2 seconds. (If you are unable to do this, kneel on the carpet next to the spot and use your fist or the palm of your hand to apply as much upper body weight to the spot as possible without hurting yourself.)

3. Lift the chamois/towel off the carpet.

4. Refold and reposition the chamois/towel over the spot so you have a clean, dry area to blot with and then stand on the spot again.

5. Repeat repositioning the chamois/towel and standing on the spot until no more is absorbed. (Replace the chamois or towel as needed to aid blotting and avoid spreading the spot or re-contaminating the spot area.)

6. Carefully put the dirty chamois or towel into your Contaminants bucket.

Section I

— 50 —

## Pinch Out Spot with a Towel or Tissue

**Purpose:** To remove soft spots, such as soft candy or crayon, by pinching the dirty carpet yarns between your towel-covered thumb and forefinger and then pulling the fingers up and off the yarns.

**Step 1**

**Step 2**

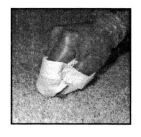
**Step 4**

**Step 5**

**Step 6**

**To do:**

1. Extend your thumb and pointer finger. Loosely curl the other fingers against your palm.

2. Put a washcloth, hand towel or disposable tissues over the thumb and pointer finger of that hand. Press the washcloth into your palm as if you were making a little puppet face.

3. Grasp the rest of the towel in your palm with the other fingers. (If needed, move any excess toweling out of the way by pulling it up around your wrist and holding it with the other hand.)

4. With your towel-covered finger and thumb nearly touching one another, firmly press them into the spot so you can grasp a few of the dirty carpet yarns between them. Avoid pressing so deep into the pile that you force spot matter further into the carpet.

5. Pinch your finger and thumb together around the dirty yarns and then pull your fingers up and off the yarns.

### Pinch Out Spot with a Towel or Tissue, continued

6. Reposition the towel on your fingers so you have a clean area to pinch with. Then pinch out more of the spot matter in a different part of the spot. **Caution:** Use a clean part of the towel each time to avoid spreading the spot or re-contaminating the yarns you've already cleaned. (Replace the towel or tissues as needed to avoid spreading the spot or re-contaminating the spot area.)

7. Repeat repositioning the towel and pinching out the spot matter in different parts of the spot until no more removes.

8. Carefully put the dirty towel or tissues into your Contaminants bucket.

## Rake Spot onto Towel with a Hard Brush

A description of this technique is under the above title on page 9 in the "Brush - Hard" section of this Chapter.

## Scoop Spot onto Towel using Spoon

A description of this technique is under the above title on page 28 in the "Spoon" section of this Chapter.

## Scrape Spot into Disposable Towel with a Dinner Knife

A description of this technique is under the above title on page 16 in the "Knife - Dinner" section of this Chapter.

# Vacuum Cleaner / Wet/Dry Shop Vac

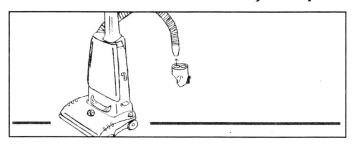

## *Vacuum Debris with Vacuum Cleaner*

-Or-

## *Vacuum, Dry Powders (Powdered Detergents, Dry Goods, Etc.)*

**Purpose: Debris:** To remove the debris left after scraping dry spots, such as dried banana, asphalt or soft cheese, out of the carpet yarns before applying spotting agents.

**Dry Powders:** To remove dry, powdered spots like detergents, baby powder, flour, sugar by vacuuming.

**Note:** Some treatment instructions say to use a shop vac rather than a regular vacuum cleaner, but you can use a shop vacuum any time you do this technique. If, however, a shop vac is specified in the treatment steps, you **must** use it to avoid clogging your regular vacuum cleaner or filling it with potentially smelly debris.

**Note:** You may be able to see the spot better and have more control over the area being vacuumed if you remove any attachments from the vacuum cleaner hose. But, you can use the crevice tool attached to the hose, if you wish, as long as the sizes of the spot particles are all small enough to fit through the opening of the tool.

  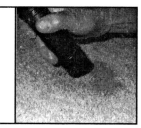 

**Step 1**          **Step 2**                              **Step 3**

***Vacuum Debris with Vacuum Cleaner* -Or- *Vacuum, Dry Powders (Powdered Detergents,***

***Dry Goods, Etc.), continued***

**To do:**

1. Lay the hose on the carpet with the opening near the outside edge of the spot furthest from you. (If you are using a crevice tool, the opening would be just outside the edge of the spot.)

2. Holding the hose at a 45° angle or less to the surface of the carpet, slowly pull the hose toward you until it reaches the opposite side of the spot. (The bottom edge of the hose opening should scrape across the surface of the carpet as you pull. This scraping action will loosen more spot matter.)

3. Lift the hose or tool off the carpet.

4. Move the opening to a slightly different place on the outside edge of the spot and slowly pull the hose toward you.

5. Repeat placing the hose opening at a slightly different place on the outside edge of the spot and pulling it towards you until the entire spot area has been vacuumed and no more spot matter removes.

6. Thoroughly clean the hose opening. (If you have used the crevice tool, carefully put it into your Contaminants bucket and clean it thoroughly after treating the spot.)

— 53 —

Section I

## *Vacuum Fine, Dry Powders with End of Vacuum Hose Only*
## *(Copier Toner, Soot, Jello® Powder)*

**Purpose:** To carefully remove fine, dry powders like copier toner, soot, powdered food coloring or Jello® powder by vacuuming. **Caution:** Use a vacuum cleaner with a micro-filtration bag or a bag-less system with a HEPA filter for this spotting technique. The fine particles may escape a wet/dry shop vacuum or any bag-less system without a filter and become airborne, resulting in further contamination of the area. **Caution:** Do this technique without any type of tool on the end of the vacuum hose. You need as much control as possible over where the hose touches the carpet, because these fine, dry powders are easily spread to clean areas of the carpet.

— 54 —

 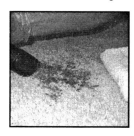  

**Step 1**   **Step 3**   **Step 4**   **Step 5**

**Step 6**   **Step 9**

### *Vacuum Fine, Dry Powders with End of Vacuum Hose Only (Copier Toner, Soot, Jello®*

### *Powder), continued*

**To do:**

1. Lay a small towel or several disposable tissues next to the spot. (It/they will be used to wipe the powder off the end of the vacuum cleaner hose after each pass at the spot.)

2. Remove any attachment from the end of the vacuum hose.

3. Lay the hose on the carpet with the opening near the outside edge of the spot furthest from you.

4. Holding the hose at a 45° angle or less to the surface of the carpet, slowly pull the hose opening from the edge into the middle of the spot. (The bottom edge of the hose opening should scrape across the surface of the carpet as you pull. This scraping action will loosen more spot matter.)

5. Lift the end of the hose off the carpet.

6. To avoid spreading the spot, carefully wipe any spot matter off the hose opening with a towel or tissue. Put the dirty tissue or towel in the Contaminants bucket so it won't soil the clean carpet.

7. Start from a different place on the edge of the spot and make another pass across it.

8. Repeat vacuuming the entire spot 8 - 10 times or until no more spot matter removes. Wipe the hose opening thoroughly after each pass.

9. Hold the hose at a 90° angle to the carpet's surface and place the entire opening on the spot. (This forms a seal that increases the sucking action of the vacuum and also moves the yarns around and opens them up so the vacuum picks up even more fine powder.)

10. Slowly move the hose opening in a circular motion clockwise and then counterclockwise over the entire spot and around the edges of it. **Caution:** Keep within the edges of the spot. Going outside them could spread the spot to clean areas of the carpet. If you see any powder on the hose opening, wipe it off with your tissue and put the tissue in the bucket.

11. Repeat until no more spot matter removes.

12. Carefully clean the hose opening and drop the dirty towel or tissues into your Contaminants bucket.

— 55 —

Section I

## *Vacuum Dry Goods with Vacuum Beater Bar*

**Purpose:** To further remove dry, powdered spots like detergents, baby powder, flour, sugar after you have vacuumed them with the end of the vacuum hose. (The beater bar is the rotating brush inside the head of your vacuum that's normally used when you're vacuuming your carpet.)

**Step 1**

**To do:**

1. Vacuum the spot area as if you were doing your regular carpet cleaning. Approach the spot from different directions to remove spot matter from all sides of the carpet yarns.

2. Repeat until it appears that no more of the spot is being removed.

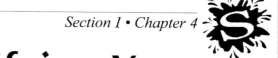

# Chapter 4 *Identifying Your Spot, Stain Or Discoloration*

## Introduction

This guide gives detailed instructions about how to treat a variety of spots, but before you take action, you must first identify what caused the spot so you can use the most effective treatment method.

If you were there when the accident occurred or have credible witnesses, then identification is easy.

If the spot is not new or there were no credible witnesses to the accident, then you must do some detective work to try to identify what caused the problem.

In this Chapter, I will give you some basic methods for identifying unknown spots, plus additional clues for determining the cause of what I call "Mystery Spots, Stains and Discolorations".

**Note:** The common term used to describe the results of an accidental spill on your carpet is a "spot" (or spots) and that is the term we will use throughout this book. But to be a little more technical, that spill can cause a "spot", a "stain", a "discoloration", or a combination spot/stain, etc.

Defining the difference between spots, stains and discolorations is like trying to differentiate between carpets, rugs and mats. The terms have been used interchangeably for so long that attempting to separate the three would be like trying to separate the Three Musketeers.

For our purposes, let's define them as follows:

**Spot** - A spot adds substance to the carpet fibers and usually changes the way the carpet feels when you touch it - greasy, crusty, sticky, etc. (Spot examples: gum, tar, oil, starch, sugar.)

**Stain** - A stain adds color to the fibers, but does not change the feel or texture of the carpet unless it is combined with another contaminant. (Stain examples: hair dye, wood stain, Sugar-Free Kool-Aid®, colored medicines.)

**Discoloration** - A discoloration causes a change in color, or movement of, or loss of color to occur in the fibers, but does not usually change the texture of the carpet. Color movement happens when the spot causes a dye buildup in some areas so the fibers are darker, and a lessening of the dye in others so they are lighter than they were originally. A loss of color means the color disappears from the affected fibers. (Discoloration examples: bleaches, strong soaps, urine, strong alcohols, gasoline.)

Discolorations are the most difficult type of spill to remedy because they generally don't leave anything behind to remove from the carpet. The spill simply changes, moves or removes what is already there. This means that neither your actions or those of a professional will reverse the dye movement and return the spot area to its original color. Instead, the pro may recommend re-dyeing or cut and plug or replacement of the carpet in the damaged area.

I mention discolorations because I want you to have realistic expectations about which spots you can effectively treat and which cannot be entirely repaired using my recommended chemicals and special application techniques.

To further complicate things, many spot and stain problems are often combined into one compound. Examples:

- Nail polish, candle wax and lipstick all have hard components that add substance (spots) to the carpet fibers and dye components that add color (stain).

- Coffee has a vegetable dye called tannin (color - stain) and may be mixed with cream and sugar (substances - spot).

- Perfumes, pesticides and fuels contain colorants (stain) as well as the ability to change, distort or move carpet dye (discoloration).

In order to do successful spot removal, you don't have to worry about whether the spill is a spot, a stain or a discoloration, because I've already considered that when I wrote the treatment steps.

Knowing the differences between the three terms can be useful for you, because it can help explain why the treatments for various spills are different, plus it influences how effective your spot removal efforts will be.

Use the following identification methods to see if you can determine exactly what your problem spot is before you start any step of the treatment phase.

## *Identification Methods*

Basically, you identify unknown spots the same way you have been identifying other things your entire life - by asking questions, using your physical senses, by general observation, and by using your good common sense.

These methods are listed in the order I have found them to be most effective:

• Ask

• Use your physical senses

• Analyze the location

• Try to match the spot

If asking doesn't work, then try using your physical senses. If that still doesn't solve the problem, keep trying the next method until you have either identified the spot or have given up and decided to call a pro.

### *Ask*

Just asking is usually the easiest method for identifying unknown spots. Ask the people who live in your home, drive your car, or work with you if they might possibly know what caused the spot on your home, car or office carpet. Hopefully, the person or persons responsible for the spot will feel bad about it and will be glad to give you all the dreadful details about what the spill is and how it happened.

**Best Practice:** It is also a good idea to ask if they have done anything to try to remove the spot. If so, find out the name of every product they used in their removal efforts. (Please, tell me they didn't try chlorine bleach!) If you must call in a pro, being able to tell him/her everything that has been done during earlier removal efforts will help the professional determine the most efficient and least expensive remedy for the problem.

**Hint:** If you own an auto detailing shop that does minor carpet spot cleanup, you can make your work more effective by asking customers before they leave:

• Do they know what's on their car carpet?
• Did they try to remove it earlier?
• If so, what did they use?

If you are lucky, asking is all that's needed to find out what the problem is so you can look up the spot in Chapter 5 in Section II and use the proper treatment method. If not, try using your physical senses to identify the spot.

Section I

— 4 —

### *Use Your Physical Senses*

Using your physical senses may give you clues as to what the spot is.

**Sight** is the first sense used to determine a spot's composition:

- What color is it?
- Does it look crusty, shiny, dull?
- Does it look lighter or darker than the surrounding carpet fibers?
- Is there any build-up?
- Have you seen something before that looked similar? What was it?

**Touch** is the second sense used:

- Does it feel sticky? Greasy? Gummy? Powdery? Hard? Soft?
- What is the texture of the spot? Rough? Smooth? No texture at all?

**Smell** is the last sense used. There are two ways to smell the problem:

- Kneel down over the spot and smell the airborne odor produced by it.
- Pinch at the spot matter firmly with your fingers, followed by rubbing your fingers together. Then smell the odor on your fingertips. (The combination of heat generated by friction and the moisture from your skin intensify the odor from the spot.)

**Caution:** If you have pets that run about the house, use caution. Those little brown lumps ground into the carpet may not be chocolate candy.

If using your physical senses doesn't solve the mystery, then maybe using the next identification method will solve the spot puzzle.

### *Analyze the Location of the Spot*

Another way to identify your spot is by analyzing it in terms of its location - exactly where it is in the house, business, etc.

Examples:

- A brown stain you see near the coffee machine is probably spilled coffee.

- Red, pink, brown or black spots in front of a vanity usually indicates cosmetics.

- A thick red spatter in front of the refrigerator or around the dining room table would suggest ketchup or some other food item.

- A yellow stain around the sofa leg that corresponds to a similar stain on the sofa's skirt . . . . looks like Spot the dog has been up to his old tricks again.

It's said in the real estate business that the location is the most important aspect of selling a home. It may also prove to be the most important aspect in identifying what your spots are as well. If not, then try matching the spot.

## *Try to Match the Spot*

If using the other spot identification methods has failed, try to match it! What I mean is, look for something that looks, feels or smells like the spot you are trying to treat.

- Check around the immediate area, on a counter top, in a cabinet, atop a table, atop a chest of drawers, in a drawer, in a toy box, in a play makeup set, a vanity, a tool chest, in a pantry or even underneath the furniture to see if there is a container or other item that could be the source of the mystery spot.

- If you have found a container that could be the source of the problem, checking the label (if available) may show you ingredients that have similar color, texture and odor to the spot.

- Consider whether there is a logical (or illogical in the case of children) reason why this potential source of the problem would have been in the spot area.

If you are reasonably sure you have located the rogue spot material, ask the person you think might be responsible if this is what the spot material might be. (Sometimes people, especially children, are reluctant to admit anything until after the evidence has been presented.)

## *The Spot Remains a Mystery*

If after using all the other identification methods, trying to match the spot does not yield satisfactory results, look in the "Mystery Spots" starting on page 6 to see if there is a match. If so, follow the directions listed with each spot.

If even looking in "Mystery Spots" does not help, nor give you enough confidence to attempt treatment, your best option is to see "Chapter 10. How Do I Find A Quality Carpet Cleaning Professional" and use the IICRC (Institute Of Inspection, Cleaning & Restoration Certification) Referral Line (800) 835-4624 to find a certified cleaning technician who may be able to identify the problem and remove it.

When you call, describe your problem and ask for a technician with a lot of experience dealing with tough and hard to identify problem spots. Also ask that the technician have experience in carpet dyeing and repair, just in case the only effective treatment option is to re-dye or cut the spot out and plug the hole with another piece of carpet (referred to as a "seamless insert").

Section I

— 6 —

# *Mystery Spots*

One of the most frustrating carpet dilemmas a person can encounter is a mysterious spot, stain or discoloration that has no apparent source. (Remember I loosely defined a spot as something that adds texture to carpet fibers, a stain as something that adds color, and a discoloration as something that moves, removes or changes the carpet dye.)

One day the carpet in your home, office or car is fine. The next day a mysterious spot, stain or discoloration appears - seemingly without cause or any relationship to the circumstances. Even your usually reliable spot makers say they don't know what it is or how it got there.

To help you identify these mystery spots, I have collected information on some of the more common and yet more perplexing (when you find them) spot, stain and discoloration-causing substances. This group of mystery spots does not include every possible puzzling spot. In fact, there are some spots that even the most well-trained professional cannot identify. (Fortunately, those are few in number, but they do exist.)

In addition to helping you identify your mystery spot, I also list the suggested treatment(s) for the problem. Some of the spots you will be able to treat yourself, others will require a professional to remove them or in the case of really problematic spots, stains or discolorations, it will be necessary for the pro to re-dye the spot area or do a seamless insert (a cut and plug). In some really bad situations, he or she may suggest replacing the carpet or just living with the spot as the best option.

The first mystery spot described is not always such a "mystery", but it can be one of the more frustrating situations - the recurring spot (or "the spot that wouldn't stay away"). After showing you how to handle these repeat problems, we'll get into the real mystery spots, stains and discolorations.

**Note**: As I mentioned in the "Introduction and Preview" at the front of the book, this guide is for synthetic carpets. I do **not** recommend your using the same home treatment processes for natural carpet fibers like wool, cotton or silk because they react differently from synthetics. In this Chapter, however, I will include some information about how these mystery spots can affect natural fiber carpets or rugs so you will have some idea what your professional will be dealing with when you call him or her.

## Recurring Spots

Of all the frustrating spots to treat, recurring spots or stains must be one of the worst. Just when you think you or the professional carpet cleaner have removed a spot or stain, it reappears within a few hours, days or weeks....

The main reasons spots recur (or seem to recur) is because:

• The spill was never completely removed in the first place. Either the proper treatment steps were not followed or the spill was too large or too difficult (like some oily or other types of spills) for you to treat effectively. Some spots are impossible to completely remove, even for a professional with his/her heavy-duty spotters and equipment.

• The spill soaked into the carpet fibers and with time and humidity, wicks back up to the surface. Any spill large enough to penetrate the backing or even further through the pad and to the subfloor (the depth of penetration partially depends on how dense the carpet pile is) can become a recurring spot.

• The spot was originally treated before you read this guide, so the wrong type of spot remover or cleaner was used to treat it. These wrong removers can leave residues behind, even though the spot or stain is gone. The residues can become so sticky that they can attract more soil to the spot area than there was before you removed the spot. Unfortunately, these residues may include high pH chemical soaps that can damage and discolor carpet dyes.

**What You Normally See**

What you will see with the recurring spot will depend on what was there in the first place.

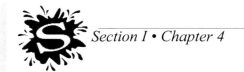 

Section I

— 8 —

**The following lists the spills most likely to cause recurring spots,** especially if the spill was a large one. If you've forgotten what caused the spot, this list may help jog your memory.

• Alcoholic Beverages

• Body Oils, Butter, Margarine, Spreads

• Cheese - Hard or Dry

• Coffee or Tea

• Cooking Oil, Salad Dressing - Oily

• Detergents, Soaps and Cleaners - Liquid or Gel, Powder

• Dry Goods - Sugar

• Eggs or Egg Beaters® - Cooked or Raw

• Furniture Polish

• Grease

• Lignin Browning: Alkaline Browning, Cellulosic Browning

• Mayonnaise, Miracle Whip®, Milk, Buttermilk, Rice or Soy Milk, Yogurt

• Oils / Thin Lubricants

• Ointments - First Aid, Petroleum Jelly, etc.

• Pasta (with meat, butter or oils)

• Peanut Butter, Other Nut Butters

• Potpourri - Liquid

• Snacks - Dry (chips, peanuts, popcorn, etc.)

• Soft Drinks, Sports Drinks, Isotonics, Energy Drinks

• Soup - Thick

• Soup - Thin, White Clam Sauce

• Spaghetti Sauce, Cheeseburger, Hamburger, Pizza

• Syrup, Honey

• Urine

• Wood Stain, Furniture Stain

**Additional Identification Tests**

If the content of the original spill is still a mystery, you can try the following test to narrow the list of possible spot materials in addition to using the Identification Methods described earlier.

**Hint:** Spray some hydrogen peroxide from your spotting kit on the recurring spot problem. Agitate it with a spoon and then scoop up some of the residue. Watch to see if it foams. Peroxide's high oxygen content causes the soapy residue in poorly formulated spotting agents and other cleaners to foam up profusely.

If you do find that soapy residue is your problem, see the spot treatments "Detergents, Soaps, Cleaners - Liquid or Gel" and "Detergents, Soaps and Cleaners - Powder" in Chapter 5 in Section II for information on how remove the residue. These treatments are the ones used for cleaners, but if you want to be even more specific in your identification of the spot material, continue the test by smelling the foam.

Since hydrogen peroxide is virtually odorless, you can smell the foam, then smell the old spot cleaner you used to use (and should have thrown away). Does the foam smell like another cleaner you use, like Pinesol®, etc., that may have dripped from a leaky bucket of cleaner? If so, you know exactly what the problem spot is.

Sugar in the makeup of a spot can also cause recurring spot problems. If spraying the hydrogen peroxide on the spot and agitating does not cause foaming, sugar may be the culprit. In that case, see the instructions for the types of spills containing sugar that most likely caused your spot.

9

Section I

*— 10 —*

**Treatment Options**

If the spot or stain is not too large (or they are not too numerous) or it has not been set by treatment using off-the-shelf spotting agents:

• Be patient.

• Retreat the spot using the treatment steps described for that particular spot in Chapter 5 in Section II. (You may have to repeat the treatment several times if the spot reappears.)

If you cannot treat the spot because it is too large or it has been set by treatment using off-the-shelf spotting agents (or the spots are too numerous):

• Call a professional.

## *The Rest of the Mystery Spots*

The rest of the mystery spots are listed in alphabetical order. To make it easier for you to identify your mystery spot, I have included a table, "Identifying Mystery Spots" on the next page. It lists the mystery spots beneath the characteristic that indicates you have a problem.

For example: If the color is gone, moved or changed in your spot area, look at all the possible causes listed under "Color Loss, Movement or Change". Then go to the individual spot information for each of the possible causes that follows the table and see which one is most likely to be the culprit in your situation.

# Identifying Mystery Spots

| Carpet Problems | | |
|---|---|---|
| **Color Loss, Movement or Change SEE:** | **Fiber Damage SEE:** | **Spots SEE:** |
| • Acne Medicine (Benzoyl Peroxide) | • Bleaches / Cleaning Products with Bleach / Mildew Removers / Hair Lighteners | • Cleaner Splashes / Dripping Trash Bag |
| • Bleaches / Cleaning Products with Bleach / Mildew Removers / Hair Lighteners | • Chlorine / Pool & Hot Tub Chemicals | • Contact Lens Solution / Denture Cleaners, Whiteners |
| • Ceiling Cleaning Compounds | • Disinfectants / Sanitizers | • Filtration |
| • Chlorine / Pool & Hot Tub Chemicals | | • Furniture Stain |
| • Cleaners | | • Graphite, Metal Shavings, and Lubricants from Door Hinges |
| • Cleaners - Very Strong | | • Lignin Browning: Alkaline or Cellulosic Browning |
| • Disinfectants / Sanitizers | | • Oil / Urine / BHT |
| • Foot Fungus Medicine | | • Plant Food |
| • Furniture Stain | | • Rust |
| • Lignin Browning: Alkaline or Cellulosic Browning | | • Tack Strip (Carpet) |
| • Oil / Urine / BHT | | • Water Spills |
| • Perfume | | • Zero-Phantoms |
| • Pesticides / Insecticides / Pet Shampoos | | |
| • Plant Food | | |
| • Soaps / Shampoos | | |
| • Toilet Bowl Cleaner / Sanitizer | | |
| • Water Spills | | |

– 11 –

### *Acne Medicine (Benzoyl Peroxide)*

Typically, nylon, wool, cotton and silk are easily discolored by Benzoyl Peroxide. Olefin, acrylic and polyester are somewhat more resistant, but not entirely.

**What You Normally See / Where You Usually See It**

Discolorations shaped like drips, hand or fingerprints (or the shape of anything else, including a Stridex® pad, that had acne medicine on it and then touched the carpet):

• Light color carpet: Light orange sherbet colored discoloration

• Dark color carpet: Small drips - Light orange sherbet colored discoloration; Large drips - There may be a creamy white center inside the orange sherbet-colored halo.

Location: Drips usually occur on the carpet near bathroom sinks, mirrors. Hand, fingerprint or other shapes may be seen on the carpet (or upholstery) in front of the television.

**Treatment Options**

See "Bleaching Products" in Chapter 5 in Section II and follow the treatment steps for the appropriate Class of spot.

**Best Practice:** Prevention is best. Benzoyl Peroxide is not water-soluble so when your teenager tries to wash this medicine off his or her hands with regular soap, it doesn't remove. Tell anyone in your house who uses acne products to wash their hands very well with liquid dish soap after applying acne medicine. The dish soap does a better job of removing the medicine and you may be able to prevent the problem.

## *Bleaches / Cleaning Products with Bleach /*
## *Mildew Removers / Hair Lighteners*

- Bleaches - Liquid or powder (Clorox®, Purex®, Javex®,) containing 5.25% - 6% sodium hypochlorite

- Home and commercial bathroom and other cleaning products containing bleach - liquid, gel or powdered (Dishwasher detergent, tub and tile cleaners such as chlorinated abrasive cleaners or Softscrub® With Bleach type cleaners containing sodium hypochlorite or lithium hypochlorite)

- Toilet bowl cleaners and sanitizers with bleach, including tablets or powders dropped into the toilet tank

- Mildew Removers - Exterior and interior (Tilex®, etc.)

- Hair lighteners and highlighters that contain 6% hydrogen peroxide

**What You Normally See / Where You Usually See It**

Bleached or discolored areas of carpet, damaged fibers. The kind of damage depends on the type of carpet fiber:

- Nylon, cotton: White to creamy white colored small to large drips, lines, splashes, etc., that are the result of rapid and permanent dye loss.

- Olefin, polyester, acrylic: The fibers themselves are fairly resistant, especially to diluted solutions; but full strength bleach can lighten the color if left for weeks and not neutralized.

- Wool: Fibers dissolve in a few hours.

— 13 —

### *Bleaches / Cleaning Products,* continued

Location: The location where you see the problem generally depends on what caused the problem:

- In or near a laundry room: Liquid or powder laundry bleach

- Kitchen, especially near the dishwasher: Liquid or powder dishwashing detergent

- Bathroom, especially along the base of the bathtub: Cleaning products with bleach or mildew removers

- Bathroom, under the shower door from the base of the shower to as far as the door will open: Cleaning products with bleach or mildew removers dripping off the shower door

- Bathroom, around the toilet: Toilet bowl sanitizers that have dripped off the cleaning brush or the toilet rim during cleaning.

- Bathroom, near the vanity: Hair lighteners or highlighters

- A traffic area outside a bathroom: People tracking cleaning products with bleach or mildew removers from the bathroom floor or rugs onto the carpet

- Throughout the house - multiple dot-sized discolorations: Solutions of bleach and water or cleaning products with bleach in a leaky bucket or bottle or a drippy mop carried through the house

- From the back door to the furnace closet or attic access door - multiple dot-sized discolorations: Bleach used by the heating / air conditioning technician to treat mold or mildew

- Inside the house or office near a window or door - spots and/or stripes of discoloration: Weather stripping has failed to keep mildew remover from entering while the remover was being applied to the outside of the house

- In entry areas from a porch or patio - discolorations are often footprint-shaped: Mildew remover being tracked in from outside

**Caution:** If small amounts of powdered bleaches like sodium perborate (the "safe bleach" in laundry detergents) or sodium dichlorosocyanurate (Comet®, swimming pool cleaning products) are spilled, you may not see anything for months that indicates you have a problem. Then, when water gets spilled on the area or your friendly, neighborhood carpet cleaner activates the bleach using any water-based carpet cleaning method, you see the damage. (In spite of your first response, the carpet professional did not add a little bleach to the cleaning solution or spill strong chemicals on your carpet, so he/she is not responsible for the problem.)

**Treatment Options**

See "Bleaching Products" in Chapter 5 in Section II and follow the treatment steps for the appropriate Class of spot.

Call a professional to determine whether the areas can be re-dyed.

• If the discolored fibers have been damaged by the bleach, it may be difficult to re-dye the areas.

• If the damaged areas are too large to re-dye, a cut and plug (seamless insert) may be the only solution.

If the carpet has unusual patterns that make color matching difficult or there are no replacement pieces of carpet to use as a plug for a large area, replacement of the carpet in the entire room may be the only repair option.

If the areas can be re-dyed, the bleach will first have to be completely neutralized with an anti-chlorinator so the replacement dye will not bleach out as well. Make sure the person who will be treating your carpet is a certified carpet dye specialist. (Call the IICRC Referral Line (800) 835-4624 to find a qualified person. Chapter 10 has more information about finding a quality professional.)

## Ceiling Cleaning Compounds

Older ceiling cleaning compounds contain sodium or lithium hypochlorite that can cause discolorations in your carpets. Newer versions of these cleaning compounds do not contain these chemicals and will not discolor carpets.

**What You Normally See / Where You Usually See It**

- Nylon, wool or cotton: Dotted areas of color loss all over the carpet or pools of color loss (areas where excess solution ran off of plastic drop cloths) after ceiling tiles have been cleaned.

- Olefin, polyester or acrylic: These fibers are not affected by these chemicals.

Location: Mostly seen in office buildings, stores or restaurants, but could be in homes that have had minor restoration work done after a small, smoky fire or water damage.

**Treatment Options**

Nylon, wool or cotton: If you start seeing these areas of color loss after having your ceiling cleaned, call a professional carpet cleaning / spot dyeing company to neutralize the bleaches and re-dye. A thorough carpet cleaning should be done within 3 days after the ceiling tile cleaning is done. (This is especially important if you cannot verify the ingredients in the ceiling cleaner and/or you saw no plastic drop cloths being used, or they were being used improperly during cleaning.) Tell the cleaning company why you're having the carpets cleaned so they can use the proper chemicals and cleaning methods to neutralize the problem.

**Caution:** Get an estimate before having the work done. Re-dyeing hundreds of tiny discolorations may not be worth the cost. Also, if the spots are not properly neutralized before re-dyeing, they could come back. In some cases, replacing the carpet may be a better option.

**Best Practice:** Prevention is best. Ask the company who will be cleaning your ceiling whether its cleaners contain sodium or lithium hypochlorite. If their cleaners contain these chemicals, get someone else. If they are not sure, ask to see the Material Safety Data Sheets or MSDS pages required by the government. These sheets will list the ingredients in the cleaners. (If they won't tell you or say they don't have the MSDS sheets for their cleaners, I suggest you find another ceiling cleaner.)

## *Chlorine / Pool & Hot Tub Chemicals*

The concentrated chlorine in pool chemicals contains up to 10% sodium hypochlorite. Nylon, cotton and wool are more susceptible to damage by chlorine. Olefin, polyester and acrylic are more resistant. The biggest problem with these chemicals is that unless you see the spill or someone tells you they've spilled pool chemicals on the carpet, you're probably not aware that chlorine is in the carpet until the fibers are already discolored or damaged.

**What You Normally See / Where You Usually See It**

Color loss or damaged carpet fibers:

- Color loss over time, especially in nylon and wool carpets that are near doorways close to any swimming pool or hot tub where chlorine algaecides are used or that are in the main traffic areas between the pool or hot tub and the rest of the house: The color loss is caused by chlorine fumes entering under doors, or people (or pets) with wet feet walking from the pool or hot tub into the house.

- People or pet footprint-shaped areas of color loss, especially on nylon and wool carpet: People or pets have been tracking particles of chlorine sticks, tablets or powder onto the carpet. A little increase in humidity or spilled water activates the bleaching properties of chlorine and you see the damage.

- Dissolved wool carpet fibers: Someone has spilled or dripped concentrated pool chemicals on the carpet. (Say goodbye to those wool fibers in the spill area, because they will be gone in a matter of hours. Unfortunately, there is nothing you can do to stop it.)

**Treatment Options**

See "Bleaching Products" in Chapter 5 in Section II and follow the treatment steps for the appropriate Class of spot.

If color loss occurs, call a certified professional carpet dye specialist to discuss neutralizing the chlorine and to determine the best option based on the size and shape of the damaged areas. Your options may be:

- Re-dyeing the discolored areas. (Get an estimate for the cost of re-dyeing before starting. Re-dyeing larger areas can be expensive, but re-dyeing smaller sized areas may be a good option.)

- Replacement of the carpet, if the cost of re-dyeing is too high.

- Cut and plug if the areas are small enough - a half dollar size or smaller. (Cut and plug is usually not an option due to the large size or unusual shapes of the areas affected by the chlorine.)

– 17 –

## Cleaner Splashes / Dripping Trash Bag

Unless you see this happen, you probably wouldn't think of either of these situations as the cause of your spot problem.

**What You Normally See / Where You Usually See It**

Dark spots through the house or office caused by:

- Cleaner splashing out of or leaking through a crack in a bucket during house-cleaning or office maintenance

- Dripping trash bag

**Treatment Options**

- Cleaner drips: See "Detergents, Soaps, Cleaners - Liquid", in Chapter 5 in Section II and follow the instructions for the appropriate Class and size of spot.

- Trash bag drips: See "Soup - Watery" in Chapter 5 in Section II and follow the instructions for the appropriate Class and size of spot.

**Note:** Even if you or a professional cleaner has removed these spots, they will often recur days or weeks later, because not all of the spot residue has been removed. Retreat using the above instructions until they go away permanently.

## *Cleaners*

Some alkaline cleaners are so strong they can chemically affect the composition of the carpet dye, resulting in a color change. (Alkalines are a necessary component of cleaners, because most soils are acid and the alkaline is needed to help break down the soil so it can be removed.) Residue from these cleaners can also cause recurring spots and soiling on the recurring spots if it is not completely removed from the carpet.

**What You Normally See / Where You Usually See It**

Greenish, fluorescent cast to lighter colored carpet. (Darker colored carpets will look somewhat lighter in the affected areas, and red carpet may appear to have more of an olive cast.)

Location: Where you see the problem depends on the cause of the spot:

• In any carpeted area:

- Off-the-shelf carpet cleaning chemicals that have been mixed too strong. (Always follow the manufacturer's instructions when diluting or using cleaning chemicals.)

- Off-the-shelf multipurpose cleaners/degreasers that list carpet cleaner as one of their uses, but are not really designed for cleaning carpets. (If it is a degreaser, the product will have a very high alkaline pH and be very soapy.)

- Concentrated laundry detergent spilled on the carpet (or used to try to clean carpet spots).

- Very strong alkaline cleaners used by inexperienced or poorly trained carpet cleaners.

• Near the washing machine:

- Concentrated liquid laundry detergent spilled on the carpet

**Treatment Options**

See "Detergents, Soaps, Cleaners - Liquid" in Chapter 5 in Section II and follow the treatment steps for the appropriate Class and size of spot.

**Note:** If not totally removed, residue can cause recurring spots and soiling on the recurring spots.

## Cleaners - Very Strong

Some cleaners (like all-purpose cleaners, hard surface floor cleaners, floor wax strippers, oven cleaners, lye, caustic soda) contain concentrated alkalines such as sodium hydroxide or ammonium hydroxide, that can cause color loss in some carpet fibers and residue problems in all types of carpet fibers.

**What You Normally See / Where You Usually See It**

• Permanent color loss over time with nylon, wool and cotton carpets. (Olefin, polyester, acrylic fibers are not likely to be affected.)

• Residue, re-soiling problems and spot recurrence problems on olefin, polyester or acrylic fibers if large amounts of strong alkaline cleaners are spilled and penetrate to the carpet backing. (Nylon and the natural fibers are also subject to these problems.)

**Note:** Large spills of dirty mop water containing regular household ammonia can also cause a recurring spot problem. (If the water is clean, the ammonia is probably diluted enough that it will self-neutralize in the carpet and be fine. You may want to dry vacuum the wet spot with a spot machine or take a large towel and soak up the water with it.)

Location: Carpet near hard surface floors or other areas such as the kitchen, where these very strong cleaners would be used.

**Treatment Options**

See "Detergents, Soaps, Cleaners - Liquid" in Chapter 5 in Section II and follow the treatment steps for the appropriate Class and size of spot.

**Caution:** If the spilled cleaner contains sodium hydroxide (lye, caustic soda), removal will require multiple professional cleanings using a de-foaming agent and very high rinse pressure.

## Contact Lens Solution / Denture Cleaners, Whiteners

Even your contact lens solution or denture cleaners can cause spots on your carpet.

**What You Normally See / Where You Usually See It**

Small dark spots on the carpet in areas where contact lenses are cleaned or dentures are cleaned / soaked. (Soil has attached to the tiny drips of contact lens or denture cleaning solution on the carpet.)

**Treatment Options**

See "Detergents, Soaps, Cleaners - Liquid" in Chapter 5 in Section II and follow the treatment steps for the appropriate Class and size of spot.

— 21 —

## Disinfectants / Sanitizers

Household disinfectants are diluted versions of chemicals that manufacturers use to dissolve some fibers and dyes. (Look for alcohol or o-pheyl in the ingredients on the label.) Repeated or heavy exposure to these chemicals can damage your carpet. Note: The alcohol used in these disinfectants and sanitizers is not the Isopropyl Alcohol you can safely use in your spot treatments.

**What You Normally See / Where You Usually See It**

Spills or overspray of household disinfectants or sanitizers in any carpet area where these chemicals are transported or used could cause the following:

- Synthetics: Carpet fibers appear to be somewhat melted and feel somewhat brittle. The fibers may even be bonded together.

- Wool, Cotton: If not removed within 2 - 3 hours of the spill, you will see permanent discoloration (color movement that looks like a water ring with a lighter center and darker ring on the outside) and weakening of the fibers (fibers look dry, have a brittle feeling).

- All fiber types: Small dark spots in bathrooms, the kitchen or the laundry room caused by residue from the chemicals attracting soils.

**Treatment Options**

Call a professional carpet cleaning company for a free in-home estimate. Have the technician test to determine if the carpet fibers have been chemically damaged. Then have the carpet professionally cleaned and thoroughly rinsed in the spill area to ensure that no further damage will occur.

*Section I*

— 22 —

## *Filtration*

Airborne contaminates - chiefly black carbon from gas heaters and car exhaust (especially from diesel fuel) entering the house from the garage - filter through the carpet fibers and can become permanently attached to them. Early detection and treatment of filtration is important. Unfortunately, it is usually unnoticed and untreated for several years, which can make it difficult to impossible to remove entirely.

**What You Normally See / Where You Usually See It**

Filtration may show up in a variety of shapes and areas:

- Black lines 1/2 to 1-1/2 inches wide on the carpet at the baseboards; lines are usually running the length of the baseboard.

- Black lines on the carpet under closet doors or closed doors to rooms that are not often used. (Lines are especially dark under doors to closets or attic doors where the hot water heater is located.)

- A black, snake-like pattern on the carpet at windows with floor-length drapes. The pattern outlines the flow of the bottom of the drapes.

- A black outline around furniture that has not been moved for a while

- Black lines on the back half of the carpet on each step of a staircase

- Wider or darker lines near walls of rooms that adjoin the garage or at the threshold to the garage. (Car exhaust, especially diesel, filters under the door from the garage into the house and/or under walls that separate rooms from the garage.)

**Treatment Options**

- Vacuum thoroughly.

- If the black lines do not vacuum away, call a professional. Note: The chemicals and tool needed to remove old filtration from the carpet fibers, especially along baseboards, are not used by all carpet cleaning companies. It would be best to contact the IICRC (Institute Of Inspection, Cleaning & Restoration Certification) Referral Line (800) 835-4624 to find a certified cleaning technician who can treat filtration problems.

**Caution:** Prevention is the best treatment. The professional chemicals needed to remove filtration can easily damage the paint on the baseboards. In addition, treating the carpet around baseboards is very expensive (about as much as having the entire carpet cleaned) and the results are often unsatisfactory, even when using a certified technician.

**Best Practices:**

- When you are doing the regular maintenance vacuuming described in "Effective Routine Carpet Maintenance" in "Chapter 7. How Often Should My Carpet Be Cleaned?", watch for filtration.

- At the first signs of filtration, carefully and thoroughly vacuum the carpet next to baseboards and any other areas where filtration appears. Use a plastic vacuum crevice tool near the baseboards, on the stairs and near doorways where a threshold prevents your running the vacuum back and forth across the carpet. Also move furniture and lift drapes. Vacuum carefully in these areas as well. Do this type of vacuuming 2 - 6 times a year; more often if needed.

- When you have your carpets cleaned, tell the carpet cleaner about the filtration areas so he/she can clean them appropriately. The filtration must be treated separately, even if you are having the carpets cleaned.

## *Foot Fungus Medicine*

If you've been wondering where that trail that looks like leftover blobs of ectoplasm came from, this may be the source.

**What You Normally See / Where You Usually See It**

Discolorations in the carpet in bathrooms, hallways just outside bathrooms, bedroom carpets in teenager's rooms, especially boys. The shape of the discoloration depends on where and how the medicine was applied to the feet. (Compare the distance between these spots with the length of the stride of the likely culprit.)

- Light color carpet: Light orange sherbet or pinkish colored discoloration

- Dark color carpet: Small drips - Light orange sherbet or pinkish colored discoloration; Large drips - There may be a creamy white center inside the sherbet colored halo.

**Treatment Options**

See "Bleaching Products" in Chapter 5 in Section II and follow the treatment steps for the appropriate Class of spot.

– 23 –

Section I

*— 24 —*

## *Furniture Stain*

Furniture stains can become permanent within:

- Minutes of making contact with nylon, wool and cotton

- Up to a day after making contact with olefin, acrylic and polyester

**What You Normally See / Where You Usually See It**

Furniture stain is a shiny, porous, reddish-brown stain that mimics rust. It is caused when water or other liquid makes contact with the legs of wooden furniture. Unfortunately, furniture stain is a much worse problem than rust.

**Treatment Options**

See "Wood Stain, Furniture Stain" in Chapter 5 in Section II and follow the treatment steps for the appropriate Class and size of spot. (The center of the spot may remove, but a reddish-brown ring often resists your best efforts. This is how you can be sure the spot is a furniture stain - not rust. To solve the stain problem, especially on nylon carpet, a carpet repair technician will often need to do a cut and plug.)

**Best Practice:** To minimize furniture stain problems, follow the preventive suggestions under "Rust" in this Chapter.

## *Graphite, Metal Shavings and Lubricants from Door Hinges*

These spots look similar to Filtration, but they are more limited location-wise.

**What You Normally See / Where You Usually See It**

Black looking, oily dust that collects below the hinges of doors

**Treatment Options**

See "Copier Toner" in Chapter 5 in Section II and follow the instructions for the appropriate Class and size of spot.

## *Lignin Browning: Alkaline or Cellulosic Browning*

Lignin is an organic substance that, along with cellulose, forms the major part of woody tissue in plants. Note: Lignin browning is also referred to as "alkaline browning" or "cellulosic browning".

Several things can cause this browning on the carpet fibers. A large water spill may start the process:

- When a large liquid spill wets jute backing on all types of carpet from the early 80's or before (or most wool carpet of any age), the jute releases lignin that wicks up to the carpet surface during drying.

- If they get wet, the wooden tack strips used along the walls to keep carpet in place can also release lignin and cause carpet browning.

- The soapy, alkaline cleaning residue left over from an improperly employed carpet cleaning method can also cause alkaline browning if it comes in contact with dirt or another type of cellulose material. (All outside soils usually contain some type of rotting plant matter.)

**Caution:** There are two other carpet spotting problems that are very similar looking to lignin/alkaline/cellulosic browning - Rust and Furniture Stain. Rust is relatively easy to remove, but Furniture Stain can be very difficult to treat especially on nylon and natural fiber carpets. Even on olefin, acrylic and polyester carpets, immediate treatment is needed to keep the stain from becoming permanent. If you're are not sure if your spot problem is lignin browning, rust or furniture stain, read the information on all three and treat as soon as possible.

**What You Normally See / Where You Usually See It**

Lignin Browning is a porous, dull brown "stain" that mimics rust. When you look closely at the spot, you can see many, tiny dull brown dots on the carpet fibers wherever the water was spilled. The lignin dots also cause a stiffness or a crusty feel to the carpet yarns.

**Treatment Options**

See "Lignin Browning" in Chapter 5 in Section II. Follow the treatment steps under the appropriate Class and size for your spot.

- 25 -

Section I

## *Oil / Urine / BHT*

Old, oxidized oil spots, urine and BHT (Butylated Hydroxy Toluene) can cause yellow spots or stains on your carpet. Each of these have different effects on carpet fibers and different spot treatment recommendations.

**Oil:**

These types of spots may become permanent and cause the fibers to yellow if the spot, especially petroleum-based spots, or oily soil is left in the carpet fiber without proper cleaning for prolonged periods of many months.

- Olefin and polyester are easily affected, especially olefin.

- Acrylic is not affected. Nylon is also not affected unless a large quantity is spilled.

- The natural fibers wool and cotton will be stained unless the oil is removed within 12 - 24 hours.

**Urine:**

- The yellow pigment in urine can stain nylon within 24 - 48 hours. This stain can usually be removed if treated within that time period. Urine can remove the dye from nylon or permanently stain it if not removed within 21 days.

- Olefin, polyester and acrylic are usually not affected by urine staining or discoloring.

- Wool and cotton carpet fibers can be discolored or permanently stained when the urine has dried (about an hour).

**Note:** Food coloring in the urine is not usually a problem, unless you have a very old animal whose liver and kidneys are failing.

**BHT:**

This is a preservative found in many food products and in plastics and rubber. In your carpet, BHT is in the latex used between the primary and secondary backings to help hold the carpet fibers in place and to cause the backings to adhere to one another.

- BHT can cause all carpet fiber types to yellow.

**What You Normally See / Where You Usually See It**

• Yellow spots or stains caused by:

- Oil: Older oil spots, especially petroleum-based oils, that have oxidized. Cooking oil spots would normally be found in or near the kitchen. Body oil spots could be found in the bathroom, bedrooms or other areas. Petroleum-based oil spot locations would usually include traffic areas coming from auto repair shop bays, a parking lot or a home garage.

- Urine: Stains could be found in the bathroom around the toilet and/or anywhere else pets or children have access to carpeted areas.

• Large yellow areas in the shape of mats or rugs placed on the carpet or just areas of yellow in the carpet caused by BHT:

- BHT: Bath mats or other area rugs with rubber or latex backings can cause yellowing when they are placed over carpet. (This yellowing also occurs when these mats are placed over vinyl floors, but unfortunately, this situation is not reparable. The carpet problem, however, can usually be treated.)

- BHT: Area rugs laid on your carpet can also cause yellowing of the carpet fibers. Note: Having one of the non-slip rug underlays between the carpet and the rug does not prevent yellowing, because humidity and a lack of oxygen can activate the BHT in the latex in the carpet directly underneath the rug.

- BHT in the latex can react with strong alkaline cleaning agents like degreaser, floor strippers, etc., if there is enough cleaner/water to cause the solution to bypass the carpet fibers and soak through the primary backing and into the latex. This reaction will turn the carpet fibers yellow. (The residue of carpet cleaners left in the carpet can also react with the BHT.) Note: Plain water will not activate the BHT, but it will help carry any residue from strong alkaline cleaners in the carpet down to the latex.

Section I

## *Oil / Urine / BHT,* continued

### Treatment Options

**Oil spots:** See "Oil - Thin Lubricants" in Chapter 5 in Section II. Follow the treatment Steps under the appropriate Class and size for your spot.

**Urine:** See "Urine - Animal, Human" in Chapter 5 in Section II. Follow the treatment Steps under the appropriate Class and size for your spot.

### Cautions:

- If you can treat a urine spot immediately on a synthetic carpet, it will respond well to the ammonia and hydrogen peroxide used in the treatment. If you wait even 3 - 4 days, it becomes more difficult to remove. After 3 weeks or less, it can remove dye from nylon and/or permanently stain it. DO NOT douse the spot with an off-the-shelf remover. You may set the spot so removal is impossible even by a pro and/or damage your carpet.

- Urine on wool and cotton can become difficult to remove as soon as it has fully dried (less than 1 hour). As soon as you find the spot on a natural fiber carpet, call your carpet professional and discuss treatment options. DO NOT douse the spot with an off-the-shelf remover. You may set the spot so removal is impossible and/or damage your carpet.

- A small animal (or human) can put down enough urine to soak into the carpet backing and pad. The spot will continuously resurface due to the sticky contaminants in urine. Your only option is to continue to retreat it using the treatment steps in Chapter 5 in Section II for your Class and size of spot.

**BHT:** Call a professional. These stains can usually be removed, but the professional's more powerful equipment and access to specialized cleaners are required for the most effective treatment. (Removing BHT from wool and cotton fibers is a bit more difficult than treating the synthetic fibers.)

## *Perfume*

When concentrated spills occur, the ethyl alcohol in some perfumes may loosen dye in the affected fibers and move it to other fibers. Fortunately, most perfume spills are small and they will evaporate before they can cause trouble.

**What You Normally See / Where You Usually See It**

Discolorations that resemble water stains with a lighter colored center and a darker ring around it on nylon, wool or cotton. (Olefin, polyester and acrylic are immune to perfume discoloration.)

Location: Carpeted areas where perfume is normally applied (or places where the children have been playing with the perfume bottle).

**Treatment Options**

If you have a large discolored area, call a pro to discuss options. A seamless insert (cut and plug) may be your only choice.

## *Pesticides / Insecticides /*

## *Pet Shampoos with Pesticides or Insecticides*

Not all pesticides or insecticides, including those in pet shampoos, affect carpet dyes; but those that do can cause discoloration problems, especially for nylon, wool and cotton carpet fibers. Olefin, polyester and acrylic are not affected.

**What You Normally See / Where You Usually See It**

Color changes in carpet in areas where the pest control man sprays or areas where pet shampoos with problematic pesticides/insecticides may be spilled or splashed on the carpet:

• Blue stains on lighter colored carpet.

• Some red dyes change to blue over a period of months, especially with heat and humidity.

• Brown carpet may turn a greenish color. (When the red dye turns blue, it plus the blue and yellow dyes that are added to red dye to create a brown color, make green.)

• Color removed entirely, usually around the perimeter of rooms (with deviations around large pieces of furniture).

### *Pesticides or Insecticides, Pet Shampoos, continued*

**Treatment Options**

**If you spill a pesticide/insecticide, put on your rubber gloves and any other protective gear you may have, and:**

- Liquid spill: Blot up as much of the pesticide/insecticide as possible. (Be especially careful with how you handle the towel you used. You may wish to dispose of it rather than wash it.) Cover the spot with a dry towel from your spotting kit and a note that says, *"Do not touch or clean!"*. Keep people and pets away from the spot. Consult a professional as soon as possible.

- Powder spill: Many vacuum cleaners allow fine dust particles to seep through the bag and into the air while you are vacuuming. These particles are spread over the carpet. Because you are dealing with a substance that could be harmful to people (including you) and pets if dispersed through the air and/or spread over the carpet, it is safer to protect the spot rather than try any sort of treatment. Cover the spot with a dry towel from your spotting kit and a note that says, *"Do not touch or clean!"*. Keep people and pets away from the spot. Consult a professional as soon as possible.

In addition to removing the pesticide, the professional will consult with you on the best way to handle the problem if the carpet is already damaged:

- Unfortunately, replacing the carpet is usually the only option.

- Cut and plug is not practical, because of the size of the damaged area.

- Dyeing is not an option because it is impossible to match the original color due to the color changes caused by the pesticide.

**If you spill a pet shampoo:**

See "Detergents, Soaps, Cleaners - Liquid" in Chapter 5 in Section II. Follow the treatment steps under the appropriate Class and size for your spot. (It may take several treatments to remove sticky residues from these spills.)

**Caution:** If a large quantity has been spilled, it may penetrate the carpet backing. This can cause a permanent recurring spot problem that will require a professional to pull up the carpet, flush and extract the residue on both sides of the carpet, plus a possible pad replacement.

After treating using the instructions under "Detergents, Soaps, Cleaners - Liquid" to remove the spill, also see "Dye - Liquid" in Chapter 5 in Section II if you have staining problems from the shampoo. Follow the treatment steps under the appropriate Class and size for your spot.

**Best Practices:** Prevention is the best treatment:

**Pesticides / Insecticides**

• The following chemicals are the problem ones: *Resmethrin [5 (phenylmethyl) 3 furanyl] methyl 2, 2-dimethyl 1-3-(2 methmethyl 1-1- propenly) cyclo-propanecurhoxylate...0.10% w/w/ and diazinon.*

• Before pesticides are applied, ask your pest control company if any of their products cause discoloration problems with carpets.

• If you do your own pest control, carefully read all directions and warning labels on all products before using them. If you are still not sure, call the 800 number or go to the company's Web site, if any, listed on the pesticide container and ask the manufacturer. (Mix the pesticide according to the container instructions. Do not make up more concentrated solutions.)

• Be especially careful to avoid spills when applying pesticides.

**Pet Shampoos**

• Carefully read all directions and warning labels on all pet shampoo products before using them. If you are still not sure, call the 800 number or go to the company's Web site, if any, listed on the shampoo container and ask the manufacturer about potential staining problems.

• If you have an animal grooming business, nylon (or wool) is not the best choice of carpet fiber for your washing area.

## *Plant Food*

Plant food is often blue colored. It becomes a carpet stain problem when there is overflow from plants that:

- Have been watered too heavily.
- Have no saucer or tray or too small a container underneath the pot.
- Have a clay saucer, instead of plastic.

Wool and cotton are immediately and permanently affected by plant food stains. Nylon is permanently affected by the time the stain dries. Olefin, polyester and acrylic are usually permanently affected if the stain is not removed within a week or less. Unfortunately, these stains are normally not found until long after the stain has become permanent.

**Best Practice:** To help prevent this problem, place a dense piece of carpet or absorbent cloth underneath the saucer and always water carefully.

**What You Normally See / Where You Usually See It**

Circular or square stains under a flower pot or saucer underneath the pot:

- Blue stains on carpet.
- Effects similar to pesticides: Red dyes change to blue. Brown carpet may turn a greenish color. (When the red turns blue, it plus the blue and yellow dyes that are added to red to create a brown color, make green.)

**Cautions:** Additional Problems

- If the carpet has been repeatedly wetted, you may also see gray or black stains on the carpet under or near the plant. This is mold and/or mildew. (In addition to producing an offensive odor, mold/mildew can spot or discolor nylon and break down cotton and wool.)
- Reddish or brownish stains under plants in wicker baskets that sit directly on the carpet.

**Treatment Options**

- Plant food stains: See "Dye - Liquid" in chapter 5 in Section II and try the treatment steps for the appropriate Class and size of the spot before calling a professional if:

  - The carpet is olefin, polyester or acrylic;

  - The stain is less than a week old;

  - No mildew or mold is present.

- Plant food stains: Call a professional as soon as possible if:

  - The carpet is nylon, wool or cotton;

  - The stain is older than a week;

  - The stain is too large for you to treat at home;

  - **Mildew or mold is present.** (It is especially important to call immediately if either of these is present.)

    **Caution:** Removing mildew and mold combined with plant food can be very difficult for even a seasoned technician. A seamless insert may be the only option OR have the mildew/mold treated by a pro and put the plant back over the stain.

- Wood stain from wicker baskets: You **may** be able to remove the stain if:

  - The carpet is olefin, polyester or acrylic;

  - The stain is only a week (or less) old;

  - There is **no** mold or mildew present.

  See "Wood Stain" in Chapter 5 in Section II and follow the instructions for the appropriate Class and size of spot.

  If you cannot treat the stain because of the carpet fiber type, age of the spot or because there is mold or mildew present (or you are unable to remove the spot if you do treat it), call a professional for options.

— 33 —

## *Rust*

Rust is caused by moisture from liquid spills, condensation, moisture leaching from outside, or pet urine reacting with metal pegs attached to the legs of household or office furniture or with file cabinets or other metal objects sitting directly on the carpet.

**What You Normally See / Where You Usually See It**

Dull-looking, reddish-brown, porous, brittle coating on the carpet. This coating will rub off on your finger or fleck off or turn to a powder if scraped with a fingernail or knife. You can barely see the carpet fibers through the coating.

**Treatment Options**

See "Rust" in Chapter 5 in Section II. Follow the treatment steps under the appropriate Class and size for your spot.

Though it is always best to remove a spot as soon as possible, normally rust can still be successfully removed months later. It can usually be easily removed after even longer periods by a knowledgeable cleaning technician using the right chemicals.

**Caution:** The "mimics" Furniture Stain and Lignin Browning are not so forgiving time-wise, so it is best to immediately treat any spot you think is rust just in case it is one of the mimics instead. (See "Furniture Stain" and "Lignin Browning" earlier in this Chapter for more information on these more problematic spots/stains.)

**Best Practices:** To minimize rust problems:
- Place rubber furniture foot cups (usually brown colored) or plastic furniture foot cups (usually clear and have spikes) underneath items that have metal pegs in the legs.

- Place fiberglass skids or plastic planks 1 - 2 inches thick under file cabinets. These are available from hardware stores or caster suppliers.

- Make sure the carpet cleaner doing a "wet" type cleaning puts protective plastic squares ("tabs") or Styrofoam blocks under the legs of tables, chairs, etc., that have been moved during cleaning. (The carpet under large pieces of furniture that are not moved does not get wet, so furniture stains are not a problem with these items.)

## *Soaps / Shampoos*

Liquid hand and bath soaps, including bubble bath and shampoo, do not have the high alkaline pH levels of the strong cleaners mentioned earlier, but they can still cause spotting and staining problems.

Drips or spills of these products can cause:

• Recurring spots on all types of carpet fibers from the residue in the carpet.

• Soiling on these recurring spots. (The soil is attracted to the sticky residue.)

• Stains on nylon, wool and cotton fibers from blue or green dandruff shampoos, colored shampoos for gray or bleached hair, and/or strongly colored bubble baths or hand soaps.

### What You Normally See / Where You Usually See It

All carpet fiber types: Recurring spots and soiling on the recurring spots in any carpeted areas, especially bathrooms, where these products may have been spilled.

Nylon, wool, cotton fibers: Stains in bathrooms around sinks, bathtubs and showers where the concentrated shampoo, bubble bath or hand soap may have splashed on the carpet.

### Treatment Options

See "Detergents, Soaps, Cleaners - Liquid" in Chapter 5 in Section II. Follow the treatment steps under the appropriate Class and size for your spot. (It may take several treatments to remove sticky residues from these spills.)

**Caution:** If a large quantity has been spilled, it may penetrate the carpet backing. This can cause a permanent recurring spot problem that will require a professional to pull up the carpet, flush and extract the residue on both sides of the carpet, plus a possible pad replacement.

After treating using the instructions under "Detergents, Soaps, Cleaners - Liquid" to remove the spill, also see "Dye - Liquid" in Chapter 5 in Section II if you have staining problems from shampoo or bubble bath, etc. Follow the treatment steps under the appropriate Class and size for your spot.

— 35 —

*Art's Ultimate Spot Cleaning • **Chapter 4 - Page 35***

Section I

## *Tack Strips (Carpet)*

If the tack strips that hold your carpet in place have been wetted, it can create a real stew of mixed spots. This wetting can be caused by moisture that has leached in from the irrigation system outside, rising water from heavy rain, a water heater or washing machine or other flood, or condensation buildup from a cold slab and warm humid conditions in the building.

The possible results of all this moisture around the tack strips are brown spots from lignin browning, black from the wetted wooden strips, rust from the tacks or nails holding the carpet and tack strips in place, and black from possible mold or mildew growth.

### What You Normally See / Where You Usually See It

Lines similar to the black lines seen with Filtration, but the lines caused by the rotting tack strips are only found along the baseboards and any other areas where tack strips would be located to hold your carpet in place.

### Caution: Additional Problem

If the carpet has been repeatedly wetted, you may also see gray or black stains on the carpet. This is mold and/or mildew. In addition to producing an offensive odor, mold/mildew can discolor nylon and break down cotton and wool. It can also rot the jute backing on wool carpets of any age. Note: If your carpet, no matter what the fiber type, was manufactured in the early 80's or before when all carpets still had jute backings, its jute backing is also susceptible to rotting.

### Treatment Options

The only treatment option, whether you have mold or mildew or not, is to call a professional. The pro may need to pull out the rotting tack strip(s), replace the pad, treat for mold/mildew if necessary and replace the carpet or repair the damaged area.

## *Toilet Bowl Cleaner / Sanitizer*

Toilet bowl cleaner/sanitizer, which is usually blue colored, can easily stain the carpet in and around the toilet area. Nylon, wool and cotton fibers are the most susceptible to permanent staining. Olefin, polyester and acrylic can be permanently affected if the cleaner/sanitizer stain is not removed promptly.

**What You Normally See / Where You Usually See It**

Blue stains on carpet or rugs around the toilet caused by toilet bowl cleaner dripping off the cleaning brush or the toilet rim during cleaning.

**Treatment Options**

- Nylon, wool and cotton: See "Bleaching Products" in Chapter 5 in Section II and follow the treatment steps for the appropriate Class of spot. Consult a professional. Once it dries, the blue color may be impossible to remove even by the pro. If so, a seamless insert (cut and plug) may be your only option.

- Olefin, polyester and acrylic: See "Bleaching Products" in Chapter 5 in Section II and follow the treatment steps for the appropriate Class of spot. Consult a professional. Caution: Even these highly stain resistant fibers are not entirely immune if the stain is not removed within a week.

## Water Spills

We don't normally think that spilling a glass of water on the carpet is that big a problem, especially if you absorb most of it with a towel. Olefin, polyester and acrylic fibers have a low absorbency rate so water spills (even smaller ones) easily bypass them and soak into the carpet backings and pad. (As you will find out in "Chapter 6. How Does One Carpet Fiber Compare To Another?", the primary and secondary backings on synthetic carpets are made of olefin, so the backings do not absorb much water either.)

Nylon, wool and cotton fibers are more absorbent, but any carpet (regardless of its fiber type, density, etc.) can be adversely affected by a larger water spill.

**These adverse effects include:**

• A dull brown "stain" caused by Lignin Browning. The browning is a result of a chemical reaction between the water and:

  - Lignin in soils in the carpet and/or in the jute carpet backing on wool or any type of older carpets manufactured during or before the early 80's (Cellulosic Browning). (All outside soils usually contain some type of rotting plant matter.)

  - Residue of alkaline cleaners (Alkaline Browning), especially those left in the carpet by an overzealous cleaning technician or carpet cleaning do-it-yourselfer that intensify the chemical reaction described above.

• A rainbow of stains caused by water spills that have activated dye in the carpet pad. The dye wicks up to the surface of the carpet as the water dries over several days. (This is a much worse problem than the dull brown "stain" caused by the cellulosic or alkaline browning.)

**What You Normally See / Where You Usually See It**

• A dull brown "stain" made up of many, tiny dull brown dots on the carpet fibers. The carpet yarns in the spot area may also have a stiff or crusty feel. This "stain" will be wherever the water was spilled.

• A rainbow of stains on the carpet fibers wherever the water was spilled.

**Treatment Options**

• Brown "stain": See "Lignin Browning" in Chapter 5 in Section II. Follow the treatment steps under the appropriate Class and size for your spot.

• Rainbow of stains: See "Dye - Liquid" in Chapter 5 in Section II and follow the instructions for the appropriate Class and size of spot.

## *Zero-Phantoms*

A Zero-Phantom is a non - spot, stain or discoloration that appears on the carpet and disappears - seemingly without any human intervention.

*Zero-Phantom* was the name I gave to one of the more interesting mystery spot "problems" I solved early in my carpet cleaning career. I had just finished cleaning a house full of relatively new carpet, when the customer called me from the formal dining room. She was quite distressed about the huge dark spot in the middle of the room where the dining room table usually sat. (She had moved the table out just prior to our arrival.) I was surprised to see this spot, because neither I nor my trusted assistant (or the lady) had noticed it earlier when we were cleaning the room.

We carefully re-cleaned the dark area, but the spot didn't budge at all. As I pondered the problem, I noticed the chandelier hanging directly over the spot. When I touched the light, causing it to gently sway back and forth, the dark spot moved as well.

The reason this shadow on the carpet had not been noticed before was because the homeowner had never used the room with the table removed, and my assistant and I had cleaned the dining room during the daylight hours before the chandelier was turned on.

### What You Normally See / Where You Usually See It

Areas that look spotted or soiled at certain times of the day or under certain light conditions, but the spots are not visible at other times. There is no specific place where Zero-Phantoms are more commonly found than others.

### "Treatment" Options

There really isn't anything to treat; you just have to find what is causing the Zero-Phantom to appear. Look for dark areas that appear under tables, ceiling fans, mirrors and places where unusual light reflections or overhead lights casting a shadow make small or large areas look spotted or soiled at only certain times of the day. Move some items around in the immediate area and see if the spot doesn't move simultaneously. You may find there wasn't a spot there at all - it was just a Zero-Phantom.

# Chapter 5
# Spot Treatment Instructions

## Introduction

Chapter 5 is the heart of this carpet spotting guide, because this is where you'll find the pages that describe how to treat over 800 different spots and stains. To make it easy for you to find your particular spot problem in the treatment pages, I've included an index called the "Alphabetical List Of Common Spots And Stains" on green-colored paper. Following the List are the treatment pages with step-by-step instructions for dealing with the most common types of spots and stains using my easy, effective methods.

On the next page, I tell you how to use the Alphabetical List and then describe the types of information you will see on the two treatment pages for each kind of spot or stain. *(No, I haven't forgotten that I promised you treatment would be easy.)* There are two pages for each type of spot, because the size of spots you can treat and the treatment steps are slightly different if you have the extra power of a spot machine (1st treatment page) versus having to rely on towels or chamois and a vacuum cleaner (2nd treatment page).

The introduction to this Chapter ends with a description of what you need to do to get ready to treat a spot, suggestions for temporarily handling a spill that occurs when you are running out the door, a short safety message and a recap of the various factors that can affect your treatment results and why.

Section II

— 1 —

# Alphabetical List Of Common Spots And Stains

This index, printed on green paper, lists the names of the majority of potential causes of carpet spots/stains in your home, office or business, vehicle, boat, etc. (To prepare this List, I reviewed hundreds of products in a variety of different stores - supermarkets, office supply, auto supply and home improvement warehouses, then added some of the more common industrial items.)

The entries in the Alphabetical List look like the following:

| Spot / Stain | Page Numbers |
|---|---|
| Paint – Oil-Based | 146 - 147 |
| Paint – Oil-Based: Aluminum, Epoxy, Latex Enamel, Paint Marker, Solvent-Based Paint (See "Paint – Oil-Based") | 146 - 147 |
| Paint – Water-Based | 148 - 149 |

*P*

As the title of the List says, the names are in alphabetical order. What you see after the spot name listed in this index depends on whether the first item in the treatment page title is the same as the name you looked up or not.
**If the names are:**

• **The same** (example below: Paint - Water-Based), you will just see the treatment page numbers listed after the name you looked up.

| Spot / Stain | Page Numbers |
|---|---|
| Paint – Oil-Based | 146 - 147 |

*P*

• **Different** (example below: Paint Strippers / Paint Thinner), you will be given the first item to look for in the title of the appropriate treatment page, as well as the treatment page numbers.

| | |
|---|---|
| Paint Strippers / Paint Thinner (See "Solvents") | 176 - 177 |

To use the List, look up the cause of your problem and then go to the two treatment pages listed. (Don't worry if some of the substances named in the List or in the corresponding treatment page title don't seem to be related to one another. The spot's ingredients, its structure - oily, crusty, gummy, etc., and other criteria were the determining factors in deciding which treatment steps would be most effective. One of the more extreme examples is Douche, where you are instructed to use the treatment steps for Dye - even though most douches are clear - not colored.)

What you'll see on those pages and how to determine the set of treatment steps you should use are described in the following two subtitles - "Treatment Page Information - Abbreviated Descriptions" and "Treatment Page Information-Detailed Descriptions".

# *Treatment Page Information - Abbreviated Descriptions*

**Caution:** The information that follows is an abbreviated version to make it easier for you to see the location of the different types of data on the treatment page. Please read the "Treatment Page Information - Detailed Version" that follows this one for important added details you need to know.

The treatment pages are in alphabetical order based on the name of the first type of spot/stain listed in the title. As mentioned earlier, there are two treatment pages for each kind of spot or stain.

• **First page:** Describes the treatment used if you have a spot machine.

• **Second page:** Describes the treatment used if you do not have a spot machine. It gives instructions for using towels/chamois to absorb liquid spills and a vacuum cleaner or shop vac for dry spills.

The same types of information are given on each of the two pages, but the second page also lists the primary ingredients in the spot or stain.

The treatment information on each of the two pages is divided into two columns (called "Classes"):

• **1st column:** Class I or III - What to do if the spot is Dried / Old.

• **2nd column:** Class II or IV - What to do if the spot is Wet / Fresh.

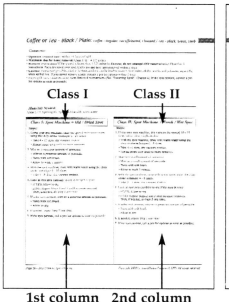

**First page:**   **Second page:**

Class I   Class II      Class III   Class IV

1st column   2nd column      1st column   2nd column

3

Section II

**① Coffee or Tea - Black / Plain:** *Coffee - Regular, Decaffeinated, Flavored / Tea - Black, Green, Herb*

② Spot / Stain Contents: Acids, Artificial Color, Possible Sugar, Tannin

③ *Comments:*

④ **Optimum removal time:** Within 24 hours of spill

**Maximum size for home removal:** Class III / IV = 3 inches

⑤ **Removal restrictions:** If the spot(s) is larger than 3 inches in diameter, **do not attempt TOTAL removal** using Class III or IV

⑥ instructions. Do Step 1 only under Class III or IV. Put a dry towel over spot. Then:
- Call a pro and have spot removed within 2 days. -OR-
- If the spot is 4 1/2 inches or less in diameter, get a spot machine and:
  - If the spot is now old/dried, do Steps 1 - 7 under Class I.
  - If the spot is still fresh/wet, do Steps 1 - 7 under Class II.

⑦ **Caution:** Tannin and possible coloring in these products can be hard to remove from nylon, olefin, acrylic and polyester, especially when spilled hot. If you cannot remove a spot, consult a pro for options within 2 days.
- Large spills may cause recurring spots that need re-treatment. (See "Recurring Spots", Chapter 4.) If the spot persists, consult a pro for options as soon as possible.

⑧ *Materials Needed:*
Class III: Spotting kit, Vacuum cleaner with attachment removed from hose
Class IV: Spotting kit

| ⑨ **Class III: Towel + Old / Dried Spot** | **Class IV: Towel + Fresh / Wet Spot** |
|---|---|
| ⑩ *Steps:* | *Steps:* |
| 1. Using your soft brush, gently brush the spot(s) in a side-to-side motion 10 - 15 times.<br>• Vacuum debris with vacuum cleaner hose. | 1. Fold a towel several times and place it over the spot(s).<br>• Step on the towel with your full weight 8 - 10 times, using a clean part of the towel each time.<br>• Repeat until no more absorbs. |
| 2. Mist on a generous amount of ammonia.<br>• Mist on a generous amount of peroxide.<br>• Tamp with soft brush.<br>• Allow to work 2 minutes. | 2. Mist on a small amount of ammonia.<br>• Mist on a small amount of peroxide.<br>• Tamp with soft brush.<br>• Allow to work 2 minutes. |
| 3. With a towel, blot 10 - 15 times, using a clean part of the towel each time. | 3. With a towel, blot 10 - 15 times, using a clean part of the towel each time. |
| 4. Look at spot area carefully to see if the spot is gone:<br>• If YES: Allow to dry.<br>• If NO: Repeat Steps 2 and 3 until no more removes. Then, if needed, do Step 5. | 4. Look at spot area carefully to see if the spot is gone:<br>• If YES: Allow to dry.<br>• If NO: Repeat Steps 2 and 3 until no more removes. Then, if needed, do Step 5. |
| 5. If color cast remains, mist on a generous amount of peroxide.<br>• Tamp with soft brush.<br>• Allow to dry. | 5. If color cast remains, mist on a generous amount of peroxide.<br>• Tamp with soft brush.<br>• Allow to dry. |
| 6. If needed, repeat Steps 2, 3 and 5 one time. | 6. If needed, repeat Steps 2, 3 and 5 one time. |
| 7. If the spot persists, call a pro for options as soon as possible. | 7. If the spot persists, call a pro for options as soon as possible. |

## *Treatment Page Headings / Descriptions*

1. **Type of Spill(s):** The more common spots or stains that are best treated using the methods on the two treatment pages.

2. **Spot or Stain Contents:** The primary ingredients in the spot or stain. This information is only listed on the 2nd treatment page for each spot. (The words "spot", "stain" or "spot/stain" before the ingredients tell you what type of problem you are dealing with.)

3. **Comments:** Items 4 - 8 that follow are listed under "Comments". They tell you whether or not you will be able to successfully treat the spot at home and what to do if you cannot.

4. **Optimum removal time:** Treating the spill within this time period will give you the best results.

5. **Maximum size for home removal:** The maximum size spot that I suggest you treat when dealing with this type of spill. The size limit is based on the type of spot material, if you are treating the spot with a spot machine or not, and the spot's condition/age.

6. **Removal restrictions:** Tells when a pro must be called because the spot's size or type prevents you from treating it safely/effectively. It also tells how to hold the spot in check and/or protect it from being spread until the pro arrives.

7. **Cautions:** Notes containing important information related to your spotting efforts and safety. They should be read carefully before you begin any spotting treatment.

8. **Materials Needed:** A brief list of the equipment, tools, chemicals, etc., needed to do the spot treatment process.

9. **Class:** The treatment steps you use for a specific type of spot depend on 1) Whether you have a spot machine for vacuuming and rinsing or must use a towel or viscose rayon chamois for blotting, and 2) The age and/or condition of the spot.

10. **Steps:** The specific instructions for treating the different Classes of spots.

— 5 —

Section II

## Treatment Page Information - Detailed Descriptions

Please carefully read this more in-depth coverage of the information that preceded this subtitle. It contains important details that were not included in the abbreviated version.

1. **Type of Spill(s):** These are some of the more common spots or stains that are best treated using one. of the four methods on the two treatment pages. (These, plus other less common spots or stains, are listed in the green pages in the "Alphabetical List Of Common Spots And Stains".)

2. **Spot or Stain Contents:** As mentioned before, the primary spot ingredients are listed directly beneath the type of spill on the second treatment page for that spot. **Note:** If you are unable to find your spot in my extensive Alphabetical List, you may be able to identify a similar spill by matching the ingredient list on the spot container with the ingredients listed on the treatment page. (The words "spot", "stain" or "spot/stain" before the ingredients tell you what type of problem you're dealing with.)

3. **Comments:** The Comments tell you whether or not you will be able to successfully treat the spot at home and what to do if you cannot. The information covered below in items 4. Optimum removal time through 8. Materials Needed is under the title "Comments".

4. **Optimum removal time:** All carpet manufacturers and cleaners will tell you that normally, the faster you can treat a spot the more successful you are likely to be. If you call their hotlines, they recommend that the spot be removed, "Within 24 hours of the spill" while it is still fresh and/or wet. (A few spots are not so time-sensitive, but it is better to be safe than wait longer and be sorry.)

   • Some spots are so time-sensitive that even an hour or so can make a difference in how successful your treatment will be. For these extremely time-sensitive spots, the **bolded** words, "**As soon as possible** within 24 hours of spill" mean exactly what they say.

   • Less sensitive spots will say "Within 24 hours of spill".

   (Experts say that starting treatment within minutes of the spill - but no longer than 24 hours later - gives the best results for the majority of spots. For 25 - 47 hours after many types of spills - you have a grace period where you can still successfully treat many spots. After 48 hours the clock really begins to work against you.)

— 6 —

**Exceptions:** Some spots such as ink and mud are better treated after they have dried, so the instructions tell you to let the spot dry completely before starting treatment. Other spots such as rust can still be successfully removed for some time after the spill. Information in the Cautions will describe these extended time periods.

5. **Maximum size for home removal:** The size limits range from No Home Removal to 1/4 inch to several inches in diameter. The size limitation is based on 1) The type of spot material - some penetrate further into the carpet fibers than others or are more damaging to the fibers, 2) Whether you are treating the spot with a spot machine or a towel/chamois, and 3) Whether the spot is old/dried or fresh/wet.

**Note: The size limit only applies to a spot that is bigger than the diameter listed.** A spot can be longer and still be home treatable as long as it is no wider than the maximum home removal size.

Examples: The instructions for your Class of spot say the **maximum size for home removal = 2 inches.**

- Example <u>A</u>: Your spot is 2 inches or less in diameter. (This means the spot is up to 2 inches wide and up to 2 inches long.) You can safely treat this spot, because it is within the size limit.

- Example <u>B</u>: Your spot is 2 1/4 inches in diameter or larger. (This means the spot is at least 2 1/4 inches wide and at least 2 1/4 inches long.) Unless you have been practicing my treatment methods for some time and are very confident, do not try to treat this spot yourself. Instead, follow the directions given in the Removal restrictions. The large concentration of spot material means it's very likely the spill has penetrated through the carpet pile and into the backing. Your equipment, even if you have a spot machine, does not have the pulling power needed to successfully treat this spill. A well-seasoned professional has more experience and stronger chemicals and equipment for dealing with these difficult spills.

- Example <u>C</u>: The spot is 2 inches wide, but 5 inches long. You can treat this spot because even though it is longer than the size restriction, it does not occupy as much concentrated area of the carpet pile as the spot in Example B. The spot material is spread out, so it is more like a smaller spot in its volume and weight displacement. This makes it easier to deal with because the spill is much less likely to have penetrated the carpet pile.

**Note:** If you've had a lot of spot removal experience and are confident of your abilities, you may **(at your own risk)** exceed the size limitation by 25%, but no greater. Otherwise, follow the size limitations exactly.

*Section II*

— 7 —

(It's interesting that there's almost no information available, except in this guide, about restrictions on home treatment of spots based on the spot's size. Some of the reasons for this lack may be a) There isn't much comprehensive written or infomercial spot removal information available at all; and b) No manufacturer wants you to think their product - spotting agent, spot machine or steam cleaning machine - cannot remove every spot you come in contact with.)

6. **Removal restrictions:** If a spot is larger than you can effectively treat or is one you can't safely / effectively handle, there are instructions for:

   • Contacting a professional.

   • Removing the top layers of spot material so the pro will be able to treat the spot more effectively. (Example: "Do Steps 1 and 2 and call a professional...")

   • Holding the spot in check until the professional arrives. (Example: "Put a dry towel over the spot." or a towel dampened with water or other specified liquid over the spot.)

   • Protecting the spot from being spread or pushed further down into the carpet until a pro can come. (Example: Put a note next to the spot that says ***"Do Not Touch Or Clean!"***) **Caution:** This note should be written in pencil - not ink. Moisture could cause the ink on a note to transfer to the carpet, causing a bigger problem than your original spot.

**Note:** It's also advisable to call a pro to discuss treatment options instead of trying to remove the spot yourself when:

   • You don't feel confident enough to remove it yourself because it looks too big or too tough or you can't identify what it is.

   • The spot is not listed in the Alphabetical List, so you don't know what treatment steps to use.

   • Your carpet is made of 100% natural fibers such as wool, silk, cotton, sea grass, etc.

**Professional Treatment Options**

The professional has several treatment options available, depending on the type, size and shape of the spot and whether or not the color has been affected or the fibers have been damaged by the spill. (If there has been a color change, the color(s) and pattern, if any in your carpet, can affect which options the professional suggests.)

These professional options are:

- **Treat the spot:** The heavier equipment and additional chemicals available to the pro make it possible for him or her to successfully remove spots that the average person cannot.

- **Re-Dye:** Depending on the type and size of damage caused by the spot and your carpet color(s)/pattern, a trained technician may suggest re-dying the damaged areas to match the rest of the carpet as your best option.

- **Cut and Plug** (also called a "seamless insert"): If the spot cannot be entirely removed or the fibers have been damaged so that even removing the spot will not fix the problem or your carpet color(s)/pattern make successful re-dying impossible, the professional may recommend cutting out the damaged part of the carpet and inserting a matching piece in the hole.

- **Replacement:** If any of the above options are not possible or will be too costly, the professional may recommend replacing the carpet in the damaged area.

7. **Cautions:** These notes contain important information related to your spotting efforts and safety. They should be read carefully before you begin any spotting treatment. The cautions include warnings of:

- Potential problems that can occur if treatment is delayed,

- Conditions where it may be necessary to consult with a professional,

- Types of spills where concentrations of bacteria or harsh substances require the use of protective wear,

- Substances that can cause immediate and permanent spotting, staining, discoloration, carpet damage or recurring spotting problems, especially on a type of carpet fiber that is sensitive to certain types of spills.

— 9 —

Section II

8. **Materials Needed:** This is a brief list of the equipment, tools, chemicals, etc., needed to do the spot treatment process. (More information on each of the items in your spotting kit is in "Chapter 2. Your Spotting Kit".)

   **Note:** If you're using a spot machine, the temperature of water that will be most effective for treating the spot will also be given here. (A description of cold, warm and hot water is in the "Getting Ready to Treat a Spot" section that follows.)

   Spots can be very sensitive to temperature and will be affected positively or negatively by the temperature of water used. **Caution:** Follow these spot machine water temperature instructions carefully. A water temperature that would cause one type of spot to break down and be easily flushed from the carpet may cause another type of spill to become more difficult to remove or could even set the spot permanently. Examples: Proteins, like blood or egg, respond well to cool water. Grease from cooking responds better to hot water. When proteins and grease are combined, as in meat gravy, it's best to use warm water.)

9. **Class:** The treatment steps you use for a specific type of spot depend on whether you have a spot machine for vacuuming and rinsing or must use a towel or viscose rayon chamois for all blotting, etc., and on the age and/or condition of the spot.

   The 1st treatment page for each spot shows the treatment steps for:

   • Class I: Spot Machine + Old and/or Dried Spot

   • Class II: Spot Machine + Fresh and/or Wet Spot

   The 2nd treatment page shows the treatment steps for:

   • Class III: Towel + Old and/or Dried Spot

   • Class IV: Towel + Fresh and/or Wet Spot

— 10 —

It's important that you use the steps for the correct Class of spot in order to get the best results. The following are the definitions for the age and/or condition of the spot:

- **Old** - The spot has been on the carpet for 48 hours or more. Most liquid spots dry within 1 - 2 days, so you may be able to guess the age by touching the spot. If you are not sure how old the spot is and no one can tell you, assume it is old and treat it using the steps for an Old / Dried Spot.

- **Dried** - When you touch a liquid spot, it's no longer fluid and has lost most of its moisture, though not necessarily all of it. A spot that was once wet can lose enough water to become sticky, gooey or tacky. It would then be classified as dried. **Note:** A spot like oil will never truly dry and will feel much the same whether it is minutes or months old. In this case it would be important to find out the spot's age if possible in order to determine the correct Class of steps to use for treatment.

- **Fresh** - The spot is up to 48 hours old. Most fresh liquid spots still feel wet or are fluid, which is a good indicator that they have not been on the carpet very long. (Some products such as correction fluid, epoxy glue activated by a catalyst, hot glue or very small quantities of solvent-based fluids may dry or harden within minutes, depending on the temperature and humidity.)

- **Wet** - The spot is still fluid and there is still a good amount of moisture present. Wet spots (except for ones like ink, nail polish, glue and paint which are better treated after they dry) are normally easily removed from the carpet fibers by dry vacuuming or rinsing with a spot machine or by blotting with a chamois or towel.

10. **Steps:** These instructions tell you exactly how to treat each Class of spot:

    - The manual method (scraping, scooping, blotting, etc.), if any, used first to remove as much spot matter as possible before applying spotting agent(s),

    - Which spotting agent(s) to apply and how much (small or generous amount),

    - The best way to agitate the spot to enhance the effectiveness of the agent(s) and the breakdown of the spot matter,

    - How long to let the spotting agent(s) work at breaking down the spot material before doing the next step, etc.

— 11 —

It's critical that these steps be followed carefully and exactly in the order in which they are listed, because:

- The specified manual removal of spot matter reduces the amount of liquids, debris to be removed and/or the bond the spot may have to the carpet fibers. It also allows the spotting agent to penetrate into the spot matter faster and further.

- The sequence and amounts in which the spotting agents are applied enhances their effectiveness at breaking down the spot material, while minimizing the quantity of spotting agents needed and reducing the potential for spreading the spot.

- The specified dwell (waiting) times and types of manual agitation after spotters have been applied also enhance their ability to break down the spot. (See "Chapter 3. Spot Treatment Techniques" for instructions for how to do each of the different treatment steps.)

## *Getting Ready to Treat a Spot*

There are several simple, but important, steps to follow when you have a spot that needs treatment, especially the first time you use my methods.

1. **Identify the type of fiber(s) your carpet is made of, if you don't already know.** Remember, the main thing you need to determine is whether or not your carpet is made of synthetic fibers or is a blend containing synthetic fibers. The treatment steps will be the same no matter what type of synthetic or synthetic blend, but your results may be affected by the type of fiber. (See "Chapter 1. Identifying Your Carpet Fiber" for instructions for how to do this.)

2. **Identify the spot(s).**

   - If you do **not** know what the "spot" is: Turn to "Chapter 4. Identifying Your Spot, Stain Or Discoloration" to refresh your memory for how to do this.

   - If you do know what the "spot" is: Go to Step 3.

3. **Find and read the treatment instructions for your type and Class of spot.** The green colored pages in this Chapter are the "Alphabetical List Of Common Spots & Stains", and the treatment pages immediately follow them.

Read the entire treatment page before going any further. It will tell you if you can successfully treat the spot, or if you should call a professional. **Caution: Always read the instructions thoroughly for your Class of spotting situation before starting (and during) treatment.** Though the tools, spotting agents and techniques used to treat many spots are similar, there could be subtle differences that could affect the success of your treatment efforts.

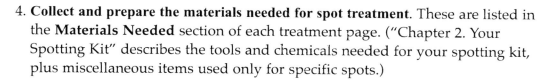

4. **Collect and prepare the materials needed for spot treatment**. These are listed in the **Materials Needed** section of each treatment page. ("Chapter 2. Your Spotting Kit" describes the tools and chemicals needed for your spotting kit, plus miscellaneous items used only for specific spots.)

Get out your spotting kit. Test the spotter bottles and spot machine, if you have one.

- **Spotter spray bottles - Testing:** Verify that the sprayers are screwed tightly to the bottles. Turn the nozzles to the ON position and verify that they are fully primed and set on "mist" by spraying each spotter into the bottom of a sink or the empty bucket from your spotting kit.

- **Spot machine - Filling:** Fill the clean water/rinse tank (called a "Clean/Solution" Tank on some models) with fresh water only. The water should be at the temperature called for in the **Materials Needed**.

  - **Cool water** - Turn on the cold water faucet and let the water run across the back of your hand. It should feel comfortably cool - just slightly cooler than your skin temperature. It should not be cold enough to cause discomfort or almost numb the skin. If the water from the faucet is too cold, adjust the hot water to bring the temperature up to the desired level.

  - **Warm water** - Turn on the cold and hot water faucets and let the water run across the back of your hand. It should feel comfortably warm, but much warmer than your skin temperature. It should not be so hot that you want to pull your hand away. If needed, adjust the cold or hot water to bring the temperature to the desired level.

  - **Hot water** - Turn on the hot water faucet and let it run until the water becomes steaming hot or as hot as it will get. (To prevent scalds or possible flooding, do not touch the water and don't leave the flowing water unattended.)

If your spot machine is being stored in a cold environment, warm up the rinse (or "Clean/Solution") tank by filling it with water of the specified temperature and dumping it at least once or twice. This will help ensure that a cold tank does not lower the water temperature too much.

**Note:** In some cases, you are also instructed to add a small amount of fresh water or your alcohol spotting agent to the dirty water/ recovery tank (called a "Dirty/Collection" Tank on some models). This will help neutralize the negative effects of certain spots or residues left behind when the wrong type of cleaner has been used in earlier spotting efforts.

— 13 —

- **Spot machine - Testing:** When the clean water tank has been filled, always test it to be sure all the spot machine systems are working properly. (Use the specific operating instructions for your type of spot machine to do the following.)

  - Plug the spot machine into an electrical outlet near a sink and turn the machine on. (I suggest using the kitchen sink if you're at home.)

  - Hold the machine's rinse tool (also called a "brush" or "cleaning" tool) over the sink and fully press the spray trigger to prime the pump. The tool should be spraying water - not dripping - when the trigger button is fully pressed. (It may take a few seconds to prime. If the pump doesn't prime quickly, turn off the machine, unplug it and read the troubleshooting section of the machine's instruction manual.)

  - Put the rinse or cleaning tool at the bottom of the sink and follow the instructions for your type of equipment to vacuum up the water. If the vacuum system sucks up all the rinse water in the bottom of the sink, then the vacuum has good air flow.

Take your spotting kit and any other needed materials to the place where the spill has occurred and set them out by the spot where you can easily reach them. **Note:** Put on your gloves and any other protective gear you choose to wear, if you are working with a spot such as feces, blood or other bodily fluids that could be contaminated with bacteria/other pathogens or with harsh chemicals such as gasoline.

5. **Carefully follow all the instruction steps listed for your type and Class of spot.** Do the recommended scraping, scooping, blotting, dry vacuuming, etc., to remove as much spot matter as possible. Apply spotting agents in the recommended sequence and amounts. Follow the recommended times for letting the spotter work by itself or for agitating the spotter into the spot. (If you are not exactly sure how to do some of the treatment steps, see "Chapter 3. Spot Treatment Techniques".)

Be patient and avoid over-treatments that cause worse problems than you started with! These include:

- Not giving the spotting agents enough time to penetrate and begin breaking down the spot, especially an old one. This can tempt you to dump more chemicals on it.

- Continuing to apply more spotting agent than instructed to speed things up. This will only spread the spot matter over a larger area and cause it to penetrate further into the carpet fibers.

- Impatient scrubbing or overly vigorous agitation. This can also spread the spot and/or result in frayed yarns that look as bad or worse than the original spot itself.

**Remember, it's much easier to retreat a spot or stain that hasn't been treated enough than it is to try to fix one that's been worked to death.**

6. **After finishing treatment, collect your spotting kit and any spot debris or other materials. Carefully clean and store the tools and other chemicals in your spotting kit.**

## Temporarily Handling a Spill When You Have Little or No Time

Whenever possible, I recommend that you follow all the treatment steps for any spot. Sometimes, however, you are in a rush to get out the door to catch a plane or something and don't have time to properly treat the spill immediately. If you are in a big hurry and have very little time when an accidental spill occurs:

• Stop!

• Calm down and take a deep breath.

• Avoid panicking and doing something like dumping cleaning chemicals on the spot. This will only make a bad situation worse.

• Instead, follow the suggestion below that best fits your circumstances:

**Suggestion #1 - Get Knowledgeable Help**

If someone else at your home, office, etc., is familiar with this guide and knows how to properly remove spots:

• Ask if they would please read the appropriate treatment page immediately, and treat the spot as per the instructions.

• Be sure they know where your spotting kit is stored.

**Suggestion #2 - Do A Mini Treatment**

If you have at least 5 to 10 minutes before you must leave:

• Grab this guide and your spotting kit.

• Turn to the proper treatment page.

• Scoop up any solid matter or blot up any liquid as per the treatment instructions. (This is especially important for a wet spill. If left without any sort of treatment, gravity will pull the spill down into the carpet fibers making it much more difficult to remove later.)

• Place a towel over the spill, unless the spot is wet glue or something equally

— 15 —

sticky that the towel would adhere to. If the spill is a dry one, use a dry towel. If the spill is a damp or wet one, use a towel moistened with water. (The Removal restrictions on the treatment page usually have a recommendation for the type of towel to use when treatment will be delayed, such as when a pro must be called.)

- Put a note next to the spill that says, *"Do Not Touch! Or Clean!"*

- Pen up or put outside any animals that run about the house, office, etc.

- Alert everyone about the spill and its location.

- When you return, finish treating the spot properly. (Be sure to use the steps under the appropriate Class, based on the spot's current age/condition.)

**Suggestion #3 - Do Damage Containment of a Liquid Spill in a Crisis Situation**

If you must be out the door almost immediately and you have no one else who can treat a liquid spill, especially one containing really bad dyes like cherry KoolAid®, unset Jello®, hair or clothing dye, quickly:

- Sprinkle enough dry baking soda or baking powder on the spot so it is completely covered and the powder extends about an inch past the edges of the spot.

- Place a towel moistened with water over the spill;

- If you have time:

  - Pen up or put outside any animals that run about the house, office, etc.

  - Alert everyone about the spill and its location.

  - Put a note next to the spill that says, *"Do Not Touch! Or Clean!"*

- When you return, break the dried powder into small particles by tapping it with the edge of a spoon and vacuum up the debris. Keep breaking and vacuuming until you have removed as much of the dried powder as possible. Then finish treating the spot using the instructions for the original spot. (Be sure to use the steps under the appropriate Class, based on the spot's current age/condition.)

— 16 —

**Note:** If left without any sort of treatment, gravity will pull the spill down into the carpet fibers, making it much more difficult to remove later. Unfortunately, quickly blotting the spot with a towel and then having to abandon treatment could result in a spot that still has enough liquid left to soak further into the fibers. The baking soda or powder continues to pull the liquid away from the carpet fibers and up to the surface, where it absorbs the spill until it almost dries out the spot.

**Caution:** Do **not** use this crisis response on oily spills or liquid spills containing semi-solids or solids. The oil and powder could make a sticky, pasty mix, and it or the liquid/solids/powder combination could be more difficult to remove later.

## *Introduction Wrap Up*

In closing this introduction to Chapter 5, I have a few comments on two topics -
1) Ensuring your **personal safety** and that of those around you, and
2) Your **potential spot treatment results**.

### *Safety*

**Caution:** Please, always read all product labels with care, especially for those spots you suspect may contain a type of chlorine bleach (usually identified as sodium hypochlorite or lithium hypochlorite in the ingredient list.) Since many of the spotting treatments in this guide require using ammonia, an accidental mixing of the chlorine bleach and ammonia can be highly dangerous.

Do **not** use ammonia to treat spills of products that contain chlorine bleach or another form of chlorine. These products include dish detergents, tub and tile cleaners, toilet bowl cleaners, mold/mildew removers, disinfectant/sanitizers, swimming pool chemicals, ceiling cleaners, etc. If you have no container or ingredient list to check, do not use ammonia with anything that you even suspect might contain chlorine.

— 17 —

### *Your Potential Spot Treatment Results*

I've given you the most in-depth information available on home treatment for carpet spots, but the quality of the results from your treatment efforts will depend on a variety of circumstances that I, unfortunately, cannot control. These include:

- **Type of carpet fibers in your carpet** - As you saw in "Synthetic Fiber Spotting / Staining Characteristics" in "Chapter 1. Identifying Your Carpet Fiber", different fiber types are more susceptible to specific types of spots and stains than others. ("Chapter 6. How Does One Carpet Fiber Compare To Another?" gives even more detailed information on this topic.)

- **Cost of the carpet** (expensive, medium or cheap) - Cheaper carpets tend to have bigger spot removal problems because the spaces between the face yarns are greater than in a more expensive carpet. The thin pile allows any spill to soak further into the carpet - sometimes even into the pad underneath the carpet. **Note:** Some carpet designs, such as frieze, can also have this problem, even though they are not necessarily cheaper carpets.

- **Soil / stain protectors** - "Chapter 9. Does My Carpet Need A Carpet Protector After Cleaning?" explains how the ability of the carpet fibers to resist spills is affected by whether the carpet has been treated with protectors against soil/stains or not and by the type of carpet protector put on by the manufacturer or replenished by a service technician after cleaning.

- **Age of the carpet** (brand new, old) / **Carpet condition** (little wear, heavy wear, clean or dirty) - The carpet fibers in a new synthetic carpet are very smooth and spot matter has few places to cling to, especially if your carpet has a good protector applied. As the carpet ages, however, abrasive soils rubbing against the "plastic-like" fibers cause scratches and pits on them, especially in high traffic areas. These scratches and pits are excellent places for spot/stain matter to penetrate, making it harder to remove. At the same time, those soils and the traffic on the carpet are wearing away the protective coat your carpet protector gives the fibers. This makes it even harder for the fibers to effectively resist or repel soil/spots/stains and for you to remove them.

- **Size of the spill** - A larger spill will soak further into the carpet, making it more difficult to remove; a smaller spill usually remains on the surface of the carpet where it is easier to treat.

- **Other spot characteristics** will affect your results. These include the spot's age and/or ingredients or if the spot was treated before - especially if it was treated with a "one size fits all" over-the-counter treatment product that has set it.

Section II

— 18 —

- **Temperature, humidity and sunlight** - These can affect both the effects of the spilled material and sometimes the effectiveness of the spotting agents.

  - Spots normally dry faster in higher temperatures. High humidity can activate the dye in dry, powdered food coloring, Jello®, or Kool-Aid®, and make what was a relatively simple treatment of vacuuming up the powder much more complex. If sunlight has been baking the spot for a prolonged period, the spot will be harder to remove.

  - Spotting agent action is accelerated by hotter temperatures and sunlight can increase the oxygen action in hydrogen peroxide.

- **Type of spot treatment equipment you have at home** - A spot machine increases your effectiveness by many times.

- **How carefully you follow the treatment steps** - This includes whether you completed all the treatment steps properly, did them in the order listed, used the correct tools and chemicals, treatment techniques, etc., etc.

◆

Even with the factors described above, my simple methods for treating your carpet spots and stains, applied as I tell you to in this guide, will enable you to keep your carpet looking its best and help maintain this valuable part of your home, office or auto. **Happy Spotting!**

— 19 —

# Chapter 5
# *Alphabetical List of Common Spots / Stains*

– 1 –

| Spot / Stain | Page Numbers |
| --- | --- |

A

**B**

| Spot / Stain | Page Numbers |
|---|---|
| Cake – Cooked: No Fruit Topping, Filling or Icing (See "Snacks") | 172 - 173 |
| Cake – Cooked: With Fruit Topping, Filling or Icing (See "Candy – Soft") | 26 - 27 |
| Cake Batters – No Candy or Fruit (See "Soup – Thick") | 180 - 181 |
| Cake Batters – With Candy or Fruit (See "Candy – Soft") | 26 - 27 |
| Cake Frosting or Icing (See "Food Coloring – Paste") | 76 - 77 |
| Candle Wax (See "Wax") | 196 - 197 |
| Candy – Hard | 24 - 25 |
| Candy – Soft | 26 - 27 |
| Candy Bars (See "Candy – Soft") | 26 - 27 |
| Canned Fish / Meats – In Mustard Sauce (See "Mustard") | 138 - 139 |
| Canned Fish / Meats – In Oil (See "Butter") | 22 - 23 |
| Canned Fish / Meats – In Tomato Sauce (See "Spaghetti Sauce") | 184 - 185 |
| Canned Fish / Meats – In Water (See "Soup – Thin") | 182 - 183 |
| Car Polish / Car Polishing Compound – Liquid or Paste (See "Metal Polish") | 128 - 129 |
| Car Wash – Liquid (See "Detergents – Liquid or Gel") | 54 - 55 |
| Car Wax – Liquid or Paste (See "Metal Polish") | 128 - 129 |
| Caramel Syrup – Cold or Hot (See "Candy – Soft") | 26 - 27 |
| Carbon Paper | 28 - 29 |
| Carbon Powder (See "Copier Toner") | 42 - 43 |
| Carburetor Cleaner – Auto (See "Solvents") | 176 - 177 |
| Carpenter's Putty (See "Putty") | 158 - 159 |
| Carpet Cleaners – Liquid (See "Detergents – Liquid or Gel") | 54 - 55 |
| Carpet Deodorizers – Powder (See "Dry Goods") | 58 - 59 |
| Carpet Dry Cleaners – Powder (See "Detergents – Powder") | 56 - 57 |
| Carpet Dry Solvent Spotters (See "Solvents") | 176 - 177 |
| Carpet Spot Remover – Liquid or Its Residue (See "Detergents – Liquid or Gel") | 54 - 55 |
| Carpet Spot Remover – Powder (See "Detergents – Powder") | 56 - 57 |
| Catsup (See "Ketchup") | 118 - 119 |

*C*

| Spot / Stain | Page Numbers |
|---|---|
| Chocolate Milk (See "Milk") | 130 - 131 |
| Chocolate Powder Mixes – Cold or Hot (See "Food Coloring – Powder") | 78 - 79 |
| Chocolate Syrup – Cold or Hot (See "Syrup") | 186 - 187 |
| Christmas Tree Water (See "Lignin Browning") | 122 - 123 |
| Chrome Polish (See "Metal Polish") | 128 - 129 |
| Clam Sauce – Red (See "Spaghetti Sauce") | 184 - 185 |
| Clam Sauce – White (See "Soup – Thin") | 182 - 183 |
| Clay Putty (See "Putty") | 158 - 159 |
| Clay Soil (See "Mud") | 136 - 137 |
| Cleaners – No Bleach: Foam, Gel or Liquid (See "Detergents – Liquid or Gel") | 54 - 55 |
| Cleaners – With Bleach: Gel or Liquid (See "Bleaching Products") | 14 - 15 |
| Cleaners – No Bleach: Powder (See "Detergents – Powder") | 56 - 57 |
| Cleaners – With Bleach: Powder (See "Bleaching Products") | 14 - 15 |
| Clothes Dye – Liquid (See "Dye") | 60 - 61 |
| Clothes Dye – Powder (See "Food Coloring – Powder") | 78 - 79 |
| Clothes Starch (See "Hair Spray") | 106 - 107 |
| Coca-Cola® (See "Soft Drinks") | 174 - 175 |
| Cocktail Sauce / Chile Sauce, Etc. (See "Ketchup") | 118 - 119 |
| Coffee – Cold: Frappuccino®, Etc. (See "Coffee or Tea – With Milk") | 38 - 39 |
| Coffee Creamer – Liquid (See "Milk") | 130 - 131 |
| Coffee Creamer – Powder (See "Dry Goods") | 58 - 59 |
| Coffee or Tea – Black / Plain | 36 - 37 |
| Coffee or Tea – With Milk, Cream | 38 - 39 |
| Coffee or Tea Grounds – Dry or Unused (See "Dry Goods") | 58 - 59 |
| Coffee or Tea Grounds – Wet or Used (See "Coffee or Tea – Black / Plain") | 36 - 37 |
| Cold Sore Medicine (See "Ointment") | 144 - 145 |
| Colloidal Minerals (See "Coffee or Tea – Black / Plain") | 36 - 37 |
| Colloidal Silver (See "Silver Nitrate") | 170 - 171 |

*C*

| Spot / Stain | Page Numbers |
|---|---|
| Cologne – Liquid (See "Solvents") | 176 - 177 |
| Concrete / Concrete Repair Putty or Caulk (See "Cement") | 30 - 31 |
| Contraceptive Foams, Gels or Jellies (See "Hair Spray") | 106 - 107 |
| Cookies – No Candies or Jelly (See "Snacks") | 172 - 173 |
| Cookies – With Candies or Jelly (See "Candy – Soft") | 26 - 27 |
| Cooking Oil | 40 - 41 |
| Cool Whip® (See "Cheese – Soft") | 34 - 35 |
| Copier Toner | 42 - 43 |
| Corn Chips (See "Snacks") | 172 - 173 |
| Corn Gluten / Corn Meal – Horticultural, Etc. (See "Snacks") | 172 - 173 |
| Correction Fluid | 44 - 45 |
| Cosmetic Wax (See "Wax") | 196 - 197 |
| Cosmetics – Creamy | 46 - 47 |
| Cosmetics – Powder: Dry, Loose or Pressed (See "Dry Goods") | 58 - 59 |
| Cosmetics – Waxy | 48 - 49 |
| Cottage Cheese (See "Cheese – Soft") | 34 - 35 |
| Cough Syrup | 50 - 51 |
| Crab Salads (See "Mayonnaise") | 126 - 127 |
| Crackers (See "Snacks") | 172 - 173 |
| Cranberries (See "Berries") | 12 - 13 |
| Cranberry Juice (See "Fruit Juice – With Dye") | 82 - 83 |
| Cranberry Sauce (See "Jam") | 114 - 115 |
| Crayolas® or Crayons | 52 - 53 |
| Cream (See "Cheese – Soft") | 34 - 35 |
| Cream Cheese (See "Cheese – Soft") | 34 - 35 |
| Credit Card Carbons (See "Carbon Paper") | 28 - 29 |
| Creosote (See "Sealers – Solvent-Based") | 164 - 165 |

**C**
●

**D**

| Spot / Stain | Page Numbers |
|---|---|
| Fabric or Fiber Protectors (See "Hair Spray") | 106 - 107 |
| Fabric Softener – Gel or Liquid (See "Detergents – Liquid or Gel") | 54 - 55 |
| Fabric Softener – Powder (See "Detergents – Powder") | 56 - 57 |
| Face Powder – Cosmetic Type (See "Dry Goods") | 58 - 59 |
| Face Tonics – With Alcohol: Astringent, Etc. (See "Solvents") | 176 - 177 |
| Facial Cold Cream (See "Ointment") | 144 - 145 |
| Feces – Liquid (See "Feces – Semi-Liquid") | 66 - 67 |
| Feces – Semi-Liquid | 66 - 67 |
| Feces – Semi-Solid Clumps | 68 - 69 |
| Feces – Solid (See "Feces – Semi-Solid Clumps") | 68 - 69 |
| Felt Tip Pen Ink (See "Magic Marker") | 124 - 125 |
| Fiber Glass Resin (Immediately Call A Pro For Advice) | |
| Finger Paint (See "Magic Marker") | 124 - 125 |
| Fingerprint Powder (See "Copier Toner") | 42 - 43 |
| Fire Extinguisher – Foam, Liquid or Powder (Immediately Call A Pro For Advice) | |
| Fire Extinguisher – Gas (No Clean-Up Necessary) | |
| Fireplace Grime (See "Soot") | 178 - 179 |
| First Aid Ointments (See "Ointment") | 144 - 145 |
| Fish Eggs, Roe, Caviar (See "Egg – Raw") | 64 - 65 |
| Fish Emulsion Fertilizer – Liquid (See "Milk") | 130 - 131 |
| Fish Guts, Intestines (See "Egg – Raw") | 64 - 65 |
| Fish Scales or Slime (See "Bodily Fluids") | 18 - 19 |
| Flat Tire Sealants (Fix-A-Flat®, Etc.) (See "Glue – Stick") | 96 - 97 |
| Flavorings – Liquid (See "Food Coloring – Liquid") | 74 - 75 |
| Flavorings – Powder (See "Food Coloring – Powder") | 78 - 79 |
| Floor Cleaner – Gel or Liquid (See "Detergents – Liquid or Gel") | 54 - 55 |
| Floor Cleaner – Powder (See "Detergents – Powder") | 56 - 57 |
| Floor Sealer or Finish – Solvent-Based (See "Sealers – Solvent-Based") | 164 - 165 |

**F**

| Spot / Stain | Page Numbers |
|---|---|

*F*

| Spot / Stain | Page Numbers |
|---|---|
| Gasket Removers (See "Solvents") | 176 - 177 |
| Gasket Sealants (See "Sealers – Solvent-Based") | 164 - 165 |
| Gasoline | 86 - 87 |
| Gasoline Treatments or Additives (See "Gasoline") | 86 - 87 |
| Gelatin – Jelled (See "Food Coloring – Paste") | 76 - 77 |
| Gelatin – Liquid (See "Food Coloring – Liquid") | 74 - 75 |
| Gelatin – Powder (See "Food Coloring – Powder") | 78 - 79 |
| Gelato (See "Ice Cream") | 108 - 109 |
| Glaze or Chutney For Meats, Fruits or Vegetables (See "Jam") | 114 - 115 |
| Glue – Airplane | 88 - 89 |
| Glue – Animal (See "Glue – Household") | 90 - 91 |
| Glue – Elmer's® | 92 - 93 |
| Glue – Furniture | 94 - 95 |
| Glue – Household | 90 - 91 |
| Glue – Latex (See "Glue – Airplane") | 88 - 89 |
| Glue – Melted Hot Glue Gun Sticks (See "Glue – Furniture") | 94 - 95 |
| Glue – Model (See "Glue – Airplane") | 88 - 89 |
| Glue – Stick | 96 - 97 |
| Glue – Super Glue (See "Glue – Airplane") | 88 - 89 |
| Glue – Washable (See "Glue – Elmer's®") | 92 - 93 |
| Glue – Wood (See "Glue – Furniture") | 94 - 95 |
| Gouda Cheese (See "Cheese – Hard or Dry") | 32 - 33 |
| Grape Juice – Red (See "Fruit Juice – With Dye") | 82 - 83 |
| Grape Juice – White (See "Fruit Juice – No Dye") | 80 - 81 |
| Grapefruit Juice (See "Fruit Juice – No Dye") | 80 - 81 |
| Graphite (See "Soot") | 178 - 179 |
| Grass Stains (See "Plant Juice") | 154 - 155 |
| Gravy – Thick or Creamy | 98 - 99 |

*G*

**G**

**H**

| Spot / Stain | Page Numbers |
|---|---|
| . . . . . . . . . . . . . . . . . . . . . . . . . . . . . . . . . . . . . . . . . . . . . . . . . . . . . . . . . . . . . . . .Honey (See "Syrup") . . . . . . . . . . . . . . . . . . . . . . . . . . . . . . . . . . . . . . . . . . . . . . | .186 - 187 |
| Horse Radish Sauce (See "Soup – Thin") . . . . . . . . . . . . . . . . . . . . . . . . . . . . . . . . . . | .182 - 183 |
| Hot Chocolate – Liquid (See "Milk") . . . . . . . . . . . . . . . . . . . . . . . . . . . . . . . . . . . . | .130 - 131 |
| Hot Chocolate – Powder (See "Food Coloring – Powder") . . . . . . . . . . . . . . . . . . . . . | .78 - 79 |
| Hot Dog / All Sausages, Etc. – Raw (See "Egg – Raw") . . . . . . . . . . . . . . . . . . . . . . . | .64 - 65 |
| Hot Dog / All Sausages, Etc. – No Condiments (See "Egg – Cooked") . . . . . . . . . . . . . | .62 - 63 |
| Hot Dog / All Sausages, Etc. – Green Condiments: Peppers, Pickle Relish, Etc. (See "Spaghetti Sauce") . . . . . . . . . . . . . . . . . . . . . . . . . . . . . . . . . . . . . . . . . . | .184 - 185 |
| Hot Dog / All Sausages, Etc. – Mustard (See "Mustard") . . . . . . . . . . . . . . . . . . . . . . | .138 - 139 |
| Hot Dog / All Sausages, Etc. – Red Condiments: Ketchup, Salsa, Etc. (See "Spaghetti Sauce") . . . . . . . . . . . . . . . . . . . . . . . . . . . . . . . . . . . . . . . . . . | .184 - 185 |
| Hot Dog / All Sausages, Etc. – White Condiments: Mayonnaise, Etc. (See "Mayonnaise") . . . . . . . . . . . . . . . . . . . . . . . . . . . . . . . . . . . . . . . . . . . . . | .126 - 127 |
| Hot Fudge or Caramel Topping – Cold or Hot (See "Candy – Soft") . . . . . . . . . . . . . . | .26 - 27 |
| Hot Glue (See "Glue – Furniture") . . . . . . . . . . . . . . . . . . . . . . . . . . . . . . . . . . . . . . | .94 - 95 |
| Hot Tub Chlorine / Cleaners – Liquid, Powder or Tablets (See "Bleaching Products") | . .14 - 15 |
| Hummus – Snack Dip (See "Peanut Butter") . . . . . . . . . . . . . . . . . . . . . . . . . . . . . . . . | .152 - 153 |
| Humus – Horticultural (See "Mud") . . . . . . . . . . . . . . . . . . . . . . . . . . . . . . . . . . . . . . | .136 - 137 |
| Hydraulic Fluids (See "Oils / Thin Lubricants") . . . . . . . . . . . . . . . . . . . . . . . . . . . . . | .142 - 143 |
| Hydrogen Peroxide 6% (See "Bleaching Products") . . . . . . . . . . . . . . . . . . . . . . . . . . | .14 - 15 |

*H*

**J, K**

| Spot / Stain | Page Numbers |
| --- | --- |
| Labels With Adhesive (See "Gum") | 102 - 103 |
| Lacquer | 120 - 121 |
| Lager (See "Beer") | 10 - 11 |
| Lantern Oil (See "Kerosene") | 116 - 117 |
| Lard (See "Grease") | 100 - 101 |
| Laser Jet Printer Ink (See "Ink") | 110 - 111 |
| Latex Paint (See "Paint – Oil-Based") | 146 - 147 |
| Lathe Oil (See "Oils / Thin Lubricants") | 142 - 143 |
| Laundry Detergent – Gel or Liquid (See "Detergents – Liquid or Gel") | 54 - 55 |
| Laundry Detergent – Powder (See "Detergents – Powder") | 56 - 57 |
| Laundry Stain Removers – Spray'n Wash®, Etc. (See "Detergents – Liquid or Gel") | 54 - 55 |
| Leather Balms (See "Sealers – Solvent-Based") | 164 - 165 |
| Leather Cleaners – Liquid or Paste: Saddle Soap, Etc. (See "Detergents – Liquid or Gel") | 54 - 55 |
| Leather or Shoe Stretch – Liquid or Spray (See "Solvents") | 176 - 177 |
| Leather Softeners or Moisturizers – Liquid, Neatsfoot Oil (See "Oils / Thin Lubricants") | 142 - 143 |
| Leather Softeners or Moisturizers – Paste, Mink Oil (See "Grease") | 100 - 101 |
| Leather Water and/or Stain Repellents – Solvent-Based (See "Sealers – Solvent-Based") | 164 - 165 |
| Leaves – Plant (See "Plant Juice") | 154 - 155 |
| Lemon Juice (See "Fruit Juice – No Dye") | 80 - 81 |
| Lighter Fluid – Charcoal or Cigarette (See "Kerosene") | 116 - 117 |
| Lignin Browning | 122 - 123 |
| Lip Balm – Greasy, in Squeeze Tube (See "Ointment") | 144 - 145 |
| Lip Balm – Waxy (See "Cosmetics – Waxy") | 48 - 49 |
| Lip Gloss (See "Ointment") | 144 - 145 |
| Lipstick (See "Cosmetics – Waxy") | 48 - 49 |

L •

**L**

| Spot / Stain | Page Numbers |
|---|---|
| Macaroni Salads (See "Mayonnaise") | 126 - 127 |
| Machine Oils – Light, Thin (See "Oils / Thin Lubricants") | 142 - 143 |
| Magic Marker | 124 - 125 |
| Manure (See "Mud") | 136 - 137 |
| Maple Syrup (See "Syrup") | 186 - 187 |
| Margarine (See "Butter") | 22 - 23 |
| Marinades (See "Food Coloring – Liquid") | 74 - 75 |
| Marshmallows (See "Candy – Soft") | 26 - 27 |
| Mascara (See "Cosmetics – Waxy") | 48 - 49 |
| Massage Oil (See "Body Oils") | 20 - 21 |
| Mayonnaise | 126 - 127 |
| Meat / Fish / Poultry – Cooked (See "Egg – Cooked") | 62 - 63 |
| Meat / Fish / Poultry – Raw (See "Egg – Raw") | 64 - 65 |
| Meat Sauce (See "Spaghetti Sauce") | 184 - 185 |
| Medicinal Silver (See "Silver Nitrate") | 170 - 171 |
| Medicines – All Capsules, Powder or Tablets (See "Dry Goods") | 58 - 59 |
| Medicines – All Liquid (See "Cough Syrup") | 50 - 51 |
| Mercurochrome / Merthiolate (See "Cough Syrup") | 50 - 51 |
| Mercury – From Thermometer (See "Silver Nitrate") | 170 - 171 |
| Metal Fillers or Putties (See "Correction Fluid") | 44 - 45 |
| Metal Joint Compound, Electrical, Etc. (See "Grease") | 100 - 101 |
| Metal Polish | 128 - 129 |
| Mildew (See "Mold") | 132 - 133 |
| Milk | 130 - 131 |
| Milk – Powdered, White (See "Dry Goods") | 58 - 59 |
| Milk Powdered Drink Mixes – All (See "Food Coloring – Powder") | 78 - 79 |
| Milkshake (See "Milk") | 130 - 131 |
| Milk Syrups – All (See "Syrup") | 186 - 187 |

M
•

| Spot / Stain | Page Numbers |
|---|---|
| Mineral Spirits (See "Solvents") | 176 - 177 |
| Miracle Whip® (See "Mayonnaise") | 126 - 127 |
| Mixed Drinks – Alcoholic or Virgin (See "Alcoholic Beverages") | 2 - 3 |
| Mixed Drinks – Powder (See "Food Coloring – Powder") | 78 - 79 |
| Moisture Absorbing Crystals or Powder (Damp Rid®, Etc.) (See "Dry Goods") | 58 - 59 |
| Moisturizer (See "Cosmetics – Creamy") | 46 - 47 |
| Molasses – Dry: Food Grade or Horticultural (See "Dry Goods") | 58 - 59 |
| Molasses – Liquid (See "Syrup") | 186 - 187 |
| Mold | 132 - 133 |
| Mold / Mildew Removers – Gel, Liquid or Powder (See "Bleaching Products") | 14 - 15 |
| Mortar (See "Cement") | 30 - 31 |
| Moth Crystals or Powder (Moth Ice®, Etc.) (See "Dry Goods") | 58 - 59 |
| Motor Oil (See "Oils / Thin Lubricants") | 142 - 143 |
| Mouthwash | 134 - 135 |
| Mucus (See "Bodily Fluids") | 18 - 19 |
| Mud | 136 - 137 |
| Mud Masque – Facial or Body (See "Mud") | 136 - 137 |
| Muffin Batters – No Candy or Fruit (See "Soup – Thick") | 180 - 181 |
| Muffin Batters – With Candy or Fruit (See "Candy – Soft") | 26 - 27 |
| Muffins – Cooked: No Fruit Topping or Icing (See "Snacks") | 172 - 173 |
| Muffins – Cooked: With Fruit Topping or Icing (See "Candy – Soft") | 26 - 27 |
| Mulch (See "Mud") | 136 - 137 |
| Musical Instrument Grease – Slide Grease (See "Grease") | 100 - 101 |
| Musical Instrument Oil – Valve Oil (See "Oils / Thin Lubricants") | 142 - 143 |
| Mustard | 138 - 139 |
| Mustard Recipes (See "Mustard") | 138 - 139 |

M

| Spot / Stain | Page Numbers |
|---|---|
| Nail Polish | 140 - 141 |
| Nail Fortifiers / Nail Top Coats / Nail Treatments (See "Nail Polish") | 140 - 141 |
| Newspaper Print Dye (See "Ink") | 110 - 111 |
| No Rinse Detergents – Liquid (See "Detergents – Liquid or Gel") | 54 - 55 |
| Nut Butters (See "Peanut Butter") | 152 - 153 |
| Nutritional Powders – Flavored: Creatine, Etc. (See "Food Coloring – Powder") | 78 - 79 |
| Nutritional Powders – Unflavored: Creatine, Etc. (See "Dry Goods") | 58 - 59 |
| Nutritional Silver (See "Silver Nitrate") | 170 - 171 |

**N, O**

| Spot / Stain | Page Numbers |
|---|---|
| Oatmeal – Cooked (See "Soup – Thick") | 180 - 181 |
| Oatmeal – Dry, Uncooked (See "Dry Goods") | 58 - 59 |
| Odor Absorbing Crystals or Powder, Odor Genie®, Etc. (See "Dry Goods") | 58 - 59 |
| Oil Crayon (See "Crayon") | 52 - 53 |
| Oil Detergents (See "Oils / Thin Lubricants") | 142 - 143 |
| Oils / Thin Lubricants | 142 - 143 |
| Ointment | 144 - 145 |
| Olive Oil – All Food-Grade Oils (See "Cooking Oil") | 40 - 41 |
| Oral Antiseptics (See "Mouthwash") | 134 - 135 |
| Orange Drinks (See "Food Coloring – Liquid") | 74 - 75 |
| Orange Juice (See "Fruit Juice – No Dye") | 80 - 81 |
| Orange Oil / Orange Polish or Wood Cleaner (See "Furniture Polish") | 84 - 85 |
| Oven Cleaner – Gel or Liquid (See "Detergents – Liquid or Gel") | 54 - 55 |
| Oxidized Metal (See "Rust") | 162 - 163 |

| Spot / Stain | Page Numbers |
|---|---|
| Paint – Oil-Based | 146 - 147 |
| Paint – Oil-Based: Aluminum, Epoxy, Latex Enamel, Paint Marker, Solvent-Based Paint (See "Paint – Oil-Based") | 146 - 147 |
| Paint – Water-Based | 148 - 149 |
| Paint – Water-Based: Acrylic, Latex, Washable, Paint Primer – Water-Based (See "Paint – Water-Based") | 148 - 149 |
| Paint Strippers / Paint Thinner (See "Solvents") | 176 - 177 |
| Pancake Batter – No Fruit or Candy (See "Soup – Thick") | 180 - 181 |
| Pancake Batter – With Fruit or Candy (See "Candy – Soft") | 26 - 27 |
| Pancake Mix – Dry (See "Dry Goods") | 58 - 59 |
| Pancakes Cooked – No Fruit Topping or Syrup (See "Snacks") | 172 - 173 |
| Pancakes Cooked – With Fruit Topping or Syrup (See "Candy – Soft") | 26 - 27 |
| Parmigiano Cheese (See "Cheese – Hard or Dry") | 32 - 33 |
| Pasta – With or Without Sauce: Linguini, Spaghetti, Etc. (See "Pasta") | 150 - 151 |
| Pastels (See "Crayon") | 52 - 53 |
| Pastries – All: Breakfast, Pop-Tarts®, Etc. (See "Candy – Soft") | 26 - 27 |
| Peanut Butter | 152 - 153 |
| Peanuts (See "Snacks") | 172 - 173 |
| Peat Moss (See "Mud") | 136 - 137 |
| Pencil – Colored or Lead (See "Crayon") | 52 - 53 |
| Peppermint Candy (See "Candy – Hard") | 24 - 25 |
| Pepsi~Cola® (See "Soft Drinks") | 174 - 175 |
| Perfume (See "Gasoline") | 86 - 87 |
| Permanent Markers (See "Magic Marker") | 124 - 126 |
| Personal Lubricants – Oil-Based (See "Body Oils") | 20 - 21 |
| Personal Lubricants – Water-Based (See "Hair Spray") | 106 - 107 |
| Pest Repellents – Animals: All Non-Insects (Immediately Call A Pro For Advice) | |
| Pesticides – Granules, Liquid or Powder: Insects Only (Immediately Call A Pro For Advice) | |
| Pet Flea & Tick Control – Powder (See "Dry Goods") | 58 - 59 |

**P**

*P*

| Spot / Stain | Page Numbers |
|---|---|
| Plumber's Putty (See "Putty") | 158 - 159 |
| Polishing Compound (See "Metal Polish") | 128 - 129 |
| Polyurethane (See "Lacquer") | 120 - 121 |
| Popcorn – With Butter, Oil or Flavored Powder Coatings (See "Snacks") | 172 - 173 |
| Popcorn – With Caramel or Candy Coating (See "Candy – Soft") | 26 - 27 |
| Popsicle – Fudge, Pudding, Yogurt (See "Ice Cream") | 108 - 109 |
| Popsicles – All: Rainbow of Colors (See "Food Coloring – Liquid") | 74 - 75 |
| Popsicle Fruit Bars – No Dye: Coconut, Peach, Etc. (See "Banana") | 8 - 9 |
| Popsicle Fruit Bars – With Dye: Blueberry, Strawberry, Etc. (See "Berries") | 12 - 13 |
| Potato Chips / Pork Rinds (See "Snacks") | 172 - 173 |
| Potato Salads – All (See "Avocado") | 6 - 7 |
| Potpourri – Dry or Liquid | 156 - 157 |
| Potting Soils (See "Mud") | 136 - 137 |
| Power Steering Fluid (See "Oils / Thin Lubricants") | 142 - 143 |
| Preserves (See "Jam") | 114 - 115 |
| Pretzels (See "Snacks") | 172 - 173 |
| Protein Bars (See "Candy – Soft") | 26 - 27 |
| Protein Powder – Dry (See "Dry Goods") | 58 - 59 |
| Protein Powder – Mixed In Any Liquid (See "Milk") | 130 - 131 |
| Prune Juice (See "Fruit Juice – With Dye") | 82 - 83 |
| Pruning Sealer – Shrub and Tree (See "Paint – Oil-Based") | 146 - 147 |
| Punch Drinks – Liquid (See "Fruit Juice – With Dye") | 82 - 83 |
| Punch Drinks – Powder (See "Food Coloring – Powder") | 78 - 79 |
| Pus (See "Blood") | 16 - 17 |
| Putty | 158 - 159 |
| PVC Pipe Cleaner / Primer (See "Solvents") | 176 - 177 |
| PVC Pipe Glue (See "Glue – Airplane") | 88 - 89 |

**P**

**Q, R**

| Spot / Stain | Page Number |
|---|---|
| Salad Dressing – Creamy (See "Mayonnaise") | 126 - 127 |
| Salad Dressing – Oily (See "Cooking Oil") | 40 - 41 |
| Saliva – Animal or Human (See "Bodily Fluids") | 18 - 19 |
| Salsa (See "Soup – Thin") | 182 - 183 |
| Salt (See "Dry Goods") | 58 - 59 |
| Sand (See "Dry Goods") | 58 - 59 |
| Sandwiches / Subs – No Condiments (See "Egg – Raw") | 64 - 65 |
| Sandwiches / Subs – Green Condiments: Peppers, Pickle Relish, Etc. (See "Spaghetti Sauce") | 184 - 185 |
| Sandwiches / Subs – Mustard (See "Mustard") | 138 - 139 |
| Sandwiches / Subs – Red Condiments: Ketchup, Salsa, Etc. (See "Spaghetti Sauce") | 184 - 185 |
| Sandwiches / Subs – White Condiments: Mayonnaise, Etc. (See "Mayonnaise") | 126 - 127 |
| Sawdust (See "Dry Goods") | 58 - 59 |
| Scotch Tape® or Any Tape (See "Gum") | 102 - 103 |
| Scratch Fix or Remover – Auto, Etc. (See "Metal Polish") | 128 - 129 |
| Seafood – Cooked (See "Egg – Cooked") | 62 - 63 |
| Seafood – Raw (See "Egg – Raw") | 64 - 65 |
| Sealers – Cream or Paste (See "Floor Wax – Paste") | 72 - 73 |
| Sealers – Liquid, Solvent-Based | 164 - 165 |
| Sealers – Liquid, Water-Based (See "Floor Wax – Liquid") | 70 - 71 |
| Seasonings – Browner, Liquid Smoke, Etc. (See "Food Coloring – Liquid") | 74 - 75 |
| Seaweed (See "Plant Juice") | 154 - 155 |
| Seeds – Bird, Grass, Sunflower, Vegetable, Etc. (See "Snacks") | 172 - 173 |
| Sewing Machine Oil (See "Oils / Thin Lubricants") | 142 - 143 |
| Shampoo (See "Detergents – Liquid or Gel") | 54 - 55 |
| Shaving Cream or Gel (See "Detergents – Liquid or Gel") | 54 - 55 |
| Sheet Rock Dust (See "Dry Goods") | 58 - 59 |
| Sheet Rock Mud or Spackle (See "Cement") | 30 - 31 |
| Shellac (See "Lacquer") | 120 - 121 |

S
•

**U,**

| Spot / Stain | Page Numbers |
| --- | --- |
| Waffle Batter – No Candy or Fruit (See "Soup – Thick") | 180 - 181 |
| Waffle Batter – With Candy or Fruit (See "Candy – Soft") | 26 - 27 |
| Waffle Mix – Dry (See "Dry Goods") | 58 - 59 |
| Waffles – Cooked: No Fruit Topping or Syrup (See "Snacks") | 172 - 173 |
| Waffles – Cooked: With Fruit Topping or Syrup (See "Candy – Soft") | 26 - 27 |
| Wallpaper Primer – Water-Based (See "Paint – Water-Based") | 148 - 149 |
| Wallpaper Stripper – Liquid (See "Detergents – Liquid or Gel") | 54 - 55 |
| Wart Treatment – Gel or Liquid (See "Hair Spray") | 106 - 107 |
| Water-Based Sealers (See "Floor Wax – Liquid") | 70 - 71 |
| Watercolor Ink Marker (See "Magic Marker") | 124 - 125 |
| Watercolor Paint (See "Magic Marker") | 124 - 125 |
| Water Spills (Blot Up or Wet-Vac And Allow To Dry) | |
| Wax – Candle, Cosmetic, Dental | 196 - 197 |
| Wax Removers (See "Solvents") | 176 - 177 |
| WD-40® (See "Oils / Thin Lubricants") | 142 - 143 |
| Weed & Feed – Granules or Liquids (Immediately Call A Pro For Advice) | |
| Weed Killer or Controller – Granules or Liquids (Immediately Call A Pro For Advice) | |
| Whipped Cream (See "Cheese – Soft") | 34 - 35 |
| Whiteboard Cleaner – Solvent-Based (See "Solvents") | 176 - 177 |
| Whiteboard Cleaner – Water-Based (See "Detergents – Liquid or Gel") | 54 - 55 |
| White Clam Sauce (See "Soup – Thin") | 182 - 183 |
| White Grape Juice (See "Fruit Juice – No Dye") | 80 - 81 |
| Wild Bird Feed Cake (See "Avocado") | 6 - 7 |
| Window Cleaner – Liquid (See "Food Coloring – Liquid") | 74 - 75 |
| Window Cleaner – No Bleach: Pills or Powder (See "Detergents – Powder") | 56 - 57 |
| Window Cleaner – With Bleach: Pills or Powder (See "Bleaching Products") | 14 - 15 |
| Windshield Rain Repellants (See "Solvents") | 176 - 177 |
| Windshield Repair Caulk (See "Glue – Airplane") | 88 - 89 |

**W**

**W, X, Y, Z**

*Art's Ultimate Spot Cleaning • Chapter 5 - Common Spots and Stains - Page 33*

# Chapter 5
# *Spot Treatment Steps*

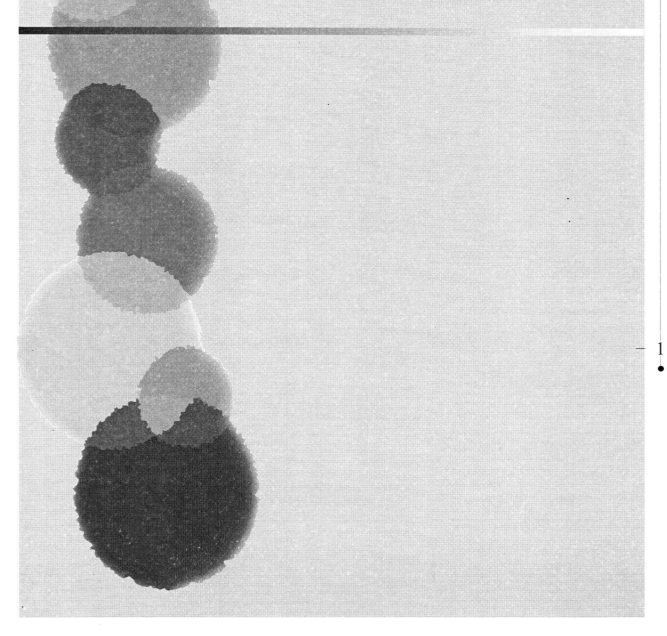

— 1 —

# Alcoholic Beverages: Mixed / Unmixed Drinks

## Comments:

- **Optimum removal time: As soon as possible** within 24 hours of spill
- **Maximum size for home removal:** Class I / II = 3 1/2 inches
- **Removal restrictions:** If the spot (or spots) is larger than 3 1/2 inches in diameter, **do not attempt TOTAL removal** using Class I or II instructions. Do Step 1 **only** under Class I or II. Mist spot(s) with a small amount of ammonia. Put a folded towel moistened with water over spot. Call a pro and have spot removed as soon as possible within 24 hours.
- Mixed drinks may contain artificial coloring that can immediately and permanently stain some nylon. If you cannot remove a spot, consult a pro for options as soon as possible.
- Large spills may cause recurring spots that need re-treatment. (See "Recurring Spots", Chapter 4.)

## Materials Needed:
Class I / II: Spotting kit, Spot machine with warm water

### Class I: Spot Machine + Old / Dried Spot

**Steps:**

1. Using your spot machine, rinse the spot(s) with warm water using the chop stroke technique 8 - 10 times.
   - Take 6 - 8 slow, dry vacuum strokes.
   - Repeat entire Step until most of the sticky residue is gone.

2. Mist on a generous amount of ammonia.
   - Agitate with hard brush.
   - Allow to work 1 minute.
   - Mist on a generous amount of peroxide.
   - Agitate with hard brush.
   - Allow to work 1 minute.

3. With the spot machine, rinse with warm water using the chop stroke technique 8 - 10 times.
   - Take 6 - 8 slow, dry vacuum strokes.

4. Look at and touch spot area carefully to see if the sticky residue is gone:
   - If YES: No further action is needed.
   - If NO: Repeat Steps 2 and 3 until no more will remove.

5. Mist on a generous amount of peroxide.
   - Mist on a small amount of ammonia.
   - Tamp with soft brush.
   - Allow to dry.

6. If needed, repeat Step 5 one time.

7. If the spot persists, call a pro for options as soon as possible.

### Class II: Spot Machine + Fresh / Wet Spot

**Steps:**

1. Using your spot machine, rinse the spot(s) with warm water using the single stroke technique 8 - 10 times.
   - Take 6 - 8 slow, dry vacuum strokes.
   - Repeat entire Step until most of the sticky residue is gone.

2. Mist on a generous amount of ammonia.
   - Agitate with hard brush.
   - Allow to work 1 minute.
   - Mist on a small amount of peroxide.
   - Agitate with hard brush.

3. With the spot machine, rinse with warm water using the chop stroke technique 8 - 10 times.
   - Take 6 - 8 slow, dry vacuum strokes.

4. Look at and touch spot area carefully to see if the sticky residue is gone:
   - If YES: No further action is needed.
   - If NO: Repeat Steps 2 and 3 until no more will remove.

5. Mist on a generous amount of peroxide.
   - Mist on a small amount of ammonia.
   - Tamp with soft brush.
   - Allow to dry.

6. If needed, repeat Step 5 one time.

7. If the spot persists, call a pro for options as soon as possible.

Section II

## *Comments:*

- **Optimum removal time: As soon as possible** within 24 hours of spill
- **Maximum size for home removal:** Class III = No home removal / Class IV = 2 inches
- **Removal restrictions - Class III:** See "Class III" instructions below.
- **Removal restrictions - Class IV:** If the spot(s) is larger than 2 inches in diameter, **do not attempt TOTAL removal** using Class IV instructions. Do Step 1 **only** under Class IV. Mist spot(s) with a small amount of ammonia. Put a folded towel moistened with water over spot. Then:
  - Call a pro and have spot removed as soon as possible within 24 hours. -OR-
  - If the spot is 3-1/2 inches or less in diameter, get a spot machine and:
    - If the spot is now old/dried, do Steps 1 - 7 under Class I.
    - If the spot is still fresh/wet, do Steps 1 - 7 under Class II.
- Mixed drinks may contain artificial coloring that can immediately and permanently stain some nylon. If you cannot remove a spot, consult a pro for options as soon as possible.
- Large spills may cause recurring spots that need re-treatment. (See "Recurring Spots", Chapter 4.)

## *Materials Needed:*

Class III: Towel
Class IV: Spotting kit

| *Class III: Towel + Old / Dried Spot* | *Class IV: Towel + Fresh / Wet Spot* |
|---|---|

### *Steps:*

1. **Do not attempt ANY removal** of a Class III spot(s).
   - Put a dry towel over spot to prevent spreading of sticky residue. Then:
     - Call a pro and have spot removed within 2 days.
       -OR-
     - If the spot is 3 1/2 inches or less in diameter, get a spot machine and do Steps 1 - 7 under Class I.

### *Steps:*

1. Fold a towel several times and place it over the spot(s).
   - Step on the towel with your full weight, using a clean part of the towel each time.
   - Repeat until no more liquid absorbs.
2. Mist on a generous amount of ammonia.
   - Agitate with hard brush.
   - Allow to work 1 minute.
   - Mist on a small amount of peroxide.
   - Agitate with hard brush.
3. With a towel, firmly blot 15 - 20 times, using a clean part of the towel each time.
4. Look at and touch spot area carefully to see if the sticky residue is gone:
   - If YES: No further action is needed.
   - If NO: Repeat Steps 2 and 3 until no more will remove.
5. Mist on a generous amount of peroxide.
   - Mist on a small amount of ammonia.
   - Tamp with soft brush.
   - Allow to dry.
6. If needed, repeat Steps 2, 3 and 5 one time.
7. If the spot persists, call a pro for options as soon as possible.

Section II

# Asphalt, Pitch, Tar, Tree Sap, Etc.

## Comments:

- **Optimum removal time:** Within 24 hours of spill
- **Maximum size for home removal:** Class I / II = 3/4 inch
- **Removal restrictions:** If the spot(s) is larger than 3/4 inch in diameter, **do not attempt ANY removal** using Class I or II instructions. Put a dry towel over spot. Call a pro and have spot removed within 7 days.
- **Caution: Do not attempt scissors removal** of spots from **any** type of looped carpet (berber, commercial glue down, etc.) unless the spot is **only on the outside fibers** of the loop(s). If in doubt, call a pro for options as soon as possible.
- **Caution:** Petroleum distillates in some products can be hard to remove from olefin or polyester carpets (due to their oil-loving nature), if left in the carpet as little as 7 days. If you cannot remove a spot, consult a pro for options as soon as possible.

---

## Materials Needed:
Class I / II: Spotting kit, Spot machine with hot water

| Class I: Spot Machine + Old / Dried Spot | Class II: Spot Machine + Fresh / Wet Spot |
|---|---|
| **Steps:** | **Steps:** |
| 1. Using your scissors, wedge the blades up under the spot(s) and snip the hardened parts from the very tip of the carpet fibers. (This will minimize the indentations caused by the removed spots.) Note: On non-looped carpets, you can also trim a few carpet fibers around the edge of the removed spot, if needed, to minimize it further. | 1. Using your scissors, wedge the blades up under the spot(s) and snip the hardened parts from the very tip of the carpet fibers. (This will minimize the indentations caused by the removed spots.) Note: On non-looped carpets, you can also trim a few carpet fibers around the edge of the removed spot, if needed, to minimize it further. |
| • On non-looped carpets, rough up the trimmed carpet fibers a little with the tips of your scissors. Trim any taller roughed up fibers so they are equal in height with the rest of the carpet. | • On non-looped carpets, rough up the trimmed carpet fibers a little with the tips of your scissors. Trim any taller roughed up fibers so they are equal in height with the rest of the carpet. |
| • Vacuum debris with spot machine. | • Vacuum debris with spot machine. |
| 2. With a towel, firmly blot 10 - 15 times, using a clean part of the towel each time. | 2. With a towel, firmly blot 10 - 15 times, using a clean part of the towel each time. |
| • Repeat until no more transfer can be observed. | • Repeat until no more transfer can be observed. |
| 3. Mist on a generous amount of alcohol. | 3. Mist on a generous amount of alcohol. |
| • Agitate with end of spoon handle. | • Agitate with end of spoon handle. |
| • Allow to work 1 minute. | • Allow to work 1 minute. |
| • Mist on a small amount of alcohol. | • Mist on a small amount of alcohol. |
| • Agitate with end of spoon handle. | • Agitate with end of spoon handle. |
| 4. With the spot machine, rinse with hot water using the chop stroke technique 5 - 7 times. | 4. With the spot machine, rinse with hot water using the chop stroke technique 5 - 7 times. |
| • Take 4 - 6 slow, dry vacuum strokes. | • Take 4 - 6 slow, dry vacuum strokes. |
| 5. Look at spot area carefully to see if the spot is gone: | 5. Look at spot area carefully to see if the spot is gone: |
| • If YES: No further action is needed. | • If YES: No further action is needed. |
| • If NO: Do Steps 6 - 8. | • If NO: Do Steps 6 - 8. |
| 6. Mist on a small amount of ammonia. | 6. Mist on a small amount of ammonia. |
| • Tamp with soft brush. | • Tamp with soft brush. |
| • Allow to work 1 minute. | • Allow to work 1 minute. |
| 7. With the spot machine, rinse with hot water using the chop stroke technique 5 - 7 times. | 7. With the spot machine, rinse with hot water using the chop stroke technique 5 - 7 times. |
| • Take 4 - 6 slow, dry vacuum strokes. | • Take 4 - 6 slow, dry vacuum strokes. |
| 8. Allow to dry. | 8. Allow to dry. |
| • If needed, repeat Steps 3 - 7 one time. | • If needed, repeat Steps 3 - 7 one time. |
| 9. If the spot persists, call a pro for options as soon as possible. | 9. If the spot persists, call a pro for options as soon as possible. |

Section II

# Asphalt, Pitch, Tar, Tree Sap, Etc.

Spot Contents: Carbon, Coal Tar, Petroleum Oil, Resins, Sulfur, Tar

## Comments:

- **Optimum removal time:** Within 24 hours of spill
- **Maximum size for home removal:** Class III / IV = 3/4 inch
- **Removal restrictions:** If the spot(s) is larger than 3/4 inch in diameter, **do not attempt ANY removal** using Class III or IV instructions. Put a dry towel over spot. Then:
  - Call a pro and have spot removed within 7 days. -OR-
  - If the spot is 3/4 inch or less in diameter, get a spot machine and:
    - If the spot is now old/dried, do Steps 1 - 9 under Class I.
    - If the spot is still fresh/wet, do Steps 1 - 9 under Class II.
- **Caution: Do not attempt scissors removal** of spots from **any** type of looped carpet (berber, commercial glue down, etc.) unless the spot is **only on the outside fibers** of the loop(s). If in doubt, call a pro for options as soon as possible.
- **Caution:** Petroleum distillates in some products can be hard to remove from olefin or polyester carpets (due to their oil-loving nature), if left in the carpet as little as 7 days. If you cannot remove a spot, consult a pro for options as soon as possible.

## Materials Needed:

Class III / IV: Spotting kit, Vacuum cleaner with attachment removed from hose

### Class III: Towel + Old / Dried Spot

**Steps:**

1. Using your scissors, wedge the blades up under the spot(s) and snip the hardened parts from the very tip of the carpet fibers. (This will minimize the indentations caused by the removed spots.) Note: On non-looped carpets, you can also trim a few carpet fibers around the edge of the removed spot, if needed, to minimize it further.
   - On non-looped carpets, rough up the trimmed carpet fibers a little with the tips of your scissors. Trim any taller roughed up fibers so they are equal in height with the rest of the carpet.
   - Vacuum debris with vacuum cleaner hose.
2. With a towel, firmly blot 10 - 15 times, using a clean part of the towel each time.
   - Repeat until no more transfer can be observed.
3. Mist on a generous amount of alcohol.
   - Agitate with end of spoon handle.
   - Allow to work 1 minute.
   - Mist on a small amount of alcohol.
   - Agitate with end of spoon handle.
4. With a towel, blot firmly 10 - 15 times, using a clean part of the towel each time.
5. Look at spot area carefully to see if the spot is gone:
   - If YES: No further action is needed.
   - If NO: Do Steps 6 - 8.
6. Mist on a small amount of ammonia.
   - Tamp with soft brush.
7. With a towel, blot firmly 10 - 15 times, using a clean part of the towel each time.
8. Allow to dry.
   - If needed, repeat Steps 3 - 7 one time.
9. If the spot persists, call a pro for options as soon as possible.

### Class IV: Towel + Fresh / Wet Spot

**Steps:**

1. Using your scissors, wedge the blades up under the spot(s) and snip the hardened parts from the very tip of the carpet fibers. (This will minimize the indentations caused by the removed spots.) Note: On non-looped carpets, you can also trim a few carpet fibers around the edge of the removed spot, if needed, to minimize it further.
   - On non-looped carpets, rough up the trimmed carpet fibers a little with the tips of your scissors. Trim any taller roughed up fibers so they are equal in height with the rest of the carpet.
   - Vacuum debris with vacuum cleaner hose.
2. With a towel, firmly blot 10 - 15 times, using a clean part of the towel each time.
   - Repeat until no more transfer can be observed.
3. Mist on a generous amount of alcohol.
   - Agitate with end of spoon handle.
   - Allow to work 1 minute.
   - Mist on a small amount of alcohol.
   - Agitate with end of spoon handle.
4. With a towel, blot firmly 10 - 15 times, using a clean part of the towel each time.
5. Look at spot area carefully to see if the spot is gone:
   - If YES: No further action is needed.
   - If NO: Do Steps 6 - 8.
6. Mist on a small amount of ammonia.
   - Tamp with soft brush.
7. With a towel, blot firmly 10 - 15 times, using a clean part of the towel each time.
8. Allow to dry.
   - If needed, repeat Steps 3 - 7 one time.
9. If the spot persists, call a pro for options as soon as possible.

Section II

# Avocado, Guacamole, Cooked Fruits or Vegetables

## Comments:

- **Optimum removal time:** Within 24 hours of spill
- **Maximum size for home removal:** Class I / II = 5 inches
- **Removal restrictions:** If the spot(s) has been pressed into the carpet fibers or is larger than 5 inches in diameter, **do not attempt TOTAL removal** using Class I or II instructions. Do Step 1 **only** under Class I or II. Put a folded towel moistened with water over spot. (Keep towel damp until pro comes.) Call a pro and have spot removed within 2 days.
- Food coloring in some products can stain some nylon. If you cannot remove a spot, consult a pro for options as soon as possible.

## Materials Needed:

Class I / II: Spotting kit, Spot machine with hot water

### Class I: Spot Machine + Old / Dried Spot

**Steps:**

1. Using your spoon, scrape out as much of the spot(s) as possible.
   - Vacuum debris with spot machine.
   - Repeat entire Step until no more removes.

2. Mist on a generous amount of ammonia.
   - Allow to work 2 minutes.
   - Mist on a small amount of alcohol.
   - Agitate with hard brush.
   - Allow to work 1 minute.
   - Mist on a small amount of ammonia.
   - Agitate with hard brush.

3. With the spot machine, rinse with hot water using the chop stroke technique 8 - 10 times.
   - Take 6 - 8 slow, dry vacuum strokes.

4. Look at spot area carefully to see if the spot is gone:
   - If YES: No further action is needed.
   - If NO: Repeat Steps 1 - 3 until no more removes. Then, if needed, do Step 5.

5. If color cast remains, mist on a generous amount of peroxide.
   - Tamp with soft brush.
   - Allow to dry.

6. If needed, repeat Step 5 one time.

7. If the spot persists, call a pro for options as soon as possible.

### Class II: Spot Machine + Fresh / Wet Spot

**Steps:**

1. Lay a small towel over the palm of your hand. Then lay your hand on the carpet so the towel is at the edge of the spot.
   - Using your spoon, scoop as much of the spot(s) as possible onto the towel. Note: After each scoop, wipe the spoon on a clean part of the towel.
   - Carefully drop the dirty towel in your empty bucket.

2. Mist on a small amount of ammonia.
   - Allow to work 1 minute.
   - Tamp with soft brush.
   - Mist on a small amount of alcohol.
   - Tamp with soft brush.

3. With the spot machine, rinse with hot water using the chop stroke technique 6 - 8 times.
   - Take 4 - 6 slow, dry vacuum strokes.

4. Look at spot area carefully to see if the spot is gone:
   - If YES: No further action is needed.
   - If NO: Repeat Steps 2 and 3 until no more removes. Then, if needed, do Step 5.

5. If color cast remains, mist on a generous amount of peroxide.
   - Tamp with soft brush.
   - Allow to dry.

6. If needed, repeat Step 5 one time.

7. If the spot persists, call a pro for options as soon as possible.

## *Comments:*

- **Optimum removal time:** Within 24 hours of spill
- **Maximum size for home removal:** Class III / IV = 2 inches
- **Removal restrictions:** If the spot(s) has been pressed into the carpet fibers or is larger than 2 inches in diameter, **do not attempt TOTAL removal** using Class III or IV instructions. Do Step 1 **only** under Class III or IV. Put a folded towel moistened with water over spot. (Keep towel damp until pro comes.) Then:
  - Call a pro and have spot removed within 2 days. -OR-
  - If the spot has not been pressed into carpet fibers and is 5 inches or less in diameter, get a spot machine and:
    - If the spot is now old/dried, do Steps 2 - 7 under Class I
    - If the spot is still fresh/wet, do Steps 2 - 7 under Class II.
- Food coloring in some products can stain some nylon. If you cannot remove a spot, consult a pro for options as soon as possible.

## *Materials Needed:*
Class III: Spotting kit, Vacuum cleaner with attachment removed from hose
Class IV: Spotting kit

| ## *Class III: Towel + Old / Dried Spot* | ## *Class IV: Towel + Fresh / Wet Spot* |
|---|---|
| ### *Steps:* | ### *Steps:* |

### *Class III: Towel + Old / Dried Spot*

#### *Steps:*

1. Using your spoon, scrape out as much of the spot(s) as possible.
   - Vacuum debris with vacuum cleaner hose.
   - Repeat entire Step until no more removes.

2. Mist on a generous amount of ammonia.
   - Allow to work 2 minutes.
   - Mist on a small amount of alcohol.
   - Agitate with hard brush.
   - Allow to work 1 minute.
   - Mist on a small amount of ammonia.
   - Agitate with hard brush.

3. Lay a small towel over the palm of your hand. Then lay your hand on the carpet so the towel is at the edge of the spot.
   - Using your spoon, scoop as much of the spot(s) as possible onto the towel. Note: After each scoop, wipe the spoon on a clean part of the towel.
   - With clean towel, blot 15 - 20 times, using a clean part of the towel each time.

4. Look at spot area carefully to see if the spot is gone:
   - If YES: No further action is needed.
   - If NO: Repeat Steps 1 - 3 until no more removes. Then, if needed, do Step 5.

5. If color cast remains, mist on a generous amount of peroxide.
   - Tamp with soft brush.
   - Allow to dry.

6. If needed, repeat Step 5 one time.

7. If the spot persists, call a pro for options as soon as possible.

### *Class IV: Towel + Fresh / Wet Spot*

#### *Steps:*

1. Lay a small towel over the palm of your hand. Then lay your hand on the carpet so the towel is at the edge of the spot.
   - Using your spoon, scoop as much of the spot(s) as possible onto the towel. Note: After each scoop, wipe the spoon on a clean part of the towel.
   - Carefully drop the dirty towel in your empty bucket.
   - With a clean towel, blot 20 - 30 times, using a clean part of the towel each time.

2. Mist on a small amount of ammonia.
   - Allow to work 1 minute.
   - Tamp with soft brush.
   - Mist on a small amount of alcohol.
   - Tamp with soft brush.
   - Allow to work 1 minute.

3. With a towel, blot 15 - 20 times, using a clean part of the towel each time.

4. Look at spot area carefully to see if the spot is gone:
   - If YES: No further action is needed.
   - If NO: Repeat Steps 2 and 3 until no more removes. Then, if needed, do Step 5.

5. If color cast remains, mist on a generous amount of peroxide.
   - Tamp with soft brush.
   - Allow to dry.

6. If needed, repeat Step 5 one time.

7. If the spot persists, call a pro for options as soon as possible.

Section II

# Banana, Banana Pie or Pudding, Plantain, Etc.

## Comments:

- **Optimum removal time:** Within 24 hours of spill
- **Maximum size for home removal:** Class I / II = 5 inches
- **Removal restrictions:** If the spot(s) has been pressed into the carpet fibers or is larger than 5 inches in diameter, **do not attempt TOTAL removal** using Class I or II instructions. Do Step 1 **only** under Class I or II. Put a folded towel moistened with water over spot. Call a pro and have spot removed within 2 days.
- Tannin in bananas can be hard to remove from some nylon. If the spot persists, consult a pro for options as soon as possible.

### Materials Needed:
Class I / II: Spotting kit, Spot machine with hot water

## Class I: Spot Machine + Old / Dried Spot

### Steps:

1. Using your spoon, scrape out as much of the spot(s) as possible.
   - Vacuum debris with spot machine.
   - Repeat entire Step until no more removes.

2. Mist on a generous amount of ammonia.
   - Allow to work 1 minute.
   - Mist on a small amount of alcohol.
   - Agitate with hard brush.
   - Allow to work 1 minute.

3. With the spot machine, rinse with hot water using the chop stroke technique 8 - 10 times.
   - Take 6 - 8 slow, dry vacuum strokes.

4. Look at spot area carefully to see if the spot is gone:
   - If YES: No further action is needed.
   - If NO: Repeat Steps 1 - 3 until no more removes. Then, if needed, do Step 5.

5. If color cast remains, mist on a generous amount of peroxide.
   - Tamp with soft brush.
   - Allow to dry.

6. If needed, repeat Step 5 one time.

7. If the spot persists, call a pro for options as soon as possible.

## Class II: Spot Machine + Fresh / Wet Spot

### Steps:

1. Lay a small towel over the palm of your hand. Then lay your hand on the carpet so the towel is at the edge of the spot.
   - Using your spoon, scoop as much of the spot(s) as possible onto the towel. Note: After each scoop, wipe the spoon on a clean part of the towel.
   - Carefully drop the dirty towel in your empty bucket.

2. Mist on a small amount of ammonia.
   - Allow to work 1 minute.
   - Agitate with hard brush.
   - Mist on a small amount of alcohol.
   - Agitate with hard brush.

3. With the spot machine, rinse with hot water using the chop stroke technique 6 - 8 times.
   - Take 4 - 6 slow, dry vacuum strokes.

4. Look at spot area carefully to see if the spot is gone:
   - If YES: No further action is needed.
   - If NO: Repeat Steps 2 and 3 until no more removes. Then, if needed, do Step 5.

5. If color cast remains, mist on a generous amount of peroxide.
   - Tamp with soft brush.
   - Allow to dry.

6. If needed, repeat Step 5 one time.

7. If the spot persists, call a pro for options as soon as possible.

Section II

## Comments:

- **Optimum removal time:** Within 24 hours of spill
- **Maximum size for home removal:** Class III / IV = 2 inches
- **Removal restrictions:** If the spot(s) has been pressed into the carpet fibers or is larger than 2 inches in diameter, **do not attempt TOTAL removal** using Class III or IV instructions. Do Step 1 **only** under Class III or IV. Put a folded towel moistened with water over spot. Then:
  - Call a pro and have spot removed within 2 days. -OR-
  - If the spot has not been pressed into carpet fibers and is 5 inches or less in diameter, get a spot machine and:
    - If the spot is now old/dried, do Steps 2 - 7 under Class I.
    - If the spot is still fresh/wet, do Steps 2 - 7 under Class II.
- Tannin in bananas can be hard to remove from some nylon. If the spot persists, consult a pro for options as soon as possible.

## Materials Needed:

Class III: Spotting kit, Vacuum cleaner with attachment removed from hose
Class IV: Spotting kit

| Class III: Towel + Old / Dried Spot | Class IV: Towel + Fresh / Wet Spot |
|---|---|
| **Steps:** | **Steps:** |
| 1. Using your spoon, scrape out as much of the spot(s) as possible.<br>• Vacuum debris with vacuum cleaner hose.<br>• Repeat entire Step until no more removes. | 1. Lay a small towel over the palm of your hand. Then lay your hand on the carpet so the towel is at the edge of the spot.<br>• Using your spoon, scoop as much of the spot(s) as possible onto the towel. Note: After each scoop, wipe the spoon on a clean part of the towel.<br>• Carefully drop the dirty towel in your empty bucket. |
| 2. Mist on a generous amount of ammonia.<br>• Allow to work 1 - 2 minutes.<br>• Mist on a small amount of alcohol.<br>• Agitate with hard brush.<br>• Allow to work 1 minute. | 2. Mist on a small amount of ammonia.<br>• Mist on a small amount of alcohol.<br>• Agitate with hard brush.<br>• Allow to work 1 minute. |
| 3. Lay a small towel over the palm of your hand. Then lay your hand on the carpet so the towel is at the edge of the spot.<br>• Using your spoon, scoop as much of the spot(s) as possible onto the towel. Note: After each scoop, wipe the spoon on a clean part of the towel.<br>• With a clean towel, blot 15 - 20 times, using a clean part of the towel each time. | 3. With a towel, blot 10 - 15 times, using a clean part of the towel each time. |
| 4. Look at spot area carefully to see if the spot is gone:<br>• If YES: No further action is needed.<br>• If NO: Repeat Steps 1 - 3 until no more removes. Then, if needed, do Step 5. | 4. Look at spot area carefully to see if the spot is gone:<br>• If YES: No further action is needed.<br>• If NO: Repeat Steps 2 and 3 until no more removes. Then, if needed, do Step 5. |
| 5. If color cast remains, mist on a generous amount of peroxide.<br>• Tamp with soft brush.<br>• Allow to dry. | 5. If color cast remains, mist on a generous amount of peroxide.<br>• Tamp with soft brush.<br>• Allow to dry. |
| 6. If needed, repeat Step 5 one time. | 6. If needed, repeat Step 5 one time. |
| 7. If the spot persists, call a pro for options as soon as possible. | 7. If the spot persists, call a pro for options as soon as possible. |

Section II

# Beer, Ale, Lager, Etc.

## Comments:

- **Optimum removal time:** Within 24 hours of spill
- **Maximum size for home removal:** Class I / II = 4 inches
- **Removal restrictions:** If the spot(s) is larger than 4 inches in diameter, **do not attempt ANY removal** using Class I or II instructions. Put a dry towel over spot. Call a pro and have spot removed within 3 days.
- Tannin in beer, etc., can be hard to remove from some nylon. If a spot persists, consult a pro for options as soon as possible.

## Materials Needed:
Class I / II: Spotting kit, Spot machine with warm water

### Class I: Spot Machine + Old / Dried Spot

#### Steps:

1. Mist a small amount of ammonia on spot(s).
   - Allow to work 1 minute.
   - Tamp with soft brush.
   - Mist on a small amount of peroxide.
   - Tamp with soft brush.
   - Allow to work 1 minute.
2. With the spot machine, rinse with warm water using the chop stroke technique 8 - 10 times.
   - Take 6 - 8 slow, dry vacuum strokes.
3. Look at spot area carefully to see if the spot is gone:
   - If YES: No further action is needed.
   - If NO: Do Steps 4 - 5.
4. Mist on a generous amount of peroxide.
   - Mist on a small amount of ammonia.
   - Tamp with soft brush.
   - Allow to work 2 minutes.
5. With the spot machine, rinse with warm water using the chop stroke technique 8 - 10 times.
   - Take 6 - 8 slow, dry vacuum strokes.
6. Look at spot area carefully to see if the spot is gone:
   - If YES: No further action is needed.
   - If NO: Do Step 7.
7. If color cast remains, mist on a generous amount of peroxide.
   - Tamp with soft brush.
   - Allow to dry.
8. If needed, repeat Step 7 one time.
9. If the spot persists, call a pro for options as soon as possible.

### Class II: Spot Machine + Fresh / Wet Spot

#### Steps:

1. Using your spot machine, dry vacuum the spot(s) 10 - 15 times taking slow, single strokes.
   - Repeat until no more removes.
2. With the spot machine, rinse with warm water using the chop stroke technique 8 - 10 times.
   - Take 6 - 8 slow, dry vacuum strokes.
3. Look at spot area carefully to see if the spot is gone:
   - If YES: No further action is needed.
   - If NO: Do Steps 4 - 5.
4. Mist on a generous amount of peroxide.
   - Mist on a small amount of ammonia.
   - Tamp with soft brush.
   - Allow to work 2 minutes.
5. With the spot machine, rinse with warm water using the chop stroke technique 8 - 10 times.
   - Take 6 - 8 slow, dry vacuum strokes.
6. Look at spot area carefully to see if the spot is gone:
   - If YES: No further action is needed.
   - If NO: Do Step 7.
7. If color cast remains, mist on a generous amount of peroxide.
   - Tamp with soft brush.
   - Allow to dry.
8. If needed, repeat Step 7 one time.
9. If the spot persists, call a pro for options as soon as possible.

Section II

## Comments:

- **Optimum removal time:** Within 24 hours of spill
- **Maximum size for home removal:** Class III / IV = 3 inches
- **Removal restrictions:** If the spot(s) is larger than 3 inches in diameter, **do not attempt ANY removal** using Class III instructions or **do not attempt TOTAL removal** using Class IV instructions. Do Step 1 **only** under Class IV. Put a dry towel over Class III or IV spot. Then:
    - Call a pro and have spot removed within 3 days. -OR-
    - If the spot is 4 inches or less in diameter, get a spot machine and:
        - If the spot is now old/dried, do Steps 1 - 9 under Class I.
        - If the spot is still fresh/wet, do Steps 1 - 9 under Class II.
- Tannin in beer, etc., can be hard to remove from some nylon. If a spot persists, consult a pro for options as soon as possible.

## Materials Needed:

Class III / IV: Spotting kit

### Class III: Towel + Old / Dried Spot

**Steps:**

1. Mist a small amount of ammonia on spot(s).
    - Allow to work 1 - 2 minutes.
    - Mist on a small amount of peroxide.
    - Tamp with soft brush.
    - Allow to work 1 minute.
2. With a towel, blot 15 - 20 times, using a clean part of the towel each time.
3. Look at spot area carefully to see if the spot is gone:
    - If YES: No further action is needed.
    - If NO: Do Steps 4 and 5.
4. Mist on a generous amount of peroxide.
    - Mist on a small amount of ammonia.
    - Tamp with soft brush.
    - Allow to work 2 minutes.
5. With a towel, blot 15 - 20 times, using a clean part of the towel each time.
    - Allow to dry.
6. Look at spot area carefully the next day to see if the spot is gone:
    - If YES: No further action is needed.
    - If NO: Repeat Steps 1 - 5 one time. Then, if needed, do Step 7.
7. If color cast remains, mist on a generous amount of peroxide.
    - Tamp with soft brush.
    - Allow to dry.
8. If needed, repeat Step 7 one time.
9. If the spot persists, call a pro for options as soon as possible.

### Class IV: Towel + Fresh / Wet Spot

**Steps:**

1. Fold a towel several times and place it over the spot(s).
    - Step on the towel with your full weight, using a clean part of the towel each time.
    - Repeat until no more absorbs.
2. Mist on a small amount of ammonia.
    - Allow to work 1 minute.
    - Mist on a small amount of peroxide.
    - Tamp with soft brush.
    - Allow to work 1 minute.
3. With a towel, blot 15 - 20 times, using a clean part of the towel each time.
4. Look at spot area carefully to see if the spot is gone:
    - If YES: No further action is needed.
    - If NO: Repeat Steps 2 and 3 one time. Allow to dry.
5. Look at spot area carefully the next day to see if the spot is gone:
    - If YES: No further action is needed.
    - If NO: Repeat Steps 2 and 3 one time. Then, if needed, do Step 6.
6. If color cast remains, mist on a generous amount of peroxide.
    - Tamp with soft brush.
    - Allow to dry.
7. If needed, repeat Step 6 one time.
8. If the spot persists, call a pro for options as soon as possible.

Section II

# Berries - All: *Blueberries, Boysenberries, Strawberries, Etc.*

## Comments:

- **Optimum removal time:** Within 24 hours of spill
- **Maximum size for home removal:** Class I / II = 5 inches
- If the spot(s) is larger than 5 inches in diameter, **do not attempt TOTAL removal** using Class I or II instructions. Do Step 1 **only** under Class I or II. Put a folded towel moistened with water over spot. Call a pro and have spot removed within 1 day.
- Strong acid dye in berries can immediately and permanently stain some nylon. If you cannot remove a spot, consult a pro for options as soon as possible.

## Materials Needed:

Class I / II: Spotting kit, Spot machine with warm water

### Class I: Spot Machine + Old / Dried Spot

**Steps:**

1. Using your spoon, scrape out as much of the spot(s) as possible.
   - Vacuum debris with spot machine.
   - Repeat entire Step until no more removes.

2. Mist on a generous amount of ammonia.
   (Red berry stains may turn blue. Do not worry.)
   - Mist on a generous amount of peroxide.
     (Blue may turn back to red.)
   - Tamp with soft brush.
   - Allow to work 1 minute.

3. With the spot machine, rinse with warm water using the chop stroke technique 8 - 10 times.
   - Take 6 - 8 slow, dry vacuum strokes.

4. Look at spot area carefully to see if the spot is gone:
   - If YES: No further action is needed.
   - If NO: Repeat Steps 2 and 3 until no more removes. Then, if needed, do Step 5.

5. If color cast remains, mist on a generous amount of peroxide.
   - Tamp with soft brush.
   - Allow to dry.

6. If needed, repeat Step 5 one time.

7. If the spot persists, call a pro for options as soon as possible.

### Class II: Spot Machine + Fresh / Wet Spot

**Steps:**

1. Lay a small towel over the palm of your hand. Then lay your hand on the carpet so the towel is at the edge of the spot.
   - Using your spoon, scoop as much of the spot(s) as possible onto the towel. Note: After each scoop, wipe the spoon on a clean part of the towel.
   - Carefully drop the dirty towel in your empty bucket.
   - Vacuum debris with spot machine.
   - Repeat entire Step until no more removes.

2. Mist on a generous amount of ammonia.
   (Red berry stains may turn blue. Do not worry.)
   - Mist on a generous amount of peroxide.
     (Blue may turn back to red.)
   - Tamp with soft brush.
   - Allow to work 1 minute.

3. With the spot machine, rinse with warm water using the chop stroke technique 8 - 10 times.
   - Take 6 - 8 slow, dry vacuum strokes.

4. Look at spot area carefully to see if the spot is gone:
   - If YES: No further action is needed.
   - If NO: Repeat Steps 2 and 3 until no more removes. Then, if needed, do Step 5.

5. If color cast remains, mist on a generous amount of peroxide.
   - Tamp with soft brush.
   - Allow to dry.

6. If needed, repeat Step 5 one time.

7. If the spot persists, call a pro for options as soon as possible.

### Comments:

- **Optimum removal time:** Within 24 hours of spill
- **Maximum size for home removal:** Class III / IV = 2 1/2 inches
- **Removal restrictions:** If the spot(s) is larger than 2 1/2 inches in diameter, **do not attempt TOTAL removal** using Class III or IV instructions. Do Step 1 **only** under Class III or IV. Put a folded towel moistened with water over spot. Then:
  - Call a pro and have spot removed within 1 day. -OR-
  - If the spot is 5 inches or less in diameter, get a spot machine and:
    - If the spot is now old/dried, do Steps 2 - 7 under Class I.
    - If the spot is still fresh/wet, do Steps 2 - 7 under Class II.
- Strong acid dye in berries can immediately and permanently stain some nylon. If you cannot remove a spot, consult a pro for options as soon as possible.

### Materials Needed:
Class III: Spotting kit, Vacuum cleaner with attachment removed from hose
Class IV: Spotting kit

## Class III: Towel + Old / Dried Spot

### Steps:

1. Using your spoon, scrape out as much of the spot(s) as possible.
   - Vacuum debris with vacuum cleaner hose.
   - Repeat entire Step until no more removes.

2. Mist on a generous amount of ammonia.
   (Red berry stains may turn blue. Do not worry.)
   - Mist on a generous amount of peroxide.
     (Blue may turn back to red.)
   - Tamp with soft brush.
   - Allow to work 1 minute.

3. With a towel, blot 10 - 15 times, using a clean part of the towel each time.

4. Look at spot area carefully to see if the spot is gone:
   - If YES: No further action is needed.
   - If NO: Repeat Steps 2 and 3 until no more removes. Then, if needed, do Step 5.

5. If color cast remains, mist on a generous amount of peroxide.
   - Tamp with soft brush.
   - Allow to dry.

6. If needed, repeat Step 5 one time.

7. If the spot persists, call a pro for options as soon as possible.

## Class IV: Towel + Fresh / Wet Spot

### Steps:

1. Lay a small towel over the palm of your hand. Then lay your hand on the carpet so the towel is at the edge of the spot.
   - Using your spoon, scoop as much of the spot(s) as possible onto the towel. Note: After each scoop, wipe the spoon on a clean part of the towel.
   - Carefully drop the dirty towel in your empty bucket.
   - With a clean towel, firmly blot spot, using a clean part of the towel each time.
   - Repeat entire Step until no more removes.

2. Mist on a small amount of ammonia.
   (Red berry stains may turn blue. Do not worry.)
   - Mist on a small amount of peroxide.
     (Blue may turn back to red.)
   - Tamp with soft brush.
   - Allow to work 1 minute.

3. With a towel, blot 10 - 15 times, using a clean part of the towel each time.

4. Look at spot area carefully to see if the spot is gone:
   - If YES: No further action is needed.
   - If NO: Repeat Steps 2 and 3 until no more removes. Then, if needed, do Step 5.

5. If color cast remains, mist on a generous amount of peroxide.
   - Tamp with soft brush.
   - Allow to dry.

6. If needed, repeat Step 5 one time.

7. If the spot persists, call a pro for options as soon as possible.

Section II

# Bleaching Products (All) - Liquid, Gel, Cream or Powder Bleach, Dish Detergent, Chlorine, Bowl, Tub and Tile Cleaners, Hair Lighteners, Acne Medicine, Etc.

## Comments:

- **Optimum removal time**: **As soon as possible: Before a wet spill dries; Within 1 to 6 hours for other spills**
- **Maximum size for home removal**: Class I/II = No total home removal
- **Removal restrictions:** See Class I or II instructions below
- **Caution:** Bleaches containing Sodium Hypochlorite and hair lighteners containing strong 6% Hydrogen Peroxide can immediately and permanently remove, lighten or discolor dye in most fibers. (See "Bleaches" in "Mystery Spots, Stains and Discolorations" in Chapter 4.)
- **Caution:** Acne medicines and some foot fungus products containing Benzoyl Peroxide can slowly and permanently remove and discolor dye in all fibers. (See "Benzoyl Peroxide" in "Mystery Spots" in Chapter 4.)

## Materials Needed:

Class I / II: Gloves, Spotting kit, Vacuum cleaner with attachment removed from hose

| Class I: Spot Machine + Old / Dried Spot | Class II: Spot Machine + Fresh / Wet Spot |
|---|---|
| **Steps:** | **Steps:** |

### Class I: Spot Machine + Old / Dried Spot

**Steps:**

1. Follow the instructions under the spot description that matches your spot:

    **The spot was a liquid:**
    - Do not attempt any removal of a Class I spot.

    **The spot is a gel or a cream:**
    - Using your spoon, scrape out as much of the carpet fibers.
    - Vacuum debris with vacuum cleaner hose.
    - Repeat entire Step until no more removes.

    **The spot is powdery:**
    - Using only the vacuum cleaner hose, vacuum up as much debris as possible.

2. Place a dry white towel over the spot and a note next to it that says, ***"Do Not Touch Or Clean!"***.

3. Call a professional immediately for options.

### Class II: Spot Machine + Fresh / Wet Spot

**Steps:**

1. Follow the instructions under the spot(s) description that matches your spot.

    **The spot is a liquid:**
    - Blot up as much of the spot as possible using a clean part of the towel each time.
    - Repeat entire Step until no more removes.
    - Carefully drop the dirty towel into your empty bucket.

    **The spot is a gel or cream:**
    - Using your spoon, scoop up as much of the spot as possible.
    - Blot up as much of the spot as possible using a clean part of the towel each time.
    - Repeat entire Step until no more removes.
    - Carefully drop the dirty towel into your empty bucket.

    **The spot is powdery:**
    - Using your vacuum cleaner hose, vacuum as much of the spot as possible.

2. Place a dry white towel over the spot and a note next to it that says, ***"Do Not Touch Or Clean!"*** .

3. Call a professional immediately for options.

Section II

# Bleaching Products (All) - Liquid, Gel, Cream or Powder Bleach, Dish Detergent, Chlorine, Bowl, Tub and Tile Cleaners, Hair Lighteners, Acne Medicine, Etc.

**Comments:** Spot contents: Sodium Hypochlorite, 6% Hydrogen Peroxide, Benzoyl Peroxide

- **Optimum removal time: As soon as possible: Before a wet spill dries; Within 1 to 6 hours for other spills**
- **Maximum size for home removal:** Class III / IV = No total home removal
- **Removal restrictions:** See Class III or IV instructions below
- **Caution:** Bleaches containing Sodium Hypochlorite and hair lighteners containing strong 6% Hydrogen Peroxide can immediately and permanently remove, lighten or discolor dye in most fibers. (See "Bleaches" in "Mystery Spots, Stains and Discolorations" in Chapter 4.)
- **Caution:** Acne medicines and some foot fungus products containing Benzoyl Peroxide can slowly and permanently remove and discolor dye in all fibers. (See "Benzoyl Peroxide" in "Mystery Spots" in Chapter 4.)

---

## Materials Needed:

Class III / IV: Gloves, Spotting kit, Vacuum cleaner with attachment removed from hose

---

### Class III: Towel + Old / Dried Spot

**Steps:**

1. Follow the instructions under the spot(s) description that matches your spot.

   **The spot was a liquid:**
   - Do not attempt any removal of a Class III spot.

   **The spot is a gel or cream:**
   - Using your spoon, scrape the spot out of the carpet fibers.
   - Vacuum debris with vacuum cleaner hose.
   - Repeat entire Step until no more removes.

   **The spot is powdery:**
   - Using your vacuum cleaner hose, vacuum as much of the spot as possible.

2. Place a dry white towel over the spot and a note next to it that says, ***"Do Not Touch Or Clean!"*** .

3. Call a professional immediately for options.

### Class IV: Towel + Wet / Fresh Spot

**Steps:**

1. Follow the instructions under the spot(s) description that matches your spot.

   **The spot is a liquid:**
   - Blot up as much of the spot as possible using a clean part of the towel each time.
   - Repeat entire Step until no more removes.
   - Carefully drop the dirty towel into your empty bucket.

   **The spot is a gel or cream:**
   - Using your spoon, scoop up as much of the spot as possible.
   - Blot up as much of the spot as possible using a clean part of the towel each time.
   - Repeat entire Step until no more removes.
   - Carefully drop the dirty towel into your empty bucket.

   **The spot is powdery:**
   - Using your vacuum cleaner hose, vacuum as much of the spot as possible.

2. Place a dry white towel over the spot and a note next to it that says, ***"Do Not Touch Or Clean!"*** .

3. Call a professional immediately for options.

Section II

**Section II**

## Comments:

- **Optimum removal time: As soon as possible** within 24 hours of spill
- **Maximum size for home removal:** Class I / II = 1 inch
- **Removal restrictions:** If the spot(s) is larger than 1 inch in diameter, **do not attempt TOTAL removal** using Class I or II instructions. Do Step 1 **only** under Class I or II. Put a folded towel moistened with water over spot and a note next to it that says, "***Blood! Do Not Touch Or Clean!***". Call a pro and have spot removed as soon as possible within 24 hours.
- **Caution:** Blood may contain large quantities of pathogens. Use your best judgment about wearing a mask, gloves and eye protection.
- Most protein stains like blood respond well with early treatment, patience and cool temperature spotting. However, blood can stain some nylon. If you cannot remove a spot, consult a pro for options as soon as possible.

## Materials Needed:

Protective mask, gloves, eye wear
Class I / II: Spotting kit, Spot machine with cool water

---

### Class I: Spot Machine + Old / Dried Spot

#### Steps:

1. Using your dinner knife and scissors, separate the spot(s) into the smallest sections possible.
   - Using your dinner knife, scrape the spot's surface in a side-to-side motion to break it up. Caution: Be careful not to fray the carpet fibers.
   - Vacuum debris with spot machine.

2. Mist on a generous amount of ammonia.
   - Allow to work 2 minutes.
   - Mist on a small amount of peroxide.
   - Allow to work 1 minute.
   - Agitate with end of spoon handle. Caution: Be careful not to fray the carpet fibers.
   - Mist on a small amount of ammonia.
   - Agitate with end of spoon handle.

3. With the spot machine, rinse with cool water using the chop stroke technique 10 - 12 times.
   - Take 6 - 8 slow, dry vacuum strokes.

4. Look at spot area carefully to see if the spot is gone:
   - If YES: No further action is needed.
   - If NO: Repeat Steps 2 and 3 until no more removes. Then, if needed, do Step 5.

5. If color cast remains, mist on a generous amount of peroxide.
   - Tamp with soft brush.
   - With the spot machine, rinse with cool water, using the single stroke technique 1 time.
   - Mist on a generous amount of peroxide.
   - Tamp with soft brush.
   - Allow to dry.

6. If needed, repeat Steps 2, 3 and 5 one time.

7. If the spot persists, call a pro for options as soon as possible.

---

### Class II: Spot Machine + Fresh / Wet Spot

#### Steps:

1. Using your spot machine, rinse spot(s) with cool water using the chop stroke technique 15 - 20 times.
   - Take 6 - 8 slow, dry vacuum strokes.

2. Mist on a generous amount of ammonia.
   - Tamp firmly with soft brush.
   - Allow to work 1 minute.
   - Mist on a generous amount of peroxide.
   - Tamp firmly with soft brush.

3. With the spot machine, rinse with cool water using the chop stroke technique 8 - 10 times.
   - Take 4 - 6 slow, dry vacuum strokes.

4. Look at spot area carefully to see if the spot is gone:
   - If YES: No further action is needed.
   - If NO: Repeat Steps 2 and 3 until no more removes. Then, if needed, do Step 5.

5. If color cast remains, mist on a generous amount of peroxide.
   - Tamp with soft brush.
   - With the spot machine, rinse with cool water, using the single stroke technique 1 time.
   - Mist on a generous amount of peroxide.
   - Tamp with soft brush.
   - Allow to dry.

6. If needed, repeat Steps 2, 3 and 5 one time.

7. If the spot persists, call a pro for options as soon as possible.

---

## *Comments:*

- **Optimum removal time: As soon as possible** within 24 hours of spill
- **Maximum size for home removal:** Class III / IV = 1/2 inch
- **Removal restrictions:** If the spot(s) is larger than 1/2 inch in diameter, **do not attempt TOTAL removal** using Class III or IV instructions. Do Step 1 **only** under Class III or IV. Put a folded towel moistened with water over spot and a note next to it that says, "***Blood! Do Not Touch Or Clean!***". Then:
  - Call a pro and have spot removed as soon as possible within 24 hours. -OR-
  - If the spot is 1 inch or less in diameter, get a spot machine and:
    - If the spot is now old/dried, do Steps 2 - 7 under Class I.
    - If the spot is still fresh/wet, do Steps 1 - 7 under Class II.
- **Caution:** Blood may contain large quantities of pathogens. Use your best judgment about wearing a mask, gloves and eye protection.
- Most protein stains like blood respond well with early treatment, patience and cool temperature spotting. However, blood can stain some nylon. If you cannot remove a spot, consult a pro for options as soon as possible.

## *Materials Needed:*

Protective mask, gloves, eye wear
Class III: Spotting kit, Vacuum cleaner with attachment removed from hose
Class IV: Spotting kit

| Class III: Towel + Old / Dried Spot | Class IV: Towel + Fresh / Wet Spot |
|---|---|
| ***Steps:*** | ***Steps:*** |
| 1. Using your dinner knife and scissors, separate the spot(s) into the smallest sections possible. | 1. Using only the edges of your towel, barely touch the spot(s) until you begin to see blood being absorbed into the towel. Caution: Do not press the towel into the spot. It will spread the spot. |
| • Using your dinner knife, scrape the spot's surface in a side-to-side motion to break it up. Caution: Be careful not to fray the carpet fibers. | • Repeat 8 - 10 times, using a clean part of the towel each time. |
| • Vacuum debris with vacuum cleaner hose. | • Blot firmly 10 - 15 times, using a clean part of the towel each time. |
| 2. Mist on a generous amount of ammonia. | 2. Mist on a generous amount of ammonia. |
| • Allow to work 2 minutes. | • Tamp with soft brush. |
| • Mist on a small amount of peroxide. | • Allow to work 1 minute. |
| • Allow to work 1 minute. | • Mist on a small amount of peroxide. |
| • Agitate with end of spoon handle. Caution: Be careful not to fray the carpet fibers. | • Tamp with soft brush. |
| • Mist on a small amount of ammonia. | • Allow to work 1 minute. |
| • Agitate with end of spoon handle. | |
| 3. With a towel, blot 15 - 20 times, using a clean part of the towel each time. | 3. With a towel, blot 15 - 20 times, using a clean part of the towel each time. |
| 4. Look at spot area carefully to see if the spot is gone: | 4. Look at spot area carefully to see if the spot is gone: |
| • If YES: No further action is needed. | • If YES: No further action is needed. |
| • If NO: Repeat Steps 2 and 3 until no more removes. Then, if needed, do Step 5. | • If NO: Repeat Steps 2 and 3 until no more removes. Then, if needed, do Step 5. |
| 5. If color cast remains, mist on a generous amount of peroxide. | 5. If color cast remains, mist on a generous amount of peroxide. |
| • Tamp with soft brush. | • Tamp with soft brush. |
| • Blot once with towel. | • Blot once with towel. |
| • Mist on a generous amount of peroxide. | • Mist on a generous amount of peroxide. |
| • Tamp with soft brush. | • Tamp with soft brush. |
| • Allow to dry. | • Allow to dry. |
| 6. If needed, repeat Steps 2, 3 and 5 one time. | 6. If needed, repeat Steps 2, 3 and 5 one time. |
| 7. If the spot persists, call a pro for options as soon as possible. | 7. If the spot persists, call a pro for options as soon as possible. |

# Bodily Fluids or Discharges: *Mammal, Bird, Fish, Insect or Reptile*
## (Any fluids or discharges except blood, feces, urine or vomit)

### Comments:

- **Optimum removal time: As soon as possible** within 24 hours of spill
- **Maximum size for removal**: Class I / II = 4 1/2 inches
- **Removal restrictions**: If the spot(s) is larger than 4 1/2 inches in diameter, **do not attempt TOTAL removal** using Class I or II instructions. Do Step 1 **only** under Class I or II. Mist spot(s) with a generous amount of alcohol. Put a dry towel over spot and a note next to it that says, ***"Do Not Touch Or Clean!"***. Call a pro and have spot removed as soon as possible within 24 hours.
- **Caution:** Some bodily fluids or discharges contain a wide variety of bacteria and/or other pathogens. Use your best judgment about wearing a mask, gloves and eye protection.
- Some fluids or discharges may contain blood. If it is in large quantities and dried, it can be very hard to remove from most nylon. If you cannot remove a spot, consult a pro for options as soon as possible.

### Materials Needed:
Protective mask, gloves, eye wear
Class I / II: Spotting kit, Spot machine with cool water

## Class I: Spot Machine + Old / Dried Spot

### Steps:

1. • Using your dinner knife, scrape the spot's surface in a side-to-side motion to break it up. Caution: Be careful not to fray the carpet fibers.
   - Vacuum debris with spot machine.
   - Repeat entire Step until no more removes.

2. Mist on a generous amount of ammonia.
   - Allow to work 2 minutes.
   - Agitate with hard brush.
   - Mist on a generous amount of peroxide.
   - Agitate with hard brush.

3. With the spot machine, rinse with cool water using the chop stroke technique 8 - 10 times.
   - Take 6 - 8 slow, dry vacuum strokes.

4. Look at spot area carefully to see if the spot is gone:
   - If YES: Allow to dry.
   - If NO: Repeat Steps 2 and 3 until no more removes. Then, if needed, do Step 5.

5. If color cast remains, mist on a generous amount of peroxide.
   - Tamp with soft brush.
   - Allow to dry.

6. If needed, repeat Steps 2, 3 and 5 one time.

7. If the spot persists, call a pro for options as soon as possible.

## Class II: Spot Machine + Fresh / Wet Spot

### Steps:

1. Lay a disposable tissue(s) over the palm of your hand. Then lay your hand on the carpet so the tissue is at the edge of the spot.
   - Using your spoon, scoop as much of the spot(s) as possible onto the tissue. Note: After each scoop, wipe the spoon on a clean part of the tissue.
   - Carefully drop the dirty tissue(s) in your bucket.
   - With the spot machine, rinse with cool water using the single stroke technique 8 - 10 times.
   - Take 6 - 8 slow, dry vacuum strokes.
   - Repeat entire Step until no more removes.

2. Mist on a generous amount of ammonia.
   - Allow to work 1 minute.
   - Agitate with soft brush.
   - Mist on a generous amount of peroxide.
   - Agitate with soft brush.

3. With the spot machine, rinse with cool water using the chop stroke technique 6 - 8 times.
   - Take 4 - 6 slow, dry vacuum strokes.

4. Look at spot area carefully to see if the spot is gone:
   - If YES: Allow to dry.
   - If NO: Repeat Steps 2 and 3 until no more removes. Then, if needed, do Step 5.

5. If color cast remains, mist on a generous amount of peroxide.
   - Tamp with soft brush.
   - Allow to dry.

6. If needed, repeat Steps 2, 3 and 5 one time.

7. If the spot persists, call a pro for options as soon as possible.

# Bodily Fluids or Discharges: Mammal, Bird, Fish, Insect or Reptile
## (Any fluids or discharges except blood, feces, urine or vomit)

**Comments:**

Spot Contents: Albumin, Protein, Serum

- **Optimum removal time: As soon as possible** within 24 hours of spill
- **Maximum size for removal:** Class III / IV = 1 1/2 inches
- **Removal restrictions:** If the spot(s) is larger than 1 1/2 inches in diameter, **do not attempt TOTAL removal** using Class III or IV instructions. Do Step 1 **only** under Class III or IV. Mist spot(s) with a generous amount of alcohol. Put a dry towel over spot and a note next to it that says, "**Do Not Touch Or Clean!**". Then:
  - Call a pro and have spot removed as soon as possible within 24 hours. -OR-
  - If the spot is 4 1/2 inches or less in diameter, get a spot machine and:
    - If the spot is now old/dried, do Steps 2 - 7 under Class I.
    - If the spot is still fresh/wet, do Steps 2 - 7 under Class II.
- **Caution:** Some bodily fluids or discharges contain a wide variety of bacteria and/or other pathogens. Use your best judgment about wearing a mask, gloves and eye protection.
- Some fluids or discharges may contain blood. If it is in large quantities and dried, it can be very hard to remove from most nylon. If you cannot remove a spot, consult a pro for options as soon as possible.

---

**Materials Needed:**

Protective mask, gloves, eye wear

Class III: Spotting kit, Shop vacuum (if you have one) with attachment removed from hose. If you do not have a shop vacuum, use a regular vacuum. As soon as you finish vacuuming the debris, remove the bag and throw it away, or clean the cartridge if you have a bagless vacuum cleaner.

Class IV: Disposable tissues or towels, spotting kit

## Class III: Towel + Old / Dried Spot

**Steps:**

1. • Using your dinner knife, scrape the spot's surface in a side-to-side motion to break it up. Caution: Be careful not to fray the carpet fibers.
   • Vacuum debris with a shop vacuum hose, if you have one.
   • Repeat entire Step until no more removes.

2. Mist on a generous amount of ammonia.
   • Allow to work 2 minutes.
   • Agitate with hard brush.
   • Mist on a generous amount of peroxide.
   • Agitate with hard brush.

3. With a towel, blot 15 - 20 times, using a clean part of the towel each time.

4. Look at spot area carefully to see if the spot is gone:
   • If YES: Allow to dry.
   • If NO: Repeat Steps 2 and 3 until no more removes. Then, if needed, do Step 5.

5. If color cast remains, mist on a generous amount of peroxide.
   • Tamp with soft brush.
   • Allow to dry.

6. If needed, repeat Steps 2, 3 and 5 one time.

7. If the spot persists, call a pro for options as soon as possible.

## Class IV: Towel + Fresh / Wet Spot

**Steps:**

1. Lay a disposable tissue(s) over the palm of your hand. Then lay your hand on the carpet so the tissue is at the edge of the spot.
   • Using your spoon, scoop as much of the spot(s) as possible onto the tissue. Note: After each scoop, wipe the spoon on a clean part of the tissue.
   • With a cloth towel, blot 15 - 20 times, using a clean part of the towel each time.
   • Repeat entire Step until no more removes.

2. Mist on a generous amount of ammonia.
   • Allow to work 2 minutes.
   • Agitate with soft brush.
   • Mist on a small amount of peroxide.
   • Agitate with soft brush.

3. With a towel, blot 10 - 12 times, using a clean part of the towel each time.

4. Look at spot area carefully to see if the spot is gone:
   • If YES: Allow to dry.
   • If NO: Repeat Steps 2 and 3 until no more removes. Then, if needed, do Step 5.

5. If color cast remains, mist on a generous amount of peroxide.
   • Tamp with soft brush.
   • Allow to dry.

6. If needed, repeat Steps 2, 3 and 5 one time.

7. If the spot persists, call a pro for options as soon as possible.

# Body Oils: Baby Oil, Massage Oil, Suntan Oil, Etc.

## Comments:

- **Optimum removal time:** Within 24 hours of spill
- **Maximum size for home removal:** Class I / II = 2 inches
- **Removal restrictions:** If the spot(s) is larger than 2 inches in diameter, **do not attempt TOTAL removal** using Class I or II instructions. Do Step 1 **only** under Class I or II. Put a dry towel over spot. Call a pro and have spot removed within 2 days.
- Large spills can soak through the carpet and pad to the subfloor and cause recurring spots. (See "Recurring Spots", Chapter 4.) Consult a pro for options as soon as possible.

## Materials Needed:
Class I / II: Spotting kit, Spot machine with hot water

| Class I: Spot Machine + Old / Dried Spot | Class II: Spot Machine + Fresh / Wet Spot |
|---|---|
| **Steps:** | **Steps:** |
| 1. Fold a towel several times and place it over the spot(s).<br> • Step on the towel with your full weight 10 - 12 times, using a clean part of the towel each time.<br> • Repeat until no more absorbs. | 1. Fold a towel several times and place it over the spot(s).<br> • Step on the towel with your full weight 10 - 12 times, using a clean part of the towel each time.<br> • Repeat until no more absorbs. |
| 2. Mist on a generous amount of alcohol.<br> • Allow to work 1 minute.<br> • Tamp with soft brush.<br> • Mist on a generous amount of alcohol.<br> • Tamp with soft brush.<br> • Allow to work 1 minute. | 2. Mist on a generous amount of alcohol.<br> • Allow to work 1 minute.<br> • Tamp with soft brush.<br> • Mist on a generous amount of alcohol.<br> • Tamp with soft brush.<br> • Allow to work 1 minute. |
| 3. With the spot machine, rinse with hot water using the chop stroke technique 6 - 8 times.<br> • Take 4 - 6 slow, dry vacuum strokes. | 3. With the spot machine, rinse with hot water using the chop stroke technique 6 - 8 times.<br> • Take 4 - 6 slow, dry vacuum strokes. |
| 4. Look at and touch spot area carefully to see if the oily residue is gone:<br> • If YES: No further action is needed.<br> • If NO: Repeat Steps 2 and 3 until no more removes. Then, if needed, do Step 5. | 4. Look at and touch spot area carefully to see if the oily residue is gone:<br> • If YES: No further action is needed.<br> • If NO: Repeat Steps 2 and 3 until no more removes. Then, if needed, do Step 5. |
| 5. If color cast remains, mist on a generous amount of peroxide.<br> • Tamp with soft brush.<br> • Blot once with clean towel.<br> • Mist on a generous amount of peroxide.<br> • Tamp with soft brush.<br> • Allow to dry. | 5. If color cast remains, mist on a generous amount of peroxide.<br> • Tamp with soft brush.<br> • Blot once with clean towel.<br> • Mist on a generous amount of peroxide.<br> • Tamp with soft brush.<br> • Allow to dry. |
| 6. If needed, repeat Steps 2, 3 and 5 one time. | 6. If needed, repeat Steps 2, 3 and 5 one time. |
| 7. If the spot persists, call a pro for options as soon as possible. | 7. If the spot persists, call a pro for options as soon as possible. |

Section II

## *Comments:*

- **Optimum removal time:** Within 24 hours of spill
- **Maximum size for home removal:** Class III / IV = 1 inch
- **Removal restrictions:** If the spot(s) is larger than 1 inch in diameter, **do not attempt TOTAL removal** using Class III or IV instructions. Do Step 1 **only** under Class III or IV. Put a dry towel over spot. Then:
  - Call a pro and have spot removed within 2 days. -OR-
  - If the spot is 2 inches or less in diameter, get a spot machine and:
    - If the spot is now old/dried, do Steps 2 - 7 under Class I.
    - If the spot is still fresh/wet, do Steps 2 - 7 under Class II.
- Large spills can soak through the carpet and pad to the subfloor and cause recurring spots. (See "Recurring Spots", Chapter 4.) Consult a pro for options as soon as possible.

## *Materials Needed:*

Class III / IV: Spotting kit

| Class III: Towel + Old / Dried Spot | Class IV: Towel + Fresh / Wet Spot |
|---|---|

*Steps:*

1. Fold a towel several times and place it over the spot(s).
   - Step on the towel with your full weight 10 - 12 times, using a clean part of the towel each time.
   - Repeat until no more absorbs.
2. Mist on a generous amount of alcohol.
   - Allow to work 1 minute.
   - Tamp with soft brush.
   - Mist on a generous amount of alcohol.
   - Tamp with soft brush.
   - Allow to work 1 minute.
3. With a towel, blot the spot 10 - 12 times, using a clean part of the towel each time.
4. Look at and touch spot area carefully to see if the oily residue is gone:
   - If YES: No further action is needed.
   - If NO: Repeat Steps 2 and 3 until no more removes. Then, if needed, do Step 5.
5. If color cast remains, mist on a generous amount of peroxide.
   - Tamp with soft brush.
   - Blot once with clean towel.
   - Mist on a generous amount of peroxide.
   - Tamp with soft brush.
   - Allow to dry.
6. If needed, repeat Steps 2, 3 and 5 one time.
7. If the spot persists, call a pro for options as soon as possible.

*Steps:*

1. Fold a towel several times and place it over the spot(s).
   - Step on the towel with your full weight 10 - 12 times, using a clean part of the towel each time.
   - Repeat until no more absorbs.
2. Mist on a generous amount of alcohol.
   - Allow to work 1 minute.
   - Tamp with soft brush.
   - Mist on a generous amount of alcohol.
   - Tamp with soft brush.
   - Allow to work 1 minute.
3. With a towel, blot the spot 10 - 12 times, using a clean part of the towel each time.
4. Look at and touch spot area carefully to see if the oily residue is gone:
   - If YES: No further action is needed.
   - If NO: Repeat Steps 2 and 3 until no more removes. Then, if needed, do Step 5.
5. If color cast remains, mist on a generous amount of peroxide.
   - Tamp with soft brush.
   - Blot once with clean towel.
   - Mist on a generous amount of peroxide.
   - Tamp with soft brush.
   - Allow to dry.
6. If needed, repeat Steps 2, 3 and 5 one time.
7. If the spot persists, call a pro for options as soon as possible.

Section II

# Butter, Margarine, Spreads, Etc.

## Comments:

- **Optimum removal time:** Within 24 hours of spill
- **Maximum size for home removal:** Class I / II = 4 inches
- **Removal restrictions:** If the spot(s) is larger than 4 inches in diameter, **do not attempt TOTAL removal** using Class I or II instructions. Do Step 1 **only** under Class I or II. Put a dry towel over spot. Call a pro and have spot removed within 2 days.
- Oils in these products can cause recurring spots on all types of fibers if not completely removed. (See "Recurring Spots", Chapter 4.) Consult a pro for options as soon as possible.

## Materials Needed:

Class I / II: Disposable towels or tissues, Spotting kit, Spot machine with hot water

### Class I: Spot Machine + Old / Dried Spot

**Steps:**

1. Lay a disposable towel over the palm of your hand. Then lay your hand on the carpet so the towel is at the edge of the spot.
   - Using your spoon, scoop as much of the spot(s) as possible onto the towel. Note: After each scoop, wipe the spoon on a clean part of the towel.
   - Carefully drop the dirty towel in your empty bucket.
   - Vacuum debris with spot machine.
   - Repeat entire Step until no more removes.

2. Mist on a generous amount of alcohol.
   - Tamp with soft brush.
   - Allow to work 1 minute.
   - Mist on a small amount of ammonia.
   - Tamp with soft brush.

3. With the spot machine, rinse with hot water using the chop stroke technique 6 - 8 times.
   - Take 4 - 6 slow, dry vacuum strokes.

4. Look at and touch spot area carefully to see if the oily residue is gone:
   - If YES: No further action is needed.
   - If NO: Repeat Steps 2 and 3 until no more removes. Then, if needed, do Step 5.

5. If color cast remains, mist on a generous amount of peroxide.
   - Tamp with soft brush.
   - Allow to dry.

6. If needed, repeat Steps 2, 3 and 5 one time.

7. If the spot persists, call a pro for options as soon as possible.

### Class II: Spot Machine + Fresh / Wet Spot

**Steps:**

1. Lay a disposable towel over the palm of your hand. Then lay your hand on the carpet so the towel is at the edge of the spot.
   - Using your spoon, scoop as much of the spot(s) as possible onto the towel. Note: After each scoop, wipe the spoon on a clean part of the towel.
   - Carefully drop the dirty towel in your empty bucket.
   - Vacuum debris with spot machine.
   - Repeat entire Step until no more removes.

2. Mist on a generous amount of alcohol.
   - Tamp with soft brush.
   - Allow to work 1 minute.
   - Mist on a small amount of ammonia.
   - Tamp with soft brush.

3. With the spot machine, rinse with hot water using the chop stroke technique 6 - 8 times.
   - Take 4 - 6 slow, dry vacuum strokes.

4. Look at and touch spot area carefully to see if the oily residue is gone:
   - If YES: No further action is needed.
   - If NO: Repeat Steps 2 and 3 until no more removes. Then, if needed, do Step 5.

5. If color cast remains, mist on a generous amount of peroxide.
   - Tamp with soft brush.
   - Allow to dry.

6. If needed, repeat Steps 2, 3 and 5 one time.

7. If the spot persists, call a pro for options as soon as possible.

### Comments:

- **Optimum removal time:** Within 24 hours of spill
- **Maximum size for home removal:** Class III / IV = 2 inches
- **Removal restrictions:** If the spot(s) is larger than 2 inches in diameter, **do not attempt TOTAL removal** using Class III or IV instructions. Do Step 1 **only** under Class III or IV. Put a dry towel over spot. Then:
  - Call a pro and have spot removed within 2 days. -OR-
  - If the spot is 4 inches or less in diameter, get a spot machine and:
    - If the spot is now old/dried, do Steps 2 - 7 under Class I.
    - If the spot is still fresh/wet, do Steps 2 - 7 under Class II.
- Oils in these products can cause recurring spots on all types of fibers if not completely removed. (See "Recurring Spots", Chapter 4.) Consult a pro for options as soon as possible.

### Materials Needed:
Class III / IV: Disposable towels or tissues, Spotting kit

| Class III: Towel + Old / Dried Spot | Class IV: Towel + Fresh / Wet Spot |
|---|---|
| **Steps:** | **Steps:** |
| 1. Lay a disposable towel over the palm of your hand. Then lay your hand on the carpet so the towel is at the edge of the spot. | 1. Lay a disposable towel over the palm of your hand. Then lay your hand on the carpet so the towel is at the edge of the spot. |
| • Using your spoon, scoop as much of the spot(s) as possible onto the towel. Note: After each scoop, wipe the spoon on a clean part of the towel. | • Using your spoon, scoop as much of the spot(s) as possible onto the towel. Note: After each scoop, wipe the spoon on a clean part of the towel. |
| • Carefully drop the dirty towel in your empty bucket. | • Carefully drop the dirty towel in your empty bucket. |
| • With a clean cloth towel, blot the spot 10 - 12 times, using a clean part of the towel each time. | • With a clean cloth towel, blot the spot 10 - 12 times, using a clean part of the towel each time. |
| • Repeat entire Step until no more removes. | • Repeat entire Step until no more removes. |
| 2. Mist on a generous amount of alcohol. | 2. Mist on a generous amount of alcohol. |
| • Tamp with soft brush. | • Tamp with soft brush. |
| • Allow to work 1 minute. | • Allow to work 1 minute. |
| • Mist on a small amount of ammonia. | • Mist on a small amount of ammonia. |
| • Tamp with soft brush. | • Tamp with soft brush. |
| 3. With a towel, blot the spot 10 - 12 times, using a clean part of the towel each time. | 3. With a towel, blot the spot 10 - 12 times, using a clean part of the towel each time. |
| 4. Look at and touch spot area carefully to see if the oily residue is gone: | 4. Look at and touch spot area carefully to see if the oily residue is gone: |
| • If YES: No further action is needed. | • If YES: No further action is needed. |
| • If NO: Repeat Steps 2 and 3 until no more removes. Then, if needed, do Step 5. | • If NO: Repeat Steps 2 and 3 until no more removes. Then, if needed, do Step 5. |
| 5. If color cast remains, mist on a generous amount of peroxide. | 5. If color cast remains, mist on a generous amount of peroxide. |
| • Tamp with soft brush. | • Tamp with soft brush. |
| • Allow to dry. | • Allow to dry. |
| 6. If needed, repeat Steps 2, 3 and 5 one time. | 6. If needed, repeat Steps 2, 3 and 5 one time. |
| 7. If the spot persists, call a pro for options as soon as possible. | 7. If the spot persists, call a pro for options as soon as possible. |

Section II

# Candy - Hard (Lollipops, Peppermints, Red Hots, Etc.)

## Comments:

- **Optimum removal time:** Within 24 hours of spill
- **Maximum size for home removal:** Class I = 1 1/2 inches / Class II = No size limit if the spot is fresh/wet.
- **Removal restrictions - Class I:** If the spot(s) is larger than 1 1/2 inches in diameter, **do not attempt TOTAL removal** using Class I instructions. Do Step 1 **only** under Class I. Put a dry towel over spot. Call a pro and have spot removed within 2 days.
- **Removal restrictions - Class II:** No size limits. Do "Class II" Steps below.
- Food coloring in some products can immediately and permanently stain most nylon. If you cannot remove a spot, consult a pro for options as soon as possible.

## Materials Needed:

Class I / II: Spotting kit, Spot machine with hot water

<table>
<tr><td>

### Class I: Spot Machine + Old / Dried Spot

</td><td>

### Class II: Spot Machine + Fresh / Wet Spot

</td></tr>
<tr><td>

**Steps:**

1. Using your spoon, scrape out as much of the spot(s) as possible.
   - Vacuum debris with spot machine.

2. With the spot machine, rinse with hot water using the chop stroke technique 8 - 10 times.
   - Take 6 - 8 slow, dry vacuum strokes.

3. Look at spot area carefully to see if the spot is gone:
   - If YES: No further action is needed.
   - If NO: Do Step 4.

4. Mist on a generous amount of ammonia.
   - Agitate with end of spoon handle.
   - Allow to work 1 minute.

5. With the spot machine, rinse with hot water using the chop stroke technique 8 - 10 times.
   - Take 6 - 8 slow, dry vacuum strokes.

6. Look at spot area carefully to see if the spot is gone:
   - If YES: No further action is needed.
   - If NO: Repeat Steps 4 and 5 until no more removes. Then, if needed, do Step 7.

7. If color cast remains, mist on a generous amount of peroxide.
   - Mist on a small amount of ammonia.
   - Tamp with soft brush.
   - Allow to dry.

8. If needed, repeat Steps 4, 5 and 7 one time.

9. If the spot persists, call a pro for options as soon as possible.

</td><td>

**Steps:**

1. Using your spoon, scrape out as much of the spot(s) as possible.
   - Vacuum debris with spot machine.

2. With the spot machine, rinse with hot water using the chop stroke technique 8 - 10 times.
   - Take 6 - 8 slow, dry vacuum strokes.

3. Look at spot area carefully to see if the spot is gone:
   - If YES: No further action is needed.
   - If NO: Do Step 4.

4. Mist on a generous amount of ammonia.
   - Agitate with end of spoon handle.
   - Allow to work 1 minute.

5. With the spot machine, rinse with hot water using the chop stroke technique 8 - 10 times.
   - Take 6 - 8 slow, dry vacuum strokes.

6. Look at spot area carefully to see if the spot is gone:
   - If YES: No further action is needed.
   - If NO: Repeat Steps 4 and 5 until no more removes. Then, if needed, do Step 7.

7. If color cast remains, mist on a generous amount of peroxide.
   - Mist on a small amount of ammonia.
   - Tamp with soft brush.
   - Allow to dry.

8. If needed, repeat Steps 4, 5 and 7 one time.

9. If the spot persists, call a pro for options as soon as possible.

</td></tr>
</table>

Section II

Spot / Stain Contents: Food Coloring, Starch, Sugar

## Comments:

- **Optimum removal time:** Within 24 hours of spill
- **Maximum size for home removal:** Class III = 3/4 inch / Class IV = No size limit if the spot is fresh/wet.
- **Removal restrictions - Class III:** If the spot(s) is larger than 3/4 inch in diameter, **do not attempt TOTAL removal** using Class III instructions. Do Step 1 **only** under Class III. Put a dry towel over spot. Then:
  - Call a pro and have spot removed within 2 days. -OR-
  - If the spot is 1 1/2 inches or less in diameter, get a spot machine and do Steps 2 - 9 under Class I.
- **Removal restrictions - Class IV:** No size limits. Do "Class IV" Steps below.
- **Caution: Do not attempt scissors removal** of spots from **any** type of looped carpet (berber, commercial glue down, etc.) unless the spot is **only on the outside fibers** of the loop(s). If in doubt, call a pro for options as soon as possible.
- Food coloring in some products can immediately and permanently stain most nylon. If you cannot remove a spot, consult a pro for options as soon as possible.

## Materials Needed:

Class III / IV: Spotting kit, Vacuum cleaner with attachment removed from hose

| Class III: Towel + Old / Dried Spot | Class IV: Towel + Fresh / Wet Spot |
|---|---|
| **Steps:** | **Steps:** |
| 1. Using your scissors, wedge the blades up under the spot(s) and snip the hardened parts from the very tip of the carpet fibers. (This will minimize the indentations caused by the removed spots.) Note: On non-looped carpets, you can also trim a few carpet fibers around the edge of the removed spot, if needed, to minimize it further. | 1. Using your scissors, wedge the blades up under the spot(s) and snip the hardened parts from the very tip of the carpet fibers. (This will minimize the indentations caused by the removed spots.) Note: On non-looped carpets, you can also trim a few carpet fibers around the edge of the removed spot, if needed, to minimize it further. |
|   • On non-looped carpets, rough up the trimmed carpet fibers a little with the tips of your scissors. Trim any taller roughed up fibers so they are equal in height with the rest of the carpet. |   • On non-looped carpets, rough up the trimmed carpet fibers a little with the tips of your scissors. Trim any taller roughed up fibers so they are equal in height with the rest of the carpet. |
|   • Vacuum debris with vacuum cleaner hose. |   • Vacuum debris with vacuum cleaner hose. |
| 2. Mist on a generous amount of ammonia. | 2. Mist on a generous amount of ammonia. |
|   • Allow to work 2 minutes. |   • Allow to work 1 minute. |
|   • Agitate with end of spoon handle. |   • Agitate with end of spoon handle. |
|   • Mist on a small amount of ammonia. |   • Mist on a small amount of ammonia. |
|   • Agitate with end of spoon handle. |   • Agitate with end of spoon handle. |
| 3. With a towel, blot 8 - 10 times, using a clean part of the towel each time. | 3. With a towel, blot 8 - 10 times, using a clean part of the towel each time. |
| 4. Look at spot area carefully to see if the spot is gone: | 4. Look at spot area carefully to see if the spot is gone: |
|   • If YES: No further action is needed. |   • If YES: No further action is needed. |
|   • If NO: Repeat Steps 2 and 3 until no more removes. Then, if needed, do Step 5. |   • If NO: Repeat Steps 2 and 3 until no more removes. Then, if needed, do Step 5. |
| 5. If color cast remains, mist on a generous amount of peroxide. | 5. If color cast remains, mist on a generous amount of peroxide. |
|   • Mist on a small amount of ammonia. |   • Mist on a small amount of ammonia. |
|   • Tamp with soft brush. |   • Tamp with soft brush. |
|   • Allow to dry. |   • Allow to dry. |
| 6. If needed, repeat Steps 2, 3 and 5 one time. | 6. If needed, repeat Steps 2, 3 and 5 one time. |
| 7. If the spot persists, call a pro for options as soon as possible. | 7. If the spot persists, call a pro for options as soon as possible. |

Section II

# Candy - Soft *(Chocolates, Jelly Beans, Marshmallows, Etc.)*

## Comments:

- **Optimum removal time:** Within 24 hours of spill
- **Maximum size for home removal:** Class I = 3 inches / Class II = No size limits as long as the spot is fresh/wet.
- **Removal restrictions - Class I:** If the spot(s) is larger than 3 inches in diameter, **do not attempt TOTAl removal** using Class I instructions. Do Steps 1 and 2 **only** under Class I. Put a towel moistened with water over spot. Call a pro and have spot removed within 2 days.
- **Removal restrictions - Class II:** No size limits. Do "Class II" instructions below.
- Food coloring in some products can immediately and permanently stain some nylon. If you cannot remove a spot, consult a pro for options as soon as possible.

## Materials Needed:

Class I / II: Spotting kit, Spot machine with hot water

<table>
<tr><td>

### Class I: Spot Machine + Old / Dried Spot

**Steps:**

1. Using your spoon, scrape out as much of the spot(s) as possible.
   - Vacuum debris with spot machine.
   - With a dry towel over your hand, pinch out more of the spot, using a clean part of the towel each time.
   - Repeat entire Step until no more removes.

2. With the spot machine, rinse with hot water using the chop stroke technique 8 - 10 times.
   - Take 6 - 8 slow, dry vacuum strokes.

3. Look at spot area carefully to see if the spot is gone:
   - If YES: Allow to dry.
   - If NO: Do Step 4.

4. Mist on a generous amount of ammonia.
   - Mist on a small amount of alcohol.
   - Agitate with hard brush.
   - Allow to work 1 minute.

5. With the spot machine, rinse with hot water using the chop stroke technique 8 - 10 times.
   - Take 6 - 8 slow, dry vacuum strokes.

6. Look at spot area carefully to see if the spot is gone:
   - If YES: Allow to dry.
   - If NO: Repeat Steps 4 and 5 until no more removes. Then, if needed, do Step 7.

7. If color cast remains, mist on a generous amount of peroxide.
   - Mist on a small amount of ammonia.
   - Tamp with soft brush.
   - Allow to dry.

8. If needed, repeat Steps 4, 5 and 7 one time.

9. If the spot persists, call a pro for options as soon as possible.

</td><td>

### Class II: Spot Machine + Fresh / Wet Spot

**Steps:**

1. Using your spoon, scrape out as much of the spot(s) as possible.
   - With a dry towel over your hand, pinch out more of the spot, using a clean part of the towel each time.
   - Repeat entire Step until no more removes.

2. With the spot machine, rinse with hot water using the chop stroke technique 8 - 10 times.
   - Take 6 - 8 slow, dry vacuum strokes.

3. Look at spot area carefully to see if the spot is gone:
   - If YES: Allow to dry.
   - If NO: Do Step 4.

4. Mist on a generous amount of ammonia.
   - Mist on a small amount of alcohol.
   - Agitate with hard brush.
   - Allow to work 1 minute.

5. With the spot machine, rinse with hot water using the chop stroke technique 8 - 10 times.
   - Take 6 - 8 slow, dry vacuum strokes.

6. Look at spot area carefully to see if the spot is gone:
   - If YES: Allow to dry.
   - If NO: Repeat Steps 4 and 5 until no more removes. Then, if needed, do Step 7.

7. If color cast remains, mist on a generous amount of peroxide.
   - Mist on a small amount of ammonia.
   - Tamp with soft brush.
   - Allow to dry.

8. If needed, repeat Steps 4, 5 and 7 one time.

9. If the spot persists, call a pro for options as soon as possible.

</td></tr>
</table>

Section II

# Candy - Soft (Chocolates, Jelly Beans, Marshmallows, Etc.)

Spot / Stain Contents: Corn Syrup, Food Coloring, Gelatin, Starch, Sugar

## Comments:

- **Optimum removal time:** Within 24 hours of spill
- **Maximum size for home removal:** Class III = 1 1/2 inches / Class IV = 2 inches in diameter.
- **Removal restrictions - Class III:** If the spot(s) is larger than 1 1/2 inches in diameter, **do not attempt TOTAL removal** using Class III instructions. Do Step 1 **only.** Put a dry towel over spot. Then:
  - Call a pro and have spot removed within 2 days. -OR-
  - If the spot is 3 inches or less in diameter, get a spot machine and do Steps 2 - 9 under Class I.
- **Removal restrictions - Class IV:** If the spot(s) is larger than 2 inches in diameter, **do not attempt TOTAL removal** using Class IV instructions. Do Step 1 **only.** Put a dry towel over spot. Then:
  - Call a pro and have spot removed within 2 days. -OR-
  - Get a spot machine and do Steps 2 - 9 under Class II.
- Food coloring in some products can immediately and permanently stain some nylon. If you cannot remove a spot, consult a pro for options as soon as possible.

## Materials Needed:
Class III / IV: Spotting kit

| Class III: Towel + Old / Dried Spot | Class IV: Towel + Fresh / Wet Spot |
|---|---|
| **Steps:** | **Steps:** |
| 1. Using your spoon, scrape out as much of the spot(s) as possible. | 1. Using your spoon, scrape out as much of the spot(s) as possible. |
| • With a dry towel over your hand, pinch out more of the spot, using a clean part of the towel each time. | • With a dry towel over your hand, pinch out more of the spot, using a clean part of the towel each time. |
| • Repeat entire Step until no more removes. | • Repeat entire Step until no more removes. |
| 2. Mist on a generous amount of ammonia. | 2. Mist on a generous amount of ammonia. |
| • Mist on a small amount of alcohol. | • Mist on a small amount of alcohol. |
| • Agitate with hard brush. | • Agitate with hard brush. |
| • Allow to work 2 minutes. | • Allow to work 2 minutes. |
| • Mist on a small amount of ammonia. | • Mist on a small amount of ammonia. |
| 3. With a towel, blot 8 - 10 times, using a clean part of the towel each time. | 3. With a towel, blot 8 - 10 times, using a clean part of the towel each time. |
| 4. Look at spot area carefully to see if the spot is gone: | 4. Look at spot area carefully to see if the spot is gone: |
| • If YES: Allow to dry. | • If YES: Allow to dry. |
| • If NO: Repeat Steps 2 and 3 until no more removes. Then, if needed, do Step 5. | • If NO: Repeat Steps 2 and 3 until no more removes. Then, if needed, do Step 5. |
| 5. If color cast remains, mist on a generous amount of peroxide. | 5. If color cast remains, mist on a generous amount of peroxide. |
| • Mist on a small amount of ammonia. | • Mist on a small amount of ammonia. |
| • Tamp with soft brush. | • Tamp with soft brush. |
| • Allow to dry. | • Allow to dry. |
| 6. If needed, repeat Steps 2, 3 and 5 one time. | 6. If needed, repeat Steps 2, 3 and 5 one time. |
| 7. If the spot persists, call a pro for options as soon as possible. | 7. If the spot persists, call a pro for options as soon as possible. |

Section II

# Carbon Paper, Credit Card or Invoice Carbons, Typewriter Ribbon, Etc.

## Comments:

- **Optimum removal time: As soon as possible** within 24 hours of spill
- **Maximum size for home removal:** Class I / II = 1 inch
- **Removal restrictions:** If the spot(s) is larger than 1 inch in diameter, **do not attempt ANY removal** using Class I or II instructions. Put a dry towel over spot and a note next to it that says, "*Do Not Touch Or Clean!*". Call a pro and have spot removed as soon as possible within 24 hours.
- Pigments in carbon paper, etc., can immediately and permanently stain some nylon. If you cannot remove a spot, consult a pro for options as soon as possible.

## Materials Needed:

Class I / II: Spotting kit, Spot machine with hot water

| Class I: Spot Machine + Old / Dried Spot | Class II: Spot Machine + Fresh / Wet Spot |
|---|---|

### Steps:

1. Using a towel, gently blot the spot(s) 10 - 15 times, using a clean part of the towel each time. Caution: Be careful not to spread the spot.
   - Repeat until no more transfer occurs.
2. Mist on a small amount of alcohol.
   - Allow to work 1 minute.
   - Gently tamp with soft brush.
   - Mist on a small amount of ammonia.
   - Gently tamp with soft brush.
3. With the spot machine, rinse with hot water using the single stroke technique 10 - 12 times.
   - Take 6 - 8 slow, dry vacuum strokes.
4. Look at spot area carefully to see if the spot is gone:
   - If YES: Allow to dry.
   - If NO: Repeat Steps 1 - 3 until no more removes. If needed, do Step 5.
5. If color cast remains, mist on a generous amount of peroxide.
   - Mist on a small amount of ammonia.
   - Tamp with soft brush.
   - Allow to dry.
6. If needed, repeat Steps 2, 3 and 5 one time.
7. If the spot persists, call a pro for options as soon as possible.

### Steps:

1. Using a towel, gently blot the spot(s) 10 - 15 times, using a clean part of the towel each time. Caution: Be careful not to spread the spot.
   - Repeat until no more transfer occurs.
2. Mist on a small amount of alcohol.
   - Allow to work 1 minute.
   - Gently tamp with soft brush.
   - Mist on a small amount of ammonia.
   - Gently tamp with soft brush.
3. With the spot machine, rinse with hot water using the single stroke technique 10 - 12 times.
   - Take 6 - 8 slow, dry vacuum strokes.
4. Look at spot area carefully to see if the spot is gone:
   - If YES: Allow to dry.
   - If NO: Repeat Steps 1 - 3 until no more removes. If needed, do Step 5.
5. If color cast remains, mist on a generous amount of peroxide.
   - Mist on a small amount of ammonia.
   - Tamp with soft brush.
   - Allow to dry.
6. If needed, repeat Steps 2, 3 and 5 one time.
7. If the spot persists, call a pro for options as soon as possible.

Section II

Spot / Stain Contents: Dyes, Oils, Pigments, Waxes

## Comments:

- **Optimum removal time: As soon as possible** within 24 hours of spill
- **Maximum size for home removal:** Class III / IV = 1/2 inch
- **Removal restrictions:** If the spot(s) is larger than 1/2 inch in diameter, **do not attempt ANY removal** using Class III or IV instructions. Put a dry towel over spot and a note next to it that says, "***Do Not Touch Or Clean!***". Then:
  - Call a pro and have spot removed as soon as possible within 24 hours. -OR-
  - If the spot is 1 inch or less in diameter, get a spot machine and:
    - If the spot is now old/dried, do Steps 1 - 7 under Class I.
    - If the spot is still fresh/wet, do Steps 1 - 7 under Class II.
- Pigments in carbon paper, etc., can immediately and permanently stain some nylon. If you cannot remove a spot, consult a pro for options as soon as possible.

## Materials Needed:
Class III / IV: Spotting kit

### Class III: Towel + Old / Dried Spot

**Steps:**

1. Using a dry towel, gently blot the spot(s) 10 - 15 times, using a clean part of the towel each time. Caution: Be careful not to spread the spot.
   - Repeat until no more transfer occurs.

2. Mist a small amount of alcohol onto a towel.
   - Gently blot the spot with the moistened part of the towel. Caution: Do not spray alcohol directly on spot; it could cause it to spread.
   - Repeat misting towel and blotting 4 - 5 times, misting a clean part of the towel each time.
   - With a dry towel, blot 10 - 15 times, using a clean part of the towel each time.

3. Look at spot area carefully to see if the spot is gone:
   - If YES: Allow to dry. Look at area next day.
   - If NO: Repeat Step 2 one time. Then do Step 4.

4. Mist a small amount of ammonia onto a towel.
   - Gently blot the spot with the moistened part of the towel. Caution: Do not spray ammonia directly on spot; it could cause it to spread.
   - Repeat misting towel and blotting 4 - 5 times, using a clean part of the towel each time.
   - With a dry towel, blot 10 - 15 times, using a clean part of the towel each time.

5. Look at spot area carefully to see if the spot is gone:
   - If YES: Allow to dry. Look at area next day.
   - If NO: Repeat Steps 2 and 4 until no more removes. Then, if needed, do Step 6.

6. If color cast remains, mist on a generous amount of peroxide.
   - Mist on a small amount of ammonia.
   - Tamp with soft brush.
   - Allow to dry.

7. If the spot persists, call a pro for options as soon as possible.

### Class IV: Towel + Fresh / Wet Spot

**Steps:**

1. Using a dry towel, gently blot the spot(s) 10 - 15 times, using a clean part of the towel each time. Caution: Be careful not to spread the spot.
   - Repeat until no more transfer occurs.

2. Mist a small amount of alcohol onto a towel.
   - Gently blot the spot with the moistened part of the towel. Caution: Do not spray alcohol directly on spot; it could cause it to spread.
   - Repeat misting towel and blotting 4 - 5 times, misting a clean part of the towel each time.
   - With a dry towel, blot 10 - 15 times, using a clean part of the towel each time.

3. Look at spot area carefully to see if the spot is gone:
   - If YES: Allow to dry. Look at area next day.
   - If NO: Repeat Step 2 one time. Then do Step 4.

4. Mist a small amount of ammonia onto a towel.
   - Gently blot the spot with the moistened part of the towel. Caution: Do not spray ammonia directly on spot; it could cause it to spread.
   - Repeat misting towel and blotting 4 - 5 times, using a clean part of the towel each time.
   - With a dry towel, blot 10 - 15 times, using a clean part of the towel each time.

5. Look at spot area carefully to see if the spot is gone:
   - If YES: Allow to dry. Look at area next day.
   - If NO: Repeat Steps 2 and 4 until no more removes. Then, if needed, do Step 6.

6. If color cast remains, mist on a generous amount of peroxide.
   - Mist on a small amount of ammonia.
   - Tamp with soft brush.
   - Allow to dry.

7. If the spot persists, call a pro for options as soon as possible.

Section II

# Cement, Concrete, Grout, Mortar, Etc.

## Comments:

- **Optimum removal time**: Within 24 hours of spill
- **Maximum size for home removal:** Class I / II = 5 inches
- **Removal restrictions:** If the spot(s) is larger than 5 inches in diameter, **do not attempt TOTAL removal** using Class I or II instructions. Do Step 1 **only** under Class I or II. Put a dry towel over spot. Call a pro and have spot removed within 2 days.
- Mixtures of concrete containing high concentrations of lime can chemically burn carpet dye and discolor (lighten) the spot area. Consult a pro for options.
- Pigments in some tile grout mixtures can permanently stain some nylon. If you cannot remove a spot, consult a pro for options as soon as possible.

## Materials Needed:

Class I: Spotting kit, Pair of pliers, Spot machine with hot water
Class II: Disposable towels or tissues, Spotting kit, Spot machine with hot water

| Class I: Spot Machine + Old / Dried Spot | Class II: Spot Machine + Fresh / Wet Spot |
|---|---|
| **Steps:** | **Steps:** |
| 1. Take your spoon by the handle and firmly slam the edge of the scoop part down onto the spot(s) 25 - 35 times to break it into tiny particles. Note: Use a pair of pliers to crush smaller, more stubborn pieces.<br>• Vacuum debris with spot machine.<br>• Repeat entire Step as many times as needed to break the spot free from the carpet fibers. | 1. Lay a disposable towel over the palm of your hand. Then lay your hand on the carpet so the towel is at the edge of the spot.<br>• Using your spoon, scoop as much of the spot(s) as possible onto the towel. Note: After each scoop, wipe the spoon on a clean part of the towel.<br>• Carefully drop the dirty towel in your empty bucket.<br>• Vacuum debris with spot machine.<br>• Repeat entire Step until no more removes. |
| 2. Mist on a generous amount of ammonia.<br>• Allow to work 1 minute.<br>• Mist on a generous amount of ammonia.<br>• Agitate with hard brush. | 2. Mist on a generous amount of ammonia.<br>• Agitate with hard brush. |
| 3. With the spot machine, rinse with hot water using the chop stroke technique 6 - 8 times.<br>• Take 4 - 6 slow, dry vacuum strokes. | 3. With the spot machine, rinse with hot water using the chop stroke technique 6 - 8 times.<br>• Take 4 - 6 slow, dry vacuum strokes. |
| 4. Look at spot area carefully to see if the spot is gone:<br>• If YES: Allow to dry.<br>• If NO: Repeat Steps 2 and 3 until no more removes. Then, if needed, do Step 5. | 4. Look at spot area carefully to see if the spot is gone:<br>• If YES: Allow to dry.<br>• If NO: Repeat Steps 2 and 3 until no more removes. Then, if needed, do Step 5. |
| 5. If color cast remains, mist on a generous amount of peroxide.<br>• Tamp with soft brush.<br>• Allow to dry. | 5. If color cast remains, mist on a generous amount of peroxide.<br>• Tamp with soft brush.<br>• Allow to dry. |
| 6. If the spot persists, call a pro for options as soon as possible. | 6. If the spot persists, call a pro for options as soon as possible. |

Section II

## Comments:

- **Optimum removal time:** Within 24 hours of spill
- **Maximum size for home removal:** Class III / IV = 3 inches
- **Removal restrictions:** If the spot(s) is larger than 3 inches in diameter, **do not attempt TOTAL removal** using Class III or IV instructions. Do Step 1 **only** under Class III or IV. Put a dry towel over spot. Then:
  - Call a pro and have spot removed within 2 days. -OR-
  - If the spot is 5 inches or less in diameter, get a spot machine and:
    - If the spot is now old/dried, do Steps 2 - 6 under Class I.
    - If the spot is still fresh/wet, do Steps 2 - 6 under Class II.
- Mixtures of concrete containing high concentrations of lime can chemically burn carpet dye and discolor (lighten) the spot area. Consult a pro for options.
- Pigments in some tile grout mixtures can permanently stain some nylon. If you cannot remove a spot, consult a pro for options as soon as possible.

## Materials Needed:

Class III: Spotting kit, Pair of pliers, Vacuum cleaner with attachment removed from hose
Class IV: Disposable towels or tissues, Spotting kit, Vacuum cleaner with attachment removed from hose

| Class III: Towel + Old / Dried Spot | Class IV: Towel + Fresh / Wet Spot |
|---|---|
| **Steps:** | **Steps:** |
| 1. Take your spoon by the handle and firmly slam the edge of the scoop part down onto the spot(s) 25 - 35 times to break it into tiny particles. Note: Use a pair of pliers to crush smaller, more stubborn pieces. | 1. Lay a disposable towel over the palm of your hand. Then lay your hand on the carpet so the towel is at the edge of the spot. |
| • Vacuum debris with vacuum cleaner hose. | • Using your spoon, scoop as much of the spot(s) as possible onto the towel. Note: After each scoop, wipe the spoon on a clean part of the towel. |
| • Repeat entire Step as many times as needed to break the spot free from the carpet fibers. | • Carefully drop the dirty towel in your empty bucket. |
| | • Vacuum debris with vacuum cleaner. |
| | • Repeat entire Step until no more removes. |
| 2. Mist on a generous amount of ammonia. | 2. Mist on a generous amount of ammonia. |
| • Allow to work 2 minutes. | • Agitate with hard brush. |
| • Mist on a generous amount of ammonia. | |
| • Agitate with hard brush. | |
| 3. With a towel, firmly blot 10 - 15 times, using a clean part of the towel each time. | 3. With a towel, firmly blot 10 - 15 times, using a clean part of the towel each time. |
| 4. Look at spot area carefully to see if the spot is gone: | 4. Look at spot area carefully to see if the spot is gone: |
| • If YES: Allow to dry. | • If YES: Allow to dry. |
| • If NO: Repeat Steps 2 and 3 until no more removes. Then, if needed, do Step 5. | • If NO: Repeat Steps 2 and 3 until no more removes. Then, if needed, do Step 5. |
| 5. If color cast remains, mist on a generous amount of peroxide. | 5. If color cast remains, mist on a generous amount of peroxide. |
| • Tamp with soft brush. | • Tamp with soft brush. |
| • Allow to dry. | • Allow to dry. |
| 6. If the spot persists, call a pro for options as soon as possible. | 6. If the spot persists, call a pro for options as soon as possible. |

Section II

# Cheese - Hard or Dry *(Cheddar, Gouda, Manchego, Parmigiano, Swiss, Etc.)*

## Comments:

- **Optimum removal time:** Within 24 hours of spill
- **Maximum size for home removal:** Class I / II = 4 inches
- **Removal restrictions:** If the spot(s) is larger than 4 inches in diameter, **do not attempt TOTAL removal** using Class I or II instructions. Do Step 1 **only** under Class I or II. Put a folded towel moistened with water over spot. (Keep towel damp until pro comes.) Call a pro and have spot removed within 2 days.
- **Caution:** Food colorings in some products can permanently stain some nylon, if left untreated as little as 7 days. If you cannot remove a spot, consult a pro for options as soon as possible.
- Oils in some products can cause recurring spots if not completely removed. (See "Recurring Spots", Chapter 4.) If a spot persists, consult a pro for options as soon as possible.

## Materials Needed:

Class I / II: Spotting kit, Spot machine with hot water

## Class I: Spot Machine + Old / Dried Spot

### Steps:

1. Using your spoon, scrape out as much of the spot as possible.
   - Vacuum debris with spot machine.
   - Repeat entire Step until no more removes.

2. Mist on a generous amount of ammonia.
   - Agitate with hard brush.
   - Allow to work 1 minute.
   - Mist on a generous amount of alcohol.
   - Agitate with hard brush.
   - Allow to work 1 minute.

3. With the spot machine, rinse with hot water using the chop stroke technique 6 - 8 times.
   - Take 4 - 6 slow, dry vacuum strokes.

4. Look at spot area carefully to see if the spot is gone:
   - If YES: Allow to dry.
   - If NO: Repeat Steps 2 and 3 until no more removes. Then, if needed, do Step 5.

5. If color cast remains, mist on a generous amount of peroxide.
   - Tamp with soft brush.
   - Allow to dry.

6. If needed, repeat Step 5 one time.

7. If the spot persists, call a pro for options as soon as possible.

## Class II: Spot Machine + Fresh / Wet Spot

### Steps:

1. Lay a small towel over the palm of your hand. Then lay your hand on the carpet so the towel is at the edge of the spot.
   - Using your spoon, scoop as much of the spot(s) as possible onto the towel. Note: After each scoop, wipe the spoon on a clean part of the towel.
   - Carefully drop the dirty towel in your empty bucket.
   - Vacuum debris with spot machine.
   - Repeat entire Step until no more removes.

2. Mist on a generous amount of ammonia.
   - Agitate with hard brush.
   - Allow to work 1 minute.
   - Mist on a generous amount of alcohol.
   - Agitate with hard brush.

3. With the spot machine, rinse with hot water using the chop stroke technique 6 - 8 times.
   - Take 4 - 6 slow, dry vacuum strokes.

4. Look at spot area carefully to see if the spot is gone:
   - If YES: Allow to dry.
   - If NO: Repeat Steps 2 and 3 until no more removes. Then, if needed, do Step 5.

5. If color cast remains, mist on a generous amount of peroxide.
   - Tamp with soft brush.
   - Allow to dry.

6. If needed, repeat Step 5 one time.

7. If the spot persists, call a pro for options as soon as possible.

Spot Contents: Albumin, Fatty Acids, Food Color, Oils

## Comments:

- **Optimum removal time:** Within 24 hours of spill
- **Maximum size for home removal:** Class III / IV = 2 inches
- **Removal restrictions:** If the spot(s) is larger than 2 inches in diameter, **do not attempt TOTAL removal** using Class III or IV instructions. Do Step 1 **only** under Class III or IV. Put a folded towel moistened with water over spot. (Keep towel damp until pro comes.) Then:
  - Call a pro and have spot removed within 2 days. -OR-
  - If the spot is 4 inches or less in diameter, get a spot machine and:
    - If the spot is now old/dried, do Steps 2 - 7 under Class I.
    - If the spot is still fresh/wet, do Steps 2 - 7 under Class II.
- **Caution:** Food colorings in some products can permanently stain some nylon, if left untreated as little as 7 days. If you cannot remove a spot, consult a pro for options as soon as possible.
- Oils in some of these products can cause recurring spots if not completely removed. (See "Recurring Spots", Chapter 4.) If a spot persists, consult a pro for options as soon as possible.

## Materials Needed:

Class III / IV: Spotting kit, Shop vacuum with attachment removed from hose

### Class III: Towel + Old / Dried Spot

**Steps:**

1. Using your spoon, scrape out as much of the spot as possible.
   - Vacuum debris with shop vacuum hose.
   - Repeat entire Step until no more removes.

2. Mist on a generous amount of ammonia.
   - Agitate with hard brush.
   - Allow to work 1 minute.
   - Mist on a generous amount of alcohol.
   - Agitate with hard brush.
   - Allow to work 1 minute.

3. With a towel, blot 10 - 15 times, using a clean part of the towel each time.

4. Look at spot area carefully to see if the spot is gone:
   - If YES: Allow to dry.
   - If NO: Repeat Steps 2 and 3 until no more removes. Then, if needed, do Step 5.

5. If color cast remains, mist on a generous amount of peroxide.
   - Tamp with soft brush.
   - Allow to dry.

6. If needed, repeat Step 5 one time.

7. If the spot persists, call a pro for options as soon as possible.

### Class IV: Towel + Fresh / Wet Spot

**Steps:**

1. Lay a small towel over the palm of your hand. Then lay your hand on the carpet so the towel is at the edge of the spot.
   - Using your spoon, scoop as much of the spot(s) as possible onto the towel. Note: After each scoop, wipe the spoon on a clean part of the towel.
   - Carefully drop the dirty towel in your empty bucket.
   - Vacuum debris with shop vacuum hose.
   - Repeat entire Step until no more removes.

2. Mist on a generous amount of ammonia.
   - Agitate with hard brush.
   - Allow to work 2 minutes.
   - Mist on a generous amount of alcohol.
   - Agitate with hard brush.

3. With a towel, blot 10 - 15 times, using a clean part of the towel each time.

4 Look at spot area carefully to see if the spot is gone:
   - If YES: Allow to dry.
   - If NO: Repeat Steps 2 and 3 until no more removes. Then, if needed, do Step 5.

5. If color cast remains, mist on a generous amount of peroxide.
   - Tamp with soft brush.
   - Allow to dry.

6. If needed, repeat Step 5 one time.

7. If the spot persists, call a pro for options as soon as possible.

Section II

# Cheese - Soft *(Brie, Cream Cheese. Etc.)*, Cream, Sour Cream, Whipped Cream, Cool Whip®, Yogurt

## Comments:

- **Optimum removal time:** Within 24 hours of spill
- **Maximum size for home removal:** Class I / II = 4 inches
- **Removal restrictions:** If the spot(s) is larger than 4 inches in diameter, **do not attempt TOTAL removal** using Class I or II instructions. Do Step 1 **only** under Class I or II. Put a dry towel over spot. Call a pro and have spot removed within 1 day.
- **Caution:** These products can create a foul odor if left untreated as little as 2 - 3 days. If odor persists after treatment, consult a pro for options as soon as possible.

## Materials Needed:

Class I / II: Spotting kit, Spot machine with warm water

### Class I: Spot Machine + Old / Dried Spot

**Steps:**

1. Using your spoon, scrape out as much of the spot as possible.
   - Vacuum debris with spot machine.
   - Repeat entire Step until no more removes.

2. Mist on a generous amount of ammonia.
   - Mist on a generous amount of alcohol.
   - Allow to work 2 minutes.
   - Agitate with hard brush.
   - Mist on a generous amount of ammonia.
   - Agitate with hard brush.

3. With the spot machine, rinse with warm water using the chop stroke technique 6 - 8 times.
   - Take 4 - 6 slow, dry vacuum strokes.

4. Look at spot area carefully to see if the spot is gone:
   - If YES: Allow to dry.
   - If NO: Repeat Steps 2 and 3 until no more removes.

5. If color cast remains, mist on a generous amount of peroxide.
   - Mist on a small amount of ammonia.
   - Tamp with soft brush.
   - Allow to dry.

6. If needed, repeat Steps 2, 3 and 5 one time.

7. If the spot persists, call a pro for options as soon as possible.

### Class II: Spot Machine + Fresh / Wet Spot

**Steps:**

1. Lay a small towel over the palm of your hand. Then lay your hand on the carpet so the towel is at the edge of the spot.
   - Using your spoon, scoop as much of the spot(s) as possible onto the towel. Note: After each scoop, wipe the spoon on a clean part of the towel.
   - Carefully drop the dirty towel into your empty bucket.

2. Mist on a small amount of ammonia.
   - Mist on a small amount of alcohol.
   - Allow to work 1 minute.
   - Agitate with hard brush.
   - Mist on a small amount of ammonia.
   - Agitate with hard brush.

3. With the spot machine, rinse with warm water using the chop stroke technique 6 - 8 times.
   - Take 4 - 6 slow, dry vacuum strokes.

4. Look at spot area carefully to see if the spot is gone:
   - If YES: Allow to dry.
   - If NO: Repeat Steps 2 and 3 until no more removes.

5. If color cast remains, mist on a generous amount of peroxide.
   - Mist on a small amount of ammonia.
   - Tamp with soft brush.
   - Allow to dry.

6. If needed, repeat Steps 2, 3 and 5 one time.

7. If the spot persists, call a pro for options as soon as possible.

Section II

# Cheese - Soft (Brie, Cream Cheese, Etc.), Cream, Sour Cream, Whipped Cream, Cool Whip®, Yogurt

Spot Contents: Albumin, Butter Fat, Gelatin, Protein, Sugar

## Comments:

- **Optimum removal time:** Within 24 hours of spill
- **Maximum size for home removal:** Class III / IV = 2 inches
- **Removal restrictions:** If the spot(s) is larger than 2 inches in diameter, **do not attempt TOTAL removal** using Class III or IV instructions. Do Step 1 **only** under Class III or IV. Put a dry towel over spot. Then:
  - Call a pro and have spot removed within 1 day. -OR-
  - If the spot is 4 inches or less in diameter, get a spot machine and:
    - If the spot is now old/dried, do Steps 2 - 7 under Class I.
    - If the spot is still fresh/wet, do Steps 2 - 7 under Class II.
- **Caution:** These products can create a foul odor if left untreated as little as 2 - 3 days. If odor persists after treatment, consult a pro for options as soon as possible.

## Materials Needed:

Class III: Spotting kit, Shop vacuum with attachment removed from hose
Class IV: Spotting kit

## Class III: Towel + Old / Dried Spot

### Steps:

1. Using your spoon, scrape out as much of the spot as possible.
   - Vacuum debris with a shop vacuum hose. Caution: Do not vacuum debris with a regular vacuum cleaner. It may foul the system.
   - Repeat entire Step until no more removes.

2. Mist on a generous amount of ammonia.
   - Mist on a generous amount of alcohol.
   - Allow to work 2 minutes.
   - Agitate with hard brush.
   - Mist on a small amount of ammonia.
   - Agitate with hard brush.

3. With a towel, blot 15 - 20 times, using a clean part of the towel each time.

4. Look at spot area carefully to see if the spot is gone:
   - If YES: Allow to dry.
   - If NO: Repeat Steps 2 and 3 until no more removes.

5. If color cast remains, mist on a generous amount of peroxide.
   - Mist on a small amount of ammonia.
   - Tamp with soft brush.
   - Allow to dry.

6. If needed, repeat Steps 2, 3 and 5 one time.

7. If the spot persists, call a pro for options as soon as possible.

## Class IV: Towel + Fresh / Wet Spot

### Steps:

1. Lay a small towel over the palm of your hand. Then lay your hand on the carpet so the towel is at the edge of the spot.
   - Using your spoon, scoop as much of the spot(s) as possible onto the towel. Note: After each scoop, wipe the spoon on a clean part of the towel.
   - Carefully drop the dirty towel into your empty bucket.

2. Mist on a small amount of ammonia.
   - Mist on a small amount of alcohol.
   - Allow to work 1 minute.
   - Agitate with hard brush.
   - Mist on a small amount of ammonia.
   - Agitate with hard brush.

3. With a towel, blot 15 - 20 times, using a clean part of the towel each time.

4. Look at spot area carefully to see if the spot is gone:
   - If YES: Allow to dry.
   - If NO: Repeat Steps 2 and 3 until no more removes.

5. If color cast remains, mist on a generous amount of peroxide.
   - Mist on a small amount of ammonia.
   - Tamp with soft brush.
   - Allow to dry.

6. If needed, repeat Steps 2, 3 and 5 one time.

7. If the spot persists, call a pro for options as soon as possible.

Section II

# Coffee or Tea - Black / Plain: Coffee - Regular, Decaffeinated, Flavored / Tea - Black, Green, Herb

## Comments:

- **Optimum removal time:** Within 24 hours of spill
- **Maximum size for home removal:** Class I / II = 4 1/2 inches
- **Removal restrictions:** If the spot(s) is larger than 4 1/2 inches in diameter, **do not attempt ANY removal** using Class I or II instructions. Put a dry towel over spot. Call a pro and have spot removed within 2 days.
- **Caution:** Tannin and possible coloring in these products can be hard to remove from nylon, olefin, acrylic and polyester, especially when spilled hot. If you cannot remove a spot, consult a pro for options within 2 days.
- Large spills may cause recurring spots that need re-treatment. (See "Recurring Spots", Chapter 4.) If the spot persists, consult a pro for options as soon as possible.

## Materials Needed:
Class I / II: Spotting kit, Spot machine with warm water

### Class I: Spot Machine + Old / Dried Spot

**Steps:**

1. Using your spot machine, rinse the spot(s) with warm water using the chop stroke technique 8 - 25 times.
   - Take 4 - 12 slow, dry vacuum strokes.
   - Repeat entire Step until no more removes.

2. Mist on a generous amount of ammonia.
   - Mist on a generous amount of peroxide.
   - Tamp with soft brush.
   - Allow to work 1 minute.

3. With the spot machine, rinse with warm water using the chop stroke technique 6 - 10 times.
   - Take 4 - 8 slow, dry vacuum strokes.

4. Look at spot area carefully to see if the spot is gone:
   - If YES: Allow to dry.
   - If NO: Repeat Steps 2 and 3 until no more removes. Then, if needed, do Step 5 one time.

5. If color cast remains, mist on a generous amount of peroxide.
   - Tamp with soft brush.
   - Allow to dry.

6. If needed, repeat Step 5 one time.

7. If the spot persists, call a pro for options as soon as possible.

### Class II: Spot Machine + Fresh / Wet Spot

**Steps:**

1. Using your spot machine, dry vacuum the spot(s) 10 - 15 times taking slow, single strokes.
   - With the spot machine, rinse with warm water using the chop stroke technique 6 - 8 times.
   - Take 4 - 6 slow, dry vacuum strokes.
   - Repeat entire Step until no more removes.

2. Mist on a small amount of ammonia.
   - Mist on a small amount of peroxide.
   - Tamp with soft brush.
   - Allow to work 1 minute.

3. With the spot machine, rinse with warm water using the chop stroke technique 4 - 6 times.
   - Take 3 - 5 slow, dry vacuum strokes.

4. Look at spot area carefully to see if the spot is gone:
   - If YES: Allow to dry.
   - If NO: Repeat Steps 2 and 3 until no more removes. Then, if needed, do Step 5 one time.

5. If color cast remains, mist on a generous amount of peroxide.
   - Tamp with soft brush.
   - Allow to dry.

6. If needed, repeat Step 5 one time.

7. If the spot persists, call a pro for options as soon as possible.

Section II

# Coffee or Tea - Black / Plain: *Coffee - Regular, Decaffeinated, Flavored / Tea - Black, Green, Herb*

Spot / Stain Contents: Acids, Artificial Color, Possible Sugar, Tannin

## Comments:

- **Optimum removal time:** Within 24 hours of spill
- **Maximum size for home removal:** Class III / IV = 3 inches
- **Removal restrictions:** If the spot(s) is larger than 3 inches in diameter, **do not attempt TOTAL removal** using Class III or IV instructions. Do Step 1 **only** under Class III or IV. Put a dry towel over spot. Then:
  - Call a pro and have spot removed within 2 days. -OR-
  - If the spot is 4 1/2 inches or less in diameter, get a spot machine and:
    - If the spot is now old/dried, do Steps 1 - 7 under Class I.
    - If the spot is still fresh/wet, do Steps 1 - 7 under Class II.
- **Caution:** Tannin and possible coloring in these products can be hard to remove from nylon, olefin, acrylic and polyester, especially when spilled hot. If you cannot remove a spot, consult a pro for options within 2 days.
- Large spills may cause recurring spots that need re-treatment. (See "Recurring Spots", Chapter 4.) If the spot persists, consult a pro for options as soon as possible.

## Materials Needed:

Class III: Spotting kit, Vacuum cleaner with attachment removed from hose
Class IV: Spotting kit

| Class III: Towel + Old / Dried Spot | Class IV: Towel + Fresh / Wet Spot |
|---|---|
| **Steps:** | **Steps:** |
| 1. Using your soft brush, gently brush the spot(s) in a side-to-side motion 10 - 15 times. <br> • Vacuum debris with vacuum cleaner hose. | 1. Fold a towel several times and place it over the spot(s). <br> • Step on the towel with your full weight 8 - 10 times, using a clean part of the towel each time. <br> • Repeat until no more absorbs. |
| 2. Mist on a generous amount of ammonia. <br> • Mist on a generous amount of peroxide. <br> • Tamp with soft brush. <br> • Allow to work 2 minutes. | 2. Mist on a small amount of ammonia. <br> • Mist on a small amount of peroxide. <br> • Tamp with soft brush. <br> • Allow to work 2 minutes. |
| 3. With a towel, blot 10 - 15 times, using a clean part of the towel each time. | 3. With a towel, blot 10 - 15 times, using a clean part of the towel each time. |
| 4. Look at spot area carefully to see if the spot is gone: <br> • If YES: Allow to dry. <br> • If NO: Repeat Steps 2 and 3 until no more removes. Then, if needed, do Step 5. | 4. Look at spot area carefully to see if the spot is gone: <br> • If YES: Allow to dry. <br> • If NO: Repeat Steps 2 and 3 until no more removes. Then, if needed, do Step 5. |
| 5. If color cast remains, mist on a generous amount of peroxide. <br> • Tamp with soft brush. <br> • Allow to dry. | 5. If color cast remains, mist on a generous amount of peroxide. <br> • Tamp with soft brush. <br> • Allow to dry. |
| 6. If needed, repeat Steps 2, 3 and 5 one time. | 6. If needed, repeat Steps 2, 3 and 5 one time. |
| 7. If the spot persists, call a pro for options as soon as possible. | 7. If the spot persists, call a pro for options as soon as possible. |

Section II

# Coffee or Tea - With Milk, Cream or Creamer:
## Coffee - Regular, Decaffeinated, Flavored / Tea - Black, Green, Herb

### Comments:

- **Optimum removal time:** Within 24 hours of spill
- **Maximum size for home removal:** Class I / II = 4 inches
- **Removal restrictions:** If the spot(s) is larger than 4 inches in diameter, **do not attempt ANY removal** using Class I or II instructions. Put a dry towel over spot. Call a pro and have spot removed within 2 days.
- **Caution:** Tannin and possible coloring in these products can be hard to remove from nylon, olefin, acrylic and polyester, especially when spilled hot. If you cannot remove a spot, consult a pro for options within 2 days.
- Large spills may cause recurring spots that need re-treatment. (See "Recurring Spots", Chapter 4.) If the spot persists, consult a pro for options as soon as possible.

### Materials Needed:
Class I / II: Spotting kit, Spot machine with warm water

## Class I: Spot Machine + Old / Dried Spot

### Steps:

1. Using your spot machine, rinse the spot(s) with warm water using the chop stroke technique 8 - 25 times.
   - Take 4 - 12 slow, dry vacuum strokes.
   - Repeat entire Step until no more removes.

2. Mist on a generous amount of ammonia.
   - Mist on a generous amount of peroxide.
   - Agitate with hard brush.
   - Allow to work 2 minutes.

3. With the spot machine, rinse with warm water using the chop stroke technique 6 - 10 times.
   - Take 4 - 8 slow, dry vacuum strokes.

4. Look at spot area carefully to see if the spot is gone:
   - If YES: Allow to dry.
   - If NO: Repeat Steps 2 and 3 until no more removes.. Then, if needed, do Step 5.

5. If color cast remains, mist on a generous amount of peroxide.
   - Tamp with soft brush.
   - Allow to dry.

6. If needed, repeat Steps 2, 3 and 5 one time.

7. If the spot persists, call a pro for options as soon as possible.

## Class II: Spot Machine + Fresh / Wet Spot

### Steps:

1. Fold a towel several times and place it over the spot(s).
   - Step on the towel with your full weight 8 - 10 times, using a clean part of the towel each time.
   - Repeat until no more absorbs.

2. Mist on a generous amount of ammonia.
   - Mist on a generous amount of peroxide.
   - Tamp with soft brush.
   - Allow to work 1 minute.

3. With the spot machine, rinse with warm water using the chop stroke technique 4 - 6 times.
   - Take 3 - 5 slow, dry vacuum strokes.

4. Look at spot area carefully to see if the spot is gone:
   - If YES: Allow to dry.
   - If NO: Repeat Steps 2 and 3 until no more removes. Then, if needed, do Step 5.

5. If color cast remains, mist on a generous amount of peroxide.
   - Tamp with soft brush.
   - Allow to dry.

6. If needed, repeat Steps 2, 3 and 5 one time.

7. If the spot persists, call a pro for options as soon as possible.

*Spot / Stain Contents: Acids, Artificial Color, Fat, Possible Sugar, Protein, Tannin*

## *Comments:*

- **Optimum removal time:** Within 24 hours of spill
- **Maximum size for home removal:** Class III / IV = 2 1/2 inches
- **Removal restrictions:** If the spot(s) is larger than 2 1/2 inches in diameter, **do not attempt TOTAL removal** using Class III or IV instructions. Do Step 1 **only** under Class III or IV. Put a dry towel over spot. Then:
  - Call a pro and have spot removed within 2 days. -OR-
  - If the spot is 4 inches or less in diameter, get a spot machine and:
    - If the spot is now old/dried, do Steps 1 - 7 under Class I.
    - If the spot is still fresh/wet, do Steps 2 - 7 under Class II.
- **Caution:** Tannin and possible coloring in these products can be hard to remove from nylon, olefin, acrylic and polyester, especially when spilled hot. If you cannot remove a spot, consult a pro for options within 2 days.
- Large spills may cause recurring spots that need re-treatment. (See "Recurring Spots", Chapter 4.) If the spot persists, consult a pro for options as soon as possible.

---

## *Materials Needed:*

Class III: Spotting kit, Vacuum cleaner with attachment removed from hose
Class IV: Spotting kit

| *Class III: Towel + Old / Dried Spot* | *Class IV: Towel + Fresh / Wet Spot* |
|---|---|
| *Steps:* | *Steps:* |
| 1. Using your soft brush, gently brush the spot(s) in a side-to-side motion 10 - 15 times.<br>• Vacuum debris with vacuum cleaner. | 1. Fold a towel several times and place it over the spot(s).<br>• Step on the towel with your full weight 8 - 10 times, using a clean part of the towel each time.<br>• Repeat until no more absorbs. |
| 2. Mist on a generous amount of ammonia.<br>• Mist on a generous amount of peroxide.<br>• Agitate with hard brush.<br>• Allow to work 2 minutes. | 2. Mist on a generous amount of ammonia.<br>• Mist on a generous amount of peroxide.<br>• Tamp with soft brush.<br>• Allow to work 2 minutes. |
| 3. With a towel, blot 10 - 15 times, using a clean part of the towel each time. | 3. With a towel, blot 10 - 15 times, using a clean part of the towel each time. |
| 4. Look at spot area carefully to see if the spot is gone:<br>• If YES: Allow to dry.<br>• If NO: Repeat Steps 2 and 3 until no more removes. Then, if needed, do Step 5. | 4. Look at spot area carefully to see if the spot is gone:<br>• If YES: Allow to dry.<br>• If NO: Repeat Steps 2 and 3 until no more removes. Then, if needed, do Step 5. |
| 5. If color cast remains, mist on a generous amount of peroxide.<br>• Tamp with soft brush.<br>• Allow to dry. | 5. If color cast remains, mist on a generous amount of peroxide.<br>• Tamp with soft brush.<br>• Allow to dry. |
| 6. If needed, repeat Steps 2, 3 and 5 one time. | 6. If needed, repeat Steps 2, 3 and 5 one time. |
| 7. If the spot persists, call a pro for options as soon as possible. | 7. If the spot persists, call a pro for options as soon as possible. |

*Section II*

# Cooking Oil, Salad Dressing - Oily

## Comments:

- **Optimum removal time:** Within 24 hours of spill
- **Maximum size for home removal:** Class I / II = 3 inches
- **Removal restrictions:** If the spot(s) is larger than 3 inches in diameter, **do not attempt TOTAL removal** using Class I or II instructions. Do Step 1 **only** under Class I or II. Put a dry towel over spot. Call a pro and have spot removed within 3 days.
- Large spills can soak through the carpet and pad to the subfloor and cause recurring spots. (See "Recurring Spots", Chapter 4.) Consult a pro for options as soon as possible.

## Materials Needed:

Class I / II: Spotting kit, Spot machine with hot water

### Class I: Spot Machine + Old / Dried Spot

**Steps:**

1. Fold a towel several times and place it over the spot(s).
   - Step on the towel with your full weight 8 - 10 times, using a clean part of the towel each time.
   - Repeat until no more absorbs.

2. Mist on a generous amount of alcohol.
   - Tamp with soft brush.
   - Allow to work 1 minute.
   - Mist on a generous amount of ammonia.
   - Tamp with soft brush.

3. With the spot machine, rinse with hot water using the chop stroke technique 6 - 8 times.
   - Take 4 - 6 slow, dry vacuum strokes.

4. Look at and touch spot area carefully to see if the oily residue is gone:
   - If YES: Allow to dry.
   - If NO: Repeat Steps 2 and 3 until no more removes. Then, if needed, do Step 5.

5. If color cast remains, mist on a generous amount of peroxide.
   - Tamp with soft brush.
   - Allow to dry.

6. If needed, repeat Steps 2, 3 and 5 one time.

7. If the spot persists, call a pro for options as soon as possible.

### Class II: Spot Machine + Fresh / Wet Spot

**Steps:**

1. Fold a towel several times and place it over the spot(s).
   - Step on the towel with your full weight 8 - 10 times, using a clean part of the towel each time.
   - Repeat until no more absorbs.

2. Mist on a generous amount of alcohol.
   - Tamp with soft brush.
   - Allow to work 1 minute.
   - Mist on a generous amount of ammonia.
   - Tamp with soft brush.

3. With the spot machine, rinse with hot water using the chop stroke technique 6 - 8 times.
   - Take 4 - 6 slow, dry vacuum strokes.

4. Look at and touch spot area carefully to see if the oily residue is gone:
   - If YES: Allow to dry.
   - If NO: Repeat Steps 2 and 3 until no more removes. Then, if needed, do Step 5.

5. If color cast remains, mist on a generous amount of peroxide.
   - Tamp with soft brush.
   - Allow to dry.

6. If needed, repeat Steps 2, 3 and 5 one time.

7. If the spot persists, call a pro for options as soon as possible.

Section II

## *Comments:*

- **Optimum removal time:** Within 24 hours of spill
- **Maximum size for home removal:** Class III / IV = 2 inches
- **Removal restrictions:** If the spot(s) is larger than 2 inches in diameter, **do not attempt TOTAL removal** using Class III or IV instructions. Do Step 1 **only** under Class III or IV. Put a dry towel over spot. Then:
  - Call a pro and have spot removed within 3 days. -OR-
  - If the spot is 3 inches or less in diameter, get a spot machine and:
    - If the spot is now old/dried, do Steps 2 - 7 under Class I.
    - If the spot is still fresh/wet, do Steps 2 - 7 under Class II.
- Large spills can soak through the carpet and pad to the subfloor and cause recurring spots. (See "Recurring Spots", Chapter 4.) Consult a pro for options as soon as possible.

## *Materials Needed:*
Class III / IV: Spotting kit

### *Class III: Towel + Old / Dried Spot*

#### *Steps:*

1. Fold a towel several times and place it over the spot(s).
   - Step on the towel with your full weight 8 - 10 times, using a clean part of the towel each time.
   - Repeat until no more absorbs.

2. Mist on a generous amount of alcohol.
   - Tamp with soft brush.
   - Allow to work 2 minutes.
   - Mist on a small amount of ammonia.
   - Tamp with soft brush.

3. Fold a towel several times and place it over the spot(s).
   - Firmly press down onto towel 8 - 10 times, using a clean part of the towel each time.

4. Look at and touch spot area carefully to see if the oily residue is gone:
   - If YES: Allow to dry.
   - If NO: Repeat Steps 2 and 3 until no more removes. Then, if needed, do Step 5.

5. If color cast remains, mist on a generous amount of peroxide.
   - Tamp with soft brush.
   - Allow to dry.

6. If needed, repeat Steps 2, 3 and 5 one time.

7. If the spot persists, call a pro for options as soon as possible.

### *Class IV: Towel + Fresh / Wet Spot*

#### *Steps:*

1. Fold a towel several times and place it over the spot(s).
   - Step on the towel with your full weight 8 - 10 times, using a clean part of the towel each time.
   - Repeat until no more absorbs.

2. Mist on a generous amount of alcohol.
   - Tamp with soft brush.
   - Allow to work 2 minutes.
   - Mist on a small amount of ammonia.
   - Tamp with soft brush.

3. Fold a towel several times and place it over the spot(s).
   - Firmly press down onto towel 8 - 10 times, using a clean part of the towel each time.

4. Look at and touch spot area carefully to see if the oily residue is gone:
   - If YES: Allow to dry.
   - If NO: Repeat Steps 2 and 3 until no more removes. Then, if needed, do Step 5.

5. If color cast remains, mist on a generous amount of peroxide.
   - Tamp with soft brush.
   - Allow to dry.

6. If needed, repeat Steps 2, 3 and 5 one time.

7. If the spot persists, call a pro for options as soon as possible.

Section II

# Copier Toner, Laser Jet Printer Ink, Carbon Powder, Finger Print Powder

## Comments:

- **Optimum removal time: As soon as possible** within 24 hours of spill
- **Maximum size for home removal:** Class I / II = 2 1/2 inches
- **Removal restrictions:** If the spot(s) is larger than 2 1/2 inches in diameter, **do not attempt TOTAL removal** using Class I or II instructions. Do Steps 1 and 2 **only** under Class I or II. Put a dry towel over spot and a note next to it that says, **"Do Not Touch Or Clean!"**. Call a pro and have spot removed within 24 hours.
- **Caution:** Do **not** use a vacuum cleaner with a beater bar on this spill. The vibration will force the fine powder deep into the carpet, making the spill even harder to remove. Note: Your vacuum's instruction booklet may tell how to temporarily disable the beater bar. If so, follow those instructions and then use the vacuum to help remove the spot.
- **Caution:** Pigments in these products, especially if exposed to water or high humidity, can permanently stain most nylon if left untreated for as little as one month. Consult a pro for options as soon as possible.

## Materials Needed:

Class I / II: Spotting kit, Vacuum cleaner, Spot machine with hot water

| Class I: Spot Machine + Old / Dried Spot | Class II: Spot Machine + Fresh / Wet Spot |
|---|---|
| **Steps:** | **Steps:** |
| 1. Prepare your vacuum cleaner: <br> • Remove the attachment, if any, from the vacuum cleaner hose. | 1. Prepare your vacuum cleaner: <br> • Remove the attachment, if any, from the vacuum cleaner hose. |
| 2. Using just the vacuum cleaner hose, vacuum the spot very slowly: <br> • Lay the hose so it is flat on the carpet with the opening near the outside edge of the spot. <br> • Slowly push the hose opening from the edge into the middle of the spot from different angles 8 - 10 times until no more will remove. <br> • Lift the hose and place it so the opening is on the carpet directly over the spot. <br> • Move the hose opening slowly in a circular motion clockwise and counterclockwise over and around the edges of the spot. Caution: Keep within the edges of the spot; going outside them could spread the spot. <br> • Repeat entire Step until no more removes. | 2. Using just the vacuum cleaner hose, vacuum the spot very slowly: <br> • Lay the hose so it is flat on the carpet with the opening near the outside edge of the spot. <br> • Slowly push the hose opening from the edge into the middle of the spot from different angles 8 - 10 times until no more will remove. <br> • Lift the hose and place it so the opening is on the carpet directly over the spot. <br> • Move the hose opening slowly in a circular motion clockwise and counterclockwise over and around the edges of the spot. Caution: Keep within the edges of the spot; going outside them could spread the spot. <br> • Repeat entire Step until no more removes. |
| 3. Mist on a small amount of alcohol. <br> • Tamp gently with soft brush. <br> • Allow to work 1 minute. | 3. Mist on a small amount of alcohol. <br> • Tamp gently with soft brush. <br> • Allow to work 1 minute. |
| 4. With the spot machine, rinse with hot water using the chop stroke technique 4 - 6 times. <br> • Take 4 - 6 slow, dry vacuum strokes. | 4. With the spot machine, rinse with hot water using the chop stroke technique 4 - 6 times. <br> • Take 4 - 6 slow, dry vacuum strokes. |
| 5. Look at spot area carefully to see if the spot is gone: <br> • If YES: Allow to dry. <br> • If NO: Repeat Steps 3 and 4 until no more removes. Allow to dry. | 5. Look at spot area carefully to see if the spot is gone: <br> • If YES: Allow to dry. <br> • If NO: Repeat Steps 3 and 4 until no more removes. Allow to dry. |
| 6. If needed, repeat Steps 3 and 4 one time. | 6. If needed, repeat Steps 3 and 4 one time. |
| 7. If the spot persists, call a pro for options as soon as possible. | 7. If the spot persists, call a pro for options as soon as possible. |

Section II

Spot / Stain Contents: Black Pigment, Carbon, Graphite, Iron, Petroleum Oil, Pumice

## Comments:

- **Optimum removal time: As soon as possible** within 24 hours of spill
- **Maximum size for home removal:** Class III / IV = 1 inch
- **Removal restrictions:** If the spot(s) is larger than 1 inch in diameter, **do not attempt TOTAL removal** using Class III or IV instructions. Do Steps 1 and 2 **only** under Class III or IV. Put a dry towel over spot and a note next to it that says, *"Do Not Touch Or Clean!"*. Then:
  - Call a pro and have spot removed within 24 hours. -OR-
  - If the spot is 2 1/2 inches or less in diameter, get a spot machine and:
    - If the spot is now old/dried, do Steps 3 - 7 under Class I.
    - If the spot is still fresh/wet, do Steps 3 - 7 under Class II.
- **Caution:** Do **not** use a vacuum cleaner with a beater bar on this spill. The vibration will force the fine powder deep into the carpet, making the spill even harder to remove. Note: Your vacuum's instruction booklet may tell how to temporarily disable the beater bar. If so, follow those instructions and then use the vacuum to help remove the spot.
- **Caution:** Pigments in these products, especially if exposed to water or high humidity, can permanently stain most nylon if left untreated for as little as one month. Consult a pro for options as soon as possible.

## Materials Needed:

Class III / IV: Ruler, Vacuum cleaner, Towel, Paper and pencil for note

## Class III: Towel + Old / Dried Spot

### Steps:

1. Prepare your vacuum cleaner:
   - Remove the attachment, if any, from the vacuum cleaner hose.

2. Using just the vacuum cleaner hose, vacuum the spot very slowly:
   - Lay the hose so it is flat on the carpet with the opening near the outside edge of the spot.
   - Slowly push the hose opening from the edge into the middle of the spot from different angles 8 - 10 times until no more will remove.
   - Lift the hose and place it so the opening is on the carpet directly over the spot.
   - Move the hose opening slowly in a circular motion clockwise and counterclockwise over and around the edges of the spot. Caution: Keep within the edges of the spot; going outside them could spread the spot.
   - Repeat entire Step until no more removes.

3. If extra fine powder remains visible within the carpet fibers, **do not continue removal** of a Class III spot(s).
   - Put a dry towel over spot and a note next to it that says, *"Do Not Touch Or Clean!"*. Then:
     - Call a pro and have spot removed as soon as possible. -OR-
     - If the spot is 2 1/2 inches or less in diameter, get a spot machine and do Steps 3 - 7 under Class I.

## Class IV: Towel + Fresh / Wet Spot

### Steps:

1. Prepare your vacuum cleaner:
   - Remove the attachment, if any, from the vacuum cleaner hose.

2. Using just the vacuum cleaner hose, vacuum the spot very slowly:
   - Lay the hose so it is flat on the carpet with the opening near the outside edge of the spot.
   - Slowly push the hose opening from the edge into the middle of the spot from different angles 8 - 10 times until no more will remove.
   - Lift the hose and place it so the opening is on the carpet directly over the spot.
   - Move the hose opening slowly in a circular motion clockwise and counterclockwise over and around the edges of the spot. Repeat until no more removes. Caution: Keep within the edges of the spot; going outside them could spread the spot.
   - Repeat entire Step until no more removes.

3. If extra fine powder remains visible within the carpet fibers, **do not continue removal** of a Class IV spot(s).
   - Put a dry towel over spot and a note next to it that says, *"Do Not Touch Or Clean!"*. Then:
     - Call a pro and have spot removed as soon as possible. -OR-
     - If the spot is 2 1/2 inches or less in diameter, get a spot machine and do Steps 3 - 7 under Class II.

# Correction Fluid, Epoxy with Catalyst

## Comments:

- **Optimum removal time:** Within 24 hours of spill
- **Maximum size for home removal:** Class I / II = 3/8 inch (pencil eraser size)
- **Removal restrictions:** See "Class I" or "Class II" instructions below.
- **Caution: Do not attempt scissors removal** of spots from **any** type of looped carpet (berber, commercial glue down, etc.) unless the spot is **only on the outside fibers** of the loop(s). If in doubt, call a pro for options as soon as possible
- These products are very hard to remove, but they are very thick and will usually dry on top of the carpet fibers. Except on some looped carpets, most of these spills can be easily trimmed away with a pair of scissors after they have hardened.

## Materials Needed:

Class I / II - 3/8 inch or less: Ruler, Scissors, Spot machine
Class I / II - larger than 3/8 inch: Ruler, Paper and pencil for note

<table>
<tr>
<td>

## Class I: Spot Machine + Old / Dried Spot

### Steps:

**Follow the instructions for your size spot(s):**

**If the spot is 3/8 inch (pencil eraser size) or smaller:**

1. Using your scissors, wedge the blades up under the spot(s) and snip the hardened parts from the very tip of the carpet fibers. (This will minimize the indentations caused by the removed spots.)
Note: On non-looped carpet, you can also trim a few carpet fibers around the edge of the removed spot, if needed, to minimize it further.
   - On non-looped carpets, rough up the trimmed carpet fibers a little with the tips of your scissors. Trim any taller roughed up fibers so they are equal in height with the rest of the carpet.
   - Vacuum debris with spot machine.

**If the spot is larger than 3/8 inch (pencil eraser size):**

1. **Do nothing but protect** the spill area! Do **not** attempt ANY removal!
   - Put a note that says, "*Do Not Touch Or Clean!*" next to the spot. Caution: Do **not** put a towel over this spot.
2. Call a pro and have the spot removed within 3 days of the spill.

</td>
<td>

## Class II: Spot Machine + Fresh / Wet Spot

### Steps:

**Follow the instructions for your size spot(s):**

**If the spot is 3/8 inch (pencil eraser size) or smaller:**

1. Allow spot to dry completely.

2. Using your scissors, wedge the blades up under the spot(s) and snip the hardened parts from the very tip of the carpet fibers. (This will minimize the indentations caused by the removed spots.)
Note: On non-looped carpet, you can also trim a few carpet fibers around the edge of the removed spot, if needed, to minimize it further.
   - On non-looped carpets, rough up the trimmed carpet fibers a little with the tips of your scissors. Trim any taller roughed up fibers so they are equal in height with the rest of the carpet.
   - Vacuum debris with spot machine.

**If the spot is larger than 3/8 inch (pencil eraser size):**

1. **Do nothing but protect** the spill area! Do **not** attempt ANY removal!
   - Put a note that says, "*Do Not Touch Or Clean!*" next to the spot. Caution: Do **not** put a towel over this spot.
   - Keep all pets and people out of the area to avoid spreading the spill.
   - Allow spot to dry.
2. Call a pro and have the spot removed within 3 days of the spill.

</td>
</tr>
</table>

Section II

# Correction Fluid, Epoxy with Catalyst

Spot Contents: Naphtha, Mineral Oil, Mustard Oil, Titanium Dioxide

## Comments:

- **Optimum removal time:** Within 24 hours of spill
- **Maximum size for home removal:** Class III / IV = 3/8 inch (pencil eraser size)
- **Removal restrictions:** See "Class III" or "Class IV" instructions below.
- **Caution: Do not attempt scissors removal** of spots from **any** type of looped carpet (berber, commercial glue down, etc.) unless the spot is **only on the outside fibers** of the loop(s). If in doubt, call a pro for options as soon as possible.
- These products are very hard to remove. However, they are very thick and will usually dry on top of the carpet fibers. Except on some looped carpets, most of these spills can be easily trimmed away with a pair of scissors after they have hardened.

## Materials Needed:

Class III / IV - 3/8 inch or less: Ruler, Scissors, Vacuum cleaner with attachment removed from hose
Class III / IV - larger than 3/8 inch: Ruler, Paper and pencil for note

## Class III: Towel + Old / Dried Spot

### Steps:
**Follow the instructions for your size spot(s):**

**If the spot is 3/8 inch (pencil eraser size) or smaller:**

1. Using your scissors, wedge the blades up under the spot(s) and snip the hardened parts from the very tip of the carpet fibers. (This will minimize the indentations caused by the removed spots.) Note: On non-looped carpet, you can also trim a few carpet fibers around the edge of the removed spot, if needed, to minimize it further.
   - On non-looped carpets, rough up the trimmed carpet fibers a little with the tips of your scissors. Trim any taller roughed up fibers so they are equal in height with the rest of the carpet.
   - Vacuum debris with vacuum cleaner hose.

**If the spot is larger than 3/8 inch (pencil eraser size):**

1. **Do nothing but protect** the spill area! Do **not** attempt ANY removal!
   - Put a note that says, "***Do Not Touch Or Clean!***" next to the spot. Caution: Do **not** put a towel over this spot.
2. Call a pro and have the spot removed within 3 days of the spill.

## Class IV: Towel + Fresh / Wet Spot

### Steps:
**Follow the instructions for your size spot(s):**

**If the spot is 3/8 inch (pencil eraser size) or smaller:**

1. Allow spot to dry completely.
2. Using your scissors, wedge the blades up under the spot and snip the hardened parts from the very tip of the carpet fibers. (This will minimize the indentations caused by the removed spots.) Note: On non-looped carpet, you can also trim a few carpet fibers around the edge of the removed spot, if needed, to minimize it further.
   - On non-looped carpets, rough up the trimmed carpet fibers a little with the tips of your scissors. Trim any taller roughed up fibers so they are equal in height with the rest of the carpet.
   - Vacuum debris with vacuum cleaner hose.

**If the spot is larger than 3/8 inch (pencil eraser size):**

1. **Do nothing but protect** the spill area! Do **not** attempt ANY removal!
   - Put a note that says, "***Do Not Touch Or Clean!***" next to the spot. Do **not** put a towel over this spot.
   - Keep all pets and people out of the area to avoid spreading the spill.
   - Allow spot to dry.
2. Call a pro and have the spot removed within 3 days of the spill

*Art's Ultimate Spot Cleaning • **Chapter 5 Treatment Steps - Page 45***

# Cosmetics - Creamy: Foundation, Lotion, Moisturizer, Etc.

## Comments:

- **Optimum removal time:** Within 24 hours of spill
- **Maximum size for home removal:** Class I / II = 2 inches
- **Removal restrictions:** If the spot(s) is larger than 2 inches in diameter, **do not attempt TOTAL removal** using Class I or II instructions. Do Step 1 **only** under Class I or II. Put a dry towel over spot. Call a pro and have spot removed within 2 days.
- Pigments in some products can immediately and permanently stain some nylon. If you cannot remove a spot, consult a pro for options as soon as possible.

## Materials Needed:

Class I / II: Spotting kit, Spot machine with hot water

## Class I: Spot Machine + Old / Dried Spot

### Steps:

1. Lay a small towel over the palm of your hand. Then lay your hand on the carpet so the towel is at the edge of the spot.
   - Using your spoon, scoop as much of the spot(s) as possible onto the towel. Note: After each scoop, wipe the spoon on a clean part of the towel.
   - Vacuum with spot machine.
   - Repeat entire Step until no more removes.

2. Mist on a generous amount of alcohol.
   - Allow to work 1 minute.
   - Agitate with hard brush.
   - Mist on a generous amount of ammonia.
   - Agitate with hard brush.
   - Allow to work 1 minute.

3. With the spot machine, rinse with hot water using the chop stroke technique 6 - 8 times.
   - Take 4 - 6 slow, dry vacuum strokes.

4. Look at spot area carefully to see if the spot is gone:
   - If YES: Allow to dry.
   - If NO: Repeat Steps 2 and 3 until no more removes. Then, if needed, do Step 5.

5. If color cast remains, mist on a generous amount of peroxide.
   - Tamp with soft brush.
   - Allow to dry.

6. If needed, repeat Steps 2, 3 and 5 one time.

7. If the spot persists, call a pro for options as soon as possible.

## Class II: Spot Machine + Fresh / Wet Spot

### Steps:

1. Lay a small towel over the palm of your hand. Then lay your hand on the carpet so the towel is at the edge of the spot.
   - Using your spoon, scoop as much of the spot(s) as possible onto the towel. Note: After each scoop, wipe the spoon on a clean part of the towel.
   - Vacuum with spot machine.
   - Repeat entire Step until no more removes.

2. Mist on a generous amount of alcohol.
   - Allow to work 1 minute.
   - Agitate with hard brush.
   - Mist on a small amount of ammonia.
   - Agitate with hard brush.

3. With the spot machine, rinse with hot water using the chop stroke technique 6 - 8 times.
   - Take 4 - 6 slow, dry vacuum strokes.

4. Look at spot area carefully to see if the spot is gone:
   - If YES: Allow to dry.
   - If NO: Repeat Steps 2 and 3 until no more removes. Then, if needed, do Step 5.

5. If color cast remains, mist on a generous amount of peroxide.
   - Tamp with soft brush.
   - Allow to dry.

6. If needed, repeat Steps 2, 3 and 5 one time.

7. If the spot persists, call a pro for options as soon as possible.

Spot Contents: Ammine, Fatty Acid, Glycerin, Lanolin, Moisturizer, Perfume, Pigment, Wax

## Comments:

- **Optimum removal time:** Within 24 hours of spill
- **Maximum size for home removal:** Class III / IV = 1 inch
- **Removal restrictions:** If the spot(s) is larger than 1 inch in diameter, **do not attempt TOTAL removal** using Class III or IV instructions. Do Step 1 **only** under Class III or IV. Put a dry towel over spot. Then:
  - Call a pro and have spot removed within 2 days. -OR-
  - If the spot is 2 inches or less in diameter, get a spot machine and:
    - If the spot is now old/dried, do Steps 2 - 7 under Class I.
    - If the spot is still fresh/wet, do Steps 2 - 7 under Class II.
- Pigments in some products can immediately and permanently stain some nylon. If you cannot remove a spot, consult a pro for options as soon as possible.

## Materials Needed:

Class III / IV: Spotting kit

### Class III: Towel + Old / Dried Spot

**Steps:**

1. Lay a small towel over the palm of your hand. Then lay your hand on the carpet so the towel is at the edge of the spot.
   - Using your spoon, scoop as much of the spot(s) as possible onto the towel. Note: After each scoop, wipe the spoon on a clean part of the towel.
2. Mist on a generous amount of alcohol.
   - Allow to work 2 minutes.
   - Agitate with hard brush.
   - Mist on a small amount of ammonia.
   - Agitate with hard brush.
   - Allow to work 1 minute.
3. With a towel, firmly blot 10 - 15 times, using a clean part of the towel each time.
4. Look at spot area carefully to see if the spot is gone:
   - If YES: Allow to dry.
   - If NO: Repeat Steps 2 and 3 until no more removes. Then, if needed, do Step 5.
5. If color cast remains, mist on a generous amount of peroxide.
   - Tamp with soft brush.
   - Allow to dry.
6. If needed, repeat Steps 2, 3 and 5 one time.
7. If the spot persists, call a pro for options as soon as possible.

### Class IV: Towel + Fresh / Wet Spot

**Steps:**

1. Lay a small towel over the palm of your hand. Then lay your hand on the carpet so the towel is at the edge of the spot.
   - Using your spoon, scoop as much of the spot(s) as possible onto the towel. Note: After each scoop, wipe the spoon on a clean part of the towel.
2. Mist on a generous amount of alcohol.
   - Allow to work 2 minutes.
   - Agitate with hard brush.
   - Mist on a small amount of ammonia.
   - Agitate with hard brush.
3. With a towel, firmly blot 10 - 15 times, using a clean part of the towel each time.
4. Look at spot area carefully to see if the spot is gone:
   - If YES: Allow to dry.
   - If NO: Repeat Steps 2 and 3 until no more removes. Then, if needed, do Step 5.
5. If color cast remains, mist on a generous amount of peroxide.
   - Tamp with soft brush.
   - Allow to dry.
6. If needed, repeat Steps 2, 3 and 5 one time.
7. If the spot persists, call a pro for options as soon as possible.

Section II

# Cosmetics - Waxy / Powder:
## Eye Liner, Lipstick, Mascara, Rouge, Blush, Eye Shadow, Etc.

### Comments:

- **Optimum removal time:** Within 24 hours of spill
- **Maximum size for home removal:** Class I / II = 1 1/2 inches
- **Removal restrictions:** If the spot(s) is larger than 1 1/2 inches in diameter, **do not attempt TOTAL removal** using Class I or II instructions. Do Step 1 **only** under Class I or II. Put a dry towel over spot. Call a pro and have spot removed within 2 days.
- **Caution: Do not attempt scissors removal** of spots from **any** type of looped carpet (berber, commercial glue down, etc.) unless the spot is **only on the outside fibers** of the loop(s). If in doubt, call a pro for options as soon as possible.
- Pigments in some products can immediately and permanently stain some nylon. If you cannot remove a spot, consult a pro for options as soon as possible.

### Materials Needed:
Class I / II: Spotting kit, Spot machine with hot water

## Class I: Spot Machine + Old / Dried Spot

### Steps:

1. Using your scissors, wedge the blades up under the spot(s) and snip it only from the very tips of the carpet fibers. (You are only trying to get the heavier matter out by cutting just the spot, not the carpet.)
   - Vacuum debris with spot machine.

2. Using your dinner knife, scrape out as much of the spot(s) as possible. Note: Clean the knife on the small towel after each scrape.
   - Repeat until no more removes.
   - Vacuum debris with spot machine.

3. With a towel, firmly blot 15 - 20 times, using a clean part of the towel each time.

4. Mist on a generous amount of alcohol.
   - Allow to work 1 minute.
   - Agitate with hard brush.
   - Mist on a generous amount of ammonia.
   - Agitate with hard brush.
   - Allow to work 1 minute.

5. With the spot machine, rinse with hot water using the chop stroke technique 8 - 10 times.
   - Take 6 - 8 slow, dry vacuum strokes.

6. Look at spot area carefully to see if the spot is gone:
   - If YES: Allow to dry.
   - If NO: Repeat Steps 4 and 5 until no more removes. Then, if needed, do Step 7.

7. If color cast remains, mist on a generous amount of peroxide.
   - Tamp with soft brush.
   - Blot once with a towel.
   - Allow to dry.

8. If needed, repeat Steps 4, 5 and 7 one time.

9. If the spot persists, call a pro for options as soon as possible.

## Class II: Spot Machine + Fresh / Wet Spot

### Steps:

1. Using your scissors, wedge the blades up under the spot(s) and snip it only from the very tips of the carpet fibers. (You are only trying to get the heavier matter out by cutting just the spot, not the carpet.)
   - Vacuum debris with spot machine.

2. Using your dinner knife, scrape out as much of the spot(s) as possible. Note: Clean the knife on the small towel after each scrape.
   - Repeat until no more removes.
   - Vacuum debris with spot machine.

3. With a towel, firmly blot 15 - 20 times, using a clean part of the towel each time.

4. Mist on a generous amount of alcohol.
   - Allow to work 1 minute.
   - Agitate with hard brush.
   - Mist on a generous amount of ammonia.
   - Agitate with hard brush.

5. With the spot machine, rinse with hot water using the chop stroke technique 8 - 10 times.
   - Take 6 - 8 slow, dry vacuum strokes.

6. Look at spot area carefully to see if the spot is gone:
   - If YES: Allow to dry.
   - If NO: Repeat Steps 4 and 5 until no more removes. Then, if needed, do Step 7.

7. If color cast remains, mist on a generous amount of peroxide.
   - Tamp with soft brush.
   - Blot once with a towel.
   - Allow to dry.

8. If needed, repeat Steps 4, 5 and 7 one time.

9. If the spot persists, call a pro for options as soon as possible.

# Cosmetics - Waxy / Powder: Eye Liner, Lipstick, Mascara, Rouge, Blush, Eye Shadow, Etc.

Spot Contents: Ammine, Fatty Acid, Glycerin, Lanolin, Moisturizer, Perfume, Pigment, Wax

## Comments:

- **Optimum removal time:** Within 24 hours of spill
- **Maximum size for removal:** Class III / IV = 1/2 inch
- **Removal restrictions:** If the spot(s) is larger than 1/2 inch in diameter, **do not attempt TOTAL removal** using Class III or IV instructions. Do Step 1 **only** under Class III or IV. Put a dry towel over spot. Then:
  - Call a pro and have spot removed within 2 days. -OR-
  - If the spot is 1 1/2 inches or less in diameter, get a spot machine and:
    - If the spot is now old/dried, do Steps 2 - 9 under Class I.
    - If the spot is still fresh/wet, do Steps 2 - 9 under Class II.
- **Caution: Do not attempt scissors removal** of spots from any type of looped carpet (berber, commercial glue down, etc.) unless the spot is **only on the outside fibers** of the loop(s). If in doubt, call a pro for options as soon as possible.
- Pigments in some products can immediately and permanently stain some nylon. If you cannot remove a spot, consult a pro for options as soon as possible.

## Materials Needed:

Class III / IV: Spotting kit, Vacuum cleaner with attachment removed from hose

### Class III: Towel + Old / Dried Spot

**Steps:**

1. Using your scissors, wedge the blades up under the spot(s) and snip it only from the very tips of the carpet fibers. (You are only trying to get the heavier matter out by cutting just the spot, not the carpet.)
   - Vacuum debris with vacuum cleaner hose.

2. Using your dinner knife, scrape out as much of the spot as possible. Note: Clean the knife on the small towel after each scrape.
   - Repeat until no more removes.
   - Vacuum debris with vacuum cleaner hose.

3. With a towel, firmly blot 15 - 20 times, using a clean part of the towel each time.

4. Mist on a generous amount of alcohol.
   - Allow to work 2 minutes.
   - Agitate with hard brush.
   - Mist on a generous amount of ammonia.
   - Agitate with hard brush.
   - Allow to work 1 minute.

5. With a towel, firmly blot 15 - 20 times, using a clean part of the towel each time.

6. Look at spot area carefully to see if the spot is gone:
   - If YES: Allow to dry.
   - If NO: Repeat Steps 4 and 5 until no more removes. Then, if needed, do Step 7.

7. If color cast remains, mist on a generous amount of peroxide.
   - Tamp with soft brush.
   - Blot once with a towel.
   - Allow to dry.

8. If needed, repeat Steps 4, 5 and 7 one time.

9. If the spot persists, call a pro for options as soon as possible.

### Class IV: Towel + Fresh / Wet Spot

**Steps:**

1. Using your scissors, wedge the blades up under the spot(s) and snip it only from the very tips of the carpet fibers. (You are only trying to get the heavier matter out by cutting just the spot, not the carpet.)
   - Vacuum debris with vacuum cleaner hose.

2. Using your dinner knife, scrape out as much of the spot as possible. Note: Clean the knife on the small towel after each scrape.
   - Repeat until no more removes.
   - Vacuum debris with vacuum cleaner hose.

3. With a towel, firmly blot 15 - 20 times, using a clean part of the towel each time.

4. Mist on a generous amount of alcohol.
   - Allow to work 1 minute.
   - Agitate with hard brush.
   - Mist on a generous amount of ammonia.
   - Agitate with hard brush.

5. With a towel, firmly blot 15 - 20 times, using a clean part of the towel each time.

6. Look at spot area carefully to see if the spot is gone:
   - If YES: Allow to dry.
   - If NO: Repeat Steps 4 and 5 until no more removes. Then, if needed, do Step 7.

7. If color cast remains, mist on a generous amount of peroxide.
   - Tamp with soft brush.
   - Blot once with a towel.
   - Allow to dry.

8. If needed, repeat Steps 4, 5 and 7 one time.

9. If the spot persists, call a pro for options as soon as possible.

Section II

# Cough Syrup, Other Liquid Medicines

## Comments:

- **Optimum removal time: As soon as possible** within 24 hours of spill
- **Maximum size for home removal:** Class I / II = 1 1/2 inches
- **Removal restrictions:** If the spot(s) is larger than 1 1/2 inches in diameter, **do not attempt TOTAL removal** using Class I or II instructions. Do Steps 1 - 2 **only** under Class I or Step 1 **only** under Class II. Put a damp, folded towel over spot. Call a pro and have spot removed as soon as possible within 24 hours.
- Coloring or Mercurochrome in these products can immediately and permanently stain nylon. If you cannot remove a spot, consult a pro for options as soon as possible.

## Materials Needed:

Class I / II: Spotting kit, Spot machine with warm water

### Class I: Spot Machine + Old / Dried Spot

#### Steps:

1. Using the tip of the blade of your dinner knife and the end of the spoon handle, gently separate stuck together fibers into as many individual tufts as possible.

2. With the spot machine, rinse the spot(s) with warm water using the chop stroke technique 8 - 10 times.
   - Take 6 - 8 slow dry vacuum strokes.

3. Mist on a generous amount of ammonia.
   - Agitate with hard brush.
   - Allow to work 2 minutes.

4. With the spot machine, rinse with warm water using the single stroke technique 6 - 8 times.
   - Take 4 - 6 slow, dry vacuum strokes.

5. Look at and touch spot area carefully to see if the sticky residue is gone:
   - If YES: Allow to dry.
   - If NO: Repeat Steps 3 and 4 until no more removes. Then, if needed, do Step 6.

6. If color cast remains, mist on a generous amount of peroxide.
   - Mist on a small amount of ammonia.
   - Tamp with soft brush.
   - Allow to dry.

7. If needed, repeat Steps 3, 4 and 6 one time.

8. If the spot persists, call a pro for options as soon as possible.

### Class II: Spot Machine + Fresh / Wet Spot

#### Steps:

1. Using your spot machine, rinse the spot(s) with warm water using the chop stroke technique 6 - 8 times.
   - Take 4 - 6 slow dry vacuum strokes.

2. Mist on a generous amount of ammonia.
   - Agitate with hard brush.
   - Allow to work 1 minute.

3. With the spot machine, rinse with warm water using the single stroke technique 10 - 15 times.
   - Take 6 - 8 slow, dry vacuum strokes.

4. Look at and touch spot area carefully to see if the sticky residue is gone:
   - If YES: Allow to dry.
   - If NO: Repeat Steps 2 and 3 until no more removes. Then, if needed, do Step 5.

5. If color cast remains, mist on a generous amount of peroxide.
   - Mist on a small amount of ammonia.
   - Tamp with soft brush.
   - Allow to dry.

6. If needed, repeat Steps 2, 3 and 5 one time.

7. If the spot persists, call a pro for options as soon as possible.

Spot / Stain Contents: Coloring, Menthol, Mercurochrome, Sugar

## *Comments:*

• **Optimum removal time: As soon as possible** within 24 hours of spill
• **Maximum size for home removal:** Class III / IV = No home removal
• **Removal restrictions:** See "Class III" or "Class IV" instructions below.
• Coloring or Mercurochrome in these products can immediately and permanently stain nylon. Consult a pro for options as soon as possible.

## *Materials Needed:*

Class III: Towel, Paper and pencil for note
Class IV: Spotting kit, Paper and pencil for note

### *Class III: Towel + Old / Dried Spot*

**Steps:**

1. **Do not attempt ANY removal** of a Class III spot(s).

   • Put a dry towel over the spot(s) to prevent spreading sticky residue.

   • Put a note next to the towel that says, ***"Do Not Touch Or Clean!"***

   • Then:
   - Call a pro and have spot removed as soon as possible within 24 hours. -OR-
   - If the spot is 1 1/2 inches or less in diameter, get a spot machine and do Steps 1 - 8 under Class I.

### *Class IV: Towel + Fresh / Wet Spot*

**Steps:**

1. **Do not attempt TOTAL removal** using Class IV instructions.

2. With a towel, blot the spot(s), using a clean part of the towel each time.

   • Repeat until no more absorbs.

3. Mist on a small amount of ammonia.

   • Tamp with soft brush.

4. Put a folded towel moistened with water over the spot(s) to prevent spreading sticky residue.

   • Put a note next to the towel that says, ***"Do Not Touch Or Clean!"***

   • Then:
   - Call a pro and have spot removed as soon as possible within 24 hours. -OR-
   - If the spot is 1 1/2 inches or less in diameter, get a spot machine and:
     - If the spot is old/dried, do Steps 1 - 8 under Class I.
     - If the spot is fresh/wet, do Steps 1 - 7 under Class II.

Section II

# Crayon, Oil Crayon, Pastels, Etc.

## Comments:

- **Optimum removal time:** Within 24 hours of spill
- **Maximum size for home removal:** Class I / II = 1 inch
- **Removal restrictions:** If the spot(s) is larger than 1 inch in diameter, **do not attempt TOTAL removal** using Class I or II instructions. Do Step 1 **only** under Class I or II. Put a dry towel over spot. Call a pro and have spot removed within 3 days.
- **Caution:** Pigments in these products can permanently stain nylon if left untreated as little as 7 days. If you cannot remove a spot, consult a pro for options as soon as possible.

## Materials Needed:

Class I / II: Spotting kit, Spot machine with hot water, Hair dryer

| Class I: Spot Machine + Old / Dried Spot | Class II: Spot Machine + Fresh / Wet Spot |
|---|---|
| **Steps:** | **Steps:** |
| 1. Using your dinner knife, scrape up as much of the spot(s) as possible. Note: After each scrape, wipe the knife on a clean part of the towel. <br> • Vacuum debris with spot machine. <br> • With a dry towel over your hand, pinch out more of the spot. <br> • Repeat entire Step until no more removes. | 1. Using your dinner knife, scrape up as much of the spot(s) as possible. Note: After each scrape, wipe the knife on a clean part of the towel. <br> • Vacuum debris with spot machine. <br> • With a clean towel over your hand, pinch out more of the spot. <br> • Repeat entire Step until no more removes. |
| 2. Put the hair dryer on the High Heat / High Fan setting and hold it 2 inches above the spot. <br> • As the spot begins to liquefy, blot it 3 - 4 times, using a clean part of the towel each time. <br> • Repeat heating and blotting until the wax residue is gone. <br> • Allow the carpet surface to cool. Touch the spot area carefully to see if the fibers are still stiff with wax. If still stiff, continue heating and blotting until stiffness is gone. | 2. Put the hair dryer on the High Heat / High Fan setting and hold it 2 inches above the spot. <br> • As the spot begins to liquefy, blot it 3 - 4 times, using a clean part of the towel each time. <br> • Repeat heating and blotting until the wax residue is gone. <br> • Allow the carpet surface to cool. Touch the spot area carefully to see if the fibers are still stiff with wax. If still stiff, continue heating and blotting until stiffness is gone. |
| 3. Mist on a generous amount of alcohol. <br> • Agitate with spoon handle end. <br> • Allow to work 2 minutes. <br> • Mist on a generous amount of alcohol. <br> • Mist on a generous amount of ammonia. <br> • Agitate with spoon handle end. | 3. Mist on a generous amount of alcohol. <br> • Agitate with spoon handle end. <br> • Allow to work 2 minutes. <br> • Mist on a generous amount of alcohol. <br> • Mist on a generous amount of ammonia. <br> • Agitate with spoon handle end. |
| 4. With the spot machine, rinse with hot water using the chop stroke technique 6 - 8 times. <br> • Take 4 - 6 slow, dry vacuum strokes. | 4. With the spot machine, rinse with hot water using the chop stroke technique 15 - 20 times. <br> • Take 4 - 6 slow, dry vacuum strokes. |
| 5. Look at spot area carefully to see if the spot is gone: <br> • If YES: Allow to dry. <br> • If NO: Repeat Steps 2 and 3 until no more removes. Then, if needed, do Step 5. | 5. Look at spot area carefully to see if the spot is gone: <br> • If YES: Allow to dry. <br> • If NO: Repeat Steps 2 and 3 until no more removes. Then, if needed, do Step 5. |
| 6. If color cast remains, mist on a generous amount of peroxide. <br> • Tamp with soft brush. <br> • Allow to dry. | 6. If color cast remains, mist on a generous amount of peroxide. <br> • Tamp with soft brush. <br> • Allow to dry. |
| 7. If needed, repeat Steps 2, 3 and 5 one time. | 7. If needed, repeat Steps 2, 3 and 5 one time. |
| 8. If the spot persists, call a pro for options as soon as possible. | 8. If the spot persists, call a pro for options as soon as possible. |

Section II

## Comments:

- **Optimum removal time:** Within 24 hours of spill
- **Maximum size for home removal:** Class III / IV = 1/2 inch
- **Removal restrictions:** If the spot(s) is larger than 1/2 inch in diameter, **do not attempt TOTAL removal** using Class III or IV instructions. Do Step 1 **only** under Class III or IV. Put a dry towel over spot. Then:
  - Call a pro and have spot removed within 3 days. -OR-
  - If the spot is 1 inch or less in diameter, get a spot machine and
    - If the spot is now old/dried, do Steps 2 - 7 under Class I.
    - If the spot is still fresh/wet, do Steps 2 - 7 under Class II.
- **Caution:** Pigments in these products can permanently stain nylon if left untreated as little as 7 days. If you cannot remove a spot, consult a pro for options as soon as possible.

## Materials Needed:

Class III / IV: Spotting kit, Vacuum cleaner with attachment removed from hose, Hair dryer

### Class III: Towel + Old / Dried Spot

**Steps:**

1. Using your dinner knife, scrape up as much of the spot(s) as possible. Note: After each scrape, wipe the knife on a clean part of the towel.
   - Vacuum debris with vacuum cleaner hose.
   - With a dry towel over your hand, pinch out more of the spot.
   - Repeat entire Step until no more removes.

2. Put the hair dryer on the High Heat / High Fan setting and hold it 2 inches above the spot.
   - As the spot begins to liquefy, blot it 3 - 4 times, using a clean part of the towel each time.
   - Repeat heating and blotting until the wax residue is gone.
   - Allow the carpet surface to cool. Touch the spot area carefully to see if the fibers are still stiff with wax. If still stiff, continue heating and blotting until stiffness is gone.

3. Mist on a generous amount of alcohol.
   - Agitate with spoon handle end.
   - Allow to work 2 minutes.
   - Mist on a generous amount of alcohol.
   - Mist on a generous amount of ammonia.
   - Agitate with spoon handle end.

4. With a towel, firmly blot 15 - 20 times, using a clean part of the towel each time.

5. Look at spot area carefully to see if the spot is gone:
   - If YES: Allow to dry.
   - If NO: Repeat Steps 2 and 3 until no more removes. Then, if needed, do Step 5.

6. If color cast remains, mist on a generous amount of peroxide.
   - Tamp with soft brush.
   - Allow to dry.

7. If needed, repeat Steps 2, 3 and 5 one time.

8. If the spot persists, call a pro for options as soon as possible.

### Class IV: Towel + Fresh / Wet Spot

**Steps:**

1. Using your dinner knife, scrape up as much of the spot(s) as possible. Note: After each scrape, wipe the knife on a clean part of the towel.
   - Vacuum debris with vacuum cleaner hose.
   - With a dry towel over your hand, pinch out more of the spot.
   - Repeat entire Step until no more removes.

2. Put the hair dryer on the High Heat / High Fan setting and hold it 2 inches above the spot.
   - As the spot begins to liquefy, blot it 3 - 4 times, using a clean part of the towel each time.
   - Repeat heating and blotting until the wax residue is gone.
   - Allow the carpet surface to cool. Touch the spot area carefully to see if the fibers are still stiff with wax. If still stiff, continue heating and blotting until stiffness is gone.

3. Mist on a generous amount of alcohol.
   - Agitate with spoon handle end.
   - Allow to work 2 minutes.
   - Mist on a generous amount of alcohol.
   - Mist on a small amount of ammonia.
   - Agitate with spoon handle end.

4. With a towel, firmly blot 10 - 20 times, using a clean part of the towel each time.

5. Look at spot area carefully to see if the spot is gone:
   - If YES: Allow to dry.
   - If NO: Repeat Steps 2 and 3 until no more removes. Then, if needed, do Step 5.

6. If color cast remains, mist on a generous amount of peroxide.
   - Tamp with soft brush.
   - Allow to dry.

7. If needed, repeat Steps 2, 3 and 5 one time.

8. If the spot persists, call a pro for options as soon as possible.

Section II

# Detergents, Soaps and Cleaners, Fabric Softener - Liquid or Gel/No Bleach:
## All Purpose Cleaners, Bubble Bath, Carpet, Dish, Floor, Laundry, Oven Cleaner

### Comments:

- **Optimum removal time: As soon as possible** within 24 hours of spill
- **Maximum size for home removal:** Class I / II = 2 1/2 inches
- **Removal restrictions:** If the spot(s) is larger than 2 1/2 inches in diameter, **do not attempt TOTAL removal** using Class I or II instructions. Do Step 1 **only** under Class I or II, but do not put alcohol or hot water in spot machine. Then put a dry towel over spot. Call a pro and have spot removed as soon as possible within 24 hours.
- Colorant in some products can immediately and permanently stain most nylon. Also, products with a high pH can cause dye loss or color change in nylon fibers. Consult a pro for options as soon as possible.
- These products will leave a soapy, sticky residue that can cause recurring spots on all fiber types if not completely removed. (See "Recurring Spots", Chapter 4.) Consult a pro for options as soon as possible.

### Materials Needed:
Class I / II: Spotting kit, Spot machine with hot water

## Class I: Spot Machine + Old / Dried Spot

### Steps:

Note: Pour 8 tablespoons of alcohol into the dirty water tank of your spot machine to prevent excess foaming as you remove the spot.

1. Using your spoon, scrape out as much of the spot(s) as possible.
   - Vacuum debris with spot machine.
   - Repeat entire Step until no more removes.

2. Mist on a generous amount of alcohol.
   - Agitate with hard brush.
   - Allow to work 1 minute.

3. With the spot machine, rinse with hot water using the single stroke technique 10 - 12 times.
   - Take 8 - 10 slow, dry vacuum strokes.

4. Look at spot area carefully to see if the spot is gone:
   - If YES: Allow to dry.
   - If NO: Repeat Steps 2 and 3 until no more removes.

5. Mist on a generous amount of peroxide.
   - Tamp with soft brush.
   - Allow to dry.

6. If foam or discoloration persists, call a pro for options as soon as possible.

## Class II: Spot Machine + Fresh / Wet Spot

### Steps:

Note: Pour 8 tablespoons of alcohol into the dirty water tank of your spot machine to prevent excess foaming as you remove the spot.

1. Lay a small towel over the palm of your hand. Then lay your hand on the carpet so the towel is at the edge of the spot.
   - Using your spoon, scoop as much of the spot(s) as possible onto the towel. Note: After each scoop, wipe the spoon on a clean part of the towel.
   - Carefully drop the dirty towel into your empty bucket.
   - With a clean towel, blot 12 - 15 times, using a clean part of the towel each time.

2. Mist on a generous amount of alcohol.
   - Agitate with hard brush.
   - Allow to work 1 minute.

3. With the spot machine, rinse with hot water using the single stroke technique 10 - 12 times.
   - Take 8 - 10 slow, dry vacuum strokes.

4. Look at spot area carefully to see if the spot is gone:
   - If YES: Allow to dry.
   - If NO: Repeat Steps 2 and 3 until no more removes.

5. Mist on a generous amount of peroxide.
   - Tamp with soft brush.
   - Allow to dry.

6. If foam or discoloration persists, call a pro for options as soon as possible.

Section II

# Detergents, Soaps and Cleaners, Fabric Softener - Liquid or Gel/No Bleach:
## All Purpose Cleaners, Bubble Bath, Carpet, Dish, Floor, Laundry, Oven Cleaner

Spot / Stain Contents: Ammonia, Alcohol, Brightener, Colorant, Fragrance, Phosphate, Surfactants

### Comments:

- **Optimum removal time: As soon as possible** within 24 hours of spill
- **Maximum size for home removal:** Class III / IV = 1 1/2 inches
- **Removal restrictions:** If the spot(s) is larger than 1 1/2 inches in diameter, **do not attempt TOTAL removal** using Class III or IV instructions. Do Step 1 **only** under Class III or IV. Put a dry towel over spot. Then:
  - Call a pro and have spot removed as soon as possible within 24 hours. -OR-
  - If the spot is 2 1/2 inches or less in diameter, get a spot machine and:
    - If the spot is now old/dried, do Steps 2 - 6 under Class I.
    - If the spot is still fresh/wet, do Steps 2 - 6 under Class II.
- Colorant in some products can immediately and permanently stain most nylon. Also, products with a high pH can cause dye loss or color change in nylon fibers. Consult a pro for options as soon as possible.
- These products will leave a soapy, sticky residue that can cause recurring spots on all fiber types if not completely removed. (See "Recurring Spots", Chapter 4.) Consult a pro for options as soon as possible.

### Materials Needed:
Class III: Spotting kit, Vacuum cleaner with attachment removed from hose
Class IV: Spotting kit

## Class III: Towel + Old / Dried Spot

### Steps:

1. Using your spoon, scrape out as much of the spot(s) as possible.
   - Vacuum debris with vacuum cleaner hose.
   - Repeat entire Step until no more removes.

2. Mist on a generous amount of alcohol.
   - Agitate with hard brush.
   - Allow to work 1 - 2 minutes.
   - Mist on a generous amount of alcohol.
   - Agitate with hard brush.

3. With a towel, firmly blot 10 - 15 times, using a clean part of the towel each time.

4. Look at spot area carefully to see if the spot is gone:
   - If YES: Allow to dry.
   - If NO: Repeat Steps 2 and 3 until no more removes.

5. Mist on a generous amount of peroxide.
   - Tamp with soft brush.
   - Allow to dry.

6. If foam or discoloration persists, call a pro for options as soon as possible.

## Class IV: Towel + Fresh / Wet Spot

### Steps:

1. Lay a small towel over the palm of your hand. Then lay your hand on the carpet so the towel is at the edge of the spot.
   - Using your spoon, scoop as much of the spot(s) as possible onto the towel. Note: After each scoop, wipe the spoon on a clean part of the towel.
   - With a clean towel, blot the spot(s) 20 - 30 times, using a clean part of the towel each time.

2. Mist on a generous amount of alcohol.
   - Agitate with hard brush.
   - Allow to work 1 minute.
   - Mist on a small amount of alcohol.
   - Agitate with hard brush.

3. With a towel, firmly blot 10 - 15 times, using a clean part of the towel each time.

4. Look at spot area carefully to see if the spot is gone:
   - If YES: Allow to dry.
   - If NO: Repeat Steps 2 and 3 until no more removes.

5. Mist on a generous amount of peroxide.
   - Tamp with soft brush.
   - Allow to dry.

6. If foam or discoloration persists, call a pro for options as soon as possible.

Section II

# Detergents, Soaps, Cleaners, Fabric Softener - Powder/No Bleach:
## All Purpose Cleaners, Bubble Bath, Carpet, Floor, Laundry

### Comments:

- **Optimum removal time: As soon as possible** within 24 hours of spill
- **Maximum size for home removal:** If the spot is powdery - no size limits / If the spot was moistened and is now dried/crusty or the spot is wet = 8 inches
- **Removal restrictions - Powdery**: None
- **Removal restrictions - Dried/Crusty or Wet:** If the spot(s) is larger than 8 inches in diameter, **do not attempt TOTAL removal** using Class I or II instructions. Do Dried/Crusty Step 1 **only** under Class I or Wet Step 1 **only** under Class II. Put a dry towel over spot. Call a pro and have spot removed as soon as possible within 24 hours.
- **Caution:** Colored specks in some products can permanently stain nylon if wetted and left in the carpet as little as 24 hours. If you cannot remove a spot, consult a pro for options as soon as possible.
- **Caution:** These products can leave a soapy, sticky residue if wetted, and can cause recurring spots on all fiber types if not completely removed. (See "Recurring Spots", Chapter 4.) Consult a pro for options as soon as possible.

### Materials Needed:

Class I / II - Powdery: Spotting kit, Vacuum cleaner, (Broom and dust pan), Spot machine with hot water
Class I - Dried/Crusty: Spotting kit, Vacuum cleaner, Spot machine with hot water
Class II - Wet: Spotting kit, Spot machine with hot water

## Class I: Spot Machine + Old / Dried Spot

### Steps:

1. Follow the instructions under the spot description that matches your spot:

   **The spot is powdery:**
   - Vacuum debris with vacuum cleaner hose. Note: If the spot is very large, use a broom to sweep up as much as you can into a dust pan and then vacuum up the remainder with the vacuum cleaner hose.
   - Repeat until no more removes.
   - Go to Step 2.

   **The spot is dried / crusty:**
   - Using your dinner knife, break up the spot(s) using a chopping action with the blade.
   - Vacuum debris with vacuum cleaner hose.
   - Repeat entire Step until no more removes.
   - Go to Step 2.

2. Mist on a generous amount of alcohol.
   - Agitate with hard brush.
   - Allow to work 1 minute.

3. With the spot machine, rinse with hot water using the single stroke technique 6 - 8 times.
   - Take 4 - 6 slow, dry vacuum strokes.

4. Look at spot area carefully to see if the spot is gone:
   - If YES: Allow to dry.
   - If NO: Repeat Steps 2 and 3 until no more removes. Then do Step 5.

5. Mist on a generous amount of peroxide.
   - Tamp with soft brush.
   - Allow to dry.

6. If foam or discoloration persists, call a pro for options as soon as possible.

## Class II: Spot Machine + Fresh / Wet Spot

### Steps:

1. Follow the instructions under the spot description that matches your spot:

   **The spot is powdery:**
   - Vacuum debris with vacuum cleaner hose. Note: If the spot is very large, use a broom to sweep up as much as you can into a dust pan and then vacuum up the remainder with the vacuum cleaner hose.
   - Repeat until no more removes.
   - Go to Step 2.

   **The spot is wet:**
   - Lay a small towel over the palm of your hand. Lay your hand on the carpet so the towel is at the edge of the spot.
     - Using your spoon, scoop as much of the spot(s) as possible onto the towel. Note: After each scoop, wipe the spoon on a clean part of the towel.
     - Carefully drop the dirty towel into your empty bucket.
     - Vacuum debris with spot machine.
     - Repeat entire Step until no more removes.
     - Go to Step 2.

2. Mist on a generous amount of alcohol.
   - Agitate with hard brush.
   - Allow to work 1 minute.

3. With the spot machine, rinse with hot water using the single stroke technique 6 - 8 times.
   - Take 4 - 6 slow, dry vacuum strokes.

4. Look at spot area carefully to see if the spot is gone:
   - If YES: Allow to dry.
   - If NO: Repeat Steps 2 and 3 until no more removes. Then do Step 5.

5. Mist on a generous amount of peroxide.
   - Tamp with soft brush.
   - Allow to dry.

6. If foam or discoloration persists, call a pro for options as soon as possible.

Section II

# Detergents, Soaps, Cleaners, Fabric Softener - Powder/No Bleach:
## All Purpose Cleaners, Bubble Bath, Carpet, Floor, Laundry

Spot / Stain Contents: Bleach, Sodium Carbonate and Silicate, Sodium Perborate, Phosphates, Brightener, Colorant, Fragrance, Surfactants

**Comments:**

- **Optimum removal time: As soon as possible** within 24 hours of spill
- **Maximum size for home removal:** If the spot is powdery - no size limits / If the spot was moistened and is now dried/crusty or the spot is wet = 4 inches
- **Removal restrictions - Powdery:** None
- **Removal restrictions - Dried/Crusty or Wet:** If the spot(s) is larger than 4 inches in diameter, **do not attempt TOTAL removal** using Class III or IV instructions. Do Dried/Crusty Step 1 **only** under Class III or Wet Step 1 **only** under Class IV. Put a dry towel over spot. Then:
  - Call a pro and have spot removed as soon as possible within 24 hours. -OR-
  - If dried/crusty or wet spot is 8 inches or less in diameter, get a spot machine and do Steps 2 - 6 under Class I.
- **Caution:** Colored specks in some products can permanently stain nylon if wetted and left in the carpet as little as 24 hours. If you cannot remove a spot, consult a pro for options as soon as possible.
- **Caution:** These products can leave a soapy, sticky residue if wetted, and can cause recurring spots on all fiber types if not completely removed. (See "Recurring Spots", Chapter 4.) Consult a pro for options as soon as possible.

## Materials Needed:

Class III / IV - Powdery: Spotting kit, Vacuum cleaner, (Broom and dust pan)
Class III / IV - Dried/Crusty or Wet: Spotting kit, Vacuum cleaner

---

### Class III: Towel + Old / Dried Spot

**Steps:**

1. Follow the instructions under the spot description that matches your spot:

   **The spot is powdery:**
   - Vacuum debris with vacuum cleaner hose. Note: If the spot is very large, use a broom to sweep up as much as you can into a dust pan and then vacuum up the remainder.
   - Repeat until no more removes.
   - Go to Step 2.

   **The spot is dried / crusty:**
   - Using your dinner knife, break up the spot(s) using a chopping action with the blade.
   - Vacuum debris with vacuum cleaner hose.
   - Repeat until no more removes.
   - Go to Step 2.

2. Mist on a generous amount of alcohol.
   - Agitate with hard brush.
   - Allow to work 1 minute.

3. With a towel, blot 10 - 12 times, using a clean part of the towel each time.

4. Look at spot area carefully to see if the spot is gone:
   - If YES: Allow to dry.
   - If NO: Repeat Steps 2 and 3 until no more removes.

5. Mist on a generous amount of peroxide.
   - Tamp with soft brush.
   - Allow to dry.

6. If foam or discoloration persists, call a pro for options as soon as possible.

---

### Class IV: Towel + Fresh / Wet Spot

**Steps:**

1. Follow the instructions under the spot description that matches your spot:

   **The spot is powdery:**
   - Vacuum debris with vacuum cleaner hose. Note: If the spot is very large, use a broom to sweep up as much as you can into a dust pan and then vacuum up the remainder.
   - Repeat until no more removes.
   - Go to Step 2.

   **The spot is wet:**
   - Lay a small towel over the palm of your hand. Then lay your hand on the carpet so the towel is at the edge of the spot.
     - Using your spoon, scoop as much of the spot(s) as possible onto the towel. Note: After each scoop, wipe the spoon on a clean part of the towel.
     - Carefully drop the dirty towel in your empty bucket.
     - Vacuum debris with vacuum cleaner hose.
     - Repeat until no more removes.
     - Go to Step 2.

2. Mist on a generous amount of alcohol.
   - Agitate with hard brush.
   - Allow to work 1 minute.

3. With a towel, blot 10 - 12 times, using a clean part of the towel each time.

4. Look at spot area carefully to see if the spot is gone:
   - If YES: Allow to dry.
   - If NO: Repeat Steps 2 and 3 until no more removes.

5. Mist on a generous amount of peroxide.
   - Tamp with soft brush.
   - Allow to dry.

6. If foam or discoloration persists, call a pro for options as soon as possible.

# Dry Goods - All:
## Baby Powder, Baking Soda, Flour, Salts, Sugar, Health Food Powders, Carpet Deodorizers, Etc.

### Comments:

- **Optimum removal time:** Within 24 hours of spill
- **Maximum size for home removal:** If the spot is still powdery - no size limits / If the spot was moistened and is now dried and crusty or the spot is wet = 8 inches
- **Removal restrictions - Powdery:** None
- **Removal restrictions - Dried/Crusty or Wet:** If the spot(s) is larger than 8 inches in diameter, **do not attempt TOTAL removal** using Class I or II instructions. Do Dried/Crusty Step 1 **only** under Class I or Wet Steps 1 and 2 **only** under Class II. Put a dry towel over spot. Call a pro and have spot removed within 3 days.
- Some products can leave a sticky residue if wetted, and can cause recurring spots on all fiber types if not completely removed. (See "Recurring Spots", Chapter 4.) Consult a pro for options.

### Materials Needed:

Class I / II - Powdery: Vacuum cleaner, (Broom and dust pan)
Class I - Dried/Crusty: Spotting kit, Vacuum cleaner, Spot machine with hot water
Class II - Wet: Hair dryer, Spotting kit, Vacuum cleaner, Spot machine with hot water

| Class I: Spot Machine + Old / Dried Spot | Class II: Spot Machine + Fresh / Wet Spot |
|---|---|

### Steps:

Follow instructions under the spot description that matches your spot:

**The spot is powdery:**

1. Using only the vacuum cleaner hose, vacuum up as much debris as possible. Then vacuum again with the vacuum cleaner's beater bar until no more removes. Note: If the spill is a large pile, use a broom to sweep up as much as you can into a dust pan. Vacuum up the remainder with the vacuum cleaner hose and then vacuum with the beater bar.
   - Repeat until no more removes.
     Note: No other Steps should be needed.

**The spot is dried and crusty:**

1. Using your dinner knife, break up the spot(s) using a chopping action with the blade.
   - Vacuum debris with the vacuum cleaner hose until no more removes.
   - Vacuum with the vacuum cleaner beater bar until no more removes.
   - Repeat entire Step until no more removes.
2. Mist on a generous amount of ammonia.
   - Agitate with hard brush.
   - Allow to work 1 minute.
3. With the spot machine, rinse with hot water using the single stroke technique 6 - 8 times.
   - Take 4 - 6 slow, dry vacuum strokes.
4. Look at spot area carefully to see if the spot is gone:
   - If YES: Allow to dry.
   - If NO: Repeat Steps 2 and 3 until no more removes. Then, if needed, do Step 5.
5. If color cast remains, mist on a generous amount of peroxide.
   - Tamp with soft brush.
   - Allow to dry.
6. If the spot persists, call a pro for options as soon as possible.

### Steps:

Follow the instructions under the spot description that matches your spot:

**The spot is powdery:**

1. Using only the vacuum cleaner hose, vacuum up as much debris as possible. Then vacuum again with the vacuum cleaner's beater bar until no more removes. Note: If the spill is a large pile, use a broom to sweep up as much as you can into a dust pan. Vacuum up the remainder with the vacuum cleaner hose and then vacuum with the beater bar.
   - Repeat until no more removes.
     Note: No other Steps should be needed.

**The spot is wet:**

1. Allow the spot(s) to dry. Note: You can speed dry it with a hairdryer. Caution: Be careful not to melt the carpet fibers.
2. Using your dinner knife, break up the spot(s) using a chopping action with the blade.
   - Vacuum debris with the vacuum cleaner hose until no more removes.
   - Vacuum with the vacuum cleaner beater bar until no more removes.
   - Repeat entire Step until no more removes.
3. Mist on a generous amount of ammonia.
   - Agitate with hard brush.
   - Allow to work 1 minute.
4. With the spot machine, rinse with hot water using the single stroke technique 6 - 8 times.
   - Take 4 - 6 slow, dry vacuum strokes.
5. Look at spot area carefully to see if the spot is gone:
   - If YES: Allow to dry.
   - If NO: Repeat Steps 3 and 4 until no more removes. Then, if needed, do Step 6.
6. If color cast remains, mist on a generous amount of peroxide.
   - Tamp with soft brush.
   - Allow to dry.
7. If the spot persists, call a pro for options as soon as possible.

Section II

# Dry Goods - All:
## Baby Powder, Baking Soda, Flour, Salts, Sugar, Health Food Powders, Carpet Deodorizers, Etc.

Spot / Stain Contents: Talc, Zinc Oxide, Baking Soda, Wheat, Barley, Minerals, Sugar

## Comments:

- **Optimum removal time:** Within 24 hours of spill
- **Maximum size for home removal:** If the spot is still powdery - no size limits / If the spot was moistened and is now dried and crusty or is wet = 4 inches
- **Removal restrictions - Powdery:** None
- **Removal restrictions - Dried/Crusty or Wet:** If the spot(s) is larger than 4 inches in diameter, **do not attempt TOTAL removal** using Class III or IV instructions. Do Dried/Crusty Step 1 **only** under Class III or Wet Steps 1 and 2 **only** under Class IV. Put a dry towel over spot. Then:
  - Call a pro and have spot removed within 3 days. -OR-
  - If spot is 8 inches or less in diameter, get a spot machine and do Steps 2 - 6 under Class I.
- Some products can leave a sticky residue if wetted, and can cause recurring spots on all fiber types if not completely removed. (See "Recurring Spots", Chapter 4.) Consult a pro for options.

## Materials Needed:

Class III / IV - Powdery: Vacuum cleaner, (Broom and dust pan)
Class III - Dried/Crusty: Spotting kit, Vacuum cleaner
Class IV - Wet: Hair dryer, Spotting kit, Vacuum cleaner

## Class III: Towel + Old / Dried Spot

### Steps:
Follow the instructions under the spot description that matches your spot:
**The spot is powdery:**

1. Using only the vacuum cleaner hose, vacuum up as much debris as possible. Then vacuum again with the vacuum cleaner's beater bar until no more removes. Note: If the spill is a large pile, use a broom to sweep up as much as you can into a dust pan. Vacuum up the remainder with the vacuum cleaner hose and then vacuum with the beater bar.
   - Repeat until no more removes.
   Note: No other Steps should be needed.

**The spot is dried and crusty:**

1. Using your dinner knife, break up the spot(s) using a chopping action with the blade.
   - Vacuum debris with the vacuum cleaner hose until no more removes.
   - Vacuum with the vacuum cleaner beater bar until no more removes.
   - Repeat entire Step until no more removes.

2. Mist on a small amount of ammonia.
   - Agitate with hard brush.
   - Allow to work 1 minute.

3. With a towel, blot 10 - 12 times, using a clean part of the towel each time.

4. Look at spot area carefully to see if the spot is gone:
   - If YES: Allow to dry.
   - If NO: Repeat Steps 2 and 3 until no more removes. Then, if needed, do Step 5.

5. Mist on a generous amount of peroxide.
   - Tamp with soft brush.
   - Allow to dry.

6. If the spot persists, call a pro for options as soon as possible.

## Class IV: Towel + Fresh / Wet Spot

### Steps:
Follow the instructions under the spot description that matches your spot:
**The spot is powdery:**

1. Using only the vacuum cleaner hose, vacuum up as much debris as possible. Then vacuum again with the vacuum cleaner's beater bar until no more removes. Note: If the spill is a large pile, use a broom to sweep up as much as you can into a dust pan. Vacuum up the remainder with the vacuum cleaner hose and then vacuum with the beater bar.
   - Repeat until no more removes.
   Note: No other Steps should be needed.

**The spot is wet:**

1. Allow the spot(s) to dry. Note: You can speed dry it with a hairdryer. Caution: Be careful not to melt the carpet fibers.

2. Using your dinner knife, break up the spot(s) using a chopping action with the blade.
   - Vacuum debris with the vacuum cleaner hose until no more removes.
   - Vacuum with the vacuum cleaner beater bar until no more removes.
   - Repeat entire Step until no more removes.

3. Mist on a small amount of ammonia.
   - Agitate with hard brush.
   - Allow to work 1 minute.

4. With a towel, blot 10 - 12 times, using a clean part of the towel each time.

5. Look at spot area carefully to see if the spot is gone:
   - If YES: Allow to dry.
   - If NO: Repeat Steps 2 and 3 until no more removes. Then, if needed, do Step 5.

6. Mist on a generous amount of peroxide.
   - Tamp with soft brush.
   - Allow to dry.

7. If the spot persists, call a pro for options as soon as possible.

# Dye - All Liquid, Water-Based Dyes *(whether edible or not)*:
## Clothes Dye, Easter Egg Dye, Plant Food

### Comments:

- **Optimum removal time: As soon as possible** within 24 hours of spill
- **Maximum size for home removal:** Class I / II = 2 1/2 inches
- **Removal restrictions:** If spot(s) is larger than 2 1/2 inches in diameter, **do not attempt TOTAL removal** using Class I or II instructions. Do Step 1 **only** under Class I or II. Mist on a small amount of ammonia. Put a folded towel moistened with water over stain. Call a pro and have spot removed as soon as possible within 24 hours.
- Strong dye in these products can immediately and permanently stain most nylon. If you cannot remove a spot, consult a pro for options as soon as possible.

### Materials Needed:
Class I / II: Spotting kit, Spot machine with warm water

## Class I: Spot Machine + Old / Dried Spot

### Steps:

1. Using your spot machine, rinse the spot(s) with warm water using the chop stroke technique 6 - 8 times.
   - Take 4 - 6 slow, dry vacuum strokes.

2. Mist on a generous amount of ammonia.
   - Tamp with soft brush.
   - Allow to work 2 minutes.
   - Mist on a generous amount of ammonia.
   - Tamp with soft brush.

3. With the spot machine, rinse with warm water using the chop stroke technique 6 - 8 times.
   - Take 4 - 6 slow, dry vacuum strokes.

4. Look at spill area carefully to see if the spot is gone:
   - If YES: Allow to dry.
   - If NO: Repeat Steps 2 and 3 until no more removes. Then, if needed, do Step 5.

5. If color cast remains, mist on a generous amount of peroxide.
   - Mist on a small amount of ammonia.
   - Tamp with soft brush.
   - Allow to dry.

6. If needed, repeat Step 5 one time.

7. If the spot persists, call a pro for options as soon as possible.

## Class II: Spot Machine + Fresh / Wet Spot

### Steps:

1. Using your spot machine, dry vacuum the spot(s) 6 - 8 times.
   - Rinse with warm water using the single stroke technique 6 - 8 times.
   - Take 4 - 6 slow, dry vacuum strokes.

2. Mist on a generous amount of ammonia.
   - Tamp with soft brush.
   - Allow to work 1 minute.
   - Mist on a small amount of ammonia.
   - Tamp with soft brush.

3. With the spot machine, rinse with warm water using the chop stroke technique 6 - 8 times.
   - Take 4 - 6 slow, dry vacuum strokes.

4. Look at spill area carefully to see if the spot is gone:
   - If YES: Allow to dry.
   - If NO: Repeat Steps 2 and 3 until no more removes. Then, if needed, do Step 5.

5. If color cast remains, mist on a generous amount of peroxide.
   - Mist on a small amount of ammonia.
   - Tamp with soft brush.
   - Allow to dry.

6. If needed, repeat Step 5 one time.

7. If the spot persists, call a pro for options as soon as possible.

Section II

# Dye - All Liquid, Water-Based Dyes *(whether edible or not)*: Clothes Dye, Easter Egg Dye, Plant Food

Stain Contents: Food Coloring, Vegetable Dye, Acid Dye, Colorants

## Comments:

- **Optimum removal time: As soon as possible** within 24 hours of spill
- **Maximum size for home removal:** Class III / IV = 2 inches
- **Removal restrictions:** If the spot(s) is larger than 2 inches in diameter, **do not attempt TOTAL removal** using Class III or IV instructions. Do Step 1 **only** under Class III or IV. Mist on a small amount of ammonia. Put a folded towel moistened with water over stain. Then:
  - Call a pro and have spot removed within 24 hours. -OR-
  - Get a spot machine and if the spot is 2 1/2 inches or less in diameter, get a spot machine and:
    - If the spot is now dried, do Steps 1 - 7 under Class I.
    - If the spot is still wet, do Steps 1 - 7 under Class II.
- Strong dye in these products can immediately and permanently stain most nylon. If you cannot remove a spot, consult a pro for options as soon as possible.

## Materials Needed:

Class III: Spotting kit, Vacuum cleaner with attachment removed from hose
Class IV: Spotting kit

## Class III: Towel + Old / Dried Spot

### Steps:

1. Using your soft brush, gently brush the spot(s) in a side-to-side motion 8 - 12 times.
   - Vacuum debris with vacuum cleaner hose.

2. Mist on a generous amount of ammonia.
   - Tamp with soft brush.
   - Allow to work 2 minutes.
   - Mist on a generous amount of ammonia.
   - Tamp with soft brush.

3. With a towel, blot 8 - 12 times, using a clean part of the towel each time.

4. Look at spot area carefully to see if the spot is gone:
   - If YES: Allow to dry.
   - If NO: Repeat Steps 2 and 3 until no more removes. Then, if needed, do Step 5.

5. If color cast remains, mist on a generous amount of peroxide.
   - Mist on a small amount of ammonia.
   - Tamp with soft brush.
   - Allow to dry.

6. If needed, repeat Steps 2, 3 and 5 one time.

7. If the spot persists, call a pro for options as soon as possible.

## Class IV: Towel + Fresh / Wet Spot

### Steps:

1. Fold a towel several times and place it over the spot(s).
   - Step on the towel with your full weight, using a clean part of the towel each time.
   - Repeat entire Step until no more absorbs.

2. Mist on a generous amount of ammonia.
   - Tamp with soft brush.
   - Allow to work 1 minute.
   - Mist on a small amount of ammonia.
   - Tamp with soft brush.

3. With a towel, blot 10 - 15 times, using a clean part of the towel each time.

4. Look at spot area carefully to see if the spot is gone:
   - If YES: Allow to dry.
   - If NO: Repeat Steps 2 and 3 until no more removes. Then, if needed, do Step 5.

5. If color cast remains, mist on a generous amount of peroxide.
   - Mist on a small amount of ammonia.
   - Tamp with soft brush.
   - Allow to dry.

6. If needed, repeat Steps 2, 3 and 5 one time.

7. If the spot persists, call a pro for options as soon as possible.

Section II

# Egg or Egg Beaters® - Cooked Well-Done
## (Fried, Hard Boiled, Poached, Scrambled)

### Comments:

- **Optimum removal time:** Within 24 hours of spill
- **Maximum size for home removal:** Class I / II = 5 inches
- **Removal restrictions:** If the spot(s) has been pressed into the carpet fibers or is larger than 5 inches in diameter, **do not attempt TOTAL removal** using Class I or II instructions. Do Step 1 **only** under Class I or II. Put a folded towel moistened with water over spot. Call a pro and have spot removed within 2 days.
- Cooked egg may contain butter or oil that can cause recurring spots. (See "Recurring Spots", Chapter 4.). Consult a pro for options as soon as possible.

### Materials Needed:

Class I / II: Spotting kit, Spot machine with warm water

## Class I: Spot Machine + Old / Dried Spot

### Steps:

1. Using your spoon, scrape out as much of the spot as possible:
   - Vacuum debris with spot machine.
   - Repeat entire Step until no more removes.

2. Mist on a generous amount of ammonia.
   - Mist on a generous amount of alcohol.
   - Agitate with hard brush.
   - Allow to work 2 minutes.

3. With the spot machine, rinse with warm water using the chop stroke technique 8 - 10 times.
   - Take 6 - 8 slow, dry vacuum strokes.

4. Look at spot area carefully to see if the spot is gone:
   - If YES: Allow to dry.
   - If NO: Repeat Steps 2 and 3 until no more removes. Then, if needed, do Step 5.

5. If color cast remains, mist on a generous amount of peroxide.
   - Tamp with soft brush.
   - Allow to dry.

6. If needed, repeat Steps 2, 3 and 5 one time.

7. If the spot persists, call a pro for options as soon as possible.

## Class II: Spot Machine + Fresh / Wet Spot

### Steps:

1. Lay a small towel over the palm of your hand. Then lay your hand on the carpet so the towel is at the edge of the spot.
   - Using your spoon, scoop as much of the spot(s) as possible onto the towel. Note: After each scoop, wipe the spoon on a clean part of the towel.
   - With the spot machine, rinse with warm water using the single stroke technique 6 - 8 times.
   - Take 4 - 6 slow, dry vacuum strokes.
   - Repeat entire Step until no more removes.

2. Mist on a generous amount of ammonia.
   - Mist on a small amount of alcohol.
   - Agitate with hard brush.
   - Allow to work 2 minutes.

3. With the spot machine, rinse with warm water using the chop stroke technique 6 - 8 times.
   - Take 4 - 6 slow, dry vacuum strokes.

4. Look at spot area carefully to see if the spot is gone:
   - If YES: Allow to dry.
   - If NO: Repeat Steps 2 and 3 until no more removes. Then, if needed, do Step 5.

5. If color cast remains, mist on a generous amount of peroxide.
   - Tamp with soft brush.
   - Allow to dry.

6. If needed, repeat Steps 2, 3 and 5 one time.

7. If the spot persists, call a pro for options as soon as possible.

Section II

Spot Contents: Fat, Vegetable Oil, Possible Butter, Protein, Salts

## Comments:

- **Optimum removal time:** Within 24 hours of spill
- **Maximum size for home removal:** Class III / IV = 2 inches
- **Removal restrictions:** If the spot(s) has been pressed into the carpet fibers or is larger than 2 inches in diameter, **do not attempt TOTAL removal** using Class III or IV instructions. Do Step 1 **only** under Class III or IV. Put a folded towel moistened with water over spot. Then:
  - Call a pro and have spot removed within 2 days. -OR-
  - If the spot has not been pressed into carpet fibers and is 5 inches or less in diameter, get a spot machine and:
    - If the spot is now old/dried, do Steps 2 - 7 under Class I.
    - If the spot is still fresh/wet, do Steps 2 - 7 under Class II.
- Cooked egg may contain butter or oil that can cause recurring spots. (See "Recurring Spots", Chapter 4.). Consult a pro for options as soon as possible.

## Materials Needed:

Class III: Spotting kit, Shop vacuum with attachment removed from hose
Class IV: Spotting kit

| Class III: Towel + Old / Dried Spot | Class IV: Towel + Fresh / Wet Spot |
|---|---|
| **Steps:** | **Steps:** |
| 1. Using your spoon, scrape out as much of the spot as possible:<br>• Vacuum debris with a vacuum cleaner hose.<br>• Repeat entire Step until no more removes. | 1. Lay a small towel over the palm of your hand. Then lay your hand on the carpet so the towel is at the edge of the spot.<br>• Using your spoon, scoop as much of the spot(s) as possible onto the towel. Note: After each scoop, wipe the spoon on a clean part of the towel.<br>• With a clean towel, gently blot 15 - 20 times, using a clean part of the towel each time.<br>• Repeat entire Step until no more removes. |
| 2. Mist on a generous amount of ammonia.<br>• Mist on a generous amount of alcohol.<br>• Agitate with hard brush.<br>• Allow to work 2 minutes. | 2. Mist on a generous amount of ammonia.<br>• Mist on a small amount of alcohol.<br>• Agitate with hard brush.<br>• Allow to work 2 minutes. |
| 3. With a towel, blot 15 - 18 times, using a clean part of the towel each time. | 3. With a towel, blot 10 - 12 times, using a clean part of the towel each time. |
| 4. Look at spot area carefully to see if the spot is gone:<br>• If YES: Allow to dry.<br>• If NO: Repeat Steps 2 and 3 until no more removes. Then, if needed, do Step 5. | 4. Look at spot area carefully to see if the spot is gone:<br>• If YES: Allow to dry.<br>• If NO: Repeat Steps 2 and 3 until no more removes. Then, if needed, do Step 5. |
| 5. If color cast remains, mist on a generous amount of peroxide.<br>• Tamp with soft brush.<br>• Allow to dry. | 5. If color cast remains, mist on a generous amount of peroxide.<br>• Tamp with soft brush.<br>• Allow to dry. |
| 6. If needed, repeat Steps 2, 3 and 5 one time. | 6. If needed, repeat Steps 2, 3 and 5 one time. |
| 7. If the spot persists, call a pro for options as soon as possible. | 7. If the spot persists, call a pro for options as soon as possible. |

Section II

# Egg or Egg Beaters®- Raw or Soft Cooked with Runny Yolks
## (Fried, Soft Boiled, Poached)

### Comments:

- **Optimum removal time:** Within 24 hours of spill
- **Maximum size for home removal:** Class I / II = 4 inches
- **Removal restrictions:** If the spot(s) has been pressed into the carpet fibers or is larger than 4 inches in diameter, **do not attempt TOTAL removal** using Class I or II instructions. Do Step 1 **only** under Class I or II. Mist spot(s) with a small amount of ammonia. Put a folded towel moistened with water over spot. Call a pro and have spot removed within 2 days.
- **Caution:** Raw egg yoke can stain some nylon carpet if left untreated as little as 10 days. If you cannot remove a spot, consult a pro for options as soon as possible.

### Materials Needed:
Class I / II: Disposable towels or tissues, Spotting kit, Spot machine with warm water

## Class I: Spot Machine + Old / Dried Spot

### Steps:

1. Using your dinner knife, scrape the surface of the spot(s) in a side-to-side motion to break up and remove as much as possible. Caution: Be careful not to fray the carpet fibers.
   - Vacuum debris with spot machine.
   - Repeat entire Step until no more removes.

2. Mist on a generous amount of ammonia.
   - Mist on a generous amount of alcohol.
   - Agitate with hard brush.
   - Allow to work 2 minutes.
   - Agitate with hard brush.

3. With the spot machine, rinse with warm water using the chop stroke technique 8 - 10 times.
   - Take 6 - 8 slow, dry vacuum strokes.

4. Look at spot area carefully to see if the spot is gone:
   - If YES: Allow to dry.
   - If NO: Repeat Steps 2 and 3 until no more removes. Then, if needed, do Step 5.

5. If color cast remains, mist on a generous amount of peroxide.
   - Tamp with soft brush.
   - Allow to dry.

6. If needed, repeat Steps 2, 3 and 5 one time.

7. If the spot persists, call a pro for options as soon as possible.

## Class II: Spot Machine + Fresh / Wet Spot

### Steps:

1. Lay a disposable towel over the palm of your hand. Then lay your hand on the carpet so the towel is at the edge of the spot.
   - Using your spoon, scrape the spot onto the towel. Note: After each scrape, wipe the spoon on a clean part of the towel.
   - Carefully drop the dirty towel in your empty bucket.
   - With the spot machine, rinse with warm water using the single stroke technique 8 - 10 times.
   - Take 6 - 8 slow, dry vacuum strokes.
   - Repeat entire Step until no more removes.

2. Mist on a generous amount of ammonia.
   - Mist on a small amount of alcohol.
   - Agitate with hard brush.
   - Allow to work 1 minute.

3. With the spot machine, rinse with warm water using the chop stroke technique 6 - 8 times.
   - Take 4 - 6 slow, dry vacuum strokes.

4. Look at spot area carefully to see if the spot is gone:
   - If YES: Allow to dry.
   - If NO: Repeat Steps 2 and 3 until no more removes. Then, if needed, do Step 5.

5. If color cast remains, mist on a generous amount of peroxide.
   - Tamp with soft brush.
   - Allow to dry.

6. If needed, repeat Steps 2, 3 and 5 one time.

7. If the spot persists, call a pro for options as soon as possible.

Section II

Spot Contents: Fat, Vegetable Oil, Possible Butter, Protein, Salts

## Comments:

- Optimum removal time: Within 24 hours of spill
- **Maximum size for home removal:** Class III / IV = 1 1/2 inches
- **Removal restrictions:** If the spot(s) has been pressed into the carpet fibers or is larger than 1 1/2 inches in diameter, **do not attempt TOTAL removal** using Class III or IV instructions. Do Step 1 **only** under Class III or IV. Mist spot(s) with a small amount of ammonia. Put a folded towel moistened with water over spot. Then:
  - Call a pro and have spot removed within 2 days. -OR-
  - If the spot has not been pressed into carpet fibers and is 4 inches or less in diameter, get a spot machine and:
    - If the spot is now old/dried, do Steps 2 - 7 under Class I.
    - If the spot is still fresh/wet, do Steps 2 - 7 under Class II.
- **Caution:** Raw egg yolk can stain some nylon carpet if left untreated as little as 10 days. If you cannot remove a spot, consult a pro for options as soon as possible.

## Materials Needed:

Class III: Spotting kit, Shop vacuum * (if you have one) with attachment removed from hose
　　　　* If you do not have a shop vacuum, use a regular vacuum. As soon as you finish vacuuming the debris, remove the bag
　　　　　and throw it away, or clean the cartridge if you have a bagless vacuum cleaner.
Class IV: Disposable towels or tissues, Spotting kit

| Class III: Towel + Old / Dried Spot | Class IV: Towel + Fresh / Wet Spot |
|---|---|
| **Steps:** | **Steps:** |
| 1. Using your dinner knife, scrape the surface of the spot(s) in a side-to-side motion to break up and remove as much as possible. Caution: Be careful not to fray the carpet fibers.<br>　• Vacuum debris with a shop vacuum hose.<br>　• Repeat entire Step until no more removes. | 1. Lay a disposable towel over the palm of your hand. Then lay your hand on the carpet so the towel is at the edge of the spot.<br>　• Using your spoon, scrape the spot onto the towel. Note: After each scrape, wipe the spoon on a clean part of the towel.<br>　• Carefully drop the dirty towel in your empty bucket.<br>　• With a clean cloth towel, gently blot 15 - 20 times using a clean part of the towel each time.<br>　• Repeat entire Step until no more removes. |
| 2. Mist on a generous amount of ammonia.<br>　• Mist on a generous amount of alcohol.<br>　• Agitate with hard brush.<br>　• Allow to work 2 minutes. | 2. Mist on a generous amount of ammonia.<br>　• Mist on a small amount of alcohol.<br>　• Agitate with hard brush.<br>　• Allow to work 1 minute. |
| 3. With a towel, blot 15 - 18 times using a clean part of the towel each time. | 3. With a towel, blot 10 - 12 times using a clean part of the towel each time. |
| 4. Look at spot area carefully to see if the spot is gone:<br>　• If YES: Allow to dry.<br>　• If NO: Repeat Steps 2 and 3 until no more removes. Then, if needed, do Step 5. | 4. Look at spot area carefully to see if the spot is gone:<br>　• If YES: Allow to dry.<br>　• If NO: Repeat Steps 2 and 3 until no more removes. Then, if needed, do Step 5. |
| 5. If color cast remains, mist on a generous amount of peroxide.<br>　• Tamp with soft brush.<br>　• Allow to dry. | 5. If color cast remains, mist on generous amount of peroxide.<br>　• Tamp with soft brush.<br>　• Allow to dry. |
| 6. If needed, repeat Steps 2, 3 and 5 one time. | 6. If needed, repeat Steps 2, 3 and 5 one time. |
| 7. If the spot persists, call a pro for options as soon as possible. | 7. If the spot persists, call a pro for options as soon as possible. |

Section II

# Feces - Semi-Liquid, Diarrhea: Human, Animal

## Comments:

- **Optimum removal time: As soon as possible** within 24 hours of spill
- **Maximum size for home removal:** Class I / II = 3 inches
- **Removal restrictions:** If the spot(s) is larger than 3 inches in diameter, **do not attempt TOTAL removal** using Class I or II instructions. Do Step 1 **only** under Class I or II. Mist spot(s) with a generous amount of ammonia. Put a folded towel moistened with water over spot(s) and a note next to it that says, ***"Do Not Touch Or Clean!"***. Call a pro and have spot removed as soon as possible within 24 hours.
- **Caution:** Feces contain large quantities of bacteria and/or other pathogens. Use your best judgment about wearing a mask, gloves and eye protection.
- Food coloring in some feces can immediately and permanently stain most nylon. If you cannot remove a spot, consult a pro for options as soon as possible.

## Materials Needed:

Protective mask, gloves, eye wear
Class I: Spotting kit, Spot machine with cool water
Class II: Disposable towels or tissues, Spotting kit, Spot machine with cool water

| Class I: Spot Machine + Old / Dried Spot | Class II: Spot Machine + Fresh / Wet Spot |
|---|---|
| **Steps:** | **Steps:** |

### Class I: Spot Machine + Old / Dried Spot

**Steps:**

1. Using your dinner knife, break up the spot(s) using a chopping action with the knife blade.
   - Using your spoon, scrape the spots out of the carpet fibers.
   - Vacuum debris with spot machine.
   - Repeat entire Step until no more removes.

2. Mist on a generous amount of ammonia.
   - Mist on a generous amount of alcohol.
   - Allow to work 2 minutes.
   - Agitate with end of spoon handle.
   - Mist on a generous amount of ammonia.
   - Agitate with end of spoon handle.

3. With the spot machine, rinse with cool water using the chop stroke technique 10 - 12 times.
   - Take 8 - 10 slow, dry vacuum strokes.

4. Look at spot area carefully to see if the spot is gone:
   - If YES: Allow to dry.
   - If NO: Repeat Steps 2 and 3 until no more removes. Then, if needed, do Step 5.

5. If color cast remains, mist on a small amount of peroxide.
   - Tamp with soft brush.
   - Allow to dry.

6. If needed, repeat Steps 2, 3 and 5 one time.

7. If the spot persists, call a pro for options as soon as possible.

### Class II: Spot Machine + Fresh / Wet Spot

**Steps:**

1. Lay a disposable towel over the palm of your hand.
   - Using your spoon, scoop as much of the spot(s) as possible into the towel. Note: After each scoop, wipe the spoon on a clean part of the towel.
   - Repeat until no more removes.
   - Carefully drop the dirty towel in your empty bucket.
   - With the spot machine, rinse with cool water using the single stroke technique 10 - 15 times.
   - Take 6 - 8 slow, dry vacuum strokes.

2. Mist on a generous amount of ammonia.
   - Mist on a generous amount of alcohol.
   - Allow to work 1 minute.
   - Mist on a generous amount of ammonia.
   - Agitate with end of spoon handle.

3. With the spot machine, rinse with cool water using the chop stroke technique 6 - 8 times.
   - Take 4 - 6 slow, dry vacuum strokes.

4. Look at spot area carefully to see if the spot is gone:
   - If YES: Allow to dry.
   - If NO: Repeat Steps 2 and 3 until no more removes. Then, if needed, do Step 5.

5. If color cast remains, mist on a small amount of peroxide.
   - Tamp with soft brush.
   - Allow to dry.

6. If needed, repeat Steps 2, 3 and 5 one time.

7. If the spot persists, call a pro for options as soon as possible.

## Comments:

- **Optimum removal time: As soon as possible** within 24 hours of spill
- **Maximum size for home removal:** Class III / IV = 1 1/2 inches
- **Removal restrictions**: If the spot(s) is larger than 1 1/2 inches in diameter, **do not attempt TOTAL removal** using Class III or IV instructions. Do Step 1 **only** under Class III or IV. Mist spot(s) with a generous amount of ammonia. Put a folded towel moistened with water over spot(s) and a note next to it that says, ***"Do Not Touch Or Clean!"***. Then:
  - Call a pro and have spot removed as soon as possible within 24 hours. -OR-
  - If the spot is 3 inches or less in diameter, get a spot machine and:
    - If the spot is now old/dried, do Steps 2 - 7 under Class I.
    - If the spot is still fresh/wet, do Steps 1 - 7 under Class II.
- **Caution:** Feces contain large quantities of bacteria and/or other pathogens. Use your best judgment about wearing a mask, gloves and eye protection.
- Food coloring in some feces can immediately and permanently stain most nylon. If you cannot remove a spot, consult a pro for options as soon as possible.

## Materials Needed:

Protective mask, gloves, eye wear

Class III: Spotting kit, Shop vacuum * (if you have one) with attachment removed from hose

* If you do not have a shop vacuum, use a regular vacuum. As soon as you finish vacuuming the debris, remove the bag and throw it away, or clean the cartridge if you have a bagless vacuum cleaner.

Class IV: Disposable towels or tissues, Spotting kit

| Class III: Towel + Old / Dried Spot | Class IV: Towel + Fresh / Wet Spot |
|---|---|

### Class III — Steps:

1. Using your dinner knife, break up the spot(s) using a chopping action with the knife blade.
   - Using your spoon, scrape the spot out of the carpet fibers.
   - Vacuum debris with shop or vacuum cleaner hose.
   - Repeat entire Step until no more removes.

2. Mist on a generous amount of ammonia.
   - Mist on a generous amount of alcohol.
   - Allow to work 2 minutes.
   - Mist on a small amount of ammonia.
   - Agitate with end of spoon handle.

3. With a clean cloth towel over your hand, pinch out the spot 10 - 15 times, using a clean part of the towel each time.
   - With a towel, blot 10 - 15 times using a clean part of the towel each time.

4. Look at spot area carefully to see if the spot is gone:
   - If YES: Allow to dry.
   - If NO: Repeat Steps 2 and 3 until no more removes. Then, if needed, do Step 5.

5. If color cast remains, mist on a small amount of peroxide.
   - Tamp with soft brush.
   - Allow to dry.

6. If needed, repeat Steps 2, 3 and 5 one time.

7. If the spot persists, call a pro for options as soon as possible.

### Class IV — Steps:

1. Lay a disposable towel over the palm of your hand.
   - Using your spoon, scoop as much of the spot(s) as possible into the towel. Note: After each scoop, wipe the spoon on a clean part of the towel.
   - Repeat until no more removes.
   - Carefully drop the dirty towel in your empty bucket.
   - With a clean cloth towel, blot 15 - 20 times using a clean part of the towel each time.
   - Repeat entire Step until no more removes.

2. Mist on a generous amount of ammonia.
   - Mist on a generous amount of alcohol.
   - Allow to work 1 minute.
   - Mist on a small amount of ammonia.
   - Agitate with end of spoon handle.

3. With a towel over your hand, pinch out the spot 10 - 15 times using a clean part of the towel each time.
   - With a towel, blot 20 - 25 times using a clean part of the towel each time.

4. Look at spot area carefully to see if the spot is gone:
   - If YES: Allow to dry.
   - If NO: Repeat Steps 2 and 3 until no more removes. Then, if needed, do Step 5.

5. If color cast remains, mist on a small amount of peroxide.
   - Tamp with soft brush.
   - Allow to dry.

6. If needed, repeat Steps 2, 3 and 5 one time.

7. If the spot persists, call a pro for options as soon as possible.

Section II

# Feces - Semi-Solid Clumps: Human, Animal

## Comments:

- **Optimum removal time: As soon as possible** within 24 hours of spill
- **Maximum size for home removal:** Class I / II = 4 inches
- **Removal restrictions:** If the spot(s) is larger than 4 inches in diameter, **do not attempt TOTAL removal** using Class I or II instructions. Do Step 1 **only** under Class I or II. Mist spot(s) with a generous amount of ammonia. Put a folded towel moistened with water over spot(s) and a note next to it that says, **"Do Not Touch Or Clean!".** Call a pro and have spot removed as soon as possible within 24 hours.
- **Caution:** Feces contain large quantities of bacteria and/or other pathogens. Use your best judgment about wearing a mask, gloves and eye protection.
- **Caution: Do not attempt scissors removal** of spots from **any** type of looped carpet (berber, commercial glue down, etc.) unless the spot is **only on the outside fibers** of the loop(s). If in doubt, call a pro for options as soon as possible.
- Food coloring in some feces can immediately and permanently stain most nylon. If you cannot remove a spot, consult a pro for options as soon as possible.

## Materials Needed:

Protective mask, gloves, eye wear
Class I / II: Disposable towel(s), Spotting kit, Spot machine with cool water

Section II

### Class I: Spot Machine + Old / Dried Spot

**Steps:**

1. Remove clumps from spot(s) with disposable towel(s).

2. Using your spoon, scrape the spots out of the carpet fibers.
   - Using your scissors, wedge the blades up under the spot and snip it from the very tips of the carpet fibers. (This will minimize the indentations caused by the removed spots.) Note: On non-looped carpet, you can also trim a few carpet fibers around the edge of the removed spot, if needed, to minimize it further.
   - On non-looped carpets, rough up the trimmed carpet fibers a little with the tips of your scissors. Trim any taller roughed up fibers so they are equal in height with the rest of the carpet.
   - Vacuum debris with spot machine until no more removes.

3. Mist on a generous amount of ammonia.
   - Mist on a generous amount of alcohol.
   - Allow to work 2 minutes.
   - Mist on a small amount of ammonia.
   - Agitate with end of spoon handle.

4. With the spot machine, rinse with cool water using the chop stroke technique 10 - 12 times.
   - Take 8 - 10 slow, dry vacuum strokes.

5. Look at spot area carefully to see if the spot is gone:
   - If YES: Allow to dry.
   - If NO: Repeat Steps 3 and 4 until no more removes. Then, if needed, do Step 6.

6. If color cast remains, mist on a small amount of peroxide.
   - Tamp with soft brush.
   - Allow to dry.

7. If needed, repeat Steps 3, 4 and 6 one time.

8. If the spot persists, call a pro for options as soon as possible.

### Class II: Spot Machine + Fresh / Wet Spot

**Steps:**

1. Remove clumps from spot(s) with disposable towel(s).

2. Lay a disposable towel over the palm of your hand.
   - Using your spoon, scoop as much of the spot(s) as possible into the towel. Note: After each scoop, wipe the spoon on a clean part of the towel.
   - Carefully drop the dirty towel in your empty bucket.
   - With the spot machine, rinse with cool water using the single stroke technique 15 - 20 times.
   - Take 6 - 8 slow, dry vacuum strokes.

3. Mist on a generous amount of ammonia.
   - Mist on a generous amount of alcohol.
   - Allow to work 1 minute.
   - Mist on a small amount of ammonia.
   - Agitate with end of spoon handle.

4. With the spot machine, rinse with cool water using the chop stroke technique 6 - 8 times.
   - Take 4 - 6 slow, dry vacuum strokes.

5. Look at spot area carefully to see if the spot is gone:
   - If YES: Allow to dry.
   - If NO: Repeat Steps 3 and 4 until no more removes. Then, if needed, do Step 6.

6. If color cast remains, mist on a small amount of peroxide.
   - Tamp with soft brush.
   - Allow to dry.

7. If needed, repeat Steps 3, 4 and 6 one time.

8. If the spot persists, call a pro for options as soon as possible.

## *Comments:*

- **Optimum removal time: As soon as possible** within 24 hours of spill
- **Maximum size for home removal:** Class III / IV = 1 1/2 inches
- **Removal restrictions:** If the spot(s) is larger than 1 1/2 inches in diameter, **do not attempt TOTAL removal** using Class III or IV instructions. Do Step 1 **only** under Class III or IV. Mist spot(s) with a generous amount of ammonia. Put a folded towel moistened with water over spot(s) and a note next to it that says, *"Do Not Touch Or Clean!"*. Then:
  - Call a pro and have spot removed as soon as possible within 24 hours or if the spot is 4 inches or less in diameter, get a spot machine and:
    - If the spot is now old/dried, do Steps 2 - 8 under Class I.
    - If the spot is still fresh/wet, do Steps 2 - 8 under Class II.
- **Caution:** Feces contain large quantities of bacteria and/or other pathogens. Use your best judgment about wearing a mask, gloves and eye protection.
- **Caution: Do not attempt scissors removal** of spots from **any** type of looped carpet (berber, commercial glue down, etc.) unless the spot is **only on the outside fibers** of the loop(s). If in doubt, call a pro for options as soon as possible.
- Food coloring in some feces can immediately and permanently stain most nylon. If you cannot remove a spot, consult a pro for options as soon as possible.

## *Materials Needed:*

Protective mask, gloves, eye wear
Class III: Disposable towel(s), Spotting kit, Shop vacuum with attachment removed from hose.
*If you must use a regular vacuum remove the bag and throw it away, or clean the cartridge in a bagless vacuum cleaner as soon as you finish vacuuming the debris.
Class IV: Disposable towels or tissues, Spotting kit

| Class III: Towel + Old / Dried Spot | Class IV: Towel + Fresh / Wet Spot |
|---|---|

### *Steps:*

1. Remove clumps from spot(s) with disposable towel(s).

2. Using your spoon, scrape the spots out of the carpet fibers.
   - Using your scissors, wedge the blades up under the spot and snip it from the very tip of the carpet fibers. (This will minimize the indentations caused by the removed spots.) Note: On non-looped carpet, you can also trim a few carpet fibers around the edge of the removed spot, if needed, to minimize it further.
   - On non-looped carpets, rough up the trimmed carpet fibers a little with the tips of your scissors. Trim any taller roughed up fibers so they are equal in height with the rest of the carpet.
   - Vacuum debris with shop or vacuum cleaner hose.
   - Repeat entire Step until no more removes.

3. Mist on a generous amount of ammonia.
   - Mist on a generous amount of alcohol.
   - Allow to work 2 minutes.
   - Mist on a small amount of ammonia.
   - Agitate with end of spoon handle.

4. With a clean cloth towel over your hand, pinch out the spot 10 - 15 times, using a clean part of the towel each time.
   - With a towel, blot 10 - 15 times using a clean part of the towel each time.

5. Look at spot area carefully to see if the spot is gone:
   - If YES: Allow to dry.
   - If NO: Repeat Steps 3 and 4 until no more removes. Then, if needed, do Step 6.

6. If color cast remains, mist on a small amount of peroxide.
   - Tamp with soft brush.
   - Allow to dry.

7. If needed, repeat Steps 3, 4 and 6 one time.

8. If the spot persists, call a pro for options as soon as possible.

### *Steps:*

1. Remove clumps from spot(s) with disposable towel(s).

2. Lay a disposable towel over the palm of your hand.
   - Using your spoon, scoop as much of the spot(s) as possible into the towel. Note: After each scoop, wipe the spoon on a clean part of the towel.
   - Repeat until no more removes.
   - Carefully drop the dirty towel in your empty bucket.
   - With a clean cloth towel, blot spot 25 - 30 times, using a clean part of the towel each time.
   - Repeat entire Step until no more removes.

3. Mist on a generous amount of ammonia.
   - Mist on a generous amount of alcohol.
   - Allow to work 1 minute.
   - Mist on a small amount of ammonia.
   - Agitate with end of spoon handle.

4. With a towel over your hand, pinch out the spot 10 - 15 times, using a clean part of the towel each time.
   - With a towel, blot 20 - 25 times using a clean part of the towel each time.

5. Look at spot area carefully to see if the spot is gone:
   - If YES: Allow to dry.
   - If NO: Repeat Steps 3 and 4 until no more removes. Then, if needed, do Step 6.

6. If color cast remains, mist on a small amount of peroxide.
   - Tamp with soft brush.
   - Allow to dry.

7. If needed, repeat Steps 3, 4 and 6 one time.

8. If the spot persists, call a pro for options as soon as possible.

# Floor Wax - Liquid: Commercial or Household

## Comments:

- **Optimum removal time:** Within 24 hours of spill
- **Maximum size for home removal:** Class I = 1 1/2 inches / Class II = 3 inches
- **Removal restriction:** If a Class I spot(s) is larger than 1 1/2 inches in diameter or a Class II spot is larger than 3 inches in diameter, **do not attempt TOTAL removal** using Class I or II instructions. Do Step 1 **only** under Class I or II. Mist on a generous amount of ammonia. Put a folded towel moistened with water over spot. (Keep towel damp until pro comes). Call a pro and have spot removed within 2 days. (A large spot soaks too deep into the carpet fibers for home removal. Higher rinse pressure and temperature are required to remove these spots.)

## Materials Needed:

Class I / II: Spotting kit, Spot machine with hot water

## Class I: Spot Machine + Old / Dried Spot

### Steps:

1. Using the tip of the blade of your dinner knife and the end of the spoon handle, separate stuck together carpet fibers into as many individual tufts as possible.

2. Mist on a generous amount of ammonia.
   - Put a very moist, but not dripping wet, towel (moistened with water) over the spot(s).
   - Allow to work 2 minutes.
   - Lift towel. (On dark carpet, you may notice that the wax may have become whitish in color. Do not worry.)
   - Mist on a generous amount of ammonia.
   - Place very moist towel back over spot.
   - Allow to work 2 minutes.
   - Mist on a small amount of alcohol.
   - Allow to work 1 minute.
   - Agitate with end of spoon handle.

3. With the spot machine, rinse with hot water using the chop stroke technique 12 - 15 times.
   - Take 4 - 6 slow, dry vacuum strokes.

4. Look at spot area carefully to see if the spot is gone:
   - If YES: Allow to dry.
   - If NO: Repeat Steps 2 and 3 until no more removes.

5. If the spot persists, call a pro for options as soon as possible.

## Class II: Spot Machine + Fresh / Wet Spot

### Steps:

1. Using your spot machine, dry vacuum the spot(s) 6 - 8 times.
   - Rinse with hot water using the chop stroke technique 6 - 8 times.
   - Take 6 - 8 slow, dry vacuum strokes.

2. Mist on a generous amount of ammonia.
   - Mist on a small amount of alcohol.
   - Tamp with soft brush.
   - Allow to work 2 minutes.

3. With the spot machine, rinse with hot water using the single stroke technique 6 - 8 times.
   - Take 6 - 8 slow, dry vacuum strokes.

4. Look at spot area carefully to see if the spot is gone:
   - If YES: Allow to dry.
   - If NO: Repeat Steps 2 and 3 until no more removes.

5. If the spot persists, call a pro for options as soon as possible.

Spot Contents: Acrylic, Ammonia, Solids, Polymers

## *Comments:*

- **Optimum removal time:** Within 24 hours of spill
- **Maximum size for home removal:** Class III = No home removal / Class IV = 1 inch
- **Removal restrictions - Class III:** See "Class III" instructions below.
- **Removal restrictions - Class IV:** If the spot(s) is larger than 1 inch in diameter, **do not attempt TOTAL removal** using Class IV instructions. Do Step 1 **only** under Class IV. Mist on a generous amount of ammonia. Put a folded towel moistened with water over spot. (Keep towel damp until pro comes). Then:
  - Call a pro and have spot removed as soon as possible. -OR-
  - If the spot is now dried and is 1-1/2 inches or less in diameter, get a spot machine and do Steps 1 - 5 under Class I.
  - If the spot is still fresh/wet and is 3 inches or less in diameter, get a spot machine and do Steps 2 - 5 under Class II.

## *Materials Needed:*

Class III / IV: Disposable towels or tissues, Spotting kit

### *Class III: Towel + Old / Dried Spot*

**Steps:**

1. **Do not attempt TOTAL removal** using Class III instructions.
   - Using the tip of the blade of your dinner knife and the end of the spoon handle, separate stuck together carpet fibers into as many individual tufts as possible.

2. Mist on a generous amount of ammonia.
   - Put a folded cloth towel moistened with water over the spot(s). (Keep towel damp until pro comes or you remove spot with spot machine.)
   - Then:
     - Call a pro and have spot removed as soon as possible within 2 days. -OR-
     - If the spot is 1 1/2 inches or less in diameter, get a spot machine and do Steps 1 - 5 under Class I.

### *Class IV: Towel + Fresh / Wet Spot*

**Steps:**

1. Using a disposable towel, firmly blot spot(s) 10 - 15 times, using a clean part of the towel each time.
   - Repeat until no more absorbs.

2. Mist on a generous amount of ammonia.
   - Tamp with soft brush.
   - Allow to work 2 minutes.
   - Mist on a small amount of alcohol.
   - Tamp with soft brush.
   - Allow to work 1 minute.

3. With a cloth towel, firmly blot 15 - 20 times using a clean part of the towel each time.

4. Look at spot area carefully to see if the spot is gone:
   - If YES: Allow to dry.
   - If NO: Repeat Steps 2 and 3 until no more removes.

5. If the spot persists, call a pro for options as soon as possible.

Section II

# Floor Wax - Paste: Commercial or Household

## Comments:

- **Optimum removal time: As soon as possible** within 24 hours of spill
- **Maximum size for home removal:** Class I / II = 1 1/2 inches
- **Removal restrictions:** If the spot(s) has been pressed into the carpet fibers or is larger than 1 1/2 inches in diameter, **do not attempt TOTAL removal** using Class I or II instructions. Do Step 1 **only** under Class I or II. Put a dry towel over spot and a note next to it that says, ***"Do Not Touch Or Clean!"***. Call a pro and have spot removed as soon as possible within 24 hours.
- **Caution:** Paste floor wax should be removed as soon as possible within 24 hours, because it may have pigments that are not usually found in liquid floor wax.
- Wood stain or pigments in most of these products can immediately and permanently stain most nylon. If you cannot remove a spot, consult a pro for options as soon as possible.
- These products may be hard to remove from loop type carpets, especially if the spill as been pressed into the loop. If you cannot remove a spot, put a dry towel over spot and consult a pro for options as soon as possible.

## Materials Needed:

Class I / II: Spotting kit, Spot machine with hot water

<table>
<tr><td>

### Class I: Spot Machine + Old / Dried Spot

**Steps:**

1. Using your spoon, scrape out loose parts of the spot(s).
   - With a dry towel over your hand, pinch out spot 10 - 15 times, using a clean part of the towel each time.
   - Repeat entire Step until no more removes.

2. Mist on a generous amount of alcohol.
   - Mist on a generous amount of ammonia.
   - Agitate with hard brush.
   - Allow to work 2 minutes.

3. With the spot machine, rinse with hot water using the chop stroke technique 10 - 12 times.
   - Take 8 - 10 slow, dry vacuum strokes.

4. Look at spot area carefully to see if the spot is gone:
   - If YES: Allow to dry.
   - If NO: Repeat Steps 2 and 3 until no more removes. Then, if needed, do Step 5.

5. If color cast remains, mist on a generous amount of peroxide.
   - Mist on a small amount of ammonia.
   - Tamp with soft brush.
   - Allow to dry.

6. If the spot persists, call a pro for options as soon as possible.

</td><td>

### Class II: Spot Machine + Fresh / Wet Spot

**Steps:**

1. Using your spoon, scrape out loose parts of the spot(s).
   - With a dry towel over your hand, pinch out spot 10 - 15 times, using a clean part of the towel each time.
   - Repeat entire Step until no more removes.

2. Mist on a generous amount of alcohol.
   - Mist on a generous amount of ammonia.
   - Agitate with hard brush.
   - Allow to work 2 minutes.

3. With the spot machine, rinse with hot water using the chop stroke technique 6 - 8 times.
   - Take 4 - 6 slow, dry vacuum strokes.

4. Look at spot area carefully to see if the spot is gone:
   - If YES: Allow to dry.
   - If NO: Repeat Steps 2 and 3 until no more removes. Then, if needed, do Step 5.

5. If color cast remains, mist on a generous amount of peroxide.
   - Mist on a small amount of ammonia.
   - Tamp with soft brush.
   - Allow to dry.

6. If the spot persists, call a pro for options as soon as possible.

</td></tr>
</table>

Section II

## Comments:

- **Optimum removal time: As soon as possible** within 24 hours of spill
- **Maximum size for home removal:** Class III = No home removal / Class IV = 3/4 inch
- **Removal restrictions - Class III:** See "Class III" instructions below.
- **Removal restrictions - Class IV:** If the spot(s) has been pressed into the carpet fibers or is larger than 3/4 inch in diameter, **do not attempt TOTAL removal** using Class IV instructions. Do Step 1 **only** under Class IV. Put a dry towel over spot and a note next to it that says, ***"Do Not Touch Or Clean!"***. Then:
  - Call a pro and have spot removed as soon as possible within 24 hours. -OR-
  - If the spot is 1 1/2 inches or less in diameter and has not been pressed into the carpet fibers, get a spot machine and if the spot is still fresh/wet, do Steps 2 - 6 under Class II.
- **Caution:** Paste floor wax should be removed as soon as possible within 24 hours, because it may have pigments that are not usually found in liquid floor wax.
- Wood stain or pigments in most of these products can immediately and permanently stain most nylon. If you cannot remove a spot, consult a pro for options as soon as possible.
- These products may be hard to remove from loop type carpets, especially if the spill has been pressed into the loop. If you cannot remove a spot, put a dry towel over spot and call a pro for options as soon as possible.

## Materials Needed:
Class III: Spotting kit, Paper and pencil for note
Class IV: Spotting kit

### Class III: Towel + Old / Dried Spot

**Steps:**

1. Using your spoon, scrape out loose parts of the spot(s).
   - With a dry towel over your hand, pinch out spot 10 - 15 times, using a clean part of the towel each time.
   - Repeat entire Step until no more removes.
2. **Do not continue removal** for a Class III spot.
   - Put a dry towel over spot(s) and a note next to it that says, ***"Do Not Touch Or Clean!"***.
   - Then:
     - Call a pro and have spot removed as soon as possible within 24 hours. -OR-
     - If the spot is 1 1/2 inches or less in diameter and has not been pressed into the carpet fibers, get a spot machine and do Steps 2 - 6 under Class I.

### Class IV: Towel + Fresh / Wet Spot

**Steps:**

1. Using your spoon, scrape out loose parts of the spot(s).
   - With a dry towel over your hand, pinch out spot 10 - 15 times, using a clean part of the towel each time.
   - Repeat entire Step until no more removes.
2. Mist on a generous amount of alcohol.
   - Mist on a generous amount of ammonia.
   - Agitate with hard brush.
   - Allow to work 1 - 2 minutes.
3. With a towel, firmly blot 15 - 20 times using a clean part of the towel each time.
4. Look at spot area carefully to see if the spot is gone:
   - If YES: Allow to dry.
   - If NO: Repeat Steps 2 and 3 until no more removes. Then, if needed, do Step 5.
5. If color cast remains, mist on a generous amount of peroxide.
   - Mist on a small amount of ammonia.
   - Tamp with soft brush.
   - Allow to dry.
6. If the spot persists, call a pro for options as soon as possible.

Copyright 2006 by AmeriChoice Partners I, LTD. All rights reserved.

Section II

# Food Coloring, Extracts, Flavorings, Jell-O®, Gelatin, Kool-Aid®, Window Cleaner - Liquid

## Comments:

- **Optimum removal time: As soon as possible** within 24 hours of spill
- **Maximum size for home removal:** Class I / II = 2 inches
- **Removal restrictions:** If the spot(s) is larger than 2 inches in diameter, **do not attempt TOTAL removal** using Class I or II instructions. Do Step 1 **only** under Class I or II. Put a folded towel moistened with water over spot(s). (Keep towel damp until pro comes.) Call a pro to remove as soon as possible within 24 hours.
- Strong dye in these products can immediately and permanently stain most nylon. If you cannot remove a spot, consult a pro for options as soon as possible.

## Materials Needed:

Class I / II: Spotting kit, Spot machine with warm water

| Class I: Spot Machine + Old / Dried Spot | Class II: Spot Machine + Fresh / Wet Spot |
|---|---|
| **Steps:** | **Steps:** |
| 1. Using your spot machine, rinse the spot(s) with warm water using the chop stroke technique 8 - 10 times. | 1. Using your spot machine, dry vacuum the spot(s) until no more removes. |
| • Take 6 - 8 slow, dry vacuum strokes. | • Rinse with warm water using the single stroke technique 8 - 10 times. |
| • Repeat entire Step until no more removes. | • Take 4 - 6 slow, dry vacuum strokes. |
| 2. Mist on a small amount of alcohol. | • Repeat entire Step until no more removes. |
| • Mist on a generous amount of ammonia. | 2. Mist on a small amount of alcohol. |
| • Tamp with soft brush. | • Mist on a generous amount of ammonia. |
| • Allow to work 2 minutes. | • Tamp with soft brush. |
| 3. With the spot machine, rinse with warm water using the chop stroke technique 6 - 8 times. | • Allow to work 1 minute. |
| • Take 4 - 6 slow, dry vacuum strokes. | 3. With the spot machine, rinse with warm water using the single stroke technique 6 - 8 times. |
| 4. Look at and touch spill area carefully to see if the sticky residue is gone: | • Take 4 - 6 slow, dry vacuum strokes. |
| • If YES: Allow to dry. | 4. Look at and touch spill area carefully to see if the sticky residue is gone: |
| • If NO: Repeat Steps 2 and 3 until no more removes. Then, if needed, do Step 5. | • If YES: Allow to dry. |
| 5. If color cast remains, mist on a generous amount of peroxide. | • If NO: Repeat Steps 2 and 3 until no more removes. Then, if needed, do Step 5. |
| • Mist on a small amount of ammonia. | 5. If color cast remains, mist on a generous amount of peroxide. |
| • Tamp with soft brush. | • Mist on a small amount of ammonia. |
| • Allow to dry. | • Tamp with soft brush. |
| 6. If the spot persists, call a pro for options as soon as possible. | • Allow to dry. |
| | 6. If the spot persists, call a pro for options as soon as possible. |

Section II

Stain Contents: Alcohol, Sugar, Food Coloring, Vegetable Dyes, Colorant

## Comments:

- **Optimum removal time: As soon as possible** within 24 hours of spill
- **Maximum size for home removal:** Class III = No home removal / Class IV = 1 inch
- **Removal restrictions - Class III:** See "Class III" instructions below.
- **Removal restrictions - Class IV:** If the spot(s) is larger than 1 inch in diameter, **do not attempt TOTAL removal** using Class IV instructions. Do Step 1 **only** under Class IV. Mist a small amount of ammonia on spot(s). Put a folded towel moistened with water over spot(s). (Keep towel damp until pro comes.) Then:
  - Call a pro and have spot removed as soon as possible within 24 hours. -OR-
  - If the spot is 2 inches or less in diameter, get a spot machine and:
    - Old/dried spot: Do Steps 1 - 6 under Class I.
    - Fresh/wet spot: Do Steps 1 - 6 under Class II.
- Strong dye in these products can immediately and permanently stain nylon. If you cannot remove a spot, consult a pro for options as soon as possible.

## Materials Needed:
Class III: Ammonia, Towel
Class IV: Spotting kit

### Class III: Towel + Old / Dried Spot

**Steps:**

1. Do not attempt ANY removal using Class III instructions.
   - Mist on a generous amount of ammonia.
   - Put a dry towel over the spot(s).
   - Then:
     - Call a pro and have spot removed as soon as possible within 24 hours. -OR-
     - If the spot is 2 inches or less in diameter, get a spot machine and do Steps 1 - 6 under Class I.

### Class IV: Towel + Fresh / Wet Spot

**Steps:**

1. Fold a towel several times and place it over the spot(s).
   - Step on the towel with your full weight, using a clean part of the towel each time.
   - Repeat until no more absorbs.
2. Mist on a small amount of alcohol.
   - Mist on a generous amount of ammonia.
   - Tamp with soft brush.
   - Allow to work 1 minute.
3. With a towel, blot 15 - 20 times using a clean part of the towel each time.
4. Look at and touch spot area carefully to see if the sticky residue is gone:
   - If YES: Allow to dry.
   - If NO: Repeat Steps 2 and 3 until no more removes. Then, if needed, do Step 5.
5. If color cast remains, mist on a generous amount of peroxide.
   - Mist on a small amount of ammonia.
   - Tamp with soft brush.
   - Allow to dry.
6. If the spot persists, call a pro for options as soon as possible.

Section II

# Food Coloring - Paste, Cake Icing, Jello®- Gelled, Etc.

## Comments:

- **Optimum removal time**: **As soon as possible** within 24 hours of spill
- **Maximum size for home removal:** Class I / II = 3 inches
- **Removal restrictions:** If the spot(s) is larger than 3 inches in diameter, **do not attempt TOTAL removal** using Class I or II instructions. Do Step 1 **only** under Class I or II. Put a dry towel over spot. Call a pro and have spot removed as soon as possible within 24 hours.
- Strong dye in these products can immediately and permanently stain most nylon. If you are unable to remove a spot, consult a pro for options as soon as possible.

---

## Materials Needed:
Class I / II: Spotting kit, Spot machine with warm water

| Class I: Spot Machine + Old / Dried Spot | Class II: Spot Machine + Fresh / Wet Spot |
|---|---|
| **Steps:** | **Steps:** |
| 1. Using your dinner knife, break up the spot(s) using a chopping action with the knife blade.<br>• Using your spoon, scrape as much of the spot as possible out of the carpet fibers.<br>• Vacuum debris with spot machine.<br>• Repeat entire Step until no more removes. | 1. Lay a small towel over the palm of your hand. Then lay your hand on the carpet so the towel is at the edge of the spot.<br>• Using your spoon, scrape the spot onto the towel. Note: After each scrape, wipe the spoon on a clean part of the towel.<br>• Carefully drop the dirty towel in your empty bucket. |
| 2. Mist on a generous amount of ammonia.<br>• Agitate with hard brush.<br>• Allow to work 2 minutes. | 2. With the spot machine, rinse with warm water using the single stroke technique 10 - 12 times.<br>• Take 6 - 8 slow, dry vacuum strokes. |
| 3. With the spot machine, rinse with warm water using the chop stroke technique 8 - 10 times.<br>• Take 6 - 8 slow, dry vacuum strokes. | 3. Mist on a generous amount of ammonia.<br>• Agitate with hard brush.<br>• Allow to work 1 minute. |
| 4. Look at and touch spot area carefully to see if the sticky residue is gone:<br>• If YES: Allow to dry.<br>• If NO: Repeat Steps 2 and 3 until no more removes. Then, if needed, do Step 5. | 4. With the spot machine, rinse with warm water using the chop stroke technique 6 - 8 times.<br>• Take 4 - 6 slow, dry vacuum strokes. |
| 5. If color cast remains, mist on a generous amount of peroxide.<br>• Mist on a small amount of ammonia.<br>• Tamp with soft brush.<br>• Allow to dry. | 5. Look at and touch spot area carefully to see if the sticky residue is gone:<br>• If YES: Allow to dry.<br>• If NO: Repeat Steps 3 and 4 until no more removes. Then, if needed, do Step 6. |
| 6. If the spot persists, call a pro for options as soon as possible. | 6. If color cast remains, mist on a generous amount of peroxide.<br>• Mist on a small amount of ammonia.<br>• Tamp with soft brush.<br>• Allow to dry. |
| | 7. If the spot persists, call a pro for options as soon as possible. |

---

# Food Coloring - Paste, Cake Icing, Jello®- Gelled Etc.

Spot Contents: Sugar, Vegetable Dyes

## Comments:

- **Optimum removal time: As soon as possible** within 24 hours of spill
- **Maximum size for home removal:** Class III / IV = 1 1/2 inches
- **Removal restrictions:** If the spot(s) is larger than 1 1/2 inch in diameter, **do not attempt TOTAL removal** using Class III or IV instructions. Do Step 1 **only** under Class III or IV. Put a dry towel over spot. Then:
  - Call a pro and have spot removed as soon as possible within 24 hours. -OR-
  - If the spot is 3 inches or less in diameter, get a spot machine and:
    - If the spot is now old/dried, do Steps 2 - 6 under Class I.
    - If the spot is still fresh/wet, do Steps 1 - 7 under Class II.
- Strong dye in these products can immediately and permanently stain most nylon. If you are unable to remove a spot, consult a pro for options as soon as possible.

## Materials Needed:

Class III / IV: Spotting kit, Vacuum cleaner with attachment removed from hose

### Class III: Towel + Old / Dried Spot

**Steps:**

1. Using your dinner knife, break up the spot(s) using a chopping action with the knife blade.
   - Using your spoon, scrape as much of the spot as possible out of the carpet fibers.
   - Vacuum debris with vacuum cleaner hose.
   - Repeat entire Step until no more removes.

2. Mist on a generous amount of ammonia.
   - Agitate with hard brush.
   - Allow to work 2 minutes.

3. With a towel, blot 8 - 10 times using a clean part of the towel each time.

4. Look at and touch spot area carefully to see if the sticky residue is gone:
   - If YES: Allow to dry.
   - If NO: Repeat Steps 2 and 3 until no more removes. Then, if needed, do Step 5.

5. If color cast remains, mist on a generous amount of peroxide.
   - Mist on a small amount of ammonia.
   - Tamp with soft brush.
   - Allow to dry.

6. If the spot persists, call a pro for options as soon as possible.

### Class IV: Towel + Fresh / Wet Spot

**Steps:**

1. Lay a small towel over the palm of your hand. Then lay your hand on the carpet so the towel is at the edge of the spot.
   - Using your spoon, scrape the spot onto the towel. Note: After each scrape, wipe the spoon on a clean part of the towel.
   - Carefully drop the dirty towel in your empty bucket.

2. Mist on a generous amount of ammonia.
   - Agitate with hard brush.
   - Allow to work 1 minute.

3. With a towel, blot 8 - 10 times using a clean part of the towel each time.

4. Look at and touch spot area carefully to see if the sticky residue is gone:
   - If YES: Allow to dry.
   - If NO: Repeat Steps 2 and 3 until no more removes. Then, if needed, do Step 5.

5. If color cast remains, mist on a generous amount of peroxide.
   - Mist on a small amount of ammonia.
   - Tamp with soft brush.
   - Allow to dry.

6. If the spot persists, call a pro for options as soon as possible.

# Food Coloring, Jell-O®, Gelatin, Kool-Aid®, Clothes Dye - Powder

## Comments:

- **Optimum removal time:** Within 24 hours of spill
- **Maximum size for home removal:** Class I = No size limit if powder is dry / II = 4 inches
- **Removal restrictions:** If spot(s) is larger than 4 inches, **do not attempt TOTAL removal** using Class II instructions. Do Step 1 **only** under Class II. Put a dry towel over spot. Call a pro and have spot removed as soon as possible within 24 hours.
- **Caution:** Do **not** use a vacuum cleaner with a beater bar on this spill. The vibration will force the fine powder deep into the carpet, making the spill even harder to remove. Note: It is very important to be patient and thorough when dry vacuuming these types of products.
- **Caution:** Strong dye in these products can immediately and permanently stain most nylon if exposed to moisture, including high humidity. If you cannot remove a spot, contact a pro for options as soon as possible.

## Materials Needed:

Class I / II: Spotting kit, Spot machine with warm water, Vacuum cleaner

| Class I: Spot Machine + Old / Dried Spot | Class II: Spot Machine + Fresh / Wet Spot |
|---|---|
| **Steps:** | **Steps:** |

### Class I: Spot Machine + Old / Dried Spot

**Steps:**

1. Prepare your vacuum cleaner:
   - Remove the attachment, if any, from the vacuum cleaner hose.
2. Using just the vacuum cleaner hose, vacuum the spot very slowly:
   - Lay the hose so it is flat on the carpet with the opening near the outside edge of the spot.
   - Slowly push the hose opening from the edge into the middle of the spot from different angles 8 - 10 times until no more will remove.
   - Lift the hose and place it so the opening is on the carpet directly over the spot.
   - Move the hose opening slowly in a circular motion clockwise and counterclockwise over and around the edges of the spot.
   - Repeat entire Step until no more removes.
3. Mist on a small amount of alcohol.
   - Tamp gently with soft brush.
4. With the spot machine, rinse with warm water using the single stroke technique 8 - 10 times.
   - Take 6 - 8 slow, dry vacuum strokes.
5. Look at spot area carefully to see if the spot is gone:
   - If YES: Allow to dry.
   - If NO: Repeat Steps 3 and 4 one time. Then, if needed, do Step 6.
6. If color cast remains, mist on a generous amount of peroxide.
   - Mist on a small amount of ammonia.
   - Tamp with soft brush.
   - Allow to dry.
7. If the spot persists, call a pro for options as soon as possible.

### Class II: Spot Machine + Fresh / Wet Spot

**Steps:**

1. Prepare your vacuum cleaner:
   - Remove the attachment, if any, from the vacuum cleaner hose.
2. Using just the vacuum cleaner hose, vacuum the spot very slowly:
   - Lay the hose so it is flat on the carpet with the opening near the outside edge of the spot.
   - Slowly push the hose opening from the edge into the middle of the spot from different angles 8 - 10 times until no more will remove.
   - Lift the hose and place it so the opening is on the carpet directly over the spot.
   - Move the hose opening slowly in a circular motion clockwise and counterclockwise over and around the edges of the spot.
   - Repeat entire Step until no more removes.
3. Mist on a small amount of alcohol.
   - Tamp gently with soft brush.
4. With the spot machine, rinse with warm water using the single stroke technique 8 - 10 times.
   - Take 6 - 8 slow, dry vacuum strokes.
5. Look at spot area carefully to see if the spot is gone:
   - If YES: Allow to dry.
   - If NO: Repeat Steps 3 and 4 one time. Then, if needed, do Step 6.
6. If color cast remains, mist on a generous amount of peroxide.
   - Mist on a small amount of ammonia.
   - Tamp with soft brush.
   - Allow to dry.
7. If the spot persists, call a pro for options as soon as possible.

Section II

# Food Coloring, Jell-O®, Gelatin, Kool-Aid®, Clothes Dye - Powder

Spot Contents: Flavoring, Sugar, Vegetable Dyes, Acid Dyes, Colorant

## Comments:

- **Optimum removal time:** Within 24 hours of spill
- **Maximum size for home removal:** Class III / IV = 2 1/2 inches
- **Removal restrictions:** If the spot(s) is larger than 2 1/2 inches in diameter, do not attempt TOTAL removal using Class III or IV instructions. Do Steps 1 and 2 **only** under Class III or IV. Put a dry towel over spot. Then:
  - Call a pro and have spot removed within 2 days. -OR-
  - If the spot is 4 inches or less in diameter, get a spot machine and:
    - If the spot is now old/dried, do Steps 3 - 7 under Class I.
    - If the spot is still fresh/wet, do Steps 3 - 7 under Class II.
- **Caution:** Do **not** use a vacuum cleaner with a beater bar on this spill. The vibration will force the fine powder deep into the carpet, making the spill even harder to remove. Note: It is very important to be patient and thorough when dry vacuuming these types of products.
- Strong dye in these products can immediately and permanently stain most nylon if exposed to moisture, including high humidity. If you cannot remove a spot, contact a pro for options as soon as possible.

## Materials Needed:

Class III / IV: Spotting kit, Vacuum cleaner

### Class III: Towel + Old / Dried Spot

**Steps:**

1. Prepare your vacuum cleaner:
   - Remove the attachment, if any, from the vacuum cleaner hose.

2. Using just the vacuum cleaner hose, vacuum the spot very slowly:
   - Lay the hose so it is flat on the carpet with the opening near the outside edge of the spot.
   - Slowly push the hose opening from the edge into the middle of the spot from different angles 8 - 10 times until no more will remove.
   - Lift the hose and place it so the opening is on the carpet directly over the spot.
   - Move the hose opening slowly in a circular motion clockwise and counterclockwise over and around the edges of the spot.
   - Repeat entire Step until no more removes.

3. Mist on a small amount of alcohol.
   - Gently tamp with soft brush.

4. With a towel, blot 15 - 20 times using a clean part of the towel each time.

5. Look at spot area carefully to see if the spot is gone:
   - If YES: Allow to dry.
   - If NO: Repeat Steps 3 and 4 one time. Then, if needed, do Step 6.

6. If color cast remains, mist on a generous amount of peroxide.
   - Mist on a small amount of ammonia.
   - Tamp with soft brush.
   - Allow to dry.

7. If the spot persists, call a pro for options as soon as possible.

### Class IV: Towel + Fresh / Wet Spot

**Steps:**

1. Prepare your vacuum cleaner:
   - Remove the attachment, if any, from the vacuum cleaner hose.

2. Using just the vacuum cleaner hose, vacuum the spot very slowly:
   - Lay the hose so it is flat on the carpet with the opening near the outside edge of the spot.
   - Slowly push the hose opening from the edge into the middle of the spot from different angles 8 - 10 times until no more will remove.
   - Lift the hose and place it so the opening is on the carpet directly over the spot.
   - Move the hose opening slowly in a circular motion clockwise and counterclockwise over and around the edges of the spot.
   - Repeat entire Step until no more removes.

3. Mist on a small amount of alcohol.
   - Gently tamp with soft brush.

4. With a towel, blot 15 - 20 times using a clean part of the towel each time.

5. Look at spot area carefully to see if the spot is gone:
   - If YES: Allow to dry.
   - If NO: Repeat Steps 3 and 4 one time. Then, if needed, do Step 6.

6. If color cast remains, mist on a generous amount of peroxide.
   - Mist on a small amount of ammonia.
   - Tamp with soft brush.
   - Allow to dry.

7. If the spot persists, call a pro for options as soon as possible.

Section II

# Fruit Juice - No Dye: Apple, Apricot, Grapefruit, Lemon, Orange, White Grape, Etc.

## Comments:

- **Optimum removal time:** Within 24 hours of spill
- **Maximum size for home removal:** Class I / II = 4 inches
- **Removal restrictions:** If the spot(s) is larger than 4 inches in diameter, **do not attempt TOTAL removal** using Class I or II instructions. Do Step 1 **only** under Class I or II. Put a folded towel moistened with water over spot. Call a pro and have spot removed within 3 days.
- **Caution:** These products can stain some nylon if left untreated as little as 3 days. If you cannot remove a spot, consult a pro for options as soon as possible.
- These products contain strong acids or tannin, can be very sticky, and/or contain lots of pulp that can be very hard to remove from loop type carpets. If you cannot remove a spot, consult a pro for options as soon as possible.

## Materials Needed:

Class I / II: Spotting kit, Spot machine with warm water

### Class I: Spot Machine + Old / Dried Spot

#### Steps:

1. Using your spot machine, rinse the spot(s) with warm water using the chop stroke technique 10 - 12 times.
   - Take 8 - 10 slow, dry vacuum strokes.
   - Repeat entire Step until no more removes.

2. Mist on a generous amount of ammonia.
   - Mist on a small amount of peroxide.
   - Allow to work 2 minutes.
   - Mist on a small amount of ammonia.
   - Agitate with hard brush.
   - Mist on a small amount of ammonia.
   - Agitate with hard brush.

3. With the spot machine, rinse with warm water using the chop stroke technique 6 - 8 times.
   - Take 4 - 6 slow, dry vacuum strokes.

4. Look at and touch spill area carefully to see if the sticky residue is gone:
   - If YES: Allow to dry.
   - If NO: Repeat Steps 2 and 3 until no more removes. Then, if needed, do Step 5.

5. If color cast remains, mist on a generous amount of peroxide.
   - Tamp with soft brush.
   - Allow to dry.

6. If needed, repeat Steps 2, 3 and 5 one time.

7. If the spot persists, call a pro for options as soon as possible.

### Class II: Spot Machine + Fresh / Wet Spot

#### Steps:

1. Using your spot machine, dry vacuum the spot(s) 6 - 8 times.
   - Rinse with warm water using the single stroke technique 8 - 10 times.
   - Take 6 - 8 slow, dry vacuum strokes.
   - Repeat entire Step until no more removes.

2. Mist on a small amount of ammonia.
   - Mist on a small amount of peroxide.
   - Allow to work 1 minute.
   - Agitate with hard brush.
   - Mist on a small amount of ammonia.
   - Agitate with hard brush.

3. With the spot machine, rinse with warm water using the chop stroke technique 6 - 8 times.
   - Take 4 - 6 slow, dry vacuum strokes.

4. Look at and touch spill area carefully to see if the sticky residue is gone:
   - If YES: Allow to dry.
   - If NO: Repeat Steps 2 and 3 until no more removes. Then, if needed, do Step 5.

5. If color cast remains, mist on a generous amount of peroxide.
   - Tamp with soft brush.
   - Allow to dry.

6. If needed, repeat Steps 2, 3 and 5 one time.

7. If the spot persists, call a pro for options as soon as possible.

Section II

# Fruit Juice - No Dye: *Apple, Apricot, Grapefruit, Lemon, Orange, White Grape, Etc.*

Spot / Stain Contents: Citric Acid, Possible Corn Syrup, Pulp, Tannin

## Comments:

- **Optimum removal time:** Within 24 hours of spill
- **Maximum size for home removal:** Class III / IV = 2 inches
- **Removal restrictions:** If the spot(s) is larger than 2 inches in diameter, do not attempt TOTAL removal using Class III or IV instructions. Do Steps 1 and 2 **only** under Class III or IV. Put a folded towel moistened with water over the stain. Then:
  - Call a pro and have spot removed within 2 days. -OR-
  - If the spot is 4 inches or less in diameter, get a spot machine and:
    - If the spot is now old/dried, do Steps 1 - 7 under Class I.
    - If the spot is still fresh/wet, do Steps 1 - 7 under Class II.
- **Caution:** These products can stain some nylon if left untreated for as little as 3 days. If you cannot remove a spot, consult a pro for options as soon as possible.
- These products contain strong acids or tannin, can be very sticky, and/or contain lots of pulp that can be especially hard to remove from loop type carpets. If you cannot remove a spot, consult a pro for options as soon as possible.

## Materials Needed:

Class III / IV: Spotting kit

### Class III: Towel + Old / Dried Spot

**Steps:**

1. Mist on a generous amount of ammonia.
   - Mist on a small amount of peroxide.
   - Allow to work 2 minutes.
   - Mist on a small amount of ammonia.
   - Agitate with hard brush.
   - Mist on a small amount of ammonia.
   - Agitate with hard brush.
2. With a towel, firmly blot 13 - 15 times, using a clean part of the towel each time.
3. Look at and touch spill area carefully to see if sticky residue is gone:
   - If YES: Allow to dry.
   - If NO: Repeat Steps 1 and 2 until no more removes. Then, if needed, do Step 4.
4. If color cast remains, mist on a generous amount of peroxide.
   - Tamp with soft brush.
   - Allow to dry.
5. If needed, repeat Steps 1, 2 and 4 one time.
6. If the spot persists, call a pro for options as soon as possible.

### Class IV: Towel + Fresh / Wet Spot

**Steps:**

1. Fold a towel several times and place it over the spot(s).
   - Step on the towel with your full weight, using a clean part of the towel each time.
   - Repeat entire Step until no more absorbs.
2. Mist on a small amount of ammonia.
   - Mist on a small amount of peroxide.
   - Allow to work 1 minute.
   - Agitate with hard brush.
   - Mist on a small amount of ammonia
   - Agitate with hard brush
3. With a towel, blot 10 - 12 times, using a clean part of the towel each time.
4. Look at and touch spill area carefully to see if sticky residue is gone:
   - If YES: Allow to dry.
   - If NO: Repeat Steps 2 and 3 until no more removes. Then, if needed, do Step 5.
5. If color cast remains, mist on a generous amount of peroxide.
   - Tamp with soft brush.
   - Allow to dry.
6. If needed, repeat Steps 2, 3 and 5 one time.
7. If the spot persists, call a pro for options as soon as possible.

Section II

# Fruit Juice - With Dye: Blueberry, Cherry, Cranberry, Prune, Red Grape, Etc.

## Comments:

- **Optimum removal time:** Within 24 hours of spill
- **Maximum size for home removal:** Class I / II = 4 inches
- **Removal restrictions:** If the spot(s) is larger than 4 inches in diameter, **do not attempt TOTAL removal** using Class I or II instructions. Do Step 1 **only** under Class I or II. Put a folded towel moistened with water over the stain. Call a pro and have spot removed within 2 days.
- Strong acid dyes in these products can immediately and permanently stain most nylon. If you cannot remove a spot, consult a pro for options as soon as possible.

## Materials Needed:

Class I / II: Spotting kit, Spot machine with warm water

| Class I: Spot Machine + Old / Dried Spot | Class II: Spot Machine + Fresh / Wet Spot |
|---|---|
| **Steps:** | **Steps:** |

### Class I: Spot Machine + Old / Dried Spot

**Steps:**

1. Using your spot machine, rinse the spot(s) with warm water using the chop stroke technique 10 - 12 times.
   - Take 6 - 8 slow, dry vacuum strokes.
   - Repeat entire Step until no more removes.

2. Mist on a generous amount of ammonia.
   (Red berry stains may turn blue. Do not worry.)
   - Mist on a generous amount of peroxide.
     (The blue may turn back to red.)
   - Allow to work 2 minutes.
   - Tamp with soft brush.

3. With the spot machine, rinse with warm water using the chop stroke technique 8 - 10 times.
   - Take 6 - 8 slow, dry vacuum strokes.

4. Look at and touch spot area carefully to see if the sticky residue is gone:
   - If YES: Allow to dry.
   - If NO: Repeat Steps 2 and 3 until no more removes. Then, if needed, do Step 5.

5. If color cast remains, mist on a generous amount of peroxide.
   - Mist on a small amount of ammonia.
   - Tamp with soft brush.
   - Allow to dry.

6. If the spot persists, call a pro for options as soon as possible.

### Class II: Spot Machine + Fresh / Wet Spot

**Steps:**

1. Using your spot machine, dry vacuum the spot(s) 8 - 10 times.
   - Rinse with warm water using the single stroke technique 8 - 10 times.
   - Take 6 - 8 slow, dry vacuum strokes.
   - Repeat entire Step until no more removes.

2. Mist on a generous amount of ammonia.
   (Red berry stains may turn blue. Do not worry.)
   - Mist on a generous amount of peroxide.
     (The blue may turn back to red.)
   - Allow to work 1 minute.
   - Tamp with soft brush.

3. With the spot machine, rinse with warm water using the single stroke technique 6 - 8 times.
   - Take 4 - 6 slow, dry vacuum strokes.

4. Look at and touch spot area carefully to see if the sticky residue is gone:
   - If YES: Allow to dry.
   - If NO: Repeat Steps 2 and 3 until no more removes. Then, if needed, do Step 5.

5. If color cast remains, mist on a generous amount of peroxide.
   - Mist on a small amount of ammonia.
   - Tamp with soft brush.
   - Allow to dry.

6. If the spot persists, call a pro for options as soon as possible.

# Fruit Juice - With Dye: *Blueberry, Cherry, Cranberry, Prune, Red Grape, Etc.*

Stain Contents: Acid Dye, Coloring, Possible Preservatives, Sugar, Tannin

## Comments:

- **Optimum removal time:** Within 24 hours of spill
- **Maximum size for home removal:** Class III / IV = 2 inches
- **Removal restrictions:** If the spot(s) is larger than 2 inches in diameter, **do not attempt TOTAL removal** using Class III or IV instructions. Do Steps 1 and 2 **only** under Class III or IV. Put a folded towel moistened with water over the stain. Then:
  - Call a pro and have spot removed within 2 days. -OR-
  - If the spot is less than 4 inches in diameter, get a spot machine and:
    - If the spot is now old/dried, do Steps 1 - 6 under Class I.
    - If the spot is still fresh/wet, do Steps 1 - 6 under Class II.
- Strong acid dyes in these products can immediately and permanently stain most nylon. If you cannot remove a spot, consult a pro for options as soon as possible.

## Materials Needed:

Class III / IV: Spotting kit

### Class III: Towel + Old / Dried Spot

#### Steps:

1. Mist on a generous amount of ammonia.
   (Red berry stains may turn blue. Do not worry.)
   - Mist on a generous amount of peroxide.
     (The blue may turn back to red.)
   - Allow to work 2 minutes.
   - Tamp with soft brush.
   - Mist on a small amount of ammonia.
2. With a towel, firmly blot 13 - 15 times using a clean part of the towel each time.
3. Look at and touch spot area carefully to see if the sticky residue is gone:
   - If YES: Allow to dry.
   - If NO: Repeat Steps 1 and 2 until no more removes. Then, if needed, do Step 4.
4. If color cast remains, mist on a generous amount of peroxide.
   - Mist on a small amount of ammonia.
   - Tamp with soft brush.
   - Allow to dry.
5. If the spot persists, call a pro for options as soon as possible.

### Class IV: Towel + Fresh / Wet Spot

#### Steps:

1. Fold a towel several times and place it over the spot(s).
   - Firmly blot the spot 10 - 12 times, using a clean part of the towel each time.
   - Repeat until no more absorbs.
2. Mist on a generous amount of ammonia.
   (Red berry stains may turn blue. Do not worry.)
   - Mist on a small amount of peroxide.
     (The blue may turn back to red.)
   - Allow to work 1 minute.
   - Tamp with soft brush.
3. With a towel, blot 10 - 12 times using a clean part of the towel each time.
4. Look at and touch spot area carefully to see if the sticky residue is gone:
   - If YES: Allow to dry.
   - If NO: Repeat Steps 2 and 3 until no more removes. Then, if needed, do Step 5.
5. If color cast remains, mist on a generous amount of peroxide.
   - Mist on a small amount of ammonia.
   - Tamp with soft brush.
   - Allow to dry.
6. If the spot persists, call a pro for options as soon as possible.

Section II

# Furniture Polish - Oil or Spray

## Comments:

- **Optimum removal time:** Within 24 hours of spill
- **Maximum size for home removal:** Class I / II = 2 inches
- **Removal restrictions:** If the spot(s) is larger than 2 inches in diameter, **do not attempt TOTAL removal** using Class I or II instructions. Do Step 1 **only** under Class I or II. Put a dry towel over spot and a note next to it that says, ***"Do Not Touch Or Clean!"***. Call a pro and have spot removed within 2 days.
- Large spills may damage latex in carpet backing and can immediately and permanently stain nylon. Consult a pro for options as soon as possible.
- Spills larger than 2 inches can soak through the carpet and pad to the subfloor and cause recurring spots. (See "Recurring Spots", Chapter 4.) Consult a pro for options as soon as possible.

## Materials Needed:
Class I / II: Spotting kit, Spot machine with hot water

| Class I: Spot Machine + Old / Dried Spot | Class II: Spot Machine + Fresh / Wet Spot |
|---|---|
| **Steps:** | **Steps:** |
| 1. Fold a towel several times and place it over the spot(s). <br> • Step on the towel with your full weight 10 - 15 times, using a clean part of the towel each time. <br> • Repeat until no more absorbs. | 1. Fold a towel several times and place it over the spot(s). <br> • Step on the towel with your full weight 10 - 15 times, using a clean part of the towel each time. <br> • Repeat until no more absorbs. |
| 2. Mist on a generous amount of alcohol. <br> • Firmly tamp with soft brush. <br> • Allow to work 2 minutes. <br> • Mist on a generous amount of alcohol. <br> • Firmly tamp with soft brush. | 2. Mist on a generous amount of alcohol. <br> • Firmly tamp with soft brush. <br> • Allow to work 1 minute. <br> • Mist on a generous amount of alcohol. <br> • Firmly tamp with soft brush. |
| 3. With the spot machine, rinse with hot water using the chop stroke technique 6 - 8 times. <br> • Take 4 - 6 slow, dry vacuum strokes. | 3. With the spot machine, rinse with hot water using the chop stroke technique 6 - 8 times. <br> • Take 4 - 6 slow, dry vacuum strokes. |
| 4. Look at and touch spot area carefully to see if the oily residue is gone: <br> • If YES: Allow to dry. <br> • If NO: Repeat Steps 2 and 3 until no more removes. Then, if needed, do Step 5. | 4. Look at and touch spot area carefully to see if the oily residue is gone: <br> • If YES: Allow to dry. <br> • If NO: Repeat Steps 2 and 3 until no more removes. Then, if needed, do Step 5. |
| 5. If color cast remains, mist on a generous amount of peroxide. <br> • Mist on a small amount of ammonia. <br> • Tamp with soft brush. <br> • Allow to dry. | 5. If color cast remains, mist on a generous amount of peroxide. <br> • Mist on a small amount of ammonia. <br> • Tamp with soft brush. <br> • Allow to dry. |
| 6. If needed, repeat Steps 2, 3 and 5 one time. | 6. If needed, repeat Steps 2, 3 and 5 one time. |
| 7. If the spot persists, call a pro for options as soon as possible. | 7. If the spot persists, call a pro for options as soon as possible. |

## Comments:

- **Optimum removal time:** Within 24 hours of spill
- **Maximum size for home removal:** Class III / IV = 1 1/4 inches
- **Removal restrictions:** If the spot(s) is larger than 1 1/4 inches in diameter, **do not attempt TOTAL removal** using Class III or IV instructions. Do Step 1 **only** under Class III or IV. Put a dry towel over spot and a note next to it that says, "*Do Not Touch Or Clean!*". Then:
  - Call a pro and have spot removed within 2 days. -OR-
  - If the spot is 2 inches or less in diameter, get a spot machine and:
    - If the spot is now old, do Steps 2 - 7 under Class I.
    - If the spot is still fresh, do Steps 2 - 7 under Class II.
- Large spills may damage latex in carpet backing and can immediately and permanently stain nylon. Consult a pro for options as soon as possible.
- Spills larger than 2 inches can soak through the carpet and pad to the subfloor and cause recurring spots. (See "Recurring Spots", Chapter 4.) Consult a pro for options as soon as possible.

## Materials Needed:

Class III / IV: Spotting kit

### Class III: Towel + Old / Dried Spot

**Steps:**

1. Fold a towel several times and place it over the spot(s).
   - Step on the towel with your full weight 10 - 15 times, using a clean part of the towel each time.
   - Repeat until no more absorbs.
2. Mist on a generous amount of alcohol.
   - Firmly tamp with soft brush.
   - Allow to work 2 minutes.
   - Mist on a generous amount of alcohol.
   - Firmly tamp with soft brush.
3. With a towel, blot the spot 13 - 15 times, using a clean part of the towel each time.
4. Look at and touch spot area carefully to see if the oily residue is gone:
   - If YES: Allow to dry.
   - If NO: Repeat Steps 2 and 3 until no more removes. Then, if needed, do Step 5.
5. If color cast remains, mist on a generous amount of peroxide.
   - Mist on a small amount of ammonia.
   - Tamp with soft brush.
   - Allow to dry.
6. If needed, repeat Step 5 one time the next day.
7. If the spot persists, call a pro for options as soon as possible.

### Class IV: Towel + Fresh / Wet Spot

**Steps:**

1. Fold a towel several times and place it over the spot(s).
   - Step on the towel with your full weight 10 - 15 times, using a clean part of the towel each time.
   - Repeat until no more absorbs.
2. Mist on a generous amount of alcohol.
   - Firmly tamp with soft brush.
   - Allow to work 2 minutes.
   - Mist on a small amount of alcohol.
   - Firmly tamp with soft brush.
3. With a towel, blot the spot 13 - 15 times, using a clean part of the towel each time.
4. Look at and touch spot area carefully to see if the oily residue is gone:
   - If YES: Allow to dry.
   - If NO: Repeat Steps 2 and 3 until no more removes. Then, if needed, do Step 5.
5. If color cast remains, mist on a generous amount of peroxide.
   - Mist on a small amount of ammonia.
   - Tamp with soft brush.
   - Allow to dry.
6. If needed, repeat Step 5 one time the next day.
7. If the spot persists, call a pro for options as soon as possible.

Section II

# Gasoline - Unmixed or Mixed with Oil

## Comments:

- **Optimum removal time: As soon as possible** within 24 hours of spill
- **Maximum size for home removal:** Class I / II = 2 1/2 inches
- **Removal restrictions:** If the spot(s) is larger than 2 1/2 inches in diameter, **do not attempt TOTAL removal** using Class I or II instructions. Do Step 1 **only** under Class I or II. Put a dry towel over spot. Call a pro and have spot removed as soon as possible within 24 hours.
- Large spills can damage latex in the carpet backing and pad and cause it to swell. These little hills in the carpet make it look as if it is loose and needs to be re-stretched. Consult a pro for options.
- Large spills may cause discoloration to polyester and nylon over time (as little as 1 - 4 weeks). Consult a pro for options.

## Materials Needed:
Class I / II: Gloves, Spotting kit, Spot machine with hot water

### Class I: Spot Machine + Old / Dried Spot

**Steps:**

1. Using your spot machine, rinse the spot(s) with hot water using the single stroke technique 10 - 12 times.
   - Take 6 - 8 slow, dry vacuum strokes.

2. Mist on a generous amount of ammonia.
   - Mist on a generous amount of alcohol.
   - Tamp with soft brush.
   - Allow to work 1 minute.

3. With the spot machine, rinse with hot water using the single stroke technique 8 - 10 times.
   - Take 6 - 8 slow, dry vacuum strokes.

4. Smell spot area carefully to see if the spot odor is gone:
   - If YES: Allow to dry.
   - If NO: Repeat Steps 2 and 3 until no more removes. Allow to dry.

5. Check for odor the next day to see if odor is still gone:
   - If YES: No further action is needed.
   - If NO: Repeat Steps 2 and 3 one time.

6. If odor persists, call a pro for options.

### Class II: Spot Machine + Fresh / Wet Spot

**Steps:**

1. Using your spot machine, dry vacuum the spot(s) 10 - 12 times taking slow, single strokes.
   - Rinse with hot water using the single stroke technique 10 - 12 times.
   - Take 6 - 8 slow, dry vacuum strokes.

2. Mist on a generous amount of ammonia.
   - Mist on a generous amount of alcohol.
   - Tamp with soft brush.
   - Allow to work 1 minute.

3. With the spot machine, rinse with hot water using the single stroke technique 8 - 10 times.
   - Take 6 - 8 slow, dry vacuum strokes.

4. Smell spot area carefully to see if the spot odor is gone:
   - If YES: Allow to dry.
   - If NO: Repeat Steps 2 and 3 until no more removes. Allow to dry.

5. Check for odor the next day to see if odor is still gone:
   - If YES: No further action is needed.
   - If NO: Repeat Steps 2 and 3 one time.

6. If odor persists, call a pro for options.

Section II

## Comments:

- **Optimum removal time: As soon as possible** within 24 hours of spill
- **Maximum size for home removal:** Class III / IV = 1 1/2 inches
- **Removal restrictions:** If the spot(s) is larger than 1 1/2 inches in diameter, **do not attempt TOTAL removal** using Class III or IV instructions. Do Steps 1 and 2 **only** under Class III or Steps 1 - 3 **only** under Class IV. Put a dry towel over spot. Then:
  - Call a pro and have spot removed as soon as possible within 24 hours. -OR-
  - If the spot is 2 1/2 inches or less in diameter, get a spot machine and:
    - If the spot is now old/dried, do Steps 1 - 6 under Class I.
    - If the spot is still fresh/wet, do Steps 1 - 6 under Class II.
- Large spills can damage latex in the carpet backing and pad and cause it to swell. These little hills in the carpet make it look as if it is loose and needs to be re-stretched. Consult a pro for options.
- Large spills may cause discoloration to polyester and nylon over time (as little as 1 - 4 weeks). Consult a pro for options.

## Materials Needed:

Class III / IV: Gloves, Disposable towels or tissues, Spotting kit

### Class III: Towel + Old / Dried Spot

**Steps:**

1. Mist a generous amount of ammonia on the spot(s).
   - Mist on a generous amount of alcohol.
   - Tamp with soft brush.
   - Allow to work 1 minute.

2. With a cloth towel, blot 13 - 15 times using a clean part of the towel each time.

3. Smell spot area carefully to see if the spot odor is gone:
   - If YES: Allow to dry.
   - If NO: Repeat Steps 1 and 2 until no more removes. Allow to dry.

4. Check for odor the next day to see if odor is still gone:
   - If YES: No further action is needed.
   - If NO: Repeat Steps 1 and 2 one time.

5. If odor persists, call a pro for options as soon as possible.

### Class IV: Towel + Fresh / Wet Spot

**Steps:**

1. Fold a disposable towel several times and place it over the spot(s).
   - Step on the towel with your full weight 10 - 15 times, using a clean part of the towel each time.
   - Repeat until no more absorbs.

2. Mist on a generous amount of ammonia.
   - Mist on a generous amount of alcohol.
   - Tamp with soft brush.
   - Allow to work 1 minute.

3. With a cloth towel, blot 13 - 15 times using a clean part of the towel each time.

4. Smell spot area carefully to see if the spot odor is gone:
   - If YES: Allow to dry.
   - If NO: Repeat Steps 2 and 3 until no more removes. Allow to dry.

5. Check for odor the next day to see if odor is still gone:
   - If YES: No further action is needed.
   - If NO: Repeat Steps 2 and 3 one time.

6. If odor persists, call a pro for options as soon as possible.

# Glue - Airplane, Model, Latex, Super Glue, Etc.

## Comments:

- **Optimum removal time: As soon as possible** within 24 hours of spill
- **Maximum size for home removal:** Class I = 3/8 inch / Class II = 1 inch
- **Removal restrictions - Class I:** See "Class I" instructions below.
- **Removal restrictions - Class II:** If the spot is larger than 1 inch in diameter, **do not attempt TOTAL removal** using Class II instructions. Do Steps 1 and 2 **only** under Class II. Mist a generous amount of alcohol on spot(s). Put a folded towel moistened with water over spot. (Keep towel damp until pro comes.) Call a pro and have spot removed as soon as possible within 24 hours.
- **Caution: Do not attempt scissors removal** of spots from **any** type of looped carpet (berber, commercial glue down, etc.) unless the spot is **only on the outside fibers** of the loop(s). If in doubt, call a pro for options as soon as possible.
- These products can be very hard to remove. If you cannot remove a spot, consult a pro for options as soon as possible.

## Materials Needed:
Class I - 3/8 inch or smaller: Ruler, Scissors, Spot machine
Class I - larger than 3/8 inch: Ruler, Paper and pencil for note
Class II: Spotting kit, Disposable towel(s), Spot machine with hot water

## Class I: Spot Machine + Old / Dried Spot

### Steps:
**Follow the instructions for your size spot(s):**

**If the spot is 3/8 inch (pencil eraser size) or smaller:**

1. Allow the spot to harden completely.

2. Using your scissors, wedge the blades up under the spot(s) and snip the hardened parts from the very tip of the carpet fibers. (This will minimize the indentations caused by the removed spots.) Note: On non-looped carpets, you can also trim a few carpet fibers around the edge of the removed spot, if needed, to minimize it further.
   - On non-looped carpets, rough up the trimmed carpet fibers a little with the tips of your scissors. Trim any taller roughed up fibers so they are equal in height with the rest of the carpet.
   - Vacuum debris with spot machine.

**If the spot is larger than 3/8 inch (pencil eraser size):**

1. **Do not attempt ANY removal** of a Class I spot.
   - Put a note next to spot(s) that says, ***"Do Not Touch Or Clean!"***.
   - (Do **not** put a towel over spot.)

2. Call a pro and have spot removed as soon as possible within 24 hours of the spill.

## Class II: Spot Machine + Fresh / Wet Spot

### Steps:
1. Mist your dinner knife blade with alcohol.

2. Hold a disposable towel at the edge of the spot.
   - Keeping the blade of your dinner knife almost flat against the carpet, scrape the spot into the towel. Note: After each scrape:
     - Wipe the knife blade on a clean part of the towel.
     - Carefully drop the dirty towel in your empty bucket.
     - Re-mist the knife blade with alcohol.
   - Repeat entire Step until no more spot matter removes.

3. Mist a generous amount of alcohol on the spot(s).
   - Agitate with end of spoon handle.
   - Allow to work 1 minute.
   - Mist on a generous amount of ammonia.
   - Agitate with end of spoon handle.

4. With the spot machine, rinse with hot water using the chop stroke technique 10 - 12 times.
   - Take 6 - 8 slow, dry vacuum strokes.

5. Look at and touch spot area carefully to see if the hard or sticky residue is gone:
   - If YES: Allow to dry.
   - If NO: Repeat Steps 3 and 4 until no more removes. Allow to dry.

6. Again, look at and touch spot area carefully to see if the hard or sticky residue is gone:
   - If YES: No further action is needed.
   - If NO: Repeat Steps 3 and 4 one time.

7. If the spot persists, call a pro for options as soon as possible.

# Glue - Airplane, Model, Latex, Super Glue, Etc.

Spot Contents: Cellulose Esters, Chlorinated and Aromatic Solvents, Hardeners, Ketone, Latex Solvent-Soluble Plastics

## Comments:

- **Optimum removal time: As soon as possible** within 24 hours of spill
- **Maximum size for home removal:** Class III = 3/8 inch / Class IV = 1/2 inch
- **Removal restrictions - Class III:** See "Class III" instructions below.
- **Removal restrictions - Class IV:** If the spot(s) is larger than 1/2 inch in diameter, do not attempt TOTAL removal using Class IV instructions. Do Steps 1 and 2 **only** under Class IV. Mist a generous amount of alcohol on spot(s). Put a folded towel moistened with water over spot. (Keep towel damp until pro comes.) Then:
  - Call a pro and have spot removed as soon as possible within 24 hours. -OR-
  - If the spot is 1 inch or less in diameter and is still fresh/wet, get a spot machine and do Steps 3 - 7 under Class II.
- **Caution: Do not attempt scissors removal** of spots from **any** type of looped carpet (berber, commercial glue down, etc.) unless the spot is only **on the outside fibers** of the loop(s). If in doubt, call a pro for options as soon as possible.
- These products can be very hard to remove. If you cannot remove a spot, consult a pro for options as soon as possible.

---

## Materials Needed:

Class III - 3/8 inch or smaller: Ruler, Scissors, Vacuum cleaner with attachment removed from hose
Class III - larger than 3/8 inch: Ruler, Paper and pencil for note
Class IV: Spotting kit, Disposable towel(s)

## Class III: Towel + Old / Dried Spot

### Steps:

**Follow the instructions for your size spot(s):**

**If the spot is 3/8 inch (pencil eraser size) or smaller:**

1. Allow the spot to harden completely.

2. Using your scissors, wedge the blades up under the spot(s) and snip the hardened parts from the very tip of the carpet fibers. (This will minimize the indentations caused by the removed spots.) Note: On non-looped carpets, you can also trim a few carpet fibers around the edge of the removed spot, if needed, to minimize it further.

   - On non-looped carpets, rough up the trimmed carpet fibers a little with the tips of your scissors. Trim any taller roughed up fibers so they are equal in height with the rest of the carpet.
   - Vacuum debris with vacuum cleaner hose.

**If the spot is larger than 3/8 inch (pencil eraser size):**

1. **Do not attempt ANY removal** of a Class III spot.
   - Put a note next to spot(s) that says,
     **"Do Not Touch Or Clean!"**.
   - (Do **not** put a towel over spot.)

2. Call a pro and have spot removed as soon as possible within 24 hours of the spill.

## Class IV: Towel + Fresh / Wet Spot

### Steps:

1. Mist your dinner knife blade with alcohol.

2. Hold a disposable towel at the edge of the spot.
   - Keeping the blade of your dinner knife almost flat against the carpet, scrape the spot into the towel.
     Note: After each scrape:
     - Wipe the knife blade on a clean part of the towel.
     - Carefully drop the dirty towel in your empty bucket.
     - Re-mist the knife blade with alcohol.
   - Repeat entire Step until no more spot matter removes.

3. Mist a generous amount of alcohol on the spot(s).
   - Agitate with end of spoon handle.
   - Allow to work 2 minutes.
   - Mist on a generous amount of ammonia.
   - Agitate with end of spoon handle.

4. With a dry towel over your hand, pinch out the spot 10 - 15 times, using a clean part of the towel each time.
   - With a towel, blot the spot 10 - 15 times, using a clean part of the towel each time.

5. Look at and touch spot area carefully to see if the hard or sticky residue is gone:
   - If YES: Allow to dry.
   - If NO: Repeat Steps 3 and 4 until no more removes. Allow to dry.

6. Again, look at and touch spot area carefully to see if the hard or sticky residue is gone:
   - If YES: No further action is needed.
   - If NO: Repeat Steps 3 and 4 one time.

7. If the spot persists, call a pro for options as soon as possible.

*Art's Ultimate Spot Cleaning • Chapter 5 Treatment Steps - Page 89*

# Glue - Household, Animal

## Comments:

- **Optimum removal time: As soon as possible** within 24 hours of spill
- **Maximum size for home removal:** Class I = 3/8 inch / Class II = 1 inch
- **Removal restrictions - Class I:** See "Class I" instructions below.
- **Removal restrictions - Class II:** If the spot is larger than 1 inch in diameter, **do not attempt TOTAL removal** using Class II instructions. Do Step 1 **only** under Class II. Mist a generous amount of ammonia on spot(s). Put a folded towel moistened with water over spot. (Keep towel damp until pro comes.) Call a pro and have spot removed as soon as possible within 24 hours.
- **Caution: Do not attempt scissors removal** of spots from **any** type of looped carpet (berber, commercial glue down, etc.) unless the spot is only **on the outside fibers** of the loop(s). If in doubt, call a pro for options as soon as possible.
- These products can be very hard to remove. If you cannot remove a spot, consult a pro for options as soon as possible.

## Materials Needed:

Class I - 3/8 inch or smaller: Ruler, Scissors, Spot machine
Class I - larger than 3/8 inch: Ruler, Paper and pencil for note
Class II: Spotting kit, Disposable towel(s), Spot machine with hot water

| Class I: Spot Machine + Old / Dried Spot | Class II: Spot Machine + Fresh / Wet Spot |
|---|---|

### Class I: Spot Machine + Old / Dried Spot

**Steps:**

**Follow the instructions for your size spot(s):**

**If the spot is 3/8 inch (pencil eraser size) or smaller:**

1. Allow the spot to harden completely.

2. Using your scissors, wedge the blades up under the spot(s) and snip the hardened parts from the very tip of the carpet fibers. (This will minimize the indentations caused by the removed spots.) Note: On non-looped carpets, you can also trim a few carpet fibers around the edge of the removed spot, if needed, to minimize it further.
   - On non-looped carpets, rough up the trimmed carpet fibers a little with the tips of your scissors. Trim any taller roughed up fibers so they are equal in height with the rest of the carpet.
   - Vacuum debris with spot machine.

**If the spot is larger than 3/8 inch (pencil eraser size):**

1. **Do not attempt ANY removal** of a Class I spot.
   - Put a note next to spot(s) that says, ***"Do Not Touch Or Clean!"***.
   - (Do **not** put a towel over spot.)

2. Call a pro and have spot removed as soon as possible within 24 hours of the spill.

### Class II: Spot Machine + Fresh / Wet Spot

**Steps:**

1. Mist your dinner knife blade with ammonia.

2. Hold a disposable towel at the edge of the spot.
   - Keeping the blade of your dinner knife almost flat against the carpet, scrape the spot into the towel.
     Note: After each scrape:
     - Wipe the knife blade on a clean part of the towel.
     - Carefully drop the dirty towel in your empty bucket.
     - Re-mist the knife blade with ammonia.
   - Repeat entire Step until no more spot matter removes.

3. Mist a generous amount of ammonia on the spot(s).
   - Agitate with end of spoon handle.
   - Allow to work 1 minute.
   - Mist on a small amount of alcohol.
   - Agitate with end of spoon handle.

4. With the spot machine, rinse with hot water using the chop stroke technique 10 - 12 times.
   - Take 6 - 8 slow, dry vacuum strokes.

5. Look at and touch spot area carefully to see if the hard or sticky residue is gone:
   - If YES: Allow to dry.
   - If NO: Repeat Steps 3 and 4 until no more removes. Allow to dry.

6. Again, look at and touch spot area carefully to see if the hard or sticky residue is gone:
   - If YES: No further action is needed.
   - If NO: Repeat Steps 3 and 4 one time.

7. If the spot persists, call a pro for options as soon as possible.

Section II

## Comments:

- **Optimum removal time: As soon as possible** within 24 hours of spill
- **Maximum size for home removal:** Class III = 3/8 inch / Class IV = 1/2 inch
- R**emoval restrictions - Class III:** See "Class III" instructions below.
- **Removal restrictions - Class IV:** If the spot(s) is larger than 1/2 inch in diameter, **do not attempt TOTAL removal** using Class IV instructions. Do Steps 1 and 2 **only** under Class IV. Mist a generous amount of ammonia on spot(s). Put a folded towel moistened with water over spot. (Keep towel damp until pro comes.) Then:
  - Call a pro and have spot removed as soon as possible within 24 hours. -OR-
  - If the spot is 1 inch or less in diameter and is still fresh/wet, get a spot machine and do Steps 3 - 7 under Class II.
- **Caution: Do not attempt scissors removal** of spots from **any** type of looped carpet (berber, commercial glue down, etc.) unless the spot is **only on the outside fibers** of the loop(s). If in doubt, call a pro for options as soon as possible.
- These products can be very hard to remove. If you cannot remove a spot, consult a pro for options as soon as possible.

## Materials Needed:

Class III - 3/8 inch or smaller: Ruler, Scissors, Vacuum cleaner with attachment removed from hose
Class III - larger than 3/8 inch: Ruler, Paper and pencil for note
Class IV: Spotting kit, Disposable towel(s)

## Class III: Towel + Old / Dried Spot

### Steps:

**Follow the instructions for your size spot(s):**

**If the spot is 3/8 inch (pencil eraser size) or smaller:**

1. Allow the spot to harden completely.

2. Using your scissors, wedge the blades up under the spot(s) and snip the hardened parts from the very tip of the carpet fibers. (This will minimize the indentations caused by the removed spots.) Note: On non-looped carpets, you can also trim a few carpet fibers around the edge of the removed spot, if needed, to minimize it further.
   - On non-looped carpets, rough up the trimmed carpet fibers a little with the tips of your scissors. Trim any taller roughed up fibers so they are equal in height with the rest of the carpet.
   - Vacuum debris with vacuum cleaner hose.

**If the spot is larger than 3/8 inch (pencil eraser size):**

1. **Do not attempt ANY removal** of a Class III spot.
   - Put a note next to spot(s) that says, **"Do Not Touch Or Clean!"**.
   - (Do **not** put a towel over spot.)

2. Call a pro and have spot removed as soon as possible within 24 hours of the spill.

## Class IV: Towel + Fresh / Wet Spot

### Steps:

1. Mist your dinner knife blade with ammonia.

2. Hold a disposable towel at the edge of the spot.
   - Keeping the blade of your dinner knife almost flat against the carpet, scrape the spot into the towel.
     Note: After each scrape:
     - Wipe the knife blade on a clean part of the towel.
     - Carefully drop the dirty towel in your empty bucket.
     - Re-mist the knife blade with ammonia.
   - Repeat entire Step until no more spot matter removes.

3. Mist a generous amount of ammonia on the spot(s).
   - Agitate with end of spoon handle.
   - Allow to work 1 minute.
   - Mist on a small amount of alcohol.
   - Agitate with end of spoon handle.

4. With a dry towel over your hand, pinch out the spot 10 - 15 times, using a clean part of the towel each time.
   - With a clean towel, blot the spot 10 - 15 times, using a clean part of the towel each time.

5. Look at and touch spot area carefully to see if the hard or sticky residue is gone:
   - If YES: Allow to dry.
   - If NO: Repeat Steps 3 and 4 until no more removes. Allow to dry.

6. Again, look at and touch spot area carefully to see if the hard or sticky residue is gone:
   - If YES: No further action is needed.
   - If NO: Repeat Steps 3 and 4 one time.

7. If the spot persists, call a pro for options as soon as possible.

# Glue - Elmer's®

## Comments:

- **Optimum removal time: As soon as possible** within 24 hours of spill
- **Maximum size for home removal:** Class I = 3/8 inch / Class II = 1 inch
- **Removal restrictions - Class I:** See "Class I" instructions below.
- **Removal restrictions - Class II:** If the spot is larger than 1 inch in diameter, **do not attempt TOTAL removal** using Class II instructions. Do Step 1 **only** under Class II. Mist a generous amount of ammonia and a generous amount of alcohol on spot(s). Put a folded towel moistened with water over spot. (Keep towel damp until pro comes.) Call a pro and have spot removed as soon as possible within 24 hours.
- **Caution: Do not attempt scissors removal** of spots from **any** type of looped carpet (berber, commercial glue down, etc.) unless the spot is only **on the outside fibers** of the loop(s). If in doubt, call a pro for options as soon as possible.
- These products can be very hard to remove. If you cannot remove a spot, consult a pro for options as soon as possible.

## Materials Needed:

Class I - 3/8 inch or smaller: Ruler, Scissors, Spot machine
Class I - larger than 3/8 inch: Ruler, Paper and pencil for note
Class II: Spotting kit, Disposable towel(s), Spot machine with hot water

| Class I: Spot Machine + Old / Dried Spot | Class II: Spot Machine + Fresh / Wet Spot |
|---|---|

**Section II**

### Class I — Steps:

**Follow the instructions for your size spot(s):**

**If the spot is 3/8 inch (pencil eraser size) or smaller:**

1. Allow the spot to harden completely.

2. Using your scissors, wedge the blades up under the spot(s) and snip the hardened parts from the very tip of the carpet fibers. (This will minimize the indentations caused by the removed spots.) Note: On non-looped carpets, you can also trim a few carpet fibers around the edge of the removed spot, if needed, to minimize it further.
   - On non-looped carpets, rough up the trimmed carpet fibers a little with the tips of your scissors. Trim any taller roughed up fibers so they are equal in height with the rest of the carpet.
   - Vacuum debris with spot machine.

**If the spot is larger than 3/8 inch (pencil eraser size):**

1. **Do not attempt ANY removal** of a Class I spot.
   - Put a note next to spot(s) that says, **"Do Not Touch Or Clean!"**.
   - (Do **not** put a towel over spot.)

2. Call a pro and have spot removed as soon as possible within 24 hours of the spill.

### Class II — Steps:

1. Mist your dinner knife blade with alcohol.

2. Hold a disposable towel at the edge of the spot.
   - Keeping the blade of your dinner knife almost flat against the carpet, scrape the spot into the towel.
     Note: After each scrape:
     - Wipe the knife blade on a clean part of the towel.
     - Carefully drop the dirty towel in your empty bucket.
     - Re-mist the knife blade with alcohol.
   - Repeat entire Step until no more spot matter removes.

3. Mist a generous amount of ammonia on the spot(s).
   - Agitate with end of spoon handle.
   - Allow to work 1 minute.
   - Mist on a generous amount of alcohol.
   - Agitate with end of spoon handle.
   - Allow to work 1 minute.

4. With the spot machine, rinse with hot water using the chop stroke technique 8 - 10 times.
   - Take 6 - 8 slow, dry vacuum strokes.

5. Look at and touch spot area carefully to see if the hard or sticky residue is gone:
   - If YES: Allow to dry.
   - If NO: Repeat Steps 3 and 4 until no more removes. Allow to dry.

6. Again, look at and touch spot area carefully to see if the hard or sticky residue is gone:
   - If YES: No further action is needed.
   - If NO: Repeat Steps 3 and 4 one time.

7. If the spot persists, call a pro for options as soon as possible.

## *Comments:*

- **Optimum removal time: As soon as possible** within 24 hours of spill
- **Maximum size for home removal:** Class III = 3/8 inch / Class IV = 1/2 inch
- **Removal restrictions - Class III:** See "Class III" instructions below.
- **Removal restrictions - Class IV:** If the spot(s) is larger than 1/2 inch in diameter, **do not attempt TOTAL removal** using Class IV instructions. Do Steps 1 and 2 **only** under Class IV. Mist a generous amount of ammonia and a generous amount of alcohol on spot(s). Put a folded towel moistened with water over spot. (Keep towel damp until pro comes.) Then:
  - Call a pro and have spot removed as soon as possible within 24 hours. -OR-
  - If the spot is 1 inch or less in diameter and is still fresh/wet, get a spot machine and do Steps 3 - 7 under Class II.
- **Caution: Do not attempt scissors removal** of spots from **any** type of looped carpet (berber, commercial glue down, etc.) unless the spot is **only on the outside fibers** of the loop(s). If in doubt, call a pro for options as soon as possible.
- These products can be very hard to remove. If you cannot remove a spot, consult a pro for options as soon as possible.

## *Materials Needed:*

Class III - 3/8 inch or smaller: Ruler, Scissors, Vacuum cleaner with attachment removed from hose
Class III - larger than 3/8 inch: Ruler, Paper and pencil for note
Class IV: Spotting kit, Disposable towel

### *Class III: Towel + Old / Dried Spot*

#### *Steps:*

**Follow the instructions for your size spot(s):**

**If the spot is 3/8 inch (pencil eraser size) or smaller:**

1. Allow the spot to harden completely.

2. Using your scissors, wedge the blades up under the spot(s) and snip the hardened parts from the very tip of the carpet fibers. (This will minimize the indentations caused by the removed spots.) Note: On non-looped carpets, you can also trim a few carpet fibers around the edge of the removed spot, if needed, to minimize it further.
   - On non-looped carpets, rough up the trimmed carpet fibers a little with the tips of your scissors. Trim any taller roughed up fibers so they are equal in height with the rest of the carpet.
   - Vacuum debris with vacuum cleaner hose.

**If the spot is larger than 3/8 inch (pencil eraser size):**

1. **Do not attempt ANY removal** of a Class III spot.
   - Put a note next to spot(s) that says, ***"Do Not Touch Or Clean!"***.
   - (Do **not** put a towel over spot.)

2. Call a pro and have spot removed as soon as possible within 24 hours of the spill.

### *Class IV: Towel + Fresh / Wet Spot*

#### *Steps:*

1. Mist your dinner knife blade with alcohol.

2. Hold a disposable towel at the edge of the spot.
   - Keeping the blade of your dinner knife almost flat against the carpet, scrape the spot into the towel. Note: After each scrape:
     - Wipe the knife blade on a clean part of the towel.
     - Carefully drop the dirty towel in your empty bucket.
     - Re-mist the knife blade with alcohol.
   - Repeat entire Step until no more spot matter removes.

3. Mist a generous amount of ammonia on the spot(s).
   - Agitate with end of spoon handle.
   - Allow to work 1 minute.
   - Mist on a generous amount of alcohol.
   - Agitate with end of spoon handle.
   - Allow to work 1 minute.

4. With a dry towel over your hand, pinch out the spot 10 - 15 times, using a clean part of the towel each time.
   - With a towel, blot the spot 10 - 15 times, using a clean part of the towel each time.

5. Look at and touch spot area carefully to see if the hard or sticky residue is gone:
   - If YES: Allow to dry.
   - If NO: Repeat Steps 3 and 4 until no more removes. Allow to dry.

6. Again, look at and touch spot area carefully to see if the hard or sticky residue is gone:
   - If YES: No further action is needed.
   - If NO: Repeat Steps 3 and 4 one time.

7. If the spot persists, call a pro for options as soon as possible.

# Glue - Furniture, Wood, Melted Glue Gun Sticks

## Comments:

- **Optimum removal time: As soon as possible** within 24 hours of spill
- **Maximum size for home removal:** Class I / II = 3/8 inch (pencil eraser size)
- **Removal restrictions:** See "Class I" or "Class II" instructions below.
- **Caution: Do not attempt scissors removal** of spots from **any** type of looped carpet (berber, commercial glue down, etc.) unless the spot is **only on the outside fibers** of the loop(s). If in doubt, call a pro for options as soon as possible.
- These products are very hard to remove because they do not break down when chemically treated. If you cannot remove a spot, call a pro to remove as soon as possible.

## Materials Needed:

Class I / II - 3/8 inch or smaller: Ruler, Scissors, Spot machine
Class I / II - larger than 3/8 inch: Ruler, Paper and pencil for note

| Class I: Spot Machine + Old / Dried Spot | Class II: Spot Machine + Fresh / Wet Spot |
|---|---|
| **Steps:** | **Steps:** |
| **Follow the instructions for your size spot(s):** | **Follow the instructions for your size spot(s):** |
| **If the spot is 3/8 inch (pencil eraser size) or smaller:** | **If the spot is 3/8 inch (pencil eraser size) or smaller:** |
| 1. Allow the spot to harden completely. | 1. Allow the spot to harden completely. |
| 2. Using your scissors, wedge the blades up under the spot(s) and snip the hardened parts from the very tip of the carpet fibers. (This will minimize the indentations caused by the removed spots.) Note: On non-looped carpets, you can also trim a few carpet fibers around the edge of the removed spot, if needed, to minimize it further. | 2. Using your scissors, wedge the blades up under the spot(s) and snip the hardened parts from the very tip of the carpet fibers. (This will minimize the indentations caused by the removed spots.) Note: On non-looped carpets, you can also trim a few carpet fibers around the edge of the removed spot, if needed, to minimize it further. |
| • On non-looped carpets, rough up the trimmed carpet fibers a little with the tips of your scissors. Trim any taller roughed up fibers so they are equal in height with the rest of the carpet. | • On non-looped carpets, rough up the trimmed carpet fibers a little with the tips of your scissors. Trim any taller roughed up fibers so they are equal in height with the rest of the carpet. |
| • Vacuum debris with spot machine. | • Vacuum debris with spot machine. |
| **If the spot is larger than 3/8 inch** (pencil eraser size): | **If the spot is larger than 3/8 inch** (pencil eraser size): |
| 1. **Do not attempt ANY removal** of a Class I spot. | 1. **Do not attempt ANY removal** of a Class II spot. |
| • Put a note next to spot(s) that says, ***"Do Not Touch Or Clean!"***. | • Put a note next to spot(s) that says, ***"Do Not Touch Or Clean!"***. |
| • (Do **not** put a towel over spot.) | • (Do **not** put a towel over spot.) |
| 2. Call a pro and have spot removed as soon as possible within 24 hours of the spill. | 2. Call a pro and have spot removed as soon as possible within 24 hours of the spill. |

Spot Contents: Amousphous Ployolefin, Tackifier Resin, Latex, Polyamide, Synthetic Rubber

## Comments:

- **Optimum removal time: As soon as possible** within 24 hours of spill
- **Maximum size for home removal:** Class III / IV = 3/8 inch (pencil eraser size)
- **Removal restrictions:** See "Class III" or "Class IV" instructions below.
- **Caution: Do not attempt scissors removal** of spots from **any** type of looped carpet (berber, commercial glue down, etc.) unless the spot is **only on the outside fibers** of the loop(s). If in doubt, call a pro for options as soon as possible.
- These products are very hard to remove because they do not break down when chemically treated. If you cannot remove a spot, call a pro to remove as soon as possible.

## Materials Needed:

Class III / IV - 3/8 inch or smaller: Ruler, Scissors, Vacuum cleaner with attachment removed from hose
Class III / IV - larger than 3/8 inch: Ruler, Paper and pencil for note

### Class III: Towel + Old / Dried Spot

**Steps:**

**Follow the instructions for your size spot(s):**

**If the spot is 3/8 inch (pencil eraser size) or smaller:**

1. Allow the spot to harden completely.

2. Using your scissors, wedge the blades up under the spot(s) and snip the hardened parts from the very tip of the carpet fibers. (This will minimize the indentations caused by the removed spots.) Note: On non-looped carpets, you can also trim a few carpet fibers around the edge of the removed spot, if needed, to minimize it further.

   - On non-looped carpets, rough up the trimmed carpet fibers a little with the tips of your scissors. Trim any taller roughed up fibers so they are equal in height with the rest of the carpet.
   - Vacuum debris with vacuum cleaner hose.

**If the spot is larger than 3/8 inch (pencil eraser size):**

1. **Do not attempt ANY removal** of a Class III spot.
   - Put a note next to spot(s) that says, **"Do Not Touch Or Clean!"**.
   - (Do **not** put a towel over spot.)

2. Call a pro and have spot removed as soon as possible within 24 hours of the spill.

### Class IV: Towel + Fresh / Wet Spot

**Steps:**

**Follow the instructions for your size spot(s):**

**If the spot is 3/8 inch (pencil eraser size) or smaller:**

1. Allow the spot to harden completely.

2. Using your scissors, wedge the blades up under the spot(s) and snip the hardened parts from the very tip of the carpet fibers. (This will minimize the indentations caused by the removed spots.) Note: On non-looped carpets, you can also trim a few carpet fibers around the edge of the removed spot, if needed, to minimize it further.

   - On non-looped carpets, rough up the trimmed carpet fibers a little with the tips of your scissors. Trim any taller roughed up fibers so they are equal in height with the rest of the carpet.
   - Vacuum debris with vacuum cleaner hose.

**If the spot is larger than 3/8 inch (pencil eraser size):**

1. **Do not attempt ANY removal** of a Class IV spot.
   - Put a note next to spot(s) that says, **"Do Not Touch Or Clean!"**.
   - (Do **not** put a towel over spot.)

2. Call a pro and have spot removed as soon as possible within 24 hours of the spill.

Section II

# Glue Stick, Removable Adhesive for Paper or Fabric

## Comments:

- **Optimum removal time: As soon as possible** within 24 hours of spill
- **Maximum size for home removal:** Class I / II = 2 1/2 inches
- **Removal restrictions:** If the spot(s) has been pressed into the carpet or is larger than 2 1/2 inches in diameter, **do not attempt TOTAL removal** using Class I or II instructions. If wet, allow spot(s) to dry completely. Do Steps 1 and 2 **only** under Class I or Steps 1 - 3 **only** under Class II. Put a dry towel over spot(s). Call a pro and have spot removed within 24 hours.
- **Caution: Do not attempt scissors removal** of spots from **any** type of looped carpet (berber, commercial glue down, etc.) unless the spot is **only on the outside fibers** of the loop(s). If in doubt, call a pro for options as soon as possible.
- Coloring in some products can permanently stain some nylon. If you cannot remove a spot, consult a pro for options as soon as possible.

## Materials Needed:

Class I / II: Spotting kit, Spot machine with hot water

### Class I: Spot Machine + Old / Dried Spot

**Steps:**

1. Using your dinner knife and fingers, separate stuck together fibers into as many individual tufts as possible.

2. Using your scissors, wedge the blades up under the spot(s) and snip the hardened parts from the very tip of the carpet fibers. (This will minimize the indentations caused by the removed spots.) Note: On non-looped carpets, you can also trim a few carpet fibers around the edge of the removed spot, if needed, to minimize it further.
   - On non-looped carpets, rough up the trimmed carpet fibers a little with the tips of your scissors. Trim any taller roughed up fibers so they are equal in height with the rest of the carpet.
   - Vacuum debris with spot machine.

3. Mist on a generous amount of alcohol.
   - Agitate with end of spoon handle.
   - Allow to work 1 minute.
   - Mist on a generous amount of ammonia.
   - Agitate with end of spoon handle.

4. With the spot machine, rinse with hot water using the chop stroke technique 6 - 8 times.
   - Take 4 - 6 slow, dry vacuum strokes.

5. Look at and touch spot area carefully to see if the sticky residue is gone:
   - If YES: Allow to dry.
   - If NO: Repeat Steps 3 and 4 until no more removes. Then, if needed, do Step 6.

6. If color cast remains, mist on a generous amount of peroxide.
   - Tamp with soft brush.
   - Allow to dry.

7. If needed, repeat Steps 3, 4 and 6 one time.

8. If the spot persists, call a pro for options as soon as possible.

### Class II: Spot Machine + Fresh / Wet Spot

**Steps:**

1. Allow spot(s) to dry completely.

2. Using your dinner knife and fingers, separate stuck together fibers into as many individual tufts as possible.

3. Using your scissors, wedge the blades up under the spot(s) and snip the hardened parts from the very tip of the carpet fibers. (This will minimize the indentations caused by the removed spots.) Note: On non-looped carpets, you can also trim a few carpet fibers around the edge of the removed spot, if needed, to minimize it further.
   - On non-looped carpets, rough up the trimmed carpet fibers a little with the tips of your scissors. Trim any taller roughed up fibers so they are equal in height with the rest of the carpet.
   - Vacuum debris with spot machine.

4. Mist on a generous amount of alcohol.
   - Agitate with end of spoon handle.
   - Allow to work 1 minute.
   - Mist on a generous amount of ammonia.
   - Agitate with end of spoon handle.

5. With the spot machine, rinse with hot water using the chop stroke technique 6 - 8 times.
   - Take 4 - 6 slow, dry vacuum strokes.

6. Look at and touch spot area carefully to see if the sticky residue is gone:
   - If YES: Allow to dry.
   - If NO: Repeat Steps 4 and 5 until no more removes. Then, if needed, do Step 7.

7. If color cast remains, mist on a generous amount of peroxide.
   - Tamp with soft brush.
   - Allow to dry.

8. If needed, repeat Steps 4, 5 and 7 one time.

9. If the spot persists, call a pro for options as soon as possible.

# Glue Stick, Removable Adhesive for Paper or Fabric

Spot Contents: Dextrin, Glycerin, Plasticisers, Possible Coloring, Sugar

## Comments:

- **Optimum removal time: As soon as possible** within 24 hours of spill
- **Maximum size for home removal:** Class III / IV = 1 inch
- **Removal restrictions:** If the spot(s) has been pressed into the carpet or is larger than 1 inch in diameter, **do not attempt TOTAL removal** using Class III or IV instructions. If wet, allow spot(s) to dry completely. Do Steps 1 and 2 **only** under Class III or Steps 1 - 3 **only** under Class IV. Put a dry towel over spot(s). Then:
  - Call a pro and have spot removed within 24 hours. - OR -
  - If the spot has not been pressed into carpet and is 2 1/2 inches or less in diameter, get a spot machine and do Steps 3 - 8 under Class I.
- **Caution: Do not attempt scissors removal** of spots from **any** type of looped carpet (berber, commercial glue down, etc.) unless the spot is **only on the outside fibers** of the loop(s). If in doubt, call a pro for options as soon as possible.
- Coloring in some products can permanently stain some nylon. If you cannot remove a spot, consult a pro for options as soon as possible.

## Materials Needed:

Class III / IV: Spotting kit, Vacuum cleaner with attachment removed from hose

Section II

## Class III: Towel + Old / Dried Spot

### Steps:

1. Using your dinner knife and fingers, separate stuck together fibers into as many individual tufts as possible.

2. Using your scissors, wedge the blades up under the spot(s) and snip the hardened parts from the very tip of the carpet fibers. (This will minimize the indentations caused by the removed spots.) Note: On non-looped carpets, you can also trim a few carpet fibers around the edge of the removed spot, if needed, to minimize it further.
   - On non-looped carpets, rough up the trimmed carpet fibers a little with the tips of your scissors. Trim any taller roughed up fibers so they are equal in height with the rest of the carpet.
   - Vacuum debris with vacuum cleaner hose.

3. Mist on a generous amount of alcohol.
   - Agitate with end of spoon handle.
   - Allow to work 2 minutes.
   - Mist on a generous amount of ammonia.
   - Agitate with end of spoon handle.

4. Using a towel, rub firmly in one direction. (The spots should curdle into little balls.)
   - Vacuum spot curdles with vacuum cleaner hose.

5. Look at and touch spot area carefully to see if the sticky residue is gone:
   - If YES: Allow to dry.
   - If NO: Repeat Steps 3 and 4 until no more removes. Then, if needed, do Step 6.

6. If color cast remains, mist on a generous amount of peroxide.
   - Tamp with soft brush.
   - Allow to dry.

7. If needed, repeat Steps 3, 4 and 6 one time.

8. If the spot persists, call a pro for options as soon as possible.

## Class IV: Towel + Fresh / Wet Spot

### Steps:

1. Allow spot(s) to dry completely.

2. Using your dinner knife and fingers, separate stuck together fibers into as many individual tufts as possible.

3. Using your scissors, wedge the blades up under the spot(s) and snip the hardened parts from the very tip of the carpet fibers. (This will minimize the indentations caused by the removed spots.) Note: On non-looped carpets, you can also trim a few carpet fibers around the edge of the removed spot, if needed, to minimize it further.
   - On non-looped carpets, rough up the trimmed carpet fibers a little with the tips of your scissors. Trim any taller roughed up fibers so they are equal in height with the rest of the carpet.
   - Vacuum debris with vacuum cleaner hose.

4. Mist on a generous amount of alcohol.
   - Agitate with end of spoon handle.
   - Allow to work 1 minute.
   - Mist on a generous amount of ammonia.
   - Agitate with end of spoon handle.

5. Using a towel, rub firmly in one direction. (The spots should curdle into little balls.)
   - Vacuum spot curdles with vacuum cleaner hose.

6. Look at and touch spot area carefully to see if the sticky residue is gone:
   - If YES: Allow to dry.
   - If NO: Repeat Steps 4 and 5 until no more removes. Then, if needed, do Step 7.

7. If color cast remains, mist on a generous amount of peroxide.
   - Tamp with soft brush.
   - Allow to dry.

8. If needed, repeat Steps 4, 5 and 7 one time.

9. If the spot persists, call a pro for options as soon as possible.

# Gravy - Thick, Creamy

## Comments:

- **Optimum removal time: As soon as possible** within 24 hours
- **Maximum size for home removal:** Class I / II = 3 1/2 inches
- **Removal restrictions:** If the spot(s) is larger than 3 1/2 inches in diameter, **do not attempt TOTAL removal** using Class I or II instructions. Do Steps 1 and 2 **only** under Class I or II. Mist a generous amount of ammonia on spot(s). Put a folded towel moistened with water over spot. Call a pro and have spot removed within 24 hours.
- Gravy may contain blood and oily fats that may immediately and permanently stain some nylon. If you cannot remove a spot, consult a pro for options as soon as possible.

## Materials Needed:

Class I / II: Spotting kit, Spot machine with warm water, Disposable towel(s) optional for Class II

### Class I: Spot Machine + Old / Dried Spot

**Steps:**

1. Using your spoon, scrape out as much of the spot(s) as possible.
   - Vacuum debris with spot machine.
   - Repeat entire Step until no more removes.
2. With the spot machine, rinse with warm water using the chop stroke technique 10 - 12 times.
   - Take 6 - 8 slow, dry vacuum strokes.
3. Mist on a generous amount of ammonia.
   - Allow to work 1 minute.
   - Mist on a generous amount of alcohol.
   - Agitate with hard brush.
   - Allow to work 1 minute.
4. With the spot machine, rinse with warm water using the chop stroke technique 8 - 10 times.
   - Take 6 - 8 slow, dry vacuum strokes.
5. Look at and touch spill area carefully to see if the stiff, oily residue is gone:
   - If YES: Allow to dry.
   - If NO: Repeat Steps 3 and 4 until no more removes. Then, if needed, do Step 6.
6. If color cast remains, mist on a generous amount of peroxide.
   - Tamp with soft brush.
   - Allow to dry.
7. Look at and touch spill area carefully to see if the stiff, oily residue is gone:
   - If YES: No further action is needed.
   - If NO: Repeat Steps 3, 4 and 6 one time.
8. If the spot persists, call a pro for options as soon as possible.

### Class II: Spot Machine + Fresh / Wet Spot

**Steps:**

1. Lay a small towel (or disposable towel) over the palm of your hand. Then lay your hand on the carpet so the towel is at the edge of the spot.
   - Using your spoon, scoop as much of the spot(s) as possible onto the towel. Note: After each scoop, wipe the spoon on a clean part of the towel.
   - Carefully drop the dirty towel in your empty bucket.
   - With a clean towel, blot 15 - 20 times, using a clean part of the towel each time.
   - Repeat entire Step until no more removes.
2. With the spot machine, rinse with warm water using the chop stroke technique 6 - 8 times.
   - Take 4 - 6 slow, dry vacuum strokes.
3. Mist on a generous amount of ammonia.
   - Allow to work 1 minute.
   - Mist on a generous amount of alcohol.
   - Agitate with hard brush.
4. With the spot machine, rinse with warm water using the chop stroke technique 6 - 8 times.
   - Take 4 - 6 slow, dry vacuum strokes.
5. Look at and touch spill area carefully to see if the stiff, oily residue is gone:
   - If YES: Allow to dry.
   - If NO: Repeat Steps 3 and 4 until no more removes. Then, if needed, do Step 6.
6. If color cast remains, mist on a generous amount of peroxide.
   - Tamp with soft brush.
   - Allow to dry.
7. Look at and touch spill area carefully to see if the stiff, oily residue is gone:
   - If YES: No further action is needed.
   - If NO: Repeat Steps 3, 4 and 6 one time.
8. If the spot persists, call a pro for options as soon as possible.

Section II

Spot / Stain Contents: Albumin, Blood, Fat, Flour, Grease, Oil

## Comments:

- **Optimum removal time: As soon as possible** within 24 hours
- **Maximum size for home removal:** Class III / IV = No home removal
- **Removal restrictions:** See "Class III" or "Class IV" instructions below.
- Gravy may contain blood and oily fats that may immediately and permanently stain some nylon. If you cannot remove a spot, consult a pro for options as soon as possible.

## Materials Needed:

Class III / IV: Spotting kit, Vacuum cleaner with attachment removed from hose, Disposable towel(s) optional for Class IV

### Class III: Towel + Old / Dried Spot

**Steps:**

1. Using your spoon, scrape out as much of the spot(s) as possible.
   - Vacuum debris with vacuum cleaner hose.
   - Repeat entire Step until no more removes.

2. **Do not continue removal** for a Class III spot(s).
   - Mist a generous amount of ammonia on spot(s).
   - Put a towel moistened with water over the spot.
   - Then:
     - Call a pro and have spot removed within 24 hours of spill.
       -OR-
     - If the spot is 3 1/2 inches or less in diameter, get a spot machine and do Steps 2 - 8 under Class I.

### Class IV: Towel + Fresh / Wet Spot

**Steps:**

1. Lay a small towel (or disposable towel) over the palm of your hand. Then lay your hand on the carpet so the towel is at the edge of the spot.
   - Using your spoon, scoop as much of the spot(s) as possible onto the towel. Note: After each scoop, wipe the spoon on a clean part of the towel.
   - Carefully drop the dirty towel in your empty bucket.
   - With a clean towel, blot 20 - 25 times, using a clean part of the towel each time.
   - Repeat entire Step until no more removes.

2. **Do not continue removal** for a Class IV spot(s).
   - Mist a generous amount of ammonia on spot(s).
   - Put a towel moistened with water over the spot.
   - Then:
     - Call a pro and have spot removed within 24 hours of spill.
       -OR-
     - If the spot is 3 1/2 inches or less in diameter, get a spot machine and:
       - If the spot is now old/dried, do Steps 2 - 8 under Class I
       - If the spot is still fresh/wet, do Steps 2 - 8 under Class II.

# Grease - Thick, Liquid or Solid, New or Used:
## Auto and Other Lubricants, Lard, Shortening, Bacon Grease

### Comments:

- **Optimum removal time:** Within 24 hours of spill
- **Maximum size for home removal:** Class I / II = 1 1/2 inches
- **Removal restrictions:** If the spot(s) is larger than 1 1/2 inches in diameter, **do not attempt TOTAL removal** using Class I or II instructions. Do Step 1 **only** under Class I or II. Put a dry towel over spot and a note next to it that says, ***"Do Not Touch Or Clean!"*** over spot(s). Call a pro and have spot removed within 2 days.
- **Caution:** Oils in these products, especially the petroleum based ones, can permanently discolor polyester and olefin (due to their oil-loving natures) if left untreated as little as 3 weeks. If you cannot remove a spot, consult a pro for options as soon as possible.
- These products can be hard to remove, even for a pro, especially if a large quantity (larger than 1 1/2 inches) has been stepped on and pressed into the carpet fibers. If you cannot remove a spot, consult a pro for options as soon as possible.
- These products may cause recurring spots if not completely removed. (See "Recurring Spots", Chapter 4.) Consult a pro for options as soon as possible.

### Materials Needed:
Class I / II: Spotting kit, Spot machine with hot water, Disposable towel(s)

| Class I: Spot Machine + Old / Dried Spot | Class II: Spot Machine + Fresh / Wet Spot |
|---|---|
| **Steps:** | **Steps:** |
| 1. 1. Lay a disposable towel over the palm of your hand. Then lay your hand on the carpet so the towel is at the edge of the spot.<br>• Using your spoon, scoop as much of the spot(s) as possible onto the towel. Note: After each scoop, wipe the spoon on a clean part of the towel.<br>• Carefully drop the dirty towel in your empty bucket.<br>• With a clean cloth towel, blot 15 - 25 times, using a clean part of the towel each time.<br>• Repeat entire Step until no more removes. | 1. Lay a disposable towel over the palm of your hand. Then lay your hand on the carpet so the towel is at the edge of the spot.<br>• Using your spoon, scoop as much of the spot(s) as possible onto the towel. Note: After each scoop, wipe the spoon on a clean part of the towel.<br>• Carefully drop the dirty towel in your empty bucket.<br>• With a clean cloth towel, blot 15 - 25 times, using a clean part of the towel each time.<br>• Repeat entire Step until no more removes. |
| 2. Mist on a generous amount of alcohol.<br>• Mist on a generous amount of ammonia.<br>• Tamp with soft brush.<br>• Allow to work 2 minutes.<br>• Mist on a generous amount of alcohol.<br>• Tamp with soft brush. | 2. Mist on a generous amount of alcohol.<br>• Mist on a generous amount of ammonia.<br>• Tamp with soft brush.<br>• Allow to work 2 minutes.<br>• Mist on a generous amount of alcohol.<br>• Tamp with soft brush. |
| 3. With the spot machine, rinse with hot water using the chop stroke technique 8 - 10 times.<br>• Take 6 - 8 slow, dry vacuum strokes. | 3. With the spot machine, rinse with hot water using the chop stroke technique 8 - 10 times.<br>• Take 6 - 8 slow, dry vacuum strokes. |
| 4. Look at and touch spot area carefully to see if the oily/greasy residue is gone:<br>• If YES: Allow to dry.<br>• If NO: Repeat Steps 2 and 3 until no more removes. Then, if needed, do Step 5. | 4. Look at and touch spot area carefully to see if the oily/greasy residue is gone:<br>• If YES: Allow to dry.<br>• If NO: Repeat Steps 2 and 3 until no more removes. Then, if needed, do Step 5. |
| 5. If color cast remains, mist on a generous amount of peroxide.<br>• Tamp with soft brush.<br>• Allow to dry. | 5. If color cast remains, mist on a generous amount of peroxide.<br>• Tamp with soft brush.<br>• Allow to dry. |
| 6. If needed, repeat Step 5 one time. | 6. If needed, repeat Step 5 one time. |
| 7. If the spot persists, call a pro for options as soon as possible. | 7. If the spot persists, call a pro for options as soon as possible. |

Section II

**Comments:**

Spot Contents: Petroleum Oils - Minimally Refined, Animal Fat, Hydrogenated Oils

- **Optimum removal time:** Within 24 hours of spill
- **Maximum size for home removal:** Class III / IV = 1/2 inch
- **Removal restrictions:** If the spot(s) is larger than 1/2 inch in diameter, **do not attempt TOTAL removal** using Class III or IV instructions. Do Step 1 **only** under Class III or IV. Put a dry towel over spot and a note next to it that says, ***"Do Not Touch Or Clean!"***. Then:
  - Call a pro and have spot removed within 2 days. -OR-
  - If the spot is 1 1/2 inches or less in diameter, get a spot machine and:
    - If the spot is now old/dried, do Steps 2 - 7 under Class I.
    - If the spot is still fresh/wet, do Steps 2 - 7 under Class II.
- **Caution:** Oils in these products, especially the petroleum based ones, can permanently discolor polyester and olefin (due to their oil-loving natures) if left untreated as little as 3 weeks. If you cannot remove a spot, consult a pro for options as soon as possible.
- These products can be hard to remove, even for a pro, especially if a large quantity (larger than 1 1/2 inches) has been stepped on and pressed into the carpet fibers. If you cannot remove a spot, consult a pro for options as soon as possible.
- These products may cause recurring spots if not completely removed. (See "Recurring Spots", Chapter 4.) Consult a pro for options as soon as possible.

---

*Materials Needed:*

Class III / IV: Spotting kit, Disposable towel(s)

## Class III: Towel + Old / Dried Spot

*Steps:*

1. Lay a disposable towel over the palm of your hand. Then lay your hand on the carpet so the towel is at the edge of the spot.
   - Using your spoon, scoop as much of the spot(s) as possible onto the towel. Note: After each scoop, wipe the spoon on a clean part of the towel.
   - Carefully drop the dirty towel in your empty bucket.
   - With a clean cloth towel, blot 15 - 25 times, using a clean part of the towel each time.
   - Repeat entire Step until no more removes.

2. Mist on a generous amount of alcohol.
   - Mist on a generous amount of ammonia.
   - Tamp with soft brush.
   - Allow to work 2 minutes.
   - Mist on a small amount of alcohol.
   - Tamp with soft brush.

3. With a cloth towel, firmly blot 15 - 20 times using a clean part of the towel each time.

4. Look at and touch spot area carefully to see if the oily/greasy residue is gone:
   - If YES: Allow to dry.
   - If NO: Repeat Steps 2 and 3 until no more removes. Then, if needed, do Step 5.

5. If color cast remains, mist on a generous amount of peroxide.
   - Tamp with soft brush.
   - Allow to dry.

6. If needed, repeat Steps 2, 3 and 5 one time.

7. If the spot persists, call a pro for options as soon as possible.

## Class IV: Towel + Fresh / Wet Spot

*Steps:*

1. Lay a disposable towel over the palm of your hand. Then lay your hand on the carpet so the towel is at the edge of the spot.
   - Using your spoon, scoop as much of the spot(s) as possible onto the towel. Note: After each scoop, wipe the spoon on a clean part of the towel.
   - Carefully drop the dirty towel in your empty bucket.
   - With a clean cloth towel, blot 15 - 25 times, using a clean part of the towel each time.
   - Repeat entire Step until no more removes.

2. Mist on a generous amount of alcohol.
   - Mist on a generous amount of ammonia.
   - Tamp with soft brush.
   - Allow to work 2 minutes.
   - Mist on a small amount of alcohol.
   - Tamp with soft brush.

3. With a towel, firmly blot 15 - 20 times using a clean part of the towel each time.

4. Look at and touch spot area carefully to see if the oily / greasy residue is gone:
   - If YES: Allow to dry.
   - If NO: Repeat Steps 2 and 3 until no more removes. Then, if needed, do Step 5.

5. If color cast remains, mist on a generous amount of peroxide.
   - Tamp with soft brush.
   - Allow to dry.

6. If needed, repeat Steps 2, 3 and 5 one time.

7. If the spot persists, call a pro for options as soon as possible.

*Section II*

# Gum: Chewing Gum, Bubble Gum

## Comments:

- **Optimum removal time**: Within 24 hours of spill
- **Maximum size for home removal:** Class I / II = 2 inches
- **Removal restrictions**: If the spot(s) is larger than 2 inches in diameter, **do not attempt ANY removal** using Class I or II instructions. Put a note that says, ***"Do Not Touch Or Clean!"*** next to the spot. (Do **not** put a towel over spot.) Call a pro and have spot removed within 3 days.
- **Caution: Do not attempt scissors removal** of spots from **any** type of looped carpet (berber, commercial glue down, etc.) unless the spot is **only on the outside fibers** of the loop(s). If in doubt, call a pro for options as soon as possible.
- These products can be hard to remove, even for a pro. This is especially true if a large quantity has been stepped on and pressed into the carpet fibers. If you cannot remove a spot, consult a pro for options as soon as possible.

## Materials Needed:

Class I / II: Spotting kit, Spot machine with hot water, WD-40 with the red spray tube (usually taped to the container)

Section II

| Class I: Spot Machine + Old / Dried Spot | Class II: Spot Machine + Fresh / Wet Spot |
|---|---|

### Steps:

**Follow the instructions below for your spot size.**

**If the spot is 3/8 inch (pencil eraser size) or smaller:**

1. Using your scissors, wedge the blades up under the spot(s) and snip the gum from the very tip of the carpet fibers. (This will minimize the indentations caused by the removed spots.) Note: On non-looped carpets, you can also trim a few carpet fibers around the edge of the removed spot, if needed, to minimize it further.
   - On non-looped carpets, rough up the trimmed carpet fibers a little with the tips of your scissors. Trim any taller roughed up fibers so they are equal in height with the rest of the carpet.
   - Vacuum debris with spot machine.

2. Look at spot area carefully to see if all gum is gone:
   - If YES: No further action is needed.
   - If NO: If any gum remains, do Steps 2 - 6 below.

**If the spot is larger than 3/8 inch (pencil eraser size):**

1. Using the point of your scissors, poke 10 - 15 holes into the spot (or each spot).

2. Mist on a generous amount of WD-40 using the red spray tube. (For each 1 inch of spot diameter, press the spray button twice for 1/2 second each time.)
   - Allow to work 3 minutes.
   - Using your spoon, scrape the edges of the spot toward the center until the spot dislodges from the carpet fibers.

3. Mist on a generous amount of alcohol.
   - Tamp with soft brush.
   - Allow to work 1 minute.

4. With the spot machine, rinse with hot water using the chop stroke technique 6 - 8 times.
   - Take 4 - 6 slow, dry vacuum strokes.

5. Look at spot area carefully to see if the spot is gone:
   - If YES: Allow to dry.
   - If NO: Do Steps 2, 3 and 4 until no more removes. Then, if needed, do Step 6.

6. If the spot persists, call a pro for options as soon as possible.

### Steps:

**Follow the instructions below for your spot size.**

**If the spot is 3/8 inch (pencil eraser size) or smaller:**

1. Using your scissors, wedge the blades up under the spot(s) and snip the gum from the very tip of the carpet fibers. (This will minimize the indentations caused by the removed spots.) Note: On non-looped carpets, you can also trim a few carpet fibers around the edge of the removed spot, if needed, to minimize it further.
   - On non-looped carpets, rough up the trimmed carpet fibers a little with the tips of your scissors. Trim any taller roughed up fibers so they are equal in height with the rest of the carpet.
   - Vacuum debris with spot machine.

2. Look at spot area carefully to see if all gum is gone:
   - If YES: No further action is needed.
   - If NO: If any gum remains, do Steps 2 - 6 below.

**If the spot is larger than 3/8 inch (pencil eraser size):**

1. Using the point of your scissors, poke 10 - 15 holes into the spot (or each spot).

2. Mist on a generous amount of WD-40 using the red spray tube. (For each 1 inch of spot diameter, press the spray button twice for 1/2 second each time.)
   - Allow to work 3 minutes.
   - Using your spoon, scrape the edges of the spot toward the center until the spot dislodges from the carpet fibers.

3. Mist on a generous amount of alcohol.
   - Tamp with soft brush.
   - Allow to work 1 minute.

4. With the spot machine, rinse with hot water using the chop stroke technique 6 - 8 times.
   - Take 4 - 6 slow, dry vacuum strokes.

5. Look at spot area carefully to see if the spot is gone:
   - If YES: Allow to dry.
   - If NO: Do Steps 2, 3 and 4 until no more removes. Then, if needed, do Step 6.

6. If the spot persists, call a pro for options as soon as possible.

Spot Contents: Carnuba Wax, Coloring, Confectioner Glaze, Corn Syrup, Sugar, Tapioca Dextrin

## Comments:

- **Optimum removal time:** Within 24 hours of spill
- **Maximum size for home removal:** Class III / IV = 1 inch
- **Removal restrictions:** If the spot(s) is larger than 1 inch in diameter, **do not attempt ANY removal** using Class III or IV instructions. Put a note that says, **"Do Not Touch Or Clean!"** next to the spot. (Do **not** put a towel over spot.) Then:
  - Call a pro and have spot removed within 3 days. -OR-
  - If the spot is 2 inches or less in diameter, get a spot machine and:
    - Old spot: Do Steps 1 - 6 for spots larger than 3/8 inch under Class I.
    - Fresh spot: Do Steps 1 - 6 for spots larger than 3/8 inch under Class II.
- **Caution: Do not attempt scissors removal** of spots from **any** type of looped carpet (berber, commercial glue down, etc.) unless the spot is **only on the outside fibers** of the loop(s). If in doubt, call a pro for options as soon as possible.
- These products can be hard to remove, even for a pro. This is especially true if a large quantity has been stepped on and pressed into the carpet fibers. If you cannot remove a spot, consult a pro for options as soon as possible.

---

### Materials Needed:

Class III / IV: Spotting kit, Vacuum cleaner with attachment removed from hose, WD-40 with red spray tube (usually taped to the container)

| Class III: Towel + Old / Dried Spot | Class IV: Towel + Fresh / Wet Spot |
|---|---|
| **Steps:** | **Steps:** |
| Follow the instructions for your size spot(s): | Follow the instructions for your size spot(s): |
| **If the spot is 3/8 inch (pencil eraser size) or smaller:** | **If the spot is 3/8 inch (pencil eraser size) or smaller:** |
| 1. Using your scissors, wedge the blades up under the spot(s) and snip the gum from the very tip of the carpet fibers. (This will minimize the indentations caused by the removed spots.) Note: On non-looped carpets, you can also trim a few carpet fibers around the edge of the removed spot, if needed, to minimize it further.<br>• On non-looped carpets, rough up the trimmed carpet fibers a little with the tips of your scissors. Trim any taller roughed up fibers so they are equal in height with the rest of the carpet.<br>• Vacuum debris with vacuum cleaner hose. | 1. Using your scissors, wedge the blades up under the spot(s) and snip the gum from the very tip of the carpet fibers. (This will minimize the indentations caused by the removed spots.) Note: On non-looped carpets, you can also trim a few carpet fibers around the edge of the removed spot, if needed, to minimize it further.<br>• On non-looped carpets, rough up the trimmed carpet fibers a little with the tips of your scissors. Trim any taller roughed up fibers so they are equal in height with the rest of the carpet.<br>• Vacuum debris with vacuum cleaner hose. |
| 2. Look at spot area carefully to see if all gum is gone:<br>• If YES: No further action is needed.<br>• If NO: If any gum remains, do Steps 2 - 6 below. | 2. Look at spot area carefully to see if all gum is gone:<br>• If YES: No further action is needed.<br>• If NO: If any gum remains, do Steps 2 - 6 below. |
| **If the spot is larger than 3/8 inch (pencil eraser size):** | **If the spot is larger than 3/8 inch (pencil eraser size):** |
| 1. Using the point of your scissors, poke 10 - 15 holes into the spot (or each spot). | 1. Using the point of your scissors, poke 10 - 15 holes into the spot (or each spot). |
| 2. Mist on a generous amount of WD-40 using the red spray tube. (For each 1 inch of spot diameter, press the spray button twice for 1/2 second each time.)<br>• Allow to work 3 minutes.<br>• Using your spoon, scrape the edges of the spot toward the center until the spot dislodges from the carpet fibers. | 2. Mist on a generous amount of WD-40 using the red spray tube. (For each 1 inch of spot diameter, press the spray button twice for 1/2 second each time.)<br>• Allow to work 3 minutes.<br>• Using your spoon, scrape the edges of the spot toward the center until the spot dislodges from the carpet fibers. |
| 3. Mist on a generous amount of alcohol.<br>• Tamp with soft brush.<br>• Allow to work 1 minute. | 3. Mist on a generous amount of alcohol.<br>• Tamp with soft brush.<br>• Allow to work 1 minute. |
| 4. With a towel over your hand, pinch out as much of the spot as possible. | 4. With a towel over your hand, pinch out as much of the spot as possible. |
| 5. Look at spot area carefully to see if the spot is gone:<br>• If YES: Allow to dry.<br>• If NO: Do Steps 2, 3 and 4 until no more removes. Then, if needed, do Step 6. | 5. Look at spot area carefully to see if the spot is gone:<br>• If YES: Allow to dry.<br>• If NO: Do Steps 2, 3 and 4 until no more removes. Then, if needed, do Step 6. |
| 6. If the spot persists, call a pro for options as soon as possible. | 6. If the spot persists, call a pro for options as soon as possible. |

Section II

# Hair Dye, Hair Coloring

## Comments:

- **Optimum removal time: As soon as possible** within 24 hours of spill
- **Maximum size for home removal**: Class I = No home removal / Class II = 1 inch
- **Removal restrictions - Class I:** See "Class I" instructions below.
- **Removal restrictions - Class II:** If the spot(s) is larger than 1 inch in diameter, **do not attempt TOTAL removal** using Class II instructions. Do Steps 1 - 3 **only** under Class II. Mist spot(s) with a generous amount of ammonia. Put a folded towel moistened with water over spot and a note next to it that says, ***"Do Not Touch Or Clean!"***. (Keep towel damp until pro comes.) Call a pro and have spot removed as soon as possible within 24 hours.
- **Caution:** Strong pigments in these products can immediately and permanently stain most nylon. Even olefin, acrylic and polyester are not immune if the spill is left in the carpet as little as 2 days. If you cannot remove a spot, consult a pro for options as soon as possible.

## Materials Needed:

Class I: Towel, Paper and pencil for note
Class II: Spotting kit, Spot machine with cool water

| Class I: Spot Machine + Old / Dried Spot | Class II: Spot Machine + Fresh / Wet Spot |
|---|---|

### Class I — Steps:

1. **Do not attempt ANY removal** of a Class I spot(s).
   - Put a dry towel over spot.
   - Put a note next to it that says, ***"Do Not Touch Or Clean!"***.
   - Call a pro and have spot removed as soon as possible within 24 hours.

### Class II — Steps:

1. Using a dry towel, firmly blot the spot(s) 15 - 20 times, using a clean part of the towel each time.
   - Repeat until no more transfer occurs.

2. Mist on a small amount of ammonia.
   - Allow to work 1 minute.
   - Tamp with soft brush.
   - Mist on a small amount of alcohol.
   - Tamp firmly with soft brush.
   - Allow to work 1 minute.

3. With the spot machine, rinse with cool water using the chop stroke technique 8 - 10 times.
   - Take 6 - 8 slow, dry vacuum strokes.

4. Look at spot area carefully to see if the spot is gone:
   - If YES: No further action is needed.
   - If NO: Repeat Steps 2 and 3 until no more removes. Then, if needed, do Step 5.

5. If color cast remains, mist on a generous amount of peroxide.
   - Mist on a small amount of ammonia.
   - Tamp with soft brush.
   - Allow to dry.

6. If the spot persists, call a pro for options as soon as possible.

Section II

## *Comments:*

- **Optimum removal time: As soon as possible** within 24 hours of spill
- **Maximum size for home removal:** Class III = No home removal / Class IV = 1/2 inch
- **Removal restrictions - Class III:** See "Class III" instructions below.
- **Removal restrictions - Class IV:** If the spot(s) is larger than 1/2 inch in diameter, **do not attempt TOTAL removal** using Class IV instructions. Do Step 1 **only** under Class IV. Mist spot(s) with a small amount of ammonia. Put a folded towel moistened with water over spot and a note next to it that says, ***"Do Not Touch Or Clean!"***. (Keep towel damp until pro comes.) Call a pro and have spot removed as soon as possible within 24 hours.
- **Caution:** Strong pigments in these products can immediately and permanently stain most nylon. Even olefin, acrylic and polyester are not immune if the spill is left in the carpet as little as 2 days. If you cannot remove a spot, consult a pro for options as soon as possible.

## *Materials Needed:*
Class III: Towel, Paper and pencil for note
Class IV: Spotting kit

| *Class III: Towel + Old / Dried Spot* | *Class IV: Towel + Fresh / Wet Spot* |
|---|---|
| **Steps:** | **Steps:** |
| 1. **Do not attempt ANY removal** of a Class III spot(s). | 1. Using a dry towel, firmly blot the spot(s) 15 - 20 times, using a clean part of the towel each time. |
|   • Put a dry towel over spot. |   • Repeat until no more transfer occurs. |
|   • Put a note next to it that says, ***"Do Not Touch Or Clean!"***. | 2. Mist on a small amount of ammonia. |
|   • Call a pro and have spot removed as soon as possible within 24 hours. |   • Allow to work 1 minute. |
| |   • Tamp with soft brush. |
| |   • Mist on a small amount of alcohol. |
| |   • Tamp firmly with soft brush. |
| |   • Allow to work 1 minute. |
| | 3. With a towel, blot 10 - 15 times, using a clean part of the towel each time. |
| | 4. Look at spot area carefully to see if the spot is gone: |
| |   • If YES: No further action is needed. |
| |   • If NO: Repeat Steps 2 and 3 until no more removes. Then, if needed, do Step 5. |
| | 5. If color cast remains, mist on a generous amount of peroxide. |
| |   • Mist on a small amount of ammonia. |
| |   • Tamp with soft brush. |
| |   • Allow to dry. |
| | 6. If the spot persists, call a pro for options as soon as possible. |

Section II

# Hair Spray, Hair Gel or Mousse, Clothes Starch - Aerosol or Pump

## Comments:

- **Optimum removal time:** Within 24 hours of spill
- **Maximum size for home removal:** Class I / II = No size limits
- **Removal restrictions:** None
- These products can cause recurring spots if not completely removed. (See "Recurring Spots", Chapter 4). Re-treat using instructions under "Class I".

## Materials Needed:

Class I / II: Spotting kit, Spot machine with hot water

### Class I: Spot Machine + Old / Dried Spot

**Steps:**

1. Using your dinner knife, scrape the spot(s) in a side-to-side motion 10 - 35 times. Caution: Be careful to not fray carpet fibers.
   - Vacuum debris with spot machine hose.
   - Repeat entire Step until no more removes.

2. Mist on a generous amount of ammonia.
   - Mist on a generous amount of alcohol.
   - Agitate with hard brush.
   - Allow to work 1 minute.

3. With the spot machine, rinse with hot water using the chop stroke technique 8 - 20 times.
   - Take 10 - 15 slow, dry vacuum strokes.

4. Look at and touch spot area carefully to see if the sticky residue is gone:
   - If YES: No further action is needed.
   - If NO: Do Steps 2 and 3 until no more will remove. Allow to dry.

5. If needed, repeat Steps 2 and 3 one time.

6. If the spot persists, call a pro for options as soon as possible.

### Class II: Spot Machine + Fresh / Wet Spot

**Steps:**

1. Allow spot(s) to dry completely.

2. Using your dinner knife, scrape the spot(s) in a side-to-side motion 10 - 35 times. Caution: Be careful to not fray carpet fibers.
   - Vacuum debris with spot machine hose.
   - Repeat entire Step until no more removes.

3. Mist on a generous amount of ammonia.
   - Mist on a generous amount of alcohol.
   - Agitate with hard brush.
   - Allow to work 1 minute.

4. With the spot machine, rinse with hot water using the chop stroke technique 8 - 20 times.
   - Take 10 - 15 slow, dry vacuum strokes.

5. Look at and touch spot area carefully to see if the sticky residue is gone:
   - If YES: No further action is needed.
   - If NO: Do Steps 3 and 4 until no more will remove. Allow to dry.

6. If needed, repeat Steps 3 and 4 one time.

7. If the spot persists, call a pro for options as soon as possible.

# Hair Spray, Hair Gel or Mousse, Clothes Starch - Aerosol or Pump

Spot Contents: Amylopectin, Polyquaternium, Planthenol, Plant Based Proteins, Gum Karaya, Oxybenzon, Va/Cotonates/Vinyl, Neodecanoate Copolymer, Bonzoate, Polysorbate

## Comments:

- **Optimum removal time:** Within 24 hours of spill
- **Maximum size for home removal:** Class III / IV = 2 1/2 inches
- **Removal restrictions:** If the spot(s) is larger than 2 1/2 inches in diameter, **do not attempt TOTAL removal** using Class III or IV instructions. Do Step 1 **only** under Class III or Steps 1 and 2 **only** under Class IV. Put a dry towel over spot. Then:
  - Call a pro and have spot removed as soon as possible within 3 days. -OR-
  - Get a spot machine and do Steps 2 - 6 under Class I.
- These products can cause recurring spots if not completely removed. (See "Recurring Spots", Chapter 4). Re-treat using instructions under "Class III".

## Materials Needed:

Class III / IV: Spotting kit, Vacuum cleaner with attachment removed from hose

## Class III: Towel + Old / Dried Spot

### Steps:

1. Using your dinner knife, scrape the spot(s) in a side-to-side motion 10 - 35 times. Caution: Be careful to not fray carpet fibers.
   - Vacuum debris with vacuum cleaner hose.
   - Repeat entire Step until no more removes.

2. Mist on a generous amount of ammonia.
   - Mist on a small amount of alcohol.
   - Agitate with hard brush.
   - Allow to work 1 minute.
   - Mist on a small amount of ammonia.
   - Agitate with hard brush.

3. With a towel, blot 10 - 15 times, using a clean part of the towel each time.

4. Look at and touch spot area carefully to see if the sticky residue is gone:
   - If YES: No further action is needed.
   - If NO: Do Steps 2 and 3 until no more will remove. Allow to dry.

5. If needed, repeat Steps 2 and 3 one time.

6. If the spot persists, call a pro for options as soon as possible.

## Class IV: Towel + Fresh / Wet Spot

### Steps:

1. Allow spot to dry completely.

2. Using your dinner knife, scrape the spot(s) in a side-to-side motion 10 - 35 times. Caution: Be careful to not fray carpet fibers.
   - Vacuum debris with vacuum cleaner hose.
   - Repeat entire Step until no more removes.

3. Mist on a generous amount of ammonia.
   - Mist on a small amount of alcohol.
   - Agitate with hard brush.
   - Allow to work 1 minute.
   - Mist on a small amount of ammonia.
   - Agitate with hard brush.

4. With a towel, firmly blot 10 - 15 times, using a clean part of the towel each time.

5. Look at and touch spot area carefully to see if the sticky residue is gone:
   - If YES: No further action is needed.
   - If NO: Do Steps 3 and 4 until no more will remove. Allow to dry.

6. If needed, repeat Steps 3 and 4 one time.

7. If the spot persists, call a pro for options as soon as possible.

Section II

# Ice Cream, Frozen Yogurt, Sorbet

## Comments:

- **Optimum removal time:** Within 24 hours of spill
- **Maximum size for home removal:** Class I / II = 4 inches
- **Removal restrictions:** If the spot(s) is larger than 4 inches in diameter, **do not attempt TOTAL removal** using Class I or II instructions. Do Step 1 **only** under Class I or II. Put a folded towel moistened with water over spot. Call a pro and have spot removed within 2 days.
- **Caution:** Food coloring in some products can immediately and permanently stain nylon if left untreated as little as 4 days. If you cannot remove a spot, consult a pro for options as soon as possible.

## Materials Needed:
Class I / II: Spotting kit, Spot machine with cool water

### Class I: Spot Machine + Old / Dried Spot

**Steps:**

1. Using your spoon, scrape out as much of the spot(s) as possible.
   - Vacuum debris with spot machine.
   - Repeat entire Step until no more removes.

2. Mist on a generous amount of ammonia.
   - Agitate with hard brush.
   - Mist on a small amount of alcohol.
   - Agitate with hard brush.
   - Allow to work 1 minute.
   - Mist on a small amount of ammonia.
   - Agitate with hard brush.

3. With the spot machine, rinse with cool water using the chop stroke technique 6 - 8 times.
   - Take 4 - 6 slow, dry vacuum strokes.

4. Look at spot area carefully to see if the spot is gone:
   - If YES: No further action is needed.
   - If NO: Repeat Steps 2 and 3 until no more removes. Then, if needed, do Step 5.

5. If color cast remains, mist on a generous amount of peroxide.
   - Mist on a small amount of ammonia.
   - Tamp with soft brush.
   - Allow to dry.

6. If needed, repeat Step 5 one time.

7. If the spot persists, call a pro for options as soon as possible.

### Class II: Spot Machine + Fresh / Wet Spot

**Steps:**

1. Lay a small towel over the palm of your hand. Then lay your hand on the carpet so the towel is at the edge of the spot.
   - Using your spoon, scoop as much of the spot(s) as possible into the towel. Note: After each scoop, wipe the spoon on a clean part of the towel.
   - Carefully drop the dirty towel in your empty bucket.
   - Repeat entire Step until no more removes.

2. With the spot machine, rinse with cool water using the chop stroke technique 6 - 8 times.
   - Take 4 - 6 slow, dry vacuum strokes.

3. Look at spot area carefully to see if the spot is gone:
   - If YES: No further action is needed.
   - If NO: Do Step 4.

4. Mist on a small amount of ammonia.
   - Agitate with hard brush.
   - Allow to work 1 minute.
   - Mist on a small amount of alcohol.
   - Tamp with soft brush.

5. With the spot machine, rinse with cool water using the chop stroke technique 4 - 6 times.
   - Take 2 - 4 slow, dry vacuum strokes.

6. Look at spot area carefully to see if the spot is gone:
   - If YES: No further action is needed.
   - If NO: Repeat Steps 4 and 5 until no more removes. Then, if needed, do Step 7.

7. If color cast remains, mist on a generous amount of peroxide.
   - Mist on a small amount of ammonia.
   - Tamp with soft brush.
   - Allow to dry.

8. If needed, repeat Step 7 one time.

9. If the spot persists, call a pro for options as soon as possible.

## Comments:

- **Optimum removal time:** Within 24 hours of spill
- **Maximum size for home removal**: Class III = No home removal / Class IV = 2 inches
- **Removal restrictions - Class III:** See "Class III" instructions below.
- **Removal restrictions - Class IV**: If the spot(s) is larger than 2 inches in diameter, **do not attempt TOTAL removal** using Class IV instructions. Do Step 1 **only** under Class IV. Put a folded towel moistened with water over spot. Then:
  - Call a pro and have spot removed within 2 days. -OR
  - If the spot is 4 inches or less in diameter, get a spot machine and:
    - If the spot is now old/dried, do Steps 2 - 7 under Class I.
    - If the spot is still fresh/wet, do Steps 2 - 9 under Class II.
- **Caution:** Food coloring in some products can immediately and permanently stain nylon if left untreated as little as 4 days. If you cannot remove a spot, consult a pro for options as soon as possible.

## Materials Needed:

Class III: Spotting kit, Vacuum cleaner with attachment removed from hose
Class IV: Spotting kit

### Class III: Towel + Old / Dried Spot

**Steps:**

1. Using your spoon, scrape out as much of the spot(s) as possible.
   - Vacuum debris with vacuum cleaner hose.
   - Repeat entire Step until no more removes.

2. **Do not continue removal** of a Class III spot(s).
   - Put a dry towel over spot.
   - Then:
     - Call a pro and have spot removed within 48 hours. -OR-
     - Get a spot machine and do Steps 2 - 7 under Class I.

### Class IV: Towel + Fresh / Wet Spot

**Steps:**

1. Lay a small towel over the palm of your hand. Then lay your hand on the carpet so the towel is at the edge of the spot.
   - Using your spoon, scoop as much of the spot(s) as possible into the towel. Note: After each scoop, wipe the spoon on a clean part of the towel.
   - Carefully drop the dirty towel in your empty bucket.
   - With a clean towel, firmly blot 15 - 20 times, using a clean part of the towel each time.
   - Repeat entire Step until no more removes.

2. Mist on a small amount of ammonia.
   - Agitate with hard brush.
   - Allow to work 1 minute.
   - Mist on a small amount of alcohol.
   - Tamp with hard brush.

3. With a towel, firmly blot 20 - 25 times, using a clean part of the towel each time.

4. Look at spot area carefully to see if the spot is gone:
   - If YES: No further action is needed.
   - If NO: Repeat Steps 2 and 3 until no more removes. Then, if needed, do Step 5.

5. If color cast remains, mist on a generous amount of peroxide.
   - Mist on a small amount of ammonia.
   - Tamp with soft brush.
   - Allow to dry.

6. If needed, repeat Steps 2, 3 and 5 one time.

7. If the spot persists, call a pro for options as soon as possible.

Section II

# Ink - Soluble or Waterproof, Permanent, Indelible:
## Ball Point Pens, Felt Tip Pens, Permanent Markers

### Comments:

- **Optimum removal time**: Between 24 - 48 hours after spill (Let wet spot, or spots, dry 24 hours and then remove.)
- **Maximum size for home removal**: Class I / II = 3/8 inch
- **Removal restrictions - Class I:** If the spot(s) is larger than 3/8 inch in diameter, **do not attempt TOTAL removal** using Class I instructions. Do Step 1 **only**. Put a dry towel over spot and a note next to it that says, *"Do Not Touch Or Clean!"*. Call a pro as soon as possible and schedule spot removal between 24 - 48 hours of spill.
- **Removal restrictions - Class II:** See "Class II" instructions below.
- **Caution: Do not attempt scissors removal** of spots from **any** type of looped carpet (berber, commercial glue down, etc.) unless the spot is **only on the outside fibers** of the loop(s). If in doubt, call a pro for options as soon as possible.
- **Caution: Do not attempt to remove wet ink spots.** The ink may disperse if treated while wet, making it harder to remove.
- **Caution:** Strong dyes in these products can immediately and permanently stain all nylon if left untreated as little as 2 days. If you cannot remove a spot, consult a pro for options as soon as possible.

### Materials Needed:

Class I: Spotting kit, Spot machine with warm water
Class II: Towel, Paper and pencil for note, Spotting kit, Spot machine with warm water

## Class I: Spot Machine + Old / Dried Spot

### Steps:

1. Using your scissors, wedge the blades up under the spot(s) and snip only the hardened parts from the very tip of the carpet fibers. Caution: Be careful not to remove too much of the fibers. Note: On non-looped carpets, you can also trim a few carpet fibers around the edge of the removed spot, if needed, to minimize it further.
   - On non-looped carpets, rough up the trimmed carpet fibers a little with the tips of your scissors. Trim any taller roughed up fibers so they are equal in height with the rest of the carpet.
   - Vacuum debris with spot machine.

2. With a towel, blot 15 - 20 times, using a clean part of the towel each time.
   - Repeat until no more transfer occurs.

3. Mist on a small amount of alcohol.
   - Tamp with soft brush.
   - Mist on a small amount of alcohol.
   - Tamp with soft brush.

4. With the spot machine, rinse with warm water using the chop stroke technique 8 - 10 times.
   - Take 6 - 8 slow, dry vacuum strokes.

5. Look at spot area carefully to see if the spot is gone:
   - If YES: No further action is needed.
   - If NO: Do Steps 3 and 4 until no more removes. Then, if needed, do Step 6.

6. If color cast remains, mist on a generous amount of peroxide.
   - Mist on a small amount of ammonia.
   - Tamp with soft brush.
   - Allow to dry.

7. If the spot persists, call a pro for options as soon as possible.

## Class II: Spot Machine + Fresh / Wet Spot

### Steps:

1. **Do not attempt IMMEDIATE removal** of a Class II spot(s).
   - Put a note next to spot that says, *"Do Not Touch Or Clean!"*.
   - Tell everyone to avoid the area to prevent spreading the spot.

   **Caution:** Allow the spot to dry 24 hours before attempting any home or pro removal.

2. Complete the Step 3 instructions below for your spot size.

**If the spot is 3/8 inch (pencil eraser size) or smaller:**

3. Do Steps 1 - 7 under Class I.

**If the spot is larger than 3/8 inch (pencil eraser size):**

3. Call a pro as soon as possible and schedule spot removal between 24 - 48 hours after spill.

4. Do Step 1 only under Class I before pro arrives.

# Ink - Soluble or Waterproof, Permanent, Indelible: Ball Point Pens, Felt Tip Pens, Permanent Markers

Spot / Stain Contents: Aniline Dye, Carbon Black/Blue, Clay, Dyes, Graphite, Gum Arabic, Oil, Pigments, Resins, Solvents

## Comments:

- **Optimum removal time:** Between 24 - 48 hours of spill (Let wet spot, or spots, dry 24 hours and then remove.)
- **Maximum size for home removal:** Class III / IV = No total home removal
- **Removal restrictions:** See "Class III" or "Class IV" instructions below.
- **Caution: Do not attempt scissors removal** of spots from **any** type of looped carpet (berber, commercial glue down, etc.) unless the spot is **only on the outside fibers** of the loop(s). If in doubt, call a pro for options as soon as possible.
- **Caution: Do not attempt to remove wet ink spots.** The ink may disperse if treated while wet, making it harder to remove.
- **Caution:** Strong dyes in these products can immediately and permanently stain all nylon if left untreated as little as 2 days. If you cannot remove a spot, consult a pro for options as soon as possible.

## Materials Needed:

Class III - 3/8 inch or smaller: Spotting kit, Vacuum cleaner with attachment removed from hose, Paper and pencil for note
Class III - larger than 3/8 inch: Towel, Paper and pencil for note
Class IV: Towel, Paper and pencil for note

## Class III: Towel + Old / Dried Spot

### Steps:

**Follow the instructions for your size spot(s):**

**If the spot is 3/8 inch (pencil eraser size) or smaller:**

1. Using your scissors, wedge the blades up under the spot(s) and snip only the hardened parts from the very tip of the carpet fibers. Caution: Be careful not to remove too much of the fibers. Note: On non-looped carpets, you can also trim a few carpet fibers around the edge of the removed spot, if needed, to minimize it further.

   - On non-looped carpets, rough up the trimmed carpet fibers a little with the tips of your scissors. Trim any taller roughed up fibers so they are equal in height with the rest of the carpet.
   - Vacuum debris with vacuum cleaner hose.

2. With a towel, blot 15 - 20 times, using a clean part of the towel each time.

   - Repeat until no more transfer occurs.

3. Put a dry towel over spot and a note next to it that says, **"Do Not Touch Or Clean!"**.

   - Tell everyone to avoid the area.
   - Then:
     - Call a pro as soon as possible and schedule spot removal between 24 - 48 hours after spill. -OR-
     - If the spot is smaller than 3/8 inch, get a spot machine and do Steps 3 - 7 under Class I.

**If the spot is larger than 3/8 inch (pencil eraser size):**

1. Put a dry towel over spot and a note next to it that says, **"Do Not Touch Or Clean!"**.

   - Tell everyone to avoid the area.
   - Call a pro as soon as possible and schedule spot removal between 24 - 48 hours after spill. (Spot should dry at least 24 hours before removal.)

## Class IV: Towel + Fresh / Wet Spot

### Steps:

**Follow the instructions for your size spot(s):**

1. **Do not attempt IMMEDIATE removal** of a Class IV spot(s).

   - Put a note next to spot that says, **"Do Not Touch Or Clean!"**.
   - Tell everyone to avoid the area.

   **Caution:** Allow the spot to dry 24 hours before attempting any home or pro removal.

2. Then:

   - Call a pro as soon as possible and schedule spot removal between 24 - 48 hours after spill. -OR-
   - If the spot is 3/8 inch or smaller, get a spot machine and do Steps 1 - 7 under Class I.

# *Iodine*

## Comments:

- **Optimum removal time: As soon as possible** within 24 hours of spill
- **Maximum size for home removal:** Class I = No home removal / Class II = 1 1/4 inches
- **Removal restrictions - Class I:** No home removal. See "Class I" instructions below.
- **Removal restrictions - Class II:** If the spot(s) is larger than 1 1/4 inches in diameter, **do not attempt TOTAL removal** using Class II instructions. Do Step 1 **only** under Class II. Mist a small amount of ammonia and a generous amount of peroxide on spot. Put a folded towel moistened with water over spot and a note next to it that says, ***"Do Not Touch Or Clean!"***. (Keep towel damp until pro comes.) Call a pro and have spot removed as soon as possible within 24 hours.
- **Caution:** Strong dyes in iodine can immediately and permanently stain all nylon, and even olefin, acrylic and polyester if left untreated as little as 12 hours. If you cannot remove a spot, consult a pro for options as soon as possible.

## Materials Needed:

Class I: Towel, Paper and pencil for note
Class II: Spotting kit, Spot machine with warm water

| Class I: Spot Machine + Old / Dried Spot | Class II: Spot Machine + Fresh / Wet Spot |
|---|---|

### Class I — Steps:

1. **Do not attempt ANY removal** of a Class I spot(s).
   - Put a dry towel over spot.
   - Put a note next to it that says, ***"Do Not Touch Or Clean!"***.
   - Call a pro and have spot removed as soon as possible within 24 hours.

### Class II — Steps:

1. Using your spot machine, dry vacuum the spot(s) 10 - 15 times taking slow, single strokes.
   - Rinse with warm water using the chop stroke technique 10 - 12 times.
   - Take 6 - 8 slow, dry vacuum strokes.
2. Mist on a generous amount of alcohol.
   - Mist on a small amount of ammonia.
   - Tamp with soft brush.
   - Allow to work 1 minute.
3. With the spot machine, rinse with warm water using the chop stroke technique 6 - 8 times.
   - Take 4 - 6 slow, dry vacuum strokes.
4. Look at spot area carefully to see if the spot is gone:
   - If YES: No further action is needed.
   - If NO: Repeat Steps 2 and 3 until no more removes. Then, if needed, do Step 5.
5. If color cast remains, mist on a generous amount of peroxide.
   - Mist on a small amount of ammonia.
   - Tamp with soft brush.
   - Allow to dry.
6. If the spot persists, call a pro for options as soon as possible.

## *Comments:*

- **Optimum removal time: As soon as possible** within 24 hours of spill
- **Maximum size for home removal:** Class III = No home removal / Class IV = 3/4 inch
- **Removal restrictions - Class III:** No home removal. See "Class III" instructions below.
- **Removal restrictions - Class IV:** If the spot(s) is larger than 3/4 inch in diameter, **do not attempt TOTAL removal** using Class IV instructions. Do Step 1 **only** under Class IV. Mist a small amount of ammonia and a generous amount of peroxide on spot. Put a folded towel moistened with water over spot and a note next to it that says, ***"Do Not Touch Or Clean!"***. (Keep towel damp until pro comes.) Call a pro and have spot removed as soon as possible within 24 hours.
- **Caution:** Strong dyes in iodine can immediately and permanently stain all nylon, and even olefin, acrylic and polyester if left untreated as little as 12 hours. If you cannot remove a spot, consult a pro for options as soon as possible.

## *Materials Needed:*

Class III: Towel, Paper and pencil for note
Class IV: Spotting kit

### *Class III: Towel + Old / Dried Spot*

*Steps:*

1. **Do not attempt ANY removal** of a Class III spot(s).
   - Put a dry towel over spot.
   - Call a pro and have spot removed as soon as possible within 24 hours.

### *Class IV: Towel + Fresh / Wet Spot*

*Steps:*

1. Using a dry towel, firmly blot spot(s) 15 - 20 times, using a clean part of the towel each time.
   - Repeat until no more transfer occurs.

2. Mist on a generous amount of alcohol.
   - Mist on a small amount of ammonia.
   - Tamp with soft brush.
   - Allow to work 1 minute.

3. With a dry towel, firmly blot spot(s) 15 - 20 times, using a clean part of the towel each time.

4. Look at spot area carefully to see if the spot is gone:
   - If YES: No further action is needed.
   - If NO: Repeat Steps 2 and 3 until no more removes. Then, if needed, do Step 5.

5. If color cast remains, mist on a generous amount of peroxide.
   - Mist on a small amount of ammonia.
   - Tamp with soft brush.
   - Allow to dry.

6. If the spot persists, call a pro for options as soon as possible.

Section II

# Jam, Jelly, Preserves

## Comments:

- **Optimum removal time**: Within 24 hours of spill
- **Maximum size for home removal**: Class I / II = 5 inches
- **Removal restrictions**: If the spot(s) is larger than 5 inches in diameter, **do not attempt TOTAL removal** using Class I or II instructions. Do Step 1 **only** under Class I or II. Put a folded towel moistened with water over spot. Call a pro and have spot removed within 2 days.
- Food coloring and/or acid dyes in some products can immediately and permanently stain some nylon. If you cannot remove a spot, consult a pro for options as soon as possible.

## Materials Needed:
Class I / II: Spotting kit, Spot machine with warm water

### Class I: Spot Machine + Old / Dried Spot

**Steps:**

1. Using your spoon, scrape out as much of the spot(s) as possible.
   - With a towel over your hand, pinch out the spot matter, using a clean part of the towel each time.
   - Repeat entire Step until no more removes.

2. Mist on a generous amount of ammonia. (Jams that are red may turn blue. Do not worry.)
   - Allow to work 2 minutes.
   - Mist on a generous amount of peroxide. (The blue may turn back to red.)
   - Agitate with hard brush.

3. With the spot machine, rinse with warm water using the chop stroke technique 8 - 10 times.
   - Take 6 - 8 slow, dry vacuum strokes.

4. Look at spot area carefully to see if the spot is gone:
   - If YES: No further action is needed.
   - If NO: Repeat Steps 2 and 3 until no more removes. Then, if needed, do Step 5.

5. If color cast remains, mist on a generous amount of peroxide.
   - Mist on a small amount of ammonia.
   - Tamp with soft brush.
   - Allow to dry.

6. If needed, repeat Step 5 one time.

7. If the spot persists, call a pro for options as soon as possible.

### Class II: Spot Machine + Fresh / Wet Spot

**Steps:**

1. Lay a small towel over the palm of your hand. Then lay your hand on the carpet so the towel is at the edge of the spot.
   - Using your spoon, scoop as much of the spot(s) as possible into the towel. Note: After each scoop, wipe the spoon on a clean part of the towel.
   - Carefully drop the dirty towel in your empty bucket.
   - With the spot machine, rinse with warm water using the chop stroke technique 4 - 6 times. Take 2 - 4 slow, dry vacuum strokes.

2. Mist on a generous amount of ammonia. (Jams that are red may turn blue. Do not worry.)
   - Allow to work 1 minute.
   - Mist on a generous amount of peroxide. (The blue may turn back to red.)
   - Agitate with hard brush.

3. With the spot machine, rinse with warm water using the single stroke technique 6 - 8 times.
   - Take 4 - 6 slow, dry vacuum strokes.

4. Look at spot area carefully to see if the spot is gone:
   - If YES: No further action is needed.
   - If NO: Repeat Steps 2 and 3 until no more removes. Then, if needed, do Step 5.

5. If color cast remains, mist on a generous amount of peroxide.
   - Mist on a small amount of ammonia.
   - Tamp with soft brush.
   - Allow to dry.

6. If needed, repeat Step 5 one time.

7. If the spot persists, call a pro for options as soon as possible.

Section II

# Jam, Jelly, Preserves

Stain / Spot Contents: Acid Dye, Coloring, Fruits, Sugar

## Comments:

- **Optimum removal time:** Within 24 hours of spill
- **Maximum size for home removal:** Class III / IV = 2 inches
- **Removal restrictions:** If the spot(s) is larger than 2 inches in diameter, **do not attempt TOTAL removal** using Class III or IV instructions. Do Step 1 **only** under Class III or IV. Put a folded towel moistened with water over spot. Then:
  - Call a pro and have spot removed within 2 days. -OR-
  - If the spot is 5 inches or less in diameter, get a spot machine and:
    - If the spot is now old/dried, do Steps 2 - 7 under Class I.
    - If the spot is still fresh/wet, do Steps 1 - 7 under Class II.
- Food coloring and/or acid dyes in some products can immediately and permanently stain some nylon. If you cannot remove a spot, consult a pro for options as soon as possible.

## Materials Needed:

Class III / IV: Spotting kit

### Class III: Towel + Old / Dried Spot

**Steps:**

1. Using your spoon, scrape out as much of the spot(s) as possible.
   - With a towel over your hand, pinch out the spot matter, using a clean part of the towel each time.
   - Repeat entire Step until no more removes.

2. Mist on a generous amount of ammonia.
   (Jams that are red may turn blue. Do not worry.)
   - Allow to work 2 minutes.
   - Mist on a generous amount of peroxide.
     (The blue may turn back to red.)
   - Agitate with hard brush.

3. With a towel, blot 15 - 20 times, using a clean part of the towel each time.

4. Look at spot area carefully to see if the spot is gone:
   - If YES: No further action is needed.
   - If NO: Repeat Steps 2 and 3 until no more removes. Then, if needed, do Step 5.

5. If color cast remains, mist on a generous amount of peroxide.
   - Mist on a small amount of ammonia.
   - Tamp with soft brush.
   - Allow to dry.

6. If needed, repeat Steps 2, 3 and 5 one time.

7. If the spot persists, call a pro for options as soon as possible.

### Class IV: Towel + Fresh / Wet Spot

**Steps:**

1. Lay a small towel over the palm of your hand. Then lay your hand on the carpet so the towel is at the edge of the spot.
   - Using your spoon, scoop as much of the spot(s) as possible into the towel. Note: After each scoop, wipe the spoon on a clean part of the towel.
   - Carefully drop the dirty towel in your empty bucket.
   - With a clean towel over your hand, pinch out the spot matter, using a clean part of the towel each time.
   - Repeat entire Step until no more removes.

2. Mist on a generous amount of ammonia.
   (Jams that are red may turn blue. Do not worry.)
   - Allow to work 1 minute.
   - Mist on a generous amount of peroxide.
     (The blue may turn back to red.)
   - Agitate with hard brush.

3. With a towel, blot 15 - 20 times, using a clean part of the towel each time.

4. Look at spot area carefully to see if the spot is gone:
   - If YES: No further action is needed.
   - If NO: Repeat Steps 2 and 3 until no more removes. Then, if needed, do Step 5.

5. If color cast remains, mist on a generous amount of peroxide.
   - Mist on a small amount of ammonia.
   - Tamp with soft brush.
   - Allow to dry.

6. If needed, repeat Steps 2, 3 and 5 one time.

7. If the spot persists, call a pro for options as soon as possible.

Section II

# Kerosene, Diesel Fuel, Lantern Oil

## Comments:

- **Optimum removal time: As soon as possible** within 24 hours of spill
- **Maximum size for home removal:** Class I / II = 2 inches
- **Removal restrictions:** If the spot(s) is larger than 2 inches in diameter, **do not attempt TOTAL removal** using Class I or II instructions. Do Step 1 **only** under Class I or II. Put a dry towel over spot. Call a pro and have spot removed as soon as possible within 24 hours.
- Large spills can damage latex in the carpet and pad and cause it to swell into little hills. This makes the carpet look as if it is loose and needs to be re-stretched. Consult a pro for options.
- These products may cause color distortion to polyester and nylon over time (as little as 2 - 3 weeks). Consult a pro for options.

## Materials Needed:

Class I / II: Spotting kit, Spot machine with hot water

| Class I: Spot Machine + Old / Dried Spot | Class II: Spot Machine + Fresh / Wet Spot |
|---|---|
| **Steps:** | **Steps:** |
| 1. Using your spot machine, rinse the spot(s) with hot water using the single stroke technique 6 - 8 times. | 1. Using your spot machine, rinse the spot(s) with hot water using the single stroke technique 6 - 8 times. |
| • Take 4 - 6 slow, dry vacuum strokes. | • Take 4 - 6 slow, dry vacuum strokes. |
| 2. Mist on a generous amount of alcohol. | 2. Mist on a generous amount of alcohol. |
| • Mist on a small amount of ammonia. | • Mist on a small amount of ammonia. |
| • Tamp with soft brush. | • Tamp with soft brush. |
| • Allow to work 1 minute. | • Allow to work 1 minute. |
| 3. Rinse with hot water using the single stroke technique 6 - 8 times. | 3. Rinse with hot water using the single stroke technique 6 - 8 times. |
| • Take 4 - 6 slow, dry vacuum strokes. | • Take 4 - 6 slow, dry vacuum strokes. |
| 4. Smell spot area carefully to see if the spot odor is gone: | 4. Smell spot area carefully to see if the spot odor is gone: |
| • If YES: Allow to dry. | • If YES: Allow to dry. |
| • If NO: Repeat Steps 2 and 3 until no more removes. Allow to dry. | • If NO: Repeat Steps 2 and 3 until no more removes. Allow to dry. |
| 5. Check for odor the next day to see if odor is still gone: | 5. Check for odor the next day to see if odor is still gone: |
| • If YES: No further action is needed. | • If YES: No further action is needed. |
| • If NO: Call a pro for options if odor persists. | • If NO: Call a pro for options if odor persists. |

Section II

Spot Contents: Refined Aliphatic Hydrocarbons, Refined Petroleum Oils

## Comments:

- **Optimum removal time: As soon as possible** within 24 hours of spill
- **Maximum size for home removal:** Class III / IV = 1 inch
- **Removal restrictions:** If the spot(s) is larger than 1 inch in diameter **do not attempt ANY removal** using Class III or IV instructions. Blot up as much of the liquid (if present) as possible by placing a folded dry towel over the spill and stepping on it until no more absorbs. Put a clean, dry towel over spot. Then:
  - Call a pro and have spot removed as soon as possible within 24 hours. -OR-
  - If the spot is 2 inches or less in diameter, get a spot machine and:
    - If the spot is now old, do Steps 1 - 5 under Class I.
    - If the spot is still fresh, do Steps 1 - 5 under Class II.
- Large spills can damage latex in the carpet and pad and cause it to swell into little hills. This makes the carpet look as if it is loose and needs to be re-stretched. Consult a pro for options.
- These products may cause color distortion to polyester and nylon over time (as little as 2 - 3 weeks). Consult a pro for options.

## Materials Needed:

Class III: Spotting kit, Vacuum cleaner with beater brush
Class IV: Disposable towels or tissues, Spotting kit

| Class III : Towel + Old / Dried Spot | Class IV: Towel + Fresh / Wet Spot |
|---|---|

### Steps:

1. Using your hard brush, brush the spot(s) in a side-to-side motion 15 - 18 times. Caution: Be careful not to fray carpet fibers.
   - Vacuum with vacuum cleaner beater brush.

2. Mist on a generous amount of alcohol.
   - Mist on a small amount of ammonia.
   - Tamp with soft brush.
   - Allow to work 2 minutes.

3. Fold a cloth towel several times and place it over the spot(s).
   - Step on the towel with your full weight 15 - 20 times, using a clean part of the towel each time.

4. Smell spot area carefully to see if the spot odor is gone:
   - If YES: Allow to dry.
   - If NO: Repeat Steps 2 and 3 until no more removes. Allow to dry.

5. Check for odor the next day to see if odor is still gone:
   - If YES: No further action is needed.
   - If NO: Call a pro for options, if odor persists.

### Steps:

1. Fold a disposable towel several times and place it over the spot(s).
   - Step on the towel with your full weight 15 - 20 times, using a clean part of the towel each time.
   - Repeat until no more absorbs.

2. Mist on a small amount of alcohol.
   - Mist on a small amount of ammonia.
   - Tamp with soft brush.
   - Allow to work 1 minute.

3. Fold a cloth towel several times and place it over the spot(s).
   - Step on the towel with your full weight 10 - 15 times, using a clean part of the towel each time.

4. Smell spot area carefully to see if the spot odor is gone:
   - If YES: Allow to dry.
   - If NO: Repeat Steps 2 and 3 until no more removes. Allow to dry.

5. Check for odor the next day to see if odor is still gone:
   - If YES: No further action is needed.
   - If NO: Call a pro for options, if odor persists.

Section II

# Ketchup (Catsup), Chili Paste, Tomato Paste / Puree / Sauce, Salsa

## Comments:

- **Optimum removal time:** Within 24 hours of spill
- **Maximum size for home removal**: Class I / II = 3 inches
- **Removal restrictions:** If the spot(s) is larger than 3 inches in diameter, **do not attempt TOTAL removal** using Class I or II instructions. Do Step 1 **only** under Class I or II. Put a folded towel moistened with water over spot. Call a pro and have spot removed within 2 days.
- Coloring in these products can immediately and permanently stain some nylon. If you cannot remove a spot, consult a pro for options as soon as possible.

## Materials Needed:

Class I / II: Spotting kit, Spot machine with hot water

| Class I: Spot Machine + Old / Dried Spot | Class II: Spot Machine + Fresh / Wet Spot |
|---|---|
| **Steps:** | **Steps:** |

**Class I: Spot Machine + Old / Dried Spot**

**Steps:**

1. Using your spoon, scrape out as much of the spot(s) as possible.
   - Vacuum debris with spot machine.
   - Repeat entire Step until no more removes.
2. Mist on a generous amount of ammonia.
   - Agitate with hard brush.
   - Mist on a generous amount of peroxide.
   - Agitate with hard brush.
   - Allow to work 2 minutes.
3. With the spot machine, rinse with hot water using the chop stroke technique 8 - 10 times.
   - Take 6 - 8 slow, dry vacuum strokes.
4. Look at spot area carefully to see if the spot is gone:
   - If YES: No further action is needed.
   - If NO: Repeat Steps 2 and 3 until no more removes. Then, if needed, do Step 5.
5. If color cast remains, mist on a generous amount of peroxide.
   - Tamp with soft brush.
   - Dry vacuum with spot machine.
   - Mist on a generous amount of peroxide.
   - Tamp with soft brush.
   - Allow to dry.
6. If needed, repeat Step 5 one time.
7. If the spot persists, call a pro for options as soon as possible.

**Class II: Spot Machine + Fresh / Wet Spot**

**Steps:**

1. Lay a small towel over the palm of your hand. Then lay your hand on the carpet so the towel is at the edge of the spot.
   - Using your spoon, scoop as much of the spot(s) as possible into the towel. Note: After each scoop, wipe the spoon on a clean part of the towel.
   - Carefully drop the dirty towel in your empty bucket.
   - With the spot machine, rinse with hot water using the chop stroke technique 6 - 8 times. Take 4 - 6 slow, dry vacuum strokes.
2. Mist on a generous amount of ammonia.
   - Agitate with hard brush.
   - Mist on a generous amount of peroxide.
   - Agitate with hard brush.
   - Allow to work 1 minute.
3. With the spot machine, rinse with hot water using the single stroke technique 6 - 8 times.
   - Take 4 - 6 slow, dry vacuum strokes.
4. Look at spot area carefully to see if the spot is gone:
   - If YES: No further action is needed.
   - If NO: Repeat Steps 2 and 3 until no more removes. Then, if needed, do Step 5.
5. If color cast remains, mist on a generous amount of peroxide.
   - Tamp with soft brush.
   - Dry vacuum with spot machine.
   - Mist on a generous amount of peroxide.
   - Tamp with soft brush.
   - Allow to dry.
6. If needed, repeat Step 5 one time.
7. If the spot persists, call a pro for options as soon as possible.

Section II

Stain / Spot Contents: Acid, Coloring, Peppers, Salt, Spices, Tannin, Tomatoes

## Comments:

- **Optimum removal time:** Within 24 hours of spill
- **Maximum size for home removal:** Class III / IV = 1 1/2 inches
- **Removal restrictions:** If the spot(s) is larger than 1 1/2 inches in diameter, **do not attempt TOTAL removal** using Class III or IV instructions. Do Step 1 **only** under Class III or IV. Put a folded towel moistened with water over spot. Then:
  - Call a pro and have spot removed within 2 days. -OR-
  - If the spot is 3 inches or less in diameter, get a spot machine and:
    - If the spot is now old/dried, do Steps 2 - 7 under Class I
    - If the spot is still fresh/wet, do Steps 1 - 7 under Class II.
- Coloring in these products can immediately and permanently stain some nylon. If you cannot remove a spot, consult a pro for options as soon as possible.

## Materials Needed:

Class III: Spotting kit, Vacuum cleaner with attachment removed from hose
Class IV: Spotting kit

### Class III: Towel + Old / Dried Spot

**Steps:**

1. Using your spoon, scrape out as much of the spot(s) as possible.
   - Vacuum debris with vacuum cleaner hose.
   - Repeat entire Step until no more removes.

2. Mist on a generous amount of ammonia.
   - Agitate with hard brush.
   - Mist on a generous amount of peroxide.
   - Agitate with hard brush.
   - Allow to work 2 minutes.

3. With a towel, blot 15 - 20 times, using a clean part of the towel each time.

4. Look at spot area carefully to see if the spot is gone:
   - If YES: No further action is needed.
   - If NO: Repeat Steps 2 and 3 until no more removes. Then, if needed, do Step 5.

5. If color cast remains, mist on a generous amount of peroxide.
   - Tamp with soft brush.
   - Blot twice with dry towel.
   - Mist on a generous amount of peroxide.
   - Tamp with soft brush.
   - Allow to dry.

6. If needed, repeat Steps 2, 3 and 5 one time.

7. If the spot persists, call a pro for options as soon as possible.

### Class IV: Towel + Fresh / Wet Spot

**Steps:**

1. Lay a small towel over the palm of your hand. Then lay your hand on the carpet so the towel is at the edge of the spot.
   - Using your spoon, scoop as much of the spot(s) as possible into the towel. Note: After each scoop, wipe the spoon on a clean part of the towel.
   - Carefully drop the dirty towel in your empty bucket.
   - With a clean towel over your hand, pinch out the spot matter, using a clean part of the towel each time.
   - Repeat entire Step until no more removes.

2. Mist on a generous amount of ammonia.
   - Agitate with hard brush.
   - Mist on a generous amount of peroxide.
   - Agitate with hard brush.
   - Allow to work 1 minute.

3. With a towel, blot 10 - 15 times, using a clean part of the towel each time.

4. Look at spot area carefully to see if the spot is gone:
   - If YES: No further action is needed.
   - If NO: Repeat Steps 2 and 3 until no more removes. Then, if needed, do Step 5.

5. If color cast remains, mist on a generous amount of peroxide.
   - Tamp with soft brush.
   - Blot twice with dry towel.
   - Mist on a generous amount of peroxide.
   - Tamp with soft brush.
   - Allow to dry.

6. If needed, repeat Steps 2, 3 and 5 one time.

7. If the spot persists, call a pro for options as soon as possible.

Section II

# Lacquer, Polyurethane, Shellac, Varnish, Etc.

## Comments:

- **Optimum removal time: As soon as possible** within 24 hours of spill
- **Maximum size for home removal:** Class I = No home removal / Class II = 1 inch
- **Removal restrictions - Class I:** See "Class I" instructions below.
- **Removal restrictions - Class II:** If the spot(s) is larger than 1 inch in diameter, **do not attempt TOTAL removal** using Class II instructions. Do Step 1 **only** under Class II. Mist a generous amount of alcohol on the spot. Put a folded towel moistened with water over spot. Call a pro and have spot removed as soon as possible within 24 hours.
- Stain in some products can immediately and permanently stain nylon. If you cannot remove a spot, consult a pro for options as soon as possible.
- Solvents in these products can damage latex in the carpet and pad if a large spill (as little as 1/2 pint) is allowed to soak into the carpet backing. Consult a pro for options as soon as possible.

## Materials Needed:

Class I: Towel
Class II: Disposable towels, Spotting kit, Spot machine with hot water

## Class I: Spot Machine + Old / Dried Spot

### Steps:

1. **Do not attempt ANY removal** of a Class I spot(s).
   - Put a dry towel over spot.
   - Call a pro and have spot removed as soon as possible within 24 hours.

## Class II: Spot Machine + Fresh / Wet Spot

### Steps:

1. Using a disposable towel, very gently blot the spot(s) 15 - 20 times, using a clean part of the towel each time.
   - Repeat until no more absorbs.

2. Mist on a generous amount of alcohol.
   - Agitate with end of spoon handle.
   - Allow to work 1 minute.
   - Mist on a generous amount of alcohol.
   - Agitate with end of spoon handle.

3. With the spot machine, rinse with hot water using the chop stroke technique 10 - 12 times.
   - Take 4 - 6 slow, dry vacuum strokes.

4. Look at and touch spot area carefully to see if the sticky residue is gone:
   - If YES: No further action is needed.
   - If NO: Repeat Steps 2 and 3 until no more removes. Then, if needed, do Step 5.

5. If color cast remains, mist on a generous amount of peroxide.
   - Tamp with soft brush.
   - Mist on a small amount of ammonia.
   - Tamp with soft brush.
   - Allow to dry.

6. If the spot persists, call a pro for options as soon as possible.

Section II

# Lacquer, Polyurethane, Shellac, Varnish, Etc.

Spot / Stain Contents: Alcohol, Aromatic Solvents, Glycol Solvents, Ketone, Nitrocellulose, Oils, Plasticizers, Resins, Silicone, Solvent Soluble Plastics, Stain, Thickeners

## Comments:

- **Optimum removal time: As soon as possible** within 24 hours of spill
- **Maximum size for home removal:** Class III = No home removal / Class IV = No size restrictions
- **Removal restrictions - Class III:** See "Class III" instructions below.
- **Removal restrictions - Class IV:** No TOTAL home removal. See "Class IV" instructions below.
- Stain in these products can immediately and permanently stain nylon. If you cannot remove a spot, consult a pro for options as soon as possible.
- Solvents in these products can damage latex in the carpet and pad if a large spill (as little as 1/2 pint) is allowed to soak into the carpet backing. Consult a pro for options as soon as possible.

## Materials Needed:

Class III: Towel
Class IV: Disposable towels, Spotting kit

## Class III: Towel + Old / Dried Spot

### Steps:

1. **Do not attempt ANY removal** of a Class III spot(s).
   - Put a dry towel over spot.
   - Call a pro and have spot removed as soon as possible within 24 hours.

## Class IV: Towel + Fresh / Wet Spot

### Steps:

1. Using a disposable towel, very gently blot the spot(s) 15 - 20 times, using a clean part of the towel each time.
   - Repeat until no more absorbs.

2. Mist on a generous amount of alcohol.
   - Gently agitate with end of spoon handle.

3. With a cloth towel, blot the spot(s) 15 - 20 times, using a clean part of the towel each time.

4. Mist on a generous amount of alcohol.

5. Put a folded towel dampened with water over spot. (Keep the towel moist until the pro arrives.) Then:
   - Call a pro and have spot removed as soon as possible within 24 hours. -OR-
   - If the spot is 1 inch or less in diameter and is still fresh/wet, get a spot machine and do Steps 2 - 6 under Class II.

Section II

# Lignin Browning: Alkaline Browning, Cellulosic Browning

## Comments:

- **Optimum removal time:** Within 24 hours of spill
- **Maximum size for home removal:** Class I = No size limit if spot is dry / Class II = Allow spot to dry, then no size limit
- **Removal restrictions:** See "Class I" or "Class II" instructions below.
- If not completely removed, this type of spot may permanently stain most nylons over a long period of time (as little as 10 months).
- Spills over 6 inches can cause recurring spots on all fiber types. (See "Recurring Spots", Chapter 4.) Consult a pro for options.

## Materials Needed:
Class I / II: Spotting kit, Spot machine with hot water

### Class I: Spot Machine + Old / Dried Spot

**Steps:**

1. Using your soft brush, brush the spot(s) in a side-to-side motion 15 - 20 times.
   - With the soft brush, brush spot in a circular motion 10 - 15 times clockwise and 10 - 15 times counterclockwise. Caution: Be careful to not fray carpet fibers.
   - Vacuum debris with spot machine.

2. Mist on a generous amount of ammonia.
   - Mist on a generous amount of peroxide.
   - Agitate with soft brush.
   - Allow to work 2 minutes.
   - Mist on a generous amount of peroxide.
   - Agitate with soft brush.
   - Allow to work 1 minute.

3. With the spot machine, rinse with hot water using the chop stroke technique 8 - 10 times.
   - Take 6 - 8 slow, dry vacuum strokes.

4. Look at spot area carefully to see if the spot is gone:
   - If YES: No further action is needed.
   - If NO: Do Steps 2 and 3 until no more will remove. If needed, do Step 5.

5. If color cast remains, mist on a generous amount of peroxide.
   - Tamp with soft brush.
   - Allow to dry.

6. If needed, repeat Steps 2, 3 and 5 one time.

7. If the spot persists, call a pro for options as soon as possible.

### Class II: Spot Machine + Fresh / Wet Spot

**Steps:**

1. Using your spot machine, dry vacuum the spot(s) 15 - 20 times.

2. Allow the spot to dry completely.

3. Using your soft brush, brush the spot(s) in a side-to-side motion 15 - 20 times.
   - With the soft brush, brush spot in a circular motion 10 - 15 times clockwise and 10 - 15 times counterclockwise. Caution: Be careful to not fray carpet fibers.
   - Vacuum debris with spot machine.

4. Mist on a generous amount of ammonia.
   - Mist on a generous amount of peroxide.
   - Agitate with soft brush.
   - Allow to work 2 minutes.
   - Mist on a generous amount of peroxide.
   - Agitate with soft brush.
   - Allow to work 1 minute.

5. With the spot machine, rinse with hot water using the chop stroke technique 8 - 10 times.
   - Take 6 - 8 slow, dry vacuum strokes.

6. Look at spot area carefully to see if the spot is gone:
   - If YES: No further action is needed.
   - If NO: Do Steps 4 and 5 until no more will remove. If needed, do Step 6.

7. If color cast remains, mist on a generous amount of peroxide.
   - Tamp with soft brush.
   - Allow to dry.

8. If needed, repeat Steps 4, 5, and 7 one time.

9. If the spot persists, call a pro for options as soon as possible.

Section II

Spot / Stain Contents: Cellulosic Plant Matter, Organic Dye, Possible Detergent and Soil

## Comments:

- **Optimum removal time:** Within 24 hours of spill
- **Maximum size for home removal:** Class III / IV = 3 inches
- **Removal restrictions:** If the spot(s) is larger than 3 inches in diameter, **do not attempt TOTAL removal** using Class III or IV instructions. Do Step 1 **only** under Class III or Steps 1 - 3 **only** under Class IV. (Note: If you will be able to get a spot machine quickly, do Step 1 only under Class IV.) Put a dry towel over spot. Then:
  - Call a pro and have spot removed as soon as possible within 3 days. -OR-
  - Get a spot machine and:
    - If the spot is now old/dried, do Steps 2 - 7 under Class I.
    - If the spot is still wet, do Steps 1 - 9 under Class II.
- If not completely removed, this type of spot may permanently stain most nylons over a long period of time (as little as 10 months).
- Spills over 6 inches can cause recurring spots on all fiber types. (See "Recurring Spots", Chapter 4.) Consult a pro for options.

## Materials Needed:

Class III / IV: Spotting kit, Vacuum cleaner with attachment removed from hose

### Class III: Towel + Old / Dried Spot

#### Steps:

1. Using your soft brush, brush the spot(s) in a side-to-side motion 15 - 20 times.
   - Then brush spot in a circular motion 10 - 15 times clockwise and 10 - 15 times counterclockwise. Caution: Be careful to not fray carpet fibers.
   - Vacuum debris with vacuum cleaner hose.

2. Mist on a generous amount of ammonia.
   - Mist on a generous amount of peroxide.
   - Agitate with soft brush.
   - Allow to work 2 minutes.
   - Mist on a small amount of peroxide.
   - Agitate with soft brush.
   - Allow to work 1 minute.

3. With a towel, blot 15 - 20 times, using a clean part of the towel each time.

4. Look at spot area carefully to see if the spot is gone:
   - If YES: No further action is needed.
   - If NO: Do Steps 2 and 3 until no more will remove. Then, if needed, do Step 5.

5. If color cast remains, mist on a generous amount of peroxide.
   - Tamp with soft brush.
   - Allow to dry.

6. If needed, repeat Steps 2, 3 and 5 one time.

7. If the spot persists, call a pro for options as soon as possible.

### Class IV: Towel + Fresh / Wet Spot

#### Steps:

1. Fold a towel several times and place it over the spot(s).
   - Step on the towel with your full weight 15 - 20 times, using a clean part of the towel each time.
   - Repeat until no more absorbs.

2. Allow spot to dry completely.

3. Using your soft brush, brush the spot(s) in a side-to-side motion 15 - 20 times.
   - Then brush spot in a circular motion 10 - 15 times clockwise and 10 - 15 times counterclockwise. Caution: Be careful to not fray carpet fibers.
   - Vacuum debris with vacuum cleaner hose.

4. Mist on a generous amount of ammonia.
   - Mist on a generous amount of peroxide.
   - Agitate with soft brush.
   - Allow to work 2 minutes.
   - Mist on a small amount of peroxide.
   - Agitate with soft brush.
   - Allow to work 1 minute.

5. With a towel, firmly blot 15 - 20 times, using a clean part of the towel each time.

6. Look at spot area carefully to see if the spot is gone:
   - If YES: No further action is needed.
   - If NO: Do Steps 4 and 5 until no more will remove. Then, if needed, do Step 7.

7. If color cast remains, mist on a generous amount of peroxide.
   - Tamp with soft brush.
   - Allow to dry.

8. If needed, repeat Steps 4, 5 and 7 one time.

9. If the spot persists, call a pro for options as soon as possible.

Section II

# Magic Marker, Ink - Fountain Pen, Finger Paint, Water Color Paint

## Comments:

- **Optimum removal time: As soon as possible** within 24 hours of spill
- **Maximum size for home removal:** Class I / II = 3/4 inch
- **Removal restrictions:** If the spot(s) is larger than 3/4 inch in diameter, **do not attempt TOTAL removal** using Class I or II instructions. Do Step 1 **only** under Class I or II. Put a dry towel over spot. Call a pro and have spot removed as soon as possible within 24 hours.
- Dye in these products can immediately and permanently stain nylon. If you cannot remove a spot, consult a pro for options as soon as possible.

## Materials Needed:
Class I / II: Spotting kit, Spot machine with warm water

### Class I: Spot Machine + Old / Dried Spot

**Steps:**

1. Using your spot machine, rinse the spot(s) with warm water using the single stroke technique 8 - 10 times.
   - Take 6 - 8 slow, dry vacuum strokes.
   - Repeat entire Step until no more removes.

2. Mist on a small amount of ammonia.
   - Tamp with soft brush.

3. Rinse with warm water using the chop stroke technique 8 - 10 times.
   - Take 6 - 8 slow, dry vacuum strokes.

4. Look at spot area carefully to see if the spot is gone:
   - If YES: Allow to dry.
   - If NO: Repeat Steps 2 and 3 until no more removes. Then, if needed, do Step 5.

5. If color cast remains, mist on a generous amount of peroxide.
   - Mist on a small amount of ammonia.
   - Tamp with soft brush.
   - Allow to dry.

6. If needed, repeat Steps 2, 3 and 5 one time.

7. If the spot persists, call a pro for options as soon as possible.

### Class II: Spot Machine + Fresh / Wet Spot

**Steps:**

1. Using your spot machine, rinse the spot(s) with warm water using the single stroke technique 8 - 10 times.
   - Take 6 - 8 slow, dry vacuum strokes.
   - Repeat entire Step until no more removes.

2. Mist on a small amount of ammonia.
   - Tamp with soft brush.

3. Rinse with warm water using the chop stroke technique 8 - 10 times.
   - Take 6 - 8 slow, dry vacuum strokes.

4. Look at spot area carefully to see if the spot is gone:
   - If YES: Allow to dry.
   - If NO: Repeat Steps 2 and 3 until no more removes. Then, if needed, do Step 5.

5. If color cast remains, mist on a generous amount of peroxide.
   - Mist on a small amount of ammonia.
   - Tamp with soft brush.
   - Allow to dry.

6. If needed, repeat Steps 2, 3 and 5 one time.

7. If the spot persists, call a pro for options as soon as possible.

Section II

## Comments:

- **Optimum removal time: As soon as possible** within 24 hours of spill
- **Maximum size for home removal:** Class III / IV = 1/2 inch
- **Removal restrictions:** If the spot(s) is larger than 1/2 inch in diameter **do not attempt TOTAL removal** using Class III or IV instructions. Do Step 1 **only** under Class III or IV. Put a dry towel over spot. Then:
  - Call a pro and have spot removed as soon as possible within 24 hours. -OR-
  - If the spot is 3/4 inch or less in diameter, get a spot machine and:
    - If the spot is now old/dried, do Steps 1 - 7 under Class I.
    - If the spot is still fresh/wet, do Steps 1 - 7 under Class II.
- Dye in these products can immediately and permanently stain nylon. If you cannot remove a spot, consult a pro for options as soon as possible.

## Materials Needed:

Class III: Spotting kit, Vacuum cleaner with beater brush
Class IV: Spotting kit

| Class III: Towel + Old / Dried Spot | Class IV: Towel + Fresh / Wet Spot |
|---|---|
| **Steps:** | **Steps:** |
| 1. Using your soft brush, brush the spot(s) in a side-to-side motion 15 - 18 times.<br>• Vacuum with vacuum cleaner beater brush. | 1. Using a towel, firmly blot the spot(s) 10 - 15 times, using a clean part of the towel each time.<br>• Repeat until no more transfer occurs. |
| 2. Mist on a small amount of ammonia.<br>• Tamp with soft brush. | 2. Mist on a small amount of ammonia.<br>• Tamp with soft brush. |
| 3. With a towel, blot 15 - 20 times, using a clean part of the towel each time. | 3. With a towel, blot 15 - 20 times, using a clean part of the towel each time. |
| 4. Look at spot area carefully to see if the spot is gone:<br>• If YES: Allow to dry.<br>• If NO: Repeat Steps 2 and 3 until no more removes. Then, if needed, do Step 5. | 4. Look at spot area carefully to see if the spot is gone:<br>• If YES: Allow to dry.<br>• If NO: Repeat Steps 2 and 3 until no more removes. Then, if needed, do Step 5. |
| 5. If color cast remains, mist on a generous amount of peroxide.<br>• Mist on a small amount of ammonia.<br>• Tamp with soft brush.<br>• Allow to dry. | 5. If color cast remains, mist on a generous amount of peroxide.<br>• Mist on a small amount of ammonia.<br>• Tamp with soft brush.<br>• Allow to dry. |
| 6. If needed, repeat Steps 2, 3 and 5 one time. | 6. If needed, repeat Steps 2, 3 and 5 one time. |
| 7. If the spot persists, call a pro for options as soon as possible. | 7. If the spot persists, call a pro for options as soon as possible. |

Section II

# Mayonnaise, Miracle Whip®

## Comments:

- **Optimum removal time:** Within 24 hours of spill
- **Maximum size for home removal:** Class I / II = 4 inches
- **Removal restrictions:** If the spot(s) has been pressed into the carpet fibers or is larger than 4 inches in diameter, **do not attempt TOTAL** removal using Class I or II instructions. Do Step 1 **only** under Class I or II. Put a dry towel over spot. Call a pro and have spot removed within 2 days.
- If stepped on, these products may deposit oils that can penetrate acrylic, nylon, olefin and polyester and cause recurring spots if not completely removed. (See "Recurring Spots", Chapter 4.) Consult a pro for options as soon as possible.

## Materials Needed:

Class I / II: Spotting kit, Spot machine with hot water

### Class I: Spot Machine + Old / Dried Spot

#### Steps:

1. Using your spoon, scrape out as much of the spot(s) as possible.
   - Vacuum debris with spot machine.
   - Repeat entire Step until no more removes.

2. Mist on a generous amount of alcohol.
   - Mist on a generous amount of ammonia.
   - Allow to work 2 minutes.
   - Agitate with hard brush.
   - Mist on a small amount of alcohol.
   - Agitate with hard brush.

3. With the spot machine, rinse with hot water using the chop stroke technique 6 - 8 times.
   - Take 4 - 6 slow, dry vacuum strokes.

4. Look at and touch spot area carefully to see if the oily residue is gone:
   - If YES: No further action is needed.
   - If NO: Repeat Steps 2 and 3 until no more removes. Then, if needed, do Step 5.

5. If color cast remains, mist on a generous amount of peroxide.
   - Tamp with soft brush.
   - Allow to dry.

6. If needed, repeat Steps 2, 3 and 5 one time.

7. If the spot persists, call a pro for options as soon as possible.

### Class II: Spot Machine + Fresh / Wet Spot

#### Steps:

1. Lay a small towel over the palm of your hand. Then lay your hand on the carpet so the towel is at the edge of the spot.
   - Using your spoon, scoop as much of the spot(s) as possible into the towel. Note: After each scoop, wipe the spoon on a clean part of the towel.
   - Carefully drop the dirty towel in your empty bucket.
   - With a clean towel, blot 15 - 20 times, using a clean part of the towel each time.
   - Repeat entire Step until no more removes.

2. Mist on a generous amount of alcohol.
   - Mist on a generous amount of ammonia.
   - Allow to work 1 minute.
   - Agitate with hard brush.
   - Mist on a small amount of alcohol.
   - Agitate with hard brush.

3. With the spot machine, rinse with hot water using the chop stroke technique 4 - 6 times.
   - Take 3 - 5 slow, dry vacuum strokes.

4. Look at and touch spot area carefully to see if the oily residue is gone:
   - If YES: No further action is needed.
   - If NO: Repeat Steps 2 and 3 until no more removes. Then, if needed, do Step 5.

5. If color cast remains, mist on a generous amount of peroxide.
   - Tamp with soft brush.
   - Allow to dry.

6. If needed, repeat Steps 2, 3 and 5 one time.

7. If the spot persists, call a pro for options as soon as possible.

Section II

## Comments:

- **Optimum removal time:** Within 24 hours of spill
- **Maximum size for home removal:** Class III / IV = 2 inches
- **Removal restrictions:** If the spot(s) has been pressed into the carpet fibers or is larger than 2 inches in diameter, **do not attempt TOTAL** removal using Class III or IV instructions. Do Step 1 **only** under Class III or IV. Put a dry towel over spot. Then:
  - Call a pro and have spot removed within 2 days. -OR-
  - If the spot has not been pressed into carpet fibers and is 4 inches or less in diameter, get a spot machine and:
    - If the spot is now old/dried, do Steps 2 - 7 under Class I.
    - If the spot is still fresh/wet, do Steps 2 - 7 under Class II.
- If stepped on, these products may deposit oils that can penetrate acrylic, nylon, olefin and polyester and cause recurring spots if not completely removed. (See "Recurring Spots", Chapter 4.) Consult a pro for options as soon as possible.

## Materials Needed:

Class III: Spotting kit, Vacuum cleaner with attachment removed from hose
Class IV: Spotting kit

| Class III: Towel + Old / Dried Spot | Class IV: Towel + Fresh / Wet Spot |
|---|---|

**Class III — Steps:**

1. Using your spoon, scrape out as much of the spot(s) as possible.
   - Vacuum debris with vacuum cleaner hose.
   - Repeat entire Step until no more removes.
2. Mist on a generous amount of alcohol.
   - Mist on a small amount of ammonia.
   - Allow to work 2 minutes.
   - Agitate with hard brush.
   - Mist on a small amount of alcohol.
   - Agitate with hard brush.
3. With a clean towel, blot 20 - 25 times, using a clean part of the towel each time.
4. Look at and touch spot area carefully to see if the oily residue is gone:
   - If YES: No further action is needed.
   - If NO: Repeat Steps 2 and 3 until no more removes. Then, if needed, do Step 5.
5. If color cast remains, mist on a generous amount of peroxide.
   - Tamp with soft brush.
   - Allow to dry.
6. If needed, repeat Steps 2, 3 and 5 one time.
7. If the spot persists, call a pro for options as soon as possible.

**Class IV — Steps:**

1. Lay a small towel over the palm of your hand. Then lay your hand on the carpet so the towel is at the edge of the spot.
   - Using your spoon, scoop as much of the spot(s) as possible into the towel. Note: After each scoop, wipe the spoon on a clean part of the towel.
   - Carefully drop the dirty towel in your empty bucket.
   - With a clean towel, blot 20 - 25 times, using a clean part of the towel each time.
   - Repeat entire Step until no more removes.
2. Mist on a generous amount of alcohol.
   - Mist on a small amount of ammonia.
   - Allow to work 1 minute.
   - Agitate with hard brush.
   - Mist on a small amount of alcohol.
   - Agitate with hard brush.
3. With a clean towel, blot 20 - 25 times, using a clean part of the towel each time.
4. Look at and touch spot area carefully to see if the oily residue is gone:
   - If YES: No further action is needed.
   - If NO: Repeat Steps 2 and 3 until no more removes. Then, if needed, do Step 5.
5. If color cast remains, mist on a generous amount of peroxide.
   - Tamp with soft brush.
   - Allow to dry.
6. If needed, repeat Steps 2, 3 and 5 one time.
7. If the spot persists, call a pro for options as soon as possible.

Section II

# Metal Polish, Car Polishing Compound, Car Wax - Liquid or Paste

## Comments:

- **Optimum removal time: As soon as possible** within 24 hours of spill
- **Maximum size for home removal:** Class I / II = 3 1/2 inches
- **Removal restrictions:** If the spot(s) is larger than 3 1/2 inches in diameter, **do not attempt TOTAL removal** using Class I or II instructions. Do Step 1 **only** under Class I or II. Mist spot(s) with a generous amount of alcohol. Put a folded towel moistened with water over spot. Call a pro and have spot removed as soon as possible within 24 hours.
- Alcohols, detergents or coloring in some of these products can discolor or permanently stain nylon. If you cannot remove a spot, consult a pro for options as soon as possible.

## Materials Needed:

Class I / II: Spotting kit, Spot machine with hot water, Disposable towels for Class II

### Class I: Spot Machine + Old / Dried Spot

**Steps:**

1. Using your spoon, scrape out as much of the spot(s) as possible.
   - Vacuum debris with spot machine.
   - Repeat entire Step until no more removes.

2. Mist on a small amount of ammonia.
   - Mist on a generous amount of alcohol.
   - Agitate with hard brush.
   - Allow to work 2 minutes.
   - Mist on a small amount of alcohol.
   - Agitate with hard brush.

3. With the spot machine, rinse with hot water using the chop stroke technique 8 - 10 times.
   - Take 6 - 8 slow, dry vacuum strokes.

4. Look at spot area carefully to see if the spot is gone:
   - If YES: No further action is needed.
   - If NO: Repeat Steps 2 and 3 until no more removes. Then, if needed, do Step 5.

5. If color cast remains, mist on a small amount of peroxide.
   - Mist on a small amount of ammonia.
   - Tamp with soft brush.
   - Allow to dry.

6. If needed, repeat Steps 2, 3 and 5 one time.

7. If the spot persists, call a pro for options as soon as possible.

### Class II: Spot Machine + Fresh / Wet Spot

**Steps:**

1. Lay a disposable towel over the palm of your hand. Then lay your hand on the carpet so the towel is at the edge of the spot.
   - Using your spoon, scoop as much of the spot(s) as possible into the towel. Note: After each scoop, wipe the spoon on a clean part of the towel.
   - Carefully drop the dirty towel in your empty bucket.
   - With a clean cloth towel, firmly blot 15 - 20 times, using a clean part of the towel each time.
   - Repeat entire Step until no more removes.

2. Mist on a small amount of ammonia.
   - Mist on a generous amount of alcohol.
   - Agitate with hard brush.
   - Allow to work 1 minute.
   - Mist on a small amount of alcohol.
   - Agitate with hard brush.

3. With the spot machine, rinse with hot water using the chop stroke technique 6 - 8 times.
   - Take 4 - 6 slow, dry vacuum strokes.

4. Look at spot area carefully to see if the spot is gone:
   - If YES: No further action is needed.
   - If NO: Repeat Steps 2 and 3 until no more removes. Then, if needed, do Step 5.

5. If color cast remains, mist on a small amount of peroxide.
   - Mist on a small amount of ammonia.
   - Tamp with soft brush.
   - Allow to dry.

6. If needed, repeat Steps 2, 3 and 5 one time.

7. If the spot persists, call a pro for options as soon as possible.

Section II

Spot / Stain Contents: Alcohol, Chalk, Colorants, Detergent, Gelatin, Gum, Oleic Acid, Petroleum Oils, Polymers, Pumice, Silica, Silicone

## Comments:

- **Optimum removal time: As soon as possible** within 24 hours of spill
- **Maximum size for home removal:** Class III / IV = 1 1/2 inches
- **Removal restrictions:** If the spot(s) is larger than 1 1/2 inches in diameter, **do not attempt TOTAL removal** using Class III or IV instructions. Do Step 1 **only** under Class III or IV. Mist spot(s) with a generous amount of alcohol. Put a folded towel moistened with water over spot. Then:
  - Call a pro and have spot removed as soon as possible within 24 hours. -OR-
  - If the spot is 3 1/2 inches or less in diameter, get a spot machine and:
    - If the spot is now old/dried, do Steps 2 - 7 under Class I.
    - If the spot is still fresh/wet, do Steps 2 - 7 under Class II.
- Alcohols, detergents or coloring in some of these products can discolor or permanently stain nylon. If you cannot remove a spot, consult a pro for options as soon as possible.

## Materials Needed:

Class III: Spotting kit, Vacuum cleaner with attachment removed from hose
Class IV: Disposable towels, Spotting kit

### Class III: Towel + Old / Dried Spot

**Steps:**

1. Using your spoon, scrape out as much of the spot(s) as possible.
   - Vacuum debris with vacuum cleaner hose.
   - Repeat entire Step until no more removes.

2. Mist on a small amount of ammonia.
   - Mist on a generous amount of alcohol.
   - Agitate with hard brush.
   - Allow to work 2 minutes.
   - Mist on a small amount of alcohol.
   - Agitate with hard brush.

3. With a towel, blot 15 - 20 times, using a clean part of the towel each time.

4. Look at spot area carefully to see if the spot is gone:
   - If YES: No further action is needed.
   - If NO: Repeat Steps 2 and 3 until no more removes. Then, if needed, do Step 5.

5. If color cast remains, mist on a small amount of peroxide.
   - Mist on a small amount of ammonia.
   - Tamp with soft brush.
   - Allow to dry.

6. If needed, repeat Steps 2, 3 and 5 one time.

7. If the spot persists, call a pro for options as soon as possible.

### Class IV: Towel + Fresh / Wet Spot

**Steps:**

1. Lay a disposable towel over the palm of your hand. Then lay your hand on the carpet so the towel is at the edge of the spot.
   - Using your spoon, scoop as much of the spot(s) as possible into the towel. Note: After each scoop, wipe the spoon on a clean part of the towel.
   - Carefully drop the dirty towel in your empty bucket.
   - With a clean cloth towel, firmly blot 20 - 30 times, using a clean part of the towel each time.
   - Repeat entire Step until no more removes.

2. Mist on a small amount of ammonia.
   - Mist on a generous amount of alcohol.
   - Agitate with hard brush.
   - Allow to work 1 minute.
   - Mist on a small amount of alcohol.
   - Agitate with hard brush.

3. With a towel, firmly blot 15 - 20 times, using a clean part of the towel each time.

4. Look at spot area carefully to see if the spot is gone:
   - If YES: No further action is needed.
   - If NO: Repeat Steps 2 and 3 until no more removes. Then, if needed, do Step 5.

5. If color cast remains, mist on a small amount of peroxide.
   - Mist on a small amount of ammonia.
   - Tamp with soft brush.
   - Allow to dry.

6. If needed, repeat Steps 2, 3 and 5 one time.

7. If the spot persists, call a pro for options as soon as possible.

Section II

# Milk (White, Flavored), Buttermilk, Egg Nog, Rice Milk, Soy Milk, Yogurt Drinks

## Comments:

- **Optimum removal time:** Within 24 hours of spill
- **Maximum size for home removal:** Class I / II = 4 inches
- **Removal restrictions:** If the spot(s) is larger than 4 inches in diameter, **do not attempt TOTAL removal** using Class I or II instructions. Do Step 1 **only** under Class I or II. Mist spot(s) with a small amount of ammonia. Put a folded towel moistened with water over spot. Call a pro and have spot removed within 2 days.
- **Caution:** Food coloring in some flavored milk can immediately and permanently stain some nylon. If you cannot remove a spot, consult a pro for options as soon as possible.
- **Caution:** Large spills can penetrate carpet and create a sticky, smelly residue and recurring spots that can be hard to remove if allowed to fester as little as 24 to 48 hours. (See "Recurring Spots", Chapter 4.) Consult a pro for options as soon as possible.

## Materials Needed:
Class I / II: Spotting kit, Spot machine with warm water

### Class I: Spot Machine + Old / Dried Spot

**Steps:**

1. Using your dinner knife, scrape out as much of the spot(s) as possible. Caution: Be careful to not fray carpet fibers.
   - Vacuum debris with spot machine.
   - Repeat entire Step until no more removes.
2. Mist on a generous amount of ammonia.
   - Agitate with hard brush.
   - Allow to work 2 minutes.
   - Mist on a generous amount of alcohol.
   - Agitate with hard brush.
3. With the spot machine, rinse with warm water using the chop stroke technique 6 - 8 times.
   - Take 4 - 6 slow, dry vacuum strokes.
4. Look at spot area carefully to see if the spot is gone:
   - If YES: No further action is needed.
   - If NO: Repeat Steps 2 and 3 until no more removes. Then, if needed, do Step 5.
5. If color cast remains, mist on a generous amount of peroxide.
   - Mist on a small amount of ammonia.
   - Tamp with soft brush.
   - Allow to dry.
6. Smell spot area carefully to see if the odor is gone:
   - If YES: No further action is needed.
   - If NO: Repeat Steps 2, 3 and 5 one time.
7. If odor persists, call a pro for options as soon as possible.

### Class II: Spot Machine + Fresh / Wet Spot

**Steps:**

1. Using a towel, blot the spot(s) 15 - 25 times, using a clean part of the towel each time.
2. Fold a towel several times and place it over the spot(s).
   - Step on the towel with your full weight 15 - 25 times, using a clean part of the towel each time.
   - Repeat until no more liquid absorbs.
3. With the spot machine, rinse with warm water using the single stroke technique 8 - 10 times.
   - Take 6 - 8 slow, dry vacuum strokes.
4. Mist on a generous amount of ammonia.
   - Agitate with hard brush.
   - Allow to work 1 minute.
   - Mist on a small amount of alcohol.
   - Agitate with hard brush.
5. With the spot machine, rinse with warm water using the single stroke technique 6 - 8 times.
   - Take 4 - 6 slow, dry vacuum strokes.
6. Look at spot area carefully to see if the spot is gone:
   - If YES: No further action is needed.
   - If NO: Repeat Steps 3, 4 and 5 until no more removes. Then, if needed, do Step 7.
7. If color cast remains, mist on a small amount of peroxide.
   - Mist on a small amount of ammonia.
   - Tamp with soft brush.
   - Allow to dry.
8. Smell spot area carefully to see if the odor is gone:
   - If YES: No further action is needed.
   - If NO: Repeat Steps 3 - 5 and 7 one time.
9. If odor persists, call a pro for options as soon as possible.

Section II

# Milk (White, Flavored), Buttermilk, Egg Nog, Rice Milk, Soy Milk, Yogurt Drinks

Spot Contents: Albumin, Butter, Carob, Chocolate, Casein, Coloring, Egg, Fats, Lactic Acid, Spices, Vanilla, Oils

## Comments:

- **Optimum removal time:** Within 24 hours of spill
- **Maximum size for home removal:** Class III = No home removal / Class IV = 2 inches
- **Removal restrictions - Class III:** See "Class III" instructions below.
- **Removal restrictions - Class IV:** If the spot(s) is larger than 2 inches in diameter, **do not attempt TOTAL removal** using "Class IV" instructions. Do Step 1 **only** under Class IV. Mist spot(s) with a small amount of ammonia. Put a folded towel moistened with water over spot. Then:
  - Call a pro and have spot removed within 2 days. -OR-
  - If the spot is 4 inches or less in diameter, get a spot machine and:
    - If the spot is now old/dried, do Steps 2 - 7 under Class I.
    - If the spot is still fresh/wet, do Steps 2 - 9 under Class II.
- Food coloring in some flavored milk can immediately and permanently stain some nylon. If you cannot remove a spot, consult a pro for options as soon as possible.
- **Caution:** Large spills can penetrate carpet and create a sticky, smelly residue and recurring spots that can be hard to remove if allowed to fester as little as 24 to 48 hours. (See "Recurring Spots", Chapter 4.) Consult a pro for options as soon as possible.

## Materials Needed:

Class III / IV: Spotting kit

## Class III: Towel + Old / Dried Spot

### Steps:

1. **Do not attempt ANY removal** of a Class III spot(s).
   - Mist spot(s) with a small amount of ammonia.
   - Put a folded towel moistened with water over spot.
   - Then:
     - Call a pro and have spot removed within 2 days. -OR-
     - If the spot is 4 inches or less in diameter, get a spot machine and do Steps 2 - 7 under Class I.

## Class IV: Towel + Fresh / Wet Spot

### Steps:

1. Using a towel, blot the spot(s) 15 - 25 times, using a clean part of the towel each time.
2. Fold a towel several times and place it over the spot(s).
   - Step on the towel with your full weight 15 - 25 times, using a clean part of the towel each time.
   - Repeat until no more liquid absorbs.
3. Mist on a generous amount of ammonia.
   - Agitate with hard brush.
   - Allow to work 1 minute.
   - Mist on a small amount of alcohol.
   - Agitate with hard brush.
4. With a towel, firmly blot 15 - 20 times, using a clean part of the towel each time.
5. Look at spot area carefully to see if the spot is gone:
   - If YES: No further action is needed.
   - If NO: Repeat Steps 3 and 4 until no more removes. Then, if needed, do Step 6.
6. If color cast remains, mist on a small amount of peroxide.
   - Mist on a small amount of ammonia.
   - Tamp with soft brush.
   - Allow to dry.
7. Smell spot area carefully to see if odor is gone:
   - If YES: No further action is needed.
   - If NO: Repeat Steps 3, 4 and 6 one time.
8. If odor persists, call a pro for options as soon as possible.

Section II

# Mold, Mildew, Fungus

## Comments:

- **Optimum removal time:** Within 24 hours of discovery of spot(s)
- **Maximum size for home removal:** No home removal
- **Removal restrictions:** See "Class I" or "Class II" instructions below.
- Mold, mildew, etc., usually grow in unusual places. They can emerge from beneath carpet and from behind walls. This makes it hard for even the most experienced technician to detect them. However, if you find or suspect that you have one of these, consult a pro for options as soon as possible.

## Materials Needed:

Class I / II: None

### Class I: Spot Machine + Old / Dried Spot

**Steps:**

1. **Do not attempt ANY removal** of a Class I spot(s).

2. Call a pro to remove within 3 days of finding spot.

### Class II: Spot Machine + Fresh / Wet Spot

**Steps:**

1. **Do not attempt ANY removal** of a Class II spot(s).

2. Call a pro to remove within 3 days of finding spot.

## *Comments:*

- **Optimum removal time:** Within 24 hours of discovery of spot(s)
- **Maximum size for home removal:** No home removal
- **Removal restrictions:** See "Class III" or "Class IV" instructions below.
- Mold, mildew, etc., usually grow in unusual places. They can emerge from beneath carpet and from behind walls. This makes it hard for even the most experienced technician to detect them. However, if you find or suspect that you have one of these, consult a pro for options as soon as possible.

## *Materials Needed:*
Class III / IV: None

### *Class III: Towel + Old / Dried Spot*

*Steps:*

1. **Do not attempt ANY removal** of a Class III spot(s).

2. Call a pro to remove within 3 days of finding spot.

### *Class IV: Towel + Fresh / Wet Spot*

*Steps:*

1. **Do not attempt ANY removal** of a Class IV spot(s).

2. Call a pro to remove within 3 days of finding spot.

# Mouthwash, Oral Disinfectants

## Comments:

- **Optimum removal time: As soon as possible** within 24 hours of spill
- **Maximum size for home removal:** Class I / II = 3 inches
- **Removal restrictions:** If the spot(s) is larger than 3 inches in diameter, **do not attempt TOTAL removal** using Class I or II instructions. Do Step 1 **only** under Class I or II. Put a folded towel moistened with water over spot. (Keep towel damp until pro comes.) Call a pro and have spot removed as soon as possible within 24 hours.
- Coloring in some products can immediately and permanently stain some nylon. If you cannot remove a spot, consult a pro for options as soon as possible.

## Materials Needed:
Class I / II: Spotting kit, Spot machine with warm water

### Class I: Spot Machine + Old / Dried Spot

**Steps:**

1. Using your spot machine, rinse the spot(s) with warm water using the chop stroke technique 6 - 8 times.
   - Take 4 - 6 slow, dry vacuum strokes.

2. Mist on a generous amount of ammonia.
   - Mist on a generous amount of peroxide.
   - Tamp with soft brush.
   - Allow to work 2 minutes.

3. With the spot machine, rinse with warm water using the chop stroke technique 8 - 10 times.
   - Take 6 - 8 slow, dry vacuum strokes.

4. Look at spot area carefully to see if the spot is gone:
   - If YES: No further action is needed.
   - If NO: Do Steps 2 and 3 until no more will remove.

5. Mist on a generous amount of peroxide.
   - Mist on a small amount of ammonia.
   - Tamp with soft brush.
   - Allow to dry.

6. If needed, repeat Step 5 one time.

7. If the spot persists, call a pro for options as soon as possible.

### Class II: Spot Machine + Fresh / Wet Spot

**Steps:**

1. Using your spot machine, dry vacuum up as much of the spot(s) as possible.
   - Rinse the spot with warm water using the single stroke technique 6 - 8 times.
   - Take 4 - 6 slow, dry vacuum strokes.

2. Mist on a generous amount of ammonia.
   - Mist on a small amount of peroxide.
   - Tamp with soft brush.
   - Allow to work 1 minute.

3. With the spot machine, rinse with warm water using the single stroke technique 8 - 10 times.
   - Take 6 - 8 slow, dry vacuum strokes.

4. Look at spot area carefully to see if the spot is gone:
   - If YES: No further action is needed.
   - If NO: Do Steps 2 and 3 until no more will remove.

5. Mist on a generous amount of peroxide.
   - Mist on a small amount of ammonia.
   - Tamp with soft brush.
   - Allow to dry.

6. If needed, repeat Step 5 one time.

7. If the spot persists, call a pro for options as soon as possible.

## Comments:

- **Optimum removal time: As soon as possible** within 24 hours of spill
- **Maximum size for home removal:** Class III / IV = 2 inches
- **Removal restrictions:** If the spot(s) is larger than 2 inches in diameter, **do not attempt TOTAL removal** using Class III or IV instructions. Do Step 1 **only** under Class III or IV. Put a folded towel moistened with water over spot. (Keep towel damp until pro comes.) Then:
  - Call a pro and have spot removed as soon as possible within 24 hours. -OR-
  - If the spot is 3 inches or less in diameter, get a spot machine and:
    - If the spot is now old/dried, do Steps 1 - 7 under Class I
    - If the spot is still fresh/wet, do Steps 1 - 7 under Class II.
- Coloring in some products can immediately and permanently stain some nylon. If you cannot remove a spot, consult a pro for options as soon as possible.

## Materials Needed:
Class III: Spotting kit, Vacuum cleaner with attachment removed from hose/
Class IV: Spotting kit

| Class III: Towel + Old / Dried Spot | Class IV: Towel + Fresh / Wet Spot |
|---|---|
| **Steps:** | **Steps:** |
| 1. Using your soft brush, gently brush the spot(s) in a side-to-side motion 10 - 15 times. Caution: Be careful to not fray carpet fibers.<br>• Vacuum debris with vacuum cleaner hose. | 1. Fold a towel several times and place it over the spot(s).<br>• Step on the towel with your full weight, using a clean part of the towel each time.<br>• Repeat until no more liquid absorbs. |
| 2. Mist on a generous amount of ammonia.<br>• Mist on a generous amount of peroxide.<br>• Tamp with soft brush.<br>• Allow to work 2 minutes. | 2. Mist on a generous amount of ammonia.<br>• Mist on a small amount of peroxide.<br>• Tamp with soft brush.<br>• Allow to work 1 minute. |
| 3. With a towel, blot 15 - 20 times, using a clean part of the towel each time. | 3. With a towel, blot 15 - 20 times, using a clean part of the towel each time. |
| 4. Look at spot area carefully to see if the spot is gone:<br>• If YES: No further action·is needed.<br>• If NO: Do Steps 2 and 3 until no more will remove. | 4. Look at spot area carefully to see if the spot is gone:<br>• If YES: No further action is needed.<br>• If NO: Do Steps 2 and 3 until no more will remove. |
| 5. Mist on a generous amount of peroxide.<br>• Mist on a small amount of ammonia.<br>• Tamp with soft brush.<br>• Allow to dry. | 5. Mist on a generous amount of peroxide.<br>• Mist on a small amount of ammonia.<br>• Tamp with soft brush.<br>• Allow to dry. |
| 6. If needed, repeat Step 5 one time. | 6. If needed, repeat Step 5 one time. |
| 7. If the spot persists, call a pro for options as soon as possible. | 7. If the spot persists, call a pro for options as soon as possible. |

Section II

# Mud, Dirt, Soil, Clay, Peat Moss, Mulch

## Comments:

- **Optimum removal time:** Within 24 hours of spill
- **Maximum size for home removal:** Class I / II = 15 inches
- **Removal restrictions:** If the spot(s) is larger than 15 inches in diameter, **do not attempt TOTAL removal** using Class I or II instructions. Do Step 1 **only** under Class I or II. Put a dry towel over spot. Call a pro and have spot removed within 3 days.
- **Caution:** Some muds, especially red clay, or wet peat moss or mulch that contain wood stain, can permanently stain some nylon if allowed to stay ground into the carpet as little as 3 days. If you cannot remove a spot, consult a pro for options as soon as possible.

## Materials Needed:

Class I: Spotting kit, Spot machine with hot water
Class II: Spotting kit, Hair dryer, Spot machine with hot water

### Class I: Spot Machine + Old / Dried Spot

#### Steps:

1. Take your spoon by the handle and tamp the edge of the scoop part down onto the spot(s) 10 - 35 times to break it into tiny particles.
   - Vacuum debris with spot machine.
   - Repeat until no more will remove.
   - With the hard brush, brush the spot in a side-to-side motion 15 - 30 times. Caution: Be careful to not fray carpet fibers.
   - Vacuum debris with spot machine.

2. Mist on a generous amount of ammonia.
   - Agitate with hard brush.
   - Allow to work 1 minute.
   - Mist on a generous amount of ammonia.
   - Agitate with hard brush.

3. With the spot machine, rinse with hot water using the chop stroke technique 8 - 20 times.
   - Take 6 - 15 slow, dry vacuum strokes.

4. Look at spot area carefully to see if the spot is gone:
   - If YES: Allow to dry.
   - If NO: Repeat Steps 2 and 3 until no more removes. Then, if needed, do Step 5.

5. If color cast remains, mist on a generous amount of peroxide.
   - Mist on a small amount of ammonia.
   - Tamp with soft brush.
   - Allow to dry.

6. If the spot persists, call a pro for options as soon as possible.

### Class II: Spot Machine + Fresh / Wet Spot

#### Steps:

1. Allow the spot(s) to dry. Note: You can speed dry it with a hairdryer. Caution: Be careful not to melt the carpet fibers.

2. Take your spoon by the handle and tamp the edge of the scoop part down onto the spot(s) 10 - 35 times to break it into tiny particles.
   - Vacuum debris with spot machine.
   - Repeat until no more will remove.
   - With the hard brush, brush the spot in a side-to-side motion 15 - 30 times. Caution: Be careful to not fray carpet fibers.
   - Vacuum debris with spot machine.

3. Mist on a generous amount of ammonia.
   - Agitate with hard brush.
   - Allow to work 1 minute.
   - Mist on a generous amount of ammonia.
   - Agitate with hard brush.

4. With the spot machine, rinse with hot water using the chop stroke technique 8 - 20 times.
   - Take 6 - 15 slow, dry vacuum strokes.

5. Look at spot area carefully to see if the spot is gone:
   - If YES: Allow to dry.
   - If NO: Repeat Steps 3 and 4 until no more removes. Then, if needed, do Step 6.

6. If color cast remains, mist on a generous amount of peroxide.
   - Mist on a small amount of ammonia.
   - Tamp with soft brush.
   - Allow to dry.

7. If the spot persists, call a pro for options as soon as possible.

Section II

# Mud, Dirt, Soil, Clay, Peat Moss, Mulch

Spot Contents: Clay, Feldspar, Gypsum, Iron Ore, Minerals, Organic Matter, Silica, Soil

## Comments:

- **Optimum removal time:** Within 24 hours of spill
- **Maximum size for home removal:** Class III / IV = 3 1/2 inches
- **Removal restrictions:** If the spot(s) is larger than 3 1/2 inches in diameter, **do not attempt TOTAL removal** using Class III or IV instructions. Do Step 1 **only** under Class III or Steps 1 and 2 **only** under Class IV. Put a dry towel over spot. Then:
  - Call a pro and have spot removed within 3 days. -OR-
  - If the spot is 15 inches or less in diameter, get a spot machine and:
    - If the spot is now old/dried, do Steps 2 - 6 under Class I.
    - If the spot is still fresh/wet, do Steps 3 - 7 under Class II.
- **Caution:** Some muds, especially red clay, or wet peat moss or mulch that contain wood stain, can permanently stain some nylon if allowed to stay ground into the carpet as little as 3 days. If you cannot remove a spot, consult a pro for options as soon as possible.

## Materials Needed:

Class III: Spotting kit, Vacuum cleaner with attachment removed from hose
Class IV: Spotting kit, Hair dryer, Vacuum cleaner with attachment removed from hose

### Class III: Towel + Old / Dried Spot

**Steps:**

1. Take your spoon by the handle and tamp the edge of the scoop part down onto the spot(s) 10 - 35 times to break it into tiny particles.
   - Vacuum debris with vacuum cleaner hose.
   - Repeat until no more will remove.
   - With the hard brush, brush the spot in a side-to-side motion 15 - 30 times. Caution: Be careful to not fray carpet fibers.
   - Vacuum debris with vacuum cleaner hose.
2. Mist on a generous amount of ammonia.
   - Agitate with hard brush.
   - Allow to work 1 minute.
   - Mist on a small amount of ammonia.
   - Agitate with hard brush.
3. With a towel, blot 15 - 40 times, using a clean part of the towel each time.
4. Look at spot area carefully to see if the spot is gone:
   - If YES: Allow to dry.
   - If NO: Repeat Steps 2 and 3 until no more removes. Then, if needed, do Step 5.
5. If color cast remains, mist on a generous amount of peroxide.
   - Mist on a small amount of ammonia.
   - Tamp with soft brush.
   - Allow to dry.
6. If the spot persists, call a pro for options as soon as possible.

### Class IV: Towel + Fresh / Wet Spot

**Steps:**

1. Allow the spot(s) to dry. Note: You can speed dry it with a hairdryer. Caution: Be careful not to melt the carpet fibers.
2. Take your spoon by the handle and tamp the edge of the scoop part down onto the spot(s) 10 - 35 times to break it into tiny particles.
   - Vacuum debris with vacuum cleaner hose.
   - Repeat until no more will remove.
   - With the hard brush, brush the spot in a side-to-side motion 15 - 30 times. Caution: Be careful to not fray carpet fibers.
   - Vacuum debris with vacuum cleaner hose.
3. Mist on a generous amount of ammonia.
   - Agitate with hard brush.
   - Allow to work 1 minute.
   - Mist on a small amount of ammonia.
   - Agitate with hard brush.
4. With a towel, blot 15 - 40 times, using a clean part of the towel each time.
5. Look at spot area carefully to see if the spot is gone:
   - If YES: Allow to dry.
   - If NO: Repeat Steps 3 and 4 until no more removes. Then, if needed, do Step 6.
6. If color cast remains, mist on a generous amount of peroxide.
   - Mist on a small amount of ammonia.
   - Tamp with soft brush.
   - Allow to dry.
7. If the spot persists, call a pro for options as soon as possible.

Section II

## Comments:

- **Optimum removal time: As soon as possible** within 24 hours of spill
- **Maximum size for home removal:** Class I / II = 2 1/2 inches
- **Removal restrictions:** If the spot(s) is larger than 2 1/2 inches in diameter, **do not attempt TOTAL removal** using Class I or II instructions. Do Steps 1 - 4 **only** under Class I or II. Put a folded towel moistened with water over spot and a note next to it that says, ***"Do Not Touch Or Clean!"***. Call a pro and have spot removed **as soon as possible** within 24 hours.
- Turmeric in mustard is very hard to remove and can immediately and permanently stain some nylon. If you cannot remove a spot, consult a pro for options as soon as possible.

## Materials Needed:

Class I: Spotting kit, Spot machine with warm water

Class II: Spotting kit, Disposable tissues, Spot machine with warm water

**Section II**

### Class I: Spot Machine + Old / Dried Spot

#### Steps:

1. Using your spoon, scrape out as much of the spot(s) as possible.
   - Vacuum debris with spot machine.
   - Repeat entire Step until no more removes.
2. Get the container of mustard that was spilled and bring it to room temperature so the oil will separate from the solids.
   - Pour **only** the oil into a cup.
   - Dip the end of your spoon handle into the oil.
   - Agitate the oil into the spot.
   - Allow to work 2 minutes.
   - Repeat 1 more time.
3. Mist on a generous amount of alcohol.
   - Tamp with soft brush.
   - Mist on a generous amount of ammonia.
   - Tamp with soft brush.
   - Allow to work 2 minutes.
4. With the spot machine, rinse with warm water using the chop stroke technique 8 - 10 times.
   - Take 6 - 8 slow, dry vacuum strokes.
5. Look at spot area carefully to see if the spot is gone:
   - If YES: No further action is needed.
   - If NO: Repeat Steps 3 and 4 until no more removes. Then, if needed, do Step 6.
6. If color cast remains, mist on a generous amount of peroxide.
   - Tamp with soft brush.
   - Mist on a small amount of ammonia.
   - Tamp with soft brush.
   - Allow to dry.
7. If stain persists, call a pro for options as soon as possible.

### Class II: Spot Machine + Fresh / Wet Spot

#### Steps:

1. Lay a disposable tissue(s) over the palm of your hand. Then lay your hand on the carpet so the tissue is at the edge of the spot.
   - Using your spoon, scoop as much of the spot(s) as possible into the tissue. Note: After each scoop, wipe the spoon on a clean part of the tissue.
   - Carefully drop the tissue in your empty bucket.
2. With your spot machine, rinse with warm water using the single stroke technique 10 - 15 times.
   - Repeat until no more removes.
3. Mist on a generous amount of alcohol.
   - Tamp with soft brush.
   - Mist on a small amount of ammonia.
   - Tamp with soft brush.
   - Allow to work 1 minute.
4. With the spot machine, rinse with warm water using the single stroke technique 8 - 10 times.
   - Take 6 - 8 slow, dry vacuum strokes.
5. Look at spot area carefully to see if the spot is gone:
   - If YES: No further action is needed.
   - If NO: Repeat Steps 3 and 4 until no more removes. Then, if needed, do Step 6.
6. If color cast remains, mist on a generous amount of peroxide.
   - Tamp with soft brush.
   - Mist on a small amount of ammonia.
   - Tamp with soft brush.
   - Allow to dry.
7. If stain persists, call a pro for options as soon as possible.

## Comments:

- **Optimum removal time: As soon as possible** within 24 hours of spill
- **Maximum size for home removal:** Class III / IV = 1 inch
- **Removal restrictions:** If the spot(s) is larger than 1 inch in diameter, **do not attempt TOTAL removal** using Class III or IV instructions. Do Steps 1 - 4 **only** under Class III or Steps 1 - 3 **only** under Class IV. Put a folded towel moistened with water over spot and a note next to it that says, ***"Do Not Touch Or Clean!"***. Then:
  - Call a pro and have spot removed **as soon as possible** within 24 hours. -OR-
  - If the spot is 2 1/2 inches or less in diameter, get a spot machine and:
    - If the spot is now old/dried, do Steps 3 - 7 under Class I.
    - If the spot is still fresh/wet, do Steps 2 - 7 under Class II.
- Turmeric in mustard is very hard to remove and can immediately and permanently stain some nylon. If you cannot remove a spot, consult a pro for options as soon as possible.

---

## Materials Needed:

Class III: Spotting kit, Vacuum cleaner with attachment removed from hose
Class IV: Spotting kit, Disposable towel(s)

### Class III: Towel + Old / Dried Spot

#### Steps:

1. Using your spoon, scrape out as much of the spot(s) as possible.
   - Vacuum debris with vacuum cleaner hose.
   - Repeat entire Step until no more removes.

2. Get the container of mustard that was spilled and bring it to room temperature so the oil will separate from the solids.
   - Pour **only** the oil into a cup.
   - Dip the end of your spoon handle into the oil.
   - Agitate the oil into the spot.
   - Allow to work 2 minutes.
   - Repeat 1 more time.

3. Mist on a generous amount of alcohol.
   - Tamp with soft brush.
   - Mist on a small amount of ammonia.
   - Tamp with soft brush.
   - Allow to work 2 minutes.

4. With a towel, blot 15 - 20 times, using a clean part of the towel each time.

5. Look at spot area carefully to see if the spot is gone:
   - If YES: No further action is needed.
   - If NO: Repeat Steps 3 and 4 until no more removes. Then, if needed, do Step 6.

6. If color cast remains, mist on a generous amount of peroxide.
   - Tamp with soft brush.
   - Mist on a small amount of ammonia.
   - Tamp with soft brush.
   - Allow to dry.

7. If stain persists, call a pro for options as soon as possible.

### Class IV: Towel + Fresh / Wet Spot

#### Steps:

1. Lay a disposable towel over the palm of your hand. Then lay your hand on the carpet so the towel is at the edge of the spot.
   - Using your spoon, scoop as much of the spot(s) as possible into the towel. Note: After each scoop, wipe the spoon on a clean part of the towel.
   - Carefully drop the towel in your empty bucket.
   - With a clean cloth towel, gently blot spot 10 - 15 times, using a clean part of the towel each time.
   - Repeat entire Step until no more removes.

2. Mist on a generous amount of alcohol.
   - Tamp with soft brush.
   - Mist on a small amount of ammonia.
   - Tamp with soft brush.
   - Allow to work 1 minute.

3. With a towel, blot 15 - 20 times, using a clean part of the towel each time.

4. Look at spot area carefully to see if the spot is gone:
   - If YES: No further action is needed.
   - If NO: Repeat Steps 2 and 3 until no more removes. Then, if needed, do Step 5.

5. If color cast remains, mist on a generous amount of peroxide.
   - Tamp with soft brush.
   - Mist on a small amount of ammonia.
   - Tamp with soft brush.
   - Allow to dry.

6. If needed, repeat Step 5 one time.

7. If spot persists, call a pro for options as soon as possible.

Section II

# Nail Polish, Nail Fortifiers, Top Coats, Treatments

## Comments:

- **Optimum removal time:** Within 48 hours of spill (Let spot dry 24 hours before removing.)
- **Maximum size for home removal:** Class I / II = 3/8 inch (pencil eraser size)
- **Removal restrictions:** See "Class I" or "Class II" instructions below.
- **Caution: Do not attempt scissors removal** of spots from **any** type of looped carpet (berber, commercial glue down, etc.) unless the spot is **only on the outside fibers** of the loop(s). If in doubt, call a pro for options as soon as possible.
- Lacquer and pigments in these products are very hard to remove, but they are very thick and will usually dry on top of the carpet fibers. Except on some looped carpets, most of these spills can be easily trimmed away with a pair of scissors after they have hardened.

## Materials Needed:

Class II: Paper and pencil for note
Class I / II - 3/8 inch or smaller: Spotting kit, Spot machine
Class I / II - larger than 3/8 inch: Paper and pencil for note

## Class I: Spot Machine + Old / Dried Spot

### Steps:

**Follow the instructions for your size spot(s):**

**If the spot is 3/8 inch (pencil eraser size) or smaller:**
1. Using your scissors, wedge the blades up under the spot(s) and snip the hardened parts from the very tip of the carpet fibers. (This will minimize the indentations caused by the removed spots.) Note: On non-looped carpets, you can also trim a few carpet fibers around the edge of the removed spot, if needed, to minimize it further.
   - On non-looped carpets, rough up the trimmed carpet fibers a little with the tips of your scissors. Trim any taller roughed up fibers so they are equal in height with the rest of the carpet.
   - Vacuum debris with spot machine.

**If the spot is larger than 3/8 inch (pencil eraser size):**
1. **Do nothing but protect the spill area! Do not attempt ANY removal!**
   - Put a note next to the spot that says,
     ***"Do Not Touch Or Clean!"***.
     **Caution:** Do **not** put a towel over this spot.

2. Call a pro as soon as possible and schedule spot removal between 24 - 72 hours after the spill.

## Class II: Spot Machine + Fresh / Wet Spot

### Steps:

1. **Do not attempt IMMEDIATE removal** of a Class II spot(s).
   - Put a note next to spot that says, ***"Do Not Touch Or Clean!"***. **Caution:** Do **not** put a towel over this spot.
   - Tell everyone to avoid the area to prevent spreading the spot.
   - Keep all pets out of the area to avoid spreading the spot.
   
   **Caution:** Allow the spot to dry 24 hours before attempting any home or pro removal.

2. Complete the Step 3 instructions below for your spot size.

**If the spot is 3/8 inch (pencil eraser size) or smaller:**
3. Do Step 1 for this size spot under Class I to the left of this page.

**If the spot is larger than 3/8 inch (pencil eraser size):**
3. Call a pro as soon as possible and schedule spot removal between 24 - 72 hours after the spill.

Section II

## Comments:

- **Optimum removal time:** Within 48 hours of spill (Let spot dry 24 hours before removing.)
- **Maximum size for home removal:** Class III / IV = 3/8 inch (pencil eraser size)
- **Removal restrictions:** See "Class III" or "Class IV" instructions below.
- **Caution: Do not attempt scissors removal** of spots from **any** type of looped carpet (berber, commercial glue down, etc.) unless the spot is **only on the outside fibers** of the loop(s). If in doubt, call a pro for options as soon as possible.
- Lacquer and pigments in these products are very hard to remove, but they are very thick and will usually dry on top of the carpet fibers. Except on some looped carpets, most of these spills can be easily trimmed away with a pair of scissors after they have hardened.

## Materials Needed:

Class IV: Paper and pencil for note
Class III / IV - 3/8 inch or smaller: Spotting kit, Vacuum cleaner with attachment removed from hose
Class III / IV - larger than 3/8 inch: Paper and pencil for note

### Class III: Towel + Old / Dried Spot

**Steps:**

**Follow the instructions for your size spot(s):**

**If the spot is 3/8 inch (pencil eraser size) or smaller:**
1. Using your scissors, wedge the blades up under the spot(s) and snip the hardened parts from the very tip of the carpet fibers. (This will minimize the indentations caused by the removed spots.) Note: On non-looped carpets, you can also trim a few carpet fibers around the edge of the removed spot, if needed, to minimize it further.

   - On non-looped carpets, rough up the trimmed carpet fibers a little with the tips of your scissors. Trim any taller roughed up fibers so they are equal in height with the rest of the carpet.
   - Vacuum debris with vacuum cleaner hose.

**If the spot is larger than 3/8 inch (pencil eraser size):**
1. **Do nothing but protect the spill area! Do not attempt ANY removal!**

   - Put a note next to the spot that says,
   **"Do Not Touch Or Clean!"**.
   **Caution:** Do **not** put a towel over this spot.

2. Call a pro as soon as possible and schedule spot removal between 24 - 72 hours after the spill.

### Class IV: Towel + Fresh / Wet Spot

**Steps:**

1. **Do not attempt IMMEDIATE removal** of a Class II spot(s).

   - Put a note next to the spot that says,
   **"Do Not Touch Or Clean!"**.
   **Caution:** Do **not** put a towel over this spot.
   - Tell everyone to avoid the area to prevent spreading the spot.
   - Keep all pets out of the area to avoid spreading the spot.

   **Caution:** Allow the spot to dry 24 hours before attempting any home or pro removal.

2. Complete the Step 3 instructions below for your spot size.

**If the spot is 3/8 inch (pencil eraser size) or smaller:**
3. Do Step 1 for this size spot under Class III.

**If the spot is larger than 3/8 inch (pencil eraser size):**
3. Call a pro as soon as possible and schedule spot removal between 24 - 72 hours after the spill.

Section II

# Oils / Thin Lubricants - New or Used:

## All Thin Auto Fluids (Brake, Power Steering, Transmission, Motor Oil), Sewing Machine, Lathe Oils

### Comments:

- **Optimum removal time:** Within 24 hours of spill
- **Maximum size for home removal:** Class I / II = 2 1/2 inches
- **Removal restrictions:** If the spot(s) is larger than 2 1/2 inches in diameter, **do not attempt TOTAL removal** using Class I or II instructions. Do Step 1 **only** under Class I or II. Put a dry towel over spot. Call a pro and have spot removed within 2 days.
- These products can permanently stain polyester and olefin due to their oil loving natures. If you are unable to remove a spot, consult a pro as soon as possible for options.
- Large spills can soak through carpet and pad to the subfloor and damage the latex carpet backing or pad and/or cause recurring spots. (See "Recurring Spots", Chapter 4.) Consult a pro for options as soon as possible.

### Materials Needed:
Class I / II: Spotting kit, Spot machine with hot water

## Class I: Spot Machine + Old / Dried Spot

### Steps:

1. Fold a towel several times and place it over the spot(s).
   - Step on the towel with your full weight 10 - 15 times, using a clean part of the towel each time.
   - Repeat until no more absorbs.
2. Mist on a generous amount of alcohol.
   - Allow to work 1 minute.
   - Mist on a small amount of alcohol.
   - Agitate with hard brush.
   - Allow to work 1 minute.
   - Mist on a generous amount of ammonia.
   - Agitate with hard brush.
3. With the spot machine, rinse with hot water using the chop stroke technique 8 - 10 times.
   - Take 6 - 8 slow, dry vacuum strokes.
4. Look at and touch spot area carefully to see if the oily residue is gone:
   - If YES: No further action is needed.
   - If NO: Repeat Steps 2 and 3 until no more removes. Then, if needed, do Step 5.
5. If color cast remains, allow to dry.
   - If needed, repeat Steps 2 and 3 one time.
6. If the spot persists, call a pro for options as soon as possible.

## Class II: Spot Machine + Fresh / Wet Spot

### Steps:

1. Fold a towel several times and place it over the spot(s).
   - Step on the towel with your full weight 10 - 15 times, using a clean part of the towel each time.
   - Repeat until no more absorbs.
2. Mist on a generous amount of alcohol.
   - Allow to work 1 minute.
   - Mist on a small amount of alcohol.
   - Agitate with hard brush.
   - Mist on a generous amount of ammonia.
   - Agitate with hard brush.
3. With the spot machine, rinse with hot water using the chop stroke technique 6 - 8 times.
   - Take 4 - 6 slow, dry vacuum strokes.
4. Look at and touch spot area carefully to see if the oily residue is gone:
   - If YES: No further action is needed.
   - If NO: Repeat Steps 2 and 3 until no more removes. Then, if needed, do Step 5.
5. If color cast remains, allow to dry.
   - If needed, repeat Steps 2 and 3 one time.
6. If the spot persists, call a pro for options as soon as possible.

Section II

## Comments:

- **Optimum removal time:** Within 24 hours of spill
- **Maximum size for home removal:** Class III / IV = 1 1/4 inches
- **Removal restrictions:** If the spot(s) is larger than 1 1/4 inches in diameter, **do not attempt TOTAL removal** using Class III or IV instructions. Do Step 1 **only** under Class III or IV. Put a dry towel over spot. Then:
  - Call a pro and have spot removed within 2 days. -OR-
  - If the spot is 2 1/2 inches or less in diameter, get a spot machine and:
    - If the spot is now old/dried, do Steps 2 - 6 under Class I.
    - If the spot is still fresh/wet, do Steps 2 - 6 under Class II.
- These products can permanently stain polyester and olefin due to their oil loving natures. If you are unable to remove a spot, consult a pro as soon as possible for options.
- Large spills can soak through carpet and pad to the subfloor and damage the latex carpet backing or pad and/or cause recurring spots. (See "Recurring Spots", Chapter 4.) Consult a pro for options as soon as possible.

---

## Materials Needed:
Class III / IV: Spotting kit

### Class III: Towel + Old / Dried Spot

**Steps:**

1. Fold a towel several times and place it over the spot(s).
   - Step on the towel with your full weight 10 - 15 times, using a clean part of the towel each time.
   - Repeat until no more absorbs.
2. Mist on a small amount of alcohol.
   - Allow to work 1 minute.
   - Mist on a small amount of alcohol.
   - Agitate with hard brush.
   - Allow to work 1 minute.
   - Mist on a small amount of ammonia.
   - Agitate with hard brush.
3. With a towel, blot the spot 15 - 20 times, using a clean part of the towel each time.
4. Look at and touch spot area carefully to see if the oily residue is gone:
   - If YES: No further action is needed.
   - If NO: Repeat Steps 2 and 3 until no more removes. Then, if needed, do Step 5.
5. If color cast remains, allow to dry.
   - If needed, repeat Steps 2 and 3 one time.
6. If the spot persists, call a pro for options as soon as possible.

### Class IV: Towel + Fresh / Wet Spot

**Steps:**

1. Fold a towel several times and place it over the spot(s).
   - Step on the towel with your full weight 10 - 15 times, using a clean part of the towel each time.
   - Repeat until no more absorbs.
2. Mist on a small amount of alcohol.
   - Allow to work 1 minute.
   - Mist on a small amount of alcohol.
   - Agitate with hard brush.
   - Mist on a small amount of ammonia.
   - Agitate with hard brush.
3. With a towel, blot the spot 15 - 20 times, using a clean part of the towel each time.
4. Look at and touch spot area carefully to see if the oily residue is gone:
   - If YES: No further action is needed.
   - If NO: Repeat Steps 2 and 3 until no more removes. Then, if needed, do Step 5.
5. If color cast remains, allow to dry.
   - If needed, repeat Steps 2 and 3 one time
6. If the spot persists, call a pro for options as soon as possible.

Section II

# Ointment:

## First Aid Ointment, Lip Balm, Petroleum Jelly, Sore Muscle Ointment, Zinc Oxide

### Comments:

- **Optimum removal time: As soon as possible** within 24 hours of spill
- **Maximum size for home removal:** Class I / II = 3 1/2 inches
- **Removal restrictions:** If the spot(s) is larger than 3 1/2 inches in diameter, **do not attempt TOTAL removal** using Class I or II instructions. Do Step 1 **only** under Class I or II. Put a dry towel over spot. Call a pro and have spot removed within 24 hours.
- **Caution:** Coloring in some of these products can permanently stain some nylon if left untreated for as little as 2 days. If you are unable to remove a spot, consult a pro for options as soon as possible.
- Acne medicines can also cause discolorations on all types of carpet. (See "Benzoil Peroxide" in "Mystery Spots, Stains and Discolorations", Chapter 4.)
- Ointments can also leave a sticky residue that can cause recurring spots on all types of fibers if not completely removed. (See "Recurring Spots", Chapter 4.) Consult a pro for options as soon as possible.

### Materials Needed:

Class I / II: Disposable towels, Spotting kit, Spot machine with hot water

| Class I: Spot Machine + Old / Dried Spot | Class II: Spot Machine + Fresh / Wet Spot |
|---|---|
| **Steps:** | **Steps:** |
| 1. Lay a disposable towel over the palm of your hand. Then lay your hand on the carpet so the towel is at the edge of the spot.<br>• Using your spoon, scoop as much of the spot(s) as possible into the towel. Note: After each scoop, wipe the spoon on a clean part of the towel.<br>• Carefully drop the dirty towel in your empty bucket.<br>• With a clean cloth towel, blot 15 - 20 times, using a clean part of the towel each time.<br>• Repeat entire Step until no more removes. | 1. Lay a disposable towel over the palm of your hand. Then lay your hand on the carpet so the towel is at the edge of the spot.<br>• Using your spoon, scoop as much of the spot(s) as possible into the towel. Note: After each scoop, wipe the spoon on a clean part of the towel.<br>• Carefully drop the dirty towel in your empty bucket.<br>• With a clean cloth towel, blot 15 - 20 times, using a clean part of the towel each time.<br>• Repeat entire Step until no more removes. |
| 2. Mist on a generous amount of alcohol.<br>• Agitate with hard brush.<br>• Allow to work 1 minute.<br>• Mist on a generous amount of alcohol.<br>• Agitate with hard brush. | 2. Mist on a generous amount of alcohol.<br>• Agitate with hard brush.<br>• Allow to work 1 minute.<br>• Mist on a generous amount of alcohol.<br>• Agitate with hard brush. |
| 3. With the spot machine, rinse with hot water using the chop stroke technique 8 - 10 times.<br>• Take 6 - 8 slow, dry vacuum strokes. | 3. With the spot machine, rinse with hot water using the chop stroke technique 8 - 10 times.<br>• Take 6 - 8 slow, dry vacuum strokes. |
| 4. Look at and touch spot area carefully to see if the oily/waxy residue is gone:<br>• If YES: No further action is needed.<br>• If NO: Repeat Steps 2 and 3 until no more removes. Then, if needed, do Step 5. | 4. Look at and touch spot area carefully to see if the oily/waxy residue is gone:<br>• If YES: No further action is needed.<br>• If NO: Repeat Steps 2 and 3 until no more removes. Then, if needed, do Step 5. |
| 5. If color cast remains, mist on a generous amount of peroxide.<br>• Tamp with soft brush.<br>• Mist on a small amount of ammonia.<br>• Tamp with soft brush.<br>• Allow to dry. | 5. If color cast remains, mist on a generous amount of peroxide.<br>• Tamp with soft brush.<br>• Mist on a small amount of ammonia.<br>• Tamp with soft brush.<br>• Allow to dry. |
| 6. If needed, repeat Steps 2, 3 and 5 one time. | 6. If needed, repeat Steps 2, 3 and 5 one time. |
| 7. If the spot persists, call a pro for options as soon as possible. | 7. If the spot persists, call a pro for options as soon as possible. |

Section II

Spot Contents: Aloe Vera, Coloring, Medication Oil or Wax Based, Zinc Oxide

## Comments:

- **Optimum removal time: As soon as possible** within 24 hours of spill
- **Maximum size for home removal:** Class III / IV = 1 3/4 inches
- **Removal restrictions:** If the spot(s) is larger than 1 3/4 inches in diameter, **do not attempt TOTAL removal** using Class III or IV instructions. Do Step 1 **only** under Class III or IV. Put a dry towel over spot. Then:
  - Call a pro and have spot removed within 24 hours. -OR-
  - If the spot is 3 1/2 inches or less in diameter, get a spot machine and:
    - If the spot is now old/dried, do Steps 2 - 7 under Class I.
    - If the spot is still fresh/wet, do Steps 2 - 7 under Class II.
- **Caution:** Coloring in some of these products can permanently stain some nylon if left untreated for as little as 2 days. If you are unable to remove a spot, consult a pro for options as soon as possible.
- Acne medicines can also cause discolorations on all types of carpet. (See "Benzoil Peroxide" in "Mystery Spots, Stains and Discolorations", Chapter 4.)
- Ointments can also leave a sticky residue that can cause recurring spots on all types of fibers if not completely removed. (See "Recurring Spots", Chapter 4.) Consult a pro for options as soon as possible.

---

## Materials Needed:

Class III / IV: Disposable towels, Spotting kit

| Class III: Towel + Old / Dried Spot | Class IV: Towel + Fresh / Wet Spot |
|---|---|
| **Steps:** | **Steps:** |
| 1. Lay a disposable towel over the palm of your hand. Then lay your hand on the carpet so the towel is at the edge of the spot. | 1. Lay a disposable towel over the palm of your hand. Then lay your hand on the carpet so the towel is at the edge of the spot. |
| • Using your spoon, scoop as much of the spot(s) as possible into the towel. Note: After each scoop, wipe the spoon on a clean part of the towel. | • Using your spoon, scoop as much of the spot(s) as possible into the towel. Note: After each scoop, wipe the spoon on a clean part of the towel. |
| • Carefully drop the dirty towel in your empty bucket. | • Carefully drop the dirty towel in your empty bucket. |
| • With a clean cloth towel, blot the spot 15 - 20 times, using a clean part of the towel each time. | • With a clean cloth towel, blot the spot 15 - 20 times, using a clean part of the towel each time. |
| • Repeat entire Step until no more removes. | • Repeat entire Step until no more removes. |
| 2. Mist on a generous amount of alcohol. | 2 Mist on a generous amount of alcohol. |
| • Agitate with hard brush. | • Agitate with hard brush. |
| • Allow to work 1 minute. | • Allow to work 1 minute. |
| • Mist on a generous amount of alcohol. | • Mist on a generous amount of alcohol. |
| • Agitate with hard brush. | • Agitate with hard brush. |
| 3. With a towel, blot the spot 15 - 20 times, using a clean part of the towel each time. | 3. With a towel, blot the spot 15 - 20 times, using a clean part of the towel each time. |
| 4. Look at and touch spot area carefully to see if the oily/waxy residue is gone: | 4. Look at and touch spot area carefully to see if the oily/waxy residue is gone: |
| • If YES: No further action is needed. | • If YES: No further action is needed. |
| • If NO: Repeat Steps 2 and 3 until no more removes. Then, if needed, do Step 5. | • If NO: Repeat Steps 2 and 3 until no more removes. Then, if needed, do Step 5. |
| 5. If color cast remains, mist on a generous amount of peroxide. | 5. If color cast remains, mist on a generous amount of peroxide. |
| • Tamp with soft brush. | • Tamp with soft brush. |
| • Mist on a small amount of ammonia. | • Mist on a small amount of ammonia. |
| • Tamp with soft brush. | • Tamp with soft brush. |
| • Allow to dry. | • Allow to dry. |
| 6. If needed, repeat Steps 2, 3 and 5 one time. | 6 If needed, repeat Steps 2, 3 and 5 one time. |
| 7. If the spot persists, call a pro for options as soon as possible. | 7. If the spot persists, call a pro for options as soon as possible. |

Section II

# Paint - Oil-Based, Solvent-Based: Acrylic, Aluminum, Enamel, Latex

## Comments:

- **Optimum removal time: As soon as possible** within 24 hours of spill
- **Maximum size for home removal:** No total home removal.
- **Removal restrictions:** See "Class I" or "Class II" instructions below.
- **Caution: Do not attempt scissors removal** of spots from **any** type of looped carpet (berber, commercial glue down, etc.) unless the spot is **only on the outside fibers** of the loop(s). If in doubt, call a pro for options as soon as possible.
- Resins and pigments in these products are very hard to remove. If you cannot remove a spot, consult a pro for options as soon as possible.

## Materials Needed:

Class I - 3/8 inch or smaller: Spotting kit, Spot machine
Class II - 3/8 inch or smaller: Spotting kit, Paper and pencil for note, Spot machine
Class II - larger than 3/8 inch: Spotting kit, Disposable towel(s), Spot machine with hot water, Paper and pencil for note

## Class I: Spot Machine + Old / Dried Spot

### Steps:

**Follow the instructions for your size spot(s):**

**If the spot is 3/8 inch (pencil eraser size) or smaller:**

1. Using your scissors, wedge the blades up under the spot(s) and snip the hardened parts from the very tip of the carpet fibers. (This will minimize the indentations caused by the removed spots.) Note: On non-looped carpets, you can also trim a few carpet fibers around the edge of the removed spot, if needed, to minimize it further.
   - On non-looped carpets, rough up the trimmed carpet fibers a little with the tips of your scissors. Trim any taller roughed up fibers so they are equal in height with the rest of the carpet.
   - Vacuum debris with spot machine.

**If the spot is larger than 3/8 inch (pencil eraser size):**

1. **Do not attempt ANY removal** of a Class I spot (or spots.)
2. Call a pro and have spot removed within 24 hours.

## Class II: Spot Machine + Fresh / Wet Spot

### Steps:

**Follow the instructions for your size spot(s):**

**If the spot is 3/8 inch (pencil eraser size) or smaller:**

1. **Do not attempt IMMEDIATE removal.** Let the spot(s) dry until the center is hard.
   - Put a note that says, **"Do Not Touch Or Clean!"** next to spot. Caution: Do **not** put a towel over this spot. Tell everyone to avoid the area to prevent spreading the spot. Keep all pets out of the area to avoid spreading the spot.

2. Using your scissors, wedge the blades up under the spot(s) and snip the hardened parts from the very tip of the carpet fibers. (This will minimize the indentations caused by the removed spots.) Note: On non-looped carpets, you can also trim a few carpet fibers around the edge of the removed spot, if needed, to minimize it further.
   - On non-looped carpets, rough up the trimmed carpet fibers a little with the tips of your scissors. Trim any taller roughed up fibers so they are equal in height with the rest of the carpet.
   - Vacuum debris with spot machine.

**If the spot is larger than 3/8 inch (pencil eraser size):**

1. Hold a disposable towel at the edge of the spot.
   - Using your spoon, scrape the spot onto the towel. Note: After each scrape wipe the spoon on a clean part of the towel.
   - Carefully drop the dirty towel in your empty bucket.
   - Repeat until no more spot(s) removes.

2. With a clean towel, blot 30 - 40 times, using a clean part of the towel each time.

3. With the spot machine, rinse with hot water using the single stroke technique 8 - 10 times.
   - Take 4 - 6 slow, dry vacuum strokes.

4. **Do not continue removal** of a Class II spot.
   - Mist the spot(s) with a generous amount of alcohol.
   - Put a folded towel moistened with water over spot and a note next to it that says, **"Do Not Touch Or Clean!"**. (Keep towel damp until pro comes.)
   - Call a pro and have spot removed within 24 hours.

### Comments:

- **Optimum removal time: As soon as possible** within 24 hours of spill
- **Maximum size for home removal:** No total home removal.
- **Removal restrictions:** See "Class III" or "Class IV" instructions below.
- **Caution: Do not attempt scissors removal** of spots from **any** type of looped carpet (berber, commercial glue down, etc.) unless the spot is **only on the outside fibers** of the loop(s). If in doubt, call a pro for options as soon as possible.
- Resins and pigments in these products are very hard to remove. If you cannot remove a spot, consult a pro for options as soon as possible.

### Materials Needed:

Class III - 3/8 inch or smaller: Spotting kit, Vacuum cleaner with attachment removed from hose

Class IV - 3/8 inch or smaller: Spotting kit, Paper and pencil for note, Vacuum cleaner with attachment removed from hose

Class IV - larger than 3/8 inch: Spotting kit, Disposable towel, Paper and pencil for note

## Class III: Towel + Old / Dried Spot

### Steps:

**Follow the instructions for your size spot(s):**

**If the spot is 3/8 inch (pencil eraser size) or smaller:**

1. Using your scissors, wedge the blades up under the spot(s) and snip the hardened parts from the very tip of the carpet fibers. (This will minimize the indentations caused by the removed spots.) Note: On non-looped carpets, you can also trim a few carpet fibers around the edge of the removed spot, if needed, to minimize it further.

   - On non-looped carpets, rough up the trimmed carpet fibers a little with the tips of your scissors. Trim any taller roughed up fibers so they are equal in height with the rest of the carpet.
   - Vacuum debris with vacuum cleaner hose.

**If the spot is larger than 3/8 inch (pencil eraser size):**

1. **Do not attempt ANY removal** of a Class III spot (or spots.)

2. Call a pro and have spot removed within 24 hours.

## Class IV: Towel + Fresh / Wet Spot

### Steps:

**Follow the instructions for your size spot(s):**

**If the spot is 3/8 inch (pencil eraser size) or smaller:**

1. **Do not attempt IMMEDIATE removal.** Let the spot(s) dry until the center is hard.

   - Put a note that says, **"Do Not Touch Or Clean!"** next to spot. Caution: Do **not** put a towel over this spot. Tell everyone to avoid the area to prevent spreading the spot. Keep all pets out of the area to avoid spreading the spot.

2. Using your scissors, wedge the blades up under the spot(s) and snip the hardened parts from the very tip of the carpet fibers. (This will minimize the indentations caused by the removed spots.) Note: On non-looped carpets, you can also trim a few carpet fibers around the edge of the removed spot, if needed, to minimize it further.

   - On non-looped carpets, rough up the trimmed carpet fibers a little with the tips of your scissors. Trim any taller roughed up fibers so they are equal in height with the rest of the carpet.
   - Vacuum debris with vacuum cleaner hose.

**If the spot is larger than 3/8 inch (pencil eraser size):**

1. Hold a disposable towel at the edge of the spot.

   - Using your spoon, scrape the spot onto the towel. Note: After each scrape wipe the spoon on a clean part of the towel.
   - Carefully drop the dirty towel in your empty bucket.
   - Repeat until no more spot(s) removes.

2. With a clean towel, blot 30 - 40 times, using a clean part of the towel each time.

3. **Do not continue removal** of a Class IV spot.

   - Mist the spot(s) with a generous amount of alcohol.
   - Put a folded towel moistened with water over spot and a note next to it that says, **"Do Not Touch Or Clean!"**. (Keep towel damp until pro comes.)
   - Call a pro and have spot removed within 24 hours.

Section II

# Paint - Water-Based

## Comments:

- **Optimum removal time: As soon as possible** within 24 hours of spill
- **Maximum size for home removal:** Class I = No total home removal / Class II = 1 1/2 inches
- **Removal restrictions - Class I:** See "Class I" instructions below.
- **Removal restrictions - Class II:** If the spot(s) is larger than 1 1/2 inches in diameter, **do not attempt TOTAL removal** using Class II instructions. Do Steps 1 and 2 **only** under Class II. Mist spot(s) with a generous amount of ammonia. Put a folded towel moistened with water over spot and a note next to it that says, "***Do Not Touch Or Clean***!". (Keep towel damp until pro comes.) Call a pro and have spot removed within 24 hours.
- **Caution: Do not attempt scissors removal** of spots from **any** type of looped carpet (berber, commercial glue down, etc.) unless the spot is **only on the outside fibers** of the loop(s). If in doubt, call a pro for options as soon as possible.
- Pigments and dyes in water-based paints can immediately and permanently stain some nylon. If you cannot remove a spot, consult a pro for options as soon as possible.

## Materials Needed:

Class I: Spotting kit, Spot machine
Class II: Spotting kit, Disposable towel(s), Spot machine with hot water

## Class I: Spot Machine + Old / Dried Spot

### Steps:

**Follow the instructions for your size spot(s):**

**If the spot is 3/8 inch (pencil eraser size) or smaller:**

1. Using your scissors, wedge the blades up under the spot(s) and snip the hardened parts from the very tip of the carpet fibers. (This will minimize the indentations caused by the removed spots.) Note: On non-looped carpets, you can also trim a few carpet fibers around the edge of the removed spot, if needed, to minimize it further.
   - On non-looped carpets, rough up the trimmed carpet fibers a little with the tips of your scissors. Trim any taller roughed up fibers so they are equal in height with the rest of the carpet.
   - Vacuum debris with spot machine.

**If the spot is larger than 3/8 inch (pencil eraser size):**

1. **Do not attempt ANY removal** of a Class I spot(s).
2. Call a pro and have spot removed within 24 hours.

## Class II: Spot Machine + Fresh / Wet Spot

### Steps:

1. Lay a disposable towel(s) over the palm of your hand. Then lay your hand on the carpet so the towel is at the edge of the spot.
   - Using your spoon, scoop as much of the spot(s) as possible into the towel. Note: After each scoop, wipe the spoon on a clean part of the towel.
   - Carefully drop the dirty towel in your empty bucket.

2. With the spot machine, rinse with hot water using the chop stroke technique 10 - 12 times.
   - Take 8 - 10 slow, dry vacuum strokes.

3. Mist with a generous amount of ammonia.
   - Agitate with hard brush.
   - Allow to work 1 minute.
   - Mist on a generous amount of alcohol.
   - Agitate with hard brush.
   - Mist on a generous amount of ammonia.
   - Agitate with hard brush.

4. With the spot machine, rinse with hot water using the chop stroke technique 10 - 12 times.
   - Take 8 - 10 slow, dry vacuum strokes.

5. Look at spot area carefully to see if the spot is gone:
   - If YES: No further action is needed.
   - If NO: Repeat Steps 3 and 4 until no more removes.

6. If the spot persists, call a pro for options as soon as possible.

**Section II**

## Comments:

- **Optimum removal time: As soon as possible** within 24 hours of spill
- **Maximum size for home removal:** No total home removal.
- **Removal restrictions:** See "Class III" or "Class IV" instructions below.
- **Caution: Do not attempt scissors removal** of spots from **any** type of looped carpet (berber, commercial glue down, etc.) unless the spot is **only on the outside fibers** of the loop(s). If in doubt, call a pro for options as soon as possible.
- Pigments and dyes in water-based paints can immediately and permanently stain some nylon. If you cannot remove a spot, consult a pro for options as soon as possible.

## Materials Needed:

Class III - 3/8 inch or smaller: Spotting kit, Vacuum cleaner with attachment removed from hose
Class IV - 3/8 inch or smaller: Spotting kit, Paper and pencil for note, Vacuum cleaner with attachment removed from hose
Class IV - larger than 3/8 inch: Spotting kit, Disposable towel, Paper and pencil for note

### Class III: Towel + Old / Dried Spot

**Steps:**

**Follow the instructions for your size spot(s):**

**If the spot is 3/8 inch (pencil eraser size) or smaller:**

1. Using your scissors, wedge the blades up under the spot(s) and snip the hardened parts from the very tip of the carpet fibers. (This will minimize the indentations caused by the removed spots.) Note: On non-looped carpets, you can also trim a few carpet fibers around the edge of the removed spot, if needed, to minimize it further.
   - On non-looped carpets, rough up the trimmed carpet fibers a little with the tips of your scissors. Trim any taller roughed up fibers so they are equal in height with the rest of the carpet.
   - Vacuum debris with vacuum cleaner hose.

**If the spot is larger than 3/8 inch (pencil eraser size):**

1. **Do not attempt ANY removal** of a Class III spot (or spots.)

2. Call a pro and have spot removed as soon as possible within 24 hours.

### Class IV: Towel + Fresh / Wet Spot

**Steps:**

**Follow the instructions for your size spot(s):**

**If the spot is 3/8 inch (pencil eraser size) or smaller:**

1. **Do not attempt IMMEDIATE removal.** Let the spot(s) dry until the center is hard.
   - Put a note that says, "***Do Not Touch Or Clean!***" next to the spot. Caution: Do **not** put a towel over this spot. Tell everyone to avoid the area to prevent spreading the spot. Keep all pets out of the area to avoid spreading the spot.

2. Using your scissors, wedge the blades up under the spot(s) and snip the hardened parts from the very tip of the carpet fibers. (This will minimize the indentations caused by the removed spots.) Note: On non-looped carpets, you can also trim a few carpet fibers around the edge of the removed spot, if needed, to minimize it further.
   - On non-looped carpets, rough up the trimmed carpet fibers a little with the tips of your scissors. Trim any taller roughed up fibers so they are equal in height with the rest of the carpet.
   - Vacuum debris with vacuum cleaner hose.

**If the spot is larger than 3/8 inch (pencil eraser size):**

1. Lay a disposable towel(s) over the palm of your hand. Then lay your hand on the carpet so the towel is at the edge of the spot.
   - Using your spoon, scoop as much of the spot(s) as possible into the towel. Note: After each scoop, wipe the spoon on a clean part of the towel.
   - Carefully drop the dirty towel in your empty bucket.

2. With clean disposable towels or a towel, blot 30 - 40 times, using a clean part of the towel each time.

3. **Do not continue removal** of a Class IV spot.
   - Mist the spot(s) with a generous amount of ammonia.
   - Put a folded towel moistened with water over spot and a note next to it that says, "***Do Not Touch Or Clean!***". (Keep towel damp until pro comes.)
   - Call a pro and have spot removed as soon as possible within 24 hours.

Section II

# Pasta: Linguini, Noodles, Spaghetti, Etc.

## Comments:

- **Optimum removal time:** Within 24 hours of spill
- **Maximum size for home removal:** Class I / II = 6 inches
- **Removal restrictions:** If the spot(s) is larger than 6 inches in diameter, **do not attempt TOTAL removal** using Class I or II instructions. Do Step 1 **only** under Class I or II. Mist spot(s) with a generous amount of ammonia. Put a folded towel moistened with water over spot. Call a pro and have spot removed within 1 day.
- Sauces in some recipes contain food coloring that can immediately and permanently stain nylon. If you cannot remove a spot, consult a pro for options as soon as possible.
- Meats, butter or oils in some recipes can soak into the fibers and cause recurring spots. (See "Recurring Spots", Chapter 4.) Consult a pro for options as soon as possible.

## Materials Needed:

Class I / II: Spotting kit, Spotting machine with hot water

<table>
<tr><td>

### Class I: Spot Machine + Old / Dried Spot

**Steps:**

1. Using your spoon, scrape out as much of the spot(s) as possible.
   - Vacuum debris with spot machine.
   - Repeat entire Step until no more removes.
2. Mist on a generous amount of ammonia.
   - Allow to work 2 minutes.
   - Mist on a generous amount of alcohol.
   - Agitate with hard brush.
   - Mist on a small amount of ammonia.
   - Agitate with hard brush.
3. With the spot machine, rinse with hot water using the chop stroke technique 6 - 10 times.
   - Take 4 - 6 slow, dry vacuum strokes.
4. Look at spot area carefully to see if the spot is gone: .
   - If YES: No further action is needed.
   - If NO: Repeat Steps 2 and 3 until no more removes. Then, if needed, do Step 5.
5. If color cast remains, mist on a generous amount of peroxide.
   - Tamp with soft brush.
   - Blot with a towel.
   - Mist on a generous amount of peroxide.
   - Tamp with soft brush.
   - Allow to dry.
6. If needed, repeat Steps 2, 3 and 5 one time.
7. If the spot persists, call a pro for options as soon as possible.

</td><td>

### Class II: Spot Machine + Fresh / Wet Spot

**Steps:**

1. Lay a small towel over the palm of your hand. Then lay your hand on the carpet so the towel is at the edge of the spot.
   - Using your hard brush, rake the spot onto the towel. Note: Use a second towel if needed to avoid spreading the spot onto clean carpet.
   - Repeat raking until no more spot removes.
   - With your spoon, scoop any remaining spot onto the towel.
   - Carefully drop the dirty towel in your empty bucket.
2. Clean your hard brush by rinsing it in the sink under hot water.
3. Mist on a generous amount of ammonia.
   - Allow to work 1 minute.
   - Mist on a generous amount of alcohol.
   - Agitate with hard brush. Caution: Clean hard brush before using it to agitate spot.
4. With the spot machine, rinse with hot water using the chop stroke technique 6 - 10 times.
   - Take 2 - 4 slow, dry vacuum strokes.
5. Look at spot area carefully to see if the spot is gone:
   - If YES: No further action is needed.
   - If NO: Repeat Steps 3 and 4 until no more removes. Then, if needed, do Step 6.
6. If color cast remains, mist on a generous amount of peroxide.
   - Tamp with soft brush.
   - Blot with a towel.
   - Mist on a generous amount of peroxide.
   - Tamp with soft brush.
   - Allow to dry.
7. If needed, repeat Steps 3, 4 and 6 one time.
8. If the spot persists, call a pro for options as soon as possible.

</td></tr>
</table>

Section II

# Pasta: Linguini, Noodles, Spaghetti, Etc.

Spot Contents: Egg, Flour, Possible Butter or Oil, Possible Meat Sauce, Salt, Starch

## Comments:

- **Optimum removal time:** Within 24 hours of spill
- **Maximum size for home removal:** Class III / IV = 3 1/2 inches
- **Removal restrictions:** If the spot(s) is larger than 3 1/2 inches in diameter, **do not attempt TOTAL removal** using Class III or IV instructions. Do Step 1 **only** under Class III or IV. Mist spot(s) with a generous amount of ammonia. Put a folded towel moistened with water over spot. Then:
  - Call a pro and have spot removed within 1 day. -OR-
  - If the spot is 6 inches or less in diameter, get a spot machine and:
    - If the spot is now old/dried, do Steps 2 - 7 under Class I.
    - If the spot is still fresh/wet, do Steps 2 - 8 under Class II.
- Sauces in some recipes contain food coloring that can immediately and permanently stain nylon. If you cannot remove a spot, consult a pro for options as soon as possible.
- Meats, butter or oils in some recipes can soak into the fibers and cause recurring spots. (See "Recurring Spots", Chapter 4.) Consult a pro for options as soon as possible.

## Materials Needed:

Class III: Spotting kit, Vacuum cleaner with attachment removed from hose
Class IV: Spotting kit

## Class III: Towel + Old / Dried Spot

### Steps:

1. Using your spoon, scrape out as much of the spot(s) as possible.
   - Vacuum debris with vacuum cleaner hose.
   - Repeat entire Step until no more removes.

2. Mist on a generous amount of ammonia.
   - Allow to work 2 minutes.
   - Mist on a small amount of alcohol.
   - Agitate with hard brush.
   - Mist on a small amount of ammonia.
   - Agitate with hard brush.

3. With a towel, blot 20 - 30 times, using a clean part of the towel each time.
   - With a towel over your hand, pinch out more of the spot, using a clean part of the towel each time.

4. Look at spot area carefully to see if the spot is gone:
   - If YES: No further action is needed.
   - If NO: Repeat Steps 2 and 3 until no more removes. Then, if needed, do Step 5.

5. If color cast remains, mist on a generous amount of peroxide.
   - Tamp with soft brush.
   - Blot with a towel.
   - Mist on a generous amount of peroxide.
   - Tamp with soft brush.
   - Allow to dry.

6. If needed, repeat Steps 2, 3 and 5 one time.

7. If the spot persists, call a pro for options as soon as possible.

## Class IV: Towel + Fresh / Wet Spot

### Steps:

1. Lay a small towel over the palm of your hand. Then lay your hand on the carpet so the towel is at the edge of the spot.
   - Using your hard brush, rake the spot onto the towel. Note: Use a second towel if needed to avoid spreading the spot onto clean carpet.
   - Repeat raking until no more spot removes.
   - With your spoon, scoop any remaining spot onto the towel.
   - Carefully drop the dirty towel in your empty bucket.

2. Clean your hard brush by rinsing it in the sink under hot water.

3. Mist on a generous amount of ammonia.
   - Allow to work 1 minute.
   - Mist on a small amount of alcohol.
   - Agitate with hard brush. Caution: Clean hard brush before using it to agitate spot.

4. With a towel, blot 20 - 30 times, using a clean part of the towel each time.
   - With a towel over your hand, pinch out more of the spot, using a clean part of the towel each time.

5. Look at spot area carefully to see if the spot is gone:
   - If YES: No further action is needed.
   - If NO: Repeat Steps 3 and 4 until no more removes. Then, if needed, do Step 6.

6. If color cast remains, mist on a generous amount of peroxide.
   - Tamp with soft brush.
   - Blot with a towel.
   - Mist on a generous amount of peroxide.
   - Tamp with soft brush.
   - Allow to dry.

7. If needed, repeat Steps 3, 4 and 6 one time.

8. If the spot persists, call a pro for options as soon as possible.

# Peanut Butter, Other Nut Butters

## Comments:

- **Optimum removal time:** Within 24 hours of spill
- **Maximum size for home removal:** Class I / II = 5 inches
- **Removal restrictions:** If the spot(s) is larger than 5 inches in diameter or has been pressed into the carpet fibers, **do not attempt TOTAL removal** using Class I or II instructions. Do Step 1 **only** under Class I or II. Put a dry towel over spot. Call a pro and have spot removed within 3 days.
- **Caution:** Excessive quantities of oil in some of these products can cause recurring spots in nylon, polyester and olefin if left untreated as little as 3 days. (See "Recurring Spots", Chapter 4.) Consult a pro for options as soon as possible.

## Materials Needed:

Class I / II: Spotting kit, Spot machine with hot water

### Class I: Spot Machine + Old / Dried Spot

#### Steps:

1. Lay a small towel over the palm of your hand. Then lay your hand on the carpet so the towel is at the edge of the spot.
   - Using your spoon, scoop as much of the spot(s) as possible into the towel. Note: After each scoop, wipe the spoon on a clean part of the towel.
   - Carefully drop the dirty towel in your empty bucket.
   - Vacuum debris with spot machine.
   - Repeat entire Step until no more removes.

2. Mist on a generous amount of ammonia.
   - Mist on a generous amount of alcohol.
   - Agitate with hard brush.
   - Allow to work 1 minute.

3. With the spot machine, rinse with hot water using the chop stroke technique 8 - 10 times.
   - Take 6 - 8 slow, dry vacuum strokes.

4. Look at and touch spot area carefully to see if the oily residue is gone:
   - If YES: No further action is needed.
   - If NO: Repeat Steps 2 and 3 until no more removes. Allow to dry.

5. If needed, repeat Steps 2 and 3 one time.

6. If the spot persists, call a pro for options as soon as possible.

### Class II: Spot Machine + Fresh / Wet Spot

#### Steps:

1. Lay a small towel over the palm of your hand. Then lay your hand on the carpet so the towel is at the edge of the spot.
   - Using your spoon, scoop as much of the spot(s) as possible into the towel. Note: After each scoop, wipe the spoon on a clean part of the towel.
   - Carefully drop the dirty towel in your empty bucket.

2. Mist on a generous amount of ammonia.
   - Mist on a generous amount of alcohol.
   - Agitate with hard brush.
   - Allow to work 1 minute.

3. With the spot machine, rinse with hot water using the chop stroke technique 6 - 8 times.
   - Take 4 - 6 slow, dry vacuum strokes.

4. Look at and touch spot area carefully to see if the oily residue is gone:
   - If YES: No further action is needed.
   - If NO: Repeat Steps 2 and 3 until no more removes. Allow to dry.

5. If needed, repeat Steps 2 and 3 one time.

6. If the spot persists, call a pro for options as soon as possible.

## Comments:

- **Optimum removal time:** Within 24 hours of spill
- **Maximum size for home removal:** Class III / IV = 3 inches
- **Removal restrictions:** If the spot(s) is larger than 3 inches in diameter or has been pressed into the carpet fibers, **do not attempt TOTAL removal** using Class III or IV instructions. Do Step 1 **only** under Class III or IV. Put a dry towel over spot. Then:
  - Call a pro and have spot removed within 3 days. -OR-
  - If the spot has not been pressed into the carpet fibers and is 5 inches or less in diameter, get a spot machine and:
    - If the spot is now old/dried, do Steps 2 - 6 under Class I.
    - If the spot is still fresh/wet, do Steps 2 - 6 under Class II.
- **Caution:** Excessive quantities of oil in some of these products can cause recurring spots in nylon, polyester and olefin if left untreated as little as 3 days. (See "Recurring Spots", Chapter 4.) Consult a pro for options as soon as possible.

## Materials Needed:

Class III: Spotting kit, Vacuum cleaner with attachment removed from hose
Class IV: Spotting kit

### Class III: Towel + Old / Dried Spot

**Steps:**

1. Lay a small towel over the palm of your hand. Then lay your hand on the carpet so the towel is at the edge of the spot.
   - Using your spoon, scoop as much of the spot(s) as possible into the towel. Note: After each scoop, wipe the spoon on a clean part of the towel.
   - Carefully drop the dirty towel in your empty bucket.
   - Vacuum debris with vacuum cleaner hose.
   - Repeat entire Step until no more removes.
2. Mist on a generous amount of ammonia.
   - Mist on a generous amount of alcohol.
   - Agitate with hard brush.
   - Allow to work 2 minutes.
   - Mist on a small amount of ammonia.
   - Agitate with hard brush.
3. With a clean towel, blot 20 - 30 times, using a clean part of the towel each time.
   - With a towel over your hand, pinch out more of the spot, using a clean part of the towel each time.
4. Look at and touch spot area carefully to see if the oily residue is gone:
   - If YES: No further action is needed.
   - If NO: Repeat Steps 2 and 3 until no more removes. Allow to dry.
5. If needed, repeat Steps 2 and 3 one time.
6. If the spot persists, call a pro for options as soon as possible.

### Class IV: Towel + Fresh / Wet Spot

**Steps:**

1. Lay a small towel over the palm of your hand.
   - Using your spoon, scoop as much of the spot(s) as possible into the towel. Note: After each scoop, wipe the spoon on a clean part of the towel.
   - Repeat until no more removes.
   - Carefully drop the dirty towel in your empty bucket.
2. Mist on a small amount of ammonia.
   - Mist on a generous amount of alcohol.
   - Agitate with hard brush.
   - Allow to work 1 minute.
   - Mist on a small amount of ammonia.
   - Agitate with hard brush.
3. With a clean towel, blot 15 - 20 times, using a clean part of the towel each time.
   - With a towel over your hand, pinch out more of the spot, using a clean part of the towel each time.
4. Look at and touch spot area carefully to see if the oily residue is gone:
   - If YES: No further action is needed.
   - If NO: Repeat Steps 2 and 3 until no more removes. Allow to dry.
5. If needed, repeat Steps 2 and 3 one time.
6. If the spot persists, call a pro for options as soon as possible.

Section II

# Plant Juice: Algae, Flowers, Grass Stains, Leaves, Seaweed, Vines

## Comments:

- **Optimum removal time:** Within 24 hours of spill
- **Maximum size for home removal:** Class I / II = 5 inches
- **Removal restrictions:** If the spot(s) is larger than 5 inches in diameter, **do not attempt TOTAL removal** using Class I or II instructions. Do Step 1 **only** under Class I or II. Put a folded towel moistened with water over spot and note next to it that says ***"Do Not Touch Or Clean!"***. (Keep towel damp until pro comes.) Call a pro and have spot removed within 2 days.
- **Caution:** Deep green or blue-green organic pigmentation in these spots can permanently stain most nylon if left untreated as little as one month. If you cannot remove a spot, consult a pro for options as soon as possible.

### Materials Needed:
Class I / II: Spotting kit, Vacuum cleaner with attachment removed from hose, Spot machine with warm water

Section II

## Class I: Spot Machine + Old / Dried Spot

### Steps:

1. Vacuum debris with vacuum cleaner hose. (Pick up larger pieces with your hands.)
   - Agitate spot(s) with soft brush.
   - Vacuum debris with vacuum cleaner hose.
   - Repeat entire step until no more removes.

2. Mist on a generous amount of ammonia.
   - Agitate with hard brush.
   - Mist on a small amount of peroxide.
   - Agitate with hard brush.
   - Allow to work 2 minutes.

3. With the spot machine, rinse with warm water using the chop stroke technique 10 - 15 times.
   - Take 6 - 8 slow, dry vacuum strokes.

4. Look at spot area carefully to see if the spot is gone:
   - If YES: No further action is needed.
   - If NO: Do Steps 2 and 3 until no more will remove. Then, if needed, do Step 5.

5. If color cast remains, mist on a generous amount of peroxide.
   - Tamp with soft brush.
   - Allow to dry.

6. If needed, repeat Steps 2, 3 and 5 one time.

7. If the spot persists, call a pro for options as soon as possible.

## Class II: Spot Machine + Fresh / Wet Spot

### Steps:

1. Vacuum debris with vacuum cleaner hose. (Pick up larger pieces with your hands.)
   - Agitate spot(s) with soft brush.
   - Vacuum debris with vacuum cleaner hose.
   - Repeat entire step until no more removes.

2. Mist on a generous amount of ammonia.
   - Agitate with hard brush.
   - Mist on a small amount of peroxide.
   - Agitate with hard brush.
   - Allow to work 1 minute.

3. With the spot machine, rinse with warm water using the chop stroke technique 10 - 15 times.
   - Take 6 - 8 slow, dry vacuum strokes.

4. Look at spot area carefully to see if the spot is gone:
   - If YES: No further action is needed.
   - If NO: Do Steps 2 and 3 until no more will remove. Then, if needed, do Step 5.

5. If color cast remains, mist on a generous amount of peroxide.
   - Tamp with soft brush.
   - Allow to dry.

6. If needed, repeat Steps 2, 3 and 5 one time.

7. If the spot persists, call a pro for options as soon as possible.

## Comments:

- **Optimum removal time:** Within 24 hours of spill
- **Maximum size for home removal:** Class III / IV = 2 inches
- **Removal restrictions:** If the spot(s) is larger than 2 inches in diameter, **do not attempt TOTAL removal** using Class III or IV instructions. Do Step 1 **only** under Class III or IV. Put a folded towel moistened with water over spot and a note next to it that says, ***"Do Not Touch Or Clean!"***. (Keep towel damp until pro comes.) Then:
  - Call a pro and have spot removed within 3 days. -OR-
  - If the spot is 5 inches or less in diameter, get a spot machine and:
    - If the spot is now old/dried, do Steps 2 - 7 under Class I.
    - If the spot is still fresh/wet, do Steps 2 - 7 under Class II.
- **Caution:** Deep green or blue-green organic pigmentation in these spots can permanently stain most nylon if left untreated as little as one month. If you cannot remove a spot, consult a pro for options as soon as possible.

## Materials Needed:

Class III / IV: Spotting kit, Vacuum cleaner with attachment removed from hose

### Class III: Towel + Old / Dried Spot

**Steps:**

1. Vacuum debris with vacuum cleaner hose. (Pick up larger pieces with your hands.)
   - Agitate spot(s) with soft brush.
   - Vacuum debris with vacuum cleaner hose.
   - Repeat entire step until no more removes.

2. Mist on a generous amount of ammonia.
   - Agitate with hard brush.
   - Mist on a small amount of peroxide.
   - Agitate with hard brush.
   - Allow to work 1 minute.

3. With a towel, blot 20 - 30 times, using a clean part of the towel each time.

4. Look at spot area carefully to see if the spot is gone:
   - If YES: No further action is needed.
   - If NO: Do Steps 2 and 3 until no more will remove. Then, if needed, do Step 5.

5. If color cast remains, mist on a generous amount of peroxide.
   - Tamp with soft brush.
   - Allow to dry.

6. If needed, repeat Steps 2, 3 and 5 one time.

7. If the spot persists, call a pro for options as soon as possible.

### Class IV: Towel + Fresh / Wet Spot

**Steps:**

1. Vacuum debris with vacuum cleaner hose. (Pick up larger pieces with your hands.)
   - Agitate spot(s) with soft brush.
   - Vacuum debris with vacuum cleaner hose.
   - Repeat entire step until no more removes.

2. Mist on a generous amount of ammonia.
   - Agitate with hard brush.
   - Mist on a small amount of peroxide.
   - Agitate with hard brush.
   - Allow to work 1 minute.

3. With a towel, blot 20 - 30 times, using a clean part of the towel each time.

4. Look at spot area carefully to see if the spot is gone:
   - If YES: No further action is needed.
   - If NO: Do Steps 2 and 3 until no more will remove. Then, if needed, do Step 5.

5. If color cast remains, mist on a generous amount of peroxide.
   - Tamp with soft brush.
   - Allow to dry.

6. If needed, repeat Steps 2, 3 and 5 one time.

7. If the spot persists, call a pro for options as soon as possible.

Section II

# Potpourri - Dry or Liquid

## Comments:

- **Optimum removal time: As soon as possible** within 24 hours of spill
- **Maximum size for home removal:** Class I / II = 3 inches
- **Removal restrictions:** If the spot(s) is larger than 3 inches in diameter, **do not attempt TOTAL removal** using Class I or II instructions. Do Steps 1 - 3 **only** under Class I or Steps 1 and 2 **only** under Class II. Mist spot(s) with a generous amount of ammonia. Put a folded towel moistened with water over spot. Call a pro and have spot removed as soon as possible within 24 hours.
- Strong dyes in these products can immediately and permanently stain most nylon. If you cannot remove a spot, consult a pro for options as soon as possible.
- Oil in some products can cause recurring spots. (See "Recurring Spots", Chapter 4.) Consult a pro for options as soon as possible.

## Materials Needed:
Class I / II: Spotting kit, Spot machine with warm water

### Class I: Spot Machine + Old / Dried Spot

**Steps:**

1. Using your spot machine, dry vacuum any loose debris.

2. Using your soft brush, agitate the spot(s) 15 - 20 times. Caution: Be careful to not fray carpet fibers.
   - Vacuum debris with spot machine.

3. With the spot machine, rinse the spot(s) with warm water using the single stroke technique 10 - 12 times.
   - Take 6 - 8 slow, dry vacuum strokes.

4. Mist on a generous amount of alcohol.
   - Mist on a generous amount of ammonia.
   - Allow to work 2 minutes.
   - Tamp with soft brush.

5. With the spot machine, rinse with warm water using the single stroke technique 10 - 12 times.
   - Take 6 - 8 slow, dry vacuum strokes.

6. Look at and touch spot area carefully to see if the oily residue is gone:
   - If YES: No further action is needed.
   - If NO: Do Steps 4 and 5 until no more will remove. Then, if needed, do Step 7.

7. If color cast remains, mist on a generous amount of peroxide.
   - Tamp with soft brush.
   - Mist on a small amount of ammonia.
   - Tamp with soft brush.
   - Allow to dry.

8. If the spot persists, call a pro for options as soon as possible.

### Class II: Spot Machine + Fresh / Wet Spot

**Steps:**

1. Using your spot machine, dry vacuum up as much of the spot(s) as possible.

2. With the spot machine, rinse the spot(s) with warm water using the single stroke technique 8 - 10 times.
   - Take 4 - 6 slow, dry vacuum strokes.

3. Mist on a generous amount of alcohol.
   - Mist on a generous amount of ammonia.
   - Allow to work 1 minute.
   - Tamp with soft brush.

4. With the spot machine, rinse with warm water using the single stroke technique 8 - 10 times.
   - Take 4 - 6 slow, dry vacuum strokes.

5. Look at and touch spot area carefully to see if the oily residue is gone:
   - If YES: No further action is needed.
   - If NO: Do Steps 3 and 4 until no more will remove. Then, if needed, do Step 6.

6. If color cast remains, mist on a generous amount of peroxide.
   - Tamp with soft brush.
   - Mist on a small amount of ammonia.
   - Tamp with soft brush.
   - Allow to dry.

7. If the spot persists, call a pro for options as soon as possible.

Section II

## Comments:

- **Optimum removal time: As soon as possible** within 24 hours of spill
- **Maximum size for home removal:** Class III = No home removal / Class IV = 1 1/2 inches
- **Removal restrictions - Class III:** See "Class III" instructions below.
- **Removal restrictions - Class IV:** If the spot(s) is larger than 1 1/2 inches in diameter, **do not attempt TOTAL removal** using Class IV instructions. Do Step 1 **only** under Class IV. Mist spot(s) with a generous amount of ammonia. Put a folded towel moistened with water over spot. Then:
  - Call a pro and have spot removed as soon as possible within 24 hours. -OR-
  - If the spot is 3 inches or less in diameter, get a spot machine and:
    - If the spot is now old/dried, do Steps 2 - 8 under Class I.
    - If the spot is still fresh/wet, do Steps 2 - 7 under Class II.
- Strong dyes in these products can immediately and permanently stain most nylon. If you cannot remove a spot, consult a pro for options as soon as possible.
- Oil in some products can cause recurring spots. (See "Recurring Spots", Chapter 4.) Consult a pro for options as soon as possible.

## Materials Needed:
Class III: Vacuum Cleaner with attachments removed from hose
Class IV: Spotting kit, Vacuum cleaner with attachments removed from hose

### Class III: Towel + Old / Dried Spot

**Steps:**

1. **Do not attempt TOTAL removal** of a Class III spot(s).
   - Using your vacuum cleaner hose, dry vacuum any loose debris.
   - Put a dry towel over spot to prevent the spreading of oily residue.
   - Then:
     - Call a pro and have spot removed as soon as possible within 24 hours. -OR-
     - If the spot is 3 inches or less in diameter, get a spot machine and do Steps 2 - 8 under Class I.

### Class IV: Towel + Fresh / Wet Spot

**Steps:**

1. Using your vacuum cleaner hose, dry vacuum any loose debris.
2. Fold a towel several times and place it over the spot(s).
   - Step on the towel with your full weight, using a clean part of the towel each time.
   - Repeat until no more liquid absorbs.
3. Mist on a small amount of alcohol.
   - Mist on a small amount of ammonia.
   - Tamp with soft brush.
   - Allow to work 1 minute.
4. With a towel, blot 10 - 15 times, using a clean part of the towel each time.
5. Look at and touch spot area carefully to see if the oily residue is gone:
   - If YES: No further action is needed.
   - If NO: Do Steps 3 and 4 until no more will remove. Then, if needed, do Step 6.
6. If color cast remains, mist on a generous amount of peroxide.
   - Tamp with soft brush.
   - Mist on a small amount of ammonia.
   - Tamp with soft brush.
   - Allow to dry.
7. If the spot persists, call a pro for options as soon as possible.

# Putty - All: Carpenters Putty, Play-Doh®, Silly Putty®

## Comments:

- **Optimum removal time:** Within 24 hours of spill
- **Maximum size for home removal:** Class I / II = 2 1/2 inches
- **Removal restrictions:** If the spot(s) is larger than 2 1/2 inches in diameter or has been pressed into the carpet fibers, **do not attempt ANY removal** using Class I or II instructions. Put a dry towel over spot. Call a pro and have spot removed within 3 days.
- **Caution: Do not attempt scissors removal** of spots from **any** type of looped carpet (berber, commercial glue down, etc.) unless the spot is only on the outside fibers of the loop(s). If in doubt, call a pro for options as soon as possible.
- Coloring in some products can immediately and permanently stain some nylon. If you cannot remove a spot, consult a pro for options as soon as possible.

## Materials Needed:

Class I: Spotting kit, Pair of pliers, Spot machine with hot water
Class II: Spotting kit, Spot machine with hot water

<table>
<tr><th>Class I: Spot Machine + Old / Dried Spot</th><th>Class II: Spot Machine + Fresh / Wet Spot</th></tr>
</table>

### Class I: Spot Machine + Old / Dried Spot

**Steps:**

1. Using your spoon, scrape out as much of the spot(s) as possible. Note: If the spot is too hard, use a pair of pliers to crush into smaller pieces or trim out tiny pieces with your scissors.
   - Using your scissors, wedge the blades up under the spot(s) and snip the hardened parts from the very tip of the carpet fibers. (This will minimize the indentations caused by the removed spots.) Note: On non-looped carpets, you can also trim a few carpet fibers around the edge of the removed spot, if needed, to minimize it further. Caution: Be careful not to remove too much of the fibers.
   - On non-looped carpets, rough up the trimmed carpet fibers a little with the tips of your scissors. Trim any taller roughed up fibers so they are equal in height with the rest of the carpet.
   - Vacuum debris with spot machine.
   - Repeat entire Step until no more removes.

2. Mist on a generous amount of ammonia.
   - Allow to work 2 minutes.
   - Mist on a generous amount of alcohol.
   - Agitate with end of spoon handle.
   - Allow to work 1 minute.

3. With the spot machine, rinse with hot water using the chop stroke technique 15 - 20 times.
   - Take 6 - 8 slow, dry vacuum strokes.

4. Look at spot area carefully to see if the spot is gone:
   - If YES: Allow to dry.
   - If NO: Repeat Steps 2 and 3 until no more removes. Then, if needed, do Step 5.

5. If color cast remains, mist on a generous amount of peroxide.
   - Tamp with soft brush.
   - Allow to dry.

6. If the spot persists, call a pro for options as soon as possible.

### Class II: Spot Machine + Fresh / Wet Spot

**Steps:**

1. With a towel over your hand, pinch out as much of the spot as possible, using a clean part of the towel each time.
   - Using the tip of your dinner knife, scrape out as much of the spot(s) as possible. Note: Wipe the tip of the knife on a clean part of the towel after each scrape.
   - Repeat entire Step until no more removes.

2. Mist on a generous amount of ammonia.
   - Allow to work 2 minutes.
   - Mist on a generous amount of alcohol.
   - Agitate with end of spoon handle.
   - Allow to work 1 minute.

3. With the spot machine, rinse with hot water using the chop stroke technique 15 - 20 times.
   - Take 6 - 8 slow, dry vacuum strokes.

4. Look at spot area carefully to see if the spot is gone:
   - If YES: Allow to dry.
   - If NO: Repeat Steps 2 and 3 until no more removes. Then, if needed, do Step 5.

5. If color cast remains, mist on a generous amount of peroxide.
   - Tamp with soft brush.
   - Allow to dry.

6. If the spot persists, call a pro for options as soon as possible.

## Comments:

- **Optimum removal time:** Within 24 hours of spill
- **Maximum size for home removal:** Class III / IV = 1 inch
- **Removal restrictions:** If the spot(s) has been pressed into the carpet fibers or is larger than 1 inch in diameter, **do not attempt TOTAL removal** using Class III or IV instructions. Do Step 1 **only** under Class III or IV. Put a dry towel over spot. Then:
  - Call a pro and have spot removed within 3 days. -OR-
  - If the spot has not been pressed into the carpet fibers and is 2 1/2 inches or less in diameter, get a spot machine and:
    - If the spot is now old/dried, do Steps 2 - 6 under Class I.
    - If the spot is still fresh/wet, do Steps 2 - 6 under Class II.
- **Caution: Do not attempt scissors removal** of spots from **any** type of looped carpet (berber, commercial glue down, etc.) unless the spot is only on the outside fibers of the loop(s). If in doubt, call a pro for options as soon as possible.
- Coloring in some products can immediately and permanently stain some nylon. If you cannot remove a spot, consult a pro for options as soon as possible.

---

## Materials Needed:

Class III: Spotting kit, Pair of pliers, Vacuum cleaner with attachment removed from hose
Class IV: Spotting kit

### Class III: Towel + Old / Dried Spot

#### Steps:

1. Using your spoon, scrape out as much of the spot(s) as possible. Note: If the spot is too hard, use a pair of pliers to crush into smaller pieces or trim out tiny pieces with your scissors.
   - Using your scissors, wedge the blades up under the spot(s) and snip the hardened parts from the very tip of the carpet fibers. (This will minimize the indentations caused by the removed spots.) Note: On non-looped carpets, you can also trim a few carpet fibers around the edge of the removed spot, if needed, to minimize it further. Caution: Be careful not to remove too much of the fibers.
   - On non-looped carpets, rough up the trimmed carpet fibers a little with the tips of your scissors. Trim any taller roughed up fibers so they are equal in height with the rest of the carpet.

2. Mist on a generous amount of ammonia.
   - Allow to work 2 minutes.
   - Mist on a generous amount of alcohol.
   - Agitate with end of spoon handle.
   - Allow to work 1 minute.

3. With a towel over your hand, pinch out the spot 20 - 25 times, using a clean part of the towel each time.
   - With a towel, blot 10 - 15 times, using a clean part of the towel each time.

4. Look at spot area carefully to see if the spot is gone:
   - If YES: Allow to dry.
   - If NO: Repeat Steps 2 and 3 until no more removes. Then, if needed, do Step 5.

5. If color cast remains, mist on a generous amount of peroxide.
   - Tamp with soft brush.
   - Allow to dry.

6. If the spot persists, call a pro for options as soon as possible.

### Class IV: Towel + Fresh / Wet Spot

#### Steps:

1. With a towel over your hand, pinch out as much of the spot as possible, using a clean part of the towel each time.
   - Using the tip of your dinner knife, scrape out as much of the spot(s) as possible. Note: Wipe the tip of the knife on a clean part of the towel after each scrape.
   - Repeat entire Step until no more removes.

2. Mist on a generous amount of ammonia.
   - Allow to work 2 minutes.
   - Mist on a generous amount of alcohol.
   - Agitate with end of spoon handle.
   - Allow to work 1 minute.

3. With a towel over your hand, pinch out the spot 20 - 25 times, using a clean part of the towel each time.
   - With a towel, blot 10 - 15 times, using a clean part of the towel each time.

4. Look at spot area carefully to see if the spot is gone:
   - If YES: Allow to dry.
   - If NO: Repeat Steps 2 and 3 until no more removes. Then, if needed, do Step 5.

5. If color cast remains, mist on a generous amount of peroxide.
   - Tamp with soft brush.
   - Allow to dry.

6. If the spot persists, call a pro for options as soon as possible.

Section II

# Rubber / Plastic - Melted: Vacuum Cleaner Belt, Etc.

## Comments:

- **Optimum removal time:** Within 24 hours of spill
- **Maximum size for home removal:** Class I / II = 3/8 inch
- **Removal restrictions:** If the spot(s) is larger than 3/8 inch in diameter or was caused by burning rubber or plastic, **do not attempt ANY removal** using Class I or II instructions. Call a pro and have spot removed within 3 days.
- **Caution: Do not attempt scissors removal** of spots from **any** type of looped carpet (berber, commercial glue down, etc.) unless the spot is **only on the outside fibers** of the loop(s). If in doubt, call a pro for options as soon as possible.
- These spots, when burning, may adhere to the carpet by actually melting into the yarns. Olefin is especially vulnerable due to its low melting point. If you cannot remove a spot, consult a pro for options as soon as possible.

## Materials Needed:

Class I / II: Spotting kit, Spot machine with hot water

<table>
<tr><td>

### Class I: Spot Machine + Old / Dried Spot

*Steps:*

1. Using your scissors, wedge the blades up under the spot(s) and snip the hardened parts from the very tip of the carpet fibers. (This will minimize the indentations caused by the removed spots.) Note: On non-looped carpets, you can also trim a few carpet fibers around the edge of the removed spot, if needed, to minimize it further.
   - On non-looped carpets, rough up the trimmed carpet fibers a little with the tips of your scissors. Trim any taller roughed up fibers so they are equal in height with the rest of the carpet.
   - Vacuum debris with spot machine until no more removes.

2. Look at spot area carefully to see if the spot is gone:
   - If YES: No further action is needed.
   - If NO: Do Step 3.

3. Mist on a generous amount of alcohol.
   - Allow to work 2 minutes.
   - Mist on a generous amount of alcohol.
   - Agitate with end of spoon handle.

4. With the spot machine, rinse with hot water using the chop stroke technique 10 - 12 times.
   - Take 8 - 10 slow, dry vacuum strokes.

5. Look at spot area carefully to see if the spot is gone:
   - If YES: No further action is needed.
   - If NO: Repeat Steps 3 and 4 until no more removes.

6. If the spot persists, call a pro for options as soon as possible.

</td><td>

### Class II: Spot Machine + Fresh / Wet Spot

*Steps:*

1. Using your scissors, wedge the blades up under the spot(s) and snip the hardened parts from the very tip of the carpet fibers. (This will minimize the indentations caused by the removed spots.) Note: On non-looped carpets, you can also trim a few carpet fibers around the edge of the removed spot, if needed, to minimize it further.
   - On non-looped carpets, rough up the trimmed carpet fibers a little with the tips of your scissors. Trim any taller roughed up fibers so they are equal in height with the rest of the carpet.
   - Vacuum debris with spot machine until no more removes.

2. Look at spot area carefully to see if the spot is gone:
   - If YES: No further action is needed.
   - If NO: Do Step 3.

3. Mist on a generous amount of alcohol.
   - Allow to work 2 minutes.
   - Mist on a generous amount of alcohol.
   - Agitate with end of spoon handle.

4. With the spot machine, rinse with hot water using the chop stroke technique 10 - 12 times.
   - Take 8 - 10 slow, dry vacuum strokes.

5. Look at spot area carefully to see if the spot is gone:
   - If YES: No further action is needed.
   - If NO: Repeat Steps 3 and 4 until no more removes.

6. If the spot persists, call a pro for options as soon as possible.

</td></tr>
</table>

Section II

## Comments:

- **Optimum removal time:** Within 24 hours of spill
- **Maximum size for home removal**: Class III / IV = 3/8 inch
- **Removal restrictions:** If the spot(s) is larger than 3/8 inch in diameter or was caused by burning rubber or plastic, **do not attempt ANY removal** using Class III or IV instructions. Call a pro and have spot removed within 3 days.
- **Caution: Do not attempt scissors removal** of spots from **any** type of looped carpet (berber, commercial glue down, etc.) unless the spot is **only on the outside fibers** of the loop(s). If in doubt, call a pro for options as soon as possible.
- These spots, when burning, may adhere to the carpet by actually melting into the yarns. Olefin is especially vulnerable due to its low melting point. If you cannot remove a spot, consult a pro for options as soon as possible.

## Materials Needed:

Class III / IV: Spotting kit, Vacuum cleaner with attachment removed from hose

<table>
<tr><td>

### Class III: Towel + Old / Dried Spot

**Steps:**

1. Using your scissors, wedge the blades up under the spot(s) and snip the hardened parts from the very tip of the carpet fibers. (This will minimize the indentations caused by the removed spots.) Note: On non-looped carpets, you can also trim a few carpet fibers around the edge of the removed spot, if needed, to minimize it further.
   - On non-looped carpets, rough up the trimmed carpet fibers a little with the tips of your scissors. Trim any taller roughed up fibers so they are equal in height with the rest of the carpet.
   - Vacuum debris with vacuum cleaner hose until no more removes.

2. Look at spot area carefully to see if the spot is gone:
   - If YES: No further action is needed.
   - If NO: Do Step 3.

3. Mist on a generous amount of alcohol.
   - Allow to work 2 minutes.
   - Mist on a generous amount of alcohol.
   - Agitate with end of spoon handle.

4. With the tip of the blade of your dinner knife, scrape the spot in a side-to-side motion 20 - 25 times.
   - Vacuum debris with vacuum cleaner hose until no more removes.

5. Look at spot area carefully to see if the spot is gone:
   - If YES: No further action is needed.
   - If NO: Repeat Steps 3 and 4 until no more removes.

6. If the spot persists, call a pro for options as soon as possible.

</td><td>

### Class IV: Towel + Fresh / Wet Spot

**Steps:**

1. Using your scissors, wedge the blades up under the spot(s) and snip the hardened parts from the very tip of the carpet fibers. (This will minimize the indentations caused by the removed spots.) Note: On non-looped carpets, you can also trim a few carpet fibers around the edge of the removed spot, if needed, to minimize it further.
   - On non-looped carpets, rough up the trimmed carpet fibers a little with the tips of your scissors. Trim any taller roughed up fibers so they are equal in height with the rest of the carpet.
   - Vacuum debris with vacuum cleaner hose until no more removes.

2. Look at spot area carefully to see if the spot is gone:
   - If YES: No further action is needed.
   - If NO: Do Step 3.

3. Mist on a generous amount of alcohol.
   - Allow to work 2 minutes.
   - Mist on a generous amount of alcohol.
   - Agitate with end of spoon handle.

4. With the tip of the blade of your dinner knife, scrape the spot in a side-to-side motion 20 - 25 times.
   - Vacuum debris with vacuum cleaner hose until no more removes.

5. Look at spot area carefully to see if the spot is gone:
   - If YES: No further action is needed.
   - If NO: Repeat Steps 3 and 4 until no more removes.

6. If the spot persists, call a pro for options as soon as possible.

</td></tr>
</table>

Section II

# Rust, Oxidized Metal

## Comments:

- **Optimum removal time:** Within 1 - 2 months of spill (See **Caution** below.)
- **Maximum size for home removal:** Class I / II = 1 1/2 inches
- **Removal restrictions:** If the spot(s) is larger than 1 1/2 inches in diameter, **do not attempt ANY removal** using Class I or II instructions. Call a pro and have spot removed.
- **Caution:** There are several stains that mimic rust, but whose optimum removal times are more time sensitive. These are Wood Furniture Stains: 1 - 2 hours, and Cellulosic Browning: 2 - 3 days. (See "Rust" in "Mystery Spots, Stains and Discolorations", Chapter 4 for more information before you treat this spot.)

## Materials Needed:

Class I / II: Spotting kit, Spot machine with hot water, Undiluted lemon juice from concentrate (not fresh)

| Class I: Spot Machine + Old / Dried Spot | Class II: Spot Machine + Fresh / Wet Spot |
|---|---|
| **Steps:** | **Steps:** |
| 1. Using your dinner knife, scrape the spot(s) in a side-to-side motion 10 - 15 times. Caution: Be careful to not fray carpet fibers.<br>  • Vacuum debris with spot machine using the chop stroke technique 6 - 8 times.<br>  • Repeat until no more removes. | 1. Using your dinner knife, scrape the spot(s) in a side-to-side motion 10 - 15 times. Caution: Be careful to not fray carpet fibers.<br>  • Vacuum debris with spot machine using the chop stroke technique 6 - 8 times.<br>  • Repeat until no more removes. |
| 2. Pour undiluted lemon juice from concentrate on spot (1/2 teaspoon juice per 1/2 inch diameter of spot).<br>  • Agitate with end of spoon handle.<br>  • Allow to work 2 minutes.<br>  • Mist on a small amount of peroxide.<br>  • Agitate with end of spoon handle.<br>  • Allow to work 1 minute. | 2. Pour undiluted lemon juice from concentrate on spot (1/2 teaspoon juice per 1/2 inch diameter of spot).<br>  • Agitate with end of spoon handle.<br>  • Allow to work 2 minutes.<br>  • Mist on a small amount of peroxide.<br>  • Agitate with end of spoon handle.<br>  • Allow to work 1 minute. |
| 3. With the spot machine, rinse with hot water using the chop stroke technique 10 - 12 times.<br>  • Take 8 - 10 slow, dry vacuum strokes. | 3. With the spot machine, rinse with hot water using the chop stroke technique 10 - 12 times.<br>  • Take 8 - 10 slow, dry vacuum strokes. |
| 4. Look at spot area carefully to see if the spot is gone:<br>  • If YES: No further action is needed.<br>  • If NO: Repeat Steps 2 and 3 until no more removes. | 4. Look at spot area carefully to see if the spot is gone:<br>  • If YES: No further action is needed.<br>  • If NO: Repeat Steps 2 and 3 until no more removes. |
| 5. If the spot persists, call a pro for options. | 5. If the spot persists, call a pro for options. |

Section II

Spot Contents: Ferrous Oxide, Hydrated Ferric Oxide, Iron Carbonates, Iron Sulfate

## Comments:

- **Optimum removal time:** Within 1 - 2 months of spill (See **Caution** below.)
- **Maximum size for home removal:** Class III / IV = No home removal
- **Removal restrictions:** See "Class III" or "Class IV" instructions below.
- **Caution:** There are several stains that mimic rust, but whose optimum removal times are more time sensitive. These are Wood Furniture Stains: 1 - 2 hours, and Cellulosic Browning: 2 - 3 days. (See "Rust" in "Mystery Spots, Stains and Discolorations", Chapter 4 for more information before you treat this spot.)

## Materials Needed:

Class III / IV: None

### Class III: Towel + Old / Dried Spot

**Steps:**

1. **Do not attempt ANY removal** of a Class III spot(s).
   - Call a pro and have spot removed. -OR-
   - If the spot is 1 1/2 inches or less in diameter, get a spot machine and do Steps 1 - 5 under Class I.

### Class IV: Towel + Fresh / Wet Spot

**Steps:**

1. **Do not attempt ANY removal** of a Class IV spot(s).
   - Call a pro and have spot removed. -OR-
   - If the spot is 1 1/2 inches or less in diameter, get a spot machine and do Steps 1 - 5 under Class II.

Section II

# Sealers: Solvent-Based, Creosote, Thompson's Water Seal®

## Comments:

- **Optimum removal time: As soon as possible** within 24 hours of spill
- **Maximum size for home removal:** Class I / II = 2 inches
- **Removal restrictions:** See "Class I" or "Class II" instructions below for your size of spot(s).
- **Caution: Do not attempt scissors removal** of spots from **any** type of looped carpet (berber, commercial glue down, etc.) unless the spot is **only on the outside fibers** of the loop(s). If in doubt, call a pro for options as soon as possible.
- These products can immediately and permanently stain most nylon. If you cannot remove a spot, consult a pro for options as soon as possible.
- Large spills can damage latex in the carpet and pad and cause it to swell into little hills. This makes the carpet look as if it is loose and needs to be re-stretched. Consult a pro for options.

## Materials Needed:

Class I / II: Spotting kit, Spot machine with hot water, Disposable towel for Class II

| Class I: Spot Machine + Old / Dried Spot | Class II: Spot Machine + Fresh / Wet Spot |
|---|---|

### Steps:

**Follow the instructions for your size spot(s):**

**If the spot is 3/8 inch (pencil eraser size) or smaller:**

1. Using your scissors, wedge the blades up under the spot(s) and snip the hardened parts from the very tip of the carpet fibers. Note: On non-looped carpets, you can also trim a few carpet fibers around the edge of the removed spot, if needed, to minimize it further.
   - On non-looped carpets, rough up the trimmed carpet fibers a little with the tips of your scissors. Trim any taller roughed up fibers so they are equal in height with the rest of the carpet.
   - Vacuum debris with spot machine until no more removes.

2. Look at and touch spot area carefully to see if the spot is gone:
   - If YES: No further action is needed.
   - If NO: Do Step 3.

3. Mist spot(s) with a generous amount of alcohol.
   - Allow to work 2 minutes.
   - Mist on a generous amount of alcohol.
   - Agitate with end of spoon handle.

4. With the spot machine, rinse with hot water using the chop stroke technique 10 - 12 times.
   - Take 6 - 8 slow, dry vacuum strokes.

5. Look at and touch spot area carefully to see if the gummy residue is gone:
   - If YES: No further action is needed.
   - If NO: Repeat Steps 3 and 4 until no more removes. Then, if needed, do Step 6.

6. If color cast remains, mist on a generous amount of peroxide.
   - Mist on a small amount of ammonia.
   - Tamp with soft brush.
   - Allow to dry.

7. If the spot persists, call a pro for options as soon as possible.

**If the spot is larger than 3/8 inch, but no more than 2 inches:**

1. Do Steps 3 - 7 **only** under "Class I". Do not trim spot from tips of fibers first.

**If the spot is larger than 2 inches:**

1. Mist spot(s) with a small amount of alcohol.

2. Put a folded towel moistened with water over spot. (Keep towel damp until pro comes.)

3. Call a pro and have spot removed as soon as possible within 24 hours.

### Steps:

**Follow the instructions for your size spot(s):**

**If the spot is 2 inches or smaller:**

1. Using a disposable towel, blot the spot(s) 15 - 20 times, using a clean part of the towel each time.
   - Repeat until no more absorbs.

2. Mist on a generous amount of alcohol.
   - Allow to work 1 minute.
   - Mist on a generous amount of alcohol.
   - Agitate with end of spoon handle.

3. With the spot machine, rinse with hot water using the chop stroke technique 10 - 12 times.
   - Take 6 - 8 slow, dry vacuum strokes.

4. Look at and touch spot area carefully to see if the gummy residue is gone:
   - If YES: No further action is needed.
   - If NO: Repeat Steps 2 and 3 until no more removes. Then, if needed, do Step 5.

5. If color cast remains, mist on a generous amount of peroxide.
   - Mist on a small amount of ammonia.
   - Tamp with soft brush.
   - Allow to dry.

6. If the spot persists, call a pro for options as soon as possible.

**If the spot is larger than 2 inches:**

1. Using a towel, blot the spot(s) 15 - 20 times, using a clean part of the towel each time.
   - Repeat until no more absorbs.

2. Mist spot(s) with a small amount of alcohol.

3. Put a folded towel moistened with water over spot. (Keep towel damp until pro comes.)

4. Call a pro and have spot removed as soon as possible within 24 hours.

# Sealers: Solvent-Based, Creosote, Thompson's Water Seal®

Spot / Stain Contents: Coal Tar, Coloring, Oil, Petroleum Distillates

## Comments:

- **Optimum removal time: As soon as possible** within 24 hours of spill
- **Maximum size for home removal:** Class III / IV = 1 inch
- **Removal restrictions:** If the spot(s) is larger than 1 inch in diameter **do not attempt TOTAL removal** using Class III (use instructions for your spot size) or Class IV instructions. Do Step 1 **only** under Class III or Class IV. Mist spot(s) with a small amount of alcohol. Put a folded towel moistened with water over spot. (Keep towel damp until pro comes.) Call a pro and have spot removed as soon as possible within 24 hours.
- **Caution: Do not attempt scissors removal** of spots from **any** type of looped carpet (berber, commercial glue down, etc.) unless the spot is **only on the outside fibers** of the loop(s). If in doubt, call a pro for options as soon as possible.
- These products can immediately and permanently stain most nylon. If you cannot remove a spot, consult a pro for options as soon as possible.
- Large spills can damage latex in the carpet and pad and cause it to swell into little hills. This makes the carpet look as if it is loose and needs to be re-stretched. Consult a pro for options.

## Materials Needed:

Class III: Spotting kit, Vacuum cleaner with attachment removed from hose
Class IV: Spotting kit, Disposable towels

## Class III: Towel + Old / Dried Spot

### Steps:

**Follow the instructions for your size spot(s):**

**If the spot is 3/8 inch (pencil eraser size) or smaller:**

1. Using your scissors, wedge the blades up under the spot(s) and snip the hardened parts from the very tip of the carpet fibers. Note: On non-looped carpets, you can also trim a few carpet fibers around the edge of the removed spot, if needed, to minimize it further.
    - On non-looped carpets, rough up the trimmed carpet fibers a little with the tips of your scissors. Trim any taller roughed up fibers so they are equal in height with the rest of the carpet.
    - Vacuum debris with vacuum cleaner hose until no more removes.

2. Look at and touch spot area carefully to see if the spot is gone:
    - If YES: No further action is needed.
    - If NO: Do Step 3.

3. Mist spot(s) with a generous amount of alcohol.
    - Allow to work 2 minutes.
    - Mist on a generous amount of alcohol.
    - Agitate with end of spoon handle.

4. With a towel, blot the spot(s) 15 - 20 times, using a clean part of the towel each time.

5. Look at and touch spot area carefully to see if the gummy residue is gone:
    - If YES: No further action is needed.
    - If NO: Repeat Steps 3 and 4 until no more removes. Then, if needed, do Step 6.

6. If color cast remains, mist on a generous amount of peroxide.
    - Mist on a small amount of ammonia.
    - Tamp with soft brush.
    - Allow to dry.

7. If the spot persists, call a pro for options as soon as possible.

**If the spot is larger than 3/8 inch, but no more than 1 inch:**

1. Do Steps 3 - 7 **only** under "Class III". Do **not** trim spot from tips of fibers first.

## Class IV: Towel + Fresh / Wet Spot

### Steps:

1. Using a disposable towel, blot the spot(s) 15 - 20 times, using a clean part of the towel each time.
    - Repeat until no more absorbs.

2. Mist on a small amount of alcohol.
    - Allow to work 2 minutes.
    - Mist on a small amount of alcohol.
    - Agitate with end of spoon handle.

3. With a clean cloth towel, blot the spot(s) 15 - 20 times, using a clean part of the towel each time.

4. Look at and touch spot area carefully to see if the gummy residue is gone:
    - If YES: No further action is needed.
    - If NO: Repeat Steps 2 and 3 until no more removes. Then, if needed, do Step 5.

5. If color cast remains, mist on a generous amount of peroxide.
    - Mist on a small amount of ammonia.
    - Tamp with soft brush.
    - Allow to dry.

6. If the spot persists, call a pro for options as soon as possible.

# Shoe Polish, Dye - Liquid

## Comments:

- **Optimum removal time: As soon as possible** within 24 hours of spill
- **Maximum size for home removal:** Class I = No home removal / Class II = 1 1/4 inches
- **Removal restrictions - Class I:** See "Class I" instructions below.
- **Removal restrictions - Class II:** If the spot(s) is larger than 1 1/4 inches in diameter **do not attempt TOTAL removal** using Class II instructions. Do Steps 1 and 2 **only** under Class II. Mist spot(s) with a small amount of ammonia. Put a folded towel moistened with water over spot. (Keep towel damp until pro comes.) Call a pro and have spot removed as soon as possible within 24 hours.
- **Caution:** Strong pigments in these products can immediately and permanently stain most nylon. These pigments may be hard to remove even from olefin, polyester and acrylic if left untreated as little as 2 days. If you cannot remove a spot, consult a pro for options as soon as possible.

## Materials Needed:

Class I: Towel, Paper and pencil for note
Class II: Spotting kit, Spot machine with warm water

| Class I: Spot Machine + Old / Dried Spot | Class II: Spot Machine + Fresh / Wet Spot |
|---|---|

### Steps:

1. **Do not attempt ANY removal** of a Class I spot(s).
   - Put a dry towel over spot and a note next to it that says, **"Do Not Touch Or Clean!"**.
   - Call a pro and have spot removed as soon as possible within 24 hours.

### Steps:

1. Using a towel, blot the spot(s) 15 - 20 times, using a clean part of the towel each time.
   - Repeat until no more absorbs.

2. With the spot machine, rinse with warm water using the single stroke technique 10 - 12 times.
   - Take 6 - 8 slow, dry vacuum strokes.

3. Mist on a generous amount of alcohol.
   - Mist on a generous amount of ammonia.
   - Tamp with soft brush.
   - Allow to work 1 minute.

4. With the spot machine, rinse with warm water using the chop stroke technique 10 - 12 times.
   - Take 8 - 10 slow, dry vacuum strokes.

5. Look at spot area carefully to see if the spot is gone:
   - If YES: No further action is needed.
   - If NO: Repeat Steps 3 and 4 until no more removes. Then, if needed, do Step 6.

6. If color cast remains, mist on a generous amount of peroxide.
   - Mist on a small amount of ammonia.
   - Tamp with soft brush.
   - Allow to dry.

7. If the spot persists, call a pro for options as soon as possible.

Section II

## Comments:

- **Optimum removal time: As soon as possible** within 24 hours of spill
- **Maximum size for home removal:** Class III = No home removal / Class IV = 3/4 inch
- **Removal restrictions - Class III:** See "Class III" instructions below.
- **Removal restrictions - Class IV:** If the spot(s) is larger than 3/4 inch in diameter **do not attempt TOTAL removal** using Class IV instructions. Do Step 1 **only** under Class IV. Put a folded towel moistened with water over spot. (Keep towel damp until pro comes.) Call a pro and have spot removed as soon as possible within 24 hours.
- **Caution:** Strong pigments in these products can immediately and permanently stain most nylon. These pigments may be hard to remove even from olefin, polyester and acrylic if left untreated as little as 2 days. If you cannot remove a spot, consult a pro for options as soon as possible.

## Materials Needed:
Class III: Towel, Paper and pencil for note
Class IV: Spotting kit

### Class III: Towel + Old / Dried Spot

**Steps:**

1. **Do not attempt ANY removal** of a Class III spot(s).
   - Put a dry towel over spot and a note next to it that says, **"Do Not Touch Or Clean!"**.
   - Call a pro and have spot removed as soon as possible within 24 hours.

### Class IV: Towel + Fresh / Wet Spot

**Steps:**

1. Using a towel, blot the spot(s) 15 - 20 times, using a clean part of the towel each time.
   - Repeat until no more absorbs.

2. Mist on a small amount of alcohol.
   - Mist on a small amount of ammonia.
   - Allow to work 1 minute.
   - Tamp with soft brush.

3. With a towel, blot the spot(s) 15 - 20 times, using a clean part of the towel each time.

4. Look at spot area carefully to see if the spot is gone:
   - If YES: No further action is needed.
   - If NO: Repeat Steps 2 and 3 until no more removes. Then, if needed, do Step 5.

5. If color cast remains, mist on a generous amount of peroxide.
   - Mist on a small amount of ammonia.
   - Tamp with soft brush.
   - Allow to dry.

6. If the spot persists, call a pro for options as soon as possible.

Section II

# Shoe Polish, Dye - Paste

## Comments:

- **Optimum removal time: As soon as possible** within 24 hours of spill
- **Maximum size for home removal:** Class I / II = 1 3/4 inches
- **Removal restrictions:** If the spot(s) is larger than 1 3/4 inches in diameter, **do not attempt TOTAL removal** using Class I or II instructions. Do Step 1 **only** under Class I or II. Mist spot(s) with a small amount of ammonia. Put a folded towel moistened with water over spot. Call a pro and have spot removed within 24 hours.
- **Caution:** Strong pigments in these products can immediately and permanently stain most nylon. These pigments may be hard to remove even from olefin, polyester and acrylic if left untreated as little as 2 days. If you cannot remove a spot, consult a pro for options as soon as possible.

## Materials Needed:

Class I / II: Spotting kit, Spot machine with hot water, Disposable towels for Class II

### Class I: Spot Machine + Old / Dried Spot

**Steps:**

1. Using your dinner knife, scrape out as much of the spot(s) as possible.
   - Vacuum debris with spot machine.
   - With a towel over your hand, pinch out more of the spot, using a clean part of the towel each time.
   - Repeat entire Step until no more removes.

2. Mist on a generous amount of alcohol.
   - Mist on a generous amount of ammonia.
   - Agitate with hard brush.
   - Allow to work 2 minutes.
   - Mist on a generous amount of alcohol.
   - Agitate with hard brush.

3. With the spot machine, rinse with hot water using the chop stroke technique 10 - 12 times.
   - Take 8 - 10 slow, dry vacuum strokes.

4. Look at spot area carefully to see if the spot is gone:
   - If YES: No further action is needed.
   - If NO: Repeat Steps 2 and 3 until no more removes. Then, if needed, do Step 5.

5. If color cast remains, mist on a generous amount of peroxide.
   - Mist on a small amount of ammonia.
   - Tamp with soft brush.
   - Allow to dry.

6. If the spot persists, call a pro for options as soon as possible.

### Class II: Spot Machine + Fresh / Wet Spot

**Steps:**

1. Using your dinner knife, scrape out as much of the spot(s) as possible. Note: After each scrape, wipe the knife on a clean part of a disposable towel.
   - Repeat until no more removes.
   - With a clean cloth towel, blot 25 - 30 times, using a clean part of the towel each time.
   - Repeat entire Step until no more removes.

2. Mist on a generous amount of alcohol.
   - Mist on a generous amount of ammonia.
   - Agitate with hard brush.
   - Allow to work 1 minute.
   - Mist on a generous amount of alcohol.
   - Agitate with hard brush.

3. With the spot machine, rinse with hot water using the chop stroke technique 6 - 8 times.
   - Take 4 - 6 slow, dry vacuum strokes.

4. Look at spot area carefully to see if the spot is gone:
   - If YES: No further action is needed.
   - If NO: Repeat Steps 2 and 3 until no more removes. Then, if needed, do Step 5.

5. If color cast remains, mist on a generous amount of peroxide.
   - Mist on a small amount of ammonia.
   - Tamp with soft brush.
   - Allow to dry.

6. If the spot persists, call a pro for options as soon as possible

Section II

# Shoe Polish, Dye - Paste

Stain / Spot Contents: Oil-Soluble Dyes, Resins, Solvents, Waxes

## Comments:

- **Optimum removal time: As soon as possible** within 24 hours of spill
- **Maximum size for home removal:** Class III = No home removal / Class IV = 1 inch
- **Removal restrictions - Class III:** See "Class III" instructions below.
- **Removal restrictions - Class IV:** If the spot(s) is larger than 1 inch in diameter, **do not attempt TOTAL removal** using Class IV instructions. Do Step 1 **only** under Class IV. Mist spot(s) with a small amount of ammonia. Put a folded towel moistened with water over spot. Then:
  - Call a pro and have spot removed as soon as possible within 24 hours. -OR-
  - If the spot is 1 3/4 inches or less in diameter, get a spot machine and:
    - If the spot is now old/dried, do Steps 2 - 6 under Class I.
    - If the spot is still fresh/wet, do Steps 2 - 6 under Class II.
- **Caution:** Strong pigments in these products can immediately and permanently stain most nylon. These pigments may be hard to remove even from olefin, polyester and acrylic if left untreated as little as 2 days. If you cannot remove a spot, consult a pro for options as soon as possible.

---

## Materials Needed:

Class III: Towel, Paper and pencil for note
Class IV: Spotting kit, Disposable towels

## Class III: Towel + Old / Dried Spot

### Steps:

1. **Do not attempt ANY removal** of a Class III spot(s).
   - Put a dry towel over spot and a note next to it that says, **"Do Not Touch Or Clean!"**.
   - Then:
     - Call a pro and have spot removed within 24 hours. -OR-
     - If the spot is 1 3/4 inches or less in diameter, get a spot machine and do Steps 2 - 6 under Class I.

## Class IV: Towel + Fresh / Wet Spot

### Steps:

1. Using your dinner knife, scrape out as much of the spot(s) as possible. Note: After each scrape, wipe the knife on a clean part of a disposable towel.
   - Repeat until no more removes.
   - With a clean cloth towel, blot 25 - 30 times, using a clean part of the towel each time.
   - Repeat entire Step until no more removes.

2. Mist on a generous amount of alcohol.
   - Mist on a generous amount of ammonia.
   - Agitate with hard brush.
   - Allow to work 1 minute.
   - Mist on a small amount of alcohol.
   - Agitate with hard brush.

3. With a clean towel, blot 20 - 25 times, using a clean part of the towel each time.

4. Look at spot area carefully to see if the spot is gone:
   - If YES: No further action is needed.
   - If NO: Repeat Steps 2 and 3 until no more removes. Then, if needed, do Step 5.

5. If color cast remains, mist on a generous amount of peroxide.
   - Mist on a small amount of ammonia.
   - Tamp with soft brush.
   - Allow to dry.

6. If the spot persists, call a pro for options as soon as possible.

Section II

# Silver Nitrate - Medicinal or Photographic, Nutritional Silver (Colloidal)

## Comments:

- **Optimum removal time: As soon as possible** within 24 hours of spill
- **Maximum size for home removal:** No home removal
- **Removal restrictions:** See "Class I" or "Class II" instructions below.
- These products can immediately and permanently stain most nylon.
- **Caution:** Microscopic silver particles in these products may be hard to remove, even from olefin, polyester and acrylic fiber carpets, if left untreated as little as 2 days.

## Materials Needed:

Class I: Towel, Paper and pencil for note
Class II: Spot machine with warm water, Towel, Paper and pencil for note

| Class I: Spot Machine + Old / Dried Spot | Class II: Spot Machine + Fresh / Wet Spot |
|---|---|
| **Steps:** | **Steps:** |
| 1. **Do not attempt ANY removal** of a Class I spot(s). | 1. **Do not attempt TOTAL removal** of a Class II spot(s). |
| • Put a dry towel over spot and a note next to it that says, **"Do Not Touch Or Clean!"**. | • With your spot machine, rinse the spot with warm water using the single stroke technique 25 - 30 times. |
| • Call a pro and have spot removed as soon as possible within 24 hours. | • Repeat until no more removes. |
| | 2. Put a folded towel moistened with water over spot and a note next to it that says, **"Do Not Touch Or Clean!"**. (Keep towel damp until pro comes.) |
| | • Call a pro and have spot removed as soon as possible within 24 hours. |

Spot Contents: Silver Compounds, Silver Salts, Silver Mineral Colloids

## Comments:

- **Optimum removal time: As soon as possible** within 24 hours of spill
- **Maximum size for home removal:** No home removal
- **Removal restrictions:** See "Class III" or "Class IV" instructions below.
- These products can immediately and permanently stain most nylon.
- **Caution:** Microscopic silver particles in these products may be hard to remove, even from olefin, polyester and acrylic fiber carpets, if left untreated as little as 2 days.

## Materials Needed:

Class III / IV: Towel(s), Paper and pencil for note

### Class III: Towel + Old / Dried Spot

**Steps:**

1. **Do not attempt ANY removal** of a Class III spot(s).
   - Put a dry towel over spot and a note next to it that says, **"Do Not Touch Or Clean!"**.
   - Call a pro and have spot removed as soon as possible within 24 hours.

### Class IV: Towel + Fresh / Wet Spot

**Steps:**

1. **Do not attempt TOTAL removal** of a Class IV spot(s).
   - With a towel, blot the spot 25 - 35 times, using a clean part of the towel each time.
   - Repeat until no more transfer occurs.
2. Put a folded towel moistened with water over spot and a note next to it that says, **"Do Not Touch Or Clean!"**.
   (Keep towel damp until pro comes.)
   - Call a pro and have spot removed as soon as possible within 24 hours.

Section II

# Snacks - Dry:
## Cheese Puffs, Corn Chips, Peanuts, Popcorn, Potato Chips, Tortilla Chips, Etc.

### Comments:

- **Optimum removal time: As soon as possible** within 24 hours of spill
- **Maximum size for home removal:** Class I: If dry = 18 inches / Class II: If wet = 8 inches
- **Removal restrictions:** If the dry spot(s) is larger than 18 inches in diameter or a wet spot is larger than 8 inches, **do not attempt TOTAL removal** using Class I or II instructions. Do Step 1 **only** under Class I or II. Put a dry towel over spot and a note next to it that says, "*Do Not Touch Or Clean!*". Call a pro and have spot removed within 2 days.
- **Caution:** Food coloring in some products can permanently stain some nylon if left untreated as little as 7 days. If you cannot remove a spot, consult a pro for options as soon as possible.
- Oils in many products can cause recurring spots if not completely removed. (See "Recurring Spots", Chapter 4.)

### Materials Needed:
Class I / II: Spotting kit, Spot machine with hot water

| Class I: Spot Machine + Old / Dried Spot | Class II: Spot Machine + Fresh / Wet Spot |
|---|---|
| **Steps:** | **Steps:** |
| 1. Lay a small towel over the palm of your hand. Then lay your hand on the carpet so the towel is at the edge of the spot. | 1. Lay a small towel over the palm of your hand. Then lay your hand on the carpet so the towel is at the edge of the spot. |
| • Using your spoon, scoop as much of the spot(s) as possible into the towel. Note: After each scoop, wipe the spoon on a clean part of the towel. | • Using your spoon, scoop as much of the spot(s) as possible into the towel. Note: After each scoop, wipe the spoon on a clean part of the towel. |
| • Carefully drop the dirty towel in your empty bucket. | • Carefully drop the dirty towel in your empty bucket. |
| • Vacuum debris with spot machine. | • Vacuum debris with spot machine. |
| • Agitate with soft brush. | • Agitate with soft brush. |
| • Vacuum debris with spot machine. | • Vacuum debris with spot machine. |
| • Repeat entire Step until no more removes. | • Repeat entire Step until no more removes. |
| 2. Mist on a generous amount of alcohol. | 2. Mist on a generous amount of alcohol. |
| • Agitate with soft brush. | • Agitate with soft brush. |
| • Mist on a small amount of ammonia. | • Mist on a small amount of ammonia. |
| • Agitate with soft brush. | • Agitate with soft brush. |
| • Allow to work 1 minute. | • Allow to work 1 minute. |
| 3. With the spot machine, rinse with hot water using the single stroke technique 10 - 25 times. | 3. With the spot machine, rinse with hot water using the single stroke technique 10 - 25 times. |
| • Take 10 - 12 slow, dry vacuum strokes. | • Take 10 - 12 slow, dry vacuum strokes. |
| 4. Look at spot area carefully to see if the spot is gone: | 4. Look at spot area carefully to see if the spot is gone: |
| • If YES: Allow to dry. | • If YES: Allow to dry. |
| • If NO: Repeat Steps 2 and 3 until no more removes. Then, if needed, do Step 5. | • If NO: Repeat Steps 2 and 3 until no more removes. Then, if needed, do Step 5. |
| 5. If color cast remains, mist on a generous amount of peroxide. | 5. If color cast remains, mist on a generous amount of peroxide. |
| • Tamp with soft brush. | • Tamp with soft brush. |
| • Allow to dry. | • Allow to dry. |
| 6. If needed, repeat Step 5 one time. | 6. If needed, repeat Step 5 one time. |
| 7. If the spot persists, call a pro for options as soon as possible. | 7. If the spot persists, call a pro for options as soon as possible. |

Section II

Spot Contents: Corn, Potato, Nuts, Oils, Spices, Possible Food Coloring

## Comments:

- **Optimum removal time: As soon as possible** within 24 hours of spill
- **Maximum size for home removal:** Class III: If dry = 8 inches / Class IV: If wet = 5 inches
- **Removal restrictions:** If the dry spot(s) is larger than 8 inches in diameter or a wet spot is larger than 5 inches, **do not attempt TOTAL removal** using Class III or IV instructions. Do Step 1 **only** under Class III or IV. Put a dry towel over spot and a note next to it that says, "***Do Not Touch Or Clean!***". Then:
  - Call a pro and have spot removed within 2 days. -OR-
  - If a dry spot is 18 inches or less in diameter or a wet spot is 8 inches or less, get a spot machine and:
    - If the spot is dry, do Steps 2 - 7 under Class I.
    - If the spot is still wet, do Steps 2 - 7 under Class II.
- **Caution:** Food coloring in some products can permanently stain some nylon if left untreated as little as 7 days. If you cannot remove a spot, consult a pro for options as soon as possible.
- Oils in many products can cause recurring spots if not completely removed. (See "Recurring Spots", Chapter 4.)

## Materials Needed:

Class III / IV: Spotting kit, Vacuum cleaner with attachment removed from hose

| Class III: Towel + Old / Dried Spot | Class IV: Towel + Fresh / Wet Spot |
|---|---|
| **Steps:** | **Steps:** |
| 1. Lay a small towel over the palm of your hand. Then lay your hand on the carpet so the towel is at the edge of the spot. | 1. Lay a small towel over the palm of your hand. Then lay your hand on the carpet so the towel is at the edge of the spot. |
| • Using your spoon, scoop as much of the spot(s) as possible into the towel. Note: After each scoop, wipe the spoon on a clean part of the towel. | • Using your spoon, scoop as much of the spot(s) as possible into the towel. Note: After each scoop, wipe the spoon on a clean part of the towel. |
| • Carefully drop the dirty towel in your empty bucket. | • Carefully drop the dirty towel in your empty bucket. |
| • Vacuum debris with vacuum cleaner hose. | • Vacuum debris with vacuum cleaner hose. |
| • Agitate with soft brush. | • Agitate with soft brush. |
| • Vacuum debris with vacuum cleaner hose. | • Vacuum debris with vacuum cleaner hose. |
| • Repeat entire Step until no more removes. | • Repeat entire Step until no more removes. |
| 2. Mist on a small amount of alcohol. | 2. Mist on a small amount of alcohol. |
| • Agitate with soft brush. | • Agitate with soft brush. |
| • Mist on a small amount of ammonia. | • Mist on a small amount of ammonia. |
| • Agitate with soft brush. | • Agitate with soft brush. |
| • Allow to work 1 minute. | • Allow to work 1 minute. |
| 3. With a towel, firmly blot 20 - 35 times, using a clean part of the towel each time. | 3. With a towel, firmly blot 20 - 35 times, using a clean part of the towel each time. |
| 4. Look at spot area carefully to see if the spot is gone: | 4. Look at spot area carefully to see if the spot is gone: |
| • If YES: Allow to dry. | • If YES: Allow to dry. |
| • If NO: Repeat Steps 2 and 3 until no more removes. Then, if needed, do Step 5. | • If NO: Repeat Steps 2 and 3 until no more removes. Then, if needed, do Step 5. |
| 5. If color cast remains, mist on a generous amount of peroxide. | 5. If color cast remains, mist on a generous amount of peroxide. |
| • Tamp with soft brush. | • Tamp with soft brush. |
| • Allow to dry. | • Allow to dry. |
| 6. If needed, repeat Step 5 one time. | 6. If needed, repeat Step 5 one time. |
| 7. If the spot persists, call a pro for options as soon as possible. | 7. If the spot persists, call a pro for options as soon as possible. |

Section II

# Soft Drinks - All Flavors / Diet and Regular, Sports Drinks, Isotonics

## Comments:

- **Optimum removal time: As soon as possible** within 24 hours of spill
- **Maximum size for home removal:** Class I / II = 3 1/2 inches
- **Removal restrictions:** If the spot(s) is larger than 3 1/2 inches in diameter, **do not attempt ANY removal** using Class I or II instructions. Put a folded towel moistened with water over spot. (Keep towel damp until pro comes.) Call a pro and have spot removed as soon as possible within 24 hours.
- Coloring in some products (especially red and orange drinks) can immediately and permanently stain some nylon. If you cannot remove a spot, consult a pro for options as soon as possible.
- Large spills can cause recurring spots that need re-treatment. (See "Recurring Spots", Chapter 4.) If a spot persists, consult a pro for options as soon as possible.

## Materials Needed:

Class I / II: Spotting kit, Spot machine with hot water

### Class I: Spot Machine + Old / Dried Spot

**Steps:**

1. Using your spot machine, rinse the spot(s) with hot water using the chop stroke technique 10 - 25 times.
   - Take 6 - 15 slow, dry vacuum strokes.
   - Repeat entire Step until sticky residue is gone.
2. Mist on a generous amount of ammonia.
   - Tamp with soft brush.
   - Mist on a generous amount of peroxide.
   - Tamp with soft brush.
   - Allow to work 1 minute.
3. With the spot machine, rinse with hot water using the chop stroke technique 6 - 10 times.
   - Take 4 - 8 slow, dry vacuum strokes.
4. Look at spot area carefully to see if the spot is gone:
   - If YES: Allow to dry.
   - If NO: Repeat Steps 2 and 3 until no more removes. Then, if needed, do Step 5.
5. If color cast remains, mist on a generous amount of peroxide.
   - Mist on a small amount of ammonia.
   - Tamp with soft brush.
   - Allow to dry.
6. If needed, repeat Step 5 one time.
7. If the spot persists, call a pro for options as soon as possible.

### Class II: Spot Machine + Fresh / Wet Spot

**Steps:**

1. Using your spot machine, dry vacuum the spot(s) 10 - 15 times taking slow, single strokes.
   - Rinse with hot water using the chop stroke technique 6 - 8 times.
   - Take 4 - 6 slow, dry vacuum strokes.
   - Repeat entire Step until sticky residue is gone.
2. Mist on a small amount of ammonia.
   - Tamp with soft brush.
   - Mist on a generous amount of peroxide.
   - Tamp with soft brush.
   - Allow to work 1 minute.
3. With the spot machine, rinse with hot water using the chop stroke technique 6 - 8 times.
   - Take 4 - 6 slow, dry vacuum strokes.
4. Look at spot area carefully to see if the spot is gone:
   - If YES: Allow to dry.
   - If NO: Repeat Steps 2 and 3 until no more removes. Then, if needed, do Step 5.
5. If color cast remains, mist on a generous amount of peroxide.
   - Mist on a small amount of ammonia.
   - Tamp with soft brush.
   - Allow to dry.
6. If needed, repeat Step 5 one time.
7. If the spot persists, call a pro for options as soon as possible.

Section II

## Comments:

- **Optimum removal time: As soon as possible** within 24 hours of spill
- **Maximum size for home removal:** Class III = No home removal / Class IV = 2 inches
- **Removal restrictions - Class III:** No home removal. See "Class III" instructions below.
- **Removal restrictions - Class IV:** If the spot(s) is larger than 2 inches in diameter, **do not attempt TOTAL removal** using Class IV instructions. Do Step 1 **only** under Class IV. Put a folded towel moistened with water over spot. (Keep towel damp until pro comes.) Then:
  - Call a pro and have spot removed as soon as possible within 24 hours. -OR-
  - If the spot is 3 1/2 inches or less in diameter, get a spot machine and:
    - If the spot is now old/dried, do Steps 1 - 7 under Class I.
    - If the spot is still fresh/wet, do Steps 1 - 7 under Class II.
- Coloring in some products (especially red and orange drinks) can immediately and permanently stain some nylon. If you cannot remove a spot, consult a pro for options as soon as possible.
- Large spills can cause recurring spots that need re-treatment. (See "Recurring Spots", Chapter 4.) If a spot persists, consult a pro for options as soon as possible.

## Materials Needed:

Class III: Dry towel
Class IV: Spotting kit

| Class III: Towel + Old / Dried Spot | Class IV: Towel + Fresh / Wet Spot |
|---|---|

### Steps:

1. **Do not attempt ANY removal** of a Class III spot.

    - Put a dry towel over the spot(s) to prevent spreading sticky residue. Then:
      - Call a pro and have spot removed as soon as possible within 24 hours. -OR-
      - If the spot is 3 1/2 inches or less in diameter, get a spot machine and do Steps 1 - 7 under Class I.

### Steps:

1. Fold a towel several times and place it over the spot(s).

    - Step on the towel with your full weight 8 - 10 times, using a clean part of the towel each time.
    - Repeat until no more absorbs.

2. Mist on a small amount of ammonia.

    - Tamp with soft brush.
    - Mist on a generous amount of peroxide.
    - Tamp with soft brush.
    - Allow to work 1 minute.

3. With a towel, blot 10 - 15 times, using a clean part of the towel each time.

4. Look at spot area carefully to see if the spot is gone:

    - If YES: Allow to dry.
    - If NO: Repeat Steps 2 and 3 until no more removes. Then if needed, do Step 5.

5. If color cast remains, mist on a generous amount of peroxide.

    - Mist on a small amount of ammonia.
    - Tamp with soft brush.
    - Allow to dry.

6. If needed, repeat Step 5 one time.

7. If the spot persists, call a pro for options as soon as possible.

Section II

# Solvents: Paint Thinner, Mineral Spirits, Engine or Carburetor Cleaners

## Comments:

- **Optimum removal time: As soon as possible** within 24 hours of spill
- **Maximum size for home removal:** Class I / II = 12 inches
- **Removal restrictions:** If the spot(s) is larger than 12 inches in diameter, **do not attempt ANY removal** using Class I instructions; **do not attempt TOTAL removal** using Class II instructions. Do Step 1 **only** under Class II. Put a note next to the spot that says, *"Do Not Touch Or Clean!"*. Call a pro and have spot removed as soon as possible.
- Large spills can damage latex in the carpet and pad and cause it to swell into little hills. This makes the carpet look as if it is loose and needs to be re-stretched. Consult a pro for options.

## Materials Needed:

Class I: Gloves, Ruler, Spot machine with hot water
Class II: Gloves, Ruler, Spot machine with hot water, Disposable towels, Fan, Paper and pencil for note

| Class I: Spot Machine + Old / Dried Spot | Class II: Spot Machine + Fresh / Wet Spot |
|---|---|
| **Steps:** | **Steps:** |
| 1. Look for bubbles due to damaged carpet backing or pad in the spot area. | 1. Prepare your spot machine: |
| 2. Prepare your spot machine: | • Put 12 oz. of water in the collection / dirty water tank of your spot machine to prevent the solvents from damaging the plastic tank. |
| • Put 8 oz. of water in the collection / dirty water tank of your spot machine to prevent the solvents from damaging the plastic tank. | 2. Fold a disposable towel several times and place it over the spot(s). |
| 3. With the spot machine, rinse the spot(s) with hot water using the single stroke technique 20 - 30 times. | • Step on the towel with your full weight 15 - 30 times, using a clean part of the towel each time. |
| 4. **Immediately dump the water** in the collection / dirty water tank of your spot machine. Caution: Solvents, even when diluted, can damage the plastic tank if left in contact with it. | • Repeat until no more absorbs. |
| 5. **Do not continue removal** of a Class I spot. | 3. With the spot machine, dry vacuum the spot(s) using the single stroke technique 40 - 50 times. |
| • Allow spot to dry. | 4. **Immediately dump the water** in the collection / dirty water tank of your spot machine. Caution: Solvents, even when diluted, can damage the plastic tank if left in contact with it. |
| 6. Smell spot area carefully to see if the spot odor is gone: | 5. **Do not continue removal** of a Class II spot. |
| • If YES: No further action is needed. | 6. Dry the spot: |
| • If NO: Call a pro for options. | • Put a fan 4 feet away from the spot. |
| | • Put the fan on the High setting to speed dry the spot. |
| | • Put a note next to the spot that says, *"Do Not Touch Or Clean!"*. (Put something heavy on the note to keep it from blowing away.) |
| | • Allow spot to dry completely. |
| | 7. Smell spot area carefully to see if the spot odor is gone: |
| | • If YES: No further action is needed. |
| | • If NO: Call a pro for options. |

Section II

# Solvents: Paint Thinner, Mineral Spirits, Engine or Carburetor Cleaners

Spot Contents: Petroleum Distillate, Methanol, Toluene, Acetone, Methyl Ethyl Ketone, Propylene Glycol, MonoMethyl

## Comments:

- **Optimum removal time: As soon as possible** within 24 hours of spill
- **Maximum size for home removal:** Class III = No home removal / Class IV = 12 inches
- **Removal restrictions:** If the spot(s) is larger than 12 inches in diameter, **do not attempt TOTAL removal** using Class IV instructions. Do Steps 1 and 2 **only** under Class IV. Put a note next to the spot that says, **"*Do Not Touch Or Clean*!"**. Call a pro and have spot removed as soon as possible.
- Large spills can damage latex in the carpet and pad and cause it to swell into little hills. This makes the carpet look as if it is loose and needs to be re-stretched. Consult a pro for options.

## Materials Needed:

Class III: Paper and pencil
Class IV: Gloves, Ruler, Disposable towels, Fan, Paper and pencil for note

## Class III: Towel + Old / Dried Spot

### Steps:

1. **Do not attempt ANY removal** of a Class III spot.
   - Put a note next to the spot(s) that says, **"*Do Not Touch Or Clean!*"**.
   - Call a pro and have spot removed as soon as possible within 24 hours.

## Class IV: Towel + Fresh / Wet Spot

### Steps:

1. Fold a disposable towel several times and place it over the spot(s).
   - Step on the towel with your full weight 15 - 30 times, using a clean part of the towel each time.
   - Repeat until no more absorbs.

2. **Do not continue removal** of a Class IV spot.

3. Dry the spot:
   - Put a fan 4 feet away from the spot.
   - Put the fan on the High setting to speed dry the spot.
   - Put a note next to the spot that says, **"*Do Not Touch Or Clean!*"**. (Put something heavy on the note to keep it from blowing away.)
   - Allow spot to dry completely.

4. Smell spot area carefully to see if the spot odor is gone:
   - If YES: No further action is needed.
   - If NO: Call a pro for options.

# Soot, Automobile Exhaust Grime, Ashes, Fireplace Grime, Face Powder

## Comments:

- **Optimum removal time:** Within 24 hours of spill
- **Maximum size for home removal:** Class I / II = 1 inch
- **Removal restrictions:** If the spot(s) is larger than 1 inch in diameter, **do not attempt TOTAL removal** using Class I or II instructions. Do Steps 1 and 2 **only** under Class I or II. Put a dry towel over spot and a note next to it that says, *"Do Not Touch Or Clean!"*. Call a pro and have spot removed within 2 days.
- **Caution:** Do **not** use a vacuum cleaner with a beater bar on this spot. The beater bar could spread the spot, making it even harder to remove. **Note:** Your vacuum's instruction booklet may tell how to temporarily disable the beater bar. If so, follow those instructions and then use the vacuum to help remove the spot.
- Very fine, sometimes oily, particles in these products can be very hard to remove from twist style carpets such as saxony. If you cannot remove a spot, consult a pro for options as soon as possible.

## Materials Needed:

Class I / II: Spotting kit, Vacuum cleaner, Spot machine with hot water

| Class I: Spot Machine + Old / Dried Spot | Class II: Spot Machine + Fresh / Wet Spot |
|---|---|
| **Steps:** | **Steps:** |
| 1. Prepare your vacuum cleaner:<br>  • Remove the attachment, if any, from the vacuum cleaner hose. | 1. Prepare your vacuum cleaner:<br>  • Remove the attachment, if any, from the vacuum cleaner hose. |
| 2. Using just the vacuum cleaner hose, vacuum the spot very slowly:<br>  • Lay the hose so it is flat on the carpet with the opening near the outside edge of the spot.<br>  • Slowly push the hose opening from the edge into the middle of the spot from different angles 8 - 10 times until no more will remove.<br>  • Lift the hose and place it so the opening is on the carpet directly over the spot.<br>  • Move the hose opening slowly in a circular motion clockwise and counterclockwise over and around the edges of the spot. Caution: Keep within the edges of the spot; going outside them could spread the spot.<br>  • With a towel, blot 15 - 20 times, using a clean part of the towel each time.<br>  • Repeat entire Step until no more removes. | 2. Using just the vacuum cleaner hose, vacuum the spot very slowly:<br>  • Lay the hose so it is flat on the carpet with the opening near the outside edge of the spot.<br>  • Slowly push the hose opening from the edge into the middle of the spot from different angles 8 - 10 times until no more will remove.<br>  • Lift the hose and place it so the opening is on the carpet directly over the spot.<br>  • Move the hose opening slowly in a circular motion clockwise and counterclockwise over and around the edges of the spot. Caution: Keep within the edges of the spot; going outside them could spread the spot.<br>  • With a towel, blot 15 - 20 times, using a clean part of the towel each time.<br>  • Repeat entire Step until no more removes. |
| 3. Mist on a small amount of alcohol.<br>  • Mist on a small amount of ammonia.<br>  • Tamp gently with soft brush.<br>  • Allow to work 2 minutes.<br>  • Mist on a small amount of alcohol.<br>  • Tamp gently with soft brush. | 3. Mist on a small amount of alcohol.<br>  • Mist on a small amount of ammonia.<br>  • Tamp gently with soft brush.<br>  • Allow to work 2 minutes.<br>  • Mist on a small amount of alcohol.<br>  • Tamp gently with soft brush. |
| 4. With the spot machine, rinse with hot water using the chop stroke technique 10 - 12 times.<br>  • Take 8 - 10 slow, dry vacuum strokes. | 4. With the spot machine, rinse with hot water using the chop stroke technique 8 - 10 times.<br>  • Take 6 - 8 slow, dry vacuum strokes. |
| 5. Look at spot area carefully to see if the spot is gone:<br>  • If YES: Allow to dry.<br>  • If NO: Repeat Steps 3 and 4 until no more removes. | 5. Look at spot area carefully to see if the spot is gone:<br>  • If YES: Allow to dry.<br>  • If NO: Repeat Steps 3 and 4 until no more removes. |
| 6. If the spot persists, call a pro for options as soon as possible. | 6. If the spot persists, call a pro for options as soon as possible. |

Section II

Spot Contents: Carbon, Oil, Soil

## Comments:

- **Optimum removal time:** Within 24 hours of spill
- **Maximum size for home removal:** No total home removal
- **Removal restrictions:** See "Class III" or "Class IV" instructions below.
- **Caution:** Do **not** use a vacuum cleaner with a beater bar on this spot. The beater bar could spread the spot, making it even harder to remove. **Note:** Your vacuum's instruction booklet may tell how to temporarily disable the beater bar. If so, follow those instructions and then use the vacuum to help remove the spot.
- Very fine, sometimes oily, particles in these products can be very hard to remove from twist style carpets such as saxony. If you cannot remove a spot, consult a pro for options as soon as possible.

## Materials Needed:

Class III / IV: Spotting kit, Vacuum cleaner, Paper and pencil for note

| Class III: Towel + Old / Dried Spot | Class IV: Towel + Fresh / Wet Spot |
|---|---|
| **Steps:** | **Steps:** |
| 1. Prepare your vacuum cleaner:<br>• Remove the attachment, if any, from the vacuum cleaner hose. | 1. Prepare your vacuum cleaner:<br>• Remove the attachment, if any, from the vacuum cleaner hose. |
| 2. Using just the vacuum cleaner hose, vacuum the spot very slowly:<br>• Lay the hose so it is flat on the carpet with the opening near the outside edge of the spot.<br>• Slowly push the hose opening from the edge into the middle of the spot from different angles 8 - 10 times until no more will remove.<br>• Lift the hose and place it so the opening is on the carpet directly over the spot.<br>• Move the hose opening slowly in a circular motion clockwise and counterclockwise over and around the edges of the spot. Caution: Keep within the edges of the spot; going outside them could spread the spot.<br>• With a towel, blot 15 - 20 times, using a clean part of the towel each time.<br>• Repeat entire Step until no more removes. | 2. Using just the vacuum cleaner hose, vacuum the spot very slowly:<br>• Lay the hose so it is flat on the carpet with the opening near the outside edge of the spot.<br>• Slowly push the hose opening from the edge into the middle of the spot from different angles 8 - 10 times until no more will remove.<br>• Lift the hose and place it so the opening is on the carpet directly over the spot.<br>• Move the hose opening slowly in a circular motion clockwise and counterclockwise over and around the edges of the spot. Caution: Keep within the edges of the spot; going outside them could spread the spot.<br>• With a towel, blot 15 - 20 times, using a clean part of the towel each time.<br>• Repeat entire Step until no more removes. |
| 3. **Do not continue removal** for a Class III spot(s).<br>• Put a dry towel over spot and a note next to it that says, **"Do Not Touch Or Clean!"**. Then:<br>  - Call a pro and have spot removed within 2 days. -OR-<br>  - If the spot is 1 inch or less in diameter, get a spot machine and do Steps 3 - 6 under Class I. | 3. **Do not continue removal** for a Class IV spot(s).<br>• Put a dry towel over spot and a note next to it that says, **"Do Not Touch Or Clean!"**. Then:<br>  - Call a pro and have spot removed within 2 days. -OR-<br>  - If the spot is 1 inch or less in diameter, get a spot machine and do Steps 3 - 6 under Class II. |

Section II

# Soup - Thick, Cream Of (All thick soups, including Tomato)

## Comments:

- **Optimum removal time:** Within 24 hours of spill
- **Maximum size for home removal:** Class I / II = 4 1/2 inches
- **Removal restrictions:** If the spot(s) is larger than 4 1/2 inches in diameter, **do not attempt TOTAL removal** using Class I or II instructions. Do Step 1 **only** under Class I or II. Mist spot(s) with a small amount of ammonia. Put a folded towel moistened with water over spot. (Keep towel damp until pro comes.) Call a pro and have spot removed within 2 days.
- Food coloring and turmeric in some products can immediately and permanently stain most nylon. If you cannot remove a spot, consult a pro for options as soon as possible.
- Oils and fats in some products can cause recurring spots. (See "Recurring Spots", Chapter 4.) Consult a pro for options as soon as possible.

## Materials Needed:

Class I / II: Spotting kit, Spot machine with warm water

### Class I: Spot Machine + Old / Dried Spot

**Steps:**

1. Using your spoon, scrape out as much of the spot(s) as possible.
   - Vacuum debris with spot machine.
   - Repeat entire Step until no more removes.

2. Mist on a generous amount of ammonia.
   - Mist on a generous amount of alcohol.
   - Agitate with hard brush.
   - Allow to work 2 minutes.

3. With the spot machine, rinse with warm water using the chop stroke technique 10 - 12 times.
   - Take 8 - 10 slow, dry vacuum strokes.

4. Look at spot area carefully to see if the spot is gone:
   - If YES: No further action is needed.
   - If NO: Repeat Steps 2 and 3 until no more removes. Then, if needed, do Step 5.

5. If color cast remains, mist on a generous amount of peroxide.
   - Tamp with soft brush.
   - Allow to dry.

6. If needed, repeat Step 5 one time.

7. If the spot persists, call a pro for options as soon as possible.

### Class II: Spot Machine + Fresh / Wet Spot

**Steps:**

1. Lay a small towel over the palm of your hand. Then lay your hand on the carpet so the towel is at the edge of the spot.
   - Using your spoon, scoop as much of the spot(s) as possible into the towel. Note: After each scoop, wipe the spoon on a clean part of the towel.
   - Carefully drop the dirty towel in your empty bucket.

2. With the spot machine, rinse with warm water using the single stroke technique 10 - 15 times.
   - Take 8 - 10 slow, dry vacuum strokes.

3. Mist on a generous amount of ammonia.
   - Mist on a generous amount of alcohol.
   - Agitate with hard brush.
   - Allow to work 1 minute.

4. With the spot machine, rinse with warm water using the single stroke technique 6 - 8 times.
   - Take 4 - 6 slow, dry vacuum strokes.

5. Look at spot area carefully to see if the spot is gone:
   - If YES: No further action is needed.
   - If NO: Repeat Steps 3 and 4 until no more removes. Then, if needed, do Step 6.

6. If color cast remains, mist on a small amount of peroxide.
   - Tamp with soft brush.
   - Allow to dry.

7. If needed, repeat Step 5 one time.

8. If the spot persists, call a pro for options as soon as possible.

## Comments:

- **Optimum removal time:** Within 24 hours of spill
- **Maximum size for home removal:** Class III / IV = 2 1/2 inches
- **Removal restrictions:** If the spot(s) is larger than 2 1/2 inches in diameter, **do not attempt TOTAL removal** using Class III or IV instructions. Do Step 1 **only** under Class III or IV. Mist spot(s) with a small amount of ammonia. Put a folded towel moistened with water over spot. (Keep towel damp until pro comes.) Then:
  - Call a pro and have spot removed within 2 days. -OR-
  - If the spot is 4 1/2 inches or less in diameter, get a spot machine and:
    - If the spot is now old/dried, do Steps 2 - 7 under Class I.
    - If the spot is still fresh/wet, do Steps 2 - 8 under Class II.
- Food coloring and turmeric in some products can immediately and permanently stain most nylon. If you cannot remove a spot, consult a pro for options as soon as possible.
- Oils or fat in some products can cause recurring spots. (See "Recurring Spots", Chapter 4.) Consult a pro for options as soon as possible.

## Materials Needed:
Class III: Spotting kit, Vacuum cleaner with attachment removed from hose
Class IV: Spotting kit

## Class III: Towel + Old / Dried Spot

### Steps:

1. Using your spoon, scrape out as much of the spot(s) as possible.
   - Vacuum debris with vacuum cleaner hose.
   - Repeat entire Step until no more removes.

2. Mist on a generous amount of ammonia.
   - Mist on a generous amount of alcohol.
   - Agitate with hard brush.
   - Allow to work 2 minutes.
   - Mist on a small amount of ammonia.
   - Agitate with hard brush.

3. With a towel, blot 20 - 25 times, using a clean part of the towel each time.

4. Look at spot area carefully to see if the spot is gone:
   - If YES: No further action is needed.
   - If NO: Repeat Steps 2 and 3 until no more removes. Then, if needed, do Step 5.

5. If color cast remains, mist on a generous amount of peroxide.
   - Tamp with soft brush.
   - Allow to dry.

6. If needed, repeat Step 5 one time.

7. If spot persists, call a pro for options as soon as possible.

## Class IV: Towel + Fresh / Wet Spot

### Steps:

1. Lay a small towel over the palm of your hand. Then lay your hand on the carpet so the towel is at the edge of the spot.
   - Using your spoon, scoop as much of the spot(s) as possible into the towel. Note: After each scoop, wipe the spoon on a clean part of the towel.
   - Carefully drop the dirty towel in your empty bucket.
   - With a clean towel, blot the spot(s) 20 - 30 times, using a clean part of the towel each time.
   - Repeat entire Step until no more removes.

2. Mist on a small amount of ammonia.
   - Mist on a generous amount of alcohol.
   - Agitate with hard brush.
   - Allow to work 2 minutes.
   - Mist on a small amount of ammonia.
   - Agitate with hard brush.

3. With a clean towel, blot 20 - 25 times, using a clean part of the towel each time.

4. Look at spot area carefully to see if the spot is gone:
   - If YES: No further action is needed.
   - If NO: Repeat Steps 2 and 3 until no more removes. Then, if needed, do Step 5.

5. If color cast remains, mist on a small amount of peroxide.
   - Tamp with soft brush.
   - Allow to dry.

6. If needed, repeat Step 5 one time.

7. If spot persists, call a pro for options as soon as possible.

Section II

# Soup - Thin, Watery (All thin soups, including Tomato), White Clam Sauce, Pickle Relish, Pico de Gallo

## Comments:

- **Optimum removal time: As soon as possible** within 24 hours of spill
- **Maximum size for home removal:** Class I / II = 3 1/2 inches
- **Removal restrictions:** If the spot(s) is larger than 3 1/2 inches in diameter, **do not attempt TOTAL removal** using Class I or II instructions. Do Step 1 **only** under Class I or II. Mist spot(s) with a small amount of ammonia. Put a folded towel moistened with water over spot. (Keep towel damp until pro comes.) Call a pro and have spot removed as soon as possible within 24 hours.
- Food coloring and turmeric in some products can immediately and permanently stain most nylon. If you cannot remove a spot, consult a pro for options as soon as possible.
- Oils or fat in some products can cause recurring spots. (See "Recurring Spots", Chapter 4.) Consult a pro for options as soon as possible.

## Materials Needed:

Class I / II: Spotting kit, Spot machine with warm water

Section II

## Class I: Spot Machine + Old / Dried Spot

### Steps:

1. Using your spoon, scrape out as much of the spot(s) as possible.
   - Vacuum debris with spot machine.
   - Using your hard brush, agitate the spot 15 - 20 times.
   - Vacuum debris with spot machine.
   - Repeat entire Step until no more removes.

2. Mist on a generous amount of ammonia.
   - Mist on a generous amount of alcohol.
   - Agitate with hard brush.
   - Allow to work 2 minutes.

3. With the spot machine, rinse with warm water using the chop stroke technique 10 - 12 times.
   - Take 8 - 10 slow, dry vacuum strokes.

4. Look at spot area carefully to see if the spot is gone:
   - If YES: No further action is needed.
   - If NO: Repeat Steps 2 and 3 until no more removes. Then, if needed, do Step 5.

5. If color cast remains, mist on a generous amount of peroxide.
   - Mist on a small amount of ammonia.
   - Tamp with soft brush.
   - Allow to dry.

6. If needed, repeat Step 5 one time.

7. If the spot persists, call a pro for options as soon as possible.

## Class II: Spot Machine + Fresh / Wet Spot

### Steps:

1. Lay a small towel over the palm of your hand. Then lay your hand on the carpet so the towel is at the edge of the spot.
   - Using your spoon, scoop as much of the spot(s) as possible into the towel. Note: After each scoop, wipe the spoon on a clean part of the towel.
   - Carefully drop the dirty towel in your empty bucket.

2. With the spot machine, dry vacuum liquid using the single stroke technique 8 - 10 times.
   - Rinse with warm water using the single stroke technique 10 - 15 times.
   - Take 6 - 8 slow, dry vacuum strokes.

3. Mist on a generous amount of ammonia.
   - Mist on a generous amount of alcohol.
   - Agitate with hard brush.
   - Allow to work 1 minute.

4. With the spot machine, rinse with warm water using the single stroke technique 6 - 8 times.
   - Take 4 - 6 slow, dry vacuum strokes.

5. Look at spot area carefully to see if the spot is gone:
   - If YES: No further action is needed.
   - If NO: Repeat Steps 3 and 4 until no more removes. Then, if needed, do Step 6.

6. If color cast remains, mist on a small amount of peroxide.
   - Mist on a small amount of ammonia.
   - Tamp with soft brush.
   - Allow to dry.

7. If needed, repeat Step 5 one time.

8. If the spot persists, call a pro for options as soon as possible.

# Soup - Thin, Watery (All thin soups, including Tomato), White Clam Sauce, Pickle Relish, Pico de Gallo

Spot / Stain Contents: Coloring, Fat, Noodles, Oil, Protein, Possible Meat, Salt, Turmeric, Vegetables

## Comments:

- **Optimum removal time: As soon as possible** within 24 hours of spill
- **Maximum size for home removal**: Class III / IV = 2 inches
- **Removal restrictions:** If the spot(s) is larger than 2 inches in diameter, **do not attempt TOTAL removal** using Class III or IV instructions. Do Step 1 **only** under Class III or IV. Mist spot(s) with a small amount of ammonia. Put a folded towel moistened with water over spot. (Keep towel damp until pro comes.) Then:
  - Call a pro and have spot removed as soon as possible within 24 hours. -OR-
  - If the spot is 3 1/2 inches or less in diameter, get a spot machine and:
    - If the spot is now old/dried, do Steps 2 - 7 under Class I.
    - If the spot is still fresh/wet, do Steps 2 - 8 under Class II.
- Food coloring and turmeric in some products can immediately and permanently stain most nylon. If you cannot remove a spot, consult a pro for options as soon as possible.
- Oils or fat in some products can cause recurring spots. (See "Recurring Spots", Chapter 4.) Consult a pro for options as soon as possible.

## Materials Needed:

Class III: Spotting kit, Vacuum cleaner with attachment removed from hose
Class IV: Spotting kit

## Class III: Towel + Old / Dried Spot

### Steps:

1. Using your spoon, scrape out as much of the spot(s) as possible.
   - Vacuum debris with vacuum cleaner hose.
   - With the hard brush, agitate the spot 15 - 20 times.
   - Vacuum debris with vacuum cleaner hose.
   - Repeat entire Step until no more removes.

2. Mist on a generous amount of ammonia.
   - Mist on a small amount of alcohol.
   - Agitate with hard brush.
   - Allow to work 2 minutes.
   - Mist on a small amount of ammonia.
   - Agitate with hard brush.

3. With a towel, blot 20 - 25 times, using a clean part of the towel each time.

4. Look at spot area carefully to see if the spot is gone:
   - If YES: No further action is needed.
   - If NO: Repeat Steps 2 and 3 until no more removes. Then, if needed, do Step 5.

5. If color cast remains, mist on a generous amount of peroxide.
   - Mist on a small amount of ammonia.
   - Tamp with soft brush.
   - Allow to dry.

6. If needed, repeat Step 5 one time.

7. If the spot persists, call a pro for options as soon as possible.

## Class IV: Towel + Fresh / Wet Spot

### Steps:

1. Lay a small towel over the palm of your hand. Then lay your hand on the carpet so the towel is at the edge of the spot.
   - Using your spoon, scoop as much of the spot(s) as possible into the towel. Note: After each scoop, wipe the spoon on a clean part of the towel.
   - Carefully drop the dirty towel in your empty bucket.
   - Fold a clean towel several times and place it over the spot(s).
   - Step on the towel with your full weight 10 - 15 times, using a clean part of the towel each time.
   - Repeat entire Step until no more absorbs.

2. Mist on a generous amount of ammonia.
   - Mist on a small amount of alcohol.
   - Agitate with hard brush.
   - Allow to work 1 minute.
   - Mist on a small amount of ammonia.
   - Agitate with hard brush.

3. With a towel, blot 20 - 25 times, using a clean part of the towel each time.

4. Look at spot area carefully to see if the spot is gone:
   - If YES: No further action is needed.
   - If NO: Repeat Steps 2 and 3 until no more removes. Then, if needed, do Step 5.

5. If color cast remains, mist on a small amount of peroxide.
   - Mist on a small amount of ammonia.
   - Tamp with soft brush.
   - Allow to dry.

6. If needed, repeat Step 5 one time.

7. If the spot persists, call a pro for options as soon as possible.

Section II

# Spaghetti Sauce *(Meat Sauce, Red Clam Sauce)*, Cheeseburger, Hamburger, Pizza

## Comments:

- **Optimum removal time: As soon as possible** within 24 hours of spill
- **Maximum size for home removal:** Class I / II = 4 inches
- **Removal restrictions:** If the spot(s) is larger than 4 inches in diameter, **do not attempt TOTAL removal** using Class I or II instructions. Do Step 1 **only** under Class I or Steps 1 and 2 **only** under Class II. Mist spot(s) with a small amount of ammonia. Put a folded towel moistened with water over spot. (Keep towel damp until pro comes.) Call a pro and have spot removed as soon as possible within 24 hours.
- Food coloring in some products can immediately and permanently stain some nylon. If you cannot remove a spot, consult a pro for options as soon as possible.
- Oils in some products can cause recurring spots. (See "Recurring Spots", Chapter 4.) Consult a pro for options as soon as possible.

## Materials Needed:

Class I / II: Spotting kit, Spot machine with warm water

### Class I: Spot Machine + Old / Dried Spot

**Steps:**

1. Using your spoon, scrape out as much of the spot(s) as possible.
   - Vacuum debris with spot machine.
   - Repeat entire Step until no more removes.

2. Mist on a generous amount of ammonia.
   - Mist on a generous amount of alcohol.
   - Agitate with hard brush.
   - Allow to work 2 minutes.
   - Mist on a small amount of ammonia.
   - Agitate with hard brush.

3. With the spot machine, rinse with warm water using the chop stroke technique 10 - 12 times.
   - Take 6 - 8 slow, dry vacuum strokes.

4. Look at spot area carefully to see if the spot is gone:
   - If YES: No further action is needed.
   - If NO: Repeat Steps 2 and 3 until no more removes. Then, if needed, do Step 5.

5. If color cast remains, mist on a generous amount of peroxide.
   - Mist on a small amount of ammonia.
   - Tamp with soft brush.
   - Allow to dry.

6. If needed, repeat Steps 2, 3 and 5 one time.

7. If the spot persists, call a pro for options as soon as possible.

### Class II: Spot Machine + Fresh / Wet Spot

**Steps:**

1. Lay a small towel over the palm of your hand. Then lay your hand on the carpet so the towel is at the edge of the spot.
   - Using your spoon, scoop as much of the spot(s) as possible into the towel. Note: After each scoop, wipe the spoon on a clean part of the towel.
   - Carefully drop the dirty towel in your empty bucket.

2. With the spot machine, rinse with warm water using the single stroke technique 6 - 8 times.
   - Take 4 - 6 slow, dry vacuum strokes.
   - Repeat until no more removes.

3. Mist on a generous amount of ammonia.
   - Mist on a generous amount of alcohol.
   - Agitate with hard brush.
   - Allow to work 1 minute.
   - Mist on a small amount of ammonia.
   - Agitate with hard brush.

4. With the spot machine, rinse with warm water using the single stroke technique 6 - 8 times.
   - Take 4 - 6 slow, dry vacuum strokes.

5. Look at spot area carefully to see if the spot is gone:
   - If YES: No further action is needed.
   - If NO: Repeat Steps 3 and 4 until no more removes. Then, if needed, do Step 6.

6. If color cast remains, mist on a small amount of peroxide.
   - Mist on a small amount of ammonia.
   - Tamp with soft brush.
   - Allow to dry.

7. If needed, repeat Steps 3, 4 and 5 one time.

8. If the spot persists, call a pro for options as soon as possible.

# Spaghetti Sauce (Meat Sauce, Red Clam Sauce), Cheeseburger, Hamburger, Pizza

Spot / Stain Contents: Oil, Meat Juices, Possible Meat, Spices, Tomatoes, Turmeric, Vegetables

## Comments:

- **Optimum removal time: As soon as possible** within 24 hours of spill
- **Maximum size for home removal:** Class III / IV = 2 inches
- **Removal restrictions:** If the spot(s) is larger than 2 inches in diameter, **do not attempt TOTAL removal** using Class III or IV instructions. Do Step 1 **only** under Class III or IV. Mist spot(s) with a small amount of ammonia. Put a folded towel moistened with water over spot. (Keep towel damp until pro comes.) Then:
  - Call a pro and have spot removed as soon as possible within 24 hours. -OR-
  - If the spot is 4 inches or less in diameter, get a spot machine and:
    - If the spot is now old/dried, do Steps 2 - 7 under Class I.
    - If the spot is still fresh/wet, do Steps 2 - 8 under Class II.
- Food coloring in some products can immediately and permanently stain some nylon. If you cannot remove a spot, consult a pro for options as soon as possible.
- Oils in some products can cause recurring spots. (See "Recurring Spots", Chapter 4.) Consult a pro for options as soon as possible.

## Materials Needed:

Class III: Spotting kit, Vacuum cleaner with attachment removed from hose
Class IV: Spotting kit

## Class III: Towel + Old / Dried Spot

### Steps:

1. Using your spoon, scrape out as much of the spot(s) as possible.
   - Vacuum debris with vacuum cleaner hose.
   - With the hard brush, agitate the spot 15 - 20 times.
   - Vacuum debris with vacuum cleaner hose.
   - Repeat entire Step until no more removes.

2. Mist on a generous amount of ammonia.
   - Mist on a small amount of alcohol.
   - Agitate with hard brush.
   - Allow to work 2 minutes.
   - Mist on a small amount of ammonia.
   - Agitate with hard brush.

3. With a towel, blot 20 - 25 times, using a clean part of the towel each time.

4. Look at spot area carefully to see if the spot is gone:
   - If YES: No further action is needed.
   - If NO: Repeat Steps 2 and 3 until no more removes. Then, if needed, do Step 5.

5. If color cast remains, mist on a generous amount of peroxide.
   - Mist on a small amount of ammonia.
   - Tamp with soft brush.
   - Allow to dry.

6. If needed, repeat Steps 2, 3 and 5 one time.

7. If the spot persists, call a pro for options as soon as possible.

## Class IV: Towel + Fresh / Wet Spot

### Steps:

1. Lay a small towel over the palm of your hand. Then lay your hand on the carpet so the towel is at the edge of the spot.
   - Using your spoon, scoop as much of the spot(s) as possible into the towel. Note: After each scoop, wipe the spoon on a clean part of the towel.
   - Carefully drop the dirty towel in your empty bucket.
   - With a clean towel, blot 20 - 25 times, using a clean part of the towel each time.
   - Repeat entire Step until no more absorbs.

2. Mist on a generous amount of ammonia.
   - Mist on a small amount of alcohol.
   - Agitate with hard brush.
   - Allow to work 1 minute.
   - Mist on a small amount of ammonia.
   - Agitate with hard brush.

3. With a clean towel, blot 20 - 25 times, using a clean part of the towel each time.

4. Look at spot area carefully to see if the spot is gone:
   - If YES: No further action is needed.
   - If NO: Repeat Steps 2 and 3 until no more removes. Then, if needed, do Step 5.

5. If color cast remains, mist on a small amount of peroxide.
   - Mist on a small amount of ammonia.
   - Tamp with soft brush.
   - Allow to dry.

6. If needed, repeat Steps 2, 3 and 5 one time.

7. If the spot persists, call a pro for options as soon as possible.

Section II

# Syrup: Honey, Maple, Strawberry, Etc.

## Comments:

- **Optimum removal time: As soon as possible** within 24 hours of spill
- **Maximum size for home removal:** Class I / II = 2 1/2 inches
- **Removal restrictions:** If the spot(s) is larger than 2 1/2 inches in diameter, **do not attempt TOTAL removal** using Class I or II instructions. Do Steps 1 and 2 **only** under Class I or II. Put a dry towel over spot. Call a pro and have spot removed as soon as possible within 24 hours.
- Food coloring in some products can immediately and permanently stain some nylon. If you cannot remove a spot, consult a pro for options as soon as possible.
- These products can leave a sticky residue that can cause recurring spots if not completely removed. (See "Recurring Spots", Chapter 4.) Consult a pro for options as soon as possible.

## Materials Needed:

Class I / II: Spotting kit, Spot machine with warm water

### Class I: Spot Machine + Old / Dried Spot

**Steps:**

1. Using the tip of the blade of your dinner knife and the end of the spoon handle, separate stuck together fibers into as many individual tufts as possible.

2. With the spot machine, rinse the spot(s) with warm water using chop stroke technique 10 - 12 times.
   - Take 10 - 12 slow dry vacuum strokes.

3. Mist on a generous amount of ammonia.
   - Agitate with hard brush.
   - Allow to work 1 minute.
   - Mist on a generous amount of peroxide.
   - Agitate with hard brush.
   - Allow to work 1 minute.

4. With the spot machine, rinse with warm water using the chop stroke technique 10 - 12 times.
   - Take 6 - 8 slow, dry vacuum strokes.

5. Look at and touch spot area carefully to see if the sticky residue is gone:
   - If YES: Allow to dry.
   - If NO: Repeat Steps 3 and 4 until no more removes. Then, if needed, do Step 6.

6. If color cast remains, mist on a generous amount of peroxide.
   - Tamp with soft brush.
   - Mist on a small amount of ammonia.
   - Tamp with soft brush.
   - Allow to dry.

7. If needed, repeat Step 6 one time.

8. If the spot persists, call a pro for options as soon as possible.

### Class II: Spot Machine + Fresh / Wet Spot

**Steps:**

1. Lay a small towel over the palm of your hand. Then lay your hand on the carpet so the towel is at the edge of the spot.
   - Using your spoon, scoop as much of the spot(s) as possible into the towel. Note: After each scoop, wipe the spoon on a clean part of the towel.
   - Carefully drop the dirty towel in your empty bucket.

2. With the spot machine, rinse the spot with warm water using single stroke technique 10 - 12 times.
   - Take 8 - 10 slow dry vacuum strokes.
   - Repeat Steps 1 and 2 until no more removes.

3. Mist on a generous amount of ammonia.
   - Agitate with hard brush.
   - Allow to work 1 minute.
   - Mist on a generous amount of peroxide.
   - Agitate with hard brush.
   - Allow to work 1 minute.

4. With the spot machine, rinse with warm water using the single stroke technique 8 - 10 times.
   - Take 4 - 6 slow, dry vacuum strokes.

5. Look at and touch spot area carefully to see if the sticky residue is gone:
   - If YES: Allow to dry.
   - If NO: Repeat Steps 3 and 4 until no more removes. Then, if needed, do Step 6.

6. If color cast remains, mist on a generous amount of peroxide.
   - Tamp with soft brush.
   - Mist on a small amount of ammonia.
   - Tamp with soft brush.
   - Allow to dry.

7. If needed, repeat Step 6 one time.

8. If the spot persists, call a pro for options as soon as possible.

Section II

## Comments:

- **Optimum removal time: As soon as possible** within 24 hours of spill
- **Maximum size for home removal:** Class III / IV = No home removal
- **Removal restrictions:** See "Class III" or "Class IV" instructions below.
- Food coloring in some products can immediately and permanently stain some nylon. If you cannot remove a spot, consult a pro for options as soon as possible.
- These products can leave a sticky residue that can cause recurring spots if not completely removed. (See "Recurring Spots", Chapter 4.) Consult a pro for options as soon as possible.

## Materials Needed:

Class III / IV: Towel(s), Paper and pencil for note

## Class III: Towel + Old / Dried Spot

### Steps:

1. **Do not attempt ANY removal** of a Class III spot(s).
   - Put a dry towel over the spot(s) to prevent spreading sticky residue.
   - Put a note next to the towel that says,
     ***"Do Not Touch Or Clean!"***.
   - Then:
     - Call a pro and have spot removed as soon as possible within 24 hours. -OR-
     - If the spot is 2 1/2 inches or less in diameter, get a spot machine and do Steps 1 - 8 under Class I.

## Class IV: Towel + Fresh / Wet Spot

### Steps:

1. **Do not attempt TOTAL removal** using Class IV instructions.

2. With a towel, gently blot the spot(s), using a clean part of the towel each time.
   - Repeat until no more absorbs.

3. Put a dry towel over the spot(s) to prevent spreading sticky residue.
   - Put a note next to the towel that says,
     ***"Do Not Touch Or Clean!"***.
   - Then:
     - Call a pro and have spot removed as soon as possible within 24 hours. -OR-
     - If the spot is 2 1/2 inches or less in diameter, get a spot machine and:
       - If the spot is now old/dried, do Steps 1 - 8 under Class I.
       - If the spot is still fresh/wet, do Steps 1 - 8 under Class II.

Section II

# Tomato Juice, Clamato® Juice, V-8® Juice

## Comments:

- **Optimum removal time:** Within 24 hours of spill
- **Maximum size for home removal:** Class I / II = 3 1/2 inches
- **Removal restrictions:** If the spot(s) is larger than 3 1/2 inches in diameter, **do not attempt TOTAL removal** using Class I or II instructions. Do Step 1 **only** under Class I or Class II. Put a folded towel moistened with water over spot. (Keep towel damp until pro comes.) Call a pro and have spot removed within 2 days.
- Food coloring in some products can immediately and permanently stain some nylon. If you cannot remove a spot, consult a pro for options as soon as possible.

## Materials Needed:

Class I / II: Spotting kit, Spot machine with warm water

### Class I: Spot Machine + Old / Dried Spot

**Steps:**

1. Using the tip of the blade of your dinner knife and the end of the spoon handle, gently separate stuck together fibers into as many individual tufts as possible.
   - Using your spoon scrape out as much of the spot(s) as possible.
   - With the spot machine hose, dry vacuum debris.
   - Repeat entire Step until no more removes.

2. Mist on a generous amount of ammonia.
   - Mist on a generous amount of peroxide.
   - Agitate with hard brush.
   - Allow to work 2 minutes.
   - Mist on a small amount of ammonia.
   - Agitate with hard brush.

3. With the spot machine, rinse with warm water using the chop stroke technique 10 - 12 times.
   - Take 6 - 8 slow, dry vacuum strokes.

4. Look at spot area carefully to see if the spot is gone:
   - If YES: Allow to dry.
   - If NO: Repeat Steps 2 and 3 until no more removes. Then, if needed, do Step 5.

5 If color cast remains, mist on a generous amount of peroxide.
   - Tamp with soft brush.
   - Allow to dry.

6. If needed, repeat Steps 2, 3 and 5 one time.

7. If the spot persists, call a pro for options as soon as possible.

### Class II: Spot Machine + Fresh / Wet Spot

**Steps:**

1. Lay a small towel over the palm of your hand. Then lay your hand on the carpet so the towel is at the edge of the spot.
   - Using your spoon, scoop as much of the spot(s) as possible into the towel. Note: After each scoop, wipe the spoon on a clean part of the towel.
   - Carefully drop the dirty towel in your empty bucket.
   - With a clean towel, blot 15 - 20 times, using a clean part of the towel each time.
   - With the spot machine, rinse the spot with warm water using the single stroke technique 8 - 10 times.
   - Repeat entire Step until no more removes.

2. Mist on a generous amount of ammonia.
   - Mist on a generous amount of peroxide.
   - Agitate with hard brush.
   - Allow to work 1 minute.

3. With the spot machine, rinse with warm water using the single stroke technique 6 - 8 times.
   - Take 4 - 6 slow, dry vacuum strokes.

4. Look at spot area carefully to see if the spot is gone:
   - If YES: Allow to dry.
   - If NO: Repeat Steps 2 and 3 until no more removes. Then, if needed, do Step 5.

5. If color cast remains, mist on a generous amount of peroxide.
   - Tamp with soft brush.
   - Allow to dry.

6. If needed, repeat Steps 2, 3 and 5 one time.

7. If the spot persists, call a pro for options as soon as possible.

## Comments:

- **Optimum removal time:** Within 24 hours of spill
- **Maximum size for home removal:** Class III = No home removal / IV = 1 1/2 inches
- **Removal restrictions - Class III:** See "Class III" instructions below.
- **Removal restrictions - Class IV:** If the spot(s) is larger than 1 1/2 inches, **do not attempt TOTAL removal** using Class IV instructions. Do Step 1 **only** under Class IV. Put a folded towel moistened with water over spot. (Keep towel damp until pro comes.) Then:
  - Call a pro and have spot removed within 2 days. -OR-
  - Get a spot machine and if the spot is 3 1/2 inches or less in diameter:
    - If the spot is now old/dried, do Steps 1 - 7 under Class I.
    - If the spot is still fresh/wet, do Steps 1 - 7 under Class II.
- Food coloring in some products can immediately and permanently stain some nylon. If you cannot remove a spot, consult a pro for options as soon as possible.

## Materials Needed:

Class III: Towel, Paper and pencil for note
Class IV: Spotting kit

### Class III: Towel + Old / Dried Spot

**Steps:**

1. **Do not attempt ANY removal** of a Class III spot(s).
   - Put a dry towel over the spot(s).
   - Put a note next to the towel that says, ***"Do Not Touch Or Clean!"***.
   - Then:
     - Call a pro and have spot removed within 2 days. -OR-
     - If the spot is 3 1/2 inches or less in diameter, get a spot machine and do Steps 1 - 7 under Class I.

### Class IV: Towel + Fresh / Wet Spot

**Steps:**

1. Lay a small towel over the palm of your hand. Then lay your hand on the carpet so the towel is at the edge of the spot.
   - Using your spoon, scoop as much of the spot(s) as possible into the towel. Note: After each scoop, wipe the spoon on a clean part of the towel.
   - Carefully drop the dirty towel in your empty bucket.
   - With a clean towel, blot 20 - 25 times, using a clean part of the towel each time.
   - Repeat entire Step until no more absorbs.
2. Mist on a small amount of ammonia.
   - Mist on a small amount of peroxide.
   - Tamp with soft brush.
   - Allow to work 1 minute.
3. With a clean towel, blot 15 - 20 times, using a clean part of the towel each time.
4. Look at spot area carefully to see if the spot is gone:
   - If YES: Allow to dry.
   - If NO: Repeat Steps 2 and 3 until no more removes. Then, if needed, do Step 5.
5. If color cast remains, mist on a generous amount of peroxide.
   - Tamp with soft brush.
   - Allow to dry.
6. If needed, repeat Steps 2, 3 and 5 one time.
7. If the spot persists, call a pro for options as soon as possible.

Section II

# Tooth Paste, Tooth Whitening Gel

## Comments:

- **Optimum removal time:** Within 24 hours of spill
- **Maximum size for home removal:** Class I / II = 5 1/2 inches
- **Removal restrictions:** If the spot(s) is larger than 5 1/2 inches in diameter, **do not attempt TOTAL removal** using Class I or II instructions. Do Step 1 **only** under Class I or Steps 1 and 2 **only** under Class II. Put a dry towel over spot. Call a pro and have spot removed within 3 days.
- Coloring in some products can stain some nylon. If you cannot remove a spot, consult a pro for options as soon as possible.

## Materials Needed:

Class I / II: Spotting kit, Spot machine with hot water

### Class I: Spot Machine + Old / Dried Spot

**Steps:**

1. Using the tip of your dinner knife, scrape out as much of the spot(s) as possible. Note: After each scrape, wipe the knife on the small towel.
   - Vacuum debris with spot machine hose.
   - Repeat entire Step until no more removes.

2. Mist on a generous amount of ammonia.
   - Agitate with hard brush.
   - Allow to work 1 minute.
   - Mist on a generous amount of ammonia.
   - Agitate with hard brush.

3. With the spot machine, rinse with hot water using the chop stroke technique 8 - 10 times.
   - Take 4 - 6 slow, dry vacuum strokes.

4. Look at spot area carefully to see if the spot is gone:
   - If YES: No further action is needed.
   - If NO: Repeat Steps 2 and 3 until no more removes. Then, if needed, do Step 5.

5. If color cast remains, mist on a generous amount of peroxide.
   - Tamp with soft brush.
   - Allow to dry.

6. If needed, repeat Steps 2, 3 and 5 one time.

7. If the spot persists, call a pro for options as soon as possible.

### Class II: Spot Machine + Fresh / Wet Spot

**Steps:**

1. Using the tip of your dinner knife, scrape out as much of the spot(s) as possible. Note: After each scrape, wipe the knife on the small towel.
   - Vacuum debris with spot machine hose.
   - Repeat entire Step until no more removes.

2. Mist on a generous amount of ammonia.
   - Agitate with hard brush.
   - Allow to work 1 minute.
   - Mist on a generous amount of ammonia.
   - Agitate with hard brush.

3. With the spot machine, rinse with hot water using the single stroke technique 8 - 10 times.
   - Take 4 - 6 slow, dry vacuum strokes.

4. Look at spot area carefully to see if the spot is gone:
   - If YES: No further action is needed.
   - If NO: Repeat Steps 2 and 3 until no more removes. Then, if needed, do Step 5.

5. If color cast remains, mist on a small amount of peroxide.
   - Mist on a small amount of ammonia.
   - Tamp with soft brush.
   - Allow to dry.

6. If needed, repeat Steps 2, 3 and 5 one time.

7. If the spot persists, call a pro for options as soon as possible.

## Comments:

- **Optimum removal time:** Within 24 hours of spill
- **Maximum size for home removal:** Class III / IV = 2 inches
- **Removal restrictions:** If the spot(s) is larger than 2 inches in diameter, **do not attempt TOTAL removal** using Class III or IV instructions. Do Step 1 **only** under Class III or IV. Put a dry towel over spot. Then:
  - Call a pro and have spot removed within 3 days. -OR-
  - If the spot is 5 1/2 inches or less in diameter, get a spot machine and:
    - If the spot is now old/dried, do Steps 2 - 7 under Class I.
    - If the spot is still fresh/wet, do Steps 2 - 7 under Class II.
- Coloring in some products can stain some nylon. If you cannot remove a spot, consult a pro for options as soon as possible.

## Materials Needed:

Class III / IV: Spotting kit, Vacuum cleaner with attachment removed from hose

### Class III: Towel + Old / Dried Spot

**Steps:**

1. Using the tip of your dinner knife, scrape out as much of the spot(s) as possible. Note: After each scrape, wipe the knife on the small towel.
   - Vacuum debris with vacuum cleaner hose.
   - Repeat entire Step until no more removes.

2. Mist on a generous amount of ammonia.
   - Agitate with hard brush.
   - Mist on a small amount of peroxide. (The spot may bubble after you apply peroxide. Do not worry.)
   - Agitate with hard brush.

3. With a clean towel, blot 10 - 15 times, using a clean part of the towel each time.

4. Look at spot area carefully to see if the spot is gone:
   - If YES: No further action is needed.
   - If NO: Repeat Steps 2 and 3 until no more removes. Then, if needed, do Step 5.

5 If color cast remains, mist on a generous amount of peroxide.
   - Tamp with soft brush.
   - Allow to dry.

6. If needed, repeat Steps 2, 3 and 5 one time.

7. If the spot persists, call a pro for options as soon as possible.

### Class IV: Towel + Fresh / Wet Spot

**Steps:**

1. Using the tip of your dinner knife, scrape out as much of the spot(s) as possible. Note: After each scrape, wipe the knife on the small towel.
   - Vacuum debris with vacuum cleaner hose.
   - Repeat entire Step until no more removes.

2. Mist on a generous amount of ammonia.
   - Agitate with hard brush.
   - Mist on a small amount of peroxide. (The spot may bubble after you apply peroxide. Do not worry.)
   - Agitate with hard brush.

3. With a clean towel, blot 10 - 15 times, using a clean part of the towel each time.

4 Look at spot area carefully to see if the spot is gone:
   - If YES: No further action is needed.
   - If NO: Repeat Steps 2 and 3 until no more removes. Then, if needed, do Step 5.

5. If color cast remains, mist on a small amount of peroxide.
   - Tamp with soft brush.
   - Allow to dry.

6. If needed, repeat Steps 2, 3 and 5 one time.

7. If the spot persists, call a pro for options as soon as possible.

Section II

# Urine: Animal, Human

## Comments:

- **Optimum removal time: As soon as possible** within 24 hours of spill
- **Maximum size for home removal:** Class I = No size limit if the spot is dry / Class II = 4 inches
- **Removal restrictions - Class I:** See "Class I" instructions below.
- **Removal restrictions - Class II:** If the spot is larger than 4 inches in diameter, **do not attempt TOTAL removal** using Class II instructions. Do Step 1 **only** under Class II. Let spot dry completely. Do Steps 1 - 7 under Class I. (If the spot persists, consult a pro for options as soon as possible.)
- **Caution:** Urine contains yellow pigment and sometimes dye from digested food coloring that can immediately and permanently stain some nylon if left untreated as little as 24 - 48 hours. If you cannot remove a spot, consult a pro for options as soon as possible.
- Urine can cause recurring spots if not completely removed. (See "Recurring Spots", Chapter 4.) Consult a pro for options as soon as possible.

## Materials Needed:
Class I / II: Spotting kit, Spot machine with warm water, Disposable towels for Class II

### Class I: Spot Machine + Old / Dried Spot

**Steps:**

1. Using your soft brush, vigorously brush the spot(s) in a side-to-side motion 10 - 15 times. Caution: Be careful to not fray carpet fibers.
   - Vacuum dust debris with spot machine hose.
2. Mist on a generous amount of peroxide.
   - Mist on a generous amount of ammonia.
   - Tamp with soft brush.
   - Allow to work 2 minutes.
3. With the spot machine, rinse with warm water using the chop stroke technique 10 - 12 times.
   - Take 8 - 10 slow, dry vacuum strokes.
4. Look at spot area carefully to see if the spot is gone:
   - If YES: No further action is needed.
   - If NO: Do Steps 2 and 3 until no more will remove. If needed, do Step 5.
5. If color cast remains, mist on a generous amount of peroxide.
   - Mist on a small amount of ammonia.
   - Tamp with soft brush.
   - Allow to dry.
6. If needed, repeat Steps 2, 3 and 5 one time.
7. If the spot persists, call a pro for options as soon as possible.

### Class II: Spot Machine + Fresh / Wet Spot

**Steps:**

1. Fold a disposable towel several times and place it over the spot(s).
   - Step on the towel with your full weight, using a clean part of the towel each time.
   - Repeat until no more liquid absorbs.
2. Mist on a generous amount of ammonia.
   - Mist on a generous amount of peroxide.
   - Tamp with soft brush.
   - Allow to work 1 minute.
3. With the spot machine, rinse with warm water using the chop stroke technique 8 - 10 times.
   - Take 6 - 8 slow, dry vacuum strokes.
4. Look at spot area carefully to see if the spot is gone:
   - If YES: No further action is needed.
   - If NO: Do Steps 2 and 3 until no more will remove. If needed, do Step 5.
5. If color cast remains, mist on a generous amount of peroxide.
   - Mist on a small amount of ammonia.
   - Tamp with soft brush.
   - Allow to dry.
6. If needed, repeat Steps 2, 3 and 5 one time.
7. If the spot persists, call a pro for options as soon as possible.

Section II

Stain / Spot Contents: Albumin, Alkaline Salts, Cholesterol, Protein, Yellow Pigment, Uric Acid

## Comments:

- **Optimum removal time: As soon as possible** within 24 hours of spill
- **Maximum size for home removal:** Class III = No size limit if the spot is dry / Class IV = 2 1/2 inches
- **Removal restrictions - Class III:** See "Class III" instructions below.
- **Removal restrictions - Class IV:** If the spot(s) is larger than 2 1/2 inches in diameter, **do not attempt TOTAL removal** using Class IV instructions. Do Step 1 **only** under Class IV. Put a dry towel over spot. Then:
  - Call a pro and have spot removed as soon as possible within 24 hours. -OR-
  - If the spot is 4 inches or less in diameter, get a spot machine and:
    - If the spot is now old/dried, do Steps 2 - 7 under Class I.
    - If the spot is still fresh/wet, do Steps 2 - 7 under Class II.
- **Caution:** Urine contains yellow pigment and sometimes dye from digested food coloring that can immediately and permanently stain some nylon if left untreated as little as 24 - 48 hours. If you cannot remove a spot, consult a pro for options as soon as possible.
- Urine can cause recurring spots if not completely removed. (See "Recurring Spots", Chapter 4.) Consult a pro for options as soon as possible.

---

## Materials Needed:

Class III: Spotting kit, Vacuum cleaner with attachment removed from hose
Class IV: Spotting kit, Disposable towels

| Class III: Towel + Old / Dried Spot | Class IV: Towel + Fresh / Wet Spot |
|---|---|
| **Steps:** | **Steps:** |
| 1. Using your soft brush, gently brush the spot(s) in a side-to-side motion 10 - 15 times. Caution: Be careful to not fray carpet fibers.<br>• Vacuum debris with vacuum cleaner hose. | 1. Fold a disposable towel several times and place it over the spot(s).<br>• Step on the towel with your full weight, using a clean part of the towel each time.<br>• Repeat until no more liquid absorbs. |
| 2. Mist on a generous amount of peroxide.<br>• Mist on a generous amount of ammonia.<br>• Tamp with soft brush.<br>• Allow to work 2 minutes.<br>• Mist on a small amount of ammonia.<br>• Agitate with hard brush. | 2. Mist on a generous amount of ammonia.<br>• Mist on a generous amount of peroxide.<br>• Tamp with soft brush.<br>• Allow to work 1 minute.<br>• Mist on a small amount of ammonia.<br>• Agitate with hard brush. |
| 3. Fold a towel several times and place it over the spot(s).<br>• Step on the towel with your full weight 15 - 20 times, using a clean part of the towel each time. | 3. Fold a clean cloth towel several times and place it over the spot(s).<br>• Step on the towel with your full weight 15 - 20 times, using a clean part of the towel each time.<br>• Repeat until no more liquid absorbs. |
| 4. Look at spot area carefully to see if the spot is gone:<br>• If YES: No further action is needed.<br>• If NO: Do Steps 2 and 3 until no more will remove. If needed, do Step 5. | 4. Look at spot area carefully to see if the spot is gone:<br>• If YES: No further action is needed.<br>• If NO: Do Steps 2 and 3 until no more will remove. If needed, do Step 5. |
| 5. If color cast remains, mist on a generous amount of peroxide.<br>• Mist on a small amount of ammonia.<br>• Tamp with soft brush.<br>• Allow to dry. | 5. If color cast remains, mist on a generous amount of peroxide.<br>• Mist on a small amount of ammonia.<br>• Tamp with soft brush.<br>• Allow to dry. |
| 6. If needed, repeat Steps 2, 3 and 5 one time. | 6. If needed, repeat Steps 2, 3 and 5 one time. |
| 7. If the spot persists, call a pro for options as soon as possible. | 7. If the spot persists, call a pro for options as soon as possible. |

# Vomit, Regurgitation, Spit-Up: Animal, Human

## Comments:

- **Optimum removal time: As soon as possible** within 24 hours of spill
- **Maximum size for home removal:** Class I / II = 4 1/2 inches
- **Removal restrictions:** If the spot(s) is larger than 4 1/2 inches in diameter, **do not attempt TOTAL removal** using Class I or II instructions. Do Step 1 **only** under Class I or Steps 1 and 2 **only** under Class II. Mist spot(s) with a small amount of ammonia. Put a folded towel moistened with water over spot. Call a pro and have spot removed as soon as possible within 24 hours.
- These spots may contain food particles with dyes that can immediately and permanently stain most nylon. If you cannot remove a spot, consult a pro for options as soon as possible.

## Materials Needed:
Class I / II: Spotting kit, Spot machine with cool water, Disposable towels for Class II

### Class I: Spot Machine + Old / Dried Spot

**Steps:**

1. Using your spoon, scrape out as much of the spot(s) as possible.
   - Vacuum debris with spot machine.
   - Repeat entire Step until no more removes.

2. Mist on a generous amount of ammonia.
   - Agitate with hard brush.
   - Allow to work 2 minutes.
   - Mist on a small amount of ammonia.
   - Agitate with hard brush.

3. With the spot machine, rinse with cool water using the chop stroke technique 10 - 12 times.
   - Take 8 - 10 slow, dry vacuum strokes.

4. Look at spot area carefully to see if the spot is gone:
   - If YES: No further action is needed.
   - If NO: Repeat Steps 2 and 3 until no more removes. Then, if needed, do Step 5.

5. If color cast remains, mist on a generous amount of peroxide.
   - Tamp with soft brush.
   - Mist on a small amount of ammonia.
   - Tamp with soft brush.
   - Allow to dry.

6. If needed, repeat Steps 2, 3 and 5 one time.

7. If the spot persists, call a pro for options as soon as possible.

### Class II: Spot Machine + Fresh / Wet Spot

**Steps:**

1. Lay a disposable towel over the palm of your hand. Then lay your hand on the carpet so the towel is at the edge of the spot.
   - Using your spoon, scoop as much of the spot(s) as possible into the towel. Note: After each scoop, wipe the spoon on a clean part of the towel.
   - Carefully drop the dirty towel in your empty bucket.

2. With the spot machine, rinse with cool water using the single stroke technique 15 - 20 times.
   - Take 6 - 8 slow, dry vacuum strokes.
   - Repeat entire Step until no more removes.

3. Mist on a generous amount of ammonia.
   - Agitate with hard brush.
   - Allow to work 1 minute.
   - Mist on a small amount of ammonia.
   - Agitate with hard brush.

4. With the spot machine, rinse with cool water using the chop stroke technique 6 - 8 times.
   - Take 4 - 6 slow, dry vacuum strokes.

5. Look at spot area carefully to see if the spot is gone:
   - If YES: No further action is needed.
   - If NO: Repeat Steps 3 and 4 until no more removes. Then, if needed, do Step 6.

6. If color cast remains, mist on a generous amount of peroxide.
   - Tamp with soft brush.
   - Mist on a small amount of ammonia.
   - Tamp with soft brush.
   - Allow to dry.

7. If needed, repeat Steps 3, 4 and 6 one time.

8. If the spot persists, call a pro for options as soon as possible.

Section II

## Comments:

- **Optimum removal time: As soon as possible** within 24 hours of spill
- **Maximum size for home removal:** Class III / IV = 2 1/2 inches
- **Removal restrictions:** If the spot(s) is larger than 2 1/2 inches in diameter, **do not attempt TOTAL removal** using Class III or IV instructions. Do Step 1 **only** under Class III or IV. Mist spot(s) with a small amount of ammonia. Put a folded towel moistened with water over spot. Then:
  - Call a pro and have spot removed as soon as possible within 24 hours. -OR-
  - If the spot is 4 1/2 inches or less in diameter, get a spot machine and:
    - If the spot is now old/dried, do Steps 2 - 7 under Class I.
    - If the spot is still fresh/wet, do Steps 2 - 8 under Class II.
- These spots may contain food particles with dyes that can immediately and permanently stain most nylon. If you cannot remove a spot, consult a pro for options as soon as possible.

## Materials Needed:

Class III: Spotting kit, Vacuum cleaner with attachment removed from hose
Class IV: Spotting kit, Disposable towels for Class IV

### Class III: Towel + Old / Dried Spot

#### Steps:

1. Using your spoon, scrape out as much of the spot(s) as possible.
   - Vacuum debris with vacuum cleaner hose.
   - Repeat entire Step until no more removes.

2. Mist on a generous amount of ammonia.
   - Agitate with hard brush.
   - Allow to work 2 minutes.
   - Mist on a small amount of ammonia.
   - Agitate with hard brush.

3. With a towel, blot 15 - 20 times, using a clean part of the towel each time.

4. Look at spot area carefully to see if the spot is gone:
   - If YES: No further action is needed.
   - If NO: Repeat Steps 2 and 3 until no more removes. Then, if needed, do Step 5.

5. If color cast remains, mist on a generous amount of peroxide.
   - Tamp with soft brush.
   - Mist on a small amount of ammonia.
   - Tamp with soft brush.
   - Allow to dry.

6. If needed, repeat Steps 2, 3 and 5 one time.

7. If the spot persists, call a pro for options as soon as possible.

### Class IV: Towel + Fresh / Wet Spot

#### Steps:

1. Lay a disposable towel over the palm of your hand. Then lay your hand on the carpet so the towel is at the edge of the spot.
   - Using your spoon, scoop as much of the spot(s) as possible into the towel. Note: After each scoop, wipe the spoon on a clean part of the towel.
   - Carefully drop the dirty towel in your empty bucket.
   - With a clean cloth towel, blot the spot 20 - 25 times, using a clean part of the towel each time.
   - Repeat entire Step until no more absorbs.

2. Mist on a generous amount of ammonia.
   - Agitate with hard brush.
   - Allow to work 1 minute.
   - Mist on a small amount of ammonia.
   - Agitate with hard brush.

3. With a clean towel, blot 15 - 20 times, using a clean part of the towel each time.

4. Look at spot area carefully to see if the spot is gone:
   - If YES: No further action is needed.
   - If NO: Repeat Steps 2 and 3 until no more removes. Then, if needed, do Step 5.

5. If color cast remains, mist on a generous amount of peroxide.
   - Tamp with soft brush.
   - Mist on a small amount of ammonia.
   - Tamp with soft brush.
   - Allow to dry.

6. If needed, repeat Steps 2, 3 and 5 one time.

7. If the spot persists, call a pro for options as soon as possible.

# Wax: Candle, Cosmetic, Dental, Paraffin

## Comments:

- **Optimum removal time:** Within 24 hours of spill
- **Maximum size for home removal:** Class I / II = 5 inches
- **Removal restrictions:** If the spot(s) is larger than 5 inches in diameter or you do not have a hair dryer, **do not attempt TOTAL removal** using Class I or II instructions. Do Step 1 **only** under Class I or II. Put a dry towel over spot. Call a pro and have spot removed within 3 days.
- Dyes in some products can immediately and permanently stain some nylon. If you cannot remove a spot, consult a pro for options as soon as possible.

## Materials Needed:
Class I / II: Spotting kit, Spot machine with hot water, Hair dryer

| Class I: Spot Machine + Old / Dried Spot | Class II: Spot Machine + Fresh / Wet Spot |
|---|---|
| **Steps:** | **Steps:** |
| 1. Using your dinner knife, cut the spot(s) into 1/4 inch squares to break it up into sections. | 1. Using your dinner knife, cut the spot(s) into 1/4 inch squares to break it up into sections. |
| • Using your spoon, scrape across the spot's surface, shaving it off in layers. | • Using your spoon, scrape across the spot's surface, shaving it off in layers. |
| • Vacuum debris with spot machine. | • Vacuum debris with spot machine. |
| • Repeat entire Step until no more removes. | • Repeat entire Step until no more removes. |
| 2. Put the hair dryer on the High Heat / High Fan setting and hold it 2 inches above the spot. | 2. Put the hair dryer on the High Heat / High Fan setting and hold it 2 inches above the spot. |
| • As the spot begins to liquefy, blot it 3 - 4 times, using a clean part of the towel each time. | • As the spot begins to liquefy, blot it 3 - 4 times, using a clean part of the towel each time. |
| • Repeat heating and blotting until the wax residue is gone. | • Repeat heating and blotting until the wax residue is gone. |
| • Allow the carpet surface to cool. Touch the spot area carefully to see if the fibers are still stiff with wax. If still stiff, continue heating and blotting until stiffness is gone. | • Allow the carpet surface to cool. Touch the spot area carefully to see if the fibers are still stiff with wax. If still stiff, continue heating and blotting until stiffness is gone. |
| 3. Mist on a generous amount of alcohol. | 3. Mist on a generous amount of alcohol. |
| • Agitate with hard brush. | • Agitate with hard brush. |
| • Allow to work 1 minute. | • Allow to work 1 minute. |
| • Mist on a small amount of alcohol. | • Mist on a small amount of alcohol. |
| 4. With the spot machine, rinse with hot water using the chop stroke technique 6 - 8 times. | 4. With the spot machine, rinse with hot water using the chop stroke technique 6 - 8 times. |
| • Take 4 - 6 slow, dry vacuum strokes. | • Take 4 - 6 slow, dry vacuum strokes. |
| 5. Look at and touch spot area carefully to see if the oily residue is gone. (Look at your fingers also.): | 5. Look at and touch spot area carefully to see if the oily residue is gone. (Look at your fingers also.): |
| • If YES: No further action is needed. | • If YES: No further action is needed. |
| • If NO: Repeat Steps 3 and 4 until no more removes. Then, if needed, do Step 6. | • If NO: Repeat Steps 3 and 4 until no more removes. Then, if needed, do Step 6. |
| 6. If color cast remains, mist on a generous amount of peroxide. | 6. If color cast remains, mist on a generous amount of peroxide. |
| • Mist on a small amount of ammonia. | • Mist on a small amount of ammonia. |
| • Tamp with soft brush. | • Tamp with soft brush. |
| • Allow to dry. | • Allow to dry. |
| 7. If the spot persists, call a pro for options as soon as possible. | 7. If the spot persists, call a pro for options as soon as possible. |

Section II

## Comments:

- **Optimum removal time:** Within 24 hours of spill
- **Maximum size for home removal:** Class III / IV = 2 1/2 inches
- **Removal restrictions:** If the spot(s) is larger than 2 1/2 inches in diameter or you do not have a hair dryer, **do not attempt TOTAL removal** using Class III or IV instructions. Do Step 1 **only** under Class III or IV. Put a dry towel over spot. Then:
  - Call a pro and have spot removed within 3 days. - OR -
  - If the spot is 5 inches or less in diameter **and** you have a hair dryer, get a spot machine and:
    - If the spot is now old/dried, do Steps 2 - 7 under Class I.
    - If the spot is still fresh/wet, do Steps 2 - 7 under Class II.
- Dyes in some products can immediately and permanently stain some nylon. If you cannot remove a spot, consult a pro for options as soon as possible.

## Materials Needed:

Class III / IV: Spotting kit, Vacuum cleaner with attachment removed from hose, Hair dryer

| Class III: Towel + Old / Dried Spot | Class IV: Towel + Fresh / Wet Spot |
|---|---|
| **Steps:** | **Steps:** |
| 1. Using your dinner knife, cut the spot(s) into 1/4 inch squares to break it up into sections. | 1. Using your dinner knife, cut the spot(s) into 1/4 inch squares to break it up into sections. |
| • Using your spoon, scrape across the spot's surface, shaving it off in layers. | • Using your spoon, scrape across the spot's surface, shaving it off in layers. |
| • Vacuum debris with vacuum cleaner hose. | • Vacuum debris with vacuum cleaner hose. |
| • Repeat entire Step until no more removes. | • Repeat entire Step until no more removes. |
| 2. Put the hair dryer on the High Heat / High Fan setting and hold it 2 inches above the spot. | 2. Put the hair dryer on the High Heat / High Fan setting and hold it 2 inches above the spot. |
| • As the spot begins to liquefy, blot it 3 - 4 times, using a clean part of the towel each time. | • As the spot begins to liquefy, blot it 3 - 4 times, using a clean part of the towel each time. |
| • Repeat heating and blotting until the wax residue is gone. | • Repeat heating and blotting until the wax residue is gone. |
| • Allow the carpet surface to cool. Touch the spot area carefully to see if the fibers are still stiff with wax. If still stiff, continue heating and blotting until stiffness is gone. | • Allow the carpet surface to cool. Touch the spot area carefully to see if the fibers are still stiff with wax. If still stiff, continue heating and blotting until stiffness is gone. |
| 3. Mist on a generous amount of alcohol. | 3. Mist on a generous amount of alcohol. |
| • Agitate with hard brush. | • Agitate with hard brush. |
| • Allow to work 1 minute. | • Allow to work 1 minute. |
| • Mist on a small amount of alcohol. | • Mist on a small amount of alcohol. |
| 4. With a towel, blot the spot 10 - 12 times, using a clean part of the towel each time. | 4. With a towel, blot the spot 10 - 12 times, using a clean part of the towel each time. |
| 5. Look at and touch spot area carefully to see if the oily residue is gone. (Look at your fingers also.): | 5. Look at and touch spot area carefully to see if the oily residue is gone. (Look at your fingers also.): |
| • If YES: No further action is needed. | • If YES: No further action is needed. |
| • If NO: Repeat Steps 3 and 4 until no more removes. Then, if needed, do Step 6. | • If NO: Repeat Steps 3 and 4 until no more removes. Then, if needed, do Step 6. |
| 6. If color cast remains, mist on a generous amount of peroxide. | 6. If color cast remains, mist on a generous amount of peroxide. |
| • Mist on a small amount of ammonia. | • Mist on a small amount of ammonia. |
| • Tamp with soft brush. | • Tamp with soft brush. |
| • Allow to dry. | • Allow to dry. |
| 7. If the spot persists, call a pro for options as soon as possible. | 7. If the spot persists, call a pro for options as soon as possible. |

Section II

# Wood Stain, Furniture Stain

## Comments:

- **Optimum removal time: As soon as possible** within 24 hours of spill
- **Maximum size for home removal:** Class I = No home removal / Class II = 2 inches
- **Removal restrictions - Class I:** See "Class I" instructions below.
- **Removal restrictions - Class II:** If the spot(s) is larger than 2 inches in diameter, **do not attempt TOTAL removal** using Class II instructions. Do Steps 1 - 3 **only** under Class II. Mist spot(s) with a generous amount of alcohol. Put a folded towel moistened with water over spot and a note next to it that says, ***"Do Not Touch Or Clean!"***. Call a pro and have spot removed as soon as possible within 24 hours.
- These products can immediately and permanently stain most nylon. If you cannot remove a spot, consult a pro for options as soon as possible.
- Large spills can damage latex in the carpet and pad and cause it to swell into little hills. This makes the carpet look as if it is loose and needs to be re-stretched. Consult a pro for options.
- Large spills can soak through the carpet and pad to the subfloor and cause recurring spots. (See "Recurring Spots", Chapter 4.) Consult a pro for options as soon as possible.

## Materials Needed:

Class I: Towel, Paper and pencil for note
Class II: Disposable towels, Spotting kit, Spot machine with hot water

| Class I: Spot Machine + Old / Dried Spot | Class II: Spot Machine + Fresh / Wet Spot |
|---|---|
| **Steps:** | **Steps:** |

### Class I: Spot Machine + Old / Dried Spot

**Steps:**

1. **Do not attempt ANY removal** of a Class I spot.
   - Put a dry towel over the spot(s) and a note next to it that says ***"Do Not Touch Or Clean!"***.
   - Call a pro and have spot removed as soon as possible within 24 hours.

### Class II: Spot Machine + Fresh / Wet Spot

**Steps:**

1. Fold a disposable towel several times and place it over the spot(s).
   - Step on the towel with your full weight 15 - 20 times, using a clean part of the towel each time.
   - Repeat until no more absorbs.

2. Mist on a generous amount of alcohol.
   - Tamp with soft brush.
   - Allow to work 2 minutes.
   - Mist on a generous amount of ammonia.
   - Tamp with soft brush.
   - Allow to work 1 minute.

3. With the spot machine, rinse with hot water using the chop stroke technique 12 - 15 times.
   - Take 8 - 10 slow, dry vacuum strokes.

4. Look at spot area carefully to see if the spot is gone:
   - If YES: No further action is needed.
   - If NO: Do Steps 2 and 3 until no more will remove. If needed, do Step 5.

5. If color cast remains, mist on a generous amount of peroxide.
   - Tamp with soft brush.
   - Mist on a small amount of ammonia.
   - Tamp with soft brush.
   - Allow to dry.

6. If the spot persists, call a pro for options as soon as possible.

Section II

# Wood Stain, Furniture Stain

Stain Contents: Oil, Possible Pigment, Possible Urethane, Solvents, Wax

## Comments:

- **Optimum removal time: As soon as possible** within 24 hours of spill
- **Maximum size for home removal:** Class III = No home removal / Class IV = 1 1/2 inches
- **Removal restrictions - Class III:** See "Class III" instructions below.
- **Removal restrictions - Class IV:** If the spot(s) is larger than 1 1/2 inches in diameter **do not attempt TOTAL removal** using Class IV instructions. Do Steps 1 - 3 **only** under Class IV. Mist spot(s) with a generous amount of alcohol. Put a folded towel moistened with water over spot and a note next to it that says, ***"Do Not Touch Or Clean!"***. Then:
  - Call a pro and have spot removed as soon as possible within 24 hours. -OR-
  - If the spot is still fresh/wet and is 2 inches or less in diameter, get a spot machine and do Steps 2 - 6 under Class II.
- These products can immediately and permanently stain most nylon. If you cannot remove a spot, consult a pro for options as soon as possible.
- Large spills can damage latex in the carpet and pad and cause it to swell into little hills. This makes the carpet look as if it is loose and needs to be re-stretched. Consult a pro for options.
- Large spills can soak through the carpet and pad to the subfloor and cause recurring spots. (See "Recurring Spots", Chapter 4.) Consult a pro for options as soon as possible.

## Materials Needed:

Class III: Towel, Paper and pencil for note
Class IV: Disposable towels, Spotting kit

| Class III: Towel + Old / Dried Spot | Class IV: Towel + Fresh / Wet Spot |
|---|---|

### Class III: Towel + Old / Dried Spot

**Steps:**

1. **Do not attempt ANY removal** of a Class III spot.
   - Put a dry towel over the spot(s) and a note next to it that says ***"Do Not Touch Or Clean!"***.
   - Call a pro and have spot removed as soon as possible within 24 hours.

### Class IV: Towel + Fresh / Wet Spot

**Steps:**

1. Fold a disposable towel several times and place it over the spot(s).
   - Step on the towel with your full weight 15 - 20 times, using a clean part of the towel each time.
   - Repeat until no more absorbs.

2. Mist on a generous amount of alcohol.
   - Tamp with soft brush.
   - Allow to work 2 minutes.
   - Mist on a generous amount of ammonia.
   - Tamp with soft brush.

3. With a cloth towel, blot 15 - 20 times, using a clean part of the towel each time.

4. Look at spot area carefully to see if the spot is gone:
   - If YES: Allow to dry.
   - If NO: Repeat Steps 2 and 3 until no more removes. Then if needed, do Step 5.

5. If color cast remains, mist on a generous amount of peroxide.
   - Tamp with soft brush.
   - Mist on a small amount of ammonia.
   - Tamp with soft brush.
   - Allow to dry.

6. If the spot persists, call a pro for options as soon as possible.

# Tips from the Tradesman

## Introduction

For many years there has been conflicting information from a variety of sources about the differences in carpet fibers, how often carpets should be cleaned, the best way to clean a carpet and even when carpet protector is really needed.

Unfortunately, most people cannot ask the independent laboratory specialists who test carpets under all types of wear and soiling conditions, the instructors who teach the professional cleaning technicians or the well-trained professionals who actually care for the carpets in a variety of real use situations.

I didn't want to end this guide without sharing this invaluable information that is often only available to the carpet professional, so I have asked the experts and done the research for you.

You can read this Section on an "as needed" basis, unless you are curious about the topics covered. These include:

- **Chapter 6. How Does One Carpet Fiber Compare To Another?**
  A comparison of the different types of synthetic and natural carpet fibers to help you decide which best fits your needs the next time you are buying carpet.

- **Chapter 7. How Often Should My Carpet Be Cleaned?**
  How often your carpets should be cleaned, based on the type and amount of traffic your carpet receives and your environment. I also describe the routine maintenance that will prolong the life and the good appearance of your carpet.

- **Chapter 8. What Is The Best Way To Clean My Carpet?**
  A comparison that tells the pros and cons of each of the different types of carpet cleaning methods, including do-it-yourself cleaning.

- **Chapter 9. Does My Carpet Need A Carpet Protector After Cleaning?**
  The truth about whether or not you really need that carpet protector the carpet cleaner is recommending.

- **Chapter 10. How Do I Find A Quality Carpet Cleaning Professional?**
  How to find real carpet cleaning professionals for all your carpet-care needs - not just someone in the business.

Section III

- 1 -

# Chapter 6 How Does One Carpet Fiber Compare To Another?

## Introduction

Buying new carpet is a major investment for most people. A knowledgeable carpet salesperson can help you pick out the carpet that has the look and feel you want, as well as one that is in the price range you want to pay. But, you still need to be an educated consumer to help ensure that you get the best carpet for your specific environmental conditions.

Each type of carpet fiber has its own characteristics related to its reaction with spot causing materials or spot cleaning solutions, its durability, etc. In this Chapter I'll share information with you that the carpet salesperson may or may not have about how the different carpet fibers compare in terms of resistance to spots or stains, resistance to wear, how well they will hold their color, how easily the fiber can be cleaned, etc.

**Note:** There is a "Fiber Comparison Chart" at the end of this Chapter that compares the different carpet fibers and how each holds up to conditions common to most carpets in homes, commercial establishments and automobiles. This information can help you decide what fiber type best suits your home or business needs the next time you purchase carpet.

Some of the information in this document is repeated from other Chapters. I duplicated it here to make it easy for you to have all the facts if you are thinking about buying new carpet.

**Note:** I have also included a "New Carpet Purchase / Installation" form at the end of this Chapter to make it easier for you to keep accurate records when you buy new carpet. (This information will also help your carpet cleaning specialist do the best job for you, because you will be able to tell him/her exactly what type of carpet and carpet protector, if any, you have.)

# Carpet Construction

As you may remember from Chapter 3, a side view of a tufted carpet looks like:

## *Tufted Carpet*

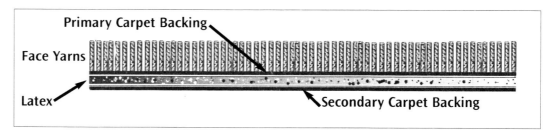

**"Face" Yarns** - Synthetic carpet fibers are manmade materials that are created in large vats, then extruded in thin filaments. Natural fibers like wool and cotton are cleaned, carded and spun into threads. The filaments or threads are twisted into yarns that are cut into short lengths. In tufted carpets these "face" yarns (your carpet pile) are then inserted into a primary carpet backing.

**Primary Carpet Backing** - In a tufted carpet the pile or face yarns are inserted into the primary carpet backing. The backing adds considerably to the strength of the carpet and it improves the "dimensional stability" - the ability of the carpet to retain its size and shape. Today, the primary backings for synthetic fiber carpets are usually made of polypropylene (olefin). It is clean, strong, chemical- and moisture-resistant plus non-allergenic. 100% wool carpets usually have jute (a natural fiber) backings.

**Latex** - Latex is used to "glue" the face yarns to the primary backing. Latex also binds the primary backing to a secondary backing.

**Secondary Carpet Backing** - The secondary backing for synthetic carpets is a fabric made of polypropylene that adheres to the underside of the carpet. It helps hold the face yarns in place and provides additional dimensional stability and strength to the carpet. (A woven carpet does not have or need a secondary carpet backing.)

**Note:** Up until the early 80's, carpet backings were normally made of natural fibers, jute or cotton (and sometimes included twisted paper yarns). These natural fiber backings support the growth of mold and mildew in high humidity environments. They also degrade or brown (cellulosic browning) in the prolonged presence of moisture, particularly alkaline moisture such as would be present during carpet cleaning.

Much of the negative talk about steam cleaning is a result of the problems caused by the natural fiber backings when the carpets were cleaned using the old steam cleaning methods. This was especially true when the cleaning was done by a poorly trained technician. Since the polypropylene used today with synthetic carpets does not mildew, the more effective cleaning methods using water and chemicals do not affect the carpet backing when properly applied.

## Carpet Fiber Types

The face yarns that make up the surface or pile of your carpet may be made of a single synthetic material, a blend or combination of different types of synthetics, a single natural fiber or a blend of natural and synthetic fibers.

There are four synthetic and two natural fibers used in home, business, automobile and other carpets:

**Synthetic Fibers**

- Nylon - Type 6, Type 6,6

- Olefin (or Polypropylene)

- Polyester

- Acrylic

**Natural Fibers**

- Wool

- Cotton*

  *Note: Cotton is seldom used for face yarns in carpets. Instead, it is mainly used for rugs.

Each type of carpet fiber has its own characteristics related to:

1. How it reacts with spot/stain causing materials (and spot cleaning solutions)

2. Durability

# 1. Reaction to Spot- / Stain-Causing Materials

The following gives important facts about how you can expect each of the fiber types to react to various spills. You know your environment and this will help you decide which fiber or fibers will be best for your specific situation the next time you buy carpet.

In addition, any special cleaning or maintenance needs, such as whether or not you will need to periodically replenish a manufacturer-applied carpet protector, are described.

## *Synthetic Fibers*

More than 85% of today's carpets are made entirely of synthetic materials and the percentage is increasing - mainly because of their easier care and lesser cost than that of natural fibers.

## *Nylon*

Nylon is used in more than 65% of the carpets on the market and is by far the most common carpet fiber.

Nylon is very resilient, meaning the yarns spring back when stepped on rather than remaining flat. It is also the most resistant of all the synthetics to abrasion. Because of these and other positive characteristics, nylon can be made into a variety of carpet styles or weaves. It is also being used more and more in auto-mobile carpets.

In the past, nylon's biggest weakness was the ease with which it is stained by a variety of spills and its susceptibility to color fading when exposed to direct sunlight for extended periods. To overcome those weaknesses and to build on nylon's strengths, a new type of nylon, called "type 6,6" or "solution dyed" was developed in the last few years.

## Nylon Spotting / Staining Characteristics

There are two types of nylon available as carpet fibers:

• **Type 6** (which we will refer to as **"regular" nylon**) - This is the original nylon, developed in 1938. "Regular" nylon is easily dyed when the color is applied to the fibers after they have been made. This is because the fibers have "dye sites", which are positively charged surface areas. Negatively charged dyes adhere to the sites when the two come in contact. Unfortunately, these dye sites also make "regular" nylon easier to stain, bleach, wear and fade than the other type of nylon - type 6,6.

• **Type 6,6** (which is also referred to as **"solution dyed"**) - This newer type of nylon has some important differences from the original. The main one is that it is always solution dyed. The dye pigment is mixed with the hot liquid polymer and is literally put inside the fiber - just like olefin, polyester and acrylic. This makes it more difficult to stain, bleach, wear or fade than "regular" nylon. **Note:** If you have "solution dyed" nylon carpet in one room of your home or business, you may find that certain spills are easily removed, while in another room with "regular" nylon carpet, the same type of spill is difficult to impossible to treat successfully.

How nylon carpet reacts to different spots may or may not be affected by whether it is type 6, "regular" nylon or type 6,6 "solution dyed".

**Nylon:**
• Generally resists spot contaminants such as cooking oils, greases, tea, coffee or cola. ("Solution dyed" nylon has an even greater resistance than "regular" nylon.) These spots are removed with little effort when treated within a reasonable amount of time using the proper technique and type / quantity of chemical spotting agents.

• Resists strong solvents such as acetone and paint thinner, acids found in white vinegar, alkalines in liquid soaps and a variety of cleaning chemicals. (Unfortunately, the dye on the type 6, "regular" nylon fibers may not be so resistant to them.)

• Is mildly "oleophilic" or oil loving, especially with petroleum-based products such as engine lubricants, tar, asphalt, etc. These types of spots may become permanent and cause the fibers to yellow if the petroleum-based spot is left in the carpet fiber for prolonged periods of many months. (Problem areas may include traffic areas coming from a home garage, auto repair shop bays or a parking lot.)

— 5 —

- Will yellow in the prolonged presence of chlorine bleach. But, "solution dyed" nylon will not lose its color easily when exposed to chlorine bleach, because the color is inside the fiber. Unfortunately, the carpet color in "regular" nylon is usually removed instantly.

- "Regular" (type 6) nylon is easily stained by spills that contain acid dyes such as the kind in fruit juices, wine, Kool-Aid®, etc., especially if the carpet does not have carpet protector applied.

- "Solution dyed" (type 6,6) resists stains by spills containing the acid dyes listed above, even if it has had no carpet protector applied or the protector has begun to wear off. **Note:** If you are buying new nylon carpet and know that spills of acid dyes will be a problem in your environment, it could be worthwhile to ensure you get a "solution dyed" nylon rather than the "original" type 6 nylon.

- Dissolves in the presence of formic acid, but unless you have a chemistry lab or a colony of ants (whose bite produces formic acid) in the house, this is an unlikely problem.

### *Nylon Ongoing Care / Maintenance Requirements*

Neither type of nylon has any special cleaning requirements other than a well-trained technician using quality products in the proper manner.

Most major manufacturers use various soil/stain-resist or repellent protective coatings on both types of nylon fibers in their higher quality carpets. Protective coatings are especially important on "regular" type 6 nylon, because it is so easily stained by a variety of foods, beverages and other products. These protective coatings further increase the "solution dyed" type 6,6 nylon's enhanced stain resistance and durability. (See "Chapter 9. Does My Carpet Need A Carpet Protector After Cleaning?" in Section III for more information on the types of carpet protectors.)

- These protective coatings are bonded to the nylon fibers or applied during the carpet manufacturing process. (If the manufacturer is going to apply a stain-resist coating to nylon fibers that will be blended with another type of fiber, the nylon will be treated before it and the other fiber are combined. Olefin, polyester and acrylic do not need the extra protection of a stain-resist coating, because they are already resistant to the acid dyes this type of protector guards against.)

- The coatings slow down the absorption of spills by the nylon fibers, but they do not prevent it. **Note:** Even though type 6,6 "solution dyed" nylon is already resistant to many types of stains and the coating further enhances its stain resistance and durability, it too can be stained by some spills if they are left on the carpet long enough.

- These carpet protectors can also repel dirt and keep it from sticking to the fibers. This can make your vacuuming more effective and efficient. If you live in a very sandy area such as the desert or near the beach, the carpet protector can reduce the wear and damage to your carpet fibers caused by soil.

- These protective coatings are not permanent and will wear off over time. You will need to have your freshly cleaned nylon carpet treated with protector in the heavy traffic lanes and spill-prone areas by its 3rd year of use, if you want to keep the stain resistant quality. After that, you will need to have carpet protector applied in the high traffic lanes and spill-prone areas every 9 - 24 months when the carpet is cleaned. (The effective life of the protector is affected by whether it is water or solvent-based. See "Chapter 9. Does My Carpet Need A Carpet Protector After Cleaning?" for more information on the types of carpet protectors.

- Unless the carpet is in excellent condition, discontinue the re-application of carpet protectors between the end of the carpet's 7th and 9th year. There is usually little benefit in continuing to have protector applied past this time. Normally, the appearance of the carpet has been so affected by abrading, fading and wear that the additional expense is not warranted. **Note:** The type of wear and care you give your carpet affects its condition. Plus, the increased resistance of "solution dyed" nylon carpet to abrading, fading and wear may cause it to remain in excellent condition longer than "regular" nylon carpets.

## *Olefin (or Polypropylene)*

Olefin or Polypropylene is more commonly known by its trade names Herculon® and Astroturf®. It is usually produced in a berber (looped) design or commercial gluedown carpet.

Olefin lacks resiliency ("spring back"), a factor that greatly affects its popularity. It has a wonderful lustrous appearance when it is new. Unfortunately, olefin is more susceptible to abrading than any of the other synthetics. In as little as two years, depending on use, that luster is dulled, especially in high traffic lanes.

Olefin is also the most heat sensitive of the synthetics. Singed tufts will easily occur around the fireplace if you have a real log-burning one.

### *Olefin Spotting / Staining Characteristics*

Olefin is always solution-dyed. The dye pigment is mixed with the hot liquid polymer and is literally put inside the carpet fiber where it cannot be contacted by bleaches. This makes it extremely colorfast.

**Olefin:**
- Does not have "dye sites" like "regular" nylon, so it is almost impossible to stain or discolor.

- Is resistant to strong alkalines or bleaches or any other types of household cleaners (including spotting agents) you are likely to use near (or on) the carpet.

- In rare instances, coloring from very hot or boiling liquids like coffee can permeate olefin. This creates a difficult to remove problem.

- In rare instances, products with strong concentrations of Benzoyl Peroxide like acne medicines can penetrate olefin and discolor the dye pigment within the fibers, if not discovered quickly and removed. This is an irreversible problem.

- Is very "oleophilic" or oil loving, especially with petroleum-based products such as engine lubricants, tar, asphalt, etc. These types of spots may become permanent and cause the fibers to yellow if the petroleum-based spot or oily soil is left in the carpet fiber without proper cleaning for prolonged periods of many months. (Problem areas may include traffic areas coming from auto repair shop bays, a parking lot or a home garage.)

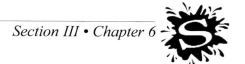

## *Olefin Ongoing Care / Maintenance Requirements*

Olefin has no special cleaning requirements other than a well-trained technician using quality products in the proper manner.

Most major manufacturers use various soil / stain repellent protective coatings on their quality olefin carpets. (Olefin does not need a stain-resist protector because it resists acid dyes already.) Unless your carpet will be exposed to the heavy concentrations of petroleum products described in olefin's spotting / staining characteristics, you may not need to replenish the carpet protector. (See "Chapter 9. Does My Carpet Need A Carpet Protector After Cleaning?" in Section III for more information on carpet protectors.)

**Note:** These carpet protectors can also repel dirt and keep it from sticking to the fibers. This can make your vacuuming more effective and efficient. If you live in a very sandy area such as in the desert regions or near the beach, the carpet protector can reduce the wear and damage to your carpet fibers caused by soil.

If you plan to do the frequent vacuuming recommended in "Effective Routine Carpet Maintenance" in "Chapter 7. How Often Should My Carpet Be Cleaned?", a soil repellent is not so necessary (especially if you don't live in a sandy area or other place where large quantities of soil may be tracked or blown in on the carpet).

## *Polyester*

Polyester is used in auto carpets because it is resistant to sun and fading. It is not so popular by itself as a home or commercial carpet fiber due to crimp loss (its bulkiness) and luster loss.

- Heavy traffic areas get flattened and stay that way.

- Abrading due to soil in the carpet makes the original smooth, shiny texture look rough and dull. Unfortunately, abrading and wear can cause this distortion in high use areas in as little as 3 years when the carpet is exposed to heavy traffic and large quantities of soil.

Polyester is often blended with nylon, because the nylon improves the crimp of the carpet face yarns and helps them maintain their luster better than polyester by itself. It also makes the fiber more versatile, because the nylon-polyester blend can be used in a variety of carpet styles such as saxony. The polyester fibers also make the nylon-polyester face yarns more stain resistant than 100% nylon yarns.

### *Polyester Spotting / Staining Characteristics*

Polyester is normally dyed with "disperse" dyes at high temperatures. A disperse dye is one that distributes evenly within the carpet filament itself rather than being on the outside. This makes polyester fibers very colorfast.

**Polyester:**
- Is excellent in terms of spot and stain removal.

- Resists most household cleaners you are likely to use, including strong alkalines such as floor stripper or oven cleaner, and most chlorine and hydrogen peroxide bleaches.

- Is difficult to stain with spills containing acid dyes (most foods and beverages).

- May be stained by organic dyes such as coffee, cola soft drinks, beer and the yellow dye (turmeric) contained in mustard, herbal tea, soup mixes, etc.

- In rare instances, products with strong concentrations of Benzoyl Peroxide like acne medicines can penetrate polyester and discolor the dye pigment within the fibers if not discovered and removed quickly. This is an irreversible problem.

- Is moderately "oleophilic" or oil loving like olefin, especially with petroleum-based products such as engine lubricants, tar, asphalt, etc. These types of spots may become permanent and cause the fibers to yellow if the petroleum-based spot or oily soil is left in the carpet fiber without proper cleaning for prolonged periods of many months. (Problem areas may include traffic areas coming from auto repair shop bays, a parking lot or a home garage.)

## *Polyester Ongoing Care / Maintenance Requirements*

Polyester has no special cleaning requirements other than a well-trained technician using quality products in the proper manner.

Most major manufacturers use various soil / stain repellent protective coatings on their quality polyester carpets. (Polyester does not need a stain-resist protector because it resists acid dyes already.) Unless your carpet will be exposed to spills of products containing organic dye or the heavy concentrations of petroleum products described in polyester's spotting / staining characteristics, you may not need to replenish the carpet protector. (See "Chapter 9. Does My Carpet Need A Carpet Protector After Cleaning?" in Section III for more information on carpet protectors.)

**Note:** These carpet protectors can also repel dirt and keep it from sticking to the fibers. This can make your vacuuming more effective and efficient. If you live in a dry sandy area such as the desert or near the beach, the carpet protector can reduce the wear and damage to your carpet fibers caused by soil.

If you plan to do the frequent vacuuming recommended in "Effective Routine Carpet Maintenance" in "Chapter 7. How Often Should My Carpet Be Cleaned?", a soil repellent is not so necessary (especially if you don't live in a sandy area or other place where large quantities of soil may be tracked or blown in on the carpet).

## *Acrylic*

Acrylic was originally designed to be the synthetic substitute for wool and to eliminate all of wool's negative characteristics. It is usually found in berber (looped) styles, including a saxony-berber style called "sculptured". Acrylic is also found in blends with nylon.

Acrylic is the least popular of the synthetic face yarns due to undesirable performance characteristics such as "nap reversal" (sections of the fibers leaning in opposite directions) and lack of resiliency ("spring back"). Blending acrylic with nylon helps reduce this problem, because the nylon fibers are more resilient.

Even when blended with nylon, acrylic still performs well with regards to spot and stain removal, because the acrylic resists most spots and stains so well.

### *Acrylic Spotting / Staining Characteristics*

Acrylic is always solution-dyed. The dye pigment is mixed with the hot liquid polymer and is literally put inside the carpet fiber where it cannot be contacted by bleaches. This makes it extremely colorfast.

**Acrylic:**

- Does not have "dye sites" like "regular" nylon, so it is almost impossible to stain or discolor.

- Resists most household cleaners you are likely to use, including strong alkalines such as floor stripper or oven cleaner, and most chlorine and hydrogen peroxide bleaches.

- In rare instances, products with strong concentrations of Benzoyl Peroxide like acne medicines can penetrate acrylic and discolor the dye pigment within the fibers if not discovered and removed quickly. This is an irreversible problem.

### *Acrylic Ongoing Care / Maintenance Requirements*

Acrylic has no special cleaning requirements other than a well-trained technician using quality products in the proper manner.

Most major manufacturers use various soil / stain repellent protective coatings on their quality acrylic carpets, but you will probably never need to replenish the carpet protector. (Acrylic does not need a stain-resist protector because it resists acid dyes already.) (See "Chapter 9. Does My Carpet Need A Carpet Protector After Cleaning?" in Section III for more information on carpet protectors.)

**Note:** These carpet protectors can also repel dirt and keep it from sticking to the fibers. This can make your vacuuming more effective and efficient. If you live in a very sandy area such as the desert or near the beach, the carpet protector can reduce the wear and damage to your carpet fibers caused by soil.

If you plan to do the frequent vacuuming recommended in "Effective Routine Carpet Maintenance" in "Chapter 7. How Often Should My Carpet Be Cleaned?", a soil repellent is not so necessary (especially if you don't live in a sandy area or other place where large quantities of soil may be tracked or blown in on the carpet).

Section III

— 13 —

## *Natural Fibers*

Natural fibers are those found in nature. Less than 5% of the total carpet sales in the U.S. are natural fibers, so you are more likely to have natural fiber rugs rather than carpets.

## *Wool*

Wool is a three-part protein fiber (epidermis - the natural protective exterior scales, cortex and medulla) from sheep. It is the most prestigious of the carpet fibers, because of its cost (wool is the most expensive of the carpet fibers), its appearance and its appealing feel to the feet.

It looks better than the synthetic fibers and it is soft, warm and very comfortable to walk on, especially in bare feet. Wool wears like iron so it holds up well to the effects of wear, but it is easily stained by a variety of foods and other products and can be damaged by bleaches and other chemicals.

### *Wool Spotting / Staining Characteristics*

Wool is always yarn-dyed.

**Wool:**

• Is easily dyed, so it is also easily stained.

• Color is easily removed when exposed to strong alkaline products like concentrated commercial spotting products or chlorine bleach.

• Degrades (dissolving of the natural protective exterior scales called the "epidermis", causing the fiber structure or color to be weakened over time) with prolonged or repeated exposure to high alkalinity such as that found in high traffic area pre-sprays made for use on synthetic carpets. **Caution:** High alkalinity is also found in other common household products like liquid hand soap, dish soap, laundry detergent and oven cleaner.

• Will dissolve in minutes when it comes in contact with chlorine bleach (products like Clorox®, Purex® or Javex® which contain 5.25 - 6% sodium hypochlorite.) It is safest to keep chlorine bleaches completely away from any possible contact with your wool carpet or rugs. (Mildew removers that contain sodium hypochlorite should also be kept away from wool.)

## *Wool Ongoing Care / Maintenance Requirements*

Cleaning costs for a wool carpet will be 25 to 35% higher than for the synthetics, because of the special chemicals needed for cleaning wool. Plus, wool carpet must be cleaned by someone who knows how to properly clean it or you will have problems with fiber degradation.

• Wool tends to be sensitive to aggressive agitation, which can cause fiber distortion called "felting". **Caution:** This condition cannot be corrected, so agitation during spot removal or cleaning must be carefully controlled.

• Any carpet pre-spray used on wool should be formulated specifically for natural fibers. (Before a new carpet cleaning technician begins to work on your wool carpet, ask him/her what types of cleaning chemicals will be used and if they are specifically for natural fibers.)

• Wool should always be rinsed with a neutral or slightly acidic solution (pH 5.5 - 6.5), since wool is slightly acidic in its natural state.

• Strong inorganic acids (acids not from plants or animals) like those found in professional acid rinsing agents formulated for synthetic carpets should be avoided. They are too strong and can weaken the fibers and their colors, and in some cases can even dissolve them over time.

**Caution:** Improperly using the high pH chemicals formulated for cleaning synthetic carpets on a wool carpet:

• Will cause the wool fibers to get brittle and to begin slowly breaking down earlier than normal.

• Can cause discoloration in large areas and even affect an entire room.

• Cause the carpet to feel sticky.

Though the wool industry does not recommend applying carpet protector to wool, it is advisable to have an odorless solvent-based (no water-based) stain repellent protector applied every two years, immediately after cleaning, in heavy traffic and spill-prone areas to give some protection against liquid spills. This protector should be applied by a trained professional. (See "Chapter 9. Does My Carpet Need A Carpet Protector After Cleaning?" in Section III for more information on carpet protectors.)

Section III

— 15 —

## *Cotton*

Cotton is strong and durable, but it is rarely used for face yarns in carpeting and is more commonly found in rugs.

**Note:** Even though cotton is not used for carpets, I thought you might be interested in how your cotton rugs will react to different spots or stains.

### *Cotton Spotting / Staining Characteristics*

Cotton is easily dyed - by both dye technicians and a 3-year old with a cup of grape juice.

**Cotton:**

• Withstands strong bleaches such as sodium hypochlorite (Clorox®, Purex® or Javex®, bleach or mildew removers), but the fibers and color will be progressively weakened if the bleach is not thoroughly rinsed out and/or neutralized with a dechlorinator from a professional carpet cleaner who is experienced in cleaning oriental rugs.

• Is easily stained.

• Will brown permanently with prolonged or repeated exposure to high alkalinity, such as that found in high traffic area pre-sprays made for use on synthetic carpets or do-it-yourself carpet cleaning chemicals that are too strong or too concentrated.

• The fibers and color will be weakened by moderate solutions of inorganic acids such as hydrochloric, sulfuric or nitric acid. (It is much more likely that some businesses rather than homes would have these chemicals present; but if you have a home mechanic who likes to work on the car, battery acid on shoes or clothing will damage your cotton rugs if it comes in contact with them.)

### *Cotton Ongoing Care / Maintenance Requirements*

The care requirements for your cotton rug depend on whether it is:

• An expensive, decorative rug with bright colors and patterns. These rugs are more safely cleaned by a professional carpet cleaner who is experienced in cleaning oriental rugs.

• A small, sturdy rug that can be washed in the washing machine without the color bleeding or fading.

**Note:** A carpet protector will provide little protection on cotton and is probably not worth the investment.

— 16 —

## *Blends or Combinations*

"Blends" are carpets made of two or more different types of fibers. For example: nylon/polyester, nylon/acrylic, acrylic/wool, etc.

Each of the fibers in the blend will be affected by the various spots and stains exactly as described in the earlier information about that fiber. How a blended fiber carpet is affected will depend on the relative percentages of the fibers in the blend.

Example: If you have a "regular" type 6 nylon / acrylic blend carpet with no carpet protector or the protector has worn off in the spot area, you may notice that after treating a spot containing acid dye, part of each yarn (the acrylic) cleaned up just fine, while the other part (the "regular" nylon) is still stained. If the percentage of nylon in the carpet yarns is low, the spot may be relatively unnoticeable and you can live with it. If the percentage of nylon is high, the spot may still be very noticeable, and you may want to get a professional out to treat the spot.

With the information I have given you about the various carpet fibers and their characteristics, you will be able to ask a knowledgeable carpet salesperson the right questions to get the facts you need about the blended-fiber carpet in order to decide if it best fits your situation. (You'll also know when a less well-trained or not so honorable carpet salesperson is giving you wrong information.)

Section III

— 17 —

## 2. Durability

Most carpet wear is caused by soils in the carpet. These soils take their toll on carpet fibers through *wear, abrading* and *fading*. These three terms describe how the soil affects the carpet's general appearance and structure.

### Wear

Wear is the reduction in carpet fiber height and density in traffic areas compared to adjacent areas along walls and under furniture. The yarns in high traffic areas become shorter and thinner as a result of the abrasive, cutting actions of glass-like soil particles.

Several carpet characteristics affect wear:

• The type of fiber(s) in the face yarns of the carpet

• The density of the pile or face yarns

• The weave or style of the carpet such as saxony, berber, frieze, etc.

### *The Type of Fiber(s) in the Face Yarns*

Some carpet fibers wear better than others. The following lists the fibers from the most resistant to the effects of wear to the most susceptible:

- Nylon (solution dyed, Type 6,6) - most resistant
- Nylon (regular, Type 6)
- Wool
- Cotton
- Polyester
- Acrylic
- Olefin - least resistant

### *The Density*

The density of the fibers affects wear and appearance. The denser the pile, the better the carpet will wear, because most of the wear will be on the tips of the fibers. Very thin pile where you can see the backing through the face yarns (apartment or builder's grade carpets) will show wear very quickly.

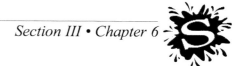

## *The Weave (Style or Design)*

How quickly and how badly a carpet will show wear is also affected by its design. Different styles expose varying amounts of each face yarn to wear when you step on them. For example: A saxony weave will generally wear better than a frieze weave, because:

• Most of the wear and tear on the yarns in a saxony style occurs on the tips of the yarns, unless it is builder's grade quality.

• The twisted loops of the frieze lay on their sides, so more of the fiber is exposed to wear.

**Note:** For more information on the wear characteristics of the different types of weaves or designs, visit our Web site at: **www.artsspotcleaning.com**

## *Abrading*

Abrading is a change in the carpet's appearance caused by a change in light reflection. This change is a result of the scratches and pits caused by abrasive soils rubbing against the "plastic-like" fibers of synthetic carpets or the natural protective exterior scales ("epidermis") of wool. Abrading is normally very noticeable in heavy use areas such as the main traffic paths throughout a home or business. It can also be more localized, such as small patches in front of a recliner or sofa or on the floorboards of your car where the soles of your shoes rub soil against the carpet fibers. It also appears under the wheels of office chairs when there is no plastic mat to protect the carpet.

**How does abrading affect the different carpet fibers?**

• Synthetic Fibers: Scratches and pits eventually dull the carpet fibers' appearance just like taking a clear piece of plastic and rubbing it with sandpaper. No matter how many times you clean the plastic, the surface will always look dull and somewhat dingy, just as your carpet will.

• Wool Fibers: These don't shred as easily as the harder, plastic manmade fibers. Instead, they fray so you don't see the effect of the abrading as easily as with the manmade fibers.

• Shiny Fibers / Dull Fibers: Shiny fibers like olefin and nylon generally show damage from abrasion faster than dull ones like wool. **Note:** Nylon is shinier than acrylic, but it wears better so the damage from abrasion does not show as quickly with nylon carpet.

– 19 –

## *Fading*

Fading or lightening of the carpet color is caused by two factors - light and acid soil. (Most soils are acidic which is why alkaline cleaners must be used to remove them most effectively.)

- Light, whether it is incandescent, fluorescent or especially ultraviolet (sunlight), has a definite affect on dyes after prolonged exposure. (Fading caused by exposure to light bulbs happens to a lesser degree and is much slower than that caused by sunlight.)

- Prolonged exposure to acid soil tends to yellow synthetic and natural carpet fibers, creating a bleached or faded look to the carpet. (The most resistant to least resistant to this yellowing are: olefin, acrylic, polyester, nylon, wool and cotton.)

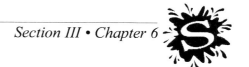

# Fiber Comparison Chart

The following "Fiber Comparison Chart" can be a very useful resource if you are buying new carpet or rugs. Comparing the fiber characteristics listed in the Chart with your needs and the environment in which the carpet or rug will be used, can help you choose the carpet fiber that will best suit your particular situation.

The Chart shows how the various carpet fibers will perform and maintain their integrity. When I say "integrity", I mean how they hold up structurally against abrasion, their resistance to fading and their resiliency ("spring back"), etc. In other words, how well they will keep those characteristics that caused you to buy that particular carpet fiber in the first place. (Again, I have included information on cotton for any rug purchases.)

**Note:** Several resources including carpet cleaning textbooks, seminars and my own experience were the sources of the information on the Fiber Comparison Chart.

# Fiber Comparison Chart Terminology Definitions

The following are the characteristics used for comparing the different carpet fiber types:

- **Cost** - The cost of a specific carpet fiber (The score is based on most expensive: 0 - 2 Poor, to least expensive: 9 - 10 Excellent.)

  **Note:** The final price per square yard of carpet is influenced by many different factors besides the fiber type. These include the grade or quality (including things you can see like the number of yarns per square inch, and things you can't see like the quality of the carpet backing, etc.) and the type of protection applied to the carpet, if any. Design features such as fancy patterns, textures, sculpting, carving, bordering and binding also affect carpet cost. Whether the carpet was manufactured domestically or imported is also a factor.

- **Resilience** - How well face yarns made of a specific carpet fiber spring back after being subjected to prolonged use

- **Abrasion Resistance** - How well a specific carpet fiber resists the sandpaper-like effects of soil, including wear, scratching and pitting

- **Chemical Resistance** - A specific carpet fiber's ability to resist the structural damage and discoloring effects of all chemicals - household and industrial

- **Heat Resistance** - A specific carpet fiber's ability to resist shrinkage or structural damage due to excessive temperatures. **Note:** All of the fibers are more than able to withstand the 180° - 190°F / 82° - 88°C water temperature used during the professional steam cleaning process.

- **Soil Hiding** - How well carpet pile made of a specific fiber hides soil particulates. (This can also be a negative trait. Since the carpet may appear cleaner than it actually is, you may delay needed cleaning and increase the wear, abrading and fading caused by the soils in the carpet.)

- **Cleaning** - How well foreign matter can be removed from a specific carpet fiber when the most effective method of cleaning - steam cleaning - is used

- **Streaking Resistance** - The ability of carpet pile made of a specific fiber to resist showing the streaking effects of dirt and cleaning chemicals caused by inconsistent or incorrect cleaning procedures

- **Spot / Stain Resistance / Removal** - Whether tough spots and stains affect a specific carpet fiber when they come in contact with it, and how easily the tough spots and stains remove when the appropriate spot treatment is used. It also includes how long you can delay treatment before the spot becomes permanent. (The longer you can delay and still remove the spot results in a better score.)

- **Color Retention** - How well a specific carpet fiber maintains its original color after prolonged exposure to cleaning, soiling, spills, flooding and sunlight

- **Color Bleeding Resistance** - A specific carpet fiber's ability to resist sudden dye loss or dye movement when exposed to strong cleaners, spotters or chemical spills

- **Sunlight Resistance** - How well a specific carpet fiber resists the fading, drying, cracking, peeling effects of the sun

- **Drying (face and backing)** - How quickly a carpet made of a specific fiber dries after cleaning or flooding

- **Mold/Mildew Resistance** - A specific carpet fiber's ability to resist this multi-species' destructive growth, feeding habits and tough spotting materials

- **Rotting Resistance** - A specific carpet fiber's ability to resist decay

- **Browning Resistance** - A specific carpet fiber's ability to resist browning activated by alkaline cleaners or moisture

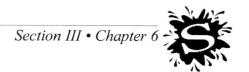

# Fiber Comparison Chart

**Rating Scores - (9 - 10 Excellent) (7 - 8 Good) (5 - 6 Fair) (3 - 4 Unimpressive) (0 - 2 Poor)**

| Fiber | Nylon Type 6,6 ("Solution Dyed") | Nylon Type 6 ("Regular") | Olefin | Polyester | Acrylic | Wool | Cotton |
|---|---|---|---|---|---|---|---|
| Cost | 9 | 9 | 10 | 5 | 5 | 0 | 6 |
| Resilience | 10 | 10 | 2 | 4 | 2 | 6 | 0 |
| Abrasion Resistance | 10 | 9 | 4 | 6 | 5 | 8 | 7 |
| Chemical Resistance | 7 | 7 | 10 | 9 | 7 | 5 | 4 |
| Heat Resistance | 8 | 7 | 6 | 7 | 7 | 4 | 4 |
| Soil Hiding | 8 | 8 | 6 | 6 | 7 | 10 | 7 |
| Cleaning | 9 | 9 | 9 | 8 | 9 | 7 | 1 |
| Streaking Resistance | 8 | 8 | 8 | 7 | 7 | 5 | 3 |
| Spot/Stain Resistance / Removal | 9 | 8 | 10 | 9 | 9 | 3 | 2 |
| Color Retention | 8 | 6 | 10 | 8 | 8 | 6 | 5 |
| Color Bleeding Resistance | 9 | 8 | 10 | 9 | 9 | 5 | 3 |
| Sunlight Resistance | 8 | 7 | 8 | 8 | 8 | 7 | 6 |
| Resistance Drying (face and backing) | 9 | 9 | 10 | 8 | 8 | 5 | 0 |
| Mold / Mildew Resistance | 8 | 8 | 9 | 9 | 9 | 3 | 0 |
| Rotting Resistance | 9 | 9 | 9 | 9 | 8 | 3 | 1 |
| Browning Resistance | 8 | 8 | 9 | 7 | 7 | 4 | 2 |
| Total Score (170 points available) | 137 | 130 | 128 | 119 | 115 | 81 | 51 |

## *Carpet Purchase And Installation Record Form*

I have included the "New Carpet Purchase / Installation Record" form to help you keep an exact record of all important information related to your purchase and installation of home or business carpets.

**Best Practice:** Keep copies of important carpet documents like the invoice for new carpet, the manufacturer's warranty, if any, in a safe place where you can find them when needed. These records, including the form I've given you, could prove invaluable in case of a warranty dispute over poor carpet construction or installation, an insurance claim, damage due to improper cleaning by a cleaning company or an emergency such as a fire or flood. This information could also be useful to you if you want to buy the same type of carpet in the future and/or to the purchaser if you sell your home or business.

There are two copies of the "Carpet Purchase and Installation" form, so you can fill out one copy and still have a "master" copy you can reproduce if additional record keeping space is needed. If you have more than one type of carpet in your home or business, fill out a form for each one.

Fill out the form as completely as possible, so you'll have the necessary information when you need it. (If you buy a nylon or nylon blend carpet, be sure to ask the salesperson if the nylon is a type 6 "original" nylon fiber or a type 6,6 "solution dyed" one. Have the salesperson write the type of nylon on the invoice and list it on your Record form.)

**Note:** There is also a "Carpet Cleaning / Restoration Record" form at the end of Chapter 7 that can help you track your cleaning schedule for your carpet, rugs, furniture, drapes and other services. It also has space to list the phone numbers of companies and service people you trust.

Section III

– 24 –

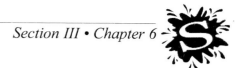

# New Carpet Purchase / Installation Record

Carpet Store: _____     Phone: _____

Address: _____

_____

Salesperson: _____     Phone: _____

Date Purchased: _____     Invoice Number: _____

Total No. of Yards: _____ ____     Cost per Yard: $_____     Total Cost: $_____

## Carpet Facts

Carpet Brand Name: _____

Manufacturer's Name: _____

Manufacturer Contact: _____     Phone: _____

Style Name / Number: _____

Color Name / Number: _____

Carpet Fiber Type(s): _____

## Carpet Protector

Factory-Applied Fiber / Carpet Protector - Yes / No

Type of Protection: _____

## Carpet Warranty

Factory Warranty - Yes / No     Length of Warranty: _____ years

Store Warranty - Yes / No     Length of Warranty: _____ years

## Installation

Date Installed: _____

Installer's Name: _____     Phone: _____

Installed in Which Room(s): _____

New Tack Board Installed - Yes / No

New Pad - Yes / No     Type of Pad & Thickness: _____

Carpet Installation Method: Power Stretched or Knee Kicked

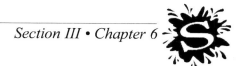

# New Carpet Purchase / Installation Record

Carpet Store: _____     Phone: _____

Address: _____

_____

Salesperson: _____     Phone: _____

Date Purchased: _____     Invoice Number: _____

Total No. of Yards: _____ _____     Cost per Yard: $_____     Total Cost: $_____

## Carpet Facts

Carpet Brand Name: _____

Manufacturer's Name: _____

Manufacturer Contact: _____     Phone: _____

Style Name / Number: _____

Color Name / Number: _____

Carpet Fiber Type(s): _____

## Carpet Protector

Factory-Applied Fiber / Carpet Protector - Yes / No

Type of Protection: _____

## Carpet Warranty

Factory Warranty - Yes / No     Length of Warranty: _____ years

Store Warranty - Yes / No     Length of Warranty: _____ years

## Installation

Date Installed: _____

Installer's Name: _____     Phone: _____

Installed in Which Room(s): _____

New Tack Board Installed - Yes / No

New Pad - Yes / No     Type of Pad & Thickness: _____

Carpet Installation Method: Power Stretched or Knee Kicked

# Chapter 7 *How Often Should My Carpet Be Cleaned?*

## Introduction

One of the questions I'm asked the most is: *"How often should my carpet be cleaned?"*

The people who ask me this question are normally thinking of carpet cleaning as being a major event involving specialized equipment, chemicals and a trained technician or a do-it-yourself person. This is an important part of carpet care, but equally critical is what we call "routine carpet maintenance". Routine carpet maintenance is the day-to-day vacuuming and spot removal you do between the major carpet cleanings.

As I mentioned in the Overview in this section, for many years there has been conflicting information from a variety of sources about how often carpets should be cleaned and the best way to clean them. I have asked the experts and done the research for you, so let's look at both routine maintenance and cleaning frequency for your carpets.

**Best Practice: Protect your investment by having your carpets cleaned as often as necessary and as often as you can afford.** (To help you keep track of your carpet cleaning, I have included a "Carpet Cleaning / Restoration Record" form at the end of this Chapter. It has spaces to list the cleaning companies and service people you trust, plus record the dates and types of cleaning service for your carpets, rugs, furniture, drapes, etc.)

## *Importance of Routine Carpet Maintenance*

The routine maintenance you give your carpet before its first cleaning and then later between cleanings is one of the most critical, yet most often neglected parts of carpet care. The useable life and appearance of carpet in your home, office or automobile are substantially affected by the type, quality and frequency of carpet maintenance procedures. (Even how often you need to clean the carpet is affected by the type and frequency of this routine maintenance.)

We are all aware of how spills and spots affect the carpet, but there is a less obvious culprit that we often underestimate - **SOIL**! The soils that are tracked onto and into your carpet cause much of the wear and damage to carpet fibers. We think of most soil as being rather soft, but if you look at minute particles of it through a microscope, you will see that they have very sharp edges, just like broken glass. It is the continual rubbing of these sharp edges against your carpet fibers as people, pets, the wheels of your office chair, etc., move across the carpet that do most of the damage.

**Caution:** The accumulation of soils also affects indoor air quality because particles become airborne as well as ground into your carpet fibers.

**Note:** From a carpet cleaning technician's point of view, soil is not just dirt. It is anything that is foreign to the carpet, including dirt, mud, hair, paper, oil, old cleaning chemical residues, spot matter, etc., etc., etc.

Most heavy, abrasive, particulate soil accumulates within the first few feet of major entries and on the floorboards of your car or other vehicle. Lighter weight, fine soils are tracked further into your home or commercial building. Once inside, these soils take their toll on carpet fibers through **abrading, fading** and **wear**. These three terms describe how the soil affects the carpet's general appearance and structure.

**Abrading** is a change in light reflection resulting from the scratches and pits caused by abrasive soils rubbing against the "plastic-like" fibers of your synthetic carpet fibers. These scratches and pits dull the carpet fibers' appearance just like taking a clear piece of plastic and rubbing it with sandpaper. No matter how many times you clean the plastic, the surface will always look dull and somewhat dingy.

Abrading is normally very noticeable in heavy use areas such as the main traffic paths throughout a home or business. It can also be more localized, such as small patches in front of a recliner or sofa or on the floorboards of your car. These localized patches are caused by the soles of your shoes rubbing soil against the carpet fibers. In offices the carpet is often dingy looking behind desks because no mats have been put under the office chairs to protect the carpet from abrading by the wheels of the desk chairs.

**Fading** of the carpet is caused by two factors - light and acid soil. Light, whether it is incandescent, fluorescent or especially ultraviolet (sunlight), has a definite affect on dyes after prolonged exposure. Prolonged exposure to acid soil tends to yellow thermoplastic synthetic carpet fibers, creating a bleached or faded look to the carpet.

**Wear** is the reduction in carpet fiber height and density in traffic areas compared to adjacent areas along walls and under furniture. The yarns in high traffic areas become shorter and thinner as a result of the abrasive, cutting actions of glass-like soil particles.

Section III

3

# *Effective Routine Carpet Maintenance*

Effective carpet maintenance involves both soil prevention and removal.

## *Step 1. Control Soil*

A key step in your maintenance program is to reduce abrading, fading and wear by keeping as much soil as possible outside your home or business and off the carpet.

The best way to do this is by placing quality entry mats both outside and inside the entrances to your home or business. These mats should collect or absorb both the soil and moisture on peoples' feet before they walk on the carpeted areas. Note: Mats outside entrances should be in a protected area like a covered porch or a foyer to a building. They should not be openly exposed to the weather.

The inside mat or mats should be placed so you step on it/them just before you step on the carpet. Avoid putting the inside mats on the carpet if possible. The rubber backing on many mats can cause yellowing on the carpet in the exact shape of the mat. If you have a colored mat, moisture or the rubbing of the mat against the carpet could result in a transfer of color to the carpet.

### *Mat Characteristics*

The type and size of the mats needed depends on the number of times people enter and exit the home or business and the type and amount of soil exposure. (Unfortunately with mats, pretty doesn't always equal effective, especially for the outside mats and sometimes for the inside ones as well. If you are not lucky enough to find a quality mat that fits with your decor, you may have to compromise based on whether protecting your carpet or mat appearance is more important to you.)

Both outside and inside mats should be at least as wide as, and preferably wider than, the entire doorway. You do not want a smaller mat that people can easily walk around and onto your carpets without having to step on the mat. An effective inside mat is long enough to cover the hard surface flooring from the doorway to the edge of the carpet without overlapping it.

Section III

### Outside Mats

A good outside mat should:

- Be synthetic so it won't deteriorate so quickly. Olefin fiber face with rubber backing is a good choice.

- Have large enough holes for moisture and soil on the soles of shoes to sift through. The holes will also help a wet mat dry faster to avoid mildewing.

- Be coarse enough to help remove soils or other matter from the soles of shoes, including treaded shoes and boots.

- Be durable enough to take stomping on, shaking or beating against a hard surface during cleaning without tearing up.

- Not have any metal on it that could rust.

With outside mats it is better to go for rugged and effective. Pretty is secondary. Effective outside mats for the home are usually found at hardware stores or higher quality garden stores. Outside and inside mats for commercial use (and possibly ones suitable for residential use) are available from companies listed under "Mats" in the yellow pages. These mats can be purchased or rented and some companies can do custom sized mats for you. They can also advise you on the best type and size of mats for your particular situation.

### Inside Mats - Homes

A good inside mat should:

- Not have a rubber backing, but should not slip on a hard surface. A good anti-slip rug underlay under the mat will keep it from skidding when someone steps on it.

- Be synthetic so it can be easily cleaned and moisture will not cause the color to bleed.

- Be low profile so people will not trip on it and it will not interfere with doors opening and closing.

### Inside Mats - Offices, Commercial Buildings

A good inside mat in a commercial location should have the same characteristics as the outside mat.

## *Mat Maintenance*

The mats must be maintained by regular vacuuming, shaking and cleaning or by periodic mat exchange if you are renting them from a mat rental company. If you have bits of litter trapped in the fibers of the mats, use a brush in a rough, scrubbing action to loosen them so they can be vacuumed up.

## *Step 2. Vacuum Frequently*

Frequent vacuuming with a quality vacuum cleaner is the most important step you can take to prolong the life and appearance of the carpet in your home, business or automobile. Thorough, frequent vacuuming reduces the quantity of soil particles in the carpet and reduces the amount of damage to the carpet fibers.

**Note:** There is no such thing as "over-vacuuming" or vacuuming too much.

**What is "frequent" vacuuming?**

The definition of "frequent vacuuming" depends on where the vacuuming is being done:

- Home - Once a week under low use conditions and up to four times a week in heavy use or traffic areas.

- Office (commercial and public facilities) - Daily regardless of amount of usage. In climates with higher levels of trackable and airborne contaminates present, vacuum more thoroughly by making two to three or more passes over the same area. This is especially important on the lower floors of a building.

- Automobile - At least once a month under low use conditions and at least every two weeks or more under heavy usage. Make four or five passes with the vacuum cleaner over the mats. If you have bits of litter trapped in the fibers of the mats, use a brush in a rough, scrubbing action to loosen them.

**What is a "quality" vacuum cleaner?**

A quality vacuum cleaner:

- Is a top-fill upright vacuum with brush/beater bar agitation or a canister vacuum with a "power head" incorporated brush agitation to loosen and remove the soil from the carpet.

— 6 —

- Has a high efficiency filtering system with a Hepa-Filter or a micro-filtration bag to minimize the amount of soil that escapes the vacuum's recovery system and reenters the air. (These particles not only pollute the air, but also fall back into the carpet fibers.)
  **Note:** If you want to see if or how much your vacuum is polluting the air, run the vacuum in a dark room. Spotlight the vacuum with a flashlight and see how much dust is swirling around the outside of the bag or filter.

- Has a 10 - 12 amp power rating.

- Has a long enough cord (25 feet or more) so you can easily vacuum the area without having to continually plug it in elsewhere.

## Step 3. Treat Spots Immediately

As you have seen in earlier portions of this guide, most spot and stain removal is more effective if the spots are treated quickly and appropriately using the directions in "Chapter 5. Spot Treatment Steps" in Section II.

If ignored, spots may bond with fiber dye sites, forming permanent stains and/or collecting additional soil to be ground into the carpet.

# Carpet Cleaning - Frequency Guidelines

How often your home, office or other business carpet should be cleaned is based on its soiling rate.

Keep in mind that the wide variety of carpet designs, types and qualities will affect the rate at which your carpet appears to soil. Other factors affecting it include:

**How your carpet is cleaned**

- If you use one of the cleaning methods that removes only the surface soil or leaves most of the soil in the carpet, you will have to clean more frequently.

- If you use the hot water extraction (steam cleaning) method and it is done by a well-trained professional, you will not have to clean your carpets as often.

**Homes**

- The amount and type of use the carpet receives
  The number of people in the home and the presence of children and/or pets affect where, as well as how much and the type of soil that accumulates in the carpet. Low use areas such as formal living and dining rooms may need less frequent cleaning, while heavy traffic areas or rooms subjected to heavy soiling need more frequent cleaning. Children or pets increase cleaning frequency. (I've been told that one child equals one pet in terms of carpet wear.)

- Occupants who have allergy or respiratory problems
  Frequent cleaning is recommended to reduce allergens and irritants.

**Commercial Establishments**

- The commercial carpet construction

- The type and amount of traffic

- The soiling conditions present - the amount and type of soil found in a fast food restaurant is generally very different from that found in the average office

- Other circumstances such as occupant activities, structure design and indoor air quality

Some areas of homes, businesses and cars normally get much heavier traffic and soiling, and therefore must be cleaned more frequently than lower traffic areas.

Examples:
- Entryways: Home/Business - Carpets in these areas soil faster because of the heavier traffic and the greater exposure to dirt, even in offices that are contained within a building or stores within a mall. This heavier soiling is an even bigger problem with entries from the outside, because of the increased quantities of and types of soils tracked in from the great outdoors.

- Homes - Depending on the number and types of rooms they lead to, hallways and staircases may receive three to five times as much traffic or more than other areas in the home. Soil and stain buildup occur more quickly in rooms used frequently by the family, especially the children and pets.

- Businesses - The areas coming from a conference area, lunch room or dirty shop floor are soiled faster.

- Cars - The front floorboard carpets may need cleaning more often than the back ones. (Unless your kids love the drive-thru at McDonald's or other fast food places.)

For your home: If you see exceptionally heavy soiling occurring in specific areas of your house, ask your carpet care professional what he/she would advise.

For commercial locations: Specialized maintenance and cleaning programs (weekly, monthly, quarterly, semi-annually) should be developed based on your business's individual needs. A program may have different areas of the office(s) or building being cleaned on different schedules. To develop a program talk with your carpet care professional and refer to the "Suggested Carpet Cleaning Frequency Chart" on page 11.

**Best Practice:** Frequent cleaning of entrances and high traffic areas will reduce the contaminants and soil particles from outside that accumulate in these areas and are tracked to other areas. It will also help control the indoor air quality.

### How do I know when my carpet needs cleaning?

The best way to judge when your carpet needs to be cleaned is to 1) review the Suggested Carpet Cleaning Frequency Chart that follows, and 2) carefully observe your main traffic lanes and high use areas for the first signs that the carpet is beginning to collect soil and spots. Look at the soiling and spots in lesser used areas as well.

- Your carpet is past due for a good cleaning if large areas of the carpet have a faint (or darker) grayish colored cast and/or approximately one fourth of the carpet in a room has spots and stains on it.

- If your carpet has fewer spots or stains, but most of them have been on the carpet for 6 months or longer, the carpet needs cleaning. (Treating a spot as soon as you can gets the best results; but if this is not possible, at least do a cleanup when you start seeing spots and stains accumulate.)

**Best Practice:** Schedule carpet cleaning before soiling or spotting becomes too apparent.

# Suggested Carpet Cleaning Frequency

The following chart gives guidelines for recommended carpet cleaning frequency based on both aesthetics and health considerations. It is a quick, easy reference that will help you determine how often you need to budget for carpet cleaning in order to maintain your carpet's good looks and prevent premature wear and other damage.

**Note:** The different environments used in the Chart are:

- Temperate climate - Temperatures are comfortable, fairly constant, and precipitation is moderate.

- Contaminated and/or dry, dusty climate - Industrial pollutants and/or dry dust are concerns.

- Extremely cold or wet climate - Heavy snowfall or frequent rain are common.

- Hot, humid, biogenic climate - High humidity environment subject to biological contamination such as mold, mildew and decomposition of organic matter occurring by natural means or from by-products of human activities.

# Suggested Carpet Cleaning Frequency Chart

| Location / Occupants | Number of Months Between Cleanings in this Climate | | | |
|---|---|---|---|---|
| | Temperate | Contaminated or Dry, Dusty | Extremely Hot, Cold/Wet | Humid, Biogenic |
| **Residence / Auto** | | | | |
| • 1 adult - no smoking | 12 - 16 | 8 - 10 | 10 - 12 | 8 - 10 |
| • 1 adult - smoking | 10 - 14 | 7 - 9 | 9 - 11 | 7 - 9 |
| • 2 adults - no smoking | 9 - 13 | 6 - 10 | 8 - 12 | 6 - 10 |
| • 2 adults - smoking | 8 - 12 | 4 - 8 | 6 - 10 | 4 - 8 |
| • 3 - 6 people (adults + kids) | 6 - 10 | 3 - 5 | 4 - 6 | 3 - 5 |
| • Up to 10 occupants (adults + kids/pets*) | 4 - 6 | 2 - 4 | 3 - 5 | 2 - 4 |
| • More than 10 occupants - Ask your cleaning professional | TBD** | TBD** | TBD** | TBD** |
| **Office Building** | | | | |
| Ground Floor | 3 - 6 | 2 - 4 | 4 - 6 | 4 - 6 |
| Higher Floors | 6 - 12 | 4 - 6 | 5 - 9 | 5 - 9 |
| **Retail Shop, Bank, Others** | | | | |
| Ground Floor | 3 - 6 | 2 | 3 | 3 |
| Higher Floors | 6 - 12 | 4 | 6 | 6 |
| **Food Service** | | | | |
| Ground Floor | 3 | 1 | 2 | 3 |
| Higher Floors | 8 | 3 | 5 | 6 |
| **Day Care Center** | 4 | 2 | 3 | 2 |
| **Nursing Home** | 4 | 2 | 3 | 2 |

* It has been said that a child and a pet are about equal in terms of the amount of carpet soil they generate.

**To Be Determined (TBD) by consulting with your cleaning professional.

Section III

– 11 –

## *Carpet Cleaning / Restoration Record Forms*

I have included the Carpet Cleaning / Restoration Record form to help you keep an exact record of all important cleaning and restoration information related to your home or business carpets (and even your car's if you want). This form helps you track your cleaning schedule for your carpet, rugs, furniture, drapes and other services. It also has space to list the phone numbers of companies and service people you trust.

There are two copies of the form so you can fill out one copy and still have a "master" copy you can reproduce if additional record keeping space is needed.

Fill the form out as completely as possible, so you will have the necessary information when you need it. (I suggest using a pencil to fill in the names of carpet technicians, etc., since personnel in the carpet cleaning industry change companies, and you may need to update names and information from time to time.) In the "Service Dates / Description" section of the form, each line can be used to record several service calls. Just put a "/" after each cleaning or other service to separate it from the next one.

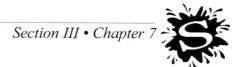

# Carpet Cleaning / Restoration Record

Carpet Cleaning Company: _____    Phone: _____

Address: _____

_____

Owner / General Manager: _____    Phone: _____

Emergency Service (Fire, Flood)

Phone: _____    Cell: _____    Pager: _____

**Services Provided**

On-Premises Estimates -                                        Yes / No

Carpet Cleaning - Synthetic Fiber Carpets -                   Yes / No

Carpet Cleaning - Natural Fiber (Wool/Cotton) Carpets -      Yes / No

Oriental, Other Area Rug Cleaning -                          Yes / No

Special Spot Cleaning -                                       Yes / No

Carpet Repair / Re-Stretching -                              Yes / No

Area or Spot Dyeing -                                         Yes / No

Hard Floor Cleaning -                                         Yes / No

Upholstery / Drapery Cleaning -                              Yes / No

Flood Restoration -                                           Yes / No

Fire Restoration -                                            Yes / No

Air Duct Cleaning -                                           Yes / No

Other Services _____

Section III

— 13 —

**Names of Estimators / Service Technicians on Staff**

Estimator(s): _____

Carpet Cleaning - Synthetic Fiber Carpets: _____

Carpet Cleaning - Natural Fiber (Wool/Cotton) Carpets: _____

Oriental, Other Area Rug Cleaning: _____

Special Spot Cleaning: _____

Carpet Repair / Re-Stretching: _____

Area or Spot Dyeing: _____

Hard Floor Cleaning: _____

Upholstery / Drapery Cleaning: _____

Flood Restoration: _____

Fire Restoration: _____

Air Duct Cleaning: _____


**Service Dates / Description**

Carpet Cleaned - Date / Rooms: _____

_____

Rugs Cleaned - Date / Rug Description: _____

_____

Upholstery / Drapes Cleaned - Date / Items Cleaned: _____

_____

Flood Restoration - Date: _____

_____

Fire Restoration - Date: _____

_____

Other Services - Date / Type: _____

_____

Section III

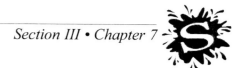

# Carpet Cleaning / Restoration Record

Carpet Cleaning Company: _____     Phone: _____

Address: _____

_____

Owner / General Manager: _____     Phone: _____

Emergency Service (Fire, Flood)

Phone: _____     Cell: _____     Pager: _____

## Services Provided

On-Premises Estimates -     Yes / No

Carpet Cleaning - Synthetic Fiber Carpets -     Yes / No

Carpet Cleaning - Natural Fiber (Wool/Cotton) Carpets -     Yes / No

Oriental, Other Area Rug Cleaning -     Yes / No

Special Spot Cleaning -     Yes / No

Carpet Repair / Re-Stretching -     Yes / No

Area or Spot Dyeing -     Yes / No

Hard Floor Cleaning -     Yes / No

Upholstery / Drapery Cleaning -     Yes / No

Flood Restoration -     Yes / No

Fire Restoration -     Yes / No

Air Duct Cleaning -     Yes / No

Other Services _____

_____

Section III

**Names of Estimators / Service Technicians on Staff**

Estimator(s): _____

Carpet Cleaning - Synthetic Fiber Carpets: _____

Carpet Cleaning - Natural Fiber (Wool/Cotton) Carpets: _____

Oriental, Other Area Rug Cleaning: _____

Special Spot Cleaning: _____

Carpet Repair / Re-Stretching: _____

Area or Spot Dyeing: _____

Hard Floor Cleaning: _____

Upholstery / Drapery Cleaning: _____

Flood Restoration: _____

Fire Restoration: _____

Air Duct Cleaning: _____


**Service Dates / Description**

Carpet Cleaned - Date / Rooms:_____

_____

Rugs Cleaned - Date / Rug Description: _____

_____

Upholstery / Drapes Cleaned - Date / Items Cleaned: _____

_____

Flood Restoration - Date: _____

_____

Fire Restoration - Date: _____

_____

Other Services - Date / Type: _____

_____

Section III

— 16 —

# Chapter 8 *What Is The Best Way To Clean My Carpet?*

## Introduction

In this Chapter we'll look at the advantages and disadvantages of the five most common professional carpet cleaning methods used today. In the segment on the hot water extraction (steam cleaning) method, I'll help end the truck mount cleaning versus portables debate. We'll wrap up by reviewing my first-hand and my customers' experiences with rental cleaning equipment and discover why do-it-yourself rent or buy machine cleaning is not such a great idea.

My goal is that you will be an educated consumer who not only selects the most effective method of carpet cleaning for you, but is able to distinguish whether the person who is offering to clean your carpets really is a professional or someone just trying to put the wool (carpet) over your eyes.

Before we begin, please put aside your current knowledge of carpet cleaning (other than what you have already learned in this guide) and bring an open mind to what I am going to tell you. The following information is based on years of study, research and asking questions of carpet manufacturers and other professionals.

During the many years I have been in the carpet cleaning business, I personally cleaned thousands of carpets in homes, businesses, automobiles, boats and airplanes, etc., in the Dallas, Texas area. My company primarily used the hot water extraction method ("steam" cleaning), although I did not use that method exclusively.

As every experienced, well-trained, certified technician does or should know, you simply must adapt to the needs of your customer in order to provide the cleaning service that best fits their particular needs. This means that you must use more than one method when necessary if you are going to satisfy a variety of customers and their varying circumstances.

That said, I am going to review the different cleaning methods from most effective to least in terms of their overall cleaning ability, when done properly by a trained professional. As I describe each method, I will tell you about the chemicals used, the steps used during the cleaning process and the pros and cons of that method.

**Note:** You will see some duplication of information in the descriptions of the cleaning methods. I wanted the information for each one to be as complete as possible in case you are only interested in one or two of them and don't want or need to read about all the rest of them.

# Carpet Cleaning Facts

Before we get to the cleaning methods themselves, we need a little background on carpet cleaning principles. The most important one is that the most effective carpet cleaning would be similar to cleaning your clothes in the washer/dryer or your dishes in the dishwasher.

**The most effective carpet cleaning would include these steps:**

1. **Dry vacuum the carpet thoroughly, especially the heavy traffic areas.**

   • Dry vacuuming is a necessary first step whether the cleaning is being done in your home, business or automobile and whether you or a technician (even a technician using a big, truck mounted unit) is doing it.

   • The less soil there is to be removed from the carpet by the cleaning method, the better the results.

   **Note:** To a cleaning technician, soil is anything that is foreign to the carpet construction (dirt, mud, hair, paper, oil, lint, old cleaning chemical residues, spot matter, etc., etc., etc.)

   • Some materials that are not water soluble, such as lint, become heavier when wet and more difficult to remove. (Extraction equipment, no matter how elaborate and powerful, is nothing more than a glorified canister vacuum that is not designed to efficiently remove particle or fibrous soil like hair or lint from carpet pile.)

   • Some dry spills such as Jell-O® powder, flour, etc., are more difficult to remove if they get wet before the majority of the spill is removed.

2. **Suspend and emulsify the soils.**

   Separate the soils from the carpet fibers, suspend and emulsify them so they are easier to remove. (The technical term for this is "deflocculation".)

   **This is done by using:**

   - **Cleaning agents** (called "pre-treatments" or "pre-conditioners") properly mixed and applied. These could be detergents with added dry solvents that help break down oxidized and oily soils, alkaline builders that enhance soil breakdown and removal, surfactants or wetting agents that enable a cleaning agent to penetrate the carpet fibers better and/or enzyme additives that digest protein soils such as body oils, animal fat and bodily fluids.

   - **Hot water** mixed with the cleaning agents to maximize their activity. Hot water not only speeds up most chemical action, but it also opens up the carpet fibers so the chemicals can soak in faster.

   - **Agitation** of the carpet and chemicals for uniform distribution of the chemicals and to enhance the chemical action. The pre-conditioning process, coupled with the agitation, causes emulsifying and suspension of the soil to occur and is crucial if the maximum benefits of the extraction process are to be realized.

   - **Dwell time** that is long enough for the chemicals to work properly. "Dwell" time is the length of time the pre-conditioner and spotting chemicals are left in the carpet to suspend and emulsify the soils before rinsing / extraction begins. 15 to 30 minutes is the normal time period. 10 to 20 minutes is okay, but 15 to 30 is better. An experienced technician will let the pre-conditioner dwell longer on more heavily soiled areas while he or she sets up the equipment, agitates, moves furnishings and cleans the furthermost areas from the traffic zones. These furthermost areas are usually the cleanest sections of the carpet unless you have pets marking there.

3. **Pre-spot extra tough spots and stains with specialty cleaners.**

   Having spotting agents formulated for specific types of spots rather than one all-purpose spotter always gives better spot removal results.

4. **Rinse / extract the suspended soil and cleaning agents.**

The rinsing could be done with clean water or water with a "rinse detergent" or rinsing agent that helps break down and wash away the pre-conditioning and pre-spotting chemicals.

**Note:** As the technician pulls out furniture, cleans underneath and returns it to its original place, he or she should immediately put protective styrofoam blocks and plastic tabs under the furniture legs to protect them from the damp carpet and to protect the carpet from possible furniture stain transfer.

5. **Groom the carpet, as necessary, using a carpet brush.**

This improves the carpet's appearance and/or aids the penetration of water-based carpet protectors, if applied. (Solvent-based protectors penetrate effectively without brushing.)

6. **Dry the carpet naturally** or, when needed, with special fans.

All of the most popular cleaning methods include many of these steps, but the degree to which the method allows them to be done in an effective manner varies. Several methods apply cleaning chemicals but do not agitate them sufficiently or do not leave them in the carpet long enough for the agents to really separate the soil from the fibers. Many methods do not include rinsing (so called "no rinse" methods), so soil and chemicals remain in the carpet. Some may rinse, but it is done with cool water which is less effective than a hot water rinse. These variations in the methods result in different "down times" for the carpet. Down time is the period during cleaning and afterwards when it is still too wet for safe (minimal chance of slips or falls) or heavy traffic. I will point out all these details during the description of each method.

**Note:** You may have noticed I did not include applying carpet protector as one of the critical steps in effective carpet cleaning. When you finish this Chapter, if you will turn to and read "Chapter 9. Does My Carpet Need A Carpet Protector After Cleaning?" later in this section, you will see that contrary to what most carpet cleaning salesmen/technicians tell you, not all types of carpet need that "...*and for $29.95 more we will protect your carpet so it stays looking good.*" It depends first on the type of fiber the carpet is made of and, in the case of some types of fibers, how old and/or worn the carpet is.

— 4 —

## Categories and Types of Cleaning Methods

There are two categories of carpet cleaning methods or systems:

- **Restorative or Restoration Cleaning Methods** - Primary focus is on soil removal. Improved carpet appearance is a result of the cleaning.

- **Maintenance Cleaning Methods** - Focus is on improving the appearance of the carpet, rather than thorough soil removal from it.

**Note:** If a technician uses variations or combinations of methods or takes extra time or uses extra cleaning agents, any maintenance method may move more toward the restorative category. On the other hand, any restorative method performed improperly moves toward the maintenance category.

| *Major U.S. Carpet Cleaning Methods* | |
|---|---|
| **Restorative** | **Maintenance** |
| • Hot Water Extraction ("Steam Cleaning")<br>• Shampoo (Rotary Shampoo) | • Absorbent Pad<br>  - Bonnet<br>  - Chem-Dry<br>  - Carbonated<br>• Absorbent Compound<br>• Dry Foam |

**Before we go into the details of each method.....**

If you are wondering which carpet cleaning method is the best, I have to say,

*"IT DEPENDS!"*

**It mainly depends on:**

• **Whether you want your carpet really clean or just looking clean.**

• **The length of time before the carpet must be ready to take normal traffic again.**

**If you want it really clean, then get a professional who has been properly trained and have him or her use the hot water extraction method on your carpet. Nearly 90% of the carpet in North America is cleaned this way. Both consumers and professionals have decided that it is the best because it is the method that most closely mimics your dishwasher or washer and dryer.**

**If you have a 24-hour establishment and do not have the luxury of waiting a number of hours before the carpet is completely dry or you must have the high traffic areas in your business cleaned nightly, then you will need one of the "maintenance" cleaning methods.**

Your circumstances determine which method will work best for your carpet, so let's look at all the methods and the pros and cons of each. We will look at each category (Restorative and Maintenance) separately, starting with the most effective cleaning method in each of the categories and working down to the least effective method.

**Note:** There are several carpet cleaning equipment manufacturers, so the machines that your cleaning professional uses may be different from the drawing included in the description of each method

## Hot Water Extraction (also called Steam Cleaning, Laundering or Jet Extraction) - "Restorative" Cleaning Method

**Note:** The water used in this method of cleaning is not heated to the point of vaporization. The name "steam" cleaning is a relative term, much like "dry" foam or "dry" absorbent compound cleaning - both of which use water-based detergent solutions.

The main advantage of the hot water extraction or steam cleaning method is the ability to physically flush out and pick up large quantities of soil during rinsing / extraction.

- This ability, however, is largely dependent on the quality of the cleaning technician and his or her application of this method.

- No matter how large or powerful, the extraction machine itself actually does minimal cleaning. The majority of the cleaning occurs when the soil is separated from the fiber's surface by the aggressive agents in the pre-conditioner, especially when combined with aggressive agitation and sufficient dwell time.

- The machine serves primarily as an efficient rinse unit when employed in proper relationship with the other essential elements of the cleaning procedure.

- **The technician, not the machine, is the crucial factor in producing quality cleaning.** The machine influences technician efficiency (mainly speed) more than quality results.

**Caution:** There are old timers or poorly trained technicians who are still using the original version of steam cleaning from the late 60's. This method is sometimes called "pure extraction" or "straight steam". It differs in two main ways from the method I so enthusiastically describe in the following pages:

1.  There is no dry vacuuming done prior to cleaning chemical application. The operators erroneously believe that the wet vacuuming during rinsing, especially if they have truck mounted equipment, is all that is needed. (As we said earlier in "Carpet Cleaning Facts", thorough dry vacuuming before chemical application is a necessary first step.)

2.  There is no pre-conditioner applied or agitation of the pre-conditioner, because they erroneously believe it is not necessary. (Do they really think that the split second of exposure the carpet fibers get to the high temperature rinsing solution between its injection and extraction will do more than erode away some of the most superficial soils? I just do not understand!)

**Caution:** There is another version of water extraction cleaning still used by some companies called "continuous flow recycle" cleaning or "CFR" that you should avoid. I describe it at the end of this section on the hot water extraction method.

### *Elements - Hot Water Extraction*

- A pre-conditioner - a detergent with a surfactant to suspend and emulsify the soils

- An alkaline builder combined with the surfactant to soften the water and enhance the emulsion / suspension of particle and oily soils

- In many cases, enzyme additives to digest protein soils are added to the detergent

- Concentrated spotting agents formulated for specific spot and stain types. A dry solvent to help break down oxidized and oily soils may be added if oily soils are present

- A mild rinse agent added to the rinse water to help further suspend the soil

### *Equipment / Methods - Hot Water Extraction*

1. Dry soil is removed by thoroughly dry vacuuming the carpet with a vacuum cleaner.

2. A hot pre-conditioner is applied, especially to the traffic lanes, using a pressurized sprayer. (The heat accelerates the chemical activity of the pre-conditioner. A cool pre-conditioner will not act as quickly.)

3. Concentrated pre-spotting agents are applied to spots and stains. (The technician should have specific spotting solutions for the various spots and stains.)

4. Agitation is done using a carpet rake and elbow grease or the rotary brushes of a rotary power scrubber machine or similar equipment. A carpet rake and elbow grease works on the 90 - 95% light to moderately soiled carpets that most technicians encounter. A carpet rake and more elbow grease works on the more heavily soiled carpet. (The main reason for using power scrubbers is to ease operator fatigue when pre-conditioning large areas of excessively soiled carpet or if the carpet pile is severely matted.)

   The aggressiveness of the agitation process depends on 1) the amount and composition of the soil present (light soil = light agitation, heavy soil = aggressive agitation) and 2) the structural condition of the carpet - should not be coming apart, be loosely installed or have ripples.

5. The chemicals are allowed a dwell time of 15 to 30 minutes between pre-conditioning and implementation of the rinsing and extraction phase. During this time, the technician sets up the equipment, agitates, etc.

6. More pre-spotting agents are applied, if necessary, to spots and stains that have not broken down during agitation.

7. A thorough extraction (rinse) process is implemented. Most technicians begin with the furthermost areas from the traffic zones, because they are usually the cleanest areas - unless you have messy pets marking there. This allows additional dwell time for preconditioner and pre-spotting agents in the areas of heaviest soiling.

   The "steam" cleaning machine pressurizes the hot water rinse solution in its tank and injects measured amounts of the solution into the carpet pile at approximately 200 - 450 psi. This further suspends and flushes out soil from the carpet fiber surface down to its base. The hot solution also re-accelerates the cleaning action of the pre-conditioning agent. As the floor wand is pulled backward, the injected solution, along with the suspended soil and a fair quantity of insoluble particulate matter such as hair, paper, fibers from the carpet pile, is picked up by the wand "shoe" and sent to a recovery tank.

   **Note:** The technician should immediately put protective styrofoam blocks and plastic tabs under the furniture legs as he or she returns each piece of furniture to its original place after pulling it out, cleaning and rinsing underneath it. This protects the furniture from the damp carpet while also protecting the carpet from possible furniture stain transfer.

8. If it is needed, carpet protector is applied. (See "Chapter 9. Does My Carpet Need A Carpet Protector?" for information on 1) whether or not your type of carpet fibers actually needs protection and 2) where the carpet protector should be applied.)

Section III

9. The damp carpet is finished with a grooming brush. (This brush is different from the carpet rake used earlier.) The brushing makes the carpet look better and if water-based carpet protector has been applied, helps ensure that the protector is evenly spread through the fibers.

10. Special fans called dryers or air movers may be used to cause the carpet to dry slightly faster. When these are used, it is normally on glue down carpet in a commercial setting. They are seldom used in homes during regular carpet cleaning.

11. Post-cleaning traffic and/or furniture moving:

   • The damp carpet can take traffic as soon as the cleaning process is done if everyone has clean, non-leather soled shoes, clean socks or bare feet. **Caution:** Any dirt on shoe soles or feet will rub off on the damp carpet. Leather soled shoes are prohibited until the carpet is dry because the dye in leather soles can bleed onto the damp carpet, leaving you with a trail of footprint stains.
   **Caution:** People should be very careful when stepping from the damp carpet onto a hard surface or vice versa.

   • Depending on the relative humidity, the carpet should be dry in approximately 14 - 24 hours after cleaning is completed. Do **not** move the furniture, and if possible, avoid walking on the carpet with dirty shoes or leather soled shoes until this has happened.

## *Pros - Hot Water Extraction*

• No other method flushes larger quantities of soil from carpet yarns as effectively and efficiently as properly executed hot water extraction.

• Hot water extraction cleans carpets so well, because when done properly, the cleaning ability of this method is amplified by the combination of soil suspension performed by the hot pre-conditioner, followed by agitation and dwell time, followed by the thorough flushing (rinsing) provided by the hot rinse solution and the injection/extraction equipment.

• When done properly, the rinse action removes excess chemicals that could cause a re-soiling residue.

• All the methods except hot water extraction must (or should) be done more frequently because they do not remove a large quantity of the soil in the carpet.

## *Pro/Con - Hot Water Extraction*

• Hot Water Extraction is the method most likely to reveal manufacturing and installation flaws in carpet. (Good news for you the carpet owner - if the flaws are discovered in time while the carpet is still under warranty.) For this reason, it is not so popular with some carpet manufacturers and retailers of cheap carpet or installers who are not correctly power stretching the carpet.

## *Cons - Hot Water Extraction*

• The 14 - 24 hour time period before the carpet is totally dry.

• It is the most complex method and the most complicated to learn, especially when using truck mount units. This makes having a well-trained, conscientious technician doing your cleaning especially critical with this method. Unfortunately, many of them in the business are not!

• Because it is such a popular cleaning method with many companies claiming to do it, you must be very careful about choosing your carpet cleaner. There are many bait and switch steam cleaning companies who promise a great job at a cheap price and either jack up the price with add-ons or give you a mediocre cleaning job. Some do both.

• Some out of date or poorly trained operators do not use pre-conditioner and think they are getting quality results because of the size of their equipment - usually truck mounts. The only cleaning chemical exposure the carpet gets is the split second between injection and extraction. (This may actually leave more soil in the carpet than a conscientious technician using one of the other "no rinse" methods.) Unfortunately, this flushing action produces just enough visible change in the appearance of the carpet that the customer thinks the carpet is really clean and does not realize that he or she has only received minimal results from the steam cleaning.

• **Caution:** The most common mistake made by operators using this method of cleaning is to turn the water heating system too high in an attempt to speed up the process. This can cause carpet to shrink or expand, depending on its makeup. If this exposure to water that is too hot is repeated too often for too long a period of time, it may cause wrinkling in the carpet.

• The technician must use proper wand stroking techniques during the rinse phase of extraction, otherwise the result is lingering soil that can result in abnormal re-soiling or streaking.

• Over-wetting the carpet may occur during the pre-conditioning procedure if the technician is poorly trained or not paying close attention. (If you see water around your shoes when you step on the carpet and/or the carpet is still wet or has a sour smell after 48 hours, you have a problem with over-wetting and should call the cleaning company to discuss the problem and solution.)

— 11 —

Section III

- Over-wetting can produce a sour odor. (If your carpet has contaminates like urine present when it is cleaned, especially if they are in large quantities, these can create a foul odor. If you have wool carpet, it will have a funky, sulfur smell as soon as it gets wet. This disappears when it dries.)

- Mold growth could occur if the carpet has jute backing. This is very unlikely these days unless you have an ancient carpet. Since most of today's synthetic carpet has 100% synthetic yarns and backing materials, browning, shrinkage and destruction by mold and mildew growth are hardly ever experienced.

- Rippling and buckling of 100% synthetic carpet may occur. These ripples and buckles can be caused by several things:

    1. If an installer fails to power stretch carpet or fails to stretch it 1 to 1-1/2% in both length and width (as required by IICRC installation standards), ripples and buckles are almost guaranteed 6 months to 1 year later.

    2. If the carpet pad is too thick or too soft, the flexing of the carpet during exposure to traffic can cause the carpet backing to weaken and eventually buckle or even de-laminate (separate). This allows the carpet to stretch even more easily.

    3. An overly thick pad can cause the carpet to pull free from the tack strips.

    4. The absorption of moisture from cleaning, and even from high humidity in the building, can cause latex laminates in the carpet backing to expand, resulting in buckling. This problem will cure itself when the carpet has completely dried or the humidity in the building returns to an acceptable level.

**Note:** The first three causes may require re-stretching of the carpet to achieve a long lasting remedy. In any case, the blame for buckles and ripples after cleaning should seldom, if ever, fall on the carpet cleaner or cleaning process. 99.9% of the time, it is caused by poor installation, an overly thick or soft carpet pad or a severe manufacturing defect in the carpet. (There is one exception - Axminster carpet found mainly in hotels usually shrinks severely under moist conditions. This creates havoc until it dries, and then it buckles and causes different problems.)

## *Continuous Flow Recycle or CFR Cleaning*

**CAUTION: Though this is a form of water extraction cleaning, I advise you to avoid it, if it is offered to you, for the reasons that follow.**

Continuous flow recycle cleaning uses a special machine that continuously recycles the water, pre-conditioner, rinsing agent and any contaminants that are extracted from the carpet. This chemical "soup" is sent through a series of filters in the machine, so the water can be reused until it is either dirty or used up. In theory, the internal filters are supposed to remove enough foreign matter to last up to five large cleaning jobs - at which time both water and filtering system cannot sustain any more contamination. (The water may be hot when it is first poured into the machine, but the machine does not reheat it as it is recycled, so this cannot really be called "hot" water extraction.)

In my experience with the equipment a number of years ago, the water appeared dark after just one cleaning of a moderately large home with lightly soiled carpet. This may have been an indication that a fair amount of cleaning was taking place, but I did wonder if some of that soil was being transferred from the more soiled traffic lanes I cleaned first to the more lightly soiled areas of the carpet that were cleaned later. Though the manufacturer assured my boss that the machine functioned as designed, I also wondered if I would be transferring contaminates, including ones like urine or feces residue, from one location to another if the filters did not work properly. .

In addition, the machine I used was seriously underpowered. This may have been because the heavier duty components needed to make it more powerful would increase the weight of the equipment. This increased machine weight plus the weight of the water in the machine would have made it too heavy for the technician lifting it in and out of the vehicle.

Another problem was the marginally effective hydro-kinetic floor wand - a variation on the highly effective upholstery cleaning hydro-kinetic tool. The upholstery cleaning tool was designed so it would not over-wet thin, smooth woven material such as upholstered furniture, drapery and wall fabric. Unfortunately, the floor wand is designed the same way so it sprays the rinse water at a 45 degree angle. This effectively wets only the surface of the carpet yarns. Normally, there is as much or more soil within the pile as there is on its surface, so the deeper soil has little exposure to the rinse water. The floor wand also does not work well on cut pile and loop carpet, because the tool design requires a fairly tightly woven surface in order to perform effectively. Unfortunately, carpet yarns, especially in looped pile construction, are not especially uniform.

**Caution:** If you are thinking about having a new company clean your carpets using the (hot) water extraction method, ask them if they use a fresh water system or do they use a recycle system. If they say, "recycle", I advise you to find someone else.

– 13 –

## *Truck Mounts Versus Portables*

The question I'm asked the most by the people who believe hot water extraction is the best way to clean their carpets is, **"Should my carpets be steam cleaned with a truck mount or a portable?"**

My answer is, *"IT DEPENDS"*.

It depends on whether an amateur or a seasoned professional is the one using the particular type of hot water extraction equipment. Most experts in the carpet cleaning industry will tell you they could rent an underpowered portable machine and clean circles around amateurs using the most powerful truck mounts.

**Note:** Relatively little cleaning is accomplished by the extraction machine. Instead, the majority of the cleaning occurs when the soil is separated from the fiber's surface by the aggressive agents in the pre-conditioner, especially when combined with aggressive agitation. The extraction machine acts primarily as an efficient rinse unit when employed in proper relationship with the other essential elements of the cleaning procedure. The technician, not the machine, is the crucial factor in producing quality cleaning. The machine influences technician efficiency (mainly speed) more than quality results.

Since you, unfortunately, may not always get an "expert" (especially if you don't use the IICRC's Referral Line), we will assume the technician you get with the equipment is at least minimally trained. In that case, the amount of power the equipment has is more important than whether it is portable or truck mounted.

## *Power*

We measure how powerful the steam cleaning equipment is based on:

• Volume of water or the more commonly used term "rinse pressure", measured in psi (pounds per square inch)

• Extraction or vacuum power - measured in both cfm (cubic feet per minute) and inches of water lift known as "hg"

In order to achieve better than acceptable results on the very thickest carpet pile, the minimum standard for hot water extraction equipment a cleaning company or consumer should be using is:

• Rinse pressure: At least 200 psi

• Water lift: 160 inches

Any increase in these standards should improve the cleaning results.
**Exception:** Rinse pressures above 750 psi used incorrectly can cause pile damage and/or distortion to cheaply manufactured synthetic carpets as well as the more expensive natural fiber - wool.

## *Water Temperature*

There is an ongoing argument that truck mounts do a better job of cleaning because they can produce hotter water than portables.

Although truck mounts can produce higher water temperatures, the hotter water speeds up the chemical processes rather than making them work better. This may or may not benefit you the consumer, but it does benefit the cleaning company and the technician doing the work by shortening the job time.

If a poorly trained technician turns the truck mount hot water system too high (in excess of 200°F / 93°C) carpet shrinking or wrinkling can happen over time with repeated exposure to the hotter water temperature.

### *The Bottom Line*

It is ultimately the experience, training and conscientiousness of the person cleaning your carpet that will determine whether you get a bad job, a great one, or something in between.

The three best ways to protect yourself and your carpet and to avoid a bad situation are to:

1. Ask someone you trust for a referral for a carpet cleaning company that he/she has had good experiences with. Be sure to get the name of the technicians or technicians who did the cleaning. Unfortunately not all people who clean carpets do outstanding work.

2. Call the IICRC (Institute Of Inspection, Cleaning And Restoration Certification) Referral Line at (800) 835 - 4624 to locate certified cleaning and restoration technicians and firms in your area.

3. If you are calling a new company for the first time, don't be afraid to ask them what psi and inches of water lift their equipment produces. If they can't tell you or the numbers they give don't meet or exceed the minimum standards given above, call someone else.

   At the very least, you should check out their machine when they show up at the door.

   - If it doesn't have two pressure gauges (one that measures psi and the other that measures vacuum or inches of water lift) or at least one of these gauges, it's probably not powerful enough to give you the cleaning job you are paying for and deserve.

   - The true test: If the machine is so small that the carpet cleaner is pulling the machine behind him/her by a hose that is 25 feet or less in length, then you'll surely know that the machine (and probably the "technician" as well) will not be able to perform up to standard. (Unless you've somehow gotten a real expert who likes the challenge of making substandard equipment perform like a champ.)

# Shampoo (Rotary Shampoo) - "Restorative" Cleaning Method

The shampoo or rotary shampoo method is possibly the most under-rated method of cleaning carpets in homes and commercial buildings that can afford the down time while the carpet dries. It does an excellent job up to the point of soil and cleaning chemical extraction. Unfortunately, the system is not designed to include the hot water rinsing that would make it a far better cleaning method.

This is also the second most complicated method to learn and to perform properly. Much of the success of this method depends on the purchase of professionally formulated detergents from reputable manufacturers and suppliers by the carpet cleaning firm. If pile distortion, over-wetting and/or uneven cleaning are to be avoided, these solutions must be uniformly applied by a certified, well-trained, conscientious technician - he or she bring the primary factor in the success of this method.

## *Elements - Rotary Shampoo*

- A water-based detergent (or shampoo) containing a surfactant to suspend and emulsify soils

- Alkaline builders combined with the surfactant to soften the water and enhance the emulsion / suspension of particle and oily soils

- Dry solvents added to the detergent help break down oxidized and oily soils

- In some shampoos, embrittling agents that crystallize with suspended soil as they dry to make it somewhat easier to remove the soil during dry vacuuming after the cleaning process

- No rinse product

## *Rotary Shampoo Equipment*

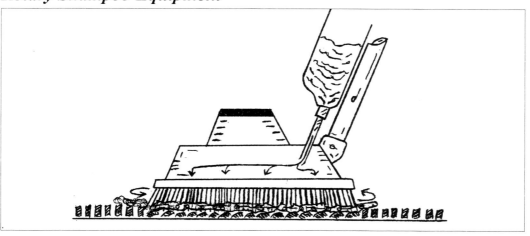

— 17 —

Section III

## *Equipment / Method - Rotary Shampoo*

1.   Dry soil is removed by a thorough dry vacuuming with a vacuum cleaner.

**Note:** Before starting step 2 on a section of the carpet in a room, the technician will move the furniture out of that area. He or she will then apply and agitate the shampoo on that section. If wet vacuuming is being done, it will be completed in the agitated area, and then the furniture will be replaced. The technician will repeat this process until the whole room has been cleaned.

2.   Shampoo is applied to the carpet and agitated using a rotary shampoo machine. To do this, diluted foaming detergent is placed in a solution tank on the machine. The solution is gravity-fed onto the brush. It flows through holes or grooves in the brush's back and then travels down the nylon bristles which are in contact with the carpet yarns. The brush moves in a revolving pattern at about 175 RPM. The interaction between the brush bristles and the carpet yarns causes the detergent to be aerated into a foam and evenly disbursed throughout the carpet pile.

Proper application provides uniform chemical dispersion and greatly increased chemical action in the emulsifying and suspension of soil particles. Proper application means:

   • The detergents are dispensed in a fore-and-aft, double lap, oval pattern. (If a side-to-side pattern is used, soil streaks may result when uneven pressure is applied on the heel and toe of the rotary brush head.)

   • The brush head is kept level. (Uneven cleaning due to uneven agitation may occur if the brush is not kept level.)

3.   It is recommended that the application / agitation part of the process be followed by wet vacuuming. Unfortunately, this rarely happens except in heavily soiled traffic or entry areas where numerous cleaning passes are necessary. (Some companies have wet vacuuming equipment that hooks up to a water source to provide a cool water rinse to the freshly shampooed carpet. The cool water rinse helps, but a hot water rinse does a better rinsing job.)

**Note:** If wet vacuuming is not done, especially in the heavily soiled areas:

   • Over-wetting may occur because the numerous passes needed to handle the heavy soil means that the carpet may be left in a very wet condition.

   • Residual soil that creates a grayish cast to the pile is left in the carpet, and/or soil streaks occur.

   • Accelerated re-soiling results from the presence of soil and sticky detergent residue that have not been extracted.

**Note:** When agitation (or wet vacuuming if done) is completed in a section of a room, the technician should put protective styrofoam blocks and plastic tabs under the furniture legs as he or she returns the furniture to its original places. This protects the furniture from the damp carpet while also protecting the carpet from possible furniture stain transfer.

4. If it is needed, carpet protector is applied. (See "Chapter 9. Does My Carpet Need A Carpet Protector?" for information on 1) whether or not your type of carpet fibers actually needs protection and 2) where the carpet protector should be applied.)

5. The damp carpet is finished with a grooming brush. (This brush is different from a carpet rake.) The brushing makes the carpet look better and if water-based carpet protector has been applied, helps ensure that the protector is evenly spread through the fibers.

6. Post-cleaning traffic and/or furniture moving:

   • The damp carpet can take traffic as soon as the cleaning process is done if everyone has clean, non-leather soled shoes, clean socks or bare feet. **Caution:** Any dirt on shoe soles or feet will rub off on the damp carpet. Leather soled shoes are prohibited until the carpet is dry because the dye in leather soles can bleed onto the damp carpet, leaving you with a trail of footprint stains.
   **Caution:** People should be very careful when stepping from the damp carpet onto a hard surface or vice versa.

   • The carpet should be completely dry in 3 - 6 hours after cleaning is completed. Do **not** move the furniture, and if possible, avoid walking on the carpet with dirty or leather soled shoes until this has happened.

7. **Best Practice: For the best soil removal results with this method, the customer should do a thorough dry vacuuming as soon as the carpet is dry - whether or not the technician has recommended it.** This dry vacuuming is when most of the actual soil is removed from the carpet.

**Note:** Some professionally formulated shampoos contain embrittling agents that form soil-trapping crystal residue flakes when they dry. These flakes make removing the soil from the carpet during dry vacuuming somewhat easier. If they are not removed from the carpet pile with a thorough dry vacuuming, however, these flakes and the soil sift down into the carpet, creating more soil.

– 19 –

Whether or not the shampoo contains embrittling agents, the key to successful soil removal is immediate and thorough dry vacuuming, preferably using a certified pile lifter vacuum (a special vacuum cleaner with two motors - one that drives a heavy pile brush and another that drives the vacuum). Otherwise, a large portion of the soil-laden detergent sifts to the base of the carpet yarn, where the buildup of soil and detergent residue occur and can create additional problems. The sticky detergent residue will attract more soil, and soil buildup can wear out carpet before its time.

### *Pros - Rotary Shampoo*

• The agitation by the rotary brush machine is probably the best feature of this method of cleaning.

  - If the brush head is kept level and the proper double-lap, fore-and-aft application pattern is applied, uniform chemical distribution and aggressive pile agitation will result.

  - Some critics of this method argue that the aggressive brush scrubbing action results in pile distortion. This is not true because enough lubrication is provided by a properly applied foaming detergent. Wool carpets and even the long shag carpets of the 60's and 70's were shampooed without problems if technicians were careful to ensure adequate lubrication of yarns during rotary brush agitation.

  "Pile distortion" is damage to the carpet that occurs when there is not enough lubrication provided between the brushes and the carpet pile. This can happen if the technician uses poorly formulated solutions with lots of residue, does not use enough solution to properly lubricate the brushes, does not keep the machine moving and the brushes are left in one place too long, or does not follow a fore-and-aft, double lap, oval pattern due to laziness or a lack of training. The damage can be a permanent discoloration due to a friction burn or unraveling of the fibers, especially in a saxony weave carpet. The carpet can look lighter and darker in the swaths or passes the technician has taken with the machine during the cleaning. (A freshly cleaned carpet often shows these lighter / darker swaths even when the cleaning is properly performed, but they disappear after people begin to walk on it and it is vacuumed. Pile distortion swaths are permanent.) If you have wool carpet, you may see frayed fibers. Though pile distortion is more likely to happen with weak or cheap carpet, any type of carpet is susceptible.

• The 3 - 6 hour drying time (depends on the amount of shampoo needed to handle the severity of soiling encountered) allows enough time for soil suspension to be maximized. (Unfortunately, soil removal is another case entirely.)

## *Pro/Con - Rotary Shampoo*

- When quality solutions are used, they have all the elements needed to emulsify and suspend soil to the fullest extent. **Unfortunately, this suspended soil and the solution stays in the carpet, because it is not really removed.**

## *Cons - Rotary Shampoo*

This method's limited soil removal is due to:

- Shampoo carpet cleaning firms eliminating necessary procedures in order to reduce prices so they can better compete with steam cleaning companies. The firms compromised the cleaning process when they eliminated the wet vacuuming that followed detergent application and agitation, especially in heavily soiled entry and high traffic areas.

- Consumers rarely have the proper equipment, and they usually do not understand the need for a thorough post-cleaning dry vacuuming to remove the dry shampoo residue. They expect to receive a completed cleaning job from the carpet cleaning company and do not follow the cleaner's recommendations for vacuuming after the technician leaves.

- As soon as traffic is re-introduced on the freshly shampooed carpet, some dry detergent residue detaches from the yarn's surface and sifts down toward the base of the pile so residue begins to accumulate.

- Depending on pile composition (the design or type of fibers) and density, this residue may be difficult to remove, even with proper vacuuming utilizing a certified pile lifter vacuum. Removing the residue is most difficult from loop carpets, wool carpet (because of its absorbency), and dense, tightly woven carpets.

- Most significantly, when large amounts of oily soils are encountered during the shampooing process, saponification of fats and oils occurs. (Alkaline builders in the detergents combine with vegetable and animal oils, when present, to form a weak, true soap.) If this true soap is not rinsed and extracted from the carpet pile, an oily scum forms. This oily scum will result in rapid re-soiling, especially in traffic lanes in restaurants, an entry from a garage, as well as the main traffic lane(s) from the kitchen of a great home cook! (Remember, this is a problem that occurs only when there are above normal amounts of oily soil in the carpets. In other situations, such as in office buildings, regularly scheduled shampoo procedures may be applied, followed by nightly vacuuming as part of building maintenance for years with no significant detergent residue or re-soiling problems.)

— 21 —

### Cons - Rotary Shampoo, *continued*

- This is a no-rinse system. If the soil is not physically removed from the carpet either during the cleaning process or later during thorough vacuuming done by the customer to remove the soil particles, then where has it gone? Unfortunately, it has gone deeper into the carpet pile.

## Absorbent Pad (also called Bonnet, Chem-Dry, Carbonated Cleaning) - "Maintenance" Cleaning Method

The absorbent pad or bonnet method has also been called "chemical dry cleaning", the "oil emulsion method" or "carbonated cleaning".

It is most effective on low pile glue down carpets - the type used in commercial sites such as offices, retail outlets, daycare centers, restaurants. It does not work so well on the higher, denser piles of residential carpets.

The absorbent pad method is a good choice for 24-hour establishments such as hospitals, hotel lobbies, airports, all-night restaurants, etc., that cannot have extended down time while the carpet is being cleaned and then dries enough to be safe for traffic.

**Note:** This is also the method most commonly used for maintenance cleaning of high traffic lanes that must be treated more often (weekly or monthly) by minimally trained personnel.

### Elements - Absorbent Pad

- Detergents added to water prior to spray application on the carpet fibers

- Small amounts of dry solvents may be added to the detergents to break down oil-based soils

- In some franchises, water containing carbon dioxide gas is used instead of the dry solvents. This is the "carbonated cleaning". The bubbling action of the cleaner does not necessarily improve the soil removal ability, but it does make for an interesting marketing tool.

- Concentrated spotting agents formulated for specific spot and stain types

## *Equipment / Method - Absorbent Pad*

1.  Dry soil is removed by a thorough dry vacuuming with a vacuum cleaner.

2.  The chemical solution is uniformly sprayed onto the carpet using a wand applicator. Enough solution should be applied so it penetrates the pile and moistens the yarns.

3.  Concentrated pre-spotting agents are applied to spots and stains. (The technician should have specific spotting solutions for the various spots and stains.)

4.  A detergent-moistened fabric pad or bonnet is spin buffed over the surface of the treated carpet area, using a rotary machine with a drive block (it holds the bonnet).

**Notes:**

• As long as adequate chemical lubrication is present, the pad provides smooth, gentle agitation to pile yarns. This aids soil suspension.

• Absorption is more uniform with a moistened pad than with a dry one.

• If the technician keeps changing the pad as it gets saturated and replaces it with a moistened one, the carpet will dry faster.

**Note:** The technician should immediately put protective styrofoam blocks and plastic tabs under the furniture legs as he or she returns each piece of furniture to its original place after pulling it out, cleaning and buffing underneath it. This protects the furniture from the damp carpet while also protecting the carpet from possible furniture stain transfer.

### *Equipment / Method - Absorbent Pad, continued*

5. If it is needed, carpet protector is applied. (See "Chapter 9. Does My Carpet Need A Carpet Protector?" for information on 1) whether or not your type of carpet fibers actually needs protection and 2) where the carpet protector should be applied.)

6. The damp carpet is finished with a grooming brush - not a rake. This makes the carpet look better and if water-based carpet protector has been applied, helps ensure that the protector is evenly spread through the fibers.

7. Post-cleaning traffic and/or furniture moving:

   • The damp carpet can take traffic as soon as the cleaning process is done if everyone has clean, non-leather soled shoes, clean socks or bare feet. **Caution:** Any dirt on shoe soles or feet will rub off on the damp carpet. Leather soled shoes are prohibited until the carpet is dry because the dye in leather soles can bleed onto the damp carpet, leaving you with a trail of footprint stains.
   **Caution:** People should be very careful when stepping from the damp carpet onto a hard surface or vice versa.

   • The carpet should be completely dry in 3 - 5 hours after cleaning is completed, depending on the amount of solution used, how often the pads were changed during buffing and the relative humidity. Do **not** move the furniture, and if possible, avoid walking on the carpet with dirty or leather soled shoes until this has happened.

### *Pros - Absorbent Pad*

• Gentle and effective in light to moderate soiling situations when used by a well-trained professional.

• The type of cleaning solutions with their non-residual nature combined with the gentle agitation of the bonnet produces uniform results without damage to carpet fibers, when the method is properly executed.

• Excellent for use in situations such as 24-hour facilities that require minimal carpet down time. The time needed for the cleaning process is reduced to a bare minimum so the carpet can be returned to use as quickly as possible.

• Because of the minimal amounts of moisture applied to the carpet, there is less chance of people slipping and falling when the still damp carpet is returned to use.
**Caution:** People should still be very careful when stepping from the damp carpet onto a hard surface or vice versa.

• This method is simple to use so it requires minimal training.

## Pro/Con - Absorbent Pad

- If insufficient detergent solution is applied, drying time may be faster, but the cleaning action may be limited to the upper half of the yarn and not down to the primary backing.

- Agitation provided is good, but it is gentle and primarily at the surface only. Carpet yarns are forced to lie down while the bonnet spins on the tops or sides of the yarns. There is no separating or combing of the pile yarns, as is the case with various forms of brush agitation.

## Cons - Absorbent Pad

- Not good in moderate to heavy (very visible) soiling conditions that demand restorative cleaning methods.

- There is little soil absorption by the bonnet or pad.

- Because much of the heavier particulate matter and soil distributed throughout the carpet is not removed by this method, there can be buildup of these damaging abrasives over time.

- Any rotary device used with insufficient lubrication supplied by the detergent solution, can cause pile distortion. (Another reason why uniform detergent application in adequate quantities is crucial.) Several carpet manufacturers do not approve bonnet cleaning for their cut pile residential carpet, mainly because the minimum moisture used may result in inadequate lubrication during agitation.

"Pile distortion" is damage to the carpet fibers that occurs when there is not enough lubrication provided between the pad and the carpet pile. This can happen if the technician does not apply enough pre-conditioner or keeps the pad in one place too long, especially on weak or cheap carpet. The pile distortion can be a permanent discoloration due to a friction burn or unraveling of the fibers, especially in a Saxony weave carpet. The carpet can look lighter and darker in the swaths or passes the technician has taken with the machine during the cleaning. (A freshly cleaned carpet often shows these lighter / darker swaths, but they disappear after people begin to walk on it again and it is vacuumed. Pile distortion swaths are permanent.)

- Chemical action is rated only fair because of the minimal quantity of cleaning solution applied. (More solution = More drying time.)

- There is minimal time for maximum soil suspension by surfactants.

# Absorbent Compound - "Maintenance" Cleaning Method

The absorbent compound or "dry powder" method (Host®, Dry-Way®, Capture®) has been around for several decades. The term "dry" is relative in that the amount of water used in this method is less than other methods to minimize drying time and to protect some natural fibers.

The absorbent compound method was developed in an effort to simplify carpet cleaning. It is promoted extensively for the "do-it-yourself" home and business owner because of the method's safety and simplicity - even when used by people with little or no training.

This method is primarily used in commercial cleaning situations including offices, retail outlets, daycare centers, restaurants, etc. Because the carpet stays relatively dry, the absorbent compound method is especially practical for use in 24-hour establishments such as all-night fast food and other restaurants, hotels, hospitals, transportation facilities, that have continuous traffic on the carpet.

## *Elements - Absorbent Compound*

- A very small amount of dry cleaning solvent to break down oily soils and cause faster drying

- A detergent combined with a water-based surfactant to suspend or emulsify other soils that may be present

- A highly absorbent carrier to distribute the cleaning chemicals

  The carrier later attracts suspended soil and holds onto it until the soil-laden carrier is vacuumed out of the carpet. These very small particles are usually easily removed from low to medium pile height carpet. They are harder to remove from deep and/or dense pile or shag carpet because the particles sift so far down into the carpet, especially in shags.

  Though the carriers may be made from different materials, the cleaning abilities and possible problems are essentially the same:

  - Host® and Dry-Way® use cellulose-based products made of ground up cellulose or wood.

  - Capture® is a synthetic polymer-based product that is a byproduct of fiber manufacturing. It is more expensive to produce than the cellulose-based products, so companies using it often charge somewhat higher prices.

## *Equipment / Method - Absorbent Compound*

1. Dry soil is removed by a thorough dry vacuuming with a vacuum cleaner.

2. Water-based pre-conditioner (pre-spray or pre-treatment) may be applied using a hand pump spray. This is especially important with moderate to heavy soiling. The pre-conditioner causes better soil suspension (and cleaning results), as well as reducing dusting. (Pre-conditioner is not usually applied in 24-hour establishments unless the carpet is really dirty, because it wets the carpet and can increase drying time by a couple of hours.)

3. The absorbent carrier is broadcast over the carpet areas to be cleaned. On large commercial jobs, this is done with a special roller drum with evenly spaced holes for uniform distribution. Otherwise, broadcasting is usually done by hand.

4. While still moist, the absorbent compound is agitated into the carpet pile using a machine similar to the drawing.

    **Caution:** Because of the type and size of particles propelled into the air during agitation, the cleaning area should be unoccupied and the technician should wear a vapor mask at all times during this phase.

5. Once the compound has been uniformly agitated into the pile, it is allowed to sit 30 - 60 minutes (dwell time), depending on the ambient humidity. During this time, the dry solvents break down oily soils while detergents or surfactants suspend the other types. The suspended soil is absorbed onto the carrier, where it is held until the vacuuming phase.

6. The still damp carpet is thoroughly vacuumed with a special upright vacuum with counter-rotating brush agitation to recover the soil-laden carrier.

   **Note:** The technician should immediately put protective styrofoam blocks and plastic tabs under the furniture legs as he or she returns each piece of furniture to its original place after pulling it out, cleaning and vacuuming underneath it. This protects the furniture from the damp carpet while also protecting the carpet from possible furniture stain transfer.

7. If it is needed, carpet protector is applied. (See "Chapter 9. Does My Carpet Need A Carpet Protector After Cleaning?" for information on 1) whether or not your carpet actually needs protection and 2) where the carpet protector should be applied.)

8. The damp carpet is finished with a grooming brush. (This brush is different from a carpet rake). The brushing makes the carpet look better and if water-based carpet protector has been applied, helps ensure that the protector is evenly spread through the fibers.

9. Post-cleaning traffic and/or furniture moving:

   • The damp carpet can take traffic as soon as the cleaning process is done if everyone has clean, non-leather soled shoes, clean socks or bare feet. **Caution:** Any dirt on shoe soles or feet will rub off on the damp carpet. Leather soled shoes are prohibited until the carpet is dry, because the dye in leather soles can bleed onto the damp carpet, leaving you with a trail of footprint stains. **Caution:** People should be very careful when stepping from the damp carpet onto a hard surface or vice versa.

   • The carpet should be completely dry in 1 - 3 hours after cleaning is completed, depending on the humidity and whether pre-conditioning solution was used. Do **not** move the furniture, and if possible, avoid walking on the carpet with dirty or leather soled shoes until this has happened.

## *Pros - Absorbent Compound*

• It is effective on light to moderate soiling.

• The machine agitation is excellent. The counter-rotating brushes separate and lift the pile, while bringing the chemical compounds into maximum contact with soils.

• The carpet should be completely dry in 1 - 3 hours. If no pre-conditioner is applied, there is no real wetness to the carpet and the carpet dries in the shorter time.

- This method offers distinct advantages on commercial level-loop carpet installations where downtime must be held to a minimum, such as a 24-hour establishment, or in areas where daily preventive maintenance is needed, such as a cafeteria line, etc.

- Because of the minimal amounts of moisture applied to the carpet, there is less chance of people slipping and falling when the damp carpet is returned to use. **Caution:** People should still be very careful when stepping from the damp carpet onto a hard surface or vice versa.

- It is safe to use on most carpet. Even in the hands of a do-it-yourself amateur carpet cleaner, it is virtually impossible to cause damage to the carpet.

- It requires little or no technical training.

- It is safe to use on poorly constructed or poorly installed carpet because this cleaning method does not make these defects apparent.

- It may be used effectively on carpets with weak dyes, because there is little chance of the dye's bleeding.

- Browning and yellowing are rarely a problem.

**The following are conditional Pros:**

- This method has received hearty recommendation from some carpet manufacturers. *"Why?"*, you ask. Because, of all the cleaning methods available, this one is the least likely to make any defects in the carpet manufacturing or installation process apparent to you, the consumer.

- A study by Racine Industries showed a reduction in dust mite population after a dry compound cleaning. However, if carpet pile is aggressively agitated and thoroughly vacuumed, a similar reduction in dust mite population will be seen even without cleaning with a dry compound. In any event, unless humidity levels are kept under control, the dust mite population will soon return to pre-cleaning levels.

## *Cons - Absorbent Compound*

- This method is not effective in heavy soiling conditions, even with the use of water-based pre-conditioners.

- There is limited soil and carrier removal. Because of the nature of crimped, looped, twisted carpet fibers, plus their mass and the physical size of the absorbent carrier, it is impossible to remove all the carrier, especially in residential cut-pile or looped carpet (saxonys, berbers, friezes, velvet plushes). Much of the soil you are hoping to remove is still attached to the carrier that remains in the carpet. With denser, longer piles, there may be even more carrier left behind than there was soil in the first place. (This has been a major source of consumer complaints about the absorbent compound method of cleaning.)

  **Note:** If the carrier and absorbed soil are not vacuumed out as completely as possible during the cleaning procedure, traffic or later vacuuming will cause it to sift further downward toward the base of the yarns and accumulate at the primary backing as another form of soil.

- Switching to another method of cleaning after using absorbent compounds may result in a sticky, somewhat tacky feel to the carpet pile that is difficult to remedy, as well as creating noticeable drag on the beater bar brushes of your vacuum cleaner.

- "Dusting" - The size of the absorbent carrier particles is important to prevent "dusting" of walls and furnishings or the possibility of fine particles of carrier residue contaminating the heating / air conditioning system in a structure.

  - Commercial customers, especially those using polymer-based carriers, complain of severe dusting occurring and the need to re-clean fixtures and furnishings within the areas cleaned when this method is used.

  - **Caution:** The dusting characteristic can also cause respiratory discomfort to the technician and/or other people or animals in confined or unventilated areas, especially during the mechanical agitation phase of the dry compound cleaning. Other people or animals should not be present and the technician should wear a vapor mask in confined or unventilated areas during the agitation phase.

- Cellulosic carriers can support the growth of microorganisms in high humidity situations (more than 70% relative humidity) when left in the carpet for as little as 10 days. This can be a problem if inhabitants of the home or workplace have severe allergies.

*Section III*

- Residual cellulosic carrier in the fibers may also create an overall white to yellowish cast that looks like baby powder has been left on the carpet.

- Absorbent compound products and equipment for the do-it-yourself person may not be available in parts of the U.S.

# Dry Foam - "Maintenance" Cleaning Method

The dry foam method has been used for decades as a rapid drying maintenance system used primarily in commercial cleaning situations, such as offices, retail outlets, daycare centers, restaurants, hospitals, hotel lobbies, airports. It is especially useful for 24-hour establishments where minimal carpet downtime is important.

The chemicals used in this method are mixed with water so it is not really "dry". It is just relatively dryer in comparison with other water-based methods such as hot water extraction and shampoo.

**Note:** Because of its limited soil removal ability, cleaning using the dry foam method must be done more frequently than the other two "maintenance" cleaning methods. It works best on lightly soiled carpet. If there are definite traffic lanes in the carpet (the carpet looks dark gray to black in the traffic lanes) and/or the carpet has spots, stains, discolorations every foot or so, this method will not give you acceptable results.

## *Elements - Dry Foam*

- A detergent containing a surfactant to emulsify and suspend soils

- An alkaline builder may be combined with the surfactant to soften the water and enhance the emulsion / suspension of particle and oily soils

- A few dry foam detergents contain dry solvent additives to help break up oxidized oils. Unfortunately, these additives may hinder production of the foam required for quick drying.

- Some quality dry foam detergents contain embrittling agents that crystallize with suspended soil. (If the customer does repeated, thorough dry vacuuming after the carpet has dried, the cleaning ability of the dry foam method increases tremendously. This increase in cleaning ability is due more to the repeated post-cleaning dry vacuuming rather than the embrittling agents. Unfortunately for the dry foam method, most customers do not want to have their carpets cleaned using a method that requires them to do heavy work after the carpet is supposedly clean. To avoid the hassles of explaining the need to do this extra work to a customer or the callback that comes if the customer does not properly vacuum, most dry foam companies do not use detergents with embrittling agents.)

— 31 —

Section III

## *Equipment / Method - Dry Foam*

Illustrations in Chapter 8 were created by Arthur D. Colo'n

1.  Dry soil is removed by a thorough dry vacuuming with a vacuum cleaner.

2.  A dry foam machine aerates the detergent solution, producing a thick, minimum moisture foam. This foam is applied onto the carpet pile directly in front of a cylindrical brush that provides reel-type brushing action. The brush action agitates the detergent foam uniformly into the soiled carpet pile. The soil and excess foam are retrieved almost immediately by the wet vacuum system in the machine. (The volume of recovered moisture and soil is so minor that some equipment manufacturers eliminate the vacuum recovery system from their machines.)

    **Note:** Numerous passes over heavily soiled carpet may be necessary.

3.  The extracted soil and excess foam is deposited in a small holding tank where it mixes with defoamer. The soil-laden foam converts back into a liquid.

4.  If the dry foam machine does not have a built-in vacuum system, separate wet vacuuming after foam agitation is important, especially if traffic areas are heavily soiled. The wet vacuuming removes some of the soil.

    **Note:** When wet vacuuming is completed in a room, the technician should immediately put protective styrofoam blocks and plastic tabs under the furniture legs as he or she returns the furniture to its original places. This protects the furniture from the damp carpet while also protecting the carpet from possible furniture stain transfer.

5.  If it is needed, carpet protector is applied. (See "Chapter 9. Does My Carpet Need A Carpet Protector?" for information on 1) whether or not your type of carpet fibers actually needs protection and 2) where the carpet protector should be applied.)

6. The damp carpet is finished with a grooming brush. (This brush is different from a rake.) The brushing makes the carpet look better and if water-based carpet protector has been applied, helps ensure that the protector is evenly spread through the fibers.

7. **Best Practice: For the best soil removal results with this method, the customer should do a thorough post-cleaning dry vacuuming as soon as the carpet is dry - whether or not the technician has recommended it**. This dry vacuuming is when most of the actual soil is removed from the carpet.

   **Note:** Some dry foam detergents contain embrittling agents that form soil-trapping crystal residue flakes when they dry. These flakes make removing the soil from the carpet during dry vacuuming somewhat easier.

   Whether or not the foam contains the embrittling agents, the key to successful soil removal with the dry foam method is immediate and thorough post-cleaning dry vacuuming, preferably using a certified pile lifter vacuum (a special vacuum cleaner with two motors - one that drives a heavy pile brush and another that drives the vacuum). Otherwise, a large portion of the soil-laden detergent sifts to the base of the carpet yarn, where the buildup of soil and detergent residue occur and can create additional problems. The sticky detergent residue will attract more soil, and soil buildup can wear out carpet before its time. If you have wool carpet, the alkaline levels in the detergent may negatively affect the fibers by causing a change in the texture (a sticky feel) and/or discoloring the carpet.

8. Post-cleaning traffic and/or furniture moving:

   • The damp carpet can take traffic as soon as the cleaning process is done if everyone has clean, non-leather soled shoes, clean socks or bare feet.
   **Caution:** Any dirt on shoe soles or feet will rub off on the damp carpet. Leather soled shoes are prohibited until the carpet is dry because the dye in leather soles can bleed onto the damp carpet, leaving you with a trail of footprint stains.
   **Caution:** People should be very careful when stepping from the damp carpet onto a hard surface or vice versa.

   • The carpet should be completely dry in 30 minutes to 3 hours after cleaning is completed, depending on the humidity and the amount of soil that was in the carpet. Do **not** move the furniture, and if possible, avoid walking on the carpet with dirty or leather soled shoes until this has happened.

— 33 —

## *Pros - Dry Foam*

- The machine brush combs, lifts and separates the yarns, bringing whatever foam is involved into maximum contact with the soils present - at least on the surface of the carpet pile.

- There is minimum down time for the carpet - drying time is 30 minutes to 3 hours depending on the humidity and amount of soil. The dry foam method is thoroughly efficient in situations where minimum down time of the carpet is a critical factor (24-hour establishments, including hospitals, hotel lobbies, airports, etc.).

- Because of the minimal amounts of moisture applied to the carpet, there is less chance of people slipping and falling when the damp carpet is returned to use. **Caution:** People should still be very careful when stepping from the damp carpet onto a hard surface or vice versa.

## *Cons - Dry Foam*

- Soil removal is marginal at best. Due to the emphasis given to rapid drying, actual cleaning is more likely to be cosmetic and will not extend all the way to the base of the yarns.

- Lack of dry solvent additives limit cleaning ability in areas with heavy concentrations of oily (especially oxidized oils) soils.

- A very small amount of rinsing actually occurs because of the minimum amount of water incorporated into the foaming detergent solution.

- There is relatively little soil picked up during extraction (wet vacuuming), because minimum detergent is used (often not enough to soak down to soils at the base of the yarns), and solutions are given only a fraction of the dwell time needed to suspend soils before extraction takes place.

- Soil extraction is superficial at best unless the customer makes an unusual effort to extract soil with repeated vacuuming after the cleaning process is completed.

- With heavily soiled carpet, repeating foam applications in order to clean the dirty carpet can result in over-wetting.

- If post-cleaning soil removal, preferably by a certified pile lifter vacuum, is not done, soil removal becomes much more difficult as detergent residues and soils sift downward in the pile. Unfortunately, the business or home owner must be depended upon to complete this critical part of the cleaning process. (Assuming the customer has the equipment and motivation to do this final step.)

• After multiple cleanings without effective extraction, a tacky buildup of detergent residue may further complicate soil removal efforts and may even attract substantially more soil.

## Do-It-Yourself Cleaning - Store Rentals And Purchased Equipment

We've just covered the most popular professional methods of carpet cleaning. Now let's look at an alternative home method - **Do It Yourself!**

Have you ever thought about going (or have actually gone) to the local grocery store, discount store or do-it-yourself hardware depot to rent or buy one of those cool little carpet cleaning machines?

Until I did it for research purposes several years ago for this guide, I had not and this is why:

• Knowing what I know today about the fundamentals of effective cleaning and adequate equipment standards,

• Plus having played the "rental customer" role with a number of these rental outlets,

• Not to mention, having read dozens of instruction manuals and brochures about their products, and

• Getting feedback from many of my own customers who have used them.

My advice to myself and you would have been before I tried it and still is, ***"YOU DO NOT WANT TO DO IT!"***.

However, if you are the curious type and would like to be shown, join me on a little trip down to the local rental center to rent a carpet cleaning machine and purchase the necessary cleaning products required to make the job go as smoothly as possible.

To make the information in this guide as comprehensive as possible, I actually did rent and use one of these machines to clean a very good friend's carpet, plus I collected reports from some of my customers who tried this route before calling my company to clean their carpets. (My friend, who has to see for himself, was very curious about how well the do-it-yourself carpet cleaning equipment would work. I have been cleaning his carpets regularly for several years so I told him I would use that method for his next cleaning.)

**Note:** I discourage do-it-yourself carpet cleaning because the results you get are a poor return on investment for the cost, time and effort needed to do it. In fact, if your budget is the issue, I would recommend that you clean the carpet less often and have it done professionally rather than doing it yourself.

However, if you know someone who must or wants to try the equipment rental or purchase route, please share the following information with him or her. It will help them avoid some of the problems caused by missing or misinformation about the chemicals, the equipment and the process.

## *Rental Machine Cleaning 101*

The following describes my experience and the outcome of my rental equipment cleaning "adventure". (If you are a person who always goes directly to the bottom line, skip "The Steps" and go to "Rental Cleaning Results". You will miss some Red Flag situations that cost the average consumer money and/or hurt the cleaning results because he or she is not aware of them. But, you will see why I strongly do not recommend do-it-yourself carpet cleaning.)

### *The Steps*

Before I actually did the rental machine cleaning, I tried to find out as much as I could about the equipment and the chemicals.

**To do this:**

1. I called around to find which stores in my area had machines available for rent. The average quote I received was $24.00 per 24 hour period.

2. Then I went to the store to see the equipment and to find out what I needed to know to use the machine. I also wanted to see what chemicals were available and to decide which ones I would need to clean my carpet.

**At the rental place:**

3. I read the instruction brochure and asked the rental agent several questions to become familiar with the equipment and chemicals available.

4. I also looked at the first product - Hi-Traffic Pre-Treatment (also known as a pre-conditioner) which comes in a 1 quart hand spray bottle for about $6.00.

According to the Hi-Traffic Pre-Treatment instructions:

- This pre-conditioner is to be sprayed full-strength on the most heavily soiled areas of the carpet (usually the traffic lanes) after the carpet has been thoroughly dry vacuumed.

- The Pre-Treatment should be allowed to sit 5 - 10 minutes after application.

  **Red Flag:** Since it takes at least 15 - 30 minutes for a pre-conditioner to effectively suspend and emulsify the soil in your carpet enough to get the best removal results, waiting only 5 - 10 minutes will mean that a lot of the soil will still be clinging to the carpet fibers.

- This product should only be used in a well-ventilated area because it contains Ethylene Glycol Monobutyl Ether. (This chemical helps break down oily soils, but it evaporates and dries quickly which is probably the reason behind the 5 - 10 minute dwell time.)

  **Red Flag:** Important information is missing from the instructions on the bottle (and from the rental agent's directions).

- The instructions do not show the size of area covered by the Pre-Treatment spray bottle. After I called Customer Service from home, they told me it will take about 1 1/2 to 2 bottles per room to properly pre-treat my traffic areas.

  **Red Flag:** This means instead of the one or two bottles I thought I would need, I should probably buy five or six to treat my five rooms of moderately soiled carpet.

- There is no mention of agitating this pre-treatment after application.

  **Red Flag:** Because I, and now you too, know that proper agitation really increases the effectiveness of the soil emulsion, suspension and later removal, I decided I would add this step on my own in order to increase the chances of a more thorough cleaning. (Doing proper agitation requires a carpet rake, which most people do not have. This could mean another potential purchase.)

5. I looked at the next cleaning product recommended - Steam Cleaner Liquid in a 1 gallon bottle for about $20.00. This will clean 1200 - 2000 square feet or about 6 - 8 average size rooms. (It also came in a 1/2 gallon size: 600 - 1000 square feet or about 3 - 4 rooms and a 1 quart size: 300 - 500 square feet or about 1 - 2 rooms.)

- According to the product instructions, the Steam Cleaner Liquid is mixed with water, poured in the rinse water tank and run through the machine. It is injected into the carpet pile and immediately picked back up by the vacuum recovery.

  **Red Flag:** As we have learned earlier, cleaners (or more accurately termed "pre-conditioners" or "pre-treatments") should be applied and allowed to soak before rinsing begins. They are not normally added to the rinse water. Besides, I already have a pre-conditioner - The Hi-Traffic Pre-Treatment mentioned earlier.

**Note:** After I returned home, I called the Customer Service Departments for several of the rental companies supplying outlets to verify how the Steam Cleaner Liquid should be used.

- **Red Flag:** The customer service reps finally admitted that if their Steam Cleaner Liquid is used as directed, it will cause a powdery residue on the carpet. This residue will have to be vacuumed up after the carpet has dried.

  **Best Practice:** Use only fresh water in the rinse water tank or if you want to use the Steam Cleaner Liquid as a rinsing agent, mix it at 1/4 the recommended strength before putting it in the rinse water tank. This diluted mixture will give you additional cleaning action without the residue problems created if you follow the bottle instructions and use the Cleaner full strength.

- **Red Flag:** Since you wouldn't know that you only needed 1/4 as much of the Cleaner as you thought, you would probably waste money by buying the gallon container instead of the quart size.

6. I read the instructions for the next product offered - an anti-foam product in a 1 quart size for about $5.00. The instructions say to add 2 - 4 ounces per two gallons of rinse water. (In my case, this product was not needed. Because the products used to clean my friend's carpet in the past leave little or no residue, I did not have to worry about foaming during the rinsing phase of the cleaning process.)

   **Red Flag:** It did make me wonder if the manufacturer was trying to tell me that I could expect foaming problems during the rinsing phase. Is this because their Hi-Traffic Pre-Treatment and Steam Cleaner Liquid or similar products leave a lot of residue in the carpet so you have foaming the next time you clean? Probably so.

7. I looked at the next products - 1 pint sizes of spot remover and stain remover at about $6.00 each.

   - It was advised to use both at full strength.

     **Red Flag:** I have heard many horror stories from my customers about the excess foam residue that these off-the-shelf spot removers leave, so I would never use them. (You know, the ones that are supposed to resolve spot problems, make spotting a glory to do or make wool carpet lighter and brighter.)

     If you decide to use the rental machine spot removers or you have already treated lots of spots and stains on your carpet with off-the-shelf spot removers, you'll most likely need the anti-foam product mentioned above.

- 38 -

Section III

8.  I examined the last product offered - a 1 pint size odor removal product for pet and other smelly accidents at about $6.00 a bottle.

    • This product is added to the machine's fresh water rinse tank.

    **Caution:** If you have numerous and/or large spots where the pets or small children have had housebreaking accidents, my advice is that smelly contaminants, especially urine and feces, are best removed by a professional with heavy duty equipment and chemicals. Home removal equipment and chemicals are simply not powerful enough to do more than a superficial removal.

**When I returned home:**

9.  I obtained all the information I could get by reviewing the materials several times and calling their Customer Service line when the instructions were not clear or complete. I then decided which chemicals would best suit my needs.

    **Note:** You are probably going to need all the products available in order to come closer to doing an adequate cleaning job, not leave too much residue, as well as being able to get the most use during the rental time.

10. I planned my cleaning day so I could leave the house at 9 a.m. to pick up all the components, get to my friend's house nearby and then begin cleaning.
    **Note:** Make sure the vehicle you plan to use to transport the equipment has a big enough compartment so you can handle the main machine, any hoses, floor wand, accessories and chemicals. Also bring something to tie it all down with. Plus, check all the bottle caps to make sure they are tight to avoid unexpected spills.

**My results are on the following page . . .**

### *Rental Equipment Cleaning Results*

The following recaps my results, but includes the chemicals that you would have needed and/or would have purchased because of the missing or inaccurate information.

**Area Cleaned:** 5 average sized, moderately soiled rooms belonging to 2 adults and 3 kids - 8, 5 and 1 years old, one dog

**Materials Needed:** You would probably have used all the chemicals offered. Because I already had them, I did not have to buy a carpet rake for agitating or the styrofoam blocks and plastic tabs that I put under the furniture legs to protect them from moisture.

**Time Needed: 6 hours**

**Cost: $ 103.00**

| | |
|---|---|
| • Machine rental for 1 day | $ 24.00 |
| • 1 gallon Steam Cleaner Liquid | $ 20.00 |
| • 6 quarts High-Traffic Lane Pre-Treatment | $ 36.00 |
| • 1 quart Anti-Foam | $ 5.00 |
| • 1 pint Spot Remover | $ 6.00 |
| • 1 pint Stain Remover | $ 6.00 |
| • 1 pint Odor Remover | $ 6.00 |
| **Total** | **$ 103.00** |

**Not bad, but:**

• It took this author, a seasoned professional, from 9 a.m. to 3:30 p.m. (minus 1/2 hour for lunch) to drive to the nearby store, pick up a machine, drive to my friend's house nearby, set up the machine, pre-treat and pre-spot the traffic lanes at different intervals to keep the chemicals from drying out, fill the machine with fresh water, dump the machine and refill it with fresh water half a dozen or so times, and accomplish all the other steps necessary. I worked at a steady pace that would get good results using all my professional experience. Finally, I packed up the equipment and returned it to the store.

**Note:** I was lucky because my machine worked as it was supposed to. One of my relatives in a small town with no professional carpet cleaning companies had to make three trips to the store before she got a machine that worked properly.

- I had at least a portion left of all the chemicals I had purchased. (These were thrown away since I would not use them on my friend's carpet again, nor would I repeat my rental cleaning experiment.)

- I knew that I would need to re-clean my friend's carpet earlier than I would normally do; because even though the carpet looked clean, it was not up to my standards for my customers' homes (or mine).

## *Professional Cleaning Results*

If I had used my professional equipment, a job of this size would have required:

- **Area Cleaned:** 5 average sized, moderately soiled rooms

- **Time Needed:** 3 hours maximum including round trip drive time

- **Cost:** $ 150.00 - $190.00 for a thorough, professional cleaning, including all the steps described earlier in the Hot Water Extraction "steam cleaning" method

## *Your Probable Results*

**Caution:** Many of my customers who have tried the rental route reported that it took them much longer - up to 10 hours, depending on how long it took to figure out how to use everything in the proper sequence, and the person's level of physical fitness.

**After all that work they only achieved mediocre results at best. Here's why:**

- The instructions given by the rental representatives, as well as the information contained in their brochures, were mostly inaccurate and incomplete.

- The fundamental principals of cleaning - pre-vacuuming, proper quantity of pre-conditioning, dwell time, agitation and rinse water temperature are **all** compromised.

- Other misinformation in their instructions such as adding a cleaner to the rinse water tank of the unit is wrong and always leads to residue left in the carpet. Only a rinsing agent, if one is available, or plain water should be used for rinsing if you are going to avoid a residue problem.

  Only after calling the Customer Service line, was I able to get the information that their brand of cleaner would leave a residue, but that it could be removed by vacuuming the carpet after it dried. The average consumer would not have known to ask and would have been stuck with even more work after he/she thought they had finished cleaning their carpet.

- The rental equipment does not meet the minimum standards needed for effective cleaning. (Remember the minimum standards I told you about in "Portables Versus Truck Mounts"?)

| Minimum Carpet Cleaning Equipment Standards | | |
|---|---|---|
| **Equipment Type** | **Pump Rinse Pressure** | **Water Lift (Vacuum Power)** |
| Professional | 200 psi - minimum | 160 inches - minimum |
| Rental | 28* psi/45** psi - maximum | 90*/101** inches - maximum |

\* Smaller model machine / \*\* Larger model machine

### Buying Carpet Cleaning Equipment Versus Renting

**Caution:** Buying a carpet cleaning machine has very little advantage over renting. It mainly eliminates the pickup and return time. The instructions are no better than the rental ones. In many cases, the purchased machine's pumps and vacuums are even less powerful than the rental one. The only real difference is that one machine you get to keep and the other you get to return.

### My Best Advice

In closing, my best advice is to find a good carpet cleaning technician you can trust by asking a friend or by using the information in this guide. You will pay a few dollars more for services rendered, but you will get a much better, longer lasting carpet cleaning job. Plus, it will allow you to kick back and enjoy the fruits of your hard earned money instead of using both the hard earned money and your valuable time to yield fewer fruits. Unless, of course, you have an entire day when you have nothing else to do but clean your carpets and the physical prowess to do it yourself.

# Chapter 9 *Does My Carpet Need A Carpet Protector After Cleaning?*

## Introduction

Carpet protectors (actually carpet *fiber* protectors) are the most popular add-ons to carpet cleaning jobs, but are also the most misused.

In this Chapter I'll give you the facts you need to:

1. Decide if you really need that carpet protector the cleaning technician is offering, and
2. Know what is a reasonable price to pay for the protector if you do need it.

Unfortunately, carpet protector is often sold to customers when they don't really need it for their particular carpet. The protector is presented as an important add-on to the carpet cleaning by untrained carpet cleaners who don't know any better or by people who are more interested in the extra commission than in giving you the honest, quality service you deserve.

To help you be a more educated consumer the next time your carpets are cleaned, the information in this Chapter will give you the true facts about carpet protection for your carpet fiber type and wear conditions.

**What do carpet protectors do?**

Used properly, carpet protectors can enhance your carpet's appearance and extend its life. They do this by slowing the rate at which a spot or stain penetrates the carpet fibers.

They can also repel dirt and keep it from sticking to the fibers. This can make your vacuuming more effective and efficient. **Note:** A carpet fiber protector is no substitute for the frequent, thorough vacuuming described in "Effective Routine Carpet Maintenance" in "Chapter 7. How Often Should My Carpet Be Cleaned?".

Carpet protectors may be applied to better quality synthetic carpets during the manufacturing process. (Lower quality, less expensive carpets costing about $12.00 dollars a yard or less installed, are normally not treated by the manufacturer.) The protective chemicals are bonded to the fibers before they are sent to the carpet mill and/or the chemicals are applied at the mill during the manufacturing process.

The manufacturer's protective products, which wear off primarily in traffic areas, can be replenished by your carpet cleaning technician with quality products. When the carpet has been properly cleaned before protector application and the protector is properly applied, this treatment can restore most of the soil-repellent and stain-repellent capabilities added by the manufacturer's original protector.

> **CAUTION: Before having carpet protector reapplied to a carpet that already has a factory-applied protector, be sure you are getting the right kind of protector to ensure that any carpet manufacturer's warranties you may have will not be voided. (You need to have the same type, though not necessarily the same brand, of protector applied that the manufacturer originally used or that he/she currently recommends be applied after cleaning.)**
>
> **Currently, the soil/stain-resist protectors such as Stainmaster®, and Locked-in-Stainblocker®, described on page 3 are only available to carpet manufacturers - not to carpet cleaning technicians. If you have a carpet with a soil/stain-resist protector and want to have some protection reapplied after cleaning, call the carpet manufacturer before scheduling the cleaning appointment. Ask if there is a protector that the cleaning technician can apply that will not void the manufacturer's warranty. If there is, get the name of the protector and any other needed information. (Write down the date, time, the name of the person you spoke to at the manufacturer's and all the details about the protector in case there is a problem later.) Call your cleaning technician to ensure that he/she has the specified protector available and will apply only that protector after cleaning your carpet.**

# *Types of Carpet Fiber Protectors*

There's a lot of confusion about what these treatment products will do for your carpet. Much of this confusion is due to salespersons who make promises and statements about their products that far exceed the products' performance capabilities (including whether they are really needed). To help you make a better decision about whether you need one of these treatments and which type to choose if you do need it, let's look at the different types of protectors.

There are two main types of carpet protectors used today:

• Soil/Stain-Resist (commonly called "Stain-Resist")

• Soil/Stain Repellent

Carpet protectors come in solvent-based and water-based formulas, but the differences between the two are covered in "Solvent-Based Versus Water-Based Protectors" later in this Chapter.

| *Carpet Fiber Protectors* | |
|---|---|
| **Type Of Protector** | **Best Choice If Your Carpet Will Be Exposed To:** |
| **Soil/Stain-Resist** ("Stain-Resist")<br>• Used on nylon fibers only<br>• Brands include Stainmaster® and Locked-in-Stainblocker®<br>• Currently not available to carpet cleaning technicians for re-application in homes, businesses | Moderate amounts of:<br>• Soils<br>• Oily soils<br>• Difficult to very difficult acid dye-based stains such as fruit juices, wine, Kool-Aid®, products containing food coloring, etc. |
| **Soil/Stain Repellent**<br>• Used on nylon, olefin, polyester and acrylic<br>• Brands include Scotchguard® and Teflon®<br>• Can be reapplied by carpet cleaning technicians | Light to moderately heavy amounts of:<br>• Soils<br>• Oily soils<br>• Light to moderately difficult stains such as coffee, cola and organic dyes like grass stain, etc. |

## *Soil/Stain-Resist ("Stain-Resist") Treatments*

The newest and most effective protection products available to carpet manufacturers (but not professional cleaners at this time) are the soil/stain-resist treatments more commonly called "stain-resist". Brand names of soil/stain resist treatments include Stainmaster® and Locked-in-Stainblocker®. This protector is only used on nylon fibers, because they are the most susceptible to acid dyes. (Olefin, polyester and acrylic fibers are not so susceptible to acid dyes, so they don't need this type of protection added.) If a manufacturer is going to put carpet protector on a blended carpet, the nylon fibers are usually treated separately from the other type of fibers in the carpet.)

These new treatments are more expensive, but more effective than the soil/stain repellents. The major difference between the two types of protectors is that the new treatments have added acid dye blockers to the fluorochemical soil/stain repellent chemicals.

• The acid dye blockers fill open dye sites on the nylon carpet fibers to provide resistance to foods and beverages containing acid dyes, which are the majority of the worst spots/stains. (Acid dyes are becoming a bigger carpet staining problem because more and more manufactured foods contain food coloring which is an inorganic acid dye.)

• The fluorochemical component coats the carpet fiber to provide resistance to particle soils and oily substances.

**Soil/stain-resist ("stain-resist") treatments:**

• Can serve as both soil retardants and stain resistors for nylon fibers at the same time.

• These protective products may be first applied to nylon carpet by the carpet manufacturer. (Only the higher quality, more expensive nylon or nylon blend carpets receive this protection. Lower quality, cheaper carpets do not.)

• Are long lasting when applied by quality-conscious mills and can be expected to last up to the carpet's third year of use. At that point, the treatment wears off, primarily in traffic areas. (Currently there is no "stain-resist" product available for on-site re-application. Before having any protector reapplied to your carpets, call the manufacter of the carpet and ask what type of protector they recommend.)

• Act as soil retardants by forming a microscopic coating over fiber surfaces. **Note:** This coating or film changes the feel of the carpet to a minor extent, though most customers cannot tell the difference.

• Resist water-based and oil-based staining materials, including acid dyes, though not indefinitely. (They slow the absorption of the staining materials into the carpet fibers, but do not stop it.)

- Because it can repel liquids, these products can also repel cleaning solutions. This does not cause too many problems as long as the protector is still intact on the carpet fibers.

The ability to repel cleaning solutions can cause problems when heavy, oily soils are ground into traffic areas over a prolonged period of 18 months or more, and the oily soils are not thoroughly removed before the carpet is retreated. In this case fluorochemical stain resistors may repel detergent solutions and make the soil more difficult to remove the next time the carpet is cleaned. (With each reapplication of protector on an improperly cleaned carpet, cleaning becomes increasingly difficult.)

**Best Practice:** The secret to having these heavily oily-soiled areas cleaned effectively is to use a knowledgeable cleaning company who uses high quality pre-conditioning agents and spot removers - particularly those compounded with dry solvents from the alcohol or glycol classification. This must be followed by a thorough cleaning using a restorative cleaning method, such as "steam" cleaning. (See "Chapter 8. What Is The Best Way To Clean My Carpet?" for a description of the more effective carpet cleaning methods.)

**Caution:** Not all carpet cleaners use these quality pre-conditioning agents and spot removers. This makes it even more important that you get a referral from someone you trust or call the **IICRC Referral Line (800) 835-4624** to locate certified cleaning and restoration technicians and firms in your area. (See "Chapter 10. How Do I Find A Quality Carpet Cleaning Professional?" for more information on how to find an ethical, well-trained professional carpet care technician.)

## *Soil/Stain Repellent Treatments*

These fluorochemical soil/stain repellent compounds, which come in both solvent-based and water-based formulas, are the most popular type of carpet protector with carpet manufacturers and cleaning technicians. (Brand names for soil/stain repellent treatments include Scotchguard® and Teflon®.) These products perform to their specifications, but the main reasons for their popularity are their lower cost than the soil/stain-resist protectors and the fact that they are used on all types of synthetic carpets. (They may also be used on wool, if applied properly by a trained technician. See "Solvent-Based Versus Water-Based Protectors" later in this Chapter for information about proper application techniques and using this protector on wool.)

**Note:** A soil/stain-resist treatment may be commonly called a "stain-resist" protector; but, as you will see later in this Chapter, a soil/stain repellent is very different from a stain repellent.

*Section III*

— 5 —

**Soil/stain repellent treatments:**

- Can serve as both soil retardants and stain repellents at the same time.

- These protective products may be first applied to carpet by the carpet manufacturer. (Only the higher quality, more expensive carpets receive this protection. Lower quality, cheaper carpets do not.)

- Are long lasting when applied by quality-conscious mills and can be expected to last up to the carpet's third year of use. The major reason for re-application of this product is because the treatment wears off, primarily in traffic areas.

- Act as soil retardants by forming a microscopic coating over fiber surfaces. **Note:** This coating or film changes the feel of the carpet to a minor extent, though most customers cannot tell the difference.

- Repel water-based and oil-based staining materials, though not indefinitely. (They slow their absorption into the carpet fibers, but do not stop it.)

- Because it can repel liquids, these products can also repel cleaning solutions. This does not cause too many problems as long as the protector is still intact on the carpet fibers.

The ability to repel cleaning solutions can cause problems when heavy, oily soils are ground into traffic areas over a prolonged period of 18 months or more, and the oily soils are not thoroughly removed before the carpet is retreated. In this case fluorochemical stain repellents may repel detergent solutions and make the soil more difficult to remove the next time the carpet is cleaned. (With each reapplication of protector on an improperly cleaned carpet, cleaning becomes increasingly difficult.)

Again, the secret to having these heavily oily-soiled areas cleaned effectively is to use a knowledgeable cleaning company who uses high quality pre-conditioning agents and spot removers - particularly those compounded with dry solvents from the alcohol or glycol classification. This must be followed by a thorough cleaning using a restorative cleaning method, such as "steam" cleaning. (See "Chapter 8. What Is The Best Way To Clean My Carpet?" for a description of the more effective carpet cleaning methods.)

**Caution:** Not all carpet cleaners use these quality pre-conditioning agents and spot removers. This makes it even more important that you get a referral from someone you trust or call the **IICRC Referral Line (800) 835-4624** to locate certified cleaning and restoration technicians and firms in your area. (See "Chapter 10. How Do I Find A Quality Carpet Cleaning Professional?" for more information on how to find an ethical, well-trained professional carpet care technician.)

## Other Types of Protectors

Because of the vast improvements in carpet protectors, these last two types are rarely, if ever, used on carpets anymore. I'll give you some information about them anyway, in case you have an older carpet.

### Soil Retardants

Soil-retardants were the first type of fiber protector developed. They are rarely used in home or commercial situations these days, but some companies may still offer them. **Caution:** Do not confuse soil retardants with stain repellents or resistors. Soil retardants have absolutely no liquid repellency characteristics and are strictly limited to repelling dry particle soil.

The first soil retardant developed was a silica-based (not silicone) compound. It works by filling the microscopic cracks, crevices and irregularities on fiber surfaces with "clean soil" (colloidal silica). The real soil is unable to penetrate into its normal hiding places because those areas are already full of the "clean soil" previously mentioned.

When the carpet is vacuumed, the real soil is removed more readily, along with a portion of the dry silica compound. Eventually, most of the silica is removed during routine maintenance and re-soiling returns to its normal level.

The soil retardant is reapplied after a thorough carpet cleaning. It is sprayed on the carpet and distributed through the carpet fibers during finishing with a carpet brush.

### Stain Repellents

The arrival of the stain-resist carpet treatments described earlier eliminated the primary advantage of silicon stain repellents for carpets. Today, nearly all silicon-based stain repellents still on the market are sold for treating upholstery fabrics.

Stain repellents have their origin in water repellent products used by dry cleaners to "waterproof" raincoats, etc. They:

• Are mostly silicon-based products that are normally suspended in odorless mineral spirits or dry solvent solutions.

• Resist water-based liquids. (The majority of staining materials are water-based.)

• Do not repel oil-based liquids, greases, etc.

• Do not repel dry particle soil. They are not "soil retardants". (A few silicon-based products do claim to have some soil and oil retarding capabilities when applied to carpets; however, the majority of the silicon-based stain repellents do not.)

## Solvent-Based Versus Water-Based Protectors

Soil/stain repellent protectors, such as Scotchguard® and Teflon®, come in both solvent-based and water-based formulas. The question of whether a solvent-based or a water-based protector is better is much like the debate about truck-mounted steam cleaning versus a portable cleaning system. Except on wool carpet, the quality of the person applying the protector is more important than the type of protector being used.

- Did the cleaning technician clean the carpet properly? (See "Carpet Cleaning Facts" in "Chapter 8. What Is The Best Way To Clean My Carpet?" for a description of the steps needed to properly clean a carpet **before** the protector is applied.)

- Is he/she using a quality product from a reputable manufacturer (and is it a protector the carpet manufacturer recommends be used on his/her carpets in order to preserve any manufacturer's warranties for the carpet)?

- Is an experienced person applying the protector?

- Is he/she carefully following the application instructions for the particular brand of protector being applied?

- Is he/she using the proper application equipment with the proper spray tip?

- Is he/she using the proper spray overlap and then brush stroking technique, when necessary?

(See "How Should A Carpet Protector Be Applied" near the end of this Chapter for a description of proper application equipment and techniques.)

> **Caution: If you are having a soil / stain repellent protector applied to your wool carpet, I recommend a high quality silicon or fluorochemical, solvent-based protector (such as an odorless mineral spirit-based formula) be used.**

**Note:** Currently, the soil/stain-resist protectors such as Stainmaster® and Locked-in-Stainblocker® described on page 3 are only available to carpet manufacturers - not to carpet cleaning technicians. If you want carpet protector reapplied to a carpet that had a soil/stain-resist protector applied during production, contact the manufacturer using the instructions on page 2 in this Chapter. Ask the manufacturer if there is a solvent-based soil/stain repellent that can be used that will not void any manufacturer's warranties. (The better fiber coverage provided by the solvent-based soil/stain repellents can make them almost as effective at repelling acid dyes stains as the water-based stain-resist formulas.)

Section III

— 8 —

**The following is a comparison of the solvent-based and water-based protectors:**

| Comparison of Solvent-Based and Water-Based Carpet Protectors | |
| --- | --- |
| **Solvent-Based Protectors** | **Water-Based Protectors** |
| • Slightly more durable and lasts up to 2 years | • Not quite as durable and lasts up to 1 year |
| • More expensive (They are sprayed on in a concentrated form so a gallon of protector covers less area.) | • Less expensive (They are diluted with water so a gallon of protector covers a much larger area.) |
| • Coat the entire yarn from tip to base more easily without brush stroking, because they have a better wicking action (are almost self-coating) | • Only coat the upper half of the yarn (When the correct amount of protector is applied using the right spray overlap, and the proper brush stroking technique is used to groom it in, penetration is adequate for sufficient coverage.) |
| • May create fumes and should be used with caution where lit gas pilot lights are present (Most solvent-based protectors are generally safe and virtually odorless when used properly.) | • Has a tolerable odor that dissipates quickly<br>• Is completely safe near pilot lights |
| Both types of protector are virtually equal in their ability to protect your carpet from everyday wear, soils, oil and stains. | |

# Deciding If You Need a Carpet Protector Applied after Cleaning

**How do I know if I need carpet protector applied after cleaning?**

Whether or not your carpet needs to be treated with a protector depends on:

1. The type of fiber your carpet is made of and the kinds of soils and spots/stains it is normally exposed to

2. The carpet's quality, age and/or condition

3. Your lifestyle

## *1. Your Carpet Fiber Type and Normal Soil / Stain Exposure*

Whether your carpet needs the extra protection of a carpet protector after cleaning depends on the soils and/or spots and stains your carpet is exposed to.

- **Soils:** If you live in a very sandy area such as the desert or a beach, the carpet protector can make your vacuuming somewhat easier, because of its dirt repellent properties. It can also reduce the wear and damage to your carpet fibers caused by soil.

  **Note:** If you are doing the frequent vacuuming recommended in "Effective Routine Carpet Maintenance" in "Chapter 7. How Often Should My Carpet Be Cleaned?", a soil repellent is not so necessary (especially if you don't live in a sandy area or other place where large quantities of soil may be tracked or blown in on the carpet).

- **Normal spot / stain exposure:** The following information describes how each of the fibers reacts to various types of spots and stains.

### *Nylon*

Nylon fibers may need protector applied if you have a quality carpet in good condition. Type 6 "regular" nylon is easily dyed during manufacturing and unfortunately, easily stained by spills containing acid dyes such as the kind in fruit juices, wine, Kool-Aid®, etc. Because of this, major manufacturers use various stain resistant or repellent coatings on their better quality nylon carpets.

Type 6,6 "solution dyed" nylon is much more resistant to staining than "regular" nylon, but it is also treated with protective coatings to further enhance its resistance to stains and wear.

The protection applied by the manufacturer wears off over time and should be replaced according to the schedule described later in this Chapter in "When and Where Protector Should Be Applied".

**Note:** Nylon is also mildly oil loving, especially with petroleum-based products such as engine lubricants, tar, asphalt, etc. (See "Olefin" below for more details.)

### *Olefin (Polypropylene)*

Olefin carpet is virtually impossible to stain or discolor with the normal items spilled around a house or office.

However, olefin is very "oleophilic" or oil loving, especially with petroleum-based products such as engine lubricants, tar, asphalt, etc. If your carpet is frequently exposed to petroleum-based products, especially in large amounts, you may choose to protect it. This would be more likely in a commercial situation such as a mechanic or repair shop where the employees walk from the service bays to the carpeted waiting room or office. (Unless, of course, you have a dedicated home mechanic who is not so careful about cleaning or removing their shoes before making numerous trips across the carpet to the kitchen or other areas of the house.)

### *Polyester*

Polyester carpet is quite difficult to stain with spills containing acid dyes. It may be stained more easily by organic dyes such as coffee, cola drinks, beer and the yellow dye turmeric contained in mustard, herbal tea and soup mixes, etc. (Fortunately, most foods and beverages contain acid dyes, which polyester resists very well.)

However, polyester is moderately oil loving, especially with petroleum-based products such as engine lubricants, tar, asphalt, etc. (See "Olefin" above for more details.)

### *Acrylic*

Acrylic carpet is very resistant to staining and is not oil loving.

### *Wool*

Wool carpet is easily dyed and therefore easily stained. Although the Wool Bureau does not recommend carpet protector on wool, you may want to have a high quality silcon or fluorochemical solvent-based carpet protector (such as an odorless mineral spirit-based soil/stain repellent) applied by a well-trained, experienced technician on heavy traffic and spill-prone areas every 2 years, immediately after cleaning.

**Caution: It is best to use a solvent-based rather than water-based protector on wool carpet. The structure of the wool fibers makes it difficult to get sufficient coverage to adequately protect the carpet with a water-based formula.**

### *Cotton*

Cotton fibers are very easily stained, but cotton is rarely used for face yarns in carpet. Besides, when cotton is used for carpets, even the best protector provides very little protection and probably isn't worth the investment.

– 11 –

### *Fiber Blends*

If your carpet has a stainable fiber like nylon or wool blended with a stain resistant fiber like olefin, polyester or acrylic, follow the carpet protector recommendations for the stainable fiber.

If your carpet has two stain resistant fibers (like olefin and polyester) blended together, decide if you need carpet protection based on whether your environmental conditions (desert / beach - sandy soil and/or exposure to petroleum-based products) will affect the fibers

## 2. Your Carpet's Quality / Age / Condition

Even if you have nylon carpet with its easy staining characteristics, you need to ask yourself the following questions before agreeing to have carpet protector applied after cleaning:

**Does your carpet quality (also referred to as "grade") and age justify it?**

Some carpets are so cheaply made that there is barely enough yarn in them to hide the primary backing. (These usually cost less than $12.00 a yard installed, are sometimes referred to as "apartment grade" or "builder's grade" carpet, and are usually found in apartments and in homes costing up to $200,000.)

• These carpet grades typically need to be replaced about every 5 - 7 years.

• They almost never come with a manufacturer's applied protector. (If the manufacturer didn't think they were worth protecting, you probably shouldn't either.)

• Carpet protector is most likely not worth the investment. Because the manufacturer did not originally apply protector, it would require wall-to-wall application to cover every potential spill zone.

Other higher quality carpets can last from 8 to 15 years, depending on the carpet construction (fiber type, weave or design, etc.), type and amount of wear on the carpet, and the maintenance and cleaning care the carpet receives, etc. These carpets are more likely to be worth the investment of re-applying carpet protector.

**Is the carpet's condition good enough to justify the expense of applying a protector?**

• Is it still in good condition? Or, is it looking tired and worn?

• Is it relatively spot and stain free? Or, is it contaminated with too many pet spots or permanent food or other stains?

A carpet in good condition that is relatively spot and stain free is probably worth treating with protector. The other is not.

### 3. Your Lifestyle

Your carpet, no matter what type of fiber, may not need protector if your lifestyle doesn't warrant it.

For example: You are retired, live alone in a high rise, do not allow shoes to be worn in the house, have no pets or visiting children, vacuum your carpets frequently and your carpet never seems to get soiled or spotted for any reason. If there's not much to clean up, there isn't much to protect your carpet from.

# When and Where Should Protector Be Applied

**When should my carpet be treated with protector, if it warrants it?**

For the best long-term results:

• Start treating carpet, especially nylon, with carpet protector by the carpet's 3rd year of use.

• Thereafter, have carpet protector applied in the high traffic lanes and heavy soiling and spill-prone areas, immediately after cleaning.

- Synthetic carpets - Apply protector every 9 months - 2 years, depending on whether water or solvent-based protector is used

- Wool carpets - Apply protector every 2 years

• Discontinue use of carpet protectors based on the type of carpet fiber and the carpet's age. At the time listed below, there is normally little benefit to reapplying protector because the carpet's appearance has usually been so affected by normal wear that the additional expense is not justified.

- Nylon carpets: Discontinue at the end of the carpet's 7th to 9th year.

- Olefin, Polyester, Acrylic carpets: Discontinue at the end of the carpet's 4th to 6th year.

- Wool carpets: Discontinue at the end of the carpet's 5th to 7th year.

**Note:** If your carpet is still in excellent condition, has few if any spots, stains or discolorations and shows little to no graying after cleaning in spite of its age, continue to have the protector applied in the high traffic lanes and heavy soiling and spill-prone areas immediately after cleaning.

**If I am having my carpets protected, how much area needs to be treated?**

Only the obvious traffic lanes and heavy soiling and highly spill-prone areas need treatment. This is because:

- About 1/3 of the protector in each room or area is lost due to soiling conditions and wear. In most cases, this is in the obvious traffic paths.

- Only about 5% of the original manufacturer's treatment (when present) is removed by each cleaning. (The next time the carpet cleaning company tells you that you will also need protector applied because their cleaning process is going to remove all the protective coating, it just isn't so.)

## How Should A Carpet Protector Be Applied?

As I mentioned in "Solvent-Based Versus Water-Based Protectors", the technician is the most critical factor in whether you will get a quality carpet protector treatment. Asking him or her is the best way to know if the person applying your carpet protector has experience, is using the right equipment and knows the proper way to apply that protector.

**The following is what he/she should say and what you should see being done:**

- **Equipment:** Both solvent-based and water-based protectors should be applied using an electric or pump-up sprayer (like the type you see in a hardware store). The tip on the spray wand should be an 8003 to 8004 T-Jet Sprayer Tip. (It should not be a cone tip like the kind you would use on a weed or bug sprayer.)

- **Application Technique:** The protector should be applied slowly, using a 50% overlap with each spray pass.

- **Brush Stroking Technique:** Water-based protector should be brushed into the carpet fibers using a carpet brush - not a carpet rake. The carpet should be brushed right to left and left to right, up and down and down and up, using a 50% overlap with each pass. (Solvent-based formulas coat the yarns more effectively and do not need to be brushed.)

**Best Practice:** Have an experienced, trained professional clean and protect your carpets (and your fine upholstery). The little aerosol spray cans of fabric protector do not give good coverage on carpet pile, because of their weaker spray volume and intensity of the spray.

## How Much Should Carpet Protector Cost?

**Best Practice:** Before having your carpets protected, get an in-house estimate, including the type and brand of protector that will be used, so you have an exact quote as to the chemicals that will be used, the size and locations of the areas that will be treated and the cost.

Most carpet cleaning companies currently charge about the following for a quality protector:

• Solvent-based soil/stain repellent (such as Scotchguard®, or Teflon®,): 30 - 35 cents per square foot

• Water-based soil/stain repellent (such as Scotchguard®, or Teflon®,): 25 - 30 cents per square foot

**Note:** For the most up-to-date information about these and other carpet protectors, visit our Web site at: **www.artsspotcleaning.com**

These products provide huge profits for the carpet cleaning company at the above prices. The markup per gallon ranges from 500 - 1000%, depending on the chemical concentrate, the amount purchased, how the company chooses to sell the protector (by the square foot or by the room) and at what price.

I personally would not pay more than the following for a quality protector:

• Solvent-based soil/stain repellent: 20 - 25 cents per square foot

• Water-based soil/stain repellent: 15 - 20 cents per square foot

**Hint:** If you are going to have carpet protector applied to a large area (about 500 square feet or more) in your home or office, ask if they give a quantity discount price of at least 5 cents off the prices I suggest you pay per square foot.

— 15 —

# Chapter 10 How Do I Find A Quality Carpet Cleaning Professional?

## Introduction

You want and deserve to get quality service when you have your carpets cleaned. Finding someone you can trust can be very difficult, given the number of people doing carpet care who may or may not be ethical, well-trained professionals.

Having the right person doing your carpet cleaning is critical, because it is the experience, training and conscientiousness of the person cleaning your carpet that largely determines whether you receive a bad job or a great one.

The best way to protect yourself and your carpet and to avoid a bad situation is to:

1. Ask someone you trust for a referral for a carpet cleaning company that he/she has had good experiences with and would call again. **Hint:** Also get the name or names of the technician(s) who did the work. (In surveys, the majority of satisfied customers said this was how they found their carpet cleaning professional.)

2. Call the IICRC (Institute Of Inspection, Cleaning & Restoration Certification) Referral Line at (800) 835-4624 to locate certified cleaning and restoration technicians and firms in your area. (More on the IICRC follows.)

3. If you are calling a new company for the first time, don't be afraid to ask them all the questions necessary to see if they can and will do a good job for you. (The types of questions you should ask are on the next page.)

**Some of the questions you might ask include:**

- How long have they been in business?

- What types of carpet cleaning jobs do they specialize in? Is it residential? Commercial? Both?

- What is their level of experience with your type of cleaning situation, especially if you have natural fiber carpets, a difficult spotting situation, or some other special needs?

- What cleaning method do they use and why do they use that method? (You already know some of the things they should tell you based on what you've learned in this guide).

- What exactly will they do to clean your carpet?

- How much do they charge? Do they give free in-home estimates? Do they have a price list you can see in advance? How and when can you see it? (Get a copy and look at it before you agree to have them clean.)

- Who will be doing your cleaning? What is the experience level of that person? What kind of training has he/she had? Is he or she certified? If so, in what and by whom?

- As you saw in "Truck Mounts Versus Portables" in the last Chapter, you should ask the psi and inches of water lift their equipment produces if you are having hot water extraction "steam" cleaning done. (If they can't tell you or the numbers they give don't meet or exceed the minimum standards - Rinse pressure: At least 200 psi, Water lift: 60 inches, call someone else.)

There are many other questions you could ask, but these are the main ones. Pay careful attention to the answers, and if you are not satisfied or you don't get a feeling of confidence in these people, find someone else. Your carpet and your time are too valuable to have an incompetent or untrustworthy person do a poor cleaning job or damage the carpet or other furnishings in your home.

# The Institute Of Inspection, Cleaning And Restoration Certification (IICRC)

The largest educational group for certifying carpet cleaning professionals is the Institute Of Inspection, Cleaning And Restoration Certification (the IICRC). The IICRC is an independent, nonprofit certifying body owned and controlled by national and regional carpet cleaning industry trade associations.

The function of the IICRC is to protect customers through:

- Work with regulatory bodies, government agencies, manufacturers and consumer groups to establish fair standards of proficiency in the carpet and upholstery cleaning industry.

- Qualify and certify 1) Technicians responsible for the carpet, upholstery and drapery cleaning, 2) Firms that employ Certified Technicians or have employees working towards Certification, and 3) Individuals serving the industry as Inspectors investigating carpet problems for carpet manufacturers or mills, retailers, installers and consumers.

- Maintain a national registry of certified Technicians, Firms and Inspectors for use by fiber companies, carpet manufacturers, insurance companies, government agencies and you, the carpet owner.

## IICRC National Directory

The IICRC has its own carpet care help line for consumers to help them locate Certified Firms and Technicians anywhere in the U.S.

**To reach the IICRC Referral Line, call (800) 835-4624.**

All listings are for Certified Firms only. When you call, explain what you need. (A list of the different categories of Certified Technicians follows.) The operator will ask for the zip code where the service is needed. In a few seconds the operator will be able to give you the name and phone number of the closest Certified Firm having a Certified Technician in the requested category.

## *Categories of Certifications*

After extensive study and work by participants, the IICRC gives the following certifications:

- Certified Commercial Carpet Maintenance Technician

- Certified Carpet Cleaning Technician

- Certified Upholstery & Fabric Cleaning Technician

- Certified Repair & Reinstallation Technician

- Certified Color Repair Technician

- Certified Water Damage Technician

- Certified Odor Control Technician

- Certified Fire & Smoke Restoration Technician

**Note:** Because the IICRC cannot control how individuals apply the techniques and information they have learned during their training and certifications, the Institute has the following disclaimer:

"The IICRC assumes no responsibility and accepts no liability for the application of the principles or techniques or conformity to the IICRC Carpet Cleaning Standard by the recommended Firms."

# "ART'S ULTIMATE SPOT CLEANING"

"YOUR CARE GUIDE FOR SYNTHETIC AND BLENDED CARPETS AND RUGS"
is a great gift for anyone who needs to know more about
spot cleaning and maintenance for their carpets and rugs.

### *NEED ADDITIONAL BOOKS?  Simply:*

NOTE: Orders to be shipped outside the Continental USA should be placed online, go to
<www.ArtsSpotCleaning.com>

**1. BILLING INFORMATION** – *Fill in YOUR ADDRESS information. Please print information.*

Name: _____

Street: _____

City, State, Zip: _____ , _____ , _____

Phone Number (required)_____

**2. SHIPPING INFORMATION** – *Fill in the SHIP information (if different from above). Please print information.*

Name: _____

Street: _____

City, State, Zip: _____ , _____ , _____

**3. PAYMENT METHOD** – *DO NOT SEND CASH*

Check One:

☐ Cashier's Check, Make payable to: AmeriChoice Partners I, LTD

☐ Money Order, Make payable to: AmeriChoice Partners I, LTD

☐ MasterCard - Number |_|_|_|_|_|_|_|_|_|_|_|_|_|_|_|_|   Exp. Date: ___/___Mo./Yr.

☐ VISA - Number |_|_|_|_|_|_|_|_|_|_|_|_|_|_|_|_|   Exp. Date: ___/___Mo./Yr.

Signature: _____ Today's Date: _____

Quantity _____ X  $26.99 per book   = $_____

Sales Tax         X  $2.23 per book   = $_____ (Texas residents ONLY add $2.23 (8.25%) sales tax)

Postage/Handling  X  $7.75 per book   = $_____

TOTAL                            $_____

**4. MAIL or FAX** *this completed order form along with your cashier's check, money order or credit card information to:*

Allow 4 - 6 weeks for delivery

**MAIL to:**

AMERICHOICE PARTNERS I, LTD.
**Attn:** Order Department
P.O. Box 875
Prosper, TX   75078

**FAX to 1-972-984-1012**

*Important*
double check information supplied under #1, #2,
for accuracy before you MAIL or FAX and order
*Thank You*